GOD IN MO
PHILOSO

GOD
IN MODERN
PHILOSOPHY

James Collins

Professor of Philosophy
at St. Louis University

GREENWOOD PRESS, PUBLISHERS
WESTPORT, CONNECTICUT

Library of Congress Cataloging in Publication Data

Collins, James Daniel.
    God in modern philosophy.

    Reprint of the ed. published by H. Regnery, Chicago.
    Bibliography: p.
    Includes index.
    1. God--History of doctrines. 2. Philosophy,
Modern. I. Title.
BT98.C64 1978   231   77-25963
ISBN 0-313-20079-3

TO
YVONNE AND MICHAEL COLLINS
My Wife and Son

CONTENTS

PREFACE

THE PRIMARY IMPETUS for undertaking this study came from observing the very close union between the modern history of the problem of God and contemporary speculation about Him. It is not that the alert philosopher today will make more progress in the study of God by consulting what his predecessors have thought on the matter, but rather that he cannot make any headway without such consultation. Unless he is willing to do his thinking about God in a complete intellectual vacuum—neither being shaped by others nor shaping them in any respect—he must take some account of the modern centuries of philosophizing about God. For they furnish the warp of most contemporary views of God, and never more so than in the case of those philosophers who claim to be indifferent toward the past and uninfluenced by it. Upon analysis, their meaning usually turns out to be that they are nurturing themselves upon that particular historical tradition which regards questions about God as lying beyond the competence of philosophers or as being emptied of significance through cultural and methodological changes. As for those thinkers who do concern themselves formally about such questions, their wide diversity of opinions is due to the effective presence of certain other historically powerful trends, whose presence is not always noticed.

A major purpose of this book, then, is to determine the main kinds of philosophical approaches taken toward God during the modern period, with emphasis upon those historical tendencies which are still actively molding our contemporary conceptions of God. It is not surprising to find some broad correlations between the general phases in postmedieval philosophy and the special developments in the theory of God. But what has been brought home to me quite vividly during the course of this investigation is the intimate penetration of the question of God to the very heart of the modern philosophical enterprise. This does not argue to any one-way influence of the doctrine of God upon the rest of a man's system. There is usually a mutual relationship, in which the general position affects the man's notion of God and is, in turn, decisively influenced by the latter. But it does mean that the theme of God's existence, nature, and bond with the world is no peripheral adornment but a central theme in most of the great modern philosophies. To understand the theme in its main tenets and ramifications is to enter deeply into the mind of the given thinker and to perceive a wide region where he is fruitfully engaged with other positions. The continuity and critical interchange in modern philosophy depend in large measure upon positions taken on the problem of God. This pattern has not been suddenly broken in our own day, but still makes meaningful the diversity among philosophers and permits some common ground of discussion.

Along with the immediate historical aim of this study, there is another one which fits into a broader framework. It is difficult to make valid generalizations about the course of modern philosophy as a whole. Our knowledge of the field is still in a pioneer condition as far as the permanent and unifying characteristics are concerned. It seems to me that any well-founded inductive descriptions must rest not only upon analyses of the individual philosophies, but also upon analyses of a common problem which can be traced through several centuries and many minds. The present work takes the problem approach to modern philosophy, by following some of the main positions on God. The key distinction between the functional use of the concept of God by rationalism and its neutralization by empiricism may provide one means of access to a general view of the pre-Kantian period. Similarly, it is hoped that the polarizing conflict between the Hegelian and the naturalistic forms of absolutism will shed some light upon the general movement of thought since the time of Kant, including our contemporary situation.

One consequence of following a common theme through a long period is to bring out more forcefully the interplay of the individual philosopher, his immediate horizon, and the function of successors in working out the implications of his thought. There is always a certain potential of meaning which remains latent in the individual philosopher because of the limiting influence of his own age and his personal, inner weather. Philosophy secures its continuity and progress by mining this hidden deposit, assaying its actual worth, and then searching elsewhere for fresh sources. But the historian of philosophy cannot safely study this interplay between explicit and potential meaning at the purely general level and in terms of consequences alone. He must always find firm anchorage in the actual doctrine of the particular thinker and his actual perspective, including his intellectual limitations. In the present study, this methodological rule means that the general account of modern positions on God has to arise inductively out of a careful, primary examination of the particular philosophical systems. The latter constitute the basis and the norm for any general conclusions about the chief modern ways of viewing God.

The limits of this book should be clearly stated. It would be foolhardy to try to embrace in a single work the vast theme of modern man's quest for God. This would involve a consideration of his religious, artistic, literary, scientific, and sociopolitical productions and would also require help from psychology, intellectual history, and theology. I have confined myself to the philosophical paths to God, without tracing out the interrelationships with these other ways. Even within the philosophical order it is necessary to make selective choices of men and issues at every stage of the investigation. I have given no detailed account of writers like Vico and Comte, Schelling and Bergson, or Weiss and Tillich, who have said some notable things about God. As for the philosophers who are discussed here, my purpose is not to make an exhaustive report of their theories of God but to seize upon the essential line of thought and relate it to the ongoing history of the question. This certainly involves some principles of selection and historical evaluation, the test for which is whether, without running contrary to the established matters of text and fact, they enable the reader to approach the original sources in a more perceptive and oriented manner. Unavoidably, the present study can cast only indirect illumination upon two other nuclear themes in modern philosophy: nature and man. Non-Western views on God are omitted.

Accompanying the historical concern to grasp some major modern approaches to God is a direct theoretical interest in the issues under discussion for their own sake. The great philosophers have about them a way of refusing to become deadwood; they present an urgent challenge to any wayfarer who looks in their direction. In taking a look, I have also incurred the obligation of giving a philosophical response to at least a few of the questions they raise. The standpoint from which my own critical views develop is that of realistic theism. Some basic metaphysical aspects of this realistic philosophy of God are found in St. Thomas, while the contribution of St. Augustine and Cardinal Newman consists in their appreciation of the concrete and personal aspects of the human intelligence when engaged in its search for God. As the final chapter of this volume points out, however, I do not regard this philosophy as ready made but as still very much in the making.

The study of modern conceptions of God can make a positive, doctrinal contribution to the development of realistic theism. Such an inquiry helps to identify the pressing issues, to work out some of the chief modes of explanation, to suggest new sources of evidence, and to render the main tenets more explicit, more philosophically ordered, and more relevant to the contemporary world. Beyond the necessary work of historical understanding and critical evaluation, however, I have refrained from entering the quicksands of disputation cultivated for its own sake. In this respect, there is wisdom packed into Newman's advice of "preferring inquiry to disputation in a question about truth." The philosophy of God cannot progress without the constant testing and creative suggestion provided by many minds and outlooks, but critical discussion must also be regulated by the primary concern of increasing our understanding of God and man.

Responsibility for this interpretation and appraisal of modern philosophical thought on God is my own, including the defects in vision, which will inevitably require other examinations of the matter. It is also clear that I have incurred many intellectual debts during the course of this investigation. I owe the basic one to the theistic traditions of Augustine, Aquinas, and Newman, together with the major sources comprising the modern philosophical approaches to God. I have benefited considerably by conversations with the Reverend George P. Klubertanz, S.J., concerning the nature of the philosophy of God and its metaphysical bases. The Reverend William L. Wade, S.J., director of the philosophy department of St. Louis University, has both encouraged the inquiry and supported it by furnishing the services of a typist and procuring a number of books. The St. Louis University Library has patiently obtained other volumes for me, and the Houghton Library of Harvard University has kindly made available some special source materials on skepticism. The graduate students in my courses during the past several years have worked through several of the historical movements with me. The Reverend Walter E. Stokes, S.J., has been cheerfully helpful in library matters. Finally, the home conditions required for sustained work have always been provided by my family, to whom this book is dedicated.

James Collins

Normandy, Missouri
January, 1959

Chapter I

NEW APPROACHES TO GOD THROUGH
FAITH AND REASON

As RESEARCH probes more deeply into the intellectual milieu of the four-teenth, fifteenth, and sixteenth centuries, it becomes increasingly evident that this crucial time of transition must be viewed as an integral whole. The conventional walls separating thinkers labeled "late medieval" from those labeled "Renaissance," "Reformation," or "early modern" are crumbling beneath the evidence of continuity and interdependence among all these groups. Nowhere is there greater need and better textual foundation for taking the synoptic path through this period than in the question of God. For one cannot understand why so much of the creative effort in modern philosophy has gone into the problem of God, unless one keeps in mind the common difficulties felt especially in this area by all types of thinkers during the preparatory years.

Among the Schoolmen in particular, the doctrinal confusion and endless warfare marking the history of the traditional schools of Thomism, Scotism, and Nominalism reached a peak with respect to God's existence and nature.[1] The controversies were concerned not with whether God actually exists and has the usually ascribed attributes, but with whether we can know these truths through philosophical means and how we should establish the inferences. Among the central issues in the dispute were the contribution which faith does or must make to the rational investigation of God and the scope of arguments taken from the philosophy of nature. Those who refused to follow Nicholas of Autrecourt in denying that natural reason can make a strict causal demonstration nevertheless often shifted their arguments from a metaphysical to a physical basis, without always being aware of the transition. The more they turned to philosophy of nature for support in establishing God's existence, the more they found it necessary to ground the inference in faith or prolong it through a series of purely formal analyses. Yet in the degree that they relied upon a conceptual dialectic of the formal essence, they tended to deprive the philosophy of God of its existential basis and also to lose the philosophical significance of the new advances in physics.

It was out of this seedbed of uncertainty and conflict over the human mind's natural ability to reach God that the doctrines of Cusanus, Calvin, and Bruno grew to maturity. Among the multiform attempts during these centuries to rethink the question of human knowledge of God, their theories had perhaps the most direct bearing upon subsequent modern developments in natural theology. Cusanus highlighted the advantages of a reflective methodology aware of the limitations of the mind in divine matters, the relevance of mathematical thinking, and the need for a synthetic principle to surmount the domestic strife in the Schools. Yet his confidence was radically tempered by the suspicion that our human approximations never do yield any strict knowledge of the infinite God and hence must take faith as their basis. From Luther and Calvin came a powerful reminder that the religious revolution of the age was not without its sharp repercussions upon philosophy, especially when the knowledge of God is seen in the perspective of their interpretation of original sin and the light of faith. As if in savage protest against the inroads of fideism upon philosophy as a human discipline, however, Bruno cut loose his speculations on God from any mooring in Christian revelation, even though this meant the repudiation of Aristotelian philosophy of nature and the sacrifice of God's absolute transcendence over nature. From these men and the intellectual movements they supported there came a good portion of the momentum toward both the skeptical and the rationalist views of God which were to figure so prominently in seventeenth-century philosophy.

1. CUSANUS AND THE METHOD OF LEARNED UNKNOWING

It is fitting to begin our study of the modern conceptions of God with Cardinal Nicholas of Cues (1401–1464). Churchman and humanist, philosopher and man of action, he combined in his original thought elements taken from both tradition and the new interests of his century. At the University of Heidelberg, he was instructed in the theories of Ockham and the terminists, while at Padua he received a sound grounding in Aristotle. The latter university also introduced him to the most recent scientific methods, the mathematical tradition, and the stream of Neo-Platonic thought. Nicholas steeped himself enthusiastically in the writings of Dionysius and Proclus, Augustine and Erigena, and the school of Chartres, as well as in Eckhart and the German mystics. Compared with that of these authors, the influence of the great thirteenth-century masters upon his mind was indeed faint and indirect.

Cusanus agreed with Petrarca before him and Erasmus shortly after him that the reigning philosophies and theologies in the universities had lost touch with the real world and had substituted a dextrous verbalism for the pursuit of truth. Yet whereas these other humanists envisaged a

"Christian philosophy" which was no different in kind from a meditative study of Scripture and the great masterpieces of the spiritual life, their German confrere admitted the need for a technically competent, speculative reconstruction of our knowledge of God.[2] That he should not consult primarily the works of St. Thomas or Duns Scotus in this reconstructive task is indicative of how thoroughly these major medieval sources were obscured by the academic rivalries of the day. Instead, Cusanus turned for aid to the Plotinian and Dionysian traditions, as well as to the mathematical procedures which had always proved to be so congenial to thinkers in this line. By analyzing the findings of the Neo-Platonic philosophers and mystics with the assistance of some techniques developed in mathematics, he hoped to place our philosophical discourse about God upon a sound footing.

In his philosophical masterpiece, *On Learned Unknowing (De Docta Ignorantia,* 1440), Cusanus poses the bedrock question of whether we can know anything at all about God. That this is not an artificially stimulated issue can be seen by inspecting our ordinary way of knowing things. Knowledge is a measuring function: It sets up a comparison between that which is already understood and the further aspects of things still under investigation.[3] In this comparative process, some relation of proportion must be discovered between the known and the unknown if the frontier of knowledge is to be advanced. Granting the Christian teaching on God as the infinitely perfect being, however, there is no determinate proportion or relation of comparison between God and the entire order of finite beings, including man, with his concepts and language. If God is truly infinite in a perfect and not a privative or indefinite sense, then He must remain unknown to us and unnamable by us. At least, our usual ways of knowing do not seem to provide any basis for reaching the truth about His being.

Cusanus is thus prepared to take seriously the uniform pronouncement of Christian mystics and theologians that the perfect and holy God is unknown to us. Yet it raises in his mind the inconvenient consequence of apparently rendering senseless man's natural intellectual desire for some true knowledge about God, as well as about finite things. Instead of paring down the difficulty, however, he makes the paradoxical suggestion that the primary datum is our own unknowing or lack of knowledge of God and that any positive solution must respect and build out from this human situation. Reflection upon the drastic limits of the human mind may provide some clue for making at least a more rigorous orientation in the direction of God, even though the infinite truth itself remains unattainable. If we cannot penetrate the infinite mystery of God, then perhaps we can make as careful and disciplined an approach toward it as our cognitive instruments will permit. A condition of unknowing that is learned or reflectively and methodically enlight-

ened about itself is thus the goal of Cusanus' philosophical inquiries.
To carry through the project of a learned unknowing, he draws upon two sources: the Christian doctrine on man as the image of God and the mathematical theory of limits. Man resembles God chiefly in his mind, or spiritual knowing power, so that he stands forth in his character as *imago Dei* primarily in his intellectual life and operations.[4] It will be granted that between even a reflectively aware finite mind and its infinite exemplar, there is not present the perfect coinciding of measured and measure required for strict knowledge. Nevertheless, the assurance we have from faith that such an image-and-exemplar relationship exists does hold out some hope that a study of our own intellectual functions can yield a method and a symbolism for ordering our thought and discourse about God. The very contrast between the divine and human minds is significant. Whereas the divine mind is a formative power which creates real beings in their own existence, the human mind is a conformative power which assimilates the likenesses of real beings. We do not remain passively related to the original data of experience, however, but involve them in the distinctively intellectual operations of abstracting and generalizing, symbolizing and inferring. The human mind brings forth a world of ideal objects, organizes the likenesses in an intelligible way, and thus strives to increase knowledge beyond the limit of our initial acquaintance with the world. In these intellectual activities, the human mind not only manifests its own nature, but also makes its closest approach to the divine exemplar. Reflection upon our mental life is thus the most promising route for approximating as closely as possible to a grasp of the incomprehensible mind of God.

As a guide in this search, Nicholas distinguishes three levels of human cognition: sense, reason, and intellect.[5] He is sufficiently realistic to insist upon the sensory foundation of knowledge and the elaboration of images by the imagination. But at the sense level, the likenesses of things remain obscure and unorganized. It is the work of reason to distinguish carefully between objects, unite similar impressions in an abstract, universal concept, and follow out the relations and implications of the data. However, reasoning is not our supreme intellectual activity, since it is confined in principle to objects which are finite and to contradictory opposites which are mutually irreconcilable. This is the standpoint of Aristotle and all Peripatetic philosophies, and it must be transcended to reach the plateau of intellect. It is only through the intellect proper that we succeed in apprehending a certain type of infinity and constructing a method for unifying the contrasts of finite experience. Surely, then, the best source for obtaining some distant analogue of the divine mind is to be found in the characteristic operations of the human intellect as it develops its world of intellectual likenesses.

Instead of following the traditional Trinitarian and mystical inter-

pretations of the summit of the mind, however, Cusanus has recourse
to mathematics for his description of intellectual activity. In part, this
choice of a guide is dictated by epistemological considerations.[6] Although the external senses and imagination are required to supply the
images of material things, these powers are so closely implicated in the
physical process that they are apt to be uncertain and deceptive. Mathematical thought abstracts as much as possible from sensible flux and
hence provides a more stable and certain starting point for the study of
God. The indestructible certitude of mathematical truths and their
removal from concrete matter make them suitable patterns for an approach to God's supremely immutable and immaterial being. Furthermore, mathematical thinking accustoms us to make a symbolical and ap-
proximative use of the figures drawn from the sensible world. Since
there can be no exact comparison between visible things and the invisible God, the former must be treated symbolically to yield any true
likeness of God. And from the approximation of different geometrical
figures to each other, we can learn to use the symbols precisely through
the method of conjectures, which is a dialectic of true and increasingly
adequate symbols for the infinite exemplar.

Cusanus is not foreshadowing symbolic logic; he is treating mathematical thinking itself as a symbol of a higher intellectual mode of
thought. There is one area in mathematics in which he notes a transition from the finite to the infinite and hence from the way of reason to
that of intellect: the method of limits in dealing with infinite figures.
When the geometer conceives of the infinite straight line as the ideal
limit toward which curved lines and angles approach, he is transcending reason and attaining an intellectual conception of a certain infinite.
Cusanus does not confuse the geometrical infinite with the unbounded
actuality of God, but he does suggest that the cognitive act and method
employed to conceive the former can also be used to symbolize the latter through finite things. The whole doctrine of learned unknowing
consists in making this transference of the mathematical method to the
symbolic study of God and rethinking the traditional doctrine on God
in terms of this common intellectual pattern. To this extent there is, by
anticipation, a Cartesian flavor about his project. But it lacks the distinctive notes of a methodical doubt, a central deduction from the
thinking self, and a separation of rational analysis from the deliverances
of faith which characterize the method of Descartes. Both poles of the
Cusanian dialectic—God as the infinite existent and man taken precisely as the image of God—are ultimately held on faith. The inquiry
does not concern them so much as it does our way of conceiving a relation between them.

The procedure which Cusanus follows is set forth in the following
text:

If then we want to reach the Absolute Maximum through the finite, we must, in the first place, study finite, mathematical figures as they are, namely a mixture of potency and act; then we must attribute the respective perfections to the corresponding infinite figures, and finally we must, in a much more sublime way, attribute the perfections of the infinite figures to the simple Infinite, which cannot possibly be expressed by any figure. Then, while we are groping in the dark, our ignorance will enlighten us in an incomprehensible fashion and enable us to form a more correct and truer notion of the Absolute [*de altissimo rectius et verius*].[7]

Cusanus does not hold out the promise that his method will remove the divine unknowability but says only that our way of naming God will become as accurate and true as possible. His theory concerns the human manner of naming God through symbols rather than the divine nature in its own actual being. The contention is that our philosophical thinking about God should not consist of pure dreaming or pious laudation but should follow the general intellectual procedure used in treating the geometrical infinite through finite figures. Just as we can determine some certain conclusions about the geometrical infinite through finite images which never manifest it, so can we use these conclusions and the method of arriving at them in order to render our thought about the supreme being more rigorous, even though God does not manifest Himself in the mathematical symbols. Cusanus does not hope to remove the darkness entirely, but only to permit a beam of light to reach us through contemplation of our own highest intellectual operation.

The clue he follows from geometry is to regard God as the absolute maximum. The most effective way of representing to ourselves the infinite being of God is to analyze the mathematical conception of the infinite straight line as a maximum limit. One then makes a *transsumptio*, or symbolical transference, of the method of limits to the infinitely actual and simple being of God, transcending the confines of a purely quantitative sort of infinite. Cusanus makes it abundantly clear that his entire doctrine on God is regulated by this geometrical kind of analogy.

The relationship of the Maximum to all things is by analogy what the infinite line is to lines. . . . In reality it [the Absolute Maximum] is not a circle, circumference, diameter or center, but by reason of its infinite simplicity we have to study it by means of these comparisons.[8]

His root metaphor is found in the relation of the indefinitely expanding polygon to the circle or in that of the infinite curve and angle to the infinite straight line.

The absolute maximum, not being confined to quantity or any other categorial order, can be defined as that which is in actuality everything which can possibly exist. Nothing can be placed in opposition to it, for

6

it is one and it is all. All things are in it as the one, simple actuality, and it is in all things as their essence and actual being. For us human beings, to see God means to see all as God and God as all. The absolute maximum embraces both the maximal limit and the minimal limit, the greatest and the smallest, since it cannot be surpassed in any relative direction. Hence it reconciles within itself all contrasts and opposites, even contradictory ones: God is the *complicatio omnium* and the *coincidentia oppositorum*.[9] We cannot discover how God contains all opposites within His own simple being, but we can see the symbolic form of such containment in the generation of finite figures from the infinite straight line.

It is of no avail for Aristotelian-inspired philosophies to object that this violates the principle of contradiction, since this principle belongs to reason but not to intellect. It applies only to things at the finite level and is radically incapable of making any pronouncement about the infinite being. Cusanus does not deny the principle of contradiction, but simply confines it to the finite order and invokes his own intellectual method of limits to interpret the relation of finite things to God. They are not in Him in their limited and opposing modes, but their entire actuality is in some way contained in His essence, just as the triangle and circle are present in the infinite straight line.

Since in the absolute maximum there is no real distinction between being and acting, it is the same thing to say that God is all things and that He creates all things. Since God is in a necessary way, Cusanus is forced to conclude that He creates necessarily. But he modifies this statement in the light of Christian revelation by adding that with respect to the divine will and not simply to the divine being in general, the production of the world is a free creation. The relation of particular geometrical figures to the infinite line also supplies him with a simile for explaining the creator-creature relationship. God, or the absolute maximum, is at once the *complicatio* and the *explicatio* of all things: their concentrated envelopment in that they are one absolute essence in God, and their differentiated development in that He is present to all existing things as their creative act and goal.[10] The universe itself is a sort of intermediary between God and individual things. Cusanus calls it the contracted maximum or great image of God. What holds for God in an absolute way also obtains for the universe, but in a derived and restricted way. Cusanus preserves the unity and connectedness of the universe not by positing God as the soul of the world (as Bruno will do), but by treating the universe as the derived or contracted maximum. It is present in all particular things in a way similar to God's universal presence as their exemplar, efficient cause, and goal. Thus the universe as a whole is both the patterned image of God's knowledge and rule and the real totality of finite beings.

Throughout his detailed study of God and the universe, Cusanus says very little about how we establish the truth of God's existence.[11] He makes brief reference to a causal argument that beings which are finite and not self-existing must have an infinite, self-existing cause. But within the context of knowledge as comparative mensuration, it is difficult to find a philosophical meaning for finitude, existence, and causation. Hence the usual procedure for Cusanus is to accept God's existence as a truth of faith and then to show, by purely formal analysis, that an absolute maximum must include the note of independent being within itself. This fideism concerning the actual existence of the infinite being is an inevitable consequence of Cusanus' description of the hierarchy of our knowing powers. The senses and reason are essentially bound to finite objects and cannot make the inference to the infinite being of God. Our faculty of the infinite is the intellect. Although it is a natural knowing power, it remains dormant within us until it is aroused by the action of supernatural faith. Only after it receives the illumination of faith can the human intellect grasp the truth about the existence of the infinite God and thus acquire a true notion of infinity. Our intellectual power then unfolds and develops in a systematic way the primary truth about the infinite which was first implanted in it by faith.

Even mathematics is a purely rational science of finite quantity until the faith-illuminated intellect makes the transition to the mathematical infinite. Thus there is a curiously circular relationship in Cusanus between the religious and the mathematical infinite. Faith assures the intellect of the real existence of the one, absolute, infinite being. This truth enables the intellect to elaborate a theory of the infinite line and to develop the method of limits for dealing geometrically with the relation of finite figures to this line. In turn, the mathematical maximum provides guidance to the philosopher in his discourse about the actual infinite being, thus rendering us enlightened in our unknowing. The interplay between faith and intellect explains why Cusanus interprets the method of limits as leading toward an actual coincidence between the infinite line and finite figures. He views the asymptotic approach of finite figures to the limit as an ultimate identification only because of an underlying notion of God as the infinite essence containing all finite things. Although the philosopher can appeal to the mathematical maximum for clarification of his language about God, it is not a completely independent source of evidence about the relation of the finite to the infinite. Cusanus succeeds in making some propositions about God more intelligible to the mathematically trained men of his day, but he does not succeed in establishing the philosophical foundations of knowledge of God.

One of the most engaging features of Cusanus' mind is its lucid and frank acknowledgment of weaknesses: he is his own best critic. He has indicated four major deficiencies in his teaching which even the open door between mathematics and learned unknowing fails to remedy.

(1) Even supposing the common principle of faith behind the geometry and the philosophy of the infinite, it is difficult to show that our philosophical discourse involves the divine names and concerns itself with God rather than some indeterminate, transgeometrical *x*. Cusanus is sure that negative theology, or saying what God is not, is more appropriate to our condition than positive theology, or saying what He is.[12] He is even tempted to say that the positive names of God are purely anthropomorphic, designating only the relation of creatures to Him. Yet he also admits that although the negative names apply more properly to God, the positive names do express perfections which are somehow included in God's absolutely simple perfection. Just as it is truer to deny that God is a stone than that He is a living mind, so is it truer to affirm life or intelligence than materiality of Him. Yet why this is so cannot be established solely within the method of mathematical limits, which prescinds from questions involving the gradations of being and value.

(2) Cusanus is not unaware that a theory of causality is required in order to explain the significance of the negative and positive ways of naming God. But he is handicapped in developing this approach by his attempt to restrict the problem of causality to what is adaptable to mathematical illustration. Although he employs the geometrical paradigms of the center and the circumference to explain efficient and final causality, respectively, Cusanus is unable to avoid the mathematical reduction of these types of causality to a formal consequence in the ideal order. To avoid the pantheistic and deterministic conclusion that God produces things as their intrinsic, formal cause, he must abandon the geometrical norm and refer to God the creator as a creative mind. God is thus explained as the exemplar cause and purposive governor of the universe rather than its inner formula. But the truth about God as the free, creative mind, like the truth about the human mind as the image of God, is a deliverance of faith which does not fit comfortably within the mathematical analogy of limits and a maximum.

(3) Closely connected with the causal problem is that of finite participation in being.[13] Cusanus himself remarks that if it is the same thing for God to create and to be all things then it is difficult to conceive of creatures as being anything other than eternal, infinite, and one. Yet experience presents us with things which exist in a temporal, finite, and plural way. This is a kind of scandal in a philosophy where participation in being is conceived after the model of lines and curves which fall away from absolute straightness. Participation is thus a sort of diminution or shrinking of the infinite perfection of God, and yet the reduced form of finite being cannot be due to any niggardliness on His part or

9

any distinctions in His causal action. The geometrical type of analogy breaks down here, since it cannot suggest any positive, internal principles in finite things to account for their diversity and finitude. Cusanus is driven to conclude that diversity, temporality, finitude, and opposition of things have no positive cause whatsoever, either in God or in creatures. They are due to "contingency," a term which remains wholly unclarified within his geometrically conceived universe, where there is no room for the internally composing principles of being. Cusanus is neither convinced by the current philosophical analyses of contingency nor able to provide a new interpretation in terms of figures and limits. Hence he assigns to faith our assurance of the derived character of finite things and declares contingency to be completely unintelligible. It is by faith that we learn that God is the sole *esse* and that every other thing is an *ab-esse*, or derivation from the maximum. The method of limits permits no basis except faith for the truth about God's existence and the participative status of finite things.

(4) Because of his remarks about God as the absolute essence of the universe, Cusanus was accused by John Wenck and other contemporaries of wiping out the substantial distinction between God and the world. But he was able to show that his philosophy is pantheistic neither in intention nor in some of its leading positions.[14] The contrast between the primary cause and its effects, between the exemplar and its image in the universe, and between the governing mind and finite agents was firmly maintained. Unlike Bruno, Cusanus never formally denied finite substances and a free creation, difficult as it was for him to allow them on any grounds except the teaching of faith. What distinguished him definitively from Bruno was precisely his acceptance of revelation as a norm for philosophizing.

Yet his defense of theism was weakened by the chosen method of his philosophy. He could show that finite figures are not identified with the infinite line in their limited and diverse aspects but only in their absolute nature as figure. Nevertheless, he was unable to develop a theory of causality, participation, and finite principles of being which could correct the univocal relation between all geometrical figures, whether taken in their absolute nature or their particular forms. The Cusanian mathematical conception of knowing and of God as the maximum limit unavoidably reduced all analogies to univocity in being. It was the absence of any metaphysical causal analogy which underlay the other difficulties about the divine names, causality, and participation. The only circumstances which prevented the doctrine of learned unknowing from being a pantheism were the influence of Christian faith and the fact that the dialectic never moved beyond the ideal operations and objects of the human mind to the truth about the infinite being.

A comparison between Cusanus and Aquinas in this respect is instructive. Both thinkers agree that God in His own essence remains unknown to us because of His infinite perfection. They further agree that the divine names are taken from perfections as found in finite things and hence that the way of negation is important. Aquinas adds that we can at least come to know that the perfection truly belongs to the divine essence in an unlimited way, even though the infinite mode of the perfection must escape our minds. Such knowledge is based on our judgment about the composed being of finite things and our recognition of the caused character of their act of existing. But Cusanus lacks the existential judgment, the knowledge of the composing principles of essence and existence in finite things, and the real efficient causality and causal analogy, which are the foundation for the Thomistic doctrine on God. His God is unknown, not only because faith alone testifies to His infinite actuality, but also because we are philosophically ignorant of the real composition in finite beings, and hence of their caused and contingent character, which would permit us to make demonstratively true judgments about God. In Cusanus, faith not only suggests aspects for philosophical elaboration, but takes the place of any philosophical demonstration concerning God as distinguished from a dialectical symbolization of His being.

2. THE FALL OF MAN AND THE KNOWLEDGE OF GOD IN CALVIN

During the century following Cusanus' death, the Protestant leaders laid the theological groundwork for a distinctive conception of human knowledge of God. Although Luther and Calvin themselves were not philosophers, they took a definite stand concerning natural knowledge of God and exerted an indirect influence upon the philosophical appraisals of natural theology made during the subsequent centuries. Despite many deep theological cleavages between the two chief Continental reformers, they were in essential agreement on the question of natural knowledge of God, especially on the need to evaluate it in terms of the doctrine of original sin.

Martin Luther (1483–1546) was not interested in exploring the noetic problem for its own sake, but only in developing its religious aspects. He readily conceded that men are in possession of some natural knowledge of God's existence and that this is an inborn truth of the mind. Without inquiring closely into the question of its validity, Luther was mainly concerned to prevent such rudimentary knowledge from being expanded into an autonomous, rational doctrine on the divine nature. Although the natural mind can know that God exists, it cannot determine with certainty who or what God is in His own nature. As a consequence of the Fall, our intellectual power is darkened and ren-

11

dered impotent in matters involving the divine perfections. The few glimmerings which philosophers do obtain by natural means are inevitably misemployed, resulting in false conceptions of God's being and our relation to Him.

Luther's bar upon a philosophy of God had a primarily religious motivation.[15] He feared that such a science might be taken as the foundation of faith and thus deprive the latter of its gratuitous and independent nature. If the unaided human mind can ascertain the truth about the divine nature, then it would seem that man is not intrinsically corrupted in his highest powers, but quite the contrary, is capable of rectifying his intellect and perhaps even his will through his own efforts. Furthermore, a philosophical fund of knowledge about God would furnish an autonomous standard for judging certain religious propositions, thus setting up an independent authority to which faith itself must conform. These consequences militated against the Lutheran view of the manner in which supernatural faith must remain a sovereign gift of God.

Even during his early years as an Augustinian monk, Luther forcefully rejected the two forms of reasoning which he thought a philosophy of God might assume. If the inferences moved in an a priori way, the human mind would be supposing itself to be in possession of a real definition of the divine essence, the mystery and freedom of which would thereby be violated. Luther agreed with Aquinas in opposing the a priori approach to God on the ground of His essential hiddenness. But Luther went his own way in denying that philosophical reason can respect the hidden God and still make an a posteriori approach to His being from a study of the created world. His opposition to this second way of philosophizing abut God was founded upon moral and religious grounds rather than epistemological or metaphysical bases. The danger here was that the inquirer would become fascinated by the wisdom, goodness, and power which abound in God's works, would eventually attribute these perfections to himself in his fallen nature, and thus would end by rejecting revelation and fashioning a god after his own image. Hence Luther concluded that "God can be found only in the cross and suffering" of Christ, since it is only here that men learn to accept God's nature as He reveals it to us and use that knowledge in the obedience of faith.[16] His frequently violent language about reason's natural inquiry into God was aroused by a fear that men might look for God elsewhere than in Christ, where He reveals Himself only to preserve His own hiddenness.

At first glance, John Calvin (1509–1564) seems to be far removed from Luther's standpoint. The first book of Calvin's *Institutes of the Christian Religion* (1536, 1559) contains a detailed and calm account of the witness to God in the visible world and stresses the agreement of Scripture with what can be gathered about Him from a study of man and the other works in nature. The problem of our knowledge of God is a central theme in this book and is therefore accorded a full-scale treatment. Calvin attaches more positive significance to the study of God in the created world than does Luther, and he gives a more generous recognition to the secular sciences. But when his complex, sinuous teaching on our knowledge of God is studied in terms of its guiding principles and ultimate intent, its affiliation with the Lutheran position becomes evident.

Calvin begins the *Institutes* with the thematic statement that our true wisdom consists in the knowledge of God and ourselves.[17] This declaration is traditional enough, but Calvin intends to explain this dual knowledge in such a way that it will set off his own views from those of Greek philosophy and Catholic theology. Recognizing the mutual bearing of our self-knowledge and our knowledge of God, he nevertheless proposes to consider first of all our knowledge of God, as both creator and redeemer. God the creator is to be treated initially to the extent that He is revealed in the visible world and then to the extent that He is revealed in Scripture. God the redeemer must be approached in the only possible way, namely, through an account of Christ as the object of faith who is specially revealed in Scripture. Throughout this exposition, moreover, constant reference is to be made to the nature of man himself, viewed as both a creature and a fallen being who stands in need of revelation and redemption.

Unless this complete order of topics is kept firmly in mind, one is apt to receive the mistaken impression that Calvin is engaged in rehabilitating a philosophy of God alongside a scriptural theology. Indeed, the plan of the *Institutes* does lend itself quite easily to a threefold detachment of partial themes. One can isolate the explanation of God the creator from that of God the redeemer; next, one can concentrate upon the testimony of finite things about God the creator to the exclusion of what the Bible reports on God the creator; finally, one can divorce the problem of knowing God from any consideration of man in his actual state of depravity and the concrete conditions under which he views nature. By making this threefold narrowing of the doctrine, one apparently comes into possession of a Calvinist philosophy of God. But the outcome is achieved only by doing violence to the integral structure and movement of Calvin's thought, which requires that all the links and qualifications be maintained in full force as a total context within which to interpret his remarks about the witness to God in the created world.

Indeed, the whole sting and originality of Calvin's treatment derive from what may be called the dialectical method of progressive disclosure of the conditions and limits for any knowledge of God.[18] Not until all the relevant principles are brought forward is the reader in a position to determine the nature and scope of our knowledge of God as manifested in His works. For it turns out that after the Fall, His objective revelation in man and nature can only be apprehended distinctly and truly by us with the aid of the general revelation of God the creator in Scripture. Furthermore, God the creator is known only in the supernatural faith which the elect have in God the redeemer as manifested in Christ. The study of theological evidences in nature is not rendered superfluous thereby but is made intrinsically dependent upon the guidance of the Bible and the regenerative power of Christian faith, if it is to give us any sure and clear knowledge of God. Only through the gradual presentation of all the qualifying conditions does Calvin make us aware of the full extent of his fideism and his repudiation of any philosophy of God. This progressive disclosure enhances the dynamic sweep of the argument in his major work, but it also raises some acute problems concerning certain admissions made along the way.

Concerning God the creator, men have inquired whether He exists, what His essence is in itself, and how He stands disposed toward us. Calvin rules out any study of the divine essence in itself: It is a transcendent mystery which remains forever hidden and inaccessible to us. No strict accommodation can be made by God to establish a proportion between His infinite nature and the finite mind, so it is futile to ask what His essence is in itself. On this score, Calvin's criticism is partially directed against contemporary disciples of Epicurus and Lucretius, whose writings were enjoying a revival in Renaissance Italy and France. When these philosophers try to represent the divine nature in itself, they waver between picturing it as a self-enclosed happiness and an utter void. The former alternative encourages the view that God has not revealed Himself as redeemer, whereas the notion of divinity as a void is only a step removed from atheism. But another target which Calvin has in mind is the standpoint of speculative theology, which Luther had already castigated for weakening the contribution of moral and religious factors to a right knowledge of God. There is no storming of the citadel of the divine essence by any boldly soaring, speculative intelligence, since God can be apprehended only upon His own terms, that is, through His own modes of manifestation. On this issue, however, Calvin is not as far removed from the leading medieval theologians as he supposes; he finds his real opponent in Giordano Bruno.

Calvin is no more inclined than Cusanus or Luther to raise special difficulties about our knowledge that God exists. In conformity with his own humanist training, however, he is much more willing than Luther to invoke pagan sources, especially Plato, Seneca, and Cicero, in explanation of the natural basis of that knowledge. Our natural knowledge of God's existence is drawn from two sources: instinct and experience. "That there exists in the human mind, and indeed by natural instinct, some sense of Deity, we hold to be beyond dispute, since God himself, to prevent any man from pretending ignorance, has endued all men with some idea of his Godhead."[19] The sense of deity is not a special organ of cognition but is itself the awareness of the true God which our natural constitution spontaneously arouses in us and fixes indelibly in our mind. Calvin draws heavily upon Seneca and Cicero here, but he also fits the idea to his own theological preoccupations. The natural character of this knowledge both guarantees its validity against skepticism and atheism and sets limits upon what we can develop from it. One reason why Calvin is careful to deny that the Fall has destroyed our essential nature is precisely in order to retain a reliable basis for the instinctive knowledge of God which is present even in the ruin-of-the-image-of-God, which is fallen man. The spontaneity of this knowledge indicates its nonmeritorious character and its universal presence in all minds without affording any ground for human pride in the prowess of our intelligence. That it is indelibly graven upon our intelligence means that all men are constantly responsible for acknowledging God and are inexcusable when they fail to do so.

Under a natural impulse, the human mind spontaneously affirms the existence of God as the one maker of the world, as being distinct from the works of His power, and as demanding the service of our worship. This is the same true God revealed in Scripture, but our sense of deity does not yield an adequate knowledge of Him. Even in fallen man there is a natural love of truth and a desire to perfect his instinctive but rudimentary apprehension of God. Hence, in addition to the internal instinct, he examines his experience of the world and human history for additional information about the divine nature. Calvin admits that although the divine essence is hidden in its own infinite majesty, God does manifest some of His perfections in the created world. There is no intrinsic obstacle against our discovering what God the creator is in His actions toward us, since the very fact of creation implies a certain accommodation of God to human intelligence. But an experiential study of this manifestation also depends upon the concrete condition of the human inquirer when he actually tries to grasp the significance of the works of God.

At this juncture, Calvin makes a crucial distinction between God's objective revelation in the world (inclusive of the visible universe, man, and human history) and our subjective apprehension of this evidence, between what God manifests and what we are here and now able to grasp about His nature. As far as the objective natural revelation is concerned, Calvin cannot be outdone in celebrating the clear witness to God in created things. Not only in the *Institutes,* but also in *The Cate-*

chism of the Church of Geneva (1545), he strongly emphasizes that along with the revealed word of God, "there is the world itself as a kind of mirror, in which we may observe him, in so far as it concerns us to know him."[20] The works of God bear the indefectible mark of their author's power, goodness, paternal love, providence, justice, and other perfections. Taken together, these attributes constitute the "powers" or displayed perfections of God, Who produces other things for His own glory and as clear witnesses to their divine source.

Yet the really decisive question is whether our human mind can discern these objective marks of God's character from our experience of the world. Calvin insists that no answer can be given without adverting to the fall of man, which the pagan philosophers did not know and which the Catholic Schoolmen did not correctly interpret. If Adam had stood firm in his original condition of rectitude of intellect, will, and passions, then man could easily have apprehended God's perfections in the mirror of His works. There would have been a sufficient proportion between the objective revelation in nature and the subjective illumination in our mind to assure a distinct and certain knowledge of what God the creator is in reference to creatures. But the sin of Adam deprived the human race of the soundness of mind and heart required for obtaining and preserving such knowledge. Man was the image of God in virtue of his original integrity. With the Fall, the image was vitiated and almost destroyed, leaving only a ruin and relic of itself. Man's intelligence was not annihilated, but it was corrupted to the point where its feeble sparks of instinctive knowledge of God were quickly and inevitably smothered by darkness and all but extinguished. In this depraved condition, it became impossible to acquire a clear and stable knowledge of God's nature and a meritorious religious relationship with Him from our experience of nature and our reasoning built thereon. The objective revelation of God in the world continued in full force, but men had forfeited the supernatural conditions which alone could enable them subjectively to perceive the divine features in this mirror.

A philosophy of God is not impossible either by reason of God's infinity or man's finitude; it is impossible by reason of historical man's sinfulness. By natural intellectual means, we cannot develop either our primal sense of deity or our reasoning from the experienced world into "any distinct, solid, or certain knowledge [*nihil certum, vel solidum, vel distinctum*]" of God.[21] This does not mean that fallen man ceases to search after evidence of God in the world or that he is fully aware of his predicament before the word of God is proposed to him. Calvin compares depraved mankind's situation to that of a traveler on a stormy night, when flashes of lightning momentarily illuminate the distant landscape but do not cast a steady beam on the path to his ultimate goal or reveal its precise shape. The sparks which our unaided mind can gather from God's works are radically incapable of constituting a clear and certain natural knowledge, either for the ordinary man or for the philosopher. The few glimmerings of truth about God which do come to us through experience are mingled with false conceptions, distorted by evil passions, and thereby rendered essentially unfit for development into a philosophy of God. Calvin is arguing not merely for the need of a supernatural revelation, but also for the impossibility of a natural, philosophical knowledge of God.

When one points to the great intellectual and cultural achievements of mankind as sign of the vitality of human intelligence, even apart from grace, Calvin counters with a distinction between earthly things and heavenly things. He readily acknowledges the competence of unredeemed intelligence in the liberal arts, the sciences and technologies, and social matters. This admission lends depth and suppleness to his description of the human condition, but it does not carry over into heavenly matters or a knowledge of God. In this sphere, Calvin frankly states that "men otherwise the most ingenious are blinder than moles. . . . In divine things it [the human mind] is altogether stupid and blind."[22] The stupidity and blindness of fallen man should not be understood in a purely passive sense, however, but as a dynamic, extremely fertile tendency to produce false and idolatrous conceptions of God. Both Montaigne and Francis Bacon were interested in the claim that the individual mind is a labyrinthine factory which ceaselessly manufactures idols and diverts worship away from the true God to its own phantoms. As evidence, Calvin adduces the attempts of philosophers to substitute chance, nature, and an immanent, cosmic mind for the transcendent God.

We have no eyes to perceive God's presence and shadow in created things until we are enlightened by faith. It is only through supernatural faith that we can truly recognize visible things to be indeed the traces and image of God the creator. Through the supernatural illumination of the Spirit, we are enabled to believe in the truth of God's word, as revealed in the Bible, and only then to understand the witness of His created works. Calvin ascribes a triple function to the Bible in regard to our knowledge of God the creator.[23] First, it focuses and stabilizes the scattered, fugitive impressions about God which we originally received in the sense of deity and our experience of visible things. Second, it not only unifies but also clarifies our natural intimations about the divine nature. It gives us a distinct and clear apprehension of the divine "powers" or manifested perfections, eliminating the distortions and uncertainties of natural speculation. Furthermore, the scriptural teaching on God the creator adds some special information which the visible works do not provide: that God is triune, that His providence is special as well as general, and that His production of the world is a genuine creation of spiritual as well as material being. Thus Holy Scripture supplies us with the indispensable spectacles for looking into the mirror of the world and also for seeing aspects of the divine nature about which the world remains silent.

The third function of faith in the word of God is perhaps the most important: to detach our mind from idols and turn it to the knowledge and worship of the true God. Only through biblically nourished faith can we surely know that the world is not ruled by chance, that nature is only the order established by the will of God, and that the transcendent God is utterly distinct from any cosmic mind or other idol of human philosophies. But just as man turns to idols out of pride in shaping his own view of things, so does the conversion away from idols depend upon overcoming our corrupted state and replacing pride with obedience to God's own testimony about Himself. This regenerating obedience is only possible, however, when we have faith in Christ as our mediator. By itself, acceptance of God the creator is worthless for salvation; it is a living faith only as an integral part of our acceptance of God the redeemer. Only then does man regain his status as an image of God and thereby acquire the light both to see and to follow God the creator.

Is there any room for a natural theology and a philosophy of God within Calvin's teaching? He himself does not provide a formal answer, but the indications are that there can be a distinctive sort of natural theology which is *not* a philosophy of God. If "natural" is taken in a purely objective sense, then provision is certainly made for the manifestation of God in visible nature and for a study of this revelation. Biblical theology does not consist only in a reading of the Bible but also in a Scripture-directed investigation of the natural world. But it is supernatural faith which provides the spectacles for reading God's presence in nature. There can be a theology or religious knowledge about nature, but it remains intrinsically dependent upon faith in the word of God and cannot develop properly from the natural light of human intelligence and the natural order of inference. A Calvinistic natural theology examines the evidence for God in the world by way of confirmation of what is already apprehended about Him from the Bible and owes its entire probative force to the presence of faith in the word of God.

In order to determine whether there can be a Calvinistic philosophy of God in any other sense, one must review the three modes of knowing God: instinct, reasoning from experience, and supernatural faith. The instinctive knowledge of God is severely restricted in its content, and in its mode it is a spontaneous conviction rather than a reasoned doctrine. Calvin refers to it as a seed of knowledge and religion, but he qualifies it as a seed which does not have the natural means to grow into a distinct and organized philosophical knowledge about God. The natural means would be provided by our reasoning from experience of the universe, but here the theological verdict intervenes to prevent any philosophical elaboration of the data. We human moles may snatch at an occasional beam of light, but it is the law of our sinful nature to distort the evidence through our own mental phantoms. With Calvin, it is not merely a historical fact but "a first principle, that as often as any form is assigned to God, his glory is corrupted by an impious lie."[24] Fallen man cannot develop in a philosophical way even the most modest body of permanent truths which demonstrates God's existence and properly distinguishes Him from the world of finite things.

Nor does the third mode of knowledge—that of supernatural faith—regenerate man in such a way that it permits him to work out a natural philosophy of God. Both in the original state of rectitude and in the regenerate state, the image of God in man is a supernatural light coming into our understanding from without. Faith is an illumination present *in* our mind, but even after its reception there is no natural light *of* the mind which can approach God through a philosophical method. The only use to which Calvin puts the instinctive knowledge and experiential intimations of God is a theological one: they have no further effect within his system than to render sinful men inexcusable in their idolatry and philosophical opinions.

Although he was well aware of the burgeoning skeptical movement in contemporary France and availed himself of the skeptical argument from the diversity of philosophical opinions, Calvin's position on the knowledge of God was a theologically inspired fideism, not a skeptically inspired one. He argued that if a saving faith brings about a total renovation of man, then the effect of the Fall must be to reduce him to a natural set of powers which cannot relate themselves permanently and distinctly to God. Hence he included in the definition of "the true and right knowledge of God" a formal submission to revelation and the Christian mode of worshiping God.[25] Anything falling short of this norm must be a confused, transient, and error-ridden glimpse, which cannot constitute a philosophical science. Through this purely theological mode of reasoning, Calvin (like Pascal a century later) fused the question of a speculatively valid knowledge of God and that of a salvific, heart-moving knowledge. Since the philosophers did not supply the latter, this was taken as grounds enough for ruling out any true, philosophical doctrine on God.

The conclusion that philosophical reasoning about God must result in contradictory and idolatrous views is not the result of a direct analysis of philosophies of God, however, but an inference from the theological premises supplied by Calvin's theory of the Fall and biblical faith. No allowance is made for such characteristically philosophical operations as self-criticism, methodological improvement, and a gradual elaboration of the sound kernel of truth about God obtained through experiential reasoning. To take these into account, one must break through Calvin's rigid theological barrier and make a direct examination of the philosophies of God in every period of human history.

3. BRUNO: A PHILOSOPHY OF GOD WITHOUT REVELATION

In the stormy course of his own life, Giordano Bruno (1548–1600) reflected the intellectual turbulence of the later Renaissance, the religious upheavals, and the scientific revolution still in the making. Starting as a Dominican friar, he left his order, as well as the Catholic church, wrote feverishly in Elizabethan England, pitted his new learning against the Aristotelianism of the Paris Arts Faculty, flirted ambiguously with Luther's Wittenberg and Calvin's Geneva, and returned to Italy, only to meet incarceration and a heretic's burning at the stake. His writings, like his life, showed a wild and rich exuberance, sometimes soaring in poetic flight, sometimes dissolving into incoherence, but never entirely obscuring the animating vision of the universe that gave them birth. Central to that vision was a conception of God's nature and man's bond with God in which Bruno broke with the Christian teaching and also outstripped the contemporary scientific standpoint. Although he was unable to feel at home in any intellectual climate of his day, he foreshadowed Spinoza in a remarkable way, giving classical expression to pantheism as a monism of substance and nature.

Bruno's loss of the Christian faith was not a passing incident but a decisive factor in shaping his philosophy of God. He did not seek to reformulate the meaning of supernatural faith or to reform its moral consequences but simply refused to give any assent to revelation as true (whether in Catholic or Protestant form) or to treat Christian morality as the way to human happiness. During his mature life, he was able to move along from one religious establishment to another only because he regarded none of them as bearers of the truth about God but only as components in civil society.[26] Similarly, he could claim that there was no conflict between his philosophy and Christian doctrines only because he regarded the former as the sole interpreter of truth. Bruno did not subscribe to the irenic thesis of two truths, one for theology and one for philosophy. On the contrary, he advocated a rigorously one-truth theory in which philosophy alone contains the clear, explicit knowledge about God, man, and nature. He saw in theology only a practical instrument for maintaining institutional Christianity and regulating public conduct, not a speculative and practical science based

on revealed truths. In this respect also, he anticipated the attitude of
Spinoza toward revelation and theology.

Bruno does mention the distinction between a supernatural light
and a natural light of the mind, but only to show that the former is both
irrelevant to philosophy and basically incompatible with it. He lays
down three canons for any would-be followers of his position: They
must be sufficiently reflective to distinguish between opinions received
through a supernatural faith and those based on the evidence of nature; they must construct a philosophy entirely from the light of their
own mind and from nature; they must have the courage to criticize
famous philosophical authorities.[27] The first two rules are directed
against the Christian theologians and the third against their chief ally,
Aristotle. Bruno is not simply pleading that philosophy be permitted
to develop in accordance with its own proper evidence and methods;
he is sealing it off from any kind of influence from revelation and is
treating the latter as essentially antagonistic toward reason and philosophy. This attitude separates Bruno definitively from Cusanus, despite
a heavy debt to his German predecessor on many points. He cannot
admit with Cusanus that revelation is either relevant to philosophy or
has a reasonable content of its own. Still less can Bruno agree with
Calvin that the scriptural interpretation of nature is the decisive one
for learning about God or that the rational study of God must be intrinsically conditioned by the light of faith. What forces him to oppose
Cusanus and Calvin concerning the bearing of faith upon philosophical reason is their clear and firm adherence to the Judaeo-Christian
testimony to a transcendent God. Fundamentally, it is not the autonomy of philosophy but his own monism of substance which dictates
Bruno's opposition to any revealed truth and any influence of faith
upon reason.

Bruno's primary aim is to close philosophy off from revelation in
such a way that it will be totally enclosed in nature, conceived precisely
as a unique, divine substance having a multiformity of finite modes or
circumstances. By definition, the philosopher who meets Bruno's requirements cannot accept anything contradicting this conception of
nature. Hence he must regard a supernatural light of faith and its
object as being not only empty but also impossible. Thus the capital
difference between a theologian and a philosopher is that the latter
recognizes no transcendent creator or first principle which is distinct
in being from the infinite universe itself. When Bruno emphasizes that
he speaks as "a mere philosopher of nature," he means that his first
negative principle is to regard a free, transcendent creator and a world
of many finite substances as incompatible with the order of natural
being and the evidence of our knowing powers.[28]

On the positive side, Bruno's philosophy treats of God, the "principle and cause, in so far as it is either nature itself, or in so far as it reveals itself to us in the extent and lap of that nature."[29] God is one with substantial nature. The only kind of revelation permitted for such a God is a natural one: The divine principle-and-cause is manifested in and through the accidents and appearances which comprise our field of experience. There is no real, substantial transcendence of God to sensible nature, but there is an endless progress of human intelligence and love toward the infinite substance of nature itself. Like Cusanus and Calvin, Bruno has an unknown and ineffable God. But his God is unknown not in virtue of His infinite actuality and real transcendence of the universe, but in virtue of the immensity of the universe itself and the relative disproportion between it and the human way of knowing and loving. Bruno's outlook rests upon an intense act of natural faith in the infinity of the universe and its identification with God as expressed in his poem *Of Love.*

> Cause, Principle, and One eternal
> From whom being, life, and movement are suspended,
> And which extends itself in length, breadth, and depth,
> To whatever is in Heaven, on Earth and Hell;
> With sense, with reason, with mind, I discern,
> That there is no act, measure, nor calculation, which can comprehend
> That force, that vastness, and that number. . . .
> Crude heart, perverse spirit, insane audacity,
> Will not be sufficient to obscure the air for me,
> Will not place the veil before my eyes,
> Will never bring it about that I shall not
> Contemplate my beautiful Sun.[30]

He displays a passionate love for the immensity and divinity of living nature, upon which he bestows all the devotion and exaltation of a religious temperament.

Bruno's transitional position between Renaissance humanism and the modern scientific era is well illustrated by the two sorts of argument he uses to defend the infinity of the universe. He makes a traditional appeal to the divine attribute of power in order to establish the point in a deductive way. If God's power as a cause is infinite and determined by His infinitely perfect nature, then the effect of that power must also be infinite. Those who deny the infinity of the universe are also denying the infinity of God as the infinitely powerful first cause. Nevertheless, Bruno strikes a modern note by appealing to the research of Copernicus as scientific corroboration of his view of the infinite cosmos. This appeal does not take the form of a circumstantial study of the methods and findings of astronomy, however, but is an analogy leading to a new sort of imagery about the universe. In point of fact, the Brunonian vision of an infinite universe containing innumerable living worlds moves far beyond the very large but still finite universe of Copernicus. Bruno is unique in having his imagination set ablaze by the nascent

modern cosmology even in the period before the discovery of the telescope aroused an image of countless worlds and vanishing borders in
the minds of Donne, Milton, and other seventeenth-century poets.[31]

What the Copernican theory actually suggested to him is the possibility of expanding the revision of our ordinary sense-based notions
about place and motion into a full-blown criticism of the "finite horizon" presented by the senses. If we are mistaken about the relation between the sun and the earth, then perhaps we are mistaken about the
entire universe in which we live. Perhaps ours is a boundless universe,
animated by a single substantial world-soul, which achieves harmony
out of the conflicting tendencies of finite worlds and forces. Bruno
transforms this surmise into the new creed of his life, exclaiming that
the vision of infinite unity enchants his mind and liberates his heart
from the petty fear of death and earthly trials. Henceforth, the philosophy of the infinite universe replaces Christianity, for him, as the sole
way of salvation and happiness. Unlike Locke and the later empiricists,
who require only that a scientifically inspired philosophy make them
reasonably content with the present life, Bruno demands that his philosophy render him beatific and satisfy all his contemplative and passional aspirations.

Not only the theological outlook but also the Aristotelian philosophy
of nature stood in the way of this project. Whereas Cusanus and Erasmus retained a Christian theism amid their most fierce assaults upon
Aristotelian natural philosophy, Bruno's attack was motivated not by
Christian piety, and not even primarily by the new scientific findings,
but by his own monistic metaphysics and ethics. He set out to show that
Aristotle misconceives the nature of being and hence fails to achieve a
metaphysical wisdom. The chief lesson he wanted to be drawn from
the polemic was that in view of this metaphysical failure, Aristotle's
explanation of the natural world presents no invincible case against
the monism of substance.

Bruno did not lunge out indiscriminately against Aristotle but explicitly praised him for distinguishing metaphysics from logic. In this
respect, Bruno preferred Aristotle himself to the self-styled Peripatetics
at Oxford and Paris who were drowning the search for reality in an
ocean of grandiloquence and nominal distinctions. The Stagirite was
also sound in moving beyond particular physical explanations to a general metaphysical theory of the real. In the course of his metaphysical inquiry, however, he lost sight of the clue provided by earlier Greek
philosophers of nature, namely, that the material and formal principles are strictly and universally correlative in the constitution of being. Aristotle failed to see that just as matter is one, eternal, and ingenerable, so must the substantial form of the universe also be really
one, eternal, and ingenerable.

The only substantial principle which Bruno concedes Aristotle to have understood is the material one.[32] Although the Greek master wrote a good deal about substantial forms, the forms in question are only accidental ones. For the so-called substantial forms of Peripatetic philosophy are always defined in terms of operations and particular determinations of matter, that is, they are given only an accidental content. Bruno interprets the Aristotelian remark that the ultimate substantial differences are hidden from us as being equivalent to a confession of absolute agnosticism about the real nature of the formal substance of things. In that case, however, that which Aristotle calls the substantial form is only a logical construct and is incapable of supplying a real solution to the problems of diversity and change. Bruno grants that there are many forms and that they undergo constant change, but these forms are accidental and so are their changes. There are not many particular substances, only the one universal substance present in many particulars. The particular things of our sense experience are modes, appearances, or circumstances of the one cosmic substance or matter-form whole. Hence there are no substantial changes. All real changes are modal alterations "on the back" or surface of this single substantial entity. Since Aristotle misunderstands so radically the true nature of substance, diversity, and change, his philosophy cannot be expected to yield the truth about God.

Lest it be answered that Aristotelian metaphysics may succeed where its philosophy of nature fails, Bruno teaches the essential dependence of the former discipline upon the latter. In this contention he can appeal to some of the contemporary Schoolmen and their founding of the theory of God upon the Aristotelian philosophy of nature. Although he does not follow Plotinus in placing unity beyond being, he does agree that a knowledge of unity is the criterion of metaphysical truth. We approach the proper meaning of being and essence in the precise proportion that we understand the unicity of substance and the indivisibility of the matter-form whole of nature. The consequence of this criterion of metaphysical wisdom is that "Aristotle, among others, who did not find unity, did not find being, and did not find the truth, because he did not recognize being as one."[33] The Greek philosopher used the term "being" a great deal, but it is empty of the truth about the unique substance of nature and hence cannot rightfully regulate our judgments about nature and the ethical life. To know being in its metaphysical truth is to know that there is but one substance in the universe and that matter and form are its necessary universal aspects.

Bruno is willing to tolerate as many different ways of philosophizing as there are ways of dealing with matter and form, just as long as they do not unsettle this primary truth. Every legitimate *via philosophandi* must admit that matter is divine or an aspect of the cosmic substance and must promote the human contemplation of truth by being reducible in principle to Bruno's own conception of nature. His philosophical toleration draws the line at a pluralism of individual souls, in the Christian sense. There is one substantial form or soul of the universe, and all individual forms or souls are its particular modes and accidental appearances.

Bruno does not criticize the Aristotelians precisely for founding their metaphysics upon the philosophy of nature but for founding it upon an erroneous philosophy of nature. He himself now makes the attempt to absolutize his own philosophy of nature or convert it into a metaphysics. This conversion can be made if it can be shown that matter and form (the principles of explanation in natural philosophy) are also the principles for explaining being in general. The crucial test is provided by showing whether or not they apply to God. Having removed the speculative objections based upon revelation and substantial pluralism, Bruno now makes a final reduction of the great union of matter and form. They are not two distinct substances but are aspects of a single substance. They have their common root in the universal substance of God, from whom they are only logically distinct.[34] The selfsame divine substance can be considered now as the fertile subject or material womb of all modal things and now as the informing soul and active design in nature. God is both matter and form, subject and soul or mind, potency and act, all in their purest condition of identity. There is no higher being or principle than the totality of nature; hence a philosophy of nature is also the only legitimate sort of metaphysics. To know the matter-form substance is to have an essential knowledge of God, even though there is still endless progress to be made with respect to His particular manifestations in nature and human history.

What seems to have driven Bruno to absolutize the philosophy of nature into a metaphysical monism is his quest for a knowledge of God that is more strictly demonstrative than the inferences of the Aristotelian philosophers, whether Arabian or Christian. His main objection against the Aristotelians is that they make God a very remote cause and transform finite things into independently existing substances, which are only accidentally dependent on God.[35] On this twofold basis, one cannot make a strict proof about God. Bruno's own remedy is not to give the metaphysical inference to God a distinctive foundation in experience but rather to modify the philosophy of nature in such manner that it yields a demonstrative knowledge of God. He performs this task by regarding all finite things as modal appearances and expressions of the infinite cause, which is also the internal substantial principle of the universe. This removes the remoteness of the divine causality, which is now identified with the internal formal principle of all things, and also removes the quasi-independence of finite things, which are not substantial existents but modes of the one divine substance. A direct and necessary inference to God can thus be made from our knowledge of matter and form, so that philosophy of nature is made not only more rigorous but actually identical with metaphysics. St. Thomas had said that if there is no substance except that of changing, sensible nature, then natural philosophy is also first philosophy or metaphysics. Bruno affirms the antecedent of this conditional proposition through his theory of matter and form and so concludes that the only metaphysical route to God lies through the monism of natural substance.

Bruno's relation with Cusanus must be viewed against the background of his claim to have an essential, demonstrative knowledge of God as the immanent nature of things. Although the philosopher of Nola borrows many leading concepts from Cusanus, he transforms them by having them yield essential knowledge about God. He castigates Cusanus for relying too heavily upon "mathematical fantasies," since the method of mathematical symbolism does not yield demonstrative knowledge of the divine being itself.[36] Bruno himself uses geometrical and physical examples to illustrate how everything is in all and how all is one. But, for him, they are only ancillary signs and verifications of an already established metaphysical truth about God, not its generative source. It is the literal, univocal doctrine of cosmic matter and form, not the dialectic of mathematical limits, which is the constitutive principle of Brunonian pantheism. God is not so unknown in His essential principles that we must found the philosophy of God upon faith and a dialectic of limits, which yields only a symbolical approximation to His nature. Bruno announces the modern rationalist thesis that to know the truth about God is to know His essential principles of being. And he has the intellectual penetration to see that this thesis can ultimately be sustained only by removing any substantial distinction between God and nature.

This does not prevent Bruno from exploiting Cusanus in order to maintain some sort of distinction between God and the modal things, as long as it is not of a substantial kind.[37] The divine infinity is intensive, comprehensive, and simple, whereas the infinity of events in the universe is unfolded, developing, and dispersed among many finite modes. Again, God as substantial form can be viewed either as the immanent principle and soul of the universe or as its external cause and intellectual force. But, at the summit of infinity, the distinction between principle and cause is only a logical, perspectival one. It does not rest upon any real and substantial otherness between God and modal appearances, so the externality of God as cause is only a relative distinction. The selfsame divine substance, in its formal aspect, is the constitutive principle, efficient cause, and final goal of its various modal expressions. Whereas Cusanus qualifies all of his propositions about God as symbolical statements pertaining primarily to our use of the divine names, Bruno founds all of his theological propositions upon his claim to have essential insight into the structure of matter and form and thus into the divine nature itself. Within this context, it is a definitive truth that God is the only substantial being and hence that all our philosophical ways of distinguishing between the divine infinity and the experienced universe are only logical distinctions, as far as His substantial nature and existence are concerned.

At the end of his chief work, *Concerning the Cause, Principle, and One* (1584), Bruno appeals to certain features of man's intellectual and moral activities as crowning proof of his pantheistic monism.[38] The intellect is our highest cognitive power, being superior to both sense and sense-bound reason. As Cusanus had already noted, the two latter powers remain fascinated by the finiteness and diversity of things, whereas the intellect reduces everything complex to the simplicity of one, underlying essence. The simplifying and reductive operation expresses the native conviction of our mind that there is a single, infinite substance beneath the multiplicity of finite circumstances. It is the very same ladder by which the divine mind or first cause descends in constituting the universe of diverse finite modes and by which the human intellect ascends in gaining its knowledge of things as a substantial unity. In the moral order as well, we find our true happiness in contemplating the universe as a divine whole. We overcome the fear of death when we reflect upon the indestructible, eternal nature of the infinite aspects of matter and form or mind. Our very contemplation of the unique, divine substance is a form of love for the One. Like Actaeon in the Greek myth, we are transformed into the object of our hunt, reconciling ourselves to all natural events as divine manifestations and soaring to the beautiful Sun of our desire.

Both the noetic and the moral sides of this argument presuppose that there is some independently known evidence for the monistic position.[39] For there is no cogent basis for arguing directly from certain aspects of our human way of thinking to the constitution of all being, unless we are already convinced by other considerations that the human mind is a determinate mode and appearance of the immanent, divine mind. This rationalistic mode of arguing from our thinking to real being is not justified by Bruno on epistemological grounds but depends on a prior metaphysics of form and matter, since intellect or the highest degree of knowledge coincides, by definition, with taking a monistic view of diversity and change. However, a purely descriptive approach to human cognition recognizes the discrepancy between our simplifications or models and the highly complex realities which they are meant to help us know in some inadequate way. Our simplifying constructs do not necessarily imply that the real universe is a simple substance but only that these constructs are a convenient means for representing and using certain chosen aspects. We do have an intellectual tendency toward unity, but it need not be interpreted in terms of Bruno's facile image of the two-way ladder of the divine cause and the reflective return of a finite mode to its substantial foundation. Indeed, the intellectual search for unity must always reckon with the consideration that the kind of causal relation between God and ourselves determines the kind of unity which is present. The causal basis of our intellectual inference to God can bring out evidence for not reducing everything to a unity of substance and its modes, as well as for not treating matter and form as aspects of the divine being. To regard finite things as substantial beings need not destroy the basis for a demonstration of God's existence. It does so within Bruno's system only because he equates substance with self-sufficient existence and because he subordinates existence itself to matter and form.

Whether or not the monism of substance satisfies our moral and religious needs depends, at least in some measure, on how these needs are being met. To still the anxiety over death by pointing to the eternity of infinite form or mind does not deal pertinently with the desire for a personal sharing in eternal life or with personal concern over the quality of one's moral actions. The lover of God seeks a share in the divine life, yet there is a capital difference between obtaining it by dissolving into an appearance of that life and by entering into a personal relationship in which the finite individual's integrity and responsibility are maintained. The God who is a free creator does not engage human persons in the same way that the necessarily acting, universal substance engages its modes, and yet Bruno does not make a comparative study of the differences.

Out of the clash between the representative minds of the Renaissance period there emerged no stable and comprehensive philosophy of God. The extreme positions of Luther and Bruno gave no encouragement to any new integration of faith and reason but suggested instead that the two must stand pitted against each other in all questions involving the divine nature and the world's relation to God. Cusanus and Calvin were more convinced of the intelligible character of revelation and its positive contribution to rational speculation about God. But Cusanus, on mathematico-philosophical grounds, and Calvin, on the theological basis of original sin, called in doubt the human mind's intrinsic ability to acquire any distinctive philosophical knowledge about God. From these conflicts came the seeds for three of the abiding tendencies in modern philosophies of God: philosophical skepticism, fideism, and rationalism. Especially toward the end of the sixteenth century, it seemed to many perspicacious men that the only way to avoid the nature-pantheism of a Bruno and still retain some certainty about God was to base all speculation about Him upon faith and the content of Scripture. When to this predisposition toward fideism was added the new awareness of epistemological difficulties surrounding our ordinary modes of knowledge, skepticism, in its Christian and unbelieving forms, spread rapidly as one dominant attitude toward the philosophical approach to God. By way of challenge, however, this position was bound to provoke the alternative of investigating the problem of God without any sort of reference to revelation but along the lines of either a theistic or a pantheistic rationalism.

Thus the modern philosophical study of God was ushered in by the portentous split between fideism and rationalism, between a faith which had lost confidence in the intellect's competence to learn something about God through philosophical principles and order of demonstration and a reason which had come to regard revelation as an irrelevant or perverting factor in this philosophical work. No impetus toward overcoming this split came through effectively from the descendants of the medieval Schoolmen, who, involved in their own difficulties, were becoming increasingly less responsive to the specific needs of the modern mind as it began philosophizing about God.

Chapter II

THE SKEPTICAL ASSAULT UPON
KNOWLEDGE OF GOD

WE WOULD be historically shortsighted to try to build a direct highway from the various Renaissance theories of God to the great speculative systems of the seventeenth century. Far from being a smooth and continuous transition, the passage from the Renaissance to the modern world was pock-marked by the deep craters of skeptical criticism. Only against the background of the skeptical contention that certain and universally valid knowledge about real beings is unattainable by the natural human mind can the rationalism and empiricism of the seventeenth century be properly understood. These latter movements were definite responses to the challenge of skepticism. Each, in its own way, attempted a reconstruction of knowledge that would successfully answer the skeptical doubt. Without some examination of the depth and extent of skeptical negation, we cannot appreciate the context and motivation behind the several modern affirmations of the mind's ability to know, as well as the significant qualifications placed upon such claims.[1]

For our own study of the problem of God, such reference to the skeptical outlook is indispensable. Clearly enough, a philosophically acceptable body of knowledge about God would undermine the case for skepticism. Hence the skeptical writers singled out this area, where the human mind has always made stubborn claims to have some respectable knowledge, for their special criticism. They also probed the philosophical relations between a doctrine on God and the questions of sensation, immortality, and the basis of morality. It is historically illuminating to consider this special cluster of problems as associated with the skeptical analysis of knowledge of God. This association helps to explain how the rationalists and empiricists viewed the connections between God and human nature. The way in which skepticism posed the problem of God deeply affected the role of God in the modern systems of philosophy.

As a major intellectual force in the formation of the modern mind, the span of skeptical thought extends from about 1575 (when Montaigne was reading the Greek skeptics) to 1706 (the death of Bayle). Of

30

course, its roots reached back into earlier years, and its effects continued to be felt long after the end of the seventeenth century and far beyond the confines of French culture. But as a distinctive and relatively cohesive movement, its strongest impact was made by a succession of French thinkers during these 130 years. Its development can be divided roughly into two main phases: the humanistic and the anti-Cartesian. The first period marked the restatement of Greek skepticism in humanist, religious, and anti-Scholastic terms by Montaigne and Charron. In its second phase, skepticism had to take account of the growth of modern science and Cartesian rationalism. Gassendi and Huet were representative spokesmen for this aspect of skeptical criticism. The lasting results of the whole movement were finally consolidated by Bayle, who provided the Enlightenment with a critical method in its campaign against traditional religious and social institutions.

1. THE REVIVAL OF CLASSICAL SKEPTICISM

It is a purely romantic and one-sided view of the Renaissance that we get when we regard it simply as an untroubled and joyous acceptance of the world, a sheer glorification of man and his powers. There were some tendencies in this direction during the earlier, Italian period. But among the humanists and philosophers of the later Renaissance, especially in France, less confident attitudes about man and his role in the cosmos were voiced. Lyrical praise of human dignity and abilities began to seem a little foolish in view of the very grim actualities of human existence. There was a dawning suspicion that man may not be endowed with such wondrous faculties, seeing that he gives himself with such enthusiasm to superstitious and inhumane practices.

Three well-defined trends in Renaissance thought seem to have prepared the soil for a reception of skepticism: the general criticism of tradition, the failure of the new philosophies, and the renewed study of ancient philosophical sources. The first of these factors characterized the transitional Renaissance age, which witnessed revolutionary changes in the social, political, religious, and scientific spheres. Despite the many solid links with the medieval past, which are continually being uncovered by modern historical scholarship, there were also many genuine repudiations of previous convictions in these areas. The question of how far negative criticism should go and where reconstructive work ought to begin was inevitably raised. Some sort of rock bottom was eventually found, at least temporarily, in such positive rallying points as the national state, the Bible, and the new mechanical physics. But in philosophy it was not so easy to call a halt to the doubting process. If past beliefs and institutions were so false and enslaving—

and yet won the firm adherence of generations of intelligent men—then how could we ever trust our mind and its claims to truth? Skepticism provided the downright answer that we should forego all attempts to reach speculative truth and concentrate our energies upon practical issues and probable rules.

This suggestion received additional support from the failure of the Renaissance philosophers to construct stable world views of their own. They found it easier to tear down the Scholastic edifice than to build livable mansions of their own. And in actual practice, they had to use many carefully disguised methods, principles, and concepts of Scholasticism, but without providing a reliable criterion for sorting out the sound timbers from the rotten. They gave no guarantee that reason and the senses would not deceive people once more. Hence in an age of little philosophies, which were basically uncritical and unable to give a comprehensive account of human experience, skepticism appeared to be the only prudent position for thoughtful men to adopt.

Direct encouragement in this path came from the Renaissance interest in ancient Greek and Roman philosophers. An integral recovery of these sources could not avoid inclusion of the classical skeptical school, which flourished from about the beginning of the third century B.C. to the end of the second century A.D. There were two main varieties of Greek skeptical thought: the Pyrrhonian and the Academic (which the modern followers usually referred to, respectively, as the Skeptics and the Academics). Pyrrhonism took its name from Pyrrho of Elis, who advised men to distrust their cognitive powers, quiet their passions, and thus attain a peaceful life. The New Platonic Academy, under Arcesilas and Carneades, positively denied the possibility of our attaining any knowledge and truth. It made a frontal attack upon the Stoic doctrines about God, providence, and virtue. Instead of strict knowledge, the Academics held for a theory of probability and consistency among our ideas. The last of the Greek skeptics was Sextus Empiricus, who was also the historian of the entire movement.[2] Except for some references in philosophers of other schools, most of our information about Greek skepticism comes from Sextus. He himself professed a radical Pyrrhonism, in which the mind suspends its judgment about knowledge and does not even risk the outright denial advocated by the Academics. But in his surviving works, *Outlines of Pyrrhonism* and *Against the Professors of the Sciences*, he faithfully recorded the arguments of all the spokesmen of skepticism.

These two works were translated into Latin in 1562 and 1569, and a standard Greek-Latin edition was issued in 1621.[3] The books appealed to a wide range of readers, who found here an arsenal of arguments and, above all, a comprehensive and workable attitude toward life. Indeed, Sextus stressed that skepticism is not so much a theoretical doctrine as a way of life and a practical ability of the mind. There are two sources from which the skeptical attitude springs: a psychological one and a logical one.[4] Its psychological principle is the unquenchable hope of all men for mental contentment or tranquillity of soul. The skeptical interpretation of this yearning is that men want peace of mind at any price. Since the claim to have objective truth about the being of things and the norm of human conduct leads unavoidably to disputes and warfare, the prudent man must renounce this fatal claim. His mental peace will come as soon as he has given up the pretense to any metaphysical and moral knowledge. But this great pearl must be defended by the logical principle of equipollence, which is a deliberate technique of balancing any given proposition against its contradictory opposite. Instead of making a direct test of the validity of any suggested proposition, the skeptical mind concentrates upon placing this proposition in antithetic relation with another one. In this way, all propositions are treated as equally probable and improbable, so that the mind is prevented from giving its firm assent to any statement about reality. Through this deliberately induced suspension of judgment, the skeptic is in the enviable position of having his cake and eating it too: He continues the search after truth, but in any given instance he withholds assent and enjoys his tranquillity of mind as a sovereign good.

The general policy of canceling out every truth-claim through equipollence is developed in detail in the famous skeptical tropes.[5] They are the typical arguments or ways of setting up a contradictory relationship between the various convictions of ordinary people and philosophers. What is significant for the problem of God is that these tropes underline the weakness and contradictory testimony of the senses. The twofold implication is that the senses do not apprehend real being and that the understanding, which is dependent upon the data of the senses, is similarly incapable of learning anything about real beings through any sense-based speculative proofs. This would eliminate any empirically grounded proofs of God's existence. In the practical order, the diversity of moral standards and religious customs is employed to undermine confidence in any universally valid moral and religious truths.

Underlying the entire skeptical attitude is the assumption that we can know only the appearances in our own mind, not the real being of things. More strictly expressed, the Pyrrhonist contention is that one can neither deny nor affirm any knowledge of the transphenomenal realm of being. All that one can be sure of is knowledge of the "appearances," i.e., the subjective perceptions or states of mind and their attendant feelings. The skeptic's favorite example is that he will readily admit that snow *seems* white and feels uncomfortable to him, but he will not rashly add that it *is* white and cold in its own intimate nature. The only "things" admitted into the skeptical outlook are these subjective sense appearances. Rational concepts and judgments about real existents and essential natures distinct from one's own sense impressions and feelings can never be substantiated within the context of skepticism, despite the formal reluctance of the Pyrrhonists to make a definite negation.

In order to understand the skeptical position on God, one further consequence must be drawn from this radical phenomenalism. It concerns the nature of evidence and proof.[6] There is an unbridgeable chasm between what is pre-evident and what is nonevident. Prior to all reasoning, the sense appearances are evident to us, and they alone are evident. They require no rational proof but only careful descriptive analysis. Our private impressions and feelings constitute a self-contained area, sealed off definitively from the presumed field of nonevident things or real extramental beings. No intellectual effort can enlarge the sphere of evidence to include beings that were originally nonevident, since there are no discoverable connections between our perceptions and a distinct real world. Hence scientific inquiry cannot obtain even mediate evidence for its objects: Demonstrative proof of real beings distinct from our own states of awareness is beyond the capacity of the human mind. Sextus likens the attempts at strict proof to an archery contest: Some shafts may hit the target, but we can never determine with certainty which arrows do, in fact, hit it and which miss their mark. On this vital issue of the impossibility of demonstration, he oversteps the attitude of neutral suspense of judgment and effectively rules out existential proof.

Given these general premises, it is not difficult to predict the position which Sextus will take toward God. His personal standpoint is neither antireligious nor antitheistic but is a sort of speculative agnosticism. In the practical order, he readily admits that the skeptic can consistently believe in God's existence and join in religious worship. This admission cheered the hearts of modern fideists like Charron and Huet, who wanted to combine skepticism in the speculative order with practical faith in God. Even in speculative matters, however, Sextus does not intend to deny God's existence and human knowledge thereof but only to preserve the skeptical suspension of judgment. Unlike Herbert Spencer and modern agnostics, Sextus is not especially or exclusively agnostic about God. He is merely applying here his universal principle of refraining from giving any sort of judgment concerning the world beyond appearances. But in the actual course of discussion, he finds it difficult to maintain this nice balance of studied noncommitment.

The analysis is carried out in two stages: the origin of our notion of God and the validity of proofs for and against God's existence.[7] The former is a psychological question, the latter a metaphysical one, although both fall within what the Stoics called physics, or philosophy of nature. It is noteworthy that Sextus himself gives the primacy to the metaphysical issue. Hence he does not anticipate the evolutionary view of Marx and Nietzsche, who regard the question of God's existence as being settled in the negative once we show the genesis of the idea of God.

In point of fact, Sextus is highly critical of all the current psychological explanations. He calls attention to their mutual disagreement, deeming this a sign that we can obtain no certainty in the matter one way or the other. He is especially severe with the view that the gods are social myths invented by shrewd lawgivers to give special sanction and authority to their ordinances. Sextus asks where the lawgivers got their own conception of God or the gods or the divine nature (terms which he uses interchangeably) and how they could count upon a response of reverence and fear from the populace. Similarly, the theory of Euhemerus the Atheist that gods are only self-divinized men is open to the criticism that this presupposes some common and widely accepted notion of divinity. As for the Epicurean account that gods are made in the image of happy and wise men, the question arises: Why does this projection of desirable human qualities not result merely in giant men instead of gods? Behind the anthropomorphic explanation lies an implicit recognition that certain perfections belong properly to the gods, and indeed belong to them in a different way than to even the most fortunate of men. Still, Sextus is not convinced by the Aristotelian comparison of the prime mover to a general whose army is the orderly firmament. This is a loose comparison and again presupposes something about the divine.

In turning to the metaphysical question of whether God really exists, Sextus sharply narrows down the scope of his inquiry. Instead of reviewing all the major Greek positions, as he does in the psychological question, he confines himself to an examination of the Stoic arguments, which were the most popular in his day.

Stoicism offers four main proofs: from common consent, from universal order, from the absurd consequences of atheism, and from direct refutation of atheistic arguments. The first point is that practically everyone agrees on the existence of God, on His nature as imperishable and perfectly happy, and on the obligation of men to worship Him. This common core of conviction remains, despite the great variations concerning God's secondary attributes and the proper way to honor Him. The special form in which Sextus presents the proof from cosmic order emphasizes the Stoic origin of these arguments. The matter of the universe is motionless and shapeless in itself; but experience reveals a world of orderly motion and definitely shaped bodies; hence there must be a universal mover, or shaper, which permeates the matter of the universe as a world soul, just as the individual soul informs the human body. This is a proof for an immanent cosmic soul, not a proof for a transcendent God. The third argument states that a denial of God would overturn all the virtues and hence would render personal and social life intolerable. The Stoic definitions of justice, wisdom, holiness, and other virtues are so framed that they include a reference to the divine nature in their meaning. In the final proof, an attempt is made to meet the atheistic objections, such as the one which maintains that God has only an ideal existence, like the notoriously non-existent Stoic sage.

Most of the counterarguments marshaled by Sextus depended upon the very low estimate which pre-Christian Greek philosophers generally placed upon infinity and incorporeality. They did not consider these to be perfections of actual being but defects. Infinity meant inchoate being and vague lack of a determinate nature, while incorporeality meant wraithlike absence of the organic basis for action. Consequently, if God were unlimited and without a body, He would also be inanimate and incapable of action. The unspoken assumption here was that life and active power are always bound up with a limited, organic body. Because of Christian developments in philosophy and theology, this line of attack had lost its original vigor by the sixteenth century, but another argument based on the nature of virtue retained its attractiveness. If God is endowed with all virtues, then He must be subject to their intrinsic conditions. He cannot possess the virtue of fortitude, for instance, without having the capacity for change and hence for corruption of His being. And if wisdom is a knowledge of things good and evil, then God cannot be wise without being directly affected by suffering and evil. Like Whitehead, Brightman, and other present-day proponents of a finite, receptive aspect in God, these sources denied that evil can be known except experientially or through an actual undergoing of suffering and limitation.

Sextus himself announces that the conflicting arguments lead to a stalemate, obliging him to conclude that the question of God's existence is an undecidable one. He presents two positive considerations to reinforce the skeptical suspension of judgment on this issue.

(1) The existence of God is nonevident, for if it were pre-evident, philosophers would not dispute about it. Yet the nonevident existence of God cannot be demonstrated from some other fact, taken as a starting point of inference. The skeptical theory of evidence precludes any demonstration of the nonevident beings that are distinct from our own perceptions. If the starting point of a proposed demonstration were itself pre-evident, then the existence of God would also have to be pre-evident, since the only valid movement of theoretical reason is in the

precise description of what is already evident prior to every attempt at inference. But if God's existence were pre-evident by inclusion within an evidential fact, no demonstration would be required and no controversy would be possible. If the point of departure for a demonstration were nonevident, it would remain unredeemably so and would prevent any inference to God from being validly grounded in such a basis of proof.

(2) Sextus next asks whether divine providence and governance of the universe are known to exist. The three possibilities are that God exercises foreknowledge and government in respect to all things, some things, or none at all. Universal providence is hastily ruled out by Sextus as being incompatible with the presence of any evil in the universe. Partial providence raises the question of why God cares only for some things and not for all. If He had both the will and the power for universal providence, He would care for all things, but the presence of evil eliminates this solution. If He had the will but not the power, He would be weaker than the evil principle; if He had the power but not the will, He would be malignant; if He had neither the will nor the power, He would be both a weak and a malignant being. Sextus presumably would not respond with much enthusiasm to William James' picture of a limited, struggling deity who needs our manly help to make the good principle prevail. Instead of accepting this hypothesis, he simply concludes that the third position is most reasonable, namely, that as far as we can discern, God has no providential concern for the universe.

What makes this dialectical argument interesting for modern readers is that Sextus (unlike Bayle and Voltaire) does not regard it primarily as a moral problem of the relation between a good God and evil in the world. He simply assumes, without argument, that the reality of evil is incompatible with God's universal providence. His proper concern is to use the analysis of divine providence as an epistemological support for the skeptical position on the unknowability of God. "But if He exercises no forethought for anything, and there exists no work nor product of His, no one will be able to name the source of the apprehension of God's existence, inasmuch as He neither appears of Himself nor is apprehended by means of any of His products."[8] If God has no foreknowledge of the universe, then the latter does not bear a likeness to Him which can be discovered by the human mind and used as the foundation for a rational demonstration of His existence. God's existence is nonevident in itself (Argument 1), and there is no ground in other things for reaching His existence by inference (Argument 2).

It is doubtful whether Sextus has remained within the limits of the Pyrrhonian suspension of judgment. His reasoning leads to an outright denial of the possibility of knowing God's existence, whatever his retrospective disavowal of making any negative commitments. It is difficult to keep Pyrrhonism from converting itself into Academic skepticism without weakening the analysis itself. The whole argument rests upon the phenomenalistic theory of evidence and the object of knowledge, and when this theory is consistently followed, it leads to a definite rejection of the possibility of making a valid demonstration of God's existence.

The phenomenalism of the Greek skeptics was fostered by the inadequacy of the Stoic and Epicurean theories of knowledge. The skeptics generalized upon the inability of these theories to explain the genesis of general concepts and their reference to real things, concluding that there is no knowledge beyond the immediate evidence of sense appearances. But one of the challenging questions raised by the modern revival of skepticism was whether some other view of evidence and the object of knowledge is not possible under different historical and speculative conditions. The initiators of the rationalist and empiricist movements were convinced that the problem of phenomenalism should be reopened in a fresh way, not merely repeated in antique terms, as was the tendency of most latter-day skeptics.

Sextus Empiricus was not the only classical source of the Renaissance skeptical attitude toward God. Pliny's *Natural History,* Lucian's *Dialogues,* and Plutarch's treatises on oracles and Egyptian deities raised many doubts about the existence of God, providence, religious worship, and the immortality of the human soul. In Lucretius' great poem *On the Nature of Things,* Renaissance readers found an atomistic world-outlook from which God and immortality were excluded. But above all, Cicero fostered a skeptical frame of mind through his *On the Nature of the Gods* and *On Divination.* Cicero, an Academic skeptic, developed with great literary skill the technique of equipollence in order to determine the more probable position on a question. He used the dialogue form to expose the weaknesses in the Stoic and Epicurean natural theologies. Montaigne and others were quick to notice the superior logic displayed by the dialogue's spokesman for skepticism as he refuted the arguments for God's existence based on common consent and the order of the universe. Elsewhere, Cicero asserted his personal belief in God, immortality, and a socially useful religion. But what impressed itself most deeply upon the imagination of many a humanist was the closing remark of the skeptical protagonist in *On the Nature of the Gods:* "My words were spoken, not to destroy belief, but to give you some conception of the obscurity of the whole matter [about God's existence and essential nature] and of the difficulties involved in any attempt to explain it."[9] To maintain that speculative certainty on this issue is beyond our reach and yet that practical life demands a working belief in God and immortality is precisely the aim of Montaigne and

Charron, the spiritual heirs of Sextus and Cicero in the Renaissance world.

2. MONTAIGNE AND CHARRON

The mind of Michel de Montaigne (1533–1592) looks in two directions. It gives consummate literary expression to a skeptical movement of thought that had been ripening in France for half a century, and it provides a watershed for the skeptical writers of the following age. The fifty years preceding the first edition of Montaigne's *Essays* (1580) were turbulent ones, both in French intellectual history and French political and religious life. At the outset of the period, France was flooded with editions of the commentaries on Aristotle written by Italian philosophers, headed by Pietro Pomponazzi, at the University of Padua. Convinced followers of Pomponazzi occupied influential chairs of philosophy at Paris and spread his Averroistic interpretation of Aristotle. Among these influential Paduans was Francisco de Vicomercato, who served as Regius professor of philosophy at Paris from 1542 until 1567. During the latter half of the century, the works of Geronimo Cardano helped to popularize the naturalism of the Paduan school.[10]

The philosophical Aristotelianism presented by Pomponazzi and his followers maintained that pure philosophy cannot defend a free creation, divine providence, and personal immortality. These doctrines must give way before the solid demonstrations of philosophy of nature, which supports the eternity of matter, the inexorable determinism of natural laws of motion, and the dissolution of the individual human soul at the death of the body. As far as philosophy can ascertain, God is not a free creator but a necessary producer of the world of material motions. His actions must conform with the general laws of nature so that providence is contracted to the vanishing point and miracles are ascribed to human ignorance of the powers of nature. Morality depends upon a purely immanent, Stoic doctrine of natural justice and not upon divine sanction or personal immortality. A certain aspect of the human intellect survives death, but it does so only through its complete merger with the nonpersonal, universal intellect. As an escape device against incurring theological censure, philosophers in the Paduan tradition usually invoked the distinction between what philosophy demonstrates and what faith teaches as true. Although creation, providence, and immortality enjoy no demonstrative standing in the philosophical order, they remain untouched as truths or articles of supernatural faith. This convenient doctrine of two utterly disparate sorts of propositions was especially advantageous in university situations, such as those at Padua and Paris, where the philosophers were anxious to avoid entanglement with the theological faculty.

Confronted with this imposing system of philosophical naturalism, many Christians in sixteenth-century France lost confidence in Aristotle's philosophy, which seemed to them to be the same as losing all confidence in human reason and the philosophical enterprise as a whole. Unwilling to accept the schizoid attitude demanded by the split between philosophical demonstrations and revealed truths, they became skeptical about the ability of natural reason and philosophy to reach any certain knowledge. Skepticism about philosophical matters thus appeared to be the safest way of safeguarding the orthodox faith. This was the motivation behind the fideistic skeptics, who sought to join doubt about the mind's natural powers with faith in supernatural revelation. A strong dose of fideism was present in such a representative work as Cornelius Agrippa's *Declamation on the Uncertainty and Vanity of the Sciences and on the Excellence of God's Word* (1527), as well as in Omer Talon's *The Academy* (1548) and Francisco Sanches' *Nothing Is Known* (1581). These writers strongly denounced Aristotle as being an enemy of Christian truth and attacked the Paduan philosophers and their followers as being robbers of the Faith. With Sanches, skepticism may also have been used as a weapon against the dogmatic assertions found in the pantheistic naturalism of Bruno.

But concern for revealed truths was not the only factor accounting for the burgeoning popularity of skepticism during the later French Renaissance. In addition to the fideistic skeptics, there was an equally strong trend in the direction of freethinking skepticism.[11] Some of the freethinkers, or libertines, were genuine atheists, but most of them were what we would today call deists or men of natural religion, that is, they believed in God and often in the Stoic moral code, but they did not believe in Christ and the Church. This group maintained that neither natural nor supernatural truths can be known by speculative reason. Hence freethinking skepticism led either to total doubt and moral chaos or to a purely practical belief in God and a natural moral law, without any supernatural revelation or worship.

In any given case of a skeptical author, it is difficult to determine whether he is a fideist or a freethinker, since the line of demarcation is vague and shifting. Montaigne is a good instance of this ambiguity, but it is more likely that his personal attitude was that of fideistic skepticism as distilled in a passionately frank and analytic intelligence. He branded the maxims of Sextus Empiricus even more deeply into his own mind and sensibility than into the rafters of his library. Although he extolled the comforts of the soft feather pillow of imagination and uncritical belief, he did not allow himself to slumber very long. Like David Hume, he alternated continually between comfortable, practical acceptance of the prevailing views and self-scrutiny of the most agonizing sort.

As Montaigne sees him, natural man is a mass of weakness and corruption, both of which are concealed by his tremendous pride. The aim of the *Essays* is to dispel any presumptuous illusions about man's power and dignity: "We must strip him to his shirt."[12] Natural reason is incompetent in attaining strict knowledge about being because it is totally dependent upon the senses, which always distort the materials they receive from the world. Since the senses reveal nothing reliable about objects but only about our private impressions, reason and all its pretended demonstrations are also held captive within human subjectivity. Reasoning is only rationalizing; our best efforts at objectivity reflect only our own passions and meanness of stature. Nothing is so holy or exalted that we do not drag it down to our own level and make it serve our selfish aims. Even religion is no exception to the overwhelmingly egocentric and utilitarian drive of human nature.

Although Montaigne does not express doubt about God's existence, he does trace whatever certainty we possess on this score to the gift of faith. From the latter source we receive assurance that God has left His imprint upon the visible world and that it testifies to the majesty of His nature. But our native reason is too weak to discern the divine likeness in things, even if it could overcome the shortcomings of sensation and apprehend the material world in its own reality. Montaigne takes comfort in quoting St. Paul on the unknown God and St. Augustine on how God is better known by not being known. He interprets these famous sentences in the Pyrrhonian sense that reason can establish nothing whatever about God, whose existence and attributes simply escape the range of our knowing powers. No ground is left in natural reasoning for either the confident affirmations of orthodox rationalists or the confident negations of the Paduan Aristotelians.

As for the doctrine of immortality, it "is the part of human knowledge that is treated of with the greatest reservation and doubt. . . . Let us candidly confess that God alone has told it to us, and Faith; for it is no lesson of Nature or of our reason."[13] Montaigne points to the great diversity of opinions on this question as eloquent testimony in favor of the skeptical policy of suspension of judgment. Man is just as ignorant of his own nature and destiny as he is of the divine being. Instead of setting himself up as the measure of all things—the foolish dream of rhetorical humanism—man should honestly admit his kinship with the animals, his complete submergence in nature or the sea of becoming, and the conventional origin of his moral standards. If he wishes to have anything more sublime, he must look to the free gift of God and faith alone.

In reading Montaigne, one sometimes wonders where to draw the line between the position of the man of faith who mocks at the pretensions of every philosophical defense of religious truths and the sort of critique which reaches even to religious beliefs themselves, to the extent that they contain a definite truth-claim. The standpoint of fideistic skepticism is more sharply etched in the case of Montaigne's spiritual and legal heir, Pierre Charron (1541–1603), a priest and famous preacher in Paris and the provinces. While residing in Bordeaux (where he had personal meetings with Montaigne), he composed a treatise on *The Three Truths* (1593), which was a defense of God against the atheists, of Christianity against the pagans or deists, and of Catholicism against the Protestants. He felt that all variations from the full Catholic faith were due to a presumptuous use of reason. Hence Charron fell back upon skeptical fideism as a radical way of undermining his opponents, a position set forth in his major work, *On Wisdom* (1601). Although he was a vigorous writer, he lacked the stylistic accomplishments and subtle nuances of Montaigne. In philosophic terms, the differences stemmed from the fact that Montaigne was a Pyrrhonian, whereas Charron was an Academic skeptic who denied outright that man can have any certain natural knowledge, although he can attain various degrees of practical probability. Since Charron lacked Montaigne's more sinuous and suspensive approach and since he outlined a Stoic morality distinct from faith and moral theology, he provided the libertines of the early seventeenth century with a thesaurus of readily detachable texts which could be used for purposes directly opposed to his own intention. This circumstance led to Charron's becoming the favorite target for attack from the Sorbonne and Scholastic quarters, but there is no solid basis for doubting his religious sincerity.

In the first book of *The Three Truths*, Charron advanced several traditional arguments for God's existence. Among the physical proofs, he included those from efficient and final causes, movement, finitude, composition, harmony of the universe, and the degrees of goodness. He also mentioned the moral proof from universal consent and one based upon miracles and prophecy. Like most of his contemporaries in all schools, he recognized no distinctive metaphysical approach to God and the soul apart from philosophy of nature. Since Charron regarded the latter discipline as having only probable assurance, these proofs of God's existence are no more than probable arguments or "veri-similitudes." But in the case of God's nature and attributes, Charron did not permit even probable reasoning: The utter disproportion between our finite nature and the infinite being of God deprives us of any natural intellectual means for determining the divine nature. Echoing Montaigne in this respect, Charron recommended that we refrain from making any detailed description of God's essence and remain content with acknowledging Him as an infinitely good, yet naturally unknowable, source of perfection.

The governing impulse behind the treatise *On Wisdom* is the resolution to preserve the divine transcendence from the tendency of human reason to debase the infinite God to our own level. Charron speaks with biting satire about those superstitious and irreverent people who treat God as though He were a minor country judge who is severe and cruel at one moment, simple minded and indulgent at the next. The majesty of God is violated by the easy affirmations we make about His nature and His way with the world. Charron even takes occasion to correct Montaigne's remark that God is the summit of our efforts to imagine complete perfection. Since this may imply that God is a sort of "limit-concept" of the human mind (as later agnosticism sometimes claims), Charron observes that "more precisely, God is infinitely above all our ultimate and highest efforts and imaginings of perfection."[14] John Dryden has compressed the pertinent thought into a couplet:

> Let reason then at her own quarry fly,
> But how can finite grasp infinity?

Whatever certitude we have about the infinite God comes to us from religious faith alone, from accepting God's word, and not at all from our own natural reasoning and aspirations toward perfection.

Nevertheless, there is a twofold office for human wisdom: to prepare the way for supernatural faith and to secure the natural moral perfection of man. The first of these functions is conceived in a way diametrically opposed to the Thomistic view of philosophy as capable of reaching some natural speculative truths about God and man and of defending the reasonableness of the Christian faith. Instead, human wisdom aids faith by confessing its utter incapacity to reach any speculative truth. Far from detecting any hostility between skepticism and Christianity, Charron praises the former as the best possible preparation of the mind for the reception of a supernatural revelation. Using an example that was to become increasingly popular in the age of exploration and cultural penetration of the East, he asks what better way there is for converting a Chinese sage than by first convincing him that all philosophical doctrines are mere doubtful opinions. The Christian missionary should approach the Eastern mind with the Bible in one hand and Sextus Empiricus in the other. Skepticism is a healing purgative which eliminates false conceptions of God and the prejudices that stand in the way of acceptance of the Christian revelation.

Charron is an enthusiastic proponent of the thesis "that God has indeed created man to know the truth, but that man cannot know it by himself or by any human means. . . . We are born to seek the truth: to possess it belongs to a higher and greater power."[15] The senses are notoriously subjective and deceptive. As for reason, the philosopher's tool, it is like the legendary slipper of Theramenes: it fits every foot.

43

Charron also likens its activity to that of a ferret, one which gets lost in the underground mazes and dark holes without ever reaching its prey. The real natures of things forever escape the philosopher's reach, since even our innate intellectual ideas have no objective validity. Having deprived man of any speculative insight into being and its causal principles, Charron then invites the searcher after truth to embrace the Christian faith, which provides the only certain truth about God and human destiny.

Only in the moral order of practical reasoning and probabilities can human wisdom perform a more constructive service. It develops the doctrine of true virtue, *la vrai prud'hommie,* which secures the natural moral perfection of man as man. Charron has a Stoic conception of morality, borrowed in large part from the two leading Renaissance exponents of Christian Stoicism: Justus Lipsius and Guillaume Du Vair. Like them, he interprets the central Stoic moral precept of following nature to mean: Follow the law of God and practical reason. He outlines the entire range of virtues regulating both personal and social life in a much more systematic way than Montaigne ever attempted. And, apparently, Charron is not unaware of the possibility that the freethinkers will try to divorce this moral teaching from his equally urgent appeal to accept Christian revelation, for he explicitly counsels the truly wise or virtuous man to unite natural morality and supernatural religion in a personal synthesis.[16] The later Renaissance sage is to be a skeptic in the speculative order, a Stoic in moral matters, and a Christian in his religion.

Whatever the personal sincerity of conviction behind this projected synthesis, however, it was intrinsically too precarious to survive criticism by the freethinking skeptics. Neither Montaigne nor Charron possessed the philosophical acumen of their Greek prototype, Sextus Empiricus. They simply accepted the premise of phenomenalism without rethinking the problem of sense perception and reasoning. Their main contribution was to reformulate skepticism within the modern context of humanism and Christianity. But the attendant opposition between natural reason and the authority of faith was easily made to appear as an admission that the act of supernatural faith is either a totally unreasonable commitment or one made solely on the grounds of convention and social amity. Montaigne's ironical comment that "we are Christians by the same title as we are Périgordians or Germans" highlighted the irrational and pragmatic basis of the fideistic conception of Christian belief.[17] Some of the more extreme libertines made the same estimate of our acceptance of a natural moral law. If natural reason is so impotent in all speculative matters, then some special justification is required before one gives it credence as a source of practical, moral wisdom. Such philosophical justification was not forthcoming from

Charron, so the net effect of his position was to endanger the two wisdoms, religious and moral, which he sought to support by skeptical means.

3. GASSENDI AND HUET

During the seventeenth century, skepticism was a flourishing yet thoroughly ambivalent force in French intellectual life. The anti-Christian strain was represented in the verses of Théophile de Viau and the anonymous deistic poem entitled *The Anti-Bigot or Quatrains of a Deist* (circulated widely before 1622). During most of this period, the radical wing of skeptical unbelief was under public ban. The commoner and safer fideistic position was that adopted by cautious men like Gabriel Naudé (who became Cardinal Mazarin's librarian and trusted adviser) and François de La Mothe le Vayer (who was in the employ of Richelieu and to whom the education of the Dauphin was entrusted).[18] These men of responsible office did publish books in which the full weight of Pyrrhonian criticism was brought to bear upon the senses, the rational inferences of metaphysics and morality, and the historical bases of religious belief, but they were prudent enough to make some reservations in favor of revealed truths and to refrain from blunt attacks on Christianity. Naudé and La Mothe le Vayer had few hesitations in the practical sphere, where they lent support to royal authority and the policy of religious unification in France. Theirs was a typical blend of theoretical skepticism and practical totalitarianism which has been recurrent in the Western world from Machiavelli to our own day. Because of their doubts about universal moral principles, the duties of the ruler toward God, and the supernatural origin of the Church, they were willing contributors to the growth of political absolutism and the skeptical version of a state religion maintained and propagated by force.

By far the most interesting and complex mind among the skeptics before 1650 is Pierre Gassendi (1592–1655), priest and canon of Digne, Regius professor of mathematics at Paris, and country host to Naudé and La Mothe le Vayer. His own version of fideistic skepticism is presented in two stages: (1) a concerted attack upon current Scholasticism; and (2) a Christian interpretation of atomism and Epicureanism which is intended to overcome the philosophical shortcomings of Charron's fideism and, simultaneously, to render Christianity attractive in a pragmatic age. His negative views are set forth in a book provocatively titled *Unconventional Arguments against the Aristotelians* (1624–1627), an offshoot of his philosophical lectures at the University of Aix. Punctuated frequently by the satirical exclamation "Oh immortal God!" this

45

work is a curious medley of humanistic criticism of Scholasticism that might have been composed by Petrarca or Erasmus or Ramus, a skeptical disparagement of the human mind after the manner of Montaigne, and an earnest, Charron-like plea for faith instead of dialectics.

The only way to break out of the prison house of Aristotelianism is through a denial of any knowledge or science—in the Aristotelian sense of "a certain, evident, abiding notion of something, gained through a necessary cause or by demonstration."[19] Gassendi proposes as the proud banner of the modern skeptic: *I know nothing Aristotelianwise*, namely, nothing about what things are in their intimate natures as determined by necessary causal inference and syllogistic demonstration. Not even the natural and mathematical sciences attain to the essential structure of things. Gassendi extends the skeptical critique to include the modern sciences, which cannot transcend the realm of appearances. The only sort of knowledge open to man is *scientia experimentalis et apparentialis*, a coherent account of perceptual facts and appearances.

Within this skeptical and phenomenalistic setting there would seem to be no way of raising the mind to God by any natural means. Paradoxically enough, however, Gassendi upbraids the Scholastics for hesitating about applying the category of substance to God and obtaining a definition thereby. Since the categories are only tools of the understanding for including different things within a common concept, the application of substance to God does not affect His own nature but concerns only the disposition of the forms in the human mind. The common feature between God and other things is *per se* existing being; the distinctive feature about God is the infinitely perfect way in which He subsists. This gives us a sort of definition of God in terms of substance: He is a subsistent, existing being who has infinite perfection. What Gassendi does not explain is how we can be sure that anything real does, in fact, correspond to the concept of an infinitely perfect substance. In this early work, he simply offers no explanation of this difficulty because he cannot yet do so without reinstating some knowledge of being and causal inference.

This problem was faced in the more positive writings of Gassendi's maturity: *Remarks on the Life, Morals, and Maxims of Epicurus* (1649) and, especially, *A Philosophical Squadron* (1658). The over-all purpose of these works was to prevent the collapse of the Christian faith as a consequence of the skeptical attack upon the logic, physics, and ethics of contemporary Scholasticism. Gassendi conceived the bold plan of making a Christian and fideistic interpretation of two of the major sources of unbelief in his day—atomism and Epicureanism.[20] The reduction of all things to their atomic constituents can be confidently made, since this reduction is not the ultimate one. The atoms themselves must be produced by God. Because our universe can arise only from atoms endowed with definite tendencies or dynamic patterns, our mind is led to affirm the existence of a supreme creator and orderer of the atoms and the composite things they constitute. Gassendi also softened and amended Epicurus in the interests of God's free creation *ex nihilo,* a universal providence, and a special divine care for man. Other Greek authorities were ransacked for evidence that although the sensitive soul in man is corruptible, the rational soul or mind is free, immortal, and ordained to the supreme happiness of contemplating God.

This rather strained exegesis of classical Greek sources in philosophy seemed very convincing to Gassendi's close circle of admirers and even to scientists, like Boyle and Newton, who approved of a reconciliation between atomism and piety. But the assertion of God's existence, which Gassendi had to justify without relapsing into the view of knowledge he had repudiated, remained the crucial point for philosophy. Gassendi was seeking a middle way between strict Pyrrhonism, which denied the possibility of a transition from the pre-evident to the nonevident, and the Aristotelian explanation based on essential knowledge and demonstration by necessary causes. He professed to find this intermediate position in the Epicurean theory of a mental "anticipation," or innate idea that antecedes and shapes experience.[21] According to this view, the mind is preconditioned by certain inborn capacities, or dynamic tendencies, which actively dispose it to affirm the existence of beings transcending our experience and the world of appearances. The anticipation of God assures us of His existence, although it gives no knowledge of His essential nature. The latter can be approached philosophically only through reflecting on man's own nature and attributing the human form to God in some analogous way.

Gassendi offers two basic proofs of God's existence: the general anticipation of God found among all peoples and the accurate contemplation of nature.[22] In the first proof, he minimizes the number and significance of atheists, calling them intellectual monstrosities or sports of nature. The fact of a widespread consent of men to the existence of a supremely happy and imperishable being can be accounted for only in terms of an anticipation or natural propensity of the mind. Upon the occasion of sense experience, the mind's capacity is aroused to conceive the notion of God and to assent to His existence. The senses are the necessary occasions for, but not the real causes of, this belief, which springs forth from the human mind as its inborn response to experience of the world. This primary conception of God fills our minds spontaneously and directly, without requiring the intervention of reasoning of any kind, especially Aristotelian demonstration.

Reasoning does enter into the second proof, which rests on a reflective study of the order and perfection of the world. Even here, however, no causal demonstration is made, and no dependence upon Scholastic logic is required. The function of theistic reasoning is to make an analysis of our orderly universe and compare the findings with the mind's anticipatory or innate notion of God, conceived as the maker and providential orderer of the world. We see plainly that the world is the work of reason and plan, and this recognition corresponds with and makes a vital response to our idea of God as the supreme ruler of all things. "Hence it is just as necessary to know that God exists as it is to become aware of the striking order of the world."[23] We are unshakably sure of God's existence because of the conjunction established between our awareness of cosmic order and our natural anticipatory conviction about the supreme governor of everything.

Gassendi's purpose in adding the second proof is not to restore causal demonstration from finality in the universe, but to make room for atomism and, at the same time, to assure the existence of God precisely as the provider and governor of our atomistic universe. As far as the logical value of the two proofs is concerned, he reduces the second one to the first. The proof from an anticipation in the human mind is not merely prior in time, but also primary in evidence and validity. The spontaneous, innate idea of God is more fundamental that any inference from order, since the purpose of a reflective contemplation of nature is simply to confirm our anticipatory notion of God and bring out the aspect of God's providence. Gassendi adds that the first proof rests upon authority or faith, divine and human, whereas the second proof rests upon reasoning. Hence the reduction of the second to the first proof is an equivalent reduction of inferential knowledge to faith as the fount of all truth.

Our natural trust in our anticipatory notions and our supernatural acceptance of divine revelation are the ultimate motives of assent to God's existence. Faith is primary and reason is secondary and confirmatory in the genesis of this conviction. This thoroughly fideistic explanation is reinforced by Gassendi's remarks about the divine nature. He agrees with Epicurus that we can conceive of God's nature only anthropomorphically or under some human forms. Yet we can know that God is immeasurably removed from our noblest concept and that He is best named as an incorporeal mind or substance and as the mover or ruler of all things. When asked how we can be sure of this choice of attributes, Gassendi replies that the Holy Catholic Faith assures us that these are the most appropriate divine names and that they are most in accord with the tendencies of our mind to conceive of the supreme being's nature.

Gassendi and Descartes exchanged acrid comments on the question of God's existence.[24] The former could not accept the distinctively Cartesian proof from the innate idea of an infinitely perfect being, both because this proof is meant as a genuine demonstration of the divine existence and because it claims to give positive philosophical knowledge of the divine nature. Although Descartes did not examine the main writings of Gassendi, his outlook was quite foreign to what they contained. From Descartes' standpoint, the appeal of Gassendi to ancient authorities and prerational beliefs was a total surrender of philosophical intelligence and no improvement over Charron's less disguised fideism. The circular relation between the fideists' proofs of God's existence and their appeal to revelation was not overcome by Gassendi's doctrine on mental anticipations, for he failed to face up to the epistemological problem of why we should trust the natural promptings of the mind and how we could distinguish the misleading tendencies from the reliable ones. Gassendi was ready to call a halt to critical analysis at just about the point where Descartes thought that such analytic reflection should begin.

Whereas the goal of Cartesianism was to achieve a rigorous reconstitution of philosophical theism, the tendency of post-Gassendian fideism was to foreswear any and all positive philosophical confirmation. This radical attitude was best exemplified in the *Philosophical Treatise on the Weakness of the Human Mind* (written *ca.* 1690, published 1723), by Pierre Daniel Huet (1630–1721), bishop of Avranches. Huet was a member of skeptical circles in Paris and Stockholm from the 1650's onward. His classic statement of fideism was sufficiently clear and unqualified to make abundantly evident the deep opposition between this whole school and the Christian tradition of Augustine and Aquinas on the living intercourse between faith and reason. The fideistic version of faith thrives only on the weakness and debasement of natural human reason and does not respect its integrity.

Among the problems brought to focus for skepticism by Cartesianism was that of the certitude of our knowledge. Huet accepted the division of human certitude into mathematical, physical, and moral kinds but declared that all of these fall short of the perfect certitude, which rests on clearly perceived evidence.[25] Only the divine light of supernatural faith conveys a perfect certitude to the human mind. Descartes' vaunted standard of clear and distinct ideas is unattainable by the native power of human reason. Indeed, Huet used the Cartesian hypothesis of a deceiving evil spirit in order to prevent the mind from ever accepting propositions as absolutely evident anad certain, even including Descartes' first indubitable truth about the existence of the thinking self. Huet cited no less than sixty-five philosophers and schools on the side of the skeptical suspension of judgment in the face of all human evidence. Not content with this suspension, however, he bettered the Pyrrhonians by giving up any philosophical search for truth. In the natural order, all we can hope for is a sufficiently high probability to enable us to conduct our practical affairs with safety.

Of course, the other side of this shield of Huet's defiance of reason is his ready acceptance of faith. Only supernatural faith gives us indubitable certainties and clear knowledge of truths. Bishop Huet can discover within himself none of Gassendi's natural anticipations of truth, Descartes' innate ideas, or Malebranche's intimate perceptions of truth. Skeptical criticism must eliminate these natural supports of reason and unceremoniously strip man to his intellectual skin. Not even first principles carry sufficient evidence of themselves; they need the light of faith for their complete certitude. Hence, although we can somehow know God through both faith and reason, "knowledge" is an equivocal term. The so-called natural demonstrations of God's existence give us just as high a probability as do mathematical proofs, but neither mode of reasoning attains perfect certitude.[26] Both the principles of philosophical demonstration and their conclusions must wait upon the light of revelation in order to provide us with the knowledge and certitude that exclude all doubt.

Through this intrinsic founding of all natural principles and inferences of God's existence on the act of supernatural faith, as well as through his surrender of the philosophical quest for truth, Huet brought fideistic skepticism to its logical conclusion. This climax also proved to be a historical dead end as far as further philosophical developments were concerned. Although fear of the Enlightenment led the French traditionalists to rely upon religious fideism a century later, this self-defeating position was bound to end in complete philosophical and theological sterility. Historically, it has always proved disastrous to try to build a living faith in God upon the ruins of our natural powers of cognition and desire.

The effective channel through which skepticism was transmitted to the eighteenth century was Bayle's *Historical and Critical Dictionary* (1697). But in the process of transmission there was also a transformation. Although Bayle was a contemporary of Huet and was perfectly familiar with all the skeptical writings mentioned in this chapter, he was even more significant as an initiator of the Enlightenment than as an heir of Montaigne and Charron. Hence his viewpoint is best considered in conjunction with our study of the Enlightenment and its outlook on God.

4. MERSENNE'S CRITIQUE OF SKEPTICISM

Vigorous but often intellectually mediocre replies to skepticism issued steadily from orthodox writers throughout the seventeenth century. Apart from the Cartesians, most of the authors were Scholastic theologians. Early in the century a substantial treatise, *On Divine Providence and the Immortality of the Soul, against the Atheists and*

Machiavellians (1613), was published by the Louvain Jesuit theologian Leonard Lessius (1554–1623).[27] He defended divine providence through proofs based upon finality in the universe and God's constant ordering of events. Lessius also stressed the importance of the doctrine of immortality for revealed religion. Perhaps his most interesting position was an emphatic refusal to follow Charron and other Catholics in using skeptical arguments in theological controversy. He regarded skepticism as a consequence of abandoning the Catholic faith, not as a convenient weapon for defending it against Calvinism. Fideism can only lead to the eventual loss of one's entire conviction in a providential God. Lessius also warned against the *politici,* or those skeptics who accepted Machiavelli's view that religion and a doctrine on God are merely a matter of policy determined by the practical needs of the state.

The most respected and astute mind among the theological critics of skepticism was Marin Mersenne (1588–1648), a priest of the Order of Minims. He was a lifelong friend of Gassendi, Hobbes, and Descartes. Through his far-flung correspondence, he was also the clearinghouse for scientific and philosophical information in the decades just prior to the appearance of the first learned journals. From 1623 to 1625, he issued three influential polemical works against the skeptical movement: *Famous Questions on Genesis; The Impiety of Deists, Atheists, and Libertines;* and *The Truth of the Sciences, against the Skeptics or Pyrrhonians.* The stated aim of this series of books was to check "the impetuous course of Pyrrhonism," which had become a practical danger to religion and morals.[28] Mersenne wrote primarily as a theologian, but one who was well informed and enthusiastic about modern mathematical physics.

One reason for Mersenne's enthusiasm about recent scientific developments was rooted in his opposition to the deterministic naturalism of those Paduan and Parisian teachers who used Aristotelian physics to deny a free creation and universal providence.[29] He agreed with Gassendi that religion is more easily reconcilable with a purely phenomenalistic theory of science than with one based on essential knowledge of bodies, whose necessary laws can be imposed on the divine will. The modern mechanistic explanation of physical appearances describes the actual arrangement of things by God, but it does not claim to penetrate to essential laws and intrinsically necessary requirements to which God Himself must conform. Mechanism is also advantageous in eliminating the pantheistic immanentism of Bruno. In a purely mechanical arrangement of physical events, there is no need for conceiving of God as the indwelling world soul. Hence Mersenne was a vigorous advocate of mechanism on specifically theistic grounds.

Since his phenomenalistic theory of scientific knowledge was bound up with a stress upon sense experience as an original, though limited, source of knowledge, Mersenne was unable to accept Descartes' critique of sensation. But the two thinkers did agree upon the voluntaristic character of natural laws in respect to God and upon the need for a new basis of certainty within the thinking self. Having repudiated the Aristotelian theory of an essential knowledge of bodily natures and yet having recognized the anachronism and skepticism surrounding Gassendi's doctrine of anticipatory ideas, Mersenne was driven to locate the basis of certainty and demonstration of God's existence mainly in the reflective experience of man. His somewhat hesitant, midway position between Gassendi and Descartes was symptomatic of the prevailing philosophical insecurity of the mid-seventeenth-century orthodox mind when confronted with the unenviable choice between naturalistic Aristotelianism, fideistic skepticism, and the untried path of Cartesianism.

On one point, however, Mersenne was firmly against both the skeptics and Descartes: A defense must be made of the essential reliability of sensation. Even though it does not enable us to reach the essence of bodies, sensation does attain the objective appearances and activities of quantitative things in space and time, and it is not confined to our purely subjective states. In his sane and plodding way, Mersenne examined all of the skeptical tropes and exposed the unreasonableness of mistrusting sense cognition.[30] His analysis had the three admirable traits of being descriptive, scientific, and reflective. He deemed the skeptical objections, based on the relativity of sense perception, to be psychologically interesting but epistemologically inconclusive. The variations do not destroy the principle of contradiction or the trustworthiness of sense, since they are only illustrations of the truism that different aspects of the object are manifested to us under different conditions. The reports of the various sense powers are distinct and complementary but not mutually contradictory. Each sense power gives a partial report, which the skeptic misreads as being in conflict with other findings.

Mersenne also hammered home the point that skeptical humanism is largely ignorant of modern science. It continues to repeat the Greek difficulties with perception as if man were an unhistorical, unprogressive creature who cannot construct sciences and use them to correct his previous mistakes. Problems arising from color perception, for instance, do not leave us helpless, provided we employ the resources of modern optics and physiology. Similarly, the well-worn monistic objection that to know a particular thing one must understand all its cosmic relations overlooks the meaning of scientific research. Far from being a hindrance, partial and relational knowledge is our best human means for understanding the material world. This world is not a big, blooming, buzzing confusion, for we are able to discriminate between different kinds of relations and partial aspects of objects.

Underlying this whole critique is a constant reference to the reflective ability of the mind. We can *know* by reflection that things appear differently under varying circumstances, that the individual sense report is incomplete, and that in dreams our temperament fashions our beliefs. It is the reflective control of reason over the senses, again, that prevents a precipitate judgment about the object. For instance, to determine whether a building which appears to us under different shapes at different distances is really round or rectangular, we deliberately employ touch, as well as sight. We use ruler, compass, and other scientific tools; we make no final estimation until allowance is made for subjective factors. Because of this reflective and critical control which reason can exercise over sense perception, there is no need to accept the famous skeptical argument based on a circular relation between sense and reason. Reason is both dependent on the senses and capable of testing and evaluating their report. "The senses serve only to apply objects to the understanding, for they [the senses] cannot judge of the conformity which it has with them [the objects], nor of the intellectual truth which surpasses every sort of body. We can nevertheless say that the truth itself is judge of the understanding."[31] Because the understanding can become reflectively conformed to the thing in its own evidence, truth and certitude are open to man. There need be no skeptical regress to infinity in search of further criteria of knowledge.

Mersenne fails to complete the rehabilitation of human knowledge, however, since he does not grant that the intellect, working along experientially with the senses, can discover anything concerning the principles of being of the material thing. He emphasizes the internal strength of the light of reason without explaining how the mind transcends the sensory level, even though it must take its start from sensation. As a consequence, his proofs of God's existence are philosophically indiscriminate and unrooted in a definite theory of being and knowing. In his *Famous Questions on Genesis,* Mersenne offers no less than thirty-five proofs, which range all the way from common consent, the grades of being, the order and motion of the universe, and the infinite capacity of our desire to appeals based on music, divination, geography, and architecture. Elsewhere, he manages to pare the list down to a round dozen arguments.[32] An astronomical inference from the ordered heavens to a sovereign architect jostles with the Augustinian proof from eternal truths and St. Anselm's true idea of the being than which no greater can be conceived. The Thomistic five ways of proof are mentioned but are not given the same prominence as these other arguments, some of which had been explicitly rejected by St. Thomas.

The total impression conveyed by these eclectic texts is that Mersenne is willing to accept any rhetorically persuasive line of theistic argument and that he has no rigorous philosophical approach to God. He betrays no awareness of the distinctively metaphysical import of the Thomistic ways of proof, since he views them in the perspective of the predominant physicalism of later Scholastic thought. This interpretation makes him chary of placing too much reliance on these Thomistic ways, since he regards them as Aristotelian physical proofs that can scarcely avoid issuing in the deterministic deity of Paduan naturalism. As a consequence, Mersenne casts a wide net to include all the traditionally proposed proofs, regardless of their philosophical bases and possible incompatibility with each other.

In addition, the French Minim gives a modern accent to two of the older arguments: that from order in the universe and that from contingency. He is a typical witness to the increasing popularity of the argument from design leading to the existence of God conceived as a supreme watchmaker, architect, or engineer-in-chief of the universe.[33] He cites the astronomical findings of Copernicus and Tycho Brahe on the distances between stars and the orderly movement of the planets as an indication of the need for an intelligent maker. One reason for the popularity of this proof from design is that it takes its point of departure in mathematically described motions and distances, without supposing any knowledge of the essential nature or other principles of being in bodily things. Scientific theism is the modern phenomenalistic substitute for both a metaphysical demonstration and an Aristotelian physical inference to God. The proof from design also has the advantage of specifying the existence of God precisely as the provider and governor of the universe—a point which was under fire from both the Averroistic naturalists and the freethinking skeptics. Mersenne's formulation of the proof from contingency is also within the modern introspective trend to be developed by Descartes. Both men take the evidence of contingency from our internal experience of man's finite and fallible mind rather than from a metaphysical or an Aristotelian physical analysis of the material world.

Thus a study of Mersenne's views on God shows that he did not entirely escape from the ambit of the skepticism he warred against. On at least three counts, he showed marked traces of the inroads of skeptical criticism: his denial of sense-grounded metaphysical knowledge of the principles of being in material things, his consequent failure to make a metaphysical approach to God based on the sense world but not on Aristotelian physics, and his ultimate substitution of persuasive, probable reasoning from scientific facts for philosophical demonstration. The case of Mersenne illustrates in a concrete way the hesitant and uncertain character of orthodox thinking on the eve of the great developments in the modern conception of God. An important negative factor favoring the emergence of the rationalist and empiricist doctrines on God in the seventeenth century was the absence of a technically competent realism capable of overcoming skepticism in a constructive philosophical way.

Chapter III

GOD AS A FUNCTION IN RATIONALIST SYSTEMS

THE PYRRHONIAN crisis that gripped so many minds during the first third of the seventeenth century was aggravated by the obvious failure of all attempts at overcoming skepticism. The Peripatetics kept on re-affirming their massive realism without realizing that their underlying noetic principles were under fire and required some explicit justification. The so-called new logicians of the Ramist school and the Paris Arts Faculty talked a good deal about making a fresh start with a new and absolutely certain method and a complete system of truths. But, in fact, the Ramist movement remained at the rhetorical and pedagogical level. Despite some interesting suggestions on the need for method and system, it never squarely faced the philosophical problem of the objective reference of its tabular schemes and the ultimate guarantee of memory.[1] Mersenne came closer to the real issues with his appeal to sensation and the scientific accomplishments of the human mind, but even he failed to establish a metaphysical foundation for the knowledge of anything beyond sense appearances. As for Gassendi's Christianized atomism and hedonism, they were kept within the bounds of orthodoxy only through an act of faith.

People were beginning to recognize that modern science raised some special difficulties for theism. Bruno had appealed to the universal character of scientific laws in support of his pantheistic identification of God with the one, infinite universe of matter and form. And the method of Galileo would seem to threaten the organic relations among things, the hierarchy of kinds of being, the rule of divine providence, and the freedom and unique destiny of man. John Donne was sensitive to the revolutionary implications of the new mechanistic world view:

> And new Philosophy calls all in doubt,
> The Element of fire is quite put out;
> The Sun is lost, and th'earth, and no mans wit
> Can well direct him where to looke for it. . . .
> 'Tis all in peeces, all cohaerence gone;
> All just supply, and all Relation.[2]

Science provided only a cold refuge from skepticism, since it raised doubts of its own about God and man, as well as about the visible universe. As described in quantitative, mechanistic terms, the universe was totally devoid of divine intent and human qualities and values. Hobbes, rather than Mersenne, seemed to be developing the consequences of the new physics. Fideism beckoned to theists as providing the only solution, albeit a suicidal one as far as inquiry goes, concerning the intellectual problems of the day.

But men are not readily convinced of the wisdom of suicide, physical or mental. During the last two-thirds of the seventeenth century, rationalism developed as a viable way of dealing with skepticism and science without abandoning human intelligence. Descartes, Spinoza, and Leibniz agreed that the soundness of human reason can be fully vindicated against the skeptical attacks and that the scientific method can be accommodated within a philosophy where this vindicated reason is given the primacy in settling issues. Furthermore, they agreed that a theory of God must play a major role in any philosophic reconstruction. At no time before or since has God occupied such an important position in philosophy. This does not mean that the rationalist systems were religious or theocentric in structure. Quite the contrary. God was made to serve the purposes of the system itself. He became a major cog, but still a cog, in the over-all program of answering skepticism, incorporating the scientific spirit, and building a rational explanation of the real. It is this functional attitude toward God which characterizes the rationalist movement in the century of genius and which must be examined here in its main forms.

A rough sketch of the action shows Descartes as the pioneer, grappling directly with skepticism and discovering thereby the dire need to press God into the service of the certitudinal sciences of metaphysics and physics. Then Spinoza proposes to remove certain hesitancies caused by Descartes' Christian faith and to work out a rigorous, deductive naturalism on a pantheistic basis. Leibniz intervenes to bring temporary peace to the rationalist house by means of a doctrine on the primacy of essences to which God is diplomatically but firmly adjusted. At last the illusion of a permanent alliance between rationalism and Christianity is reluctantly dispelled by Malebranche, who retains a transcendent God only at the price of introducing some fideist and phenomenalist factors which undermine the functionalist position.

1. THE CARTESIAN GOD AS THE FOUNDATION OF CERTITUDE

Against the charge that his methodic doubt led to skepticism, René Descartes (1596–1650) made an indignant protest. Writing to a Jesuit critic, Father Bourdin, he asserted not only that he had frequently refuted Pyrrhonism, but also—a surprising claim—that he was the very first philosopher to have done so.[3] Certainly no philosopher since Augustine was so thoroughly soaked in the skeptical writings and so deeply aware of their radical criticism of accepted convictions. He felt the futility of appealing to philosophical, scientific, and religious authority in philosophical matters or of offering merely dialectical, probable arguments. For skepticism had called these authorities into question and was attracting adherents among people who despaired of ever finding demonstrative proofs of God and immortality. Instead, Descartes saw that there was only one way to arrest the drift toward skepticism: by supplying indubitable evidence and demonstrations.

As a preliminary move, he challenged the two chief principles of Pyrrhonism: the psychological principle of the pre-eminent desire for peace of mind and the logical principle of equipollence. A close study of human drives shows that the desire for wisdom is at least as fundamental as that for peace of mind. Indeed, the former urge is more characteristic of man, who may justly be described as a thinking animal in quest of wisdom. Undoubtedly, he is also seeking tranquillity and happiness, but they depend upon his growth in wisdom. Skepticism is an inhumane standpoint, not because it calls for peace of mind, but because it fails to recognize that this good comes as the proper fruit of wisdom. Unless the rightful order is maintained, men will be exchanging human tranquillity of spirit for the blissful nescience of the plant or for a mere subjective feeling of equilibrium.

On the logical side, Descartes took pains to distinguish between his own methodic withholding of assent and that of the skeptic. The skeptic is mainly interested in establishing a neutral balance between contradictory propositions; his ideal in speculative matters is the attitude of noncommitment. For Descartes, however, equipollence is only a preliminary technique for liberating the mind from the senses and putting it on guard against mere probabilities.[4] His main concern is to test propositions, with the positive hope of finding one that can resist doubt and force the mind to assent to it. Cartesian doubt is animated by a readiness to accept indubitable evidence, should it be found, and a willingness to assent to the truth of anything that can resist the most rigorous test of doubting. Pyrrhonians are guilty of the negative dogmatism of refusing assent, even in the face of nonprobable, tested evidence. Descartes uncovered this hidden dogmatism in the skeptical resolve not to accept speculative truths about reality, and thus he disqualified the skeptical claim to maintain an impartial suspense of judgment.

Although Descartes himself accepted quite uncritically the skeptical equipollential arguments against the senses, he refused to conclude that these arguments also established the unreliability of the intellectual power in man. This inference assumed that there is an intrinsic dependence of intellect upon the senses, and Descartes challenged the assumption. He set out to show that even after the data of the senses have been ruled out as doubtful, the intellect can still arrive at an indubitable truth. The test he devised to prove this point was the famous hypothesis of a deceiving demon—a mind that is very intelligent and powerful (although not infinitely powerful) and also malevolent toward man. Could not such a malignant spirit so construct the human mind that it could force the mind's assent to falsehoods as though they were evident truths? The answer is firmly in the negative, once the intellect has disciplined itself to be on guard against the senses and even against the possible deceits of physics and mathematics. For in the purely interior and spiritual zone of its own existence, the thinking self cannot be deceived. If deception should be attempted here, the existence of the intellectual self is revealed in the very act of deceit and is revealed in an unmistakably clear and distinct way. The intellect is coerced by its own self-presented evidence to assent to the existence of the Cogito, or thinking self. A speculative and existential truth about real being is thereby acquired, and, simultaneously, the hold of skepticism on the mind is forever broken. As long as one remains cautious about accepting only clear, distinct, and purely intellectual evidence, the prospect of developing a complete system of truths having a priori certainty will also remain.

Descartes soon found, however, that the discovery of an unassailable ontological truth does not automatically assure the growth of a philosophical system. The truth about the Cogito is the unconditional principle of his philosophy, in that it is the first truth attained with certainty by the inquiring mind and is therefore not derived from any prior knowledge. But a principle must also be fruitful, i.e., it must be such that it gives rise causally to the entire chain of subsequently known truths. Rationalist principles must cause, as well as order, the system of knowledge.[5] From this aspect, the isolated, finite, thinking self is not an adequate principle of philosophical synthesis out of which to derive, by deduction, the entire body of human wisdom. Hence Descartes was obliged to include God among the principles of his system. He referred to the existence of the all-perfect and all-powerful God as the first and principal intuitive truth, upon which the whole fabric of his thought depends.

As the science of the first principles of deductive knowledge, Cartesian metaphysics was primarily concerned with establishing the existence and nature of the Cogito and God. Although he was not unaware of the parallel with St. Augustine's aim—"I desire to know God and the soul" —Descartes was quite conscious of the capital differences separating his concept of metaphysics from the conventional Augustinianism of his friend Cardinal Bérulle and other members of the French Oratory. His aim was to elaborate a purely human wisdom in accord with the teachings of faith but apart from all theological schools and all influence of revelation. Moreover, his desire to escape skepticism and achieve a certitude equal to that of mathematics led him to place unique stress upon the principles of systematic knowledge. He gave impetus to the modern rationalist view that the main business of metaphysics is to establish noetically efficacious first principles of deduction for an entire system of truths derived a priori or from analysis of the conceptual necessities. Finally, Descartes took the decisive step of including God as a noetic principle of the deductive system and as a part of the proper subject matter of metaphysics. This contrasted sharply not only with the Augustinian movement of mounting gradually to God as the terminal point in the quest of wisdom, but also with the Thomistic position that God is not the subject matter of metaphysics but enters into this science only as the cause of the being of finite things. In the deductive enterprise of Descartes, God had work to do and was thus included among the principles and subject matter of metaphysics precisely because of His functional contribution to the whole system. Without God, the certitude, comprehensiveness, and deductive fertility of Cartesian metaphysics would be absent. And without a metaphysics having these traits, there would be no hope for a rigorously demonstrated physics or the practical fruits of wisdom.

Descartes has no option about proceeding directly from the Cogito to God rather than passing from the Cogito to the external world. He has called into question our ordinary knowledge of the existence of the material world, and he must make some sort of inference in order to recover this certitude. Yet the finite self alone is too fragile a starting point to supply coercive proof of an existent material world, since this self is limited in power and exists in discrete instants of time without having an intrinsic, continuous duration of its own. It is truly known only at the very moment of attending to the intuition of a thinking existent. As soon as the mind shifts to a state of remembrance of a previous intuition, it loses its perfect surety and its principles cease to give indubitable demonstrations. Some independent guarantee of memory is needed in order to forge the links in the chain of deduced truths. God is the obvious remedy for these shortcomings of the Cogito. He has the infinite power and eternal duration required to produce the material world and set uniform laws for all things. He is also a veracious creator of our knowing powers who can vouch for the reliability of our natural belief in the existence of the world, as well as for the use of memory and the criterion of clear and distinct ideas, which are needed in demonstrative reasoning. If Descartes is to construct a total philosophy, he must move at once from the self to God.

The way in which this movement of thought is to be accomplished is also dictated by the starting point in the finite, thinking self. Descartes is the initiator of three typical trends in the rationalistic method of proving God's existence: the depreciation of the sensible world as a starting point, the coalescence of demonstrative reasoning with an intuition, and the subordination of a posteriori inference to a priori. The visible things in the physical universe cannot furnish data for the proof, since our ordinary assurance in their existence has been called into doubt and can only be restored to the status of knowledge subsequent to proving the existence of a truth-dealing God. Since the bodiless, thinking self is the only reality known initially to exist, every proof of God's existence must begin with the interior and immaterial world of pure thought. With Descartes, this is not a matter of religious temperament or even of an introspective bent of mind; it is an overruling demand of his order and method of obtaining truths.[6]

Similarly, he can never be contented with a process of reasoning to God but must always try to assimilate it to an intuition of the truth of God's existence. If the proof of God's existence were an ordinary, discursive process of reasoning, it would seem to be vitiated by the general condition that the Cogito is not perfectly sure about any use of memory or any extension of the criterion of clarity and distinctness beyond the atomic moment of its own self-intuition. But the inference seems much more solid when it is presented as a continuous expansion or explication of the given content of the first intuitive truth about the Cogito. This way of viewing it also conforms to the rule that every step in deduction must be reduced to the status of an intuition by being immediately and necessarily linked with the preceding truth. At the very outset of the systematic construction, then, there is special need to establish as close a bond as possible between the truth of the Cogito and that of the existent God. Finally, the necessity and rational lucidity of this intuitive transition are more favored by the a priori sort of proof than by the a posteriori sort. As a theist who accepts a transcendent creator, however, Descartes cannot entirely rule out the latter type of reasoning.

Roughly, the three Cartesian proofs start from the idea of the infinite, the mind having this idea, and the idea of the supremely perfect being.[7] The first two proofs are a posteriori, aiming to show that the mind and its idea of the infinite are effects demanding the existence of an infinite cause. The third one is a priori, based on the inherent, rational necessities in the true idea of God as the supremely perfect being.

Descartes depreciates the proof from the contingent nature of the mind, or thinking self, remarking that its chief use is to convince those Scholastic readers who are accustomed to argue from the contingency of the sensible world. Nevertheless, this proof (which reappears in Leibniz) fulfills the important function of eliminating the possibility that the Cogito is a self-caused being. This is a real possibility because of the apparent omnipotence of the thinking self, which can call everything into doubt, and because of the self's primacy as the first-known truth.

Descartes emphatically reaffirms the theistic distinction between the first truth known by man and the first creative cause of all things. The Cogito is first in the order of knowledge but not in the order of being and real causality. Descartes cites the very facts which lead to the truth of the Cogito as additional proof of its finite, and therefore caused, nature. The thinking self is often deceived, is hampered by a faulty memory, is constantly trying to improve its knowledge, and is never sure of its continued existence from moment to moment. These traits establish the imperfect and finite nature of the self. But a self-caused being would be infinitely powerful and hence would endow itself with just as much perfection as it could conceive. Since the Cogito can conceive of infinite perfection and yet remains finite, it is caused by some infinitely powerful and self-caused being, God.

Similarly, the representative reality or objective content of our idea of the infinite does not come from any finite cause, not even from the limited mind of man. It can be accounted for only by the infinite, existent reality of God. To Gassendi's objection that we cannot comprehend the infinite and therefore have only a verbal notion of it, Descartes replies that the infinite God is certainly incomprehensible in His own being. Yet the human mind can have a true and complete idea of the infinite by understanding it as something whose being is bounded by no limits.[8] This is not merely a negation of finitude; it is a positive understanding of the divine essence as affirming itself without hindrance. Although we cannot comprehend this infinite self-affirmation after its own manner, we can at least ascertain that such is the nature of the infinite being, just as we can firmly feel and gauge a stout tree without being able to encircle it with our arms. Moreover, our own free will, or power of choice, has a certain infinite intensity about it which gives us some inkling of the divine infinity and constitutes our most intimate likeness to God. In admitting the incomprehensibility of God, Descartes is following the common Christian tradition in philosophy. But his association of infinity primarily with a powerful self-positing of essence is in the line of a voluntarist and essentialist approach to God.

The distinctively rationalist conception of God as *causa sui* (cause of Himself or self-positing power of essence) is embodied in the a priori proof from the true idea of a supremely perfect being.

It is certain that I find in my mind the idea of God, of a supremely perfect Being, no less than that of any shape or number whatsoever; and I recognize that an [actual and] eternal existence belongs to his nature no less clearly and distinctly than I recognize that all I can demonstrate about some figure or number actually belongs to the nature of that figure or number. . . . From the fact alone that I cannot conceive God except as existing, it follows that existence is inseparable from him, and consequently that he does, in truth, exist. Not that my thought can bring about this result or that it imposes any necessity upon things; on the contrary, the necessity which is in the thing itself—that is, the necessity of the existence of God—determines me to have this thought.[9]

The comparison between the idea of God and the idea of a number or shape is essential to the Cartesian program of supplying demonstrations having at least as much certainty as mathematical reasoning. In fact, metaphysics has more certainty than mathematics, both because it can overcome universal doubt and because it does so in existential terms. The mathematician can draw no existential inference from inspection of his numbers and figures, but the metaphysician does make such an inference from his examination of the idea of God.

Descartes is well aware of the distinction between conceptual and real existence, so that Kant's criticism of the so-called ontological argument does not do historical justice to his position. The Cartesian contention is that just as the idea of God concerns His real essence, so does it enable us to know His real and eternal existence. The latter is established through the *true* idea of the divine essence, i.e., the one which manifests to us the objective exigencies of His own being. When Descartes says that he recognizes "clearly and distinctly" that existence belongs necessarily to the nature of a perfect being, he means that his idea of God satisfies the criterion of true existential knowledge and that existence in the real order is therefore truly known to belong to the divine essence. Hence he insists that his thought is not foolishly trying to impose a necessity upon being but that it is in conformity with the real essence of God and hence is simply reflecting the necessity of being itself. The very necessity with which the divine essence posits itself in existence is communicated to our true, innate idea of God's essence. Just as that essence causes itself or affirms its existence through its own infinite power, so does our true idea of that essence effectively and validly establish our knowledge of the divine existence. Thus the attentive mind is coerced by an objective necessity to assent to the truth about the real existence of the divine nature.

Whatever their divergence from Descartes on other points, Spinoza and Leibniz at least agree with him in basing the primary or a priori proof upon the theory of a true idea expressing the real structure and dynamic thrust of the divine essence as it posits its own existential reality. Hence the rationalists maintain that the transition in the proof is not from a constructed idea to reality, but from the known real essence of God to the necessarily entailed real truth of His existence, and therefore that the transition is a licit one establishing a truth about being.

To be maximally effective, realist criticism should not concentrate primarily upon whether or not the idea of God is innate but upon the crucial truth-claim made for this idea, whatever its origin. The rationalist supposition is that the human mind can come into possession of a real and valid definition of God's essence prior to proof of the truth of His existence, and indeed as the generating basis for that latter truth. This would mean that the human mind already knows the divine essence in its real being, either through a direct vision or through analysis of some proposed idea about that essence. This claim has to be measured against pertinent evidence about man's ways of knowing. The finite character of our intellect prevents it from having any natural proportion and intuitive access to the infinite being of God. Furthermore, in questions involving a real nature, we have to be able to show some connection of implication with the directly experienced world. We cannot settle the question of the real validity of any proposed definition of God solely by analysis of its ideal components and their state of clarity and distinctness, and hence we cannot start off with the assurance of having a true idea of God that is valid for the real order.

Another rationalist postulate of the a priori argument is that existence is nothing more than the terminal act of the self-affirmation of essence itself. We must make another test at this point by considering what we know about the relation between the essential and existential principles in beings within the range of our direct experience. In finite beings of our acquaintance, the existential act does not manifest itself simply as a property or terminal expansion of the essential structure. Hence there is not available to us a way for vindicating the real validity of a proposed definition of the divine essence in which the existential act is treated as an essential property or terminus of the essence. The rationalists remain irremediably vague about the type of causing, affirming, positing, thrusting, or other means by which the divine essential power is to be truly conceived as establishing itself in existence. The claim to be already in possession of a real and valid definition of the divine essence prior to establishing the truth about God's existence involves something about the human mind, as well as the divine nature, and a study of the former does not sustain the view that we can have such a natural knowledge of the latter.

With the existence of God established to his own satisfaction, however, Descartes was now in full possession of all the means for building his philosophical system.

The certainty and truth of all knowledge depends solely on the knowledge of the true God, so that before I knew him I could not know any other thing perfectly. . . . The certainty of all other things depends upon this so [absolutely] that, without this knowledge, it is impossible ever to be able to know anything perfectly.[10]

This emphatic statement led many of Descartes' early critics to prefer the charge of circular reasoning against him: The Cogito proves God's existence, and then the latter truth certifies the Cogito and the principles used to demonstrate God's existence. In reply, Descartes called attention to the qualifying words "all" and "perfectly" in the above-quoted text. The truth of the Cogito as an existing mind is known directly in its own self-evidence, and it brings along with it the basic principles of demonstration and the evidence for God's existence. But the bare truth of the Cogito cannot, by itself, give rise to the tree of wisdom, with its full, systematic splendor. In this sense, the Cogito is not known in a perfect way, and thus it cannot issue forth alone in the consolidation of all the links in the chain of philosophic truths. Only after the truth about God's existence and infinitely perfect and veracious nature is established can the full task of philosophy be carried through to completion by explicitly establishing in proper order the great body of certitudes or human wisdom.

Methodologically, God must be invoked to enable us to place full confidence in memory, to apply the criterion of clear and distinct ideas universally, and to base some inferences upon the unavoidable natural beliefs arising from our God-given, composite nature of mind and body, pure intelligence and sense. In other words, our assurance that a perfect and good God would not allow a deceiving demon to hold complete sway over us is a liberating truth that enables us to use our powers and evidence to the fullest extent. Our certitude about the thinking self can then be safely expanded into the wonderful science of concatenated truths, about which the young Descartes had dreamed.

2. THE CARTESIAN GOD AS THE FOUNDATION OF PHILOSOPHICAL PHYSICS

To make his dream a reality, Descartes had to secure the connection between metaphysics and the practical disciplines of medicine, mechanics, and ethics. Until these latter disciplines were joined in vital union with the first principles of metaphysics, they would have no strict standing as sciences but would remain at the level of skills and maxims. And the only adequate medium for linking them together was a fully developed philosophical physics. Hence the problem of rounding out a complete physics became a crucial one for Descartes; upon its resolution depended the success of his entire search for a unified body of natural wisdom.[11]

That a doctrine on God has anything vital to contribute to such a project was by no means evident to Descartes' contemporaries. For instance, the Scholastic theologians and philosophers whom Mersenne consulted on the soundness of Cartesian philosophy observed that an atheist can know that the three angles of a triangle are equal to two right angles. In the same vein, Hobbes felt sure that an atheist can employ memory to ascertain whether he is waking or not. Descartes readily granted that a mathematician does not need a theory of God in order to develop his science, or even to have certain knowledge about it, as long as he does not attend to the Pyrrhonian arguments or to the Cartesian demon-hypothesis. Once he has attended to them, however, he cannot be perfectly sure that he is not being deceived. Similarly, the man who uses memory to distinguish between sleep and the waking state cannot defend himself against skeptical and methodic doubt about the reliability of memory. In both instances, the skeptical uncertainty can be removed only through recognition of the existence of an infinitely perfect and nondeceiving God. Hence it does matter a good deal whether one is a theist or an atheist, not for determining the specific content of knowledge, but for assuring its certainty and objectivity in an age of skepticism and methodic doubt.[12]

Descartes aims to make a smooth transition from metaphysics to philosophical physics so that the last word in the former science will be, at the same time, the first word in systematic physics. It is the proper task of metaphysics to establish these three propositions, which are needed by physics as an integral part of philosophy: a body is an extended thing substantially distinct from a mind or thinking thing; a world of extension or bodily things can exist; and such a world does in fact exist. On all three scores, the shortcomings of a mathematical physics not yet radicated in Cartesian metaphysics are apparent. And in every case, the positive, certitude-yielding contribution of God is a notable one.

Thus, although Galileo resolves bodies to their extended figure and motion, his descriptive method cannot determine whether extension is the special property or essence of all bodies and, consequently, whether mind and body are really distinct substances. Only the Cartesian method can ascertain these truths, especially the substantial real distinction of mind and body. This latter truth will not generate any mathematical formulas, but it will provide a philosophically significant interpretation of the findings of physics and will delimit its sphere. The criterion of clear and distinct ideas (fully guaranteed by God) is brought to bear here, since Descartes clearly and distinctly perceives that the ideas of thought and extension are mutually exclusive and therefore concludes that there is a real substantial distinction between mind and body. Again, mathematics is an abstract, nonexistential science and cannot determine whether extended objects can exist and actually do exist. Modern mathematical physics must appeal to metaphysics for assurance that its explanations bear upon a world of possible and actual existents. Rationalist metaphysics bases the possibility of a world of extension upon the fact that the essence of an extended thing can be clearly and distinctly perceived and hence can be rendered existent by the divine power. God is also the basis for knowing that the material world exists in fact, since He implants in our nature the ineluctable persuasion that our sensations and passions come from, or at least are proportioned to, a really existing world of bodies. Thus God's power over the possible essences and His veracity in constituting human nature are the ultimate grounds for holding that the physical explanation concerns a world that is really possible and actually existent.

Descartes goes even farther than this in exploiting his theory of God for the ends of an integrated, philosophical physics. Abstract geometry is capable of analyzing the bodily world into its essential property of extension. But abstract, general extension is completely inert and devoid of real motion, which is the transference of an individual parcel of extension from one place to another. Real motion is communicated to extension from without by a moving force, thus producing the composite natures, which are the particular extended bodies in motion, as we experience them in their individuality and contingency. Unless reference is made to God as the ultimate, universal origin of motion, there is no intelligible way of explaining the difference between pure mathematics, the more concrete science of mechanics elaborated by Galileo, and our actual world of individual, moving bodies.

Furthermore, Descartes offers a deductive proof for the law of inertia, considered as a universal principle governing actual, moving bodies.[13] God's agency is needed not only for the creation or first imparting of motion, but also for its conservation and continuity. The attribute of divine immutability means both that God is unchangeable in His own being and that He always acts in the same way with respect to the created world. Hence we have a priori certainty about the conservation of the quantity of motion or momentum (mv). Because the conservation of momentum is rooted in the divine immutability itself, the law of inertia is deductively established as a general law of nature or a secondary cause of all particular movements of actual bodies.

Having gone this far, Descartes might be expected to make the further claim of a complete deduction of all the proposition in physics. This ideal undoubtedly had a strong appeal for him and was essential to the fulfillment of his philosophical synthesis, but, in point of fact, he denied that it could be given realization. Instead, he qualified the procedure of physics to such an extent that a total deduction of the body of physical truths could never be achieved within the context of his philosophy.

When I wanted to descend to particulars, it seemed to me that there were so many different kinds that I believed it impossible for the human mind to distinguish the forms or species found on earth from an infinity of others which might have been there if God had so willed. It thus appeared impossible to proceed further deductively, and if we were to understand and make use of things, we would have to discover causes by their effects, and make use of many experiments. . . . I must also admit that the powers of nature are so ample and vast, and that these principles are so simple and general, that I hardly ever observed a particular effect without immediately recognizing several ways in which it could be deduced. My greatest difficulty usually is to find which of these is the true explanation, and to do this I know no other way than to seek several experiments such that their outcomes would be different according to the choice of hypotheses.[14]

The more that physical research deals with our actual world of particular kinds of bodies and motions, the more it must depart from a simple, unilinear deduction from the general laws of nature and God as the ultimate source of motion. There is an inverse increase of hypotheses and verifying experiments; this can yield no absolute certitude but only the moral certitude required for the practical control of nature for our human welfare. Descartes himself took a much more tentative and empirical view of the special developments in physics than either the later Cartesians or their Newtonian foes cared to admit.

The reasons for this extraordinary shift of attitude can be traced back to Descartes' integrity, both as a scientist and as a theist. He wanted to preserve intact the mechanistic explanation of the material world solely in terms of efficient causality. He did not deny the presence of finality in nature, but he did deny our ability to know it and to use it to complete the physical deduction. In this context, he meant by "final cause" the overarching purpose for which the universe as a whole was produced. Only the infinite wisdom of God can comprehend this purpose, and His concern in producing the world embraces many other things besides human welfare. For us to invoke reasons based on finality in the explanation of physical events is equivalent to making the claim to infinite wisdom and placing man's welfare on a par with the glory of God. Both scientific method and human good sense and humility demand the elimination of finality from the area of physical research.

Even from the standpoint of a legitimate use of efficient and mechanical causes, the physical deduction is bound to remain incomplete. Here, the decisive consideration for Descartes is that a total mechanical deductive system would endanger the immensity, infinite power, and freedom of God. This was the actual outcome of Galileo's mathematicism, in which God was given no choice but to embody in nature the very laws discovered by mathematical analysis. No such necessity regulates the infinite power and freedom of the Cartesian God, who can combine the general laws of motion in many different ways to produce many different universes. A knowledge of these laws tells us only what obtains indeterminately for any possible physical universe, not which particular combination of laws holds good for this actual universe of ours. Hence the deductive method must be supplemented by experience, hypothesis, and verifying experiment. The latter procedures enable us to give a coherent and comprehensive explanation which contradicts none of the experiential facts but which does not have a rigorous necessity. To preserve the divine immensity of essence and freedom, Descartes tempers his claims for an absolutely certain and necessary chain of deductive truths about the visible world.[15]

This revision of the mathematical world-picture extends as far as the general laws of motion, the basic propositions in pure mathematics, and other eternal truths. Descartes does not grant to them any autonomy or unconditional necessity, remarking that this smacks of the tyrany of the pagan Fates over Jupiter.[16] On the basis of the incomprehensible power of God and the lack of any sort of distinction between His intellect and will, there can be no quasi-independent order of essences (such as Suarez had supposed) by which His knowledge is specified and to which His will must conform. Since the human mind can fully comprehend the eternal truths, they are finite realities and are just as thoroughly dependent on God's sovereign power as any other created things. Just as God could have abstained from creating our world or could have created one of another structure, so could He have decreed another set of eternal verities contradictory to the prevailing ones.

Yet to stress the arbitrariness of the divine power without any qualifications would spell the destruction of all scientific certitude. Hence Descartes grants to the mathematical and general physical laws a consequent kind of necessity. Once God wills them to be, He abides by His own decision and is not going to change His decree in favor of another set of truths. This follows from the immutability of God: Given a free act of the divine will, God remains unchangeably and uniformly faithful to His actual choice of laws and truths. In this way, both the infinity of the divine power and the stability of human scientific knowledge are assured.

The full extent of Descartes' functional approach to God can now be measured. He set the pattern for the rationalist exploitation of God by transforming the doctrine on the divine attributes from an abstruse and remote theological exercise into a startlingly pertinent component of modern philosophy. The divine veracity and causal power were invoked in establishing the existence of the material world and in achieving epistemological confidence in the criterion of clear and distinct ideas. The immutability of God provided a demonstration for the universal law of inertia and a reliable foundation for the first truths in mathematics and physics. God's omnipotence and freedom furnished the ultimate reason for finding a place for the hypothetico-experimental method within the deductive movement. Thus it was impossible for Descartes to conceive of a metaphysics or a physics from which God is missing. To leave Him out would be equivalent to depriving philosophy of its universal demonstrative force, its basis in certitude, and its relevance to experience.

Yet despite all these uses of divinity, Descartes did not succeed in generating the complete body of wisdom. In safeguarding the ultimate divine attribute of unhindered essential power, he simultaneously cut off the movement toward a total deduction of physical truths. The bridge-making office of physics was consequently left incomplete, and its termination in the practical disciplines was prevented. Since the linkage of physical and ethical explanations was never welded with absolute, a priori certainty, the unimpaired vigor of Cartesian metaphysics was never communicated to ethics.[17] The provisional morality was never converted into a strict ethical science, an integral part of philosophy, and hence the happiness of man was never guaranteed with metaphysical certainty. Not having attained to a well-rounded natural wisdom, Cartesian man had to be satisfied with a working, moral certainty and seek any further illumination in supernatural faith.

3. SPINOZA'S GOD AS THE TOTALITY OF NATURE

It was the considered verdict of Benedict Spinoza (1632–1677) that Descartes' philosophy represented a brilliant but unsuccessful venture. The fragmentary character of Cartesian ethics was a sure index of some deep-seated internal failure, a sign that the Frenchman had presented no system at all but only the abortive sketch of one. For what Spinoza demanded of a philosophy above all else was assurance of human happiness and ethical perfection on a fully scientific or demonstrative basis. It was not simply that his predecessor had overlooked a few chapters at the end of the treatise on philosophy, but rather that he had left out the very heart of every genuine philosophical system: the elevation of man to his ethical goal of eternal beatitude.

Spinoza was confident that he could place his finger unerringly upon the exact spot in the Cartesian philosophy whence its shortcomings sprang: the doctrine on God. The notion of an incomprehensible and free creator was its first and greatest error, for it stood in the way of completing the rationalist deduction of all basic truths. The trouble lay in the fact that Descartes' speculations were still covertly regulated by the Judaeo-Christian conception of God and the teachings of the Scholastic theologians. In a thoroughgoing rationalism, there could be no place for even the possibility of a supernatural revelation of truths having any significance for philosophy. For Spinoza, then, the Scriptures were not sources of speculative truth, and institutional religions were primarily the instruments of social organization and practical morality. As for the theological tradition, Spinoza admitted to his friend Henry Oldenburg, first secretary of the Royal Society in London:

I hold an opinion about God and Nature very different from that which modern Christians are wont to defend. For I maintain that God is, as they say, the immanent cause of all things, but not the transitive cause. . . . I say that many attributes which they and all others at least who are known to me attribute to God, I regard as things created; and on the other hand, things which they, on account of their prejudices, regard as created, I contend to be attributes of God, and as misunderstood by them; and also that I could not separate God from Nature as all of whom I have any knowledge have done.[18]

In capsule form, this passage indicates the major reforms which Spinoza introduced into the rationalist conception of God. His transcendence as the infinite, free cause of a world of finite substances was abolished in favor of an identification between God and the totality of nature *(Deus sive Natura)*. This entailed both denying that such things as understanding and will are genuine attributes of God, in His substantial nature, and attributing to that nature extension, as well as thought.

Leibniz once said that Spinoza began where Descartes ended: in naturalism. Descartes ended in naturalism only in the sense that he eliminated final cause from physical explanation and sometimes referred to God's infinite causal power as nature, since this power was the creative and conserving source of all real motion and general laws of motion in physical nature. Yet he did hold a real, substantial distinction between God, the only absolute substance, and finite things as relative substances. Such a distinction seemed senseless to Spinoza, who identified substantial being with completely independent and self-caused being. Since Descartes admitted that the mental and bodily things in our universe are caused by God, Spinoza concluded that they are therefore not substances at all but modes or determinations of the only true substance, God Himself. Behind this denial of a plurality of substantial beings lay Spinoza's resolute plan to safeguard at all costs the rationalist ideal of a complete deductive system, which would be endangered unless God were the substantial essence of all things in nature. With God as the unique substance entering into the intrinsic constitution of all things, it was impossible to gain a true knowledge of them without conceiving them through God and in God. Expressed more positively, it now became possible to gain a unified knowledge of nature in its essential connections and thus insure the moral perfection of man, which consists precisely in this synoptic knowledge and union with God as the totality of nature.

The import and degree of Spinoza's naturalization of God can be gauged by analyzing three areas in which he openly clashed with Descartes: the unity of philosophy, the nature of extension, and the connection between divine causality and human happiness.

(1) *The unity of philosophy.* There has been more sheer nonsense written about Spinoza's views on God than about any other modern philosopher. During his own lifetime and for a century after his death, he was reviled as an atheist because of his denial of divine transcendence and freedom and because of his attribution of extension to God. During the latter part of the eighteenth century, there was an enthusiastic revival of Spinoza among the German idealists, who sketched a romantic picture of him as a feverish, God-intoxicated mystic. The man himself conformed with neither extreme description. He was firmly convinced of God's existence, but he also wanted a God in whose beatitude man

can be methodically assured of a share. He did not conceive of God or nature in a vague, emotional way but through a systematic vision, which was working out the ultimate consequences of a certain notion of the unity of wisdom.

The aim of all philosophizing is to attain our supreme happiness. Descartes was right in asserting, against the skeptics, that true happiness cannot be divorced from philosophical wisdom. But he misstated their relationship by regarding happiness as the fruit of wisdom, whereas in fact it is the very same as wisdom. The wise man is happy, not by means of his philosophical knowledge, but precisely in the possession of it. Spinoza is doing more than defending the primacy of intellect over will; he is denying any real distinction between them. Against both the Scholastics and Descartes, he teaches the complete identity of understanding and will in man.[19] This closes the gap between knowing the truth and following it to fruition. Human freedom is too dangerous a power for Spinoza to allow in man's possession, for it might wreck the entire effort to bring unalloyed happiness within human reach. Only a thoroughly logicized and deterministic view of the search after wisdom can guarantee that perfect unity between metaphysics, ethics, and the happy life which Descartes had failed to secure.

To find happiness, then, one must become aware of man's true condition, his genuine ontological status. As we find him, the ordinary man is completely engrossed in the material world and is subject to its demands. He feels himself to be at the mercy of external forces and placed at a great distance from God. In a word, the average person is estranged from himself and has lost sight of his real nature. The only way to change the situation is through a systematic healing of his understanding, to the point where it will become conscious of the real union existing between the mind and the whole of nature. Philosophy as a search for happiness is inescapably an attempt to recapture this sense of the all-embracing unity of nature and thus give a man the knowledge that is his salvation. In Spinoza, there is a complete merger between metaphysical, ethical, and religious values because they are all identified with this vision of *tota Natura,* or nature as a divine totality.

This program required Spinoza to emphasize the unity and consequence of thought even more than the clarity and distinctness of ideas. Descartes' criterion of truth was inadequate by itself, since its emphasis upon the thinking self and upon sharply distinct ideas jeopardized the union of the self with nature and the continuity of deduction among ideas. Unless this tendency toward atomization were halted, it would be impossible to achieve the geometrical derivation of knowledge as a unified and systematic whole. Hence Spinoza took the drastic step of making a theory of God serve the new epistemological function of guaranteeing the completeness and perfect continuity of a rationalist deduction. The monism of knowledge was now given a foundation in the monism of being for the sake of achieving a closed and complete system. The new standard of truth and basis of unified philosophy had to be located precisely in a monistic doctrine on God: "The first principle is a single being, and infinite. It is the totality of being, outside of which there is nothing."[20] With God as the sum total of reality, it was now possible to claim an objective basis for a complete reduction of our true ideas to a priori unity. Such a tight organization of knowledge was only a counterpart of the unity of nature, with God's substantial essence and power providing the rational links in both orders.

God became not only the ground of unity but also the starting point for Spinoza's system. Spinoza rejected both the realistic point of departure in sensible things and the Cartesian beginning in the Cogito, because they were not powerful enough to carry the systematic burden of a total vision of nature elaborated through analysis of necessary concepts and definitions. Since a deductive process is only as valid and complete as its starting point, Spinoza concluded that the most perfect philosophical deduction must begin with the idea of the most perfect being. The true definition of God's essence must be the sole point of departure in philosophy, so that our thought can express in the order of deductive inference the same active power, universal scope, and necessary sequence as God Himself expresses in nature. Descartes had required of philosophical principles that they be noetic causes of the system of knowledge; Spinoza added that this causation of systematic deductive knowledge is assured only when the first cause of being is also the first principle of our knowledge of being. The distinction between the order of being and the order of knowing had to be wiped out as much as possible for the sake of systematic completeness and certainty.

In conformity with this demand, Spinoza reduces the a posteriori proofs of God's existence to the a priori proof, which he treats as a reflective meditation upon our idea of God. Because man is a modal part of nature, his very being consists in a spontaneous expression of a certain idea of God. The Spinozistic system begins with the formulation of this basic idea in the definition of God as "the Being absolutely infinite and consummately perfect, . . . that is to say, substance consisting of infinite attributes, each one of which expresses eternal and infinite essence."[21] This is a proper and adequate definition of the divine essence, and the proof of God's existence is nothing more than an explicit recognition that existence follows necessarily from this true definition of God. Spinoza does not so much establish the existence of God as the absurdity of denying the definition of His essence. For according to the given definition, God is eternal substance, infinite essence, self-causing power —all of which signify necessity of existence.

This clarification does tell us what is implied in the defining idea of

God, but there remains the further question of whether this idea is indeed a true one, in the sense that it is one which the human mind knows to be existentially grounded. In order to justify the relevance of his definition to real being, Spinoza is obliged to invoke the pantheistic postulate that finite things exist as modes of one divine substance and the rationalistic postulate that essence produces existence in proportion to the power of essence.[22] These are precisely the points at issue, however, and they cannot simply be appealed to as evidence of the real bearing of the proposed idea of God. Spinoza notes that some of our ideas refer immediately to existing material things. But, although the existence of material things is immediately known by us, the initial evidence does not specify that they exist precisely in the modal status of affections of the one divine substance. It cannot be argued that their modal being is included in the meaning of their existence, considered under the aspect of the eternal, since there must be some independent justification of the transition from temporal existence to the meaning assigned for eternal existence within the Spinozistic outlook. The question of the relation between essence and existence also requires specific treatment before the meaning assigned for this relation in the proposed definition of the divine substance can function as a priori proof of God's existence. When this problem is dealt with in Spinoza's discussion of the nature and method of knowledge, essence and existence are already interpreted within the framework of a philosophy of a single substantial reality identical with the totality of nature. What is not shown is that this interpretative setting imposes itself intellectually upon everyone seeking philosophical knowledge of nature, man, and God.

(2) *The nature of extension.* Spinoza was sufficiently well informed about the manner and tempo of contemporary scientific discoveries to recognize that a total deduction of the scientific truths about the physical and biological worlds was an impossibility. Instead of concluding with Descartes, however, that this rendered impossible the completion of the philosophical system, he advocated another viewpoint on the relation between the sciences and philosophy. The proper office of the latter is not to incorporate and complete the findings of science but to transcend them. Scientific reason is higher than mere common sense, but it is also lower than philosophical intuitive knowledge. By introducing the concept of levels of understanding, Spinoza sought to free philosophy from the empirical dependencies and hypothetical procedure of the sciences. Using its own method and criterion of truth, philosophy must concentrate upon its distinctive task of raising the mind to the intuitive knowledge of the divine essence, apprehended as the core of nature. Thus the problem of scientific research can be safely relativized by establishing the superior, eternal view of things.

This does not mean, however, that philosophy can ignore the material world. There has to be a complete philosophical deduction of the material world in its general features, but it must be one which rests upon metaphysical principles and is regulated by the aim of philosophy to bring the mind to its ultimate happiness.[23] Descartes' definition of the material thing solely in terms of extension does not satisfy these requirements. For one thing, it leads to the view that the extended world is a substantial reality, quite distinct from mental substance and from God. This violates the monistic conditions for a deductive system as laid down by Spinoza. Hence he denies that extension is the essential property of matter in the sense that it constitutes a distinct finite substance. The unity of man is also threatened in describing him as a composite of both material and mental substance. More seriously still, the Cartesian view of extension as an inert something-in-itself means that the connection between extension and the actual motions of material things is a purely extrinsic one, dependent upon the free decree of God. Such a view stands in the way of an analytic account of the necessary structure of the physical world of moving bodies.

All three defects in the Cartesian account of extension are remedied by the simple expedient of defining extension as a proper attribute of the divine substance itself.[24] God's complete functional subordination to the demands of the Spinozistic deduction is never more evident than in this doctrine. Spinoza sets up an elaborate machinery of divine attributes and modes in order to provide himself with an a priori explanation of the diversified, actual world. The attributes are the real constituents of the divine essence, as conceived by the intellect. They are infinite in number because the divine essence is infinite in power. But (and this is an indelible mark of the difference between the order of being and that of human knowledge which Spinoza never quite succeeds in erasing) we can know only two attributes, namely, the thought and extension which constitute our own world. From each of these two known attributes there flows, with absolute necessity, an independent series of infinite and finite modes. Thus the finite modes under the attribute of extension make up the bodies of our world, while the finite modes under the attribute of thought constitute the minds or ideas of these bodies. There is a perfect correlation in structure between a given body and its corresponding mental mode, but there is not mutual causality of one upon the other. Modes as such are affections or modifications of the one divine substance, formal ways in which this substance exists and operates.

This theory of extension as a divine attribute removes the Cartesian grounds for failing to make a philosophical deduction of the physical world. Extension is not the defining property of a finite substance but of the one divine substance, and it underlies the variety of bodily things. Hence the continuity of our analysis is not interrupted by a leap from

one substantial essence to another. God enters into the essential definition of finite things as the whole enters into its component parts, thus
permitting an analytic derivation of everything from God, whose power
is the generative principle of both the philosophic system and the universe. In the case of man, there is no need to abandon the homogeneous
naturalistic explanation. He is not a composition of two finite substances
but only of two corresponding modes of the one divine substance. Spinoza's answer to the Cartesian dualism of mind-substance and body-sub-
stance is to deny the substantial character of the two terms and to achieve
the harmony of mind and body through their mutual expression of the
same substance, even though they do so under different attributes.

Finally, the revised theory of attributes and modes overcomes the objection that there can be no deduction of a free creative act. Spinoza
simply redefines creation as "an operation in which no causes except an
efficient one concur" and freedom as "free necessity" or that which "exists
from the necessity of its own nature alone, and is determined to action
by itself alone."[25] The new definition of creation does not merely affirm
the need for an efficient cause, it also excludes the possibility that God
creates as a final cause. Neither understanding nor will belongs to the
divine substance as its attribute. They are a mode of being that issues
forth from the divine substance under the attribute of thought, and
hence they are the product of creation and not its principle. Spinoza
rules them out of the creative act so that the latter will not be a free
and purposive operation. "Thought" is present in this impersonal God,
but only after the manner of a servomechanism's regulation of its own
necessary operations.

The several series of modes emerge from the absolute power and necessity of the divine nature, not from a free act of intellect and will. God is
an infinite nature, or active essence, which cannot but well over with
impersonal spontaneity in the production of an infinite number of
modal effects. He is a free cause only in the accommodated sense that
his compulsion is entirely internal. He is not necessitated externally by
any other causal principle. But He can no more help giving rise to the
modal world than a triangle can exercise any choice about the properties that flow from it.

The comparison between God's creative action and the logical consequence between a mathematical figure and its properties is not an accidental choice, but it is even more indispensable to Spinoza than it was
to Descartes. The process began with the Cartesian merging of efficient
with formal cause in the case of God's self-causation. The only way in
which the rationalist goal of a complete deductive system can be reached
is through the reduction of real *causes* to logical *reasons*. Spinoza transforms the real relation between an existing cause and its effect into the
logical entailment of ground and consequent. This transformation is

facilitated by the rationalist conception of being as essence and of essence itself as self-asserting power. Both efficient and final cause disappear, in so far as they are real extrinsic principles contributing to the distinctive act of existing of some given thing in experience. Divine efficient causality is reduced to a purely formal dynamism and analytic relation between the essence and its properties and modes. No purposive intelligence and no free decision are permitted to spoil the deductive necessity of entailment of modes from the divine attributes. God is thereby reduced to the wholly immanent definition of nature as a totality of active, essential power from which it is not surprising to find that all natural things proceed, with inexorable rational necessity, as its modal determinations.

Whereas recent naturalists like Dewey and Nagel have accustomed us to think of naturalism as a philosophy that dispenses with God, Spinoza's naturalism depends on a theory of God for its animating principle. This is due to the alliance between seventeenth-century naturalism and the rationalist method. Spinoza employs the technique of "redefining" extension, thought, and freedom so that they can be applied to God in such a way that they permit a deduction of the finite world from Him. This process of redefinition leads, however, to an equivocal use of terms and thus renders the desired deduction questionable. Considered as an attribute of God, Spinoza's intelligible extension is utterly different from the divisible dimensions of matter in our actual world. Only the name and the presumed deductive relationship are held in common. This led a contemporary geologist and anatomist (Niels Stensen, later a Catholic bishop) to propose a pertinent question from the scientific standpoint: "But of matter itself, do you, I ask, give us any other knowledge beyond a mathematical examination of quantity relating to figures not yet proved of any kind of particles except hypothetically?"[26] Unless one already concedes the metaphysical system of Spinoza, then, his notion of extension remains suppositional with respect to actual extended things. In any doctrine on God based upon an experiential study of such things, there is no warrant for saying any more than that God has the causal actuality required for production of the extended, material world. This does not imply that the divine actuality has a kind of intelligible extension but that it is a causal agency which is adequate to account for extended things and is thus distinct from them in its own actual being.

Despite Spinoza's reduction of Judaeo-Christian revelation to a practical function, its influence upon his conception of God is deep and pervasive. This is especially evident in his effort to maintain some distinction between God as substance and His modal expressions as the world, as well as in his application of thought and freedom, in some sense, to God. But the unity of God as all-embracing nature relativizes all distinctions drawn within the totality, so that the world is the modal aspect of the divine power itself under its attributes of thought and extension. As for thought and freedom, they lose their personal significance of reflective control in being predicated of God. At most there is an impersonal spontaneity which is somehow conscious of its own necessary expansion into the forms of the modal world. Hegel and the later idealists will adapt this hint about an impersonal, divine basis of being to their own dialectic of absolute spirit and its relative moments of development.

(3) *Divine causality and human happiness.* Spinoza entitled his major work an *Ethics* (1677) not only to signalize his main intent, but also to serve as a reminder that there is no ultimate distinction between metaphysics and ethics. Instead, there is a preliminary way and a plenary way of stating the same truth about nature as a whole. What appears at first to be only a transition from metaphysical error to truth turns out in fact to be a moral journey from the slavery of the passions to virtue and happiness.

An ethical meaning can now be given to the doctrine on substance-attributes-modes. Taken together, the divine substance and its infinite number of attributes constitute *natura naturans,* or nature in its dynamic, productive aspect; the totality of modes constitutes *natura naturata,* or nature in its explicated and produced aspect. When Spinoza sets the goal of philosophy to be the discovery of the union of the mind with the whole of nature, he means the knowledge of the totality of nature as both *naturans* and *naturata,* for this constitutes the full reality of God. The mind which fails to see God or nature in this integral way is taking an imaginative and erroneous view of things. It thinks that individual things are contingent, temporal substances, that man is a free agent, and that he is subject to external forces and chance events. To take this imaginative view of nature is to be subject to the passions, to be the hapless victim of all the miseries of life.

Liberation from the passions comes when we abandon this false outlook and embrace the true doctrine on substance-attributes-modes.[27] The modal world is then seen in proper, eternal perspective, and a change takes place in the individual's moral condition. He is no longer at the mercy of every external circumstance, for he has learned to regard *natura naturata* precisely as it stems from *natura naturans* and hence to see it in the true light of eternity. The total determination of the modal world and everything in it springs from its very definition as a reality caused by another. Far from leading to a depressing fatalism, however, this conception is the basis for whatever hope and enthusiasm may enliven the human breast. For this "other," this causal principle of the world of modes, is none other than the omnipotent and wholly immanent God. Hence the causal determination of things is really from within and is an expression of the divine rationality and power themselves. To pass from an imaginative to a true or eternal view of the universe is nothing more than to share in Spinoza's own vision of God's identity with the necessary unfolding of nature. And to gain this vision means to acquire a portion of God's own power and dominance over worldly events.

The human mind is an automaton, like all other modal expressions of divinity, but it is nevertheless a spiritual or reflective automaton. It can improve its state of knowledge, become aware of the divine immanence in and as nature, and thus penetrate through the world of bodily and mental modes to their source and center in God. The climax of metaphysical speculation coincides with the instant of our ethical rebirth to eternity. The man who has healed his understanding by getting an adequate knowledge of nature has simultaneously overcome the passions and entered upon the active life. Its characteristic expression is an abiding love directed toward God, in whose rational necessity and driving power we all participate. This love toward God has its counterpart in a joyous acquiescence of the mind to our human condition as a mode of the divine substance. Here we find our freedom and our immortality in surrender to the universal determinism of the rational laws of nature and to our status as modes of the divine attributes. What Spinoza defends so warmly is not personal immortality but the eternal and necessary being of an impersonal, general mode of understanding, under the attribute of thought.

This solution to the problem of human happiness is reached through a series of axiomatic definitions of God, freedom, and will. But the method of geometrical demonstration fails to obliterate the emphatic experiential difference between recognition of a situation and joyful acquiescence to it, between finding out the truth about human nature and patterning our lives in accordance with such knowledge. There remains a gap between the two which cannot be explained purely in terms of degrees of knowledge. It must include a reference to man's ability to say "nay" in the face of a known obligation and make a free acceptance distinct from knowing what he should accept. Spinoza's world is bereft of obligation, formally speaking, and yet his philosophy is an implicit plea to embrace our responsibility for overcoming the unaccountable discrepancy which exists between the necessary laws and the actual conditions of human nature. Such a discrepancy, together with the consequent obligation of healing the understanding and converting oneself to the true view of God, should have no place in the world described by his monistic metaphysics.

Another unresolved tension in Spinoza's system results from his effort to link together the universal religious sense of God's immanence and the rationalist project of a deductive system. The Spinozistic God is close to man, but only in the way that an impersonal, cosmic formula is present to the natural events regulated by it. However powerful and energetic this formula is represented as being, it cannot take the initiative in the form of a personal act of love of God for man. There can be no relation of dialogue or communication of person with person between man and God. God in His infinite substance or as *natura naturans* cannot love man. The only love He can have for man is in and through His modal expressions, but then there is a strict identity rather than a mutual communion of love between man and God. Paradoxically, the pantheistic theory of the unique divine substance leads to a God that is either equivocally related to modal things or suffocatingly identified with the world to the point of breaking down the conditions of distinction under which alone human fellowship with God can flourish.

Spinoza's portrait of the wise man surrendering himself confidently into the hands of universal reason and the necessary laws of nature exercized a strong attraction over the poetic imagination of Goethe, who, in turn, kindled Albert Schweitzer's reverence for God-Nature:

> He rightly is the world's deep-centered motion,
> Nature and He in mutual devotion,
> So that what lives and moves and is in Him,
> Will never find His strength or spirit dim.[28]

Even Nietzsche and Sartre, who have attempted to reserve lucidity about man's condition as an exclusively atheistic virtue, have drawn inspiration from Spinoza and have been unable to eliminate all traces of the relationship of man to God.

4. LEIBNIZ: GOD AND THE PRIMACY OF ESSENCE

It was left for Gottfried Leibniz (1646–1716), the lawyer and diplomat among philosophers, as well as in political life, to attempt to resolve the tensions between his rationalist forbears concerning God and the world. With his genius for discerning a common ground, he proposed a reconciliation in terms of the underlying premise of rationalism which he now brought into full focus: *the primacy of essence*. It is fashionable among historians of philosophy today to classify philosophers as essentialists or existentialists. This division can be misleading if by "essentialism" is meant ignorance or depreciation of the problem of existence. In this sense, the rationalists do not fit into this category; a concern for existence lies behind Descartes' view of the Cogito, Spinoza's theory of the production of the world, and Leibniz' principle of sufficient reason. But these thinkers do qualify as essentialists if by that is meant their systematic effort to award the primacy to essence over existence in the order of being, as well as of thought. Far from regarding this designation as a reproach, however, Leibniz would glory in the primacy of essence as providing the backbone of every truly philosophical explanation of the real.

To explain something is nothing more than to determine its reason for being or (what amounts to the same thing) its essential structure and relations. What characterizes rationalism as a distinctive philosophical current is its dedication to the task of assigning the reasons in the essence for events that occur or truths that are uncovered. Karl Jaspers has said that every philosophy operates upon a fund of capital acquired through some prephilosophical act of faith. The act of faith upon which rationalism rests is the presumption that the intelligibility of being consists primarily in the radication of all perfections in the essence and that the human mind enjoys the corresponding ability to work out all significant truths through analysis of essential concepts and principles. Leibniz' contribution is to formulate this presumption in a definitive, logically rigorous way and to adapt the doctrine on God to it.

Leibniz does not regard essences in a static and purely abstract way, for then they would have no explanatory value for generating a system of thought. On the contrary, the essence of a thing is what is most dynamic and concrete about it. The essence is the same as the substance, and the latter, in turn, is the active center of all operations and relations.[29] Hence the essence is the real basis which precontains all the events, qualities, and actions which will happen to the thing throughout its career in the world. To find a reason for something, then, is to trace out the connections of some given aspect of the thing with its essential nature or substance. We have a priori certainty that the reason is present, for otherwise the given aspect would not emerge into being and come within the scope of our experience. Indeed, what makes a proposition true is precisely its ability to express the necessary relation actually obtaining between the real essence and its dynamic consequences.

Granted this theory of the correspondence between logical reasons and real essential connections, we might expect all the true propositions in a human science to be strictly analytic in nature. That such is not actually the case had forced Descartes to modify his claims for a deductive physics and had even compelled Spinoza to establish an unwonted dualism between scientific and metaphysical explanation. But Leibniz sought after a way of admitting hypothesis and conjecture in certain areas of science and morality without disturbing in the least the theory of essential reasons. This he accomplished through a distinction between the real foundation of true propositions and our ways of ascertaining the truth in different instances. Just as the universal structure of being demands the containment of all properties and events in the real essence, so is there no exception to the rule that the predicates of all true propositions are contained necessarily in the concept of the proper subject. This exigency of being and thought is the *principle of sufficient reason*.[30] It states that nothing is without a reason why it is rather than is not, or that the concept of the subject necessarily contains all the predicates validly attributed to it. Demonstration depends on taking the essence as the causal principle of knowledge, as well as of being, and on locating in the essence the total intelligibility of being.

But our limited minds cannot always see this analytic inclusion by direct insight or by simple appeal to the principle of contradiction. Such direct verification can be achieved in necessary propositions expressing ideal relations or purely possible essences. In existential problems, however, no amount of direct conceptual analysis or appeal to violations of the principle of contradiction can settle the issue. The contingent fact of a present downpour cannot be given proof solely through analysis of the necessities of time and weather in general or by maintaining that sunshine is impossible. To determine the truth of contingent, existential matters, we require something more than direct analysis, not because the latter is inadequate in itself, but only because our minds cannot pursue it with sufficient depth and vigor to reach the relation of inclusion between the essence and its properties. Instead of making a realistic appeal to experience and a distinctive grasp of existential act, however, Leibniz has to deduce the intelligibility of the existing, sensible world from some purely a priori source. He must look outside finite existents, not only for their ultimate explanation, but also for their initial intelligibility as existents.

Once more, God is called to the rescue and given a function in saving the rationalist mode of explanation. "The first principle concerning existents is this proposition: *God wills to choose the most perfect*."[31] This criterion of existential verification is therefore termed the principle of perfection, or the *principle of the best,* in the sense that God chooses the maximum of perfection or the best possible world to exist. Even though we may be unable to see the direct connection between a thing's essence and some one of its qualities or events, we have this a priori surety that the connection does obtain. For God produces a particular event only in view of its contribution to the harmonious perfection or essential interrelatedness of the universe. This gives a more determinate meaning to the "sufficient" reason for something. This reason does not consist in the individual essence and its properties alone but in the harmony holding among all the essences entering into the existent world. A reason is sufficient when it expresses that combination of things which will insure the greatest amount of perfection or essences in the world. Although we cannot always see how the prevailing order is the best and most intelligible, we can deduce this to be so by an appeal to God's adherence to the principle of the best in His creative activity.

Alongside the physical or mechanistic explanation of nature in terms of efficient cause, Leibniz proposes this metaphysical explanation in terms of final cause or the motivation of producing the maximum of perfection. Because this motive is attributed to God, the universal creator, the metaphysical interpretation of events is comprehensive and certain. Leibniz quietly adds that the principle of the best is itself indemonstrable and that this is the same as saying that God is free. By making this equation between the indemonstrability of the principle and the divine freedom, he implies that the latter is not so much a perfection of God's will as an imperfection in our vision of the motives moving God's will. That God's choices are regulated by motives or sufficient reasons is required by the Leibnizian interpretation of the intelligibility of being in terms of essential connections and reasons. According to this view, God would be acting irrationally and the foundation of the sciences would be destroyed were His creative actions not determined by the principle of the best and hence by sufficient reasons.

In this way, Leibniz claimed to synthesize Spinoza's rational deduction of the world with Descartes' free creation. He expressed his compromise position in the key term "moral necessity."[32] God's action is ruled by a certain necessity, as Spinoza taught. The divine will does not have arbitrary control over the internal structure of essences and eternal truths but respects their own nature. Furthermore, God always acts according to the rule of the best and permits no exception to it, thus assuring us of the harmony and essential perfection of the world. Yet Descartes is right in defending the freedom of creation. For the world proceeds from the divine intellect and will, not from the necessity of God's nature. The motives or reasons for creation do not compel God with an absolute necessity, since the nonexistence of the world is not an impossibility. But they do exercise an inclining or persuasive power over the divine will. Their necessity is moral in that they appeal to the personal God's fidelity to His own choice of the rule of the best. Since the nonexistence of the world is not a contradiction and since the reasons for creation move God only on the supposition of His choice of them in accord with the rule of perfection, the creative act is free or only morally necessary.

The success of the mediating doctrine of a "Christian Fate" can be tested by inquiring whether another universe might exist and whether God might follow a principle which is different from that of the best. Leibniz cannot allow that God might create another world except on the supposition that His action is regulated by a new principle and not by the production of maximum perfection. But God is never granted any real alternative to this latter principle. As Kant once remarked, Leibniz' theory of moral necessity specifies one source for necessary action but does not lessen its compelling force. When Leibniz says that God chooses this principle freely, he is referring only to our way of looking at the divine acts of will as if they constituted an isolated series. Our human minds cannot fathom the divine will, and hence there is indeterminacy in our knowledge of the ultimate ground for the choice of the principle of the best. Taken in itself, however, the divine will is subject to a two-fold determination from the divine essence and from the essential objects of the divine intellect. "It follows from the supreme perfection [i.e., essence or power] of God, that in creating the universe he has chosen the best possible plan, in which there is the greatest variety together with the greatest order."[33] Having accepted the common rationalist equation between the perfection of God and His amount of essence or power, Leibniz struggles in vain to escape from Spinoza's inference that the divine essence affirms itself with infinite necessity, both in positing its own existence and in producing the existence of other essences. Hence the distinction between moral and absolute necessity reduces to one between a proximate freedom of God (based on the imperfection of our knowledge) and His ultimate, internal determinism in being and acting. Without an unconditioned determinism of God, the certainty of the principle of sufficient reason would disappear and the universal application of the principle of the best to the existent universe would be groundless.

On the side of the objects of the divine understanding and will, the subordination of God to the primacy of essence is equally manifest. Galileo's notion of a geometrizing God, who calculates and then brings forth a world, is given a fresh lease on life. Leibniz endows the realm of essences with a twilight reality of its own, so that it will be safe from the arbitrariness of the divine freedom as conceived by Descartes. Since to be an essence is to exert some power and generate some being, each essence is a living force in the divine mind and embodies a conatus, or dynamic tendency toward existence, as the ultimate mode of essential perfection. But just as no man is an island unto himself, so no essence is completely discrete or unrelated to its fellow centers of striving toward existence. The amount of harmony among various essences determines the perfection and power of their joint claim on existence.

The ultimate rivalry is not between individual essences but between sets or systems of essences jockeying for the privilege of constituting the finite, existing universe.

It being once posited that being is better than not being, or that there is a reason why something rather than nothing should be, or that we must pass from the possible to the actual, it follows that, *even if nothing further is determined,* the quantity of existence must be as great as possible, regard being had to the capacity of the time and of the place (or to the possible order of existence), exactly as tiles are disposed in a given area in such a way that it shall contain the greatest number of them possible.[34]

Here we have all the elements in the Leibnizian notion of the creative process. The principle of sufficient reason is the graven law of the divine essence and is posited with an infinite and necessary force. Consequently, the strife among the other essences for existential standing can be settled according to only one standard: the realization of the maximum of perfection. God is the cosmic bricklayer, and His intellect calculates which group of essences will fill out the limited available space and time to the fullest. Once this judgment of plenitude is passed, the divine will must make its creative choice and give existence to the best possible world. The essential components in the maximum system require only this acquiescence, or consent decree, on the part of God's will in order to burst into existence. Existence is the climactic moment in which the most perfect or powerful set of essences fixes the divine will upon itself and thus breaks through the barrier of possibility into actuality.

Leibniz' theory of monads is only an application of this general doctrine to the actual universe. Since the condition for the appearance of the existing world is the mutual compatibility of a certain group of dynamic essences, the pre-established harmony of things is assured on a priori grounds. A deductive explanation can then be given for the relation between the soul-monad and the body-monads, as well as between our innate ideas and the objective universe.

On the question of whether God is the prime monad or above all monads, Leibniz attempted a characteristically diplomatic compromise between pantheism and a transcendent God. He agreed with Descartes that God is utterly distinct from the created monads, both because He is the self-caused and perfectly actual essence and because the monads themselves are substances or active agents and not modes of His nature. Yet He is also the apex of the continuous pyramid of monads, the heart of the single interconnecting system of realized essences. Spinoza was right in warning that if the transcendence of God were overstressed, the a priori certainty about the principles ruling our universe would be weakened through a too remote foundation. Leibniz had the univocal conception of being as self-affirming essence wherever real beings are found. Hence he could distinguish between God and the world only in degree or quantity of essence and power, in the way that general space differs from limited spatial things. Like Cusanus and Malebranche, he accepted the mathematical metaphor of God as a given limit and finite things as figures asymptotically approaching that limit, or of God as the infinite curve and the kinds of beings as co-ordinates of that curve.

Behind this reluctance to interpret the analogy of being as anything more than a theory of degrees and mathematical proportions lay the Leibnizian ideal of founding a universal jurisprudence, or science of the metaphysical and ethical rules of justice, governing all things and events.[35] The two requirements for such a science were: (1) the universal primacy of essence and the principle of sufficient reason over every existent reality; and (2) the inclusion of all beings within the generic structure of being. The first rule led Leibniz to regard even God's existence as the outcome of the assertion of divine power of essence and to treat sufficient reason as a universal essential law imposing itself upon every aspect of the divine activity and will. The second requirement led him to take being as a genus whose specific differences or modes are the infinite substance and finite substances. Leibniz thought that God's distinction from the world could be adequately safeguarded by affirming His personal nature and by restoring substantial reality to finite monads. And with God included as one species of being, the general laws of being, goodness, and justice could apply univocally to Him and thus secure the a priori foundation for a universal jurisprudence. But if being is fundamentally generic and therefore univocal, God and finite things differ only in degree of essence and not in the very manner of existing itself. Hence this universal science has a monistic implication despite Leibniz' desire to avoid it.

Leibniz' famous *Theodicy* (1710) reflected this quandary of reconciling a universal deductive science with divine transcendence and freedom. He conceived of theodicy as an immediate application of the general definition of justice given in the universal jurisprudence and therefore as requiring the same primacy of essence and univocity of being. The task of theodicy was to vindicate God's justice with respect to the world against Bayle's doubts based on widespread suffering and evil in this presumably best possible world. When Leibniz remarked dryly that Bayle "has on his side all the advantages except that of the root of the matter,"[36] he meant that the eloquence, erudition, and factual data of Bayle could not counterbalance Leibniz' own metaphysical principles. But this remark was inadvertently indicative of something deeper: the growing split between the principles and system of rationalism and the field of empirical facts. Sufficient reasons were demonstrative, but they did not alleviate stubborn facts or illuminate historical and moral aspects of human existence. It was becoming more and more apparent that the deductive approach could not cope with the existing world at its own level and in terms of its own givenness. Evil is something more terrible than an artful shadowing or a clever atonal note. The Leibnizian theodicy was magnificent as a dialectical analysis of concepts of grace and will and wisdom and justice, but as a demonstration, it minimized the savage bite of human suffering and moral evil and endangered God as a unique existent and free agent.

5. THE SEEDS OF DISSOLUTION IN MALEBRANCHE

Even in the barest outline, it is apparent that the speculation of Nicholas Malebranche (1638–1715), priest of the French Oratory, carries the tensions between the Christian God and the rationalist system beyond the point of compromise union. His position is that of Christian rationalism *in extremis*. It is not so much an instance of Christian philosophy as the use of Christian belief to avoid the consequences of a philosophical tradition. Malebranche wants to defend both religion and scientific knowledge, but he finds that the defense cannot be made on the philosophical basis of rationalism without leading to the pantheistic naturalism of Spinoza. Hence he shifts to a fideistic view which is saved from being identical with the older skepticism only because of its speculative theological content and its respect for the sciences. The three main teachings where this process can be observed are: occasionalism, or the sole causality of God; the intuitive vision of God; and the vision of other things in God

Malebranche's occasionalism consisted in a denial of finite causality and an ascription of all real causality to God alone within a framework of finite "occasions." An explicitly religious motive prompted him to refuse all causal power to finite things. He agreed with Hobbes and the entire rationalist line that there is something divine about power and that men direct their worship toward things that can exert power over their lives. Hence Malebranche felt it necessary to reserve all causal power for God, so that all religious devotion would likewise be directed toward Him alone. He regarded the Scholastics and the Cambridge Platonists as sheer pagans in philosophy because they accepted the Aristotelian teaching on substantial forms, faculties, qualities, and other active powers inherent in creatures. He would have concurred heartily with Karl Barth and the crisis theologians of our day about the paganizing influence of Greek philosophy upon Christian religion. Against any doctrine of secondary causes he held that "all the forces of nature are nothing but the will of [the solely efficacious] God."[37] In this respect he was forced to disagree with his own masters, St. Augustine and Descartes, who had distinguished between the causal power of finite things and its ultimate source in the creator of nature.

But like other thinkers who failed to see in finite causality a manifestation of God's power and goodness, Malebranche was eventually obliged to make a covert restitution of some type of agency to finite things. God's general laws of motion are ineffective until they are determined by particular circumstances or finite modes of mind and body. Thus finite things provide the indispensable occasions, or "natural causality," for enabling the divine power to operate in the actual world along definite lines. The human will has not only the negative ability to arrest its tendency toward the perfect good but also the positive ability to give moral consent to the inclination toward other objects. This relieves God of responsibility for moral evil, but it also restores secondary causality in everything but name. Indeed, Malebranche overcompensated by making God's action in the world inherently dependent on the disposition of finite things and regulated by the autonomous principle of simplicity or economy of means.[38] He conceived of God as being bound to act in the most simple and uniform way, just as though He were following the set rules of a superior mathematical physicist. Although this gave a stable basis to the mathematical interpretation of natural laws, it also provided an easy opportunity for Hume (who made a careful study of Malebranche) to draw from occasionalism the paradoxical conclusion that God can be dispensed with in our philosophical explanation of the physical and moral worlds.

Malebranche cannot accept the realistic point of departure for proof of God's existence. He does not openly admit that there are any instances of finite causality, and he denies both that we know the existing material world through direct sensory apprehension and that it can be demonstrated Cartesianwise. For him, the sensible world is bereft of causal power, and its existence is only a matter of faith; hence it cannot provide initial evidence of God's existence. Not even the Cartesian Cogito can do this, since the human self is not lucidly self-evident but is veiled in obscurity and unintelligibility. We are aware of our own existence by an interior sentiment or act of natural faith, but we are totally ignorant of the essential nature of the self. Although we do know our states of mind and feeling, they are subjective and cannot lead us to God. Malebranche is just as skeptical as Bishop Huet about the ability of the Cogito to overcome the hypothesis of a malign spirit. Any strict reasoning to God's existence is subject to doubt, deception, and the pitfalls of a weak memory.

The only thing Malebranche can do is to convert Descartes' first proof from the idea of the infinite into an intuition or vision of the infinite being of God. He distinguishes between two meanings of the term "idea": as a subjective modification of the mind and as an objective content. In the former sense we have no idea of God, and in the latter sense we do not understand God through any finite, intelligible content. Our idea of the infinite can be nothing more than the infinite reality itself as manifested to the human mind. Only the infinite itself can represent the infinite being of God, so that the only idea of God is God Himself, the Word, or Second Person of the Trinity. The very fact of the existence of the idea of God reveals God's existence, for they are one and the same. "If we think of God, it follows that He exists."[39] This is the clearest existential proposition, and it is just as intuitively certain as the Cartesian Cogito. But in order to see its force, we have to accept two points: the identity between the idea of the infinite and the infinite being of God Himself and the identity of both of these with the Word as our interior light and master. This supposes that we already know God by faith. Consequently, Malebranche admits that philosophical knowledge of God rests ultimately upon supernatural assent to the basic truths of faith—a thoroughly fideistic conclusion.

The doctrine of the vision of other things in God was an extension of the position on God's existence, since it hinged on the distinction between ideas as modifications of our mind and as objective contents.[40] Malebranche feared that if the immediate terminus of the pure understanding were a mental mode, the objective reality of intellectual knowledge could never be established. He pushed to the extreme the rationalist policy of making God serve as the underpinning for an epistemology. Descartes used the divine power and veracity to guarantee his criterion of knowledge and his use of human cognitive faculties; Spinoza based the objectivity of knowledge on the fact that every mental mode is precisely correlated with a material mode by virtue of their mutual presence in the one divine substance; Leibniz appealed to God as the harmonizer of both the monads constituting the world and the ideas constituting states of our mind. In order to close the gap completely between idea and object, and thus achieve the rationalist goal of a perfect coincidence between the intelligible form and the reality known, Malebranche now located the objective content of ideas of pure understanding in the divine essence itself. He referred to God as the place of minds, just as space is the place of bodies. We have a direct vision of the divine essence, if not in its absolute nature, then at least to the extent that it is sharable by other things. Hence we see the same exemplar ideas according to which God creates the finite world. Since God cannot produce a contradiction, our vision of the ideal essences and eternal truths provides an unshakable mooring for the sciences.

But Malebranche could not push this intuitive vision too far without endangering the freedom of creation. Hence he maintained that the archetypal idea of intelligible extension, as seen in God, reveals to us only the essence of the material world and not its existence. The divine creative decision is not coerced by any Spinozistic overflow of power or any Leibnizian calculus of essences; hence no deduction of the existential reality of the extended universe is possible. It can be known only through faith based on a study of the account of creation in Genesis and miracles in the New Testament. Thus the existential reference of scientific knowledge is grounded in faith and not in a deductive philosophy. Our strict knowledge of material things is confined to their ideal possibility and essential relations, whereas faith is our only avenue of access to their empirical existence and the real bearing of scientific deduction.

In the case of the thinking self, the human understanding is still more restricted because the danger of Spinozism is still more imminent. Although we have an interior sentiment that the self exists in function of its perceptions and feelings, we have no knowledge of its essence.

God has not chosen to manifest to us that aspect of His essence containing the exemplar idea of the essence of the human self.[41] Contrary to the teaching of Descartes, then, Malebranche maintained that we must remain totally in the dark about our own essential nature. He encouraged a purely phenomenalistic view of the self as a series of perceptions in order to evade the pantheistic identification of the idea of the self and its objective reality in God, a position toward which his principles tended. Once more Hume was the heir of a refusal to accept the integral consequences of rationalism. Just as one can describe the natural order without a functional use of God, so can one dispense with the substantial essence in an empirical description of the self. From his reading in Malebranche, Hume concluded that God and the substantial self are surplus beliefs and not the organizing principles of philosophy.

Classical rationalism sought to overcome skepticism by freeing the intellect from dependence upon sense data and focusing it toward the essential structures and their power of self-affirmation. In order to construct a philosophical system which would be both comprehensive and relevant to actual things, however, classical rationalism had to take an increasingly instrumentalist position on God. It made certain claims about the real definition of the divine essence, the a priori proof of the divine existence, and the deductive implications of the divine attributes which could only be substantiated within a pantheistic monism. The effort of Leibniz and Malebranche to avoid this outcome was not radically enough conceived, since it did not restore the basic role of sensation and hence did not eliminate the functional subordination of God to the requirements of the philosophical system. Within the rationalist context, a fissure developed between the essential principles of deduction and the content of experience which no appeal to the laws governing God's essential exercise of power was able to close. A restoration of reason and the object of knowledge to their foundation in human experience was clearly needed. In meeting this need, however, the empiricists not only reacted against the deductive employment of God in the essentialist systems, but also made any kind of doctrine on God seem less and less pertinent to the philosophical inquiry.

Chapter IV

EMPIRICISM AND THE NEUTRALIZING
OF GOD

A FUNCTIONAL deity is a highly expendable commodity once its functions can be explained by some other principles. It was the long-range purpose of British empiricism to account for human knowledge and conduct in ways that would not require a theological guarantee. The great negative theme of this movement of thought was that a philosophy based on experience can safely dispense with God or at least reduce His role to a minimum. Empiricism made sure that if God were ever again to assume a significant place in philosophy, this would not mean a simple restoration of the Instrumental Guarantor of the rationalist systems.

The neutralizing of God as a prime philosophical influence was effected only in gradual stages and was never quite completed. In the first phase, Bacon and Hobbes concentrated chiefly on evacuating all speculative philosophical content from a natural theology. Locke's contribution was the elaboration of a theory of knowledge in which God did not figure as a principle, although His existence was demonstrated and His importance in ethics acknowledged. These last two points were challenged by Hume, who sought to reduce the doctrine on God to a bare speculative belief in His existence, without any demonstrative knowledge or ethical implications. Berkeley and the Scottish school were partial exceptions to the general trend, since they aimed at restoring strict knowledge of God and according Him an important place in moral life. But their efforts fell short of this declared aim because they employed the very premises which had already convinced the other empiricists of the precariousness of any doctrine on God within the accepted method of inquiry.

1. FRANCIS BACON ON NATURAL THEOLOGY

Even before opposition to Continental rationalism developed in England, the future of the scientific approach to nature seemed to many investigators to be bound up with the removal of natural theology as a speculative norm in philosophy. A glance at the philosophy courses being taught at Oxford and Cambridge universities during the early part of the seventeenth century makes this attitude intelligible.[1] Nominally, the curriculum was Aristotelian, but in actual practice it was supported by numberless modern commentaries, textbooks, and tutors' notes which seldom encouraged the student to undertake an independent study of man and nature. A premium was placed upon memory devices and tabular schemes for arranging everything under artificial divisions. Mathematics was scarcely cultivated at the universities until after mid-century, and the natural sciences were held strictly subordinate to philosophical categories. An attempt was made to organize all scientific findings hierarchically within various departments of "special physics." The latter, in turn, was regarded as the field of application for the general principles of metaphysics and philosophy of nature. In the process of categorizing our knowledge of natural phenomena and making it digestible for the undergraduate mind, large drafts were made on the theory of God's creative activity and providential governance of all things. This seemed to provide a safe and orderly framework within which to fit the scientific study of nature. In fact, however, the sciences were unduly confined by this deductive ordering. The predictable result was a reaction against all metaphysical concepts, with the philosophy of God as the readiest victim.

As befitted an astute politician serving under a king who fancied himself an expert theologian, Francis Bacon (1561–1626) never made an outright denial of natural theology. Instead of attempting any intrinsic discussion of its various theses, he shifted the whole problem to the terrain of the divisions and method of philosophy. He restated the nature and aim of philosophy in such a fashion that little except the name and the ancient glory remained for natural theology to claim. He calculated correctly that by undermining its methodological position, he could nullify the influence of this discipline without ever engaging in a pitched battle over particular issues.

In his report to King James I of England on how to improve the general state of learning, Bacon made the basic recommendation that a deep gulf be maintained between the natural disciplines on the one side and religion and sacred theology on the other. Both social harmony and scientific integrity demand the rigid separation of these fields. The philosopher who dabbles in theology gives birth to a fabulous, uncontrollable system, whereas the theologian who takes too much interest in philosophical distinctions and scientific discoveries ends in heresy. The only safe path is to foster a sharp dichotomy between the natural and the revealed orders. Unfortunately, natural theology seems to provide a bridge from the one domain of learning to the other, and hence it must be deprived of this intermediary role.

The most fundamental Baconian divisions of knowledge are revealed and natural, the truths received from above through divine illumination and those that come through the natural light of reason and the senses.[2] Both sacred theology and philosophy are perfections of reason, but they differ in their source and object. Sacred theology is based upon the revealed word of God contained in Scripture and deals with the divine mysteries of our redemption; philosophy is drawn from the natural report of the senses and reason and concerns itself with the structure of nature or the works of God. In line with his Calvinist upbringing, Bacon sharply distinguished between the two books of knowledge: Scripture, or the word of God, and nature, or the works of God. Although a reading of the one book may help us to appreciate better the content of the other, there are no truths which can be both revealed and arrived at independently by natural cognition. There is a possibility of mutual illumination, once the content of each is known, but no possibility of sharing any portion of the content of truth in common.

The older theological tradition of some truths discoverable through both reason and revelation was thereby removed, and with it went the conception of a philosophical knowledge of the existence and attributes of God and His causality in the world. This radical consequence was not immediately evident in Bacon's subdivision of philosophy, however, since he phrased it in venerable terminology.

There are three main branches of philosophy, depending upon where the mind's light is focused. Its direct ray shines upon nature and generates philosophy of nature; its reflected light illuminates man in terms of philosophy of man; its refracted beam mounts from creatures to God, who is studied in philosophy of God or natural theology. Bacon does little more than rough in a few headings for the content of a philosophy of man. In this area, his most remarkable achievement is the negative one of excluding entirely from philosophical inquiry the questions of the nature, origin, and immortality of the soul. He appeals to unassailable religious considerations in order to justify this exclusion. The rational soul is directly infused by God through a special act and hence entirely escapes a direct natural analysis. While it is a revealed truth that the image of God is found in man, this likeness has still been ruined by the Fall. Therefore, the light of faith is required to discern the presence of God's image and to investigate man in his rational nature. Through this appeal to Calvinist theology once more, Bacon is able to refer all skeptical difficulties about immortality to the professors of sacred theology and, at the same time, secure the total confinement of philosophical intelligence to problems involving only our material world of bodies in motion. The steady beam of human reason must be concentrated upon nature and the development of philosophy of nature, without any distraction from the other parts of philosophy.

Bacon's next step in this direction is to prevent any alliance between metaphysics and natural theology. The former is a part of philosophy of nature, whereas the latter is a totally different branch of philosophy, if, indeed, it can be said to have any standing. "Natural Science or Theory is divided into Physics and Metaphysics. . . . Natural Theology, which heretofore has been handled confusedly with Metaphysics, I have inclosed and bounded by itself."[3] Bacon conceives of metaphysics as the farthest extension of philosophy of nature, but still it cannot transcend the general object of all physical reasoning: the natural world of matter in motion. Consequently, there is no portion of metaphysics which can give knowledge of the wholly immaterial reality of God and the rational soul. "What is left remaining for Metaphysics? Certainly nothing beyond nature; but of nature itself much the most excellent part."[4] Bacon sees that the best way to keep metaphysics and natural theology apart is to physicize the former, so that it can provide no valid foundation for investigating the transcendent being of God, and then to treat the latter as a completely separate and metaphysically unfounded discipline. Baconian metaphysics is an internal division of the philosophy of nature, and therefore it cannot make the separative judgment that being is not confined to the material condition of nature in which we first encounter it. Thus there is no way in which metaphysics can culminate and complete itself in a philosophically grounded study of God.

Nevertheless, Bacon makes two observations about metaphysics which seem to contradict this last statement. He defines metaphysics as that part of natural philosophy which treats of the formal and final causes. Since the finality of nature provides one of the usual routes to God, a transition can apparently be made from the metaphysical study of final cause to natural theology. Actually, a distinction is made at once between a valid and an illegitimate search after final causes. The only type of final cause that philosophy can discover pertains to man's actions and to the subordination of science and technology to human welfare. These valid meanings for final cause refer exclusively to philosophy of man and philosophy of nature and provide no ground for going beyond the finite world. On the contrary, Bacon lists the attempt to find universal, final causes, operative in nature itself, as one of the idols, or typical fallacies, of the human mind. He does not deny that some sort of universal law or cosmic purpose is instilled by God into nature, but he insists that it remains totally unknowable by natural means. Only Scripture can assure us that God made all things according to an orderly plan and imbued them with a tendency toward the perfection of the whole. Hence the philosophical study of nature will sustain no inference to God's existence or providence.

The second apparent softening of the contrast between metaphysics and natural theology is contained in Bacon's remark that there is only a short step from the one science to the other.[5] The significant thing is, however, that to take the step, one must leave metaphysics entirely behind and enter a completely different field. Furthermore, Bacon provides no way of making even this one short step under philosophical propulsion. Since the formal and final causes studied by metaphysics are wholly immanent in material nature, they do not enable the inquirer to mount in a continuous way from the reaches of metaphysical thought to natural theology. The latter must sink or swim on its own strength, and Bacon sees to it that it cannot swim. It receives no support whatsoever from the recognized philosophical disciplines, and it ultimately cannot maintain itself except on the basis of faith.

The indefensible position of natural theology becomes manifest as soon as Bacon describes its content and scope.[6] It cannot deal with anything proper to revelation. This rules out not only the inner life of God and the redemption but also everything pertaining to God's essence, will, and design, which are reserved for sacred theology. All that a study of the book of nature can establish is that God exists and is powerful and wise. Consequently, natural theology is strictly limited to the existence, power, and wisdom of God. Even this concession is not allowed to stand, however, but is relentlessly whittled down until it becomes a meaningless admission without philosophical significance.

Bacon begins the whittling process by acknowledging that the mind which learns to view natural causes in conjunction rather than singly is inevitably led to accept God as a providential creator. Yet he qualifies in an extraordinary way every statement he makes about how the passage from nature to God is made. Contemplation of nature does not give us knowledge of God as much as it does the rudiment of knowledge. It fills us with the emotion of *wonder* (which is "broken knowledge") instead of supplying a demonstrative basis for affirming God's existence and power. For God does not really manifest His wisdom and power to our intellect in its study of nature, but He does make these perfections strongly sensible to our feelings. If natural theology has any foundation, it is emotional and not intellectual, so that it does not fit in properly among the divisions of philosophy. Natural philosophy may attune our sensibility to expect a total cause of the totality of nature, but only God's revealed word can give the certainty. Once faith assures us about God, we can view the natural world in a new way and see therein the vestiges of the divine wisdom, will, and power. But the original illumination cannot come from the side of natural philosophy. Natural theology is thus placed on a thoroughly fideistic basis. It does not signify a distinct part of philosophy as much as it reveals a distinctive way in which the man of faith can look at the findings of natural philosophy.

Behind Bacon's careful circumlocutions lies a positive conviction about matter which is perfectly incompatible with any philosophical knowledge of God, even the slender amount formally ascribed to the province of natural theology.

The *natural motion of the atom* ... is indeed the most ancient and unique force that constitutes and fashions all things out of matter. ... Of this primary matter and its proper power and action there can be no cause in nature (for we always except God), for nothing is prior to matter itself. Thus there can be no efficient cause of it, nor anything better known in nature; therefore there can be neither genus nor form. Hence whatever this matter and its power and operation may be, it is a positive and inexplicable thing, and must be taken precisely as it is found, and not judged by any previous conception. For if it were possible to be known, yet it cannot be known through a cause, since after God it is the cause of causes, and itself incapable of having a cause [*ipsa incausabilis*]. ... There seem to be three doctrines with regard to this subject which we know by faith. First, that matter is created from nothing. Second, that the development of a system was through the word of omnipotence, and not that matter developed itself out of chaos into this configuration. Third, that this configuration (before the Fall) was the best of which matter (as it had been created) was susceptible.[7]

This passage tells us clearly that as far as philosophical knowledge of the book of nature is concerned, matter is underived and self-moved. The contingent and created nature of matter and atomic motion cannot be demonstrated, since all our natural reasoning leads back to matter-in-motion as an absolute given. To seek a cause behind this primary principle and universal cause is philosophically futile because it is the ultimate fact requiring no further explanation. Every cause to which we can attain is itself caused and contained within material nature. Thus to refer to God as the naturally knowable first cause is blasphemous in Bacon's eyes—hence his insistence that the senses shut off God rather than manifest Him to us and that causal inference on the part of reason remains confined to the material world. Since a nature-centered sense and reason constitute the entire resources of man's natural light, there can be no philosophical knowledge of God. The mind's refracted ray is simply inadequate for the task. Faith is required to assure us of the three main articles of so-called natural theology: that there is a creator of the material world, that He is the all-powerful orderer of the universe, and that He is wise and benevolent in His disposition of things.

Although our natural powers cannot lead us beyond the atomism of Democritus, Bacon does not accept the inference that the scientific study of nature must therefore lead to atheism. In his report to James I, he protests against this conclusion and embodies his own view in the famous apothegm: "A little philosophy inclines man's mind to atheism; but depth in philosophy brings men's minds about to religion."[8] What this maxim noticeably does not say, however, is that philosophical study brings us a natural knowledge of God. A deeper study of the concatenation of natural causes arouses in us both awe and an expectation of grasping the comprehensive law underlying all events. The expectation is never quite realized in the philosophical sphere, however, and the summary law remains an ideal for further research. It requires the revealed word of God to assure us of His providential design and the reality of the eternal, causal order governing all things.

If there is any function for natural theology, then, it is not to discover philosophical truths but to apply revealed truths to the natural world. It gives substance to the emotional response of the scientist to the order of nature and enables him to see the footprints of God which the Fall of Adam had concealed from our natural vision. In this way, Bacon vindicates the autonomy of philosophy and the natural sciences without committing them to an irreligious viewpoint. To do this, he conceives of natural theology as a pastoral branch of sacred theology devoted to the welfare of the scientific mind. It is "natural" only with respect to the point of application of theological principles and not with respect to their origin. For Bacon, as well as for Calvin, natural theology is not a philosophical study of God but a special analysis of those deliverances of revelation which concern the natural world and which are considered as derived from God.

Thomas Hobbes (1588–1679) did not advance the case against natural theology appreciably beyond Bacon's position. His major contribution was a restatement of the conception of a self-sufficient material world in the language of Galileo's mechanics. Hobbes proposed that the scientific method of Galileo should be rendered absolute and thus identified with the philosophical method. Philosophy must then be defined as a study of the generation of bodies through natural motion. God is either a bodiless being and hence is entirely foreign to philosophical investigation, or He is known philosophically because he possesses a corporeal (albeit a very pure and infinite) nature.[9] Hobbes allowed, with Bacon, that a study of natural causes inclines men to believe in an eternal power called God but that what we prove is only our desire and belief, not God's existence.

As for the nature of God, no inferentially founded judgments can be made about it by the human mind. The attributes we ascribe to God are only names, expressive of our incapacity to know Him and our desire to describe Him in honorific terms, such as might pacify an unknown power. The whole of natural theology is thus reduced to a system of *emotive names* contrived by man to piece out his ignorance and terror before the power of the universe. Every advance in scientific and philosophical knowledge means a proportionate narrowing of the scope for theological names.

Hobbes took a much less conciliatory attitude toward the relation of natural theology with the sciences than did Bacon, since he did not acknowledge any distinctive speculative content of revealed, religious truth. On the personal side, religion's mainspring is not in the apprehension of any truths but in the individual's fear of an unknown, threatening force in the universe. And as a social manifestation, religion is a branch of the body politic, an arm of the sovereign in his governance of citizens. On this point, Hobbes agreed conclusively with Machiavelli.

On public matters of creed, cult, and interpretation of Scripture, the political ruler must have the final word, and the temporal good must be the decisive consideration.

This thorough subordination of religion to political ends is the inevitable consequence of eliminating a philosophy of God and a supernatural revelation. Wherever natural and revealed knowledge of God is excluded, religion has only a pragmatic justification as serving personal ends or those of the state. By concentrating upon the emotive and social aspects of human discourse about God, Hobbes reduces every natural doctrine on God to what St. Augustine calls a poetic and civil theology, in contradistinction to a natural or philosophical theology.

2. LOCKE'S EMPIRICAL METHOD AND THEISM

From his very early Oxford essays (which were not published until 1954) to the last writings of his career, John Locke (1632–1704) was steadily engaged with the problem of God. His preoccupation with this theme had deep moral roots, since morality was to him inconceivable without some reference to a transcendent creator and lawgiver. He read widely in the four dominant traditions of university Scholasticism, Cartesianism, Cambridge Platonism, and the naturalism of Bacon and Hobbes. Locke was indebted to all these sources for his theory of God, but he sought to evaluate the borrowed materials and produce, with the aid of his empirical method, a new synthesis of them. His own views on theism can be formulated in two negative propositions and two affirmative ones. The negative theses state that God does not serve as a deductive principle in the theory of knowledge and that there is no innate idea of God, while the affirmative ones express Locke's conviction that the existence of God can be philosophically demonstrated and that God has an important bearing upon the empirical conception of man and morality. Approximately, we may say that the negative theses embody Locke's critical reaction away from rationalism and his Scholastic environment at Oxford, whereas the affirmative propositions are a reconstruction of the doctrine on God within the empiricist context.

(1) *God is not an epistemological principle.* Locke does accept the Cartesian premise that the immediate objects of knowledge are the images or ideas in our mind and that we know things themselves only through the objective mediation of our ideas. Nevertheless, he maintains against rationalism that the senses are an indispensable and primary source of our original ideas rather than a mere stimulus or occasion for the operation of pure reason. The only reliable touchstone for knowledge is a traceable connection of an idea with something directly given through the human activity of sensation and reflection. Derivation from

these empirical sources, rather than from a purely rational set of first principles, provides the only surety for human reasoning. Hence the empirical method consists in the "historical, plain" analysis of the actual contents of sense perception and the operations of reflective reason in dependence upon sense data.

As Locke portrays him, the typical empirical thinker is not an arm-chair explorer, but conducts a field expedition to examine our mental life in its natural setting. He is prepared for trial runs, tentative find-ings, and constant revisions of his last report. During the rainy season, indeed, he delights in systematizing his results and proposing general explanations. But he never expects to achieve a total system of deductive truths, for he recognizes vast areas in which he must be content with probability and not press for a definitive solution. He always bears in mind the twofold purpose of knowledge: to control nature for our ma-terial welfare and to perform our duties worthily in this life in order to attain an everlasting happiness.[10] For such purposes, a judicious admix-ture of a few rock-bottom certainties and many safe probabilities is suf-ficient. A physics reaching to the sensible qualities but not to the real essences, a moral philosophy embodying the natural law and prudent maxims but not identical with a metaphysics of salvation, a theory of knowledge which is scrupulously descriptive of the actual operations of our mind and yet avoids a priori deductions—these are the humanly attainable goals of philosophical empiricism. They stand in marked contrast to the rationalist efforts to bring the highest conceivable system of knowledge within the scope of a human philosophy.

In pursuit of such modest aims, there is no need to make extravagant demands upon God as the motor force of our reasoning and philosophi-cal system. Locke is by no means ready to concede to Bacon and Hobbes, however, that a philosophy stressing sense experience can ascertain noth-ing about God. Rather, his precise contention is that empiricism can readily dispense with the deductive function ascribed to God by the rationalists. Elimination of this function does not entail the complete removal of God from philosophy but only a new way of conceiving His position in it. Locke wants to *defunctionalize* the doctrine on God with-out excluding it from philosophy entirely. This is a delicate position to maintain, and (historically considered) the balance is usually upset in favor of one extreme or the other. Certain aspects of the empiricist theory of knowledge were soon to lead Hume to reduce God's philo-sophical significance far beyond the limit which Locke sets for it.

Lest anyone be reluctant to forego the deductive use of God because of its purported advantages for bolstering human certitude, Locke makes an object lesson of Malebranche's theory of vision in God. To say that I see things or ideas in God does not clarify the meaning and validity of the ideas which are in my own mind. The vision in God is empirically meaningless as an explanation of human knowledge, since it never establishes the connection between ideas taken as eternal objects of cognition and ideas taken as the actual ways in which the human knower perceives things.[11] No matter what ontological reality the objective contents of the ideas may have in the divine mind, they remain irrelevant to our knowing process until we are able to entertain them through individual acts of perception. The only observable and decisive difference between seeing and not seeing a marigold is that of having or not having a determinate modification of the finite mind. The appeal to eternal objects in God does nothing to relieve the situation of the temporal, perceiving subject.

Locke broadens his polemic to embrace other versions of the rationalist epistemology. He charges that every employment of God as guarantor of knowledge is superfluous, unfruitful, and incapable of demonstration, even by rationalist standards. It is superfluous because the scope and reliability of knowledge can be fully determined through direct analysis of our knowing powers and their given operations. They are not transmuted by being brought into relation with God, considered either as their ultimate source in the order of being or as one of their objects. A theological epistemology is also unfruitful because it does not supply a method for enlarging our knowledge of the real world. For instance, the Cartesian physicists were deductively committed to the view that extension is the only special attribute of bodies, whereas Newton's way of analysis and experiment showed that solidity belongs to the nature of bodies just as properly as extension. Every new advance in our understanding of the world depends upon a direct examination of things in their own mode of being, with experience, rather than a deductive appeal to the divine power, serving as the source of real increment.

Finally, Locke denies the rationalist claim to establish a deductively demonstrative link between the divine nature and our way of knowing. No necessary inference about human knowledge can be drawn from the need for archetypal ideas in God's creative act. If this act is genuinely free and not determined by the demands of the rationalist deduction, then God is under no constraint to implant ideas in our mental faculties or to make His archetypal ideas serve also as the representative ideas in our cognition. Granted that the ultimate origin of our ideas is in God, it need not follow with any demonstrative rigor that their proximate origin must be innate (as Descartes held) or that their immediate referent must be the divine exemplar ideas themselves (as Malebranche claimed). The only way to secure a necessary inference here would be to empty the divine freedom of all humanly ascertainable meaning through a Spinozistic technique of "redefinition."

Locke discerns the presence of both universal determinism and pantheism behind the attitude of the rationalist, "who thinks he knows

God's understanding so much better than his own, that he will make use of the divine intellect to explain the human."[12] Rationalism accepts the old Platonic assumption that the objects of true knowledge must be of the same sort as our ideas so that a perfect fusion can be effected. Hence it tends to reduce real objects to aspects of the divine essence in order to give them the maximum stability, intelligibility, and conformity to the desired pattern of deduction. There is a corresponding identification of our ideas with the divine exemplars. God then becomes the total guarantor of our knowledge and happiness simply because there remains no substantial distinction between the divine and human modes of being, knowing, and acting. Spinozism is the logical outcome of the rationalist use of God as a deductive principle.

(2) *There is no innate idea of God.* In his general criticism of innatism, Locke pays special attention to the innate idea of God.[13] If God were to implant in our mind any idea antecedent to experience, it would presumably be that of His own nature. The rationalist proofs of God's existence and of purely intellectual knowledge depend upon this presumption, as does the claim to have an innate moral knowledge. In attacking innatism at this point, therefore, Locke is striking the rationalist enterprise at dead center. He attempts to show both that there is no innate idea of God and that a satisfactory empirical explanation of its origin can be given.

His negative argument is disappointingly weak and imprecise. He appeals mainly to the tales of travelers and missionaries about tribes in Africa and the Americas which are quite innocent of any notion of God. But since some primitive peoples are notoriously reticent before strangers or employ an alien symbolism to express their belief in God, the reports which Locke cites are inconclusive from an anthropological standpoint. He also points to the practical atheists in civilized countries who give only lip service to God because of their fear for civil sanctions. Descartes had already suggested, however, that attentive reflection on our part is required in order to grasp the truth contained in the idea of God and to make it practically effective in our lives.

Nevertheless, Locke does bring home a point against his university tutors, Gassendi, and the Cambridge Platonists, who argued from common consent to the innateness of the idea of God. If by common consent is meant acceptance by literally everyone, then we cannot maintain the universality of the idea of God. If it means acceptance by the wise men everywhere, then the idea of God is by no means engraved in our nature but requires a right use of reason and hence is an acquired idea. The widespread belief in God can be sufficiently explained, without requiring any innate origin for it, by the common evidence furnished by our experienced world. Locke is careful to add that absence of the idea of God in particular cases is not an argument against His reality but simply a salutary warning that we have to make a responsible inferential use of our faculties in order to come to the knowledge of God.

On the positive side, Locke describes how the idea of God is empirically formed. It is a complex idea resulting from the union of several simple ideas. It has a fully experiential foundation, for its simple components are drawn from both sensation and reflection. Both these sources of experience co-operate to provide us with the relevant ideas of unity, power, duration, and happiness. Moreover, reflection on our inner life adds the notes of thinking, willing, and spiritual being. The next step is to remove all imperfections and limits from these simple ideas through an application of the idea of infinity. Finally, we combine the various notes into the complex idea of a unique, thinking, willing, spiritual being who is both infinite in power and duration (the eternal creator) and the source of all human bliss. Since the idea of God has an observable empirical origin, it is not an innate idea and cannot bolster a system of purely intellectual, deductive knowledge.

The crux of this explanation lies in the idea of infinity, without which the other notes cannot apply to God. Locke stresses the twofold fact that we have no direct experience of the infinite God and that we have no perfect idea of infinity. Spinoza's supposition of a perfectly adequate idea of the infinite is empirically unverifiable in man. Even the Cartesian distinction between comprehending and understanding the infinite is not accurate, if it means that we have a positive understanding of God's own infinite mode of being. The entire positive content of our notion of infinity is drawn from finite things, whereas the removal of limits from this positive content is due to an act of our own mind.[14]

Our senses tell us about a certain reach of extension and number, while our reason is familiar with the operation of adding still more to any given parts of quantity. Spurred on by the indeterminate fringe-awareness that one may go yet farther or may add a still greater expanse and succession of parts, the mind learns to negate every definite terminus of quantity. Thus it gains an imperfect notion of infinity. It conceives of the divine duration as an endless succession, or eternity, and of the divine presence to things as a boundless expanse, or ubiquity. Infinity applies most properly to God's eternity and ubiquity and more figuratively to His power, wisdom, and goodness. Yet in both cases the disproportion between our idea of the infinite and God's own perfection is painfully apparent.

Locke scores two direct hits against rationalism: by showing the non-innate character of the idea of infinity and by emphasizing the specially limited application of it to divine power, which is the mainspring in the rationalist deductive scheme. In doing so, however, he reduces the human conception of the infinite to the mathematical, quantitative order. How such a restricted idea can apply, in any legitimate way, to the non-quantitative being of God is never shown. The Lockean infinite signifies the indefiniteness of our act of counting places or moments, not the unlimited act of God's own being. The quantitative and operational view of infinity is a univocal one, confined by its entire content to finite, temporal, and material things. Since Locke takes his start in our ideas and not in the actual being of finite things, he has no intellectual means at his disposal for transcribing his sound conviction that there is some foundation in experience for our true but inadequate knowledge that God is infinite. If the rationalists are too generous about the mind's ability to grasp the divine infinity in its own nature, Locke is too sparing in confining us to an operational and mathematical concept of the infinite.

Still, he is lucidly aware of the difference between explaining the psychological origin of our idea of the divine nature and demonstrating the truth about God's own existence. Even if every man had the same empirically derived idea of God,

it would not prove the existence of a God. The ideas of our minds by being there, giving us no assurance of the existence of anything but themselves, though when actually brought in by our senses they do. . . . And, therefore, though we come by the idea of him by the way above mentioned, we must yet come by the knowledge of his existence (i.e., that something answering that idea does exist) by some other way, which I think is not hard to do.[15]

Because of this conviction, Locke is under no systematic pressure to read the note of self-causation into the idea of God or to overstress the note of infinite power as the rationalists had been forced to do in order to draw the proof of His existence from the very idea of God.

(3) *There is an a posteriori demonstration of God's existence.* For many years Locke had to ponder the problem of a valid a posteriori proof. At first he was content with making an adaptation of Pascal's famous wager argument.[16] If atheism is true, it leads to our annihilation or everlasting insensibility; if it is false, the consequence is everlasting misery. If theism is true, it brings eternal happiness, whereas its falsity entails our annihilation. The odds presented to our practical assent are challenging. The best that a choice of atheism could bring for us is no better than the worst that we could expect from adherence to theism: total annihilation. Acceptance of atheism risks the loss of happiness and the danger of misery in exchange for—precisely nothing. With his customary deftness, Alexander Pope sums up the wager case for theism:

> The joy unequal'd, if its end it gain,
> And if it lose, attended with no pain.

As far as our practical judgment is concerned, atheism represents a far less probable and less reasonable choice than theism.

Locke freely admitted that this is a probable argument, and yet he added two useful observations. Against Cartesians, he defended the proper role of probability in philosophy as long as it is honestly acknowledged to be such. Thus a probable argument in favor of God's existence deserves some consideration, although one should not pretend that it is demonstrative. Furthermore, probable reasoning is quite appropriate for the order of practical assent, which cannot always wait for absolute certainty before deciding upon matter for action. It would be both unreasonable and imprudent to make an exception precisely in the case where our eternal happiness is at stake. Like Pascal, Locke was not appealing merely to the betting habits of men but mainly to the prevailing rule of probability in practical life. However, he also held that at least the fundamental points in morality are capable of demonstration, and he was therefore dissatisfied with having only this probable argument for God's existence.

Making circumspect use of the Port-Royal essays of Pierre Nicole and Ralph Cudworth's Cambridge Platonist arguments, Locke finally worked out a line of reasoning which he regarded as demonstrative or equal in certainty to, although not identical in kind with, mathematical demonstrations. It contained three main points: there must be some being or substance from eternity; this eternal being is all powerful, all knowing, and immaterial; this being is what men call God.[17]

The starting point of the inference must be either the sensible world or oneself, since they are the only existential points of departure we have. Locke does recognize the validity of the proof from the order, beauty, and motion of the sensible world. Without prejudice to this starting point, however, he usually prefers to begin with the existential intuition of one's own existence. I exist or am a real something. I also had a beginning or was really produced, as the fact of my imperfection and constant improvement testifies. The source of my production is either nothingness, myself, or some other real being. Unlike Hegel and recent existentialists, Locke sees no mysterious creative power in the nought: nothingness can produce no real being. Furthermore, Descartes had already shown that I cannot be self-made, for otherwise I would confer on myself all the perfections of knowledge, power, and everlasting duration which I can conceive. This leaves only some other real being as the productive source of my existence. Either this other thing is, in turn, brought into existence by still another being, or it is the eternally existing being. There cannot be an unending series of produced producers, for then the totality of real things would rest upon pure nothing, i. e., things would never come into existence in the first place and present themselves to my experience. Hence there must exist an eternal first being or producer of both my own existence and that of the experienced world.

There are some internal difficulties concerning the point of departure and the principle of inference involved in this proof. What makes Locke somewhat chary about starting with the sensible world is that his theory of existential perception of material things does not permit us to have full, intuitive certainty about their existence. In the case of the self, he claims to have intuitive certainty, but he fails to show how it can have strict existential import. His own definition of intuitive knowledge as the perception of an immediate relation of agreement between two ideas limits such knowledge to the ideal, nonexistential order. He attempts to modify it to fit the present case by describing intuition as the reflective perception of an immediate connection between a given idea or other mental state and the existing self. But precisely how the understanding can know either its own ideas or the self as existents is never explained or reconciled with the underlying ordination of the mind directly to ideas. If the reflective apprehension of the individual, existing self is an instance of general knowledge, then it is purely ideal and does not reach the self as an individual existent. If it is a piece of particular knowledge, then it agrees with sensations in bearing only upon material things and in failing to yield the intuitive certainty required for the basis of the theistic demonstration.

Even granting the existential basis, however, Locke avoids the issue of whether the causal principle of inference can take us beyond the existents within the world of sense and internal experience. His only formal analysis of active, causal power reduces its empirical origin to the psychological experience of will-effort. Hence he raises, but leaves unanswered, the question of whether the axiom "Nothing can cause itself to begin to be" can be given a valid extrapsychological use in reasoning to a transcendent God. Here, as well as in the instance of divine infinity, Locke remains enclosed within the way of finite ideas. Berkeley will convert these ideas into real things and thus attain to God, but Hume will question the conversion and hence decline to make the final step to God through any demonstration.

Locke gave a much more careful treatment to the question of God's immateriality and eternity. He took the negative approach of showing that neither the human self nor matter is eternal. This thesis was double pronged, since it enabled him to correct a shortcoming in Descartes and, simultaneously, to criticize the naturalism of Bacon and Hobbes. Although Descartes proved that the finite thinker is not self-existent, he did not exclude the philosophical possibility that God might have caused this self to exist from eternity. Similarly, the Cartesian view of matter as all-pervasive, substantial extension could easily lead to the position of an eternal, self-subsisting matter. Bacon, Hobbes, and some followers of Gassendi did, indeed, hold that matter is eternal and uncaused, as far as philosophy can tell, and hence that there can be no philosophical demonstration of God's existence. Therefore, Locke felt obliged to defend his demonstration by showing that matter cannot be eternal and uncaused. It is significant that he did not attempt to argue, with Aquinas and Descartes, that the material world might be eternal and yet also eternally caused and completely dependent on God. Since Locke took a psychological view of eternity and causation, he had to establish the noneternity and the caused character of matter in conjunction.

Locke's method was not to show that matter has a temporal beginning but only that it cannot be identified with the eternal mind or first cause of all things. Taken by itself, matter is inert and incapable of being the absolute origin of the motion, sensation, and intellectual activities found in our world. The primal source of the universe must be an eternal mind. Matter cannot enter into any composition with this eternal mind in order to share in its causal primacy. Locke did not deny that thought and matter can be joined in finite beings but only that they can be joined in the eternal and infinite being. If every particle of matter were supposed to be imbued with eternal mind, then the eternal source of things would consist of "an infinite number of eternal, finite, cogitative beings, independent one of another, of limited force, and distinct thoughts, which could never produce that order, harmony, and beauty which are to be found in nature."[18] If some one special particle of matter had eternal thought, its productive power is indeed due solely to that unique aspect of it which could think and will. That aspect would be transcendent of the matter itself, which would be just as much produced and temporal as the finite, thinking self. Hence in its own being, the eternal mind is completely immaterial and distinct from the world; it is one with the God of rational religious belief.

(4) *The theory of God has a bearing upon our conception of man and morality.* Locke did not want his demonstration of God's existence to open the floodgates once again to a rationalist deduction of the theory of man. Throughout his sinuous and bitter controversy with Bishop Stillingfleet of Worcester, he repulsed every attempt to settle problems about human nature by some a priori appeal to God and first principles. His remedy was to combine demonstrative knowledge of God's existence with a phenomenalistic approach to the leading questions about man. This can be illustrated by his stand on the immateriality and immortality of the soul.[19]

If God is an infinitely powerful person and not an automatically unfolding formula, He remains free in regard to the structure of finite things. We can be sure that there is a substantial nature in man, but we cannot dictate to God what the composition of this nature must be. Given the divine freedom and the limitation of our ideas to phenomenal qualities, we are unable to determine whether man's essence consists of a material substance alone or of a material substance joined with an immaterial one. We are ignorant of whether God chose to add the *power* of thinking to a fitly disposed system of matter or to add a thinking, immaterial *substance* to man's material substance. Neither possibility involves a contradiction, and yet within the context of an empirical and phenomenalist philosophy, there is no means available for deciding the issue with complete certainty. Locke felt that it is more likely that man is composed of two substances, but he rejected the rationalist efforts to demonstrate this fact on the basis of God's veracity, His pre-established harmony, or our knowledge of essences.

Although the materialists of the Enlightenment hailed Locke's hypothesis of "thinking matter" as a forerunner, he himself was at pains to distinguish his position from that of Hobbes and materialism. Of itself, matter is inert, void of perception, and incapable of originating the power of thought. Matter can be endowed with this power by God, but only after it has been disposed by Him in a special way. Locke was vague, however, about how radical the reorganization of matter has to be in order to sustain the operation of thinking and how the unity of man can be preserved in the presence of either an added power or an added substance.

When Stillingfleet objected that a lack of demonstration of the immaterial substance in man destroys belief in immortality, Locke countered by dissociating the two problems. Even if the substance of the soul were not immaterial, it could still be immortal. To sustain this contention, Locke gave a special meaning to immortality as a restoration, by God, of the same conditions prevailing in this life. This is a nonmetaphysical, purely descriptive meaning which invokes the power of God without either using Him for a deductive demonstration or involving any definite view of the substantial nature of man. Given the metaphysically neutral description of man as "a thinking, material thing" (whether thought be only a power or a distinct substance), God can give this thing a new span of life after the interruption of death. Immortality is not capable of demonstration but rests on our belief in the power of God as lord of life.

For his own dialectical purposes, then, Locke was ready enough to call upon the power of God. But he did so in order to establish the probability of belief in immortality rather than to fashion a deductive demonstration. Having cast off the rationalist metaphysics of man, with its sharp dualism and its deductive use of God, he took refuge in phenomenalism. Locke was too closely joined in battle with the Cartesians to risk exploring the road to an experiential-metaphysical study of man. Instead of taking the realistic approach to the question, he stressed the phenomenalist implications of his own theory of knowledge.

One reason why Locke was content to have demonstrative knowledge of God's existence and only probability about immortality stemmed from the different role of each in his ethics. He held that the basic ethical propositions can be demonstrated just as rigorously as mathematical ones, but with the difference that ethics is existentially grounded in the lawgiver and the moral agent. Hence ethics demands a strict demonstration of the existence of God, the source of law. Immortality is also required, since we must have assurance of an afterlife in which there is personal responsibility and appropriate sanctions. But this conviction rests upon prior knowledge of the lawmaker's existence and hence can consist in a highly probable belief. Locke's evident reluctance to speak about immortality except as a simple prolongation or restoration of the conditions of present existence was likewise controlled by his primarily moral view of immortality. He thought that responsibility might be lessened if stress were placed on a new state of life which differed markedly from the conditions under which we now act.

Locke's wide readings in the jurisprudential philosophies of Suarez, Pufendorf, Hooker, and Sanderson predisposed him toward a theistic and voluntarist view of natural law. He regarded it mainly as the expression of God's will and traced its obligation to the right of a superior power to command us to do something. But he also detected the danger of arbitrariness in the emphasis upon the divine will. Hence he pointed out that whereas God is the effective or causal source of the natural law, its terminative or embodying source is our own nature. The moral law is "natural" in the twofold sense of being known by the natural light of sense and reason and of expressing rules in conformity with our own nature. "We can infer the principle and a definite rule of our duty from man's own constitution and the faculties with which he is equipped."[20] Furthermore, Locke brought to bear the psychological fact that the will is strongly inclined by motives of pleasure and pain, without which the knowledge of a divine norm and our rational nature would have no practical effect. He regarded these hedonic factors as God's strategy for attracting our interest and holding our allegiance to the commands of natural law. Yet Locke never completed his ethical synthesis between God as the source of law and obligation, the inherent suitability of certain actions to human nature, and the compelling attraction of pleasure and pain. He left the door open for the eventual detachment of morality from reference to God, as carried out by Hume and the utilitarians.

3. THE THEISTIC IMMATERIALISM OF BERKELEY

As a student at Trinity College in Dublin, George Berkeley (1685–1753) immersed himself in Locke and Newton, Descartes and Malebranche. His readings were stimulated by a religious concern to find a remedy against the Pyrrhonism of Bayle, the materialism of Hobbes, atheism, and the general decline of religion as a social influence at the outset of the eighteenth century. As he himself phrased it, "the main drift and design of my labours . . . is the consideration of *God*, and our *duty*."[21] What puzzled Berkeley the most was that even the most capable theistic philosophers of the previous century were unable to provide a satisfactory refutation of skepticism and atheism, which continued to flourish as vigorously as ever. It occurred to him that the reason for the ineffectiveness of the theists was that they accepted one premise in common with their opponents: the reality of matter. A definitive settlement of the issue might be reached by disposing of this common assumption about matter.

The Bishop of Cloyne's denial of matter was not due, then, to some quixotic turn of mind, to an instinct of flight, or even (as one psychoanalytically inclined critic recently suggested) to a repugnance toward his own bodily functions. Rather, it resulted from a shrewd appraisal of the contemporary philosophical situation, in which many noble minds were becoming deadlocked about the reality of knowledge and God. To understand how the elimination of matter might seem to provide the only solution, Berkeley's definition of it has to be pondered.

> Philosophers vulgarly hold, that the sensible qualities exist in an inert, extended, unperceiving substance, which they call *matter,* to which they attribute a natural subsistence, exterior to all thinking beings, or distinct from being perceived by any mind whatsoever, even the eternal mind of the Creator, wherein they suppose only ideas of the corporeal substances created by him: if indeed they allow them to be at all created. . . . The question between the materialists and me is not, whether things have a real existence out of the mind of this or that person, but whether they have an absolute existence, distinct from being perceived by God, and exterior to all minds.[22]

If matter is an unknown something that nevertheless exists "absolutely" or apart from any relation to any mind, two consequences are unavoidable: (1) There is a reality which we affirm to exist and yet which is completely inaccessible to our understanding. (2) This entity exists apart from any causal dependence on God or the first creative mind. The first of these conclusions breeds skepticism, since it places the real nature of sensible things entirely beyond our reach. The second point leads to naturalism and atheism. Locke would certainly challenge the latter inference, but Berkeley would retort that he has no good grounds for doing so. Since the nature of this material substance remains unknowable, we have no way of showing that it has a real relation of causal dependence on God, any more than that it has a noetic relation of accessibility to our mind. Grant the reality of matter so defined, and there is no way to overcome skeptical doubt or to offer demonstrative proof of the causal dependence of the sensible world on a first cause.

Alternate ways were open for Berkeley to deal with this issue. He might have challenged the accepted definition of matter and proposed one that would allow jointly for the reality of matter, its knowability by the human mind, and its causal dependence upon God. To follow this route, however, he would have had to repudiate the Cartesian and Lockean assumption about the immediate object of the understanding, and this he was not prepared to do. Instead, he accepted both the current notion of the understanding and the usual definition of matter and then showed the meaninglessness of the latter within the perspective of the former. If the qualities of things are themselves ideas, they can never reside in an unperceiving substratum, and this inert substratum can never affect the human mind in order to reveal itself. Hence there is no ground for supposing a mysterious, material substance in addition to the sense qualities. We do experience sensible things, but they are identically one with the ideas or sense qualities, without any remainder. The real world is that of sensible things so described, not of unknown material substances. Since we know sensible things just as thoroughly and certainly as we know our ideas, the case for skepticism disappears with the disappearance of matter.

Spearheading the attack upon matter is what Berkeley calls his New Principle of existential meaning. Instead of seeking the first principle of his philosophy in the rationalist realm of essences, he looks for it in an existential direction, albeit one that is still confined to the context of knowledge. The New Principle states that there are only two modes of existence: that of perceived sensible things or ideas and that of perceiving immaterial substances or minds. Ideas are wholly inert and nonsubstantial things which have their being only as objects in and for the perceiving mind. Only the latter is a genuine substance and agent having the capacity for willing and perceiving.

Because of this opposition between ideas and minds, Berkeley concludes that they are simply equivocal modes of discourse about existent being. "When we say, *they exist, they are known,* or the like, these words must not be thought to signify any thing common to both natures. There is nothing alike or common in them."[23] He is quite ready to sacrifice the analogical unity of predication of being so that he can bring home a striking proof of the mind's immortality. If the mind exists according to an entirely different mode of being than the body (which is a sensible thing), then the mind is in no way dependent upon the body and can survive its dissolution. Time, with its wearing effect upon sensible things, is reducible to the succession of ideas and leaves the mind unaffected. Similarly, extension is only an object for the mind, not its very substance. Hence the human soul is an unextended and indivisible substance enjoying an unchanging and immortal existence.

Up to this point, the New Principle would seem to seal off the universe of finite minds and their ideas so completely that God can enter only by way of intrusion and superfluity. Indeed, some Berkeleyan scholars have claimed that God is an afterthought or a pious appendix to his philosophy. But the testimony of his own student notebooks shows that Berkeley always related his New Principle to the central problems of theism. His aim was to describe our knowledge of the sensible world in such fashion that it would lead directly and necessarily to the existence of a providential God or infinite mind.[24] He set out to show that certain insoluble difficulties are encountered in the analysis of knowledge unless God's existence is allowed. Three major instances of this procedure are: the permanence of external existents, the criterion of reality, and the relation between the scientific and religious views of the sensible universe.

Our ordinary conviction is that the sensible world enjoys a continuous, uninterrupted, and exterior sort of existence, that an object does not pulsate in and out of existence in rhythm with our individual acts of perceiving it. The Dutch tulip does not cease to be when I shut my eyes, and neither does my next glance at it mean its fresh creation in being. And yet this intermittent kind of being seems to be an inevitable consequence if the entire to-be of the sensible thing is its to-be-perceived by the mind. The problem and the Berkeleyan answer are neatly expressed in the following exchange of limericks between Monsignor Knox and Mr. Leslie Paul:

There was a young man who said "God
Must think it exceedingly odd
    If he finds that this tree
    Continues to be
When there's no one about in the Quad."

Dear Sir,
    Your astonishment's odd:
I am always about in the Quad
    And that's why the tree
    Will continue to be,
Since observed by
      Yours faithfully,
         GOD.[25]

The only way to reconcile the immaterialist view of sensible things with the common sense assurance about the permanence of things is to distinguish between three sorts of perceivers: oneself, other finite minds, and the infinite mind. What I am not now perceiving may well be the object of perception for some other human mind. And yet the Berkeley who explored the Cave of Dunmore in Ireland and reflected on the formation of petrified wood and salt crystals was well aware that many sensible things exist during long periods of time without being objects of actual perception on the part of any finite minds. Hence sensible things must be actually perceived at all times by the eternal, divine mind. Their permanence and externality are sufficiently secured through their objective presence in God's mind, without supposing any material entity.

Berkeley makes another dialectical ascent to God from the question of how to preserve the distinction between reality and fantasy, verified existence and hypothesis. The New Principle would seem to encourage sheer subjectivism by lending real existence to any idea which our mind can entertain. But immaterialism recognizes a psychological difference between ideas of sense and ideas of imagination. The former are more vivid, distinct, constant, and coherent; the latter are comparatively faint, vague, unsteady, and incoherent. A man is aware of himself as being the master of the ideas of imagination, which are combined according to the dictate of his own will. Yet with respect to the ideas of sense, the human mind is primarily passive, and our will is powerless to specify their content. They come to us from an external source. The psychological distinction is founded upon an ontological difference of origin: Images are of our own making, whereas sense perceptions are given to us by another. This external source cannot be matter (which is nonexistent) or another finite mind (since infinite power is required to furnish me with the entire sensible world). Hence the only adequate origin for ideas of sense is a really existent, infinite mind. The ultimate grounding of ideas of sense in God provides a criterion of reality upon which both the ordinary man and the philosophical immaterialist can agree.

Finally, Berkeley turns the presumed conflict between mechanistic science and the religious outlook to the advantage of the latter. He grants the complete competence of mathematical physics to correlate the phenomena of nature under general laws. But he insists, with even more rigor than Newton himself, upon the distinction between mechanical laws and real, efficient causes. Scientific natural laws are neither causal nor necessary in the strict sense. They do not express the causal agencies in nature but are mathematical descriptions of constant correlations among sensible things or inert ideas. There is a steady sequence of one sensible event or idea after another, but such events are entirely bereft of causal power and involve no process of actual production. Although Newton himself (in contradistinction to the Newtonians) would concede this account of mechanical laws, he would add that his natural philosophy can nevertheless arrive at a knowledge of the universal efficient cause, God. Berkeley's reply is that this knowledge is not obtained by means of the scientific method, which is confined in principle to a study of noncausal sensible things in their quantitative correlations, but only by means of the properly philosophical method. The latter is founded on the New Principle, which alone gives access to the real causal agents or minds and thus to the first cause of the entire order of nature.

Gravity and other forces used in scientific explanation are principles of knowledge but not principles of existence. Berkeley removes all causal efficacy from natural laws and events in order to prevent any pantheistic confusion between God and nature, conceived as an active being which immanently contains all causality. Similarly, the causal-essential necessity of connection among natural events is denied, lest it should be presumed that "Nature were any thing but the Ordinance of the free Will of God."[26] Against Spinoza, Berkeley defends the presence of the personal traits of intellect, freedom, and will in God. Only a spiritual being or *person* is truly active and a cause. To affirm that sensible things or ideas are caused is implicitly to affirm that they are presented to our minds by an intelligent and free agent, for a blind and determined agent is a contradiction in a context where agency concerns the communicating of ideas. That God is an infinite, personal mind follows from the requirements needed to produce the totality of sensible things in their variety, harmony, and natural laws. The latter are only the stable ways according to which God chooses to communicate the ideas of sense to our minds. By meditating on this causal relationship between God and nature, men can learn to regard natural events as the language of God, the symbols whereby He communicates with finite minds and reveals to them His personal presence, goodness, and constant providential care.

The philosophy of empirical immaterialism is designed to integrate the scientific and religious conceptions of nature and thus provide an answer to the criticism leveled against modern scientific research concerning the concentration of the human mind upon natural events to the extent that God is completely excluded from view. It is a question of educating the intelligence of man to become responsive to several levels of significance in nature itself. Berkeley would agree with Newman and Coleridge that the decisive factor is the interpretative range of awareness with which one approaches the study of natural things.

> So shalt thou see and hear
> The lovely shapes and sounds intelligible
> Of that eternal language, which thy God
> Utters, who from eternity doth teach
> Himself in all, and all things in himself.

The challenge to intelligence in the scientific age is to learn to view the natural world as both an immanent pattern of sensible events and laws and a theophany, or manifestation of God. Through this multivalent approach, a close and fruitful union can be developed between the scientific outlook and the philosophicoreligious view of natural things as the signs and language of God, as His assurance of providential care and powerful action in our regard.

It is Berkeley's proud claim not only to draw science and theistic philosophy closer together, but also to make his philosophical theism continuous with our ordinary thinking. He stresses that his several proofs of God's existence are rooted in everyday experience of sensible things, proceed in a way that can be grasped easily by any attentive person, and nevertheless achieve demonstrative rigor. It would be more precise to say, however, that his starting point in the ideas of sense agrees with ordinary conviction only after the latter has been submitted to a strenuous immaterialist cleansing and reformation. His attempt to find a common footing for both informal and philosophic reasoning to God is admirable, but it fails to respect one capital aspect of the ordinary view of sensible things, namely, that they exist in their own actuality and not merely as objects of our perception. On this crucial point, Berkeley is obliged to distinguish between the way the vulgar speak and the way the philosophers think. But more is involved in this conflict than a linguistic puzzle, which falls into proper form once the immaterialist hypothesis is applied to our discourse. At the bottom, there is the conviction that things manifest themselves not primarily as objects-to-be-perceived but as beings that have an act of existing proper to their own nature. Thus the New Principle fails to include the ground-floor meaning for existence, and it cannot appeal to any antitheistic consequences of this meaning to alleviate the failure. Since the basic grasp of sensible things as existent does not stipulate that the act of existing must be caused efficiently by the nature of the sensible thing, as well as be perfective of it, an existential realism can rehabilitate the material world without ushering in materialistic naturalism or atheism.

These alternative philosophies are not demonstratively refuted, in any case, by Berkeley's immaterialism. His arguments for God's existence are dialectical ones depending upon one's acceptance of the New Principle as a comprehensive theory of the meanings for existence. The precise relation between the New Principle and the truth of God's existence is never clarified. The truth about God's existence is presented at times as a consequence of the New Principle and other times as a presupposition for rendering it adequate to our experience. For instance, in treating the problem of the criterion of reality, Berkeley admits that there are instances in which the contrast between ideas of sense and ideas of imagination breaks down. Many images are more vivid and steady than sense perceptions.[27] This means that without the ontological basis in a difference of origin between God-derived sense perceptions and man-derived images, the psychological notes are inconclusive. But then the existence of God must be presupposed if the New Principle is to interpret our experience in an adequate way. There is an undeclared circular relation between the New Principle and the truth of God's existence, each serving as a foundation for the other at different stages in the analysis.

Berkeley declares that there are "two great Principles of Morality: the Being of a God and the Freedom of Man."[28] Like John Locke, he regards the moral law not as an impersonal code but as a declaration of the will of God, an appeal from the infinite person to finite persons, in their use of freedom. The aim of human existence is to participate in the eternal life of God to one's fullest capacity. Happiness and duty are not in any necessary conflict, since our happiness is found in following our duty, i. e., in seeking the end prescribed for human nature by God.

> God alone is maker and preserver of all things. He is, therefore, with the most undoubted right, the great legislator of the world; and mankind are, by all the ties of duty, no less than interest, bound to obey His laws. . . . It is not therefore the private good of this or that man, nation, or age, but the general well-being of all men, of all nations, of all ages of the world, which God designs should be procured by the concurring actions of each individual.[29]

In the key notion of "concurring actions," Berkeley consolidates his moral philosophy with his metaphysics. The perfection of finite minds is attained by such joint and harmonious actions as befit those personal beings who jointly participate in existence from the infinite mind. The City of God comes down from heaven to earth in the lives of men who respond with gratitude to the Father of all spiritual natures and who permeate their social relations with a family sense of respect and responsibility for others within the great community of persons.

4. HUME: THE SKEPTICAL MINIMUM OF EMPIRICAL THEISM

David Hume (1711–1776) was just as deeply concerned with the problem of God as was Berkeley, but from the opposite arm of the compass. The Scotsman was in full tide of reaction against his strict Calvinist upbringing and the ethos of predestination. His purpose was to isolate religion, or what he dryly referred to as "the established superstition," from all effective control over the moral life of individual and social man. He found plenty of ammunition in the skeptical writings of Cicero and Bayle, as well as in the naturalism propounded by Bacon and Hobbes. He agreed with these authors that there can be no demonstrative knowledge of God, but he did not share their attitude of relegating belief in God entirely to the supernatural order. Instead, Hume tried to work out the minimal sort of philosophical theism which is warranted by the empirical method. Thus he took a position midway between the complete philosophical agnosticism of Bacon and Hobbes and the efforts of Locke and Berkeley to supply a demonstration of God's existence and a theistic ethics.

(1) *No demonstrative knowledge of God.* Among Hume's earliest memoranda was a series of questions, suggested by Bayle, concerning the foundations of theism.[30] Hume inquired whether the origin of the world from God can ever be proved if matter is conceived as being imbued with a natural motion of its own. Implied in this question was another one concerning the need for supposing a cause of motion and the pos-

sibility of arguing causally from natural motion to the eternal being. Hume also consulted Bishop Fénelon's *Treatise on the Existence and Attributes of God* (1713) in order to acquaint himself with the Cartesian arguments. These proofs failed to convince him, however, partly because he agreed with Locke about the experiential origin of the idea of God and partly because he came to question the possibility of making any existential and causal demonstration.

The idea of God is no exception to the empirical rule of tracing all our ideas back to some original impression. "The idea of God, as meaning an infinitely intelligent, wise, and good Being, arises from reflecting on the operations of our own mind, and augmenting, without limit, those qualities of goodness and wisdom."[31] Hume was no more successful than Locke in explaining our ability to augment or enlarge our ideas beyond the finite limit. The only way in which the problem of infinity interested him was in connection with the mathematical paradoxes of indefinite divisibility, but this was not the relevant sort of infinity involved in predications about God. Instead of merely repeating Locke's arguments against innatism and the a priori proofs based on it, however, Hume made a highly original use of the experiential origin of the idea of God in order to give a radical criticism of the function of God in rationalist systems. The specific targets of his attack were Descartes' justification of sensation, Malebranche's occasionalism, and the appeal of Spinoza and Leibniz to the divine causal power.

If the idea of God is constructed out of data of our experience, its value depends on the prior validity of the sources of our experience. When Descartes called into doubt the trustworthiness of the senses, which are a major source of our experience, he cut off the possibility of invoking God as a guarantor of sensation. Hume poses two objections against the Cartesian use of the divine veracity to restore confidence in sensation.[32] If God does back up the senses, then they ought to be infallible and should never give rise to the illusions upon which skepticism flourishes. Furthermore, once the existence of the external world is called into question, there is no way of proving God's existence or attributes. Hume's first objection supposes, however, that the human will is not free and exerts no influence over the interpretative judgments founded on sense perception. Since Descartes explained error in terms of freedom, this criticism is insufficient by itself. The second objection is indicative of the dividing line between rationalism and empiricism, since Hume's point is that there must be some evidence in our sensory experience to warrant any existential judgment or attribution of perfections to God. To be existentially meaningful, every inference to God must take its start in sense experience, which therefore cannot be justified in terms of the divine veracity without involving a circular procedure.

Hume's attack on occasionalism is an integral moment in his general critique of causality. His denial that our idea of causal power is derived from an objective source is carried out in three stages, in the first two of which he relies heavily upon Malebranche's own rejection of secondary causality. First, Hume rules out material bodies as the source on the strength of the Malebranchean and empiricist contention that inert extension cannot give rise to any notion of an active power. Then he invokes Malebranche's analysis of man's inner life to show that Locke and Berkeley are mistaken in tracing the notion of causal power to a supposed experience of will-effort. In the third stage, Hume repudiates even Malebranche's attempt to ground the knowledge of causal power in God. Although God may well be a real cause, our minds are too weak to get their notion of a cause from any direct observation of the divine mode of acting. As far as the empirical account of the human mind is concerned, the occasionalist theory of God as the sole cause of events is a fairy tale, an engaging and coherent story which entirely escapes our ability to check against the evidence. There is also a serious moral consequence to this theory. Malebranche's verbal qualifications in the case of the human will do not obviate the fact that occasionalism makes the sole causal agent, God, responsible for vicious human actions and evil in the world.

Hume is now in a position to broaden his antirationalist polemic to include the crucial appeal of Spinoza and Leibniz to the infinite power of God. To their contention that at least we know God's will to be omnipotent and hence to be the real cause of the world, Hume responds with a purely empiricist interpretation of divine omnipotence.

In saying that the idea of an infinitely powerful being is connected with that of every effect, which he wills, we really do no more than assert, that a being, whose volition is connected with every effect, is connected with every effect; which is an identical proposition, and gives us no insight into the nature of this power or connexion. . . . The order of the universe proves an omnipotent mind; that is, a mind whose will is *constantly attended* with the obedience of every creature and being. Nothing more is requisite to give a foundation to all the articles of religion, nor is it necessary we should form a distinct idea of the force and energy of the supreme Being.[33]

Without an inquiry at present about whether cosmic order proves God's existence or about the content of religion, it is evident that Hume is now sapping the underpinnings of the functional role of God in rationalism. Any statement about the relation between the divine will and its effects is either an abstract tautology, barren of existential significance and consequences, or is reducible to the assertion of constant conjunction, without any causal dependence. We have no clear and distinct idea of the infinite causal power in its actual exercise. Hence it is futile to try to prove God's existence as cause of Himself or to base a deduction of the finite world upon the principles which are supposed to regulate divine causality. God is thus placed definitively beyond the ability of the human mind to make an a priori inference from the first cause to the world of experience. The functional deity of rationalism is rendered inoperative in British philosophy as a result of Hume's analysis of the idea of divine power.

Finally, Hume parted company with his fellow empiricists, Locke and Berkeley, over the possibility of an a posteriori demonstration of God's existence from the sensible world. He applied to this instance his two general theses—that all demonstrative reasoning is nonexistential and that causal reasoning about existents is never more than probable.[34] Since he limited demonstration to the mathematical analysis of quantitative relations, he could find no place for any sort of existential demonstration, especially when it seeks to transcend the quantitative sphere in the direction of God. The proof of God's existence is doubly handicapped, since it is not only existential but also causal reasoning.

Having eliminated an objective origin for the idea of active power and the causal bond, Hume had to trace them to purely subjective conditions within the perceiver. The objects of perception are atomic, unconnected units which may, nevertheless, follow one another in a temporal sequence and pattern. Through repeated experience of such sequences, the imagination is gradually habituated to connect antecedent and consequent objects in a necessary way. The necessity does not arise from any productive force or dependence on the side of the objects so related but comes solely from the subjective laws of association operating upon the imagination to compel it to recall one member of the sequence when the other is presented. The causal bond consists entirely in our feeling of necessity in making the transition, in thought, from one object to the other. The philosophical inference from effect to cause is abstract and empty until it is strengthened by the natural relation set up by the workings of habit and association upon the imagination.

Given this all-embracing psychological basis, however, causal inference can have nothing stronger than a probable import. Absolute certainty cannot be achieved, since the mind is not dealing with dependencies in being, on the side of the real things, but is confined phenomenalistically to its own perceptions and their relations. It is very likely that our habitual connection among ideas corresponds to some causal link among real things, but this can never be verified. Hence causal inference can yield only probability and belief, not certainty and strict knowledge. Hume rigidly applied this conclusion to the a posteriori argument for God's existence, maintaining that it is, at the very most, a probable inference and nowise a demonstration.

Since Hume brought to a climax the empiricist neutralizing of God, it may be useful to make several comments on his critique. Coming at the precise historical juncture that it did, Hume's negative position was singularly effective, for it exposed the purely abstract and essentialist mode of reasoning which characterized the rationalist doctrine on God. Hume showed that such reasoning may be very coherent and comprehensive and still not have any existential significance or relevance to our experience. At the same time, he brought out the latent agnosticism of the empirical method, as developed by his British antecedents. But the very pertinence of this criticism to the contemporary intellectual situation sharply limited its significance. On a strict reckoning, all that he could validly conclude was that the historical materials at his disposal did not lend support to a demonstrative knowledge of God.

Hume's dialectical use of a restricted historical situation to establish his own position is clearly illustrated by his method of disqualifying all the objective sources of the idea of active, causal power. Only within the context of the Cartesian definition of matter as inert extension and the occasionalist analysis of finite consciousness as noncausal thought does it seem that the causal relation has no other knowable source than our own mental habits. Hume also relies upon his limitation of the understanding to its own perceptions. Since, by definition, the latter are noninformative about any distinct existent thing, a sheer analysis of them can never reveal the real composition of existential act and nature which supplies the metaphysical groundwork for the causal inference to God. But Hume does not criticize his own phenomenalist limitation of the human understanding to its own impressions and ideas. The only warranted result of his dialectic is the statement that real causation and a real basis for the causal inference to God cannot be obtained either within the framework of the rationalist conception of bodies and minds or within the empiricist conception of the direct object of the understanding.

Hume performed a definite service in stressing the unique significance of the existential judgment and the need to have a basis in sense experience for all our existential knowledge. The a priori proofs of God's existence and the use of essential principles to predetermine the nature of the actual world were procedures resting on a confusion between mathematical reasoning and the human way of approaching existence. Nevertheless, the Humean critique of rationalism on this score was not as radical as the problem required. It stopped short with the observation that existential meaning is achieved when our ideas are referred to sense impressions or at least to the systematic connections rendered stable by association and habit. Hume refused to press the empirical analysis beyond the "ultimates" of the laws of association and mental impressions, but the meaning intended in our existential judgments does not respect these artificial boundaries. These judgments express an act of being that is more than just the condition of being perceived. Hence the meaning of existence is not confined to the percept-object of

Hume's philosophy but breaks through to the thing exercising its act of being as distinct from our perception of it. Existential knowledge is the precise point where a man discovers that to know a being is to grasp it in its otherness or its own act of existing. Hume's phenomenalist prem- ise blinded him to the ultimate basis for the irreducibility of existential knowledge: the irreducibility of the act of existing either to essence (as rationalism hoped) or to the conditions of perception (as empiricism suspected).

Given Hume's commitments on cause and existence, his appraisal of the a posteriori demonstration of God's existence was inevitable. He had to restrict demonstrative reasoning to the abstract, mathematical realm because his theory of experience embraced only the percept- object and not the existing being of material things. This led him to adopt a highly rationalistic conception of demonstration.

Nothing is demonstrable, unless the contrary implies a contradiction. Nothing, that is distinctly conceivable, implies a contradiction. Whatever we conceive as existent, we can also conceive as non-existent. There is no Being, therefore, whose non-existence implies a contradiction. Consequently there is no Being, whose existence is demonstrable.[35]

This theory of demonstration is proportioned to the essentialist view of the object of knowledge and is not applicable to the existential order, whose distinctive character Hume sought to defend. Counterfactual propositions which are conceivable but not experientially warranted do not render existential demonstration impossible. For the latter is not based upon the mind's ability to conceive of a percept-object as existent or nonexistent. It rests on the mind's discovery of the implications in a given finite existent which compel recognition of the present existence and causal action of some other being. Just as the given existent does not dissolve under the mental experiment of distinctly conceiving it as nonexistent, so does the causal inference to an existing agent not dis- solve in the face of a mental experiment about this agent's nonexistence. The a posteriori inference to God is not wiped out by application of the rationalist test of conceiving the opposite, since it rests upon the actual composition of a finite existent and not upon an abstract conception of opposing relations among concepts and essential possibilities.

Finally, Hume himself falls back upon the a priori form of reasoning when he tries to rule out beforehand any causal demonstration of God's existence. He permits his position to solidify too rapidly and too simply by way of partial contrast with contemporary rationalists. His in- stances of supposed proofs are taken exclusively from the Cartesian writers and Samuel Clarke. He has no difficulty in showing that their claim to have mathematical demonstration of God's existence is con- tradictory in view of the nonexistential nature of mathematical think- ing. But he is not equally critical of the rationalist assumption that the only kind of necessary inference is based on essential relations and that causal reasoning belongs to this class if it has a real foundation apart from our mind. Since he can find no experiential source containing the type of essential necessity claimed by the rationalists for the causal relation, Hume concludes that its only accessible basis is in our psycho-logical associations.

What the empirical orientation of his thought called for, however, was a thorough revision of the meaning of causal necessity and a new rooting of it in sensible beings. Hume's phenomenalism blocked this revision, leaving him with only mental propensities which obviously could not be applied with certainty in the inference to God. Since his account of experience did not extend to a grasp of the participated act of being on the part of a finite sensible thing, he missed the experiential source of a necessary causal relation leading demonstratively to God. Hume's philosophy remained too closely specified by the rationalist doctrine on existence and cause instead of transcending the split be-tween reason and experience, essence and existence, and doing so in the sphere of speculative knowledge of experienced beings.

(2) *Empirical belief in God.* Hume grants that the argument from design in nature is the strongest theistic proof. Yet its strength does not lie in objectively cogent grounds, as Newton and the English deists claimed. As far as the reasoning from analogy between a human artisan and the divine maker is concerned, we are in no position to gain repeated experiences of divine creative acts, and hence we cannot determine how precise the likeness is. On the contrary, this argument draws its persuasive power from the nonrational tendencies in human nature to accept the existence of an intelligent and powerful maker of the entire universe. One of Hume's favorite maxims is that "philosophy would render us entirely *Pyrrhonian,* were not nature too strong for it."[36] Our emotions and practical drives force us to adhere strongly to the exist-ence of God, even though philosophical analysis assures us that we lack the means to ascend to a knowledge of Him with demonstrative certainty. The necessity of belief in God is due to this subjective inclination of our nature rather than to the coercive character of the evidence of cosmic order and internal design adduced by the mind.

Having admitted the psychological force of our common belief in a powerful, intelligent maker of the universe, Hume then made a strenu-ous effort to limit philosophical theism entirely to this single tenet.[37] What Bacon and Hobbes had said about the emotional springs for the belief in God shows that it has a natural foundation and is not the same as supernatural faith. Yet it is an instance of a strongly held probability and not demonstrative knowledge. Furthermore, it informs us only about what Samuel Clarke and the deists called God's *natural* (or morally neutral) attributes of intelligence and power. Hume surmised that the limited amount of order and the evil in the world may mean that God is finite in respect to these attributes or even that He is a cosmic soul working upon a matter that is partially intractable. Because of the intermingling of good and evil in the world, we cannot enlarge our natural belief to include God's *moral* attributes of providence and justice, love and mercy. They may well be present in God, but they are so remote and obscure that there is no likeness between them and our moral nature, and hence they escape even our probable reasoning.

The underlying reason for excluding the moral attributes of God from our natural belief is Hume's intent of divorcing theism entirely from the practical regulation of human life. Belief in God *arises from* the influence of the practical and passional tendencies in human nature, but it is not properly *directed toward* them as materials to be ordered. The philosophical theist must give "a plain, philosophical assent" to the proposition about an intelligent and powerful God, i.e., his belief must be purely speculative and untainted by the least practical bearing.[38] Hume liked to quote Seneca to the effect that to know God is to worship Him. This does not mean that knowledge of God should prompt us to practical acts of worship but rather that the speculative knowledge is itself the entire substance of worship.

Hume identified true religion with his own philosophy of religion. His speculative theism led to no further religious doctrines, institutions, or practices. Hume traced popular religion to the passions of hope, fear, and self-interest, which function in a religious form through one's thought of being in the presence of an overwhelming and intangible power. He hoped that his minimizing of the empirical idea of God would contribute toward counterbalancing the practical effects of ordinary religious life, which he continued to view through the eyes of a rebel against Scottish Calvinist predestination and rigid supervision of conduct.

The sanitary cordon was drawn tightly around belief in God not only to reduce formal religious practices, but also to liberate morality from religious motivation entirely. Hume was a pioneer proponent of a completely nonreligious or secular morality. He wanted to eliminate extramoral considerations based on freedom and providence, immortality and future judgment. His moral philosophy was constructed around the factors of passion and association, which are immanent in human nature, and it centered upon this-worldly objectives. Because speculative theism is exhausted in the bare assent to God's existence as an invisible and incomprehensible mind, "He is not the natural object of any passion or affection. He is no object either of the senses or imagination, and very little of the understanding, without which it is impossible to excite any affection."[39] Hume's disagreement with Locke and Berkeley about the indemonstrability of God's existence was thus carried over into the practical order, where he denied that moral relations can be demonstrated or moral decisions influenced by reference to the remote deity of speculative belief. Minimal theism was thus isolated entirely from Hume's purely immanent account of moral obligation and the springs of conduct.

5. THE COMMON-SENSE REACTION

A valiant but ultimately unsuccessful effort to broaden theism beyond the Humean minimum was made by another Scotsman, Thomas Reid (1710-1796). He admired the resolute way in which Hume drew out the full skeptical consequences of modern philosophy as a whole. All the modern thinkers are "Cartesians" in the sense of agreeing that the immediate objects of knowledge are ideas, that our basic certainty is of our own consciousness, and that the existence of the material world stands in need of proof.[40] But these assumptions run counter to the convictions of ordinary men, and hence previous philosophers are guilty of the anti-Newtonian procedure of arguing from a hypothesis against the fact. Reid proposed to return to the facts of knowledge as observable in the attitude of everyday life.

The root fact of human cognition is that we know existing things in a direct way, not by first inspecting their ideas. Indeed, Reid denies the reality of intermediary ideas or mental resemblances. The operations of our mind *suggest* to us the real things, but these operations are neither strictly caused by real things nor used by us as likenesses and inferential means of knowing things. We have a common-sense or intuitively evident assurance of the existence of the material world, whose qualities exist as we know them to be. Hence the a posteriori proof of God's existence is restored, at least in its point of departure.

As for the causal principle, Reid accepts the negative part of Hume's doctrine: It cannot be derived from abstract reasoning based on the material world, where there are sequences of events but not causal agencies. But Hume's psychological explanation in terms of experience is also inacceptable, since it misunderstands the sort of universality and necessity involved in causal judgments. Reid regards the causal principle as an immediate deliverance of human nature apprehended by common sense or the intuitive judgment of reason. We are obliged to assent to it because it is supplied by the intrinsic constitution of our nature. The connection between designed effects and an intelligent cause is also a metaphysically necessary principle of which common sense affords us an immediate intuition.

Fortified by these principles, which arise from the essential structure of human nature, Reid is confident of gaining demonstrative knowledge about God.

If it be evident to the human understanding, as I take it to be, that what begins to exist must have an efficient cause, which had power to give or not to give it existence; and if it be true, that effects well and wisely fitted for the best purposes, demonstrate intelligence, wisdom, and goodness, in the efficient cause, as well as power, the proof of a Deity from these principles is very easy and obvious to all men that can reason.[41]

The order of the universe leads us to God's moral attributes, as well as to His natural ones. Reid traces Hume's reluctance to admit the moral attributes to his failure to recognize God as a free agent in creation. A similar defective view of divine freedom is at the root of Leibniz' inadequate handling of the problem of evil and the dilemma of a finite or a malevolent God. Reid is strongly critical of the Leibnizian principle of sufficient reason, which he regards as a threat to the doctrine of a free creation. If this principle refers to the reason for the existence of things, its function is already supplied by the principle of causality; if it refers to the reason for true propositions, there is none beyond the intrinsic evidence and truth. In either case, the principle of sufficient reason is vague and superfluous. It does not belong to the content of common sense and is not needed in the proof of God's existence.

Perhaps the best way to test the strength of Reid's position on God is to observe what is done with it by his loyal follower, Dugald Stewart (1753–1828). Instead of developing a complete natural theology, as we might expect, Stewart reduces the discussion on God to a chapter in ethics.[42] He refrains from calling the knowledge of God a demonstrative reasoning, but instead regards it as an immediate and necessary consequence aroused in our mind by the conjunction between the causal principle and the evidence of order in nature. The reason for this modification is not difficult to find. Reid had denied that we gain any knowledge of real causation from nature, which is the realm of settled sequences between antecedent sign and consequent thing signified. How, then, can we use the material world as a basis for an existential demonstration from really perceived effects to a real causal agent? There is no way to know that the adaptation of means to ends in nature is a *caused* adaptation requiring an actually existing, intelligent cause. Hence Stewart must fall back upon the mind's natural suggestion of a causal source for the world, even in the absence of an experience of material things as caused. But this is precisely the sort of leap beyond the evidence to which Hume condemns the empiricist mind, if it engages to seek God, and which is not far removed from Gassendi's theory of a mental "anticipation" of God.

The Scottish school of common sense remained well within the ambit of empiricism despite its repudiation of the "Cartesian" premises of modern philosophy. Its substitution of the function of mental suggestion for ideas did not resolve problems in a satisfactory way, since it left the precise nature of this suggestion a mystery. How the operations of the mind can suggest the existence of the material world and how the evidence of order in nature can suggest a first cause received no explanation at the hands of Reid and Stewart. Their appeal to the sanction of the intrinsic constitution of human nature for the causal principle could be accommodated within Hume's theory of nature or habits of association and thus could be readily deprived of transsubjective import. It could also open the way to Kant's explanation of universality and necessity as functions of the mental forms or structures of the mind.

Stewart did try to restore the bearing of the doctrine on God upon ethics, but his was a theistic ethics without any speculative foundation. Hence when Kant surveyed the writings of the empiricist school, he could conclude that they furnish no speculative knowledge of God and no safe ground for basing ethics upon God. Hume's minimal theism brought to completion the neutralizing of God in philosophy. The protest of the so-called common-sense philosophers did not change the net impact of empiricism upon the question of God's role in philosophy.

The contribution of empiricism to the problem of God was remarkably incisive on the polemical side. It put a halt to the use of God as a mathematical principle of deduction in philosophy. This it did by making an enlightening comparison between the epistemological requirements for such a deductive use and the actual capacities of our mind. A descriptive study of the human understanding and its liaison with sense experience showed the futility of attempting to prove God's existence in an a priori way or to predetermine the nature of man and the world through a theological deduction.

It was in its reconstructive phase, however, that empiricism faltered in its search for an experientially grounded doctrine on God. Its undeclared dependence on the rationalist view of the understanding was still too extensive to permit it to develop a thoroughgoing, realistic metaphysics of finite beings and the infinite being. The empiricists recognized the importance of sensible, existent things enough to outlaw a purely intellectual approach to God but not enough to achieve a new synthesis between intelligence and sense in the inferential way to God. Since the empiricist version of human experience remained enclosed phenomenalistically within our perceptions and did not include a grasp of the essential nature and existential act of sensible beings, it failed to secure a demonstrative knowledge of God's existence and the basis for a philosophy of God. It brought out the important role of the emotions and our natural inclinations in shaping our convictions about God, but it did so at the expense of our speculative apprehension of Him.

In the final estimate, then, rationalism and empiricism abetted each other in keeping alive the opposition between reason and experience, the possible essence and the actual existent, and inferential necessity and existential relation. On both sides of the dichotomy, the chief casualty was the doctrine on God, in the extreme and mutually specified forms of functionalism and neutralization. The full depth of the crisis in the modern philosophical discussion about God became visible in the bitter controversies between the leaders of the Enlightenment on whether to retain even a minimal theism. By clarifying the problem of God from various and often clashing perspectives, they cleared a pathway for the more comprehensive syntheses of Kant and Hegel.

Chapter V

THE ENLIGHTENMENT: BATTLEGROUND
OVER GOD

THE AGE of the Enlightenment is, like the Renaissance, a sprawling epoch wherein sharply opposing tendencies collide. It is difficult to make any significant generalizations without contradicting many representative cases which point in another direction. Agreement is strongest on the negative side, in a repudiation of the claims of the Christian churches to a supernatural origin and a valid use of authority in religious and moral matters. Common appeal is indeed made to the use of natural evidence and rational argument, but there is no settled opinion concerning the precise import of the evidence or the precise relation between rational inference, scientific findings, and man's affective life.

Consequently, in trying to understand the mind of the Enlightenment toward God, we must avoid imposing any rigidly simple pattern on the individual thinkers. It would be misleading to suppose that there was a monolithic, one-way process which began with the denial of Christian revelation, lingered for a while in a compromise deism, and culminated in complete materialism. The major defect in this dialectical scheme is that it evacuates the actual historical circumstances of eighteenth-century enlightened thought, with its contending crosscurrents. It would be equally far from the facts to imagine a solid front of the men of light against the obscurantist forces defending tradition. Some exponents of Christian principles—notably the two generations of Jesuit editors of the *Journal de Trévoux*—made an informed appraisal of the new ideas but continued to stress the points of honest difference concerning God and religion. Within the company of the *philosophes* themselves, these same issues led to radical cleavages and severe mutual criticism. Here, as at every other stage in the modern philosophical experience, the problem of God introduced deep divisions among the leading minds.

Perhaps the least misleading way of expressing the situation is to use the image of the battlefield, with its swirling and interlacing lines of combat.[1] Two of the protagonists continue the seventeenth-century contest between skepticism and rationalism under a somewhat new form. Bayle is a legitimate descendant of Montaigne, although his use of historical criticism introduces a novel element into fideistic skepticism. He

126

declares the bankruptcy of philosophical theism and the independence of morality from religious premises but nevertheless leaves a place for religious faith and some sort of moral and historical conviction. As the grand systematizer of rationalism in the new era, Christian Wolff rounds out his conception of metaphysics with a long treatise on natural theology. He reaffirms the a priori demonstration of God's existence and nature by mathematically cogent arguments.

The influence of Locke's empiricism and the Newtonian natural philosophy is strongly felt at the height of the Enlightenment in France. As far as the problem of God is concerned, this influence is thoroughly ambivalent, since it leads both to a strengthening of a minimal natural doctrine on God and to an outlook from which God is eliminated. Both the theistic and the atheistic appeals to Locke and Newton can be regarded as "scientific." As employed here, the term "scientific" does not refer to the demonstrative character of the reasoning involved on either side of the dispute but rather to the source of the evidence. Both Voltaire the theist and Holbach the atheist make primary use of the current scientific data in physics and biology, and in this sense there is a sharp clash between scientifically based theism and atheism. Voltaire does not regard his acceptance of God as a halfway house to anything else; he sees it as the only reasonable interpretation of nature and man in an age increasingly aware of the relevance of scientific findings to basic issues. But for Holbach and Diderot, the elimination of God functions as a necessary condition of scientific progress. Materialistic naturalism rests on the denial that God is at all entailed by the scientific findings or that He is required for the moral ordering of human society.

The latter contention receives a sharp challenge from Rousseau, who regards atheism as the result of divorcing reason from its natural union with moral will and the feelings. When all these factors are unified, man can have the certitude of natural faith in the personal reality of God and the spiritual freedom of man. Thus the Enlightenment presents itself as a battleground where contending views on God meet headlong in an unresolved struggle.

1. BAYLE ON THE GREAT COMBATS OF REASON AND FAITH

The industrious and complicated mind of Pierre Bayle (1647–1706) was Janus faced in structure. It looked backward to the seventeenth-century dialogue between skeptics and Cartesians and forward to the age of criticism and illuminism. We are accustomed to study only the latter visage in the light of Voltaire's remark that Bayle was father to the community of savants and solicitor-general for all the *philosophes*. While Bayle certainly did lay the foundation for the Enlightenment's critical approach to sacred history, ecclesiastical authority, and religiously sanctioned morality, he did so within the context of fideistic skepticism. To a Voltaire and a Diderot, fideism could not be a seriously held position; it was only a convenient dodge in the game with the censor and the consistory. Hence they took a purely ironical view of Bayle's frequent juxtaposition of the critical findings of reason and the nonrational certitudes of faith. But to a man nourished on Montaigne, Charron, and the Calvinistic divines, supernatural faith could well remain intact amidst the destructions wrought by a critical reason.

Writing from the vantage point of the nineteenth century, Ludwig Feuerbach perhaps came closer to the truth with his remark that Bayle still believed in believing and that he employed skepticism to complete the split between Protestantism as faith and Protestantism as a rationalized system. In this purpose, he opposed the rationalizing tendencies of Leibniz and the Protestant school-philosophy in Germany and Holland. Bayle took the Calvinist notion of the absolute autonomy of faith to mean not only that faith rests upon no prior basis in philosophy, but also that it entails no philosophical system and admits of no rational defense whatsoever. To believe and to know are utterly independent, disparate, and even antagonistic acts. Against any irenic efforts to find a common ground for mutual support, Bayle emphasized the impossibility of a speculative reconciliation.

One must necessarily choose between philosophy and the Gospel. If you wish to believe only that which is evident and in conformity with the common notions, take philosophy and leave Christianity. If you wish to believe the incomprehensible mysteries of religion, take Christianity and leave philosophy. For one cannot possess evidence and incomprehensibility together.[2]

At least one cannot possess them together in terms of any doctrinal synthesis, such as is claimed by the systems of sacred theology and philosophical theism. For himself, Bayle accepted only a bare faith, unsupported by any theological framework, and an equally bare minimum of natural evidence which never grows into a philosophy. He composed a dictionary, but never a *Summa* or an encyclopedia. His parsimony was a scandal to the Christian divines of his day and an annoyance to the Encyclopedist philosophers of the new age. But it suited his underlying conviction that reason should always remain skeptical toward religious affirmations and that the man of faith should forswear all concords and remain content with naturally inevident and unintelligible mysteries.

As a young professor of philosophy at Sedan, Bayle had expounded Descartes' metaphysics and natural philosophy. He regarded the latter as a plausible account of appearances but denied that it penetrated to the real nature of motion, time, and bodies. His further readings in the history of philosophy inclined him toward the Pyrrhonian position, especially after he studied the nest of controversies surrounding the various proofs of God's existence. After briefly reviewing the Thomistic five ways of proof, he set forth in some detail the Cartesian arguments from the motion and conservation of bodies and from the idea of the infinite being.[3] By way of critical comment, he noted that if we do not know the real essence of motion and time, we cannot be certain about the real foundation for inferring a prime mover and conserver of bodies. As for the idea of the infinite being, it is actively formed by the finite mind itself, when it strips off the imperfections from its prior idea of a spiritual being. But then the objection of Hobbes becomes serious, since it may follow from the sensuous origin of our ideas that we cannot really conceive of anything spiritual and hence anything infinite. Reason is never able to decide, with certainty, between the sensist theory of ideas and the fragile chain of inferences constructed by the rationalist metaphysicians upon the Cartesian notion of purely spiritual ideas. Hence one must remain in skeptical suspense of judgment concerning the demonstrability of God's existence, as well as His relationship as creator and provider for the world.

Yet Bayle did admit conditionally that if God's existence could be established philosophically, the proof would depend solely upon the natural light of the mind and would be prior to the knowledge of a divine revelation. His examination of the problem of the natural light and the types of truth and evidence led him to modify his skepticism to some degree. Even after the sin of Adam, there remains something good in our nature (although not meritorious for salvation): "an invincible and undiscardable determination toward the truth in general, a determination which prevents our mind from ever adhering to a doctrine which seems false to it."[4] Bayle's own pertinacious exposure of errors supposed that the human mind has a preference for truth. Nevertheless, this native bent is only toward the truth in general and away from the appearance of falsity. One cannot deduce from this inclination alone the validity of any special set of propositions. A distinctive sort of evidence must be presented if the mind is to assent to any particular proposition as true.

One way to specify this problem is to distinguish between contingent and necessary truths, the former being grounded upon events in human history or free divine decrees. Necessary truths are evident either immediately or mediately. Unlike the stricter Pyrrhonists, Bayle admits the presence of some immediately evident, necessary truths. They are the common notions and first principles, which carry their own evidence and produce certitude through their own clarity. Among the examples mentioned by Bayle are the very notion of the effective truth of objects as a conformity between the mind and real natures, the principle of contradiction, and the proposition that the whole is greater than its part. Such truths are given by the natural light, are intrinsically incontestable, and, at least among wise men, are universally admitted. The mind can use these truths as perfectly certain principles for proving mediate truths, either through a reasoning process or through an analysis of experience. The two requirements for mediate inference are that the proofs be rigorous in themselves and that they be clearly incontestable or sufficiently accessible for the disciplined mind to know that nothing can be said in favor of any contradictory assertions.

Bayle points out at once, however, that whereas objective rigor and subjective lucidity always coincide in the case of immediately evident truths, they seldom coincide in our inferential efforts. Necessary inference is achieved in such purely abstract disciplines as logic and mathematics but not in natural philosophy and metaphysics, where really existing things are in question. Here the connection between the supposed real object and the first principles of thought cannot be incontestably established. "Evidence is a relative quality. That is why we can scarcely tell—if it does not concern the common notions—whether what seems evident to us must also appear thus to another."[5] Whether it be the relation between body and space or between body and soul, the subjective requirement of a lucid connection with evident principles can never be satisfied. The skeptics have shown by their technique of equipollence that something reasonable can be said for both sides, so that certainty cannot be attained in metaphysical and physical inferences. There is a similar lack of perfect certitude in contingent matters of historical fact or divine decree. Bayle's famous method of "historical Pyrrhonism" is chiefly a polemical insistence on the merely probable character of all inferences in history, without distinction between the sacred and the secular.

With this epistemological foundation, Bayle can now systematically exclude philosophical theism. The error of Descartes was not in admitting some absolutely certain principles but in regarding them as existential and fruitful of subsequent demonstrations about real beings. Instead, the absolutely certain metaphysical principles of our speculative reason are both abstract and incapable of generating any necessary consequences. They are abstract or nonexistential because Descartes failed to penetrate beyond the idea of thought to the real thinking self, which remains mysterious and opaque to speculation. And they are systematically sterile, once one admits that the skeptical method of equipollence makes it impossible to assign rational cogency wholly on one side of any issue. At most, metaphysical inferences lead to probability and not to a system of deductively demonstrated truths.

Metaphysical knowledge of God's existence and nature was thus ruled out for lack of any necessary existential truths gained through demonstration. The only way to escape this conclusion would be either to revise the entire theory of existential demonstration or else to show that

God is included among the innate and immediately known truths. Since there was no effort at a revision of the theory of existential demonstration visible upon his intellectual horizon, Bayle concentrated upon weakening the latter alternative. His eager and uncritical acceptance of travelers' reports about the absence of religion and the concept of God among remote peoples was partially motivated by a desire to show that there is no innate knowledge of God anteceding all demonstrations. His interest in atheistic arguments and the naturalistic hypothesis of a self-sufficient, material universe was likewise dictated by the skeptical technique of finding counterbalancing arguments to offset any theistic affirmations. The truth of God's existence was thereby shown to be neither immediately evident nor capable of demonstration.

The purpose of Bayle's critical attitude was not, however, to foster atheism. His negative aim was to undermine any philosophical and theological defense of religious faith. On the positive side, he sought to advance a secular morality which would be independent of both speculative theism and religious revelation.

If the existence of God escapes our natural reasoning power, it is all the more likely that philosophy and theology are helpless to explain the divine nature, the creation of the world, and the problem of evil. Our experience of appearances gives us one pole of the comparison—a world having certain perfections and certain evils—but it provides us with no access to God, the creator and providential governor. Given the skeptical bar upon a knowledge of essential natures, finite and infinite, there is no basis for the theodicies of the rationalist theologians and Leibniz.

In his *Historical and Critical Dictionary* (1697), Bayle makes clever use of a system of cross references to establish a network of articles dealing with evil. After criticizing all attempts to minimize evil or to sweep it up into a Leibnizian cascade of essences and legal analogies, he concludes that the most consistent philosophical position is the Manichean doctrine of a cosmic war between the coeternal principles of good and evil. The Christian cannot overcome this view by any philosophical means but only by the deliverances of revelation, where the benevolence of the one, eternal God is given as a truth of sheer faith. This accords with the Baylean description of Christian faith as "the obligation to submit oneself to the authority of God and to believe humbly the mysteries which it has pleased Him to reveal to us, however inconceivable they may be and however impossible they may appear to our reason. . . . Let us say also that the most precious faith is that which, on the divine testimony, embraces the truths most opposed to reason."[6] Whether this declaration be taken ironically or fideistically, the upshot is that on the problem of evil and all other natural issues involving God, the probabilities of rational argumentation will always lean in the favor of unbelievers.

Although this situation may provide a purifying crucible for one's act of faith, it also indicates to Bayle the imprudence of seeking a religious basis for the moral rules governing the individual and society. He goes farther than most of his skeptical predecessors in maintaining the complete independence of morality, both from religious faith and from every sort of philosophical and theological doctrine on the relation between God and man. With his conception of faith and reason, there can be no theistic and religious ground of a natural moral law. Hence Bayle admits the possibility of a morally upright (although religiously non-meritorious) atheist society, provided that it be regulated by stringent and just laws. His defense of an almost complete toleration in civil society is based partly upon skeptical despair of any intellectual content in theism and religion and partly upon a respect for individual integrity in a pluralist world of many creeds and none. These two motives are never carefully distinguished throughout the long discussion of toleration by the leaders of the Enlightenment.

Bayle pioneered the way for Diderot, Hume, and Kant in detaching morality from rationalistic metaphysics and speculative theism. He denied that the removal of metaphysics must lead to the total subversion of moral principles, since there can be some ethical knowledge entirely apart from metaphysical speculation on God and immortality.[7] It now becomes clear why Bayle modified Pyrrhonism to the extent of allowing certitude about some first principles, even though he prevented their expansion into a metaphysical system. He did not want to declare the understanding totally incompetent and devoid of truths, since that would rule out any ethical truths. Our natural light reveals to us not only some speculative principles but also some practical ones, and indeed, its clear and distinct notions are principally in the moral order. Just as certain as our few speculative principles are such practically evident truths as the obligation to be grateful to benefactors, to keep one's word, and to act according to conscience. All of this natural moral insight is summed up in the idea of equity, which is common to all men and serves as the universal norm for moral decisions. We have a natural, certain knowledge of its three basic precepts for individual and social living: to live honestly, to do no injury, and to give everyone his due. Although speculative reason cannot construct a valid metaphysical system, practical reason has here an autonomous source for its moral judgments. Although Bayle granted that God is the ultimate causal source of this moral illumination, he did not want to make moral convictions hinge upon any revealed or natural knowledge of this source.

An autonomous, secular morality must rest upon the idea of equity and the appeal to "the supreme Parliament of reason and of the natural light . . . in respect to morality."[8] But Bayle fails to make much progress in developing a moral philosophy in accord with these general notions.

He does suggest that the moral agent must aim to do justice, simply because of its conformity with conscience or reason in the practical order, and thus his position is a precursor of the Kantian philosophy. Yet he does not explain why equity should be sought for its own sake. Having liberated morality from God, he then fails to determine any precise ground for disciplining personal life and taming social power according to a universal rule of justice. Through his historical studies of individual cases, he is able to show that men often act without any reference to their general moral principles. Within the skeptical framework, however, Bayle cannot establish why our moral ideals should ever be preferred obligatorily over selfish passions and unjust customs. And because he confines demonstrative inference to the abstract, essential order, he also finds it difficult to show the concrete and existential significance of his moral precepts.

Bayle's contribution to the eighteenth-century controversy on God revolves around three main points. Religious faith in God can and should have no rational defense, whether philosophical or theological; the human mind cannot make a metaphysical demonstration of God's existence, nature, and providence; morality is independently founded in the natural light of the practical understanding and needs no sanction from religion and speculative theism. Thus Bayle offers a highly personal blend of religious fideism, speculative skepticism, and secular moralism.

2. WOLFF'S "NATURAL THEOLOGY TREATED BY THE SCIENTIFIC METHOD"

The year 1706 marked not only the death of Bayle but also the call of Christian Wolff (1679–1754) to a professorship at Halle University. From then until Voltaire's visit to Berlin at mid-century, when the French influence became paramount, Wolff was the leading representative of the Enlightenment in Germany.[9] Through his more than sixty volumes in the physical and mathematical sciences and philosophy, he served as the schoolmaster of the German universities and the chief exponent of a rationalist system of universal knowledge. Glancing at the interminable demonstrations and numbered paragraphs of his writings, it is not difficult to picture Wolff as a complacent pedant, spinning out his thoughts in a dreamworld of his own. Yet this image is unfair to the man whom Kant sincerely hailed for his spirit of thoroughness and his rigor of scientific method. The fine-print notes appended to most of his formal proofs reveal a mind constantly critical of itself and, in some measure, aware of the need for empirical research. Wolff's dogmatic confidence in his method was qualified by a deep-seated hesitancy about its ability to encompass the empirical world. This doubt left its imprint upon all his writings, including his treatises on natural theology.

One cannot plunge directly into Wolffian natural theology, however, since it must be viewed within the closely knit context of a certain conception of philosophy and ontology. From Wolff's opening definition of philosophy as "the science of possibles, in so far as they can be" or have an essential nature, it is evident that his is a system of possibility and essence in which the role of existence is a subordinate one.[10] It is not a totally de-existentialized philosophy; it is one in which knowable and systematically exploitable being primarily means the possible essence and in which existence is admitted only by virtue of some correlation it has with this essence. What does not stand out so clearly is the reason why Wolff settled upon this essentialist viewpoint and yet never totally submerged the distinctive reality of existence.

Part of the explanation comes from Wolff's complex intellectual heritage. He was just as thoroughly familiar with the critical work of the skeptics and empiricists as with the rationalist tradition. The skeptical arguments convinced him of the impossibility of demonstratively defending our knowledge of the existing external world, either through a rationalist deduction or through an empiricist inference. Hence he concluded that it was too risky to base his philosophy upon the thesis of the reality of the material universe; his fundamental definitions remained deliberately neutral about the independent existence of a world corresponding with our ideas. This skeptically generated neutrality inclined him to focus upon the essential and the possible, without making any primary commitments about sensible existents. Nevertheless, the British scientists and philosophers also convinced him of the danger of entirely ignoring the existential aspect.

As a compromise, Wolff calls for a union in holy matrimony of three kinds of human knowledge: historical, philosophical, and mathematical.[11] Historical knowledge means the empirical assurance, gained mainly through sense experience and experiments, that certain things exist or occur. Wolff hails it as the foundation of all philosophy and the constant guide of all inferential reasoning. Yet he wavers between saying that empirical knowledge assures us indubitably that certain things actually *do* exist and saying that it merely makes us reflectively aware of having the *ideas* of things that *can* exist or come to be. This ambiguity about the import of sense experience stems from his basic epistemological neutrality and leads him to depreciate its certainty. Experiential certainty concerns the bare fact (real or ideal) and does not extend to the sufficient reason for the fact. Hence philosophical certainty must be nonexperiential in its own proper form. Every ounce of it (to use Wolff's own emphatic phrase) derives from the use of the mathematical method, which risks nothing on the real existent but concentrates upon the determinate quantity of possible objects and essential relations. This method enables philosophy to determine with perfect certainty the reasons why objects may come to be or why being is possible. Hence philosophy is primarily a study of the internal *essentialia,* or essential components, and the external reasons, or causes of the possibility of these essential components. Existence is studied properly in philosophy only to the extent that it can be drawn out with certainty from the known essential structure.

Wolff never removes the radical dichotomy between empirical and mathematico-philosophical certainties, between knowledge of fact and of possible essence. Their matrimonial bond is not based upon some unifying doctrinal principle but rests solely upon Wolff's personal awareness of the need for both approaches. His desire to found philosophy on an existential basis in experience is blocked by the skeptical critique, and he is thereby forced to locate philosophical certainty in the possible essences and their sufficient reasons. And yet he is also unwilling to follow Leibniz in overcoming the distinction between truths of fact and truths of essence by means of the principle of sufficient reason. Leibniz accords the primacy to this principle, since it expresses the dynamic law of quasi-autonomous essences, to which God must give a consent decree governing His creation of the existing world. For Wolff, however, the essences are unequivocally grounded in the divine intellect and enjoy no quasi-independence. Hence the principle of sufficient reason can give essential connections or reasons for facts, but it cannot furnish any deductive certitude concerning the actual facts themselves or existential productions of the divine will. There is no objectively determining ground which shapes God's existential decisions and closes the gap in man's philosophical system. Hence the principle of sufficient reason must remain subordinate to the principle of contradiction, which provides an indubitable certainty, at least, about the internal consistency and possibility of the essential traits as such.

In conformity with this view of philosophy, Wolff then defines ontology as the science of being, i.e., of that which can exist or that to which existence is not repugnant. In the main, it is the science of essence, namely, "that which is first of all conceived about being, and in which is contained the sufficient reason why other aspects either actually belong to it or can belong to it."[12] Ontology is a strict science precisely because it confines itself to a general study of being as possible or essentially constituted—the sphere where a mathematically rigorous certitude is obtainable. Existence figures in ontology either obliquely, as the complement of possibility, or negatively, as the furnisher of a norm of nonrepugnance. As the directly known act of a thing, it does not come within the scope of ontology, which remains a nonexistential discipline.

Because of the nonexistential character of ontology or general metaphysics, Wolff requires three special parts of metaphysics to determine the principles of the possibility of existence in the three main areas of being. Cosmology studies the reasons of being in the contingent, material world; psychology deduces the soul as the sufficient reason for the existence of mental acts; natural theology demonstrates God as the ground of existence for His own attributes and modes, as well as for the existence of the world. Natural theology presupposes these other sciences. From ontology, it draws its general principles and orientation; from cosmology, a factual basis in the material world; from psychology, a basis in the soul and also some special insight into the spiritual perfections which help us to know God's nature.

Yet Wolff disturbs this neat ordering of the metaphysical sciences by remarking that natural theology is the first to demonstrate an existing reality and that only through the primary cause can we gain philosophical knowledge of other objects as existent. Once more he is dogged by the rift between an empirical acquaintance with existing things and a philosophical knowledge of existents which must be based upon prior understanding of their essential, sufficient reasons. However close an association cosmology and rational psychology may establish with the empirical disciplines, they are unable to acquire by themselves anything more than a knowledge of the possibility of existence in the material and mental modes. Only after natural theology establishes the necessary, actual existence of the ultimate sufficient reason of things can the special metaphysical understanding of things as actually existing, or of finite essences as actually entailing the contingent mode of existence, be achieved in some measure in cosmology and psychology and extended into practical philosophy.

Through a systematic necessity, then, Wolff attached crucial importance to the question of how to prove God's existence within the framework of heretofore nonexistential certitudes. His concern is indicated by the fact that he composed two entirely distinct textbooks on natural theology in his Latin series, one to give an a posteriori demonstration of God's existence and attributes from the contingency of the world and the other to prove God's existence from the notion of the most perfect being and His attributes from the nature of the soul.[18] He was reluctant to regard the latter way as unqualifiedly a priori because it rests on a proof of the possibility of the most perfect being and because we derive the notion of the most perfect being from a contemplation of our own soul. It *is* a priori, however, in the sense that the existence of God is drawn from a knowledge of the exigency of His own essence to entail this act of existing.

Wolff prefaced his own two proofs with a critical survey of some current arguments. His contention was that they either begged the issue or were reducible to the Cartesian ontological proof. Thus the popular appeal of the Pietists to the evidences of finality in the world covertly presupposed a theistic view of God as making the world. Although Wolff did not deny the presence of finality, he insisted that any teleological interpretation of nature must follow after natural theology and not serve as a proof of God's existence. As for the stress which the New-tonians placed upon cosmic order, it could not be employed decisively in natural theology until this order was shown to be contingent and the analogy of the artisan shown to be applicable to the infinite creator. Moreover, Wolff agreed with Leibniz that the Cartesian proof from the idea of the most perfect being is defective until the possibility of such a nature is established.

The a posteriori proof can be simply stated:

> The human soul exists, or we exist. Since nothing is without a sufficient reason why it is rather than is not, a sufficient reason must be given why our soul exists, or why we exist. Now this reason is contained either in ourselves or in some other being diverse from us. But if you maintain that we have the reason of our existence in a being which, in turn, has the reason of its existence in another, you will not arrive at the sufficient reason until you come to a halt at some being which does have the sufficient reason of its own existence in itself. Therefore, either we ourselves are the necessary being, or there is given a necessary being other and diverse from us. Consequently, a necessary being exists.[14]

However, certain aspects of this proof render it more complex and more doubtfully a posteriori than may seem at first sight. Since it has served historically for Kant and his successors as the prototype of all a posteriori arguments, the proof is deserving of close, critical analysis.

Wolff himself calls attention immediately to the epistemological neu-trality of the starting point. Although he labels it a proof from the con-tingency of the world and our souls, it makes no commitment about the real existence of the sensible world. Even with regard to man the proof remains indeterminately poised between a starting point in the human soul (having a real body) and one in the self (having ideas of sensible things). What it starts with is the affirmation of an alternative about an existing something whose existential act remains unclarified. Wolff recommends this indeterminacy as a means of bypassing the dis-pute between idealists, materialists, and skeptics. But, in fact, his am-bivalence about the existing something deprives him of a philosophically specified point of departure in an actual existent. The affirmation of the existing something is an infraphilosophical one whose philosophical standing is not established. Moreover, the existential affirmation does not rule out the skeptical alternative of remaining in suspense and for-ever enclosed in a private experience which cannot decide between the self and the soul as existent.

The present proof depends upon the existential validity of the prin-ciple of sufficient reason. As defined in Wolff's ontology, the sufficient reason is that whence it is known why something is. Since a condition of knowledge is read into the very meaning of the sufficient reason, it is most perfectly exemplified in our clear grasp of the essential determinants of a possible thing. Consequently, in his ontology, Wolff bases his formal acceptance of the general principle of sufficient reason upon such nonexistential grounds as mathematical abstraction, lack of repugnance to experience, and, especially, the natural impetus of the human mind to posit a reason.[15] Yet in his natural theology it is given an existential import. Prior to the demonstration of God's existence, the only source for knowledge of existence, and hence for the existential significance of this principle, would be our ordinary empirical awareness of causal influxes. This awareness remains infraphilosophical, however, and cannot be assumed to become transformed into a philosophically warranted knowledge of the application of the principle of sufficient reason to existential cases of connection.

As the proof stands, it terminates in some necessary being but not yet formally in God. The Wolffian proof leads to the attribute of necessity, which must then be shown to belong to the existent God. To make this transition, Wolff first establishes that a necessary being is also an *ens a se,* or a being enjoying independence of existence with respect to anything else. A necessary being has the sufficient reason of existence in its own essence, and hence it exists through its own power or has independence of existence (aseity). It follows that the independent being has the sufficient reason of its existence "in and from itself" in the sense of "in and from its own essence." It is right here that the Wolffian philosophical knowledge of existence suddenly burgeons out—when we know that the divine essence necessarily gives rise to its own existence from itself. From our mental constraint of being unable to conceive *ens a se* except as existing, we conclude with philosophical certitude to its real necessity of existence. We are so constrained not because of some implications in our starting point in the soul or self, but solely because of the distinctive essential determinations known to make up the essence of this *ens a se.*

That is why Wolff inserts, at the heart of his a posteriori approach to God, the proposition that *"ens a se exists, because it is possible."*[16] Wolff warns, in opposition to Leibniz, that real existence cannot be inferred from possibility in general or from just any really possible essence. Only the particular notes making up the essence of the independent being give it the special privilege of existing simply because it is *this* possible essence. This means, however, that Wolff is subordinating his a posteriori starting point to the a priori analysis of the essential determinations of *ens a se* and is resting his knowledge of God's real, necessary existence upon the mental constraint to which this conceptual analysis leads. The existential conclusion is not inferred from some finite existent but is deduced from the necessary, infinite essence. His proof is a posteriori only to the extent that it builds a mounting pile of essential sufficient reasons; it becomes a priori in its derivation of the divine existence from the requirements of the ultimate essential reason. As an existential demonstration of God, it proceeds from the special demands of the divine essence and hence is covertly a priori.

Before identifying the independent being with the transcendent God, however, Wolff must also show that neither the visible world nor the human soul is *ens a se*. The contingency of the world follows from its being composed of elements which are not the only elements that may conceivably exist and from its successive being in time. The soul's contingency (or that of the self and its representations) follows from the correlation of its ideas with a particular world whose nonexistence is possible. In both cases, Wolff relies upon extrinsic arguments and a criterion of abstract conceivability, since he does not yet have available means for examining the intrinsic relation between the essence and the act of existing of things in experience. He does not actually show that aseity must belong to a being which is free from successive duration and from the potentiality for other constituents in its nature or that knowledge of the contingent is itself a contingent act.

Finally, the identification is made between the necessary, independent being and the God of Scripture, whose nominal definition is: the *ens a se* in which is contained the sufficient reason of the existence of this visible world and of our souls. Wolff brings this part of his investigation to a triumphant close with the conclusion that "consequently, once the divine essence is posited, its existence also is simultaneously posited."[17] Still, this does not answer Kant's pertinent question of whether our finite minds can know, with certainty, that the process of positing is in the actual order of being and not in the purely conceptual order.

The common conclusion toward which these critical observations point is that Wolff had to fall back upon a conceptual positing of existence. This was not due to some intrinsic exigency affecting every sort of a posteriori inference to God but to the fact that his first proof was not genuinely a posteriori in its structure. Because his philosophical starting point and principles of demonstration were not founded upon the sensuous and intellectual experience of the existent, material world, he had to make a covert appeal to the a priori power of a necessary, independent essence in order to posit existence. Kant did a service in exposing this procedure, but he drew from it the unwarranted generalization that every a posteriori inference to God from the sensible world must conform with the Wolffian pattern.

In order to prepare for his ontological or admittedly a priori demonstration of God's existence, Wolff uses the key concept of a "reality" to show that the most perfect being is possible and that there are grades of existences.[18] A "reality" is that which is truly understood to belong to some being rather than that which seems to belong to it according to our confused perceptions. Thus it is defined in terms of pure intellect's knowledge of that which pertains to the intrinsic possibility or essence of a thing. Wolff then goes on to define a most perfect being, *ens perfectissimum,* as that to which belong all compossible realities in the absolutely highest degree. A most perfect being is, therefore, *ens realissimum* in the quite literal and technical sense of an essential nature which gives rise to the fullest combination of realities. In this latter definition, Wolff suppresses the reference to the norm of pure, nonsensuous knowledge. He can thereby pass imperceptibly from mental to real conditions or affirmations of realities and can establish the real possibility of the most perfect being simply by noting that (our concept of) the supreme grade of reality excludes all defects and permits nothing of itself to be negated. The most perfect being is really possible, since it involves no contradiction and is sheer affirmative reality, without negation of itself.

As for existence, it is one of the realities or truly known perfections appertaining to the essential being. Just as there are grades of beings or essential natures, so are there grades of existences or realities in those natures. The main divisions are contingent and necessary existence. The existence of a contingent thing is reducible to a contingent mode of its essence, whereas the existence of a necessary being is conceived after the manner of a necessary attribute of such an essential nature. In the scale of existential realities, necessary existence holds the highest rank, since our mind cannot conceive of a greater one. The criterion of conceivability is here openly invoked.

Having taken these preparatory steps, Wolff can now present his amended ontological proof, granted the nominal definition of God as the most perfect being.

God contains all compossible realities in the absolutely highest degree. But He is possible. Wherefore, since the possible can exist, existence can appertain to it. Consequently, since existence is a reality, and since realities are compossible which can appertain together to a being, existence is in the class of compossible realities. Moreover, necessary existence is of the absolutely highest degree. Therefore, necessary existence belongs to God or, what amounts to the same thing, God necessarily exists.[19]

In his prolegomena to this proof, Wolff fails to supply an existential basis for the grades of reality, the compossible presence of existence with other realities, and the supremacy of necessary or attributive existence. By this time, however, he no longer hesitates about whether we conceive only the ideally necessary connection of existence with the divine essence or whether we know that the divine essence truly exists. The two viewpoints are firmly coalesced in natural theology, which treats existence as a "reality" of a necessary essence and hence as conceivable in terms of an attribute flowing from that essence. His philosophy is at last in possession of the only type of existential knowledge consonant with its tendency to essentialize knowable existence through and through rather than totally evacuate it. Only this "essentiality of the divine existence" enables Wolff to infer the existence of God from the concept of His essence: *existentia ipsi [Deo] essentialis est*.[20] But existence so considered is obtained from the abstract definition of a reality and not from our experience of existing things and their implications.

Kant's subsequent critique of natural theology was directed historically against Wolff, although Kant himself thought that it applied to every speculative doctrine on God. He agreed with Wolff that all other proofs are reducible to those from contingency (and order) and the idea of the most perfect being. But he pointed out that the Wolffian proofs are a posteriori only in the Pickwickian sense that they draw materials from our own mind. Kant had no difficulty in exposing their basic similarity and a priori character, even though he did not analyze sufficiently the Wolffian notion of *ens a se* or consider other types of inference to God. He went to the heart of the issue when he noted Wolff's failure to make any liaison between empirically knowable existence and the theory of existence as a reality appertaining to the essence. This lacuna left Kant wondering whether humanly knowable existence can extend beyond the existents of our empirical world. In reference to the final statement in Wolff's second proof, Kant inquired whether it is so obviously true that for our human mind to *conceive* existence in a purely intellectual and nonexperiential way, as a necessary reality in the most perfect essence, is the same as to *know* that God does necessarily exist.

Wolff also developed a very detailed theory of the divine attributes and creative power in order to insert an existential filling into cosmology, psychology, and the practical moral sciences. But the more he probed into the problem of a demonstration of the existent world through God as its sufficient reason, the more he came to agree with the empiricists and his contemporaries of the Enlightenment that a strict existential deduction is impossible. To explain the finite universe as existent, one must have simultaneous recourse to three divine attributes: intellect, power, and will. The divine intellect can account for the intrinsic possibility of things, the divine power for their extrinsic possibility or grounding in an adequate, existing cause. But Wolff defined God's power only as "the possibility of bringing into act that which, considered in itself, is possible."[21] The transition from this possibility to the actual producing is made only by the divine will, and Wolff parted company with Leibniz by denying that the will is a mere ratifier of the divine power. Will is God's radically existential power for the production of existents, and it is totally inscrutable to us. Our mind cannot understand, or bring within the ontology of sufficient reasons, a will that is purely actual and simultaneous in its operation. Hence the ultimate reason for the actual existence of contingent things eludes a strictly scientific method.

Yet philosophy is not left entirely powerless before this task. There is a distinction between supplying rigorously deductive reasons for the existence of *a* world and supplying fitting reasons for the production of *this* given world. Although we have no philosophically certain principle for penetrating God's free decision to create a world, we can suppose this decision and then offer an appropriate reason—*ratio quaedam convenientiae*—for His choosing to realize this particular world.[22] This fitting reason, or quasi-motive, consists in the representation of the best, i.e., the combination of what is best objectively, or in itself, and subjectively, or with respect to God. Instead of following Leibniz' description of the objective reason in terms of a plenitude of essences, Wolff treats it as that group of ideas which most satisfies His intellect and pleases His will by serving as a natural sign and visible symbol of the divine perfection. Ultimately, then, the objective reason is not coercive of divine action and is measured by the subjective motive of convenience, which we may fittingly suppose (without ever rigorously knowing) to be the greatest visible expression of divine perfection or glory.

We can then formulate the appropriate law for God's particular choice of things: "Whatever God represents to Himself as the best, both in itself and in relation to Himself, this He wills."[23] That this remains irremediably a formal principle of appropriateness and not a means of deductive demonstration is indicated by Wolff's claim (in opposition, again, to Leibniz) that God can bring into simultaneous, actual existence other worlds in addition to the best one and can even realize all the possibles. Since He is absolutely self-sufficient, God remains free from the objective coercion of essential combinations. The objectively best world does agree with His own perfection, but the creative act remains a miracle, a free positing of something whose sufficient reason for existence lies hidden in the transcendent will of a free God. Hence Wolff refused to base obligation, virtue, and the highest moral good upon the will of God but gave them a totally immanent basis in human nature and its self-perfection, even though moral activity does refer us to God.

The post-Kantian idealists were fascinated by the functional role of Wolff's natural theology for his entire system. When he was not plagued by the problem of contingent, empirical existence and the divine freedom, Wolff was enthusiastic about the retroactive effect of natural theology upon the speculative sciences and its constructive work in practical philosophy (even though it does not furnish the foundation of our duty). He hoped to use the divine attributes or realities as the primary possibles whereby all knowledge of things can be derived entirely a priori from their ultimate reasons. Natural theology can endow the pure intellect with a special light and enable it to follow the complete evolution of the notion of being and its sufficient reasons.[24] Thereby, one can develop a complete system of philosophy embracing the essential structures and connections of all things, the divine existence, the possibility of the contingent modes of other beings, and perhaps some unified explanation of their actual existence. That Wolff fell far short of this ideal was due, in Hegel's eyes, to his retention of an inscrutable, free divine will, as well as to his scruples about reducing empirical existence to the theory of realities or modes of the essential actuality. Hegel therefore removed these reservations by submitting God and existence to the dialectical law of the absolute.

Yet the strangest chapter in the history of Wolffian philosophy was neither its rough handling by Kant nor its transformation by Hegel but its victorious impenetration into the Christian Scholastic philosophies of the eighteenth and nineteenth centuries.[25] Although the Scholastics were suspicious about Wolff's position on divine freedom and some strictly theological points involving rationalism, many of them welcomed his divisions of philosophy, his conception of ontology and psychology, his use of sufficient reason, and his basic natural theology. Restated in more a posteriori fashion, the latter seemed to provide an ark of security precisely when the radical wing of the Enlightenment was denying God and Kant was questioning all speculative demonstrations of God's existence. Wolff's epistemological neutrality and his ambivalent attitude toward existence did not seem important to many harassed authors of class manuals. At the very moment when the rationalist adventure in natural theology was drawing to a close, many Scholastic writers began using the discredited Wolffian approach to God through sufficient reasons and essential necessities. In doing so, they not only violated the method of realism but also estranged themselves needlessly from the mainstream of philosophical inquiry on God.

3. VOLTAIRE'S SCIENTIFIC THEISM

The gradual shift of the Enlightenment from a mathematico-deductive conception of pure intellect to an empirical view of reason modeled after the physical and biological sciences can be observed in Voltaire (1694–1778). This transition had a marked effect upon the claims made for humanly attainable knowledge of God, since they are much more modest in Voltaire than in Wolff. Although the former speaks about demonstrating God's existence, his notion of proof is that of a course of empirical reasoning which successfully avoids any formal contradictions and achieves a high degree of probability as an interpretation of our experience. Voltaire remains unconvinced by the chain of essential reasons demonstrating the nature and attributes of God, as well as by the attempts of rationalist theodicies to explain evil and God's dealings with the world. Still, he ventures some speculations of his own in this area and arrives at a somewhat wavering, probable notion of the divine nature.

Three serious obstacles hamper any attempt to gain a precise understanding of Voltaire's doctrine on God. The first is his own fluctuation of opinion concerning certain aspects of the divine nature and operation, notably the freedom of God and His presence in the world. Despite his lifelong preoccupation with the problem of God, Voltaire never makes a definitive and systematic formulation of his position. A second difficulty is provided by the polemical setting within which he imbeds most of his philosophical speculation on God. Churchmen have found it difficult to believe that Voltaire's destructive policy against revelation stops short of outright denial of God's existence and general activity in the world, and their skeptical attitude toward him is shared by various freethinkers. Yet the sum of evidence indicates his sincere commitment to a type of philosophical theism which is equally antagonistic toward both Christianity and atheism. From his books and correspondence, as well as from the acid test of willingness to accept ridicule from his fellow *philosophes,* Voltaire emerges as a theist who is inimical to supernatural revelation and yet also opposed to any reduction of his convictions to atheistic naturalism. Along with Rousseau, he attempts to steer a perilous course between the Church and Holbach's synagogue of atheists.

A third factor which makes it difficult to grasp Voltaire's position is the complex historical heritage upon which it feeds. Voltaire agreed with Bayle's strictures against a rationalist metaphysics and natural theology, but he did not accept the skeptical counsel to forego all natural speculations concerning God. Instead of following Bayle into skeptical fideism or Wolff into a refurbished rationalism of sufficient reasons, he turned to the British empirical and deistic thinkers for a fresh impulse in natural theology. From his personal visit to England (1726–1729) and his intensive program of readings, Voltaire made himself sufficiently familiar with the theological views of Locke, Newton, Clarke, and such later deists as Anthony Collins. On the question of God's existence, he could receive little help from the deists, who were mainly interested in defending their several conceptions of natural religion and morality. Hence he relied chiefly upon Locke, Newton, and Clarke on this issue, although he did not agree with their speculations concerning the divine nature. He adapted Malebranche's theory of divine causality to his own way of explaining evil. Where the English deists did make a decisive contribution to his thought was in respect to God's attributes and relation with the world, the notion of natural religion and morality, and the anti-Christian arguments which filled his last fifteen years of writing.[26]

Thus Voltaire served as the main channel for transmitting the theological ideas of the English Newtonians and deists into the French Enlightenment. The earliest and most sustained expression of his scientifically based theism was in the *Treatise on Metaphysics* (written in 1734 and published posthumously) and the *Elements of Newton's Philosophy* (1741 edition). With some significant changes, his doctrine on God was reaffirmed in the *Philosophical Dictionary* (1764) and such other later writings as *The Ignorant Philosopher* (1766). Although his metaphysical reasoning was not very deep or always consistent, Voltaire made the most persistent and effective case for a philosophical acceptance of God, apart from any revealed doctrine, in eighteenth-century France. His method was to avoid a priori reasoning, which was especially vulnerable to the skeptical critique, and to present a minimal theism as the most probable inference to be drawn from Newtonian science and an empirical inspection of the physical and moral worlds. He set out to explore the alternative which Bayle and Hume never developed: a metaphysics that is probable and yet firmly grounded in some empirical evidence.

In stressing the theistic implications of the new natural philosophy, Voltaire was following the example of both Newton himself and the first generation of his British admirers. Newton set a twofold task for natural philosophy: to ascertain the most general mechanical laws or mathematical correlations of phenomena and to establish the existence of the nonmechanical first cause of all the laws and forces in the universe. The natural philosopher was engaged in the only valid sort of metaphysical reasoning when he concluded that

this most beautiful system of the sun, planets, and comets could only proceed from the counsel and dominion of an intelligent and powerful Being. . . . To compare and adjust all these things together, in so great a variety of bodies, argues that cause to be, not blind and fortuitous, but very well skilled in mechanics and geometry.[27]

The first cause is at least as scholarly—added Voltaire, with a typical blend of naïveté and satire—as the learned gentlemen of the London Royal Society. Newton argued that the beginning of motion in the universe and the correction of deficiencies in the subsequent, natural operation of the gravitational system require the action of a supreme intelligence and will. Furthermore, the power and will of the first cause are discernible in the orderly motion and uniform direction of the planets, as well as in the fact that the system of fixed stars does not collapse inwards. Joseph Addison's well-known verse expressed the popular Newtonian attitude toward the heavenly bodies:

> In reason's ear, they all rejoice,
> And utter forth a glorious voice,
> Forever singing, as they shine,
> The hand that made us is divine.[28]

Not only on this cosmic scale but also in the orderly adaptation and conformity of organs in living bodies is the design of a planning intelligence visibly present.

Voltaire restates these arguments in his own terse style so that the inference from the universe, as a work, to the divine workman will seem easy and inevitable to any mind well informed about the current scientific outlook. Whatever the doubts raised about the need for God in the Cartesian physics, "the entire philosophy of Newton leads necessarily to the knowledge of a supreme being, who has created everything, arranged everything freely. For if according to Newton (and according to reason) the world is finite, if there is a vacuum, then matter does not exist necessarily. Hence it has received existence from a free cause."[29] This confident declaration is the highlight in Voltaire's relatively orthodox scientific grounding of theism, although he fails to give it any metaphysical consolidation.

Cartesian physics leads to the conception of nature as an infinite plenum, and from this notion it is but a short step to conclude that matter is self-sufficient and God superfluous. But the contingency of matter is assured in the Newtonian system and with it the need for a free, intelligent cause transcending the order of nature. Although the laws of mathematical physics are abstractly immutable, they are not causally effective by themselves, and hence our world need not have been produced in accordance with them. The use of mathematics in Newton's system does not dispense with the requirement for a deliberate choice of a set of laws by a supreme mind and will. Moreover, these laws become operative in the actual universe only through the mediation of motion and gravitational power (which Voltaire and most Newtonians interpret as a real physical force and not merely as a functional law). Subject to variation and loss, motion and gravitation are not inherent in stable matter but come to it as an effect of an intelligent, free agent existing outside the material world.

Similarly, the internal order and purposive direction of material agents are a causal gift of God. So convinced is Voltaire of the need to posit a purposive mind that he is ready to accept ridicule as a *"final-causer,* i.e., an imbecile," just as long as he is in Newton's company.[30] He also reformulates the more metaphysical argument of Locke and Clarke, from the existing self to the eternal being. But the complexities of this proof overwhelm him, and he eventually contents himself with simply declaring the self-evidence or indisputably high probability of the proposition that "I exist, therefore something necessarily exists from all eternity." He chides Pascal for not allowing reason to see God in His works of nature and man. At the properly human level, the presence of definite moral tendencies, especially the peremptory ideal of justice toward others, provides reason with sufficient natural evidence to affirm the existence of a good and moral God. Thus empirical reason is able to break the dilemma between skepticism and rationalism.

Voltaire drew a sharp line, however, between the existence of God and questions about His nature and causal activity. He sought to prevent the unavoidable obscurity and uncertainty which surround the latter questions from unsettling the truth of God's existence. Difficulties in understanding how creation occurs, where God is, and why He permits evil should not be allowed to weaken one's assent to the existence of a supremely good and intelligent first cause. This *rule of discriminating* among theological issues and judging each one separately by its own proper evidence was Voltaire's chief polemical weapon against the materialists in the Encyclopedist group. Emphasis upon it often led him to maintain the total inability of human reason to treat of God's nature and operations: "The infinite attributes of the supreme being are abysses, where our weak lights are snuffed out."[31] He declared that Samuel Clarke's descriptions of God as resting, repenting, and talking were presumptuous caricatures, worthy only of *Punch* and completely vulnerable to the ridicule of the materialists. We should maintain a respectful agnosticism about any question beyond the bare existence of God and our duty to worship Him in spirit. A man can only know that God wants him to adore Him and to be just toward his fellow men.

It was difficult for Voltaire to restrict himself within this narrow confine, however, since his affirmation of God's existence entailed at least a minimal position on His nature as well. By the term "God," he always meant an eternal, necessarily existing being who is the intelligent and benevolent first cause of the universe. Because of his readings in Anthony Collins and other radical deists, as well as the moral shock administered by the Lisbon earthquake of 1755, however, he modified his original position on the freedom of divine causality and its total creation of the material world. God is free only in the sense of having a very powerful nature and of doing His own will, without coercion from any other agent. Yet there is an internal necessity determining the divine productive activity: "The world has always emanated from this primitive and necessary cause, just as light emanates from the sun."[32] God does not make the world through the free creation taught by Christianity but through a physically necessary and eternal emanation of orderly laws from His own attribute of action. Although he was always a vigorous critic of Spinoza (or at least of the contemporary materialistic version of Spinozism), Voltaire diminished the transcendence of God through his deterministic theory of divine causality. He allowed some distinction to remain between the eternally necessary cause and its equally necessary and eternal effects, but he also occasionally entertained the hypothesis of God as the animating soul of the world-machine. Voltaire found it difficult to reconcile divine transcendence with the necessary overflow of God's productive action.

Prompting this importation of determinism into God is Voltaire's concern over the presence of physical and moral evil in the world. Although evil cannot be minimized or harmonized away, it can be regarded as a necessary outcome of the divine action rather than as the result of a lucid and unconstrained choice. Voltairean theodicy consists in a denial that divine freedom accounts for our world. God is to be exculpated from any moral responsibility for evil by treating pain or physical evil as the unavoidable outcome of His internally determined, causal action and by restricting moral distinctions to the human level. Voltaire thus radicalizes Malebranche's assertion that everything in our universe is an action of God on creatures. Voltaire even speculates about whether the necessity of the divine action may not betoken some limitation upon God's power. The divine power may be relatively supreme, in that it is not subject to any foreign agency, and yet it may also be limited in an internal way to what can be done in accordance with Newtonian mechanical laws. Thus the benevolent God can be regarded as infinite in durational existence, yet finite in power, knowledge, and presence. At other times, when he is comparing God and man rather than seeking a solution to the problem of evil, Voltaire states categorically that "God alone can be perfect; or—better expressed—man is limited, and God is not limited."[33] His thought oscillates between stressing the finite determinism of both man and God and vindicating the infinite perfection and transcendence of God, in contradistinction to everything finite and human.

Fundamentally, this indecision arises from the nonmetaphysical nature of Voltaire's entire reasoning about the existence and attributes of God. It is based upon the evidences of order and purposive design furnished by the mechanical and biological sciences and ordinary observation, but the data are not submitted to any distinctively metaphysical analysis in terms of component principles of existent beings and their tendency toward a proper perfection or good. Hence, as Wolff had already remarked, the Newtonian scientific theists fail to establish the radical contingency of the world with respect to its entire being. Correlative with Voltaire's acceptance of divine determinism of action was his view that matter itself is an eternal, unproduced substrate in which God introduces the forms and orderly adaptations of the world we experience and scientifically describe. But in that case, God is a maker rather than a total cause or creator. The affirmation of His causality remains probable only as long as immanent scientific explanations of matter are incomplete. Consequently, Voltaire exposed his position to the criticism of Holbach, who admitted the contingent character of particular things but simply denied it of nature as a whole. Even granting a high scientific presumption that the order of our material system depends on a cause existing outside the world, Voltaire's inference to God's nature is no stronger than his approach to the material world. Because order means to him primarily the mechanical arrangement of parts in pre-existent matter, he cannot infer anything more from the finite world-machine than a finite artisan and a necessitated one at that. Only the latent resonance of the Christian tradition on God keeps his mind dissatisfied with such a deity and open at times to an infinite, free, and creative cause, whom he nevertheless cannot rigorously establish from his starting point and method.

The natural theology of Voltaire and the Newtonians is metaphysical only in the restricted sense assigned by Newton himself: It arrives at a primary real cause which is distinct from the mathematical laws and hypothetical physical agents in the material universe. In this meaning, however, "metaphysical" designates only the object of the inference and specifies nothing about the precise way of viewing the experiential data and making the inference to the being of God. Because his reasoning about the divine existence is simply a highly probable extension of natural philosophy into the region of ultimate agency, Voltaire has no demonstrative sort of metaphysical means for resolving any disputed issues about the nature and activity of God. Despite his fierce dislike of anthropomorphism, he is finally left with no other recourse than to assign to God the same determinism of action and limitation of power which belong to his conception of man.

The inconclusiveness of a natural theology erected upon Newtonian mechanics forced Voltaire to seek reinforcement of his position in the moral needs of man. He supplemented his scientific theism with some practical considerations. As he wrote to Frederick the Great, metaphysics must eventually be brought back to morality. Morality itself rests upon the intrinsic tendencies of human nature, not upon theism. Theism, on the contrary, profits in two distinct ways from its association with ethical reality. First, it finds in the moral drives of man an added argument in favor of God, the primary existing cause. He is the ultimate source of our universal tendencies toward self-love, justice, mutual help, and concord. In the second place, the moral concerns of man stabilize the mind which is adrift in the sea of controversies concerning the divine nature. As Pascal and Rousseau also observe, our moral needs can affect decisively the probable reasonings in natural theology, thus enabling us to disregard certain issues and give a morally firm assent to certain positions on God.

Although it does not constitute the basis of morality, there is one definite view of the divine nature which lends a strong support to moral decisions and hence indicates the relevance of God to this area of our experience, which lies beyond the scope of the physical sciences. "The great object, the great interest, it seems to me, is not in arguing metaphysically, but in weighing whether one must, for the common good of us other miserable and thinking animals, admit a rewarding and punishing God, who serves us both as restraint and as consolation, or reject this idea in abandoning ourselves to our calamities without hope and our crimes without remorse."[34] God Himself is the ultimate source of this universal, morally effective *idea* of God, considered as the good and powerful governor of the world, the moral judge of our good and bad secret actions. Although he remained personally unconvinced about the immateriality of the soul and immortality, Voltaire also granted that the idea of immortality has a high moral utility in regulating the average social group. But he never reduced his conviction in God merely to a helpful fiction of individual or social morality, despite its admitted usefulness.

Whatever the difficulty of reconciling universal determinism with a moral conception of God as judge and man as being under obligation to be just, Voltaire drew the implication that a general providence is operative in the world. He even agreed with his declared enemy, Pascal, that the heart opens up a special access to God as a good, just, and providential master. Hence he parted company with those few deists who regarded God merely as a far-off first cause, one who gives man no moral law and remains unconcerned about man's present conduct. In contradistinction to this type of deist, Voltaire classified himself as a theist or "a man firmly persuaded of the existence of a supreme being, just as good as he is powerful, who has formed all the extended, vegetative, sentient, and reflective beings; who perpetuates their species, who punishes crimes without cruelty, and rewards virtuous actions with kindness."[35] Providence remains a general activity, however, within the framework of the divinely founded laws of nature. Men cannot know any special ordinances of providence, beyond the universal morality of reason and nondogmatic theism, which would establish positive religion.

Here the polemical edge of Voltaire's theory of God becomes plainly visible. His hostility to any systematic, metaphysical study of God's nature was partly motivated by his deistic rejection of any revelation distinct from the evidence of the natural world. Hence he took as the sole sources of truth concerning God the evidences of mechanical and biological science and the moral code of justice common to all men. He held his theistic position down to this minimum, not only because of philosophical caution, but also because of the controversial requirements of his final campaign against Christianity. Thus Voltaire furnishes a prime instance of the impoverishing effect which a nonmetaphysical approach, joined with a hostile attitude toward supernatural revelation, has upon the philosophy of God.

Voltaire's chief antagonist among the Encyclopedists was Baron Paul Henri Thiry d'Holbach (1723–1789), who prided himself upon being "the personal enemy of God." It was Holbach who also took delight in shocking David Hume (who had reportedly never met a real atheist) by introducing him to a dinner company of fifteen atheists and three undecided minds.[36] Hume was not quite so much of a British bumpkin as Holbach thought, however, since his point was that belief of some sort usually overpowers doubt, that the passionate atheist makes a definite commitment, and hence that a consistent skepticism is rarely found. Like the historian, Edward Gibbon, Hume was astonished by the dogmatic quality of the atheism professed by Holbach's club. To this coterie, the evidence of God's nonexistence was so overpowering that only the fool and the coward could assent to theism or even maintain a skeptical reserve.

For both Voltaire and Holbach, the natural sciences were decisive for determining one's position on God, but they disagreed violently over the precise implications for natural theology. Whereas Voltaire advocated a cautious probability of theism, Holbach was anxious to base a definitive system of atheism upon the contemporary stage of scientific research. He regarded the new developments in mechanics and biology not only as indicating that the rationalistic, functional conception of God had outlived its usefulness but also as positively excluding any proof of God's existence. His most sustained defense of scientific atheism was in the celebrated *System of Nature* (1770), a book that crystallized the clandestine materialistic literature of the eighteenth century.

Some of the criticism is jejune, since it deals with Cartesian positions no longer central in philosophy.[37] Holbach shows, for instance, that the idea of God is not innate and suggests that universal assent to God's existence may mean nothing more than universal terror before natural calamities, together with ignorance of natural laws. Against Descartes, he argues that we can no more conclude to God's existence from our idea of Him than we can draw an existential conclusion from our idea of a sphinx. To the retort that the idea of God is distinctive in necessarily entailing existence, he replies that a finite, material being like man cannot form a positive and true idea of the infinite, immaterial being. This reply rests on the supposition that our intellectual power is a complicated form of sense perception totally confined to matter. Holbach also discusses the circular reasoning in Malebranche, who makes our knowledge of the existence of the material world depend upon faith in God's word and then proves God's existence from the material world. The vital center of eighteenth-century theism is affected, however, by another line of criticism directed against Newton and Clarke. Holbach treats the former almost superciliously, remarking that "the sublime Newton is no more than an infant, when he quits physics and demonstration, to lose himself in the imaginary regions of theology."[38] For Holbach, nature need not be regarded as a work which requires an intelligent and transcendent workman. On the contrary, it is axiomatic with him that nature is not a work but a self-existent totality. The so-called order of things in nature is nothing more than a projection of our subjective inclinations into a series of purposeless, mechanical actions which happen to favor our inclinations. Everything can be sufficiently accounted for by the attractive and repulsive forces of matter itself, without supposing any God in the theanthropic form of a powerful spiritual despot lording it over his slaves. When he turns to Clarke's circumstantial treatment of the divine existence and nature, Holbach performs a tour de force. He maintains that everything which Clarke and others say about God becomes intelligible and true as soon as it is transferred to his own conception of material nature. It is matter alone which exists from all eternity and performs all the works ascribed to God.

Underlying this critique of a scientifically founded theism is the conception of nature, which Holbach lays down in a series of definitions and postulates at the beginning of his *System*. His initial notion of nature as the great, self-sustaining whole beyond which nothing else can exist is a materialist version of Spinozism. By axiomatic definition, the real is equated with the natural totality of matter and motion, so that anything spiritual and transcendent of nature is ruled out in advance as a chimera. Once this Hobbesian premise is accepted, Holbach can easily decide upon the origin of motion. Since material nature is the great whole embracing all causal agencies, the original source of motion can only be matter itself.

Thus, the idea of nature necessarily includes that of motion. But, it will be asked, from whence did she receive her motion? Our reply is, from herself, since she is the great whole, beyond which, consequently, nothing can exist. We say this motion is a manner of existence that flows necessarily out of the essence of matter; that matter moves by its own peculiar energies; that its motion is to be attributed to the force which is inherent in itself; that the variety of motion and the phenomena which result, proceed from the diversity of the properties, of the qualities, and of the combinations, which are originally found in the primitive matter, of which nature is the assemblage.[39]

Matter is the immense eternal laboratory which supplies its own materials, energies, patterns of action, and products. The order of nature is nothing more than the regular and necessary series of material causes without any intelligent originator.

As far as Newtonian theism was concerned, the most challenging claim was that motion owes its primary origin to matter alone. Holbach owed this suggestion directly to the radical Irish deist John Toland, who rejected the Cartesian notion of matter as an inert extension which is only extrinsically receptive of motion. It also meant a correction of Newton, since motion is not only inherent in matter but is an essential property of matter and owes to the latter its primary impulsion. Coupling this view with his psychological explanation of the order of nature, Holbach concluded that an amended Newtonian mechanics eliminates the need for God. He sought further confirmation of his atheistic naturalism in the biological researches of John Needham and the chemical theories of G. E. Stahl. From the former, Holbach warmly and uncritically welcomed the theory of spontaneous generation as proof of the intrinsic vital force in nature. And in Stahl's views on atomism, chemical affinity, and phlogiston, he saw striking evidence of the inherent power of matter to furnish its own patterns of diversity and dynamic powers.

To these arguments, Holbach added a theory of human knowledge which is somewhat circularly and ambiguously related to the main thesis of materialism.[40] In the given definition of nature, the human intellect is only a developed mode of material process. Nature itself does not think, but it gives rise to thinking beings through the organization of matter into animated bodies having sense powers. Holbach agreed with La Mettrie that our ideas are intrinsically dependent upon sense organs and, consequently, that man has no intellectual power or spiritual nature transcending matter. There is a double consequence favoring atheism. Man cannot really conceive an immaterial divine being through his ideas but can only personify human qualities in a magnified form. Conversely, an immaterial God could not communicate knowledge of Himself to man, since He would be unable to stimulate the sense organs in order to supply the appropriate ideas. The circularity in this reasoning lies in the fact that Holbach founded his theory of the human mind on atheistic materialism and then used this theory as a major weapon against theism. A certain ambiguity also creeps into the argumentation, since one may conclude either to God's nonexistence or merely to the mutual inability of God and man to communicate with each other in knowledge. The latter, an agnostic alternative, remains open, despite Holbach's own vigorous choice of atheism.

The mind of Denis Diderot (1713–1784) was considerably more complex and supple than Holbach's in all areas. In his *Philosophical Thoughts* (1746), he presented the deistic case primarily in terms of biological finalism rather than cosmic mechanism. But several factors soon led him to adhere to atheistic naturalism.[41] Like most of his collaborators on the *Encyclopedia,* he accepted pure and applied scientific knowledge as the standard. Measured by this criterion, the idea of God seems very sterile. No inferences can be drawn from it for the increase of scientific knowledge and the control of nature; indeed, the functional God of the Cartesians is a positive hindrance to scientific advancements. Hence God must be removed from the field of scientific inquiry in order to permit the latter to achieve its autonomy and intrinsic method.

Diderot accepted the hypothesis of the creative self-movement of nature and the universal sensitivity of matter. He appealed to Needham's spontaneous generation, Buffon's organic molecules, and Trembley's polyp as evidence that nature supplies its own fermenting power, structural organization, and continuity of forms. He wanted to replace the Newtonian machine with the self-creative, sensitive organism as the dominant metaphor for interpreting the universe. This biological bias led him both to deny any scientific ground for the empirical inference to God and to revere evolving nature with a religious devotion. Nevertheless, Diderot was more aware than Holbach of the contribution of romantic imagination to this conception of an eternal, self-moving plenum of sensitive matter. Hence he usually clothed his atheistic and cosmic speculations in the tentative form of a dream or a dialogue.

In the moral order, Diderot and Holbach agreed that human conduct is determined by motives of pleasure and pain, as well as by social needs. The dynamic determinism of nature expresses itself in human esthetic and moral impulses, so that God and religion need not be invoked for moral obligation and civil order. Diderot would eliminate the natural religion of the deists, as well as Christianity, in the interests of social harmony and the exploitation of natural resources. Yet Diderot never fully shared Holbach's satisfaction with atheistic naturalism as a total explanation of reality. He retained uneasy doubts about whether it was really adequate to human experience in its total range and to other historical conditions besides those of his own age. In a letter to his mistress, he candidly admitted: "I am maddened at being entangled in a devilish philosophy that my mind can't help approving and my heart refuting."[42] This conflict between mind and heart was never resolved by Diderot, who proved himself thereby to be typical of the Enlightenment predicament on God.

Voltaire could not allow the case for atheism to go unchallenged. In *Questions on the Encyclopedia* (1770–1772) and other later writings, he analyzed Holbach's position with customary acerbity. His fundamental objection was that Holbach pretends to achieve geometrical certainty in the field of metaphysics and morality, where an absolutely certain system is impossible. On all crucial issues, Holbach begs the issue that he is apparently proving. For instance, he shows that nature is not a work of intelligence simply by positing its self-existence, which is precisely the point in dispute. Moreover, he keeps his notion of matter and life so conveniently vague that one cannot test it by reference to any definite evidence or norm of proof. The scientific examples cited by Holbach are sometimes unreliable, and they never permit a universal generalization about the nature of matter. His explanation of the origin of motion and life remains a hypothetical, indeterminate "perhaps," with no precise explanation of how unintelligent matter can produce intelligence or what the ultimate origin and causal scope of the diverse, formal patterns in matter may be. Although Voltaire was unable to furnish strict proof of the world's contingency, he could at least challenge Holbach's unwarranted assumption that scientific evidence demonstrates its self-sufficiency.

Voltaire concentrated particularly upon the noetic and moral arguments in favor of atheism. The one based upon the need to agitate the senses, in order to arouse ideas in us, presupposes that there is only one type of causal activity: material motion. There is nothing contradictory in, and considerable evidence indeed to support, the view that "if He [God] is an all-powerful being to whom we owe our life, we [also] owe Him our ideas and our senses, like everything else."[43] The fact that we cannot ascertain anything more about the nature of the eternal, intelligent, first cause and cannot deduce anything from His nature about the material world provides no ground for denying His existence and general causal activity. The scientific uselessness of the idea of God for serving as a deductive tool in the natural sciences (a point stressed by Diderot) does not remove the necessity to make an inductive, causal inference to God's real existence and to pay Him some reverence. Voltaire did not deny that morality can be established on an entirely naturalistic footing, but he added once more that our inherent moral tendencies still demand a causal inference to God as their author. He found it unreasonable to exchange the high probabilities supporting theism for the sheerly postulatory claims of atheistic naturalism.

5. ROUSSEAU'S PROFESSION OF FAITH

In his many self-revelations, Jean-Jacques Rousseau (1712–1778) depicted himself as a solitary walker and dreamer in the field of thought, an unsystematic mind lacking in consistency and often overcome by lively feelings. Yet his moral criticism worked as a powerful solvent of both the old social order and the Encyclopedist movement. Against them he used his key distinction between the *artificial* man, corrupted by the devices of an unjust society and an abstract reason, and the *natural* man, who follows the promptings of his heart both in his social dealings and in his rational speculation. Rousseau's appeal to the natural, moral man was not prompted by a wild primitivism or irrationalism but by the need for a critical norm in evaluating modern society and its philosophy. It served to emphasize the dynamic factors of freedom, conscience, feeling, and concrete reason for the remolding of man.

In the course of presenting his image of the natural man, Rousseau broke with Voltaire and the Encyclopedist group around Diderot and Holbach. Their well-aired quarrels were due not only to real and imaginary personal grievances but also to formal philosophical disagreements. Significantly, the problem of God was in the forefront of the controversies around Rousseau, since it was a principal theoretical cause of the ruptures that occurred. As early as 1756, in a letter to Voltaire, he disagreed with the Sage of Ferney's handling of evil and providence in the poem on the Lisbon earthquake. Granted that the extreme optimist solution ("all is good") is fatuous in the face of all too real evils, one need not be driven to deny God's freedom and infinite power. A moderate optimism ("the whole is good") can be sustained, once one reflects on the implications of freedom and order. The sole source of moral evil is human freedom. God gives us this power irrevocably and places in our hands the responsibility for our own improvement and also for our follies and misdeeds. Some physical evil is involved in the very existence of a given material world-system, and yet the whole sensitivity of man to the question of evil can arise only within the context of belief in a world order and a divine providence.

At the very end of his letter to Voltaire, Rousseau affirms that "all the subtleties of metaphysics will not make me doubt for a moment the immortality of the soul and a beneficent providence. I feel it, I believe it, I wish it, I hope it, I will defend it to my last breath."[44] There are two remarkable features about this credo: its content and the manner in which it is affirmed. Rousseau agrees with Malebranche and Voltaire that God governs the world by general laws and that within the temporal perspective it is unreasonable to expect Him to make special allowances for man. Nevertheless, the moral conception of God does require that the divine concern reach down to the individual man and ultimately assure him a just treatment. God is like Plato's shepherd of souls: His providence embraces not only humanity in general but also the individual person in his eternal destiny. In view of the determined laws of nature and the moral demand for ultimate justice, personal immortality is entailed by God's providential ordering of the world. Whereas Voltaire regarded immortality as a purely social and fictitious sanction, Rousseau accepts it as a truth of personal moral-religious concern, bound up with the unique worth of the individual man and the justice and goodness of God.

Rousseau made his adhesion to immortality, as well as to God's existence and providence, an act of *interior sentiment* or *natural faith*.[45] His aim was to shift the entire discussion about God and man away from the terrain of "enlightened reason," which is our intellectual power employed in artificial isolation from the feelings, conscience, and will. Such isolation is a useful methodological device in the scientific study of material objects, but it is not adapted to the study of the personal being of God and man. Abstract reason remains in equilibrium between the various probabilities, being unable by itself to give a firm assent to any position. Reason cannot produce conviction concerning the main issues in theism until it is restored to the context of man's affective tendencies and conscience. Rousseau appealed to these subjective factors, rather than to a metaphysical study of the evidence, in order to overcome the Enlightenment stalemate concerning God.

When it is a question of establishing the existence and personal nature of God, reason must accept the guidance of the heart, permitting itself to be influenced by the principles and testimony of our sentiments and moral experience as they are brought to bear upon nature and man. Rousseauvian faith is a natural force and not a supernatural virtue; it is not opposed to reason but endows reason with a certitude which cannot come from abstract, objective reasoning alone. In his appeal to the heart and interior feeling, Rousseau found an answer to both Bayle and the Encyclopedists. Because of the natural character of faith and its integration with reason, Rousseau's appeal rendered obsolete Bayle's position on the perpetual combat between supernatural faith and reason. And its inclusion of an affective and voluntary element supplied the factor of certitude needed to break the deadlock between the probabilities of Voltaire and those of Holbach and Diderot. As Rousseau saw the situation, it was not so much the probable character of the evidence as the artificial estrangement of reason from the roots of assent to available evidence about God and the soul which had caused the deadlock. Faith does not transform the theistic inference into a demonstration, but it does enable reason to assent firmly and certainly to this interpretation of existence as being most consonant with our religious feeling and moral need.

On no other issue in philosophy is Rousseau more at pains to set his thoughts in order than on the existence and nature of God. He presents his position in the long treatise, "Profession of Faith of the Savoyard Vicar," inserted at a strategic point in *Émile* (1762), his novel on the principles of education.[46] The novel form enables him to express himself in concrete fashion and thus arouse a personal response in his readers, whom he asks to verify the arguments in their own hearts or interior experiences. That *Émile* also describes the author's educational ideal has an important bearing on the role of reason in the theistic inquiry. Rousseau often disparages reason as the source of all sophisms and illusions, but this refers only to the corrupted or artificial use of reason in theological matters, when it tries to function without any support from moral conscience and sentiment. It can be purified and rendered effective for theism through a reincorporation into its complete human matrix. God did not give us reason so that we would misuse or extinguish it; He wanted us to learn to use it as a divine torch illuminating man's way toward recognition of God and moral responsibility.

In Rousseau's novel, the youth, Émile, is not taught anything about God and religion until he is entering young manhood. This postponement is due to the slow development of reason, which follows long after the passions and imagination are in full operation. If the child is told about God at too young an age, he will remain forever content with verbalisms or, at most, with an anthropomorphic conception of the infinite being. With the dawning of rational reflection, however, the evidences for God's existence and nature can be presented. Yet the instruction must always be kept on a friendly, personal basis and must be associated with the youth's other interests. Thus the instruction devolves upon a priest from Savoy—a man whom Émile admires for his moral qualities, his valiant struggle with personal defects, and his proved integrity throughout their friendship. The priest does not attempt any technical demonstrations or make any elaborate refutations of atheism. Instead, he offers his direct testimony about his personal approach to God and asks only that his listener consult his own heart.

Nor does the wise teacher forget the influence of landscape and imagination on the mind. To make his appeal all the more effective, he brings his young friend early one morning to a romantically beautiful hill overlooking the valley of the Po. There he recounts his own journey through the wasteland of doubt and his minimal assurance about his own existence and that of his sensations. The receptive relation of the self to these sensations also insures the existence of an adequate external cause of sensations: the nonself, or world of matter (although Rousseau agrees with Wolff against being drawn into any dispute between idealism and realism on the precise constitution of material being).

Next, the priest notices within himself not only the passive power of sensation but also the active power of comparing, judging, willing. Only the understanding can express the proper meaning of "is," or existence, in a judgment, and only the will can initiate motion. Man—the being who can judge and choose—contains a spiritual principle which is not reducible to matter. Furthermore, since both motion and rest are present in matter in varying degrees, they are not essential to it. Unlike Holbach and Diderot, then, the man of spontaneous intelligence understands that the cause of bodily motion and unified organization must lie in some intelligent, willing agent who is distinct from the material universe.

With the aid of his perception of sensible objects and his inner reflection, the Savoyard vicar is able to establish three fundamental principles of existence or articles of natural faith:

Inanimate bodies have no action but motion, and there is no real action without will. This is my first principle. I believe, therefore, that there is a will which sets the universe in motion and gives life to nature. . . . If matter in motion points me to a will, matter in motion according to fixed laws points me to an intelligence; that is the second article of my creed. To act, to compare, to choose, are the operations of an active, thinking being; so this being exists. . . . There is no will properly so-called without freedom. Man is therefore free to act, and as such he is animated by an immaterial substance; that is the third article of my creed.[47]

On this basis, he then concludes that the free human agent is solely responsible for moral evil and that the immaterial soul can survive death and thus justify divine providence. Theodicy thereby subordinates itself to a more comprehensive doctrine on God and man.

Voltaire once grudgingly admitted that he would like to have written the "Profession of Faith," since in content it was not too far removed from his own theism and in personal stress it indicated one way to resolve the Enlightenment debate over God. The special attention paid to physical circumstances, moral will, and affective influences suggested that the mind must be suitably prepared before it attempts an inference leading beyond finite, material nature to God. Like Augustine and Malebranche, Pascal and Newman, Rousseau held that real assent to God arises only within the carefully prepared situation where heart talks with heart and where the searcher philosophizes with his entire soul. Sentiment and moral will are not to be shunned as an antirational force, since they are the natural means of strengthening our rational conviction about the orderly unity of nature and the need for a primary, intelligent will. The evidence for theism is adhered to with certainty through the operation of faith or interior sentiment.

Rousseau established the presence of will and freedom in God, even before His intellect, in order to underline his approach to God as a personal, just, and benevolent agent. After wavering briefly on the problem of evil, he also affirmed the infinite power of God but refused to go beyond this nucleus of attributes. In answer to the charge of anthropomorphism in attributing the personal traits of will and intellect to God, he replied simply that we *get* our initial meanings for these perfections unavoidably from our inner experience but *apply* them to God precisely as the primary cause existing beyond man and nature. Concerning the manner of divine causality, Rousseau disclaimed any knowledge and stated specifically that he found the Christian notion of creation unintelligible. He posited a coeternal matter as a passive principle, with God as the only supreme active principle. Lacking the Christian metaphysics of creation, he never arrived at the conception of a total derivation of finite being from God.

Unlike other theists of the Enlightenment, however, Rousseau held that God and immortality provide the indispensable sanction and purifying principle of all morality. In order to have the complete basis of morality, the love of oneself and of order must be expanded to include the love of God.[48] Rousseau sought to reduce true Christianity to his minimal creed of a good and just God and an immortal, free principle in man; the only faith he accepted was that of moral reason and inner feeling. Behind this reductive policy toward revealed religion lay the persuasion, which he shared with the other leading minds of the age, that the official Christian teaching on man and the Fall is found in .Pascal, the Jansenist theologians, and Calvin. Despite his bitter social criticism, Rousseau deemed our natural powers to be fully adequate for the task of perfecting man morally, religiously, and politically. He gave no serious consideration to the moderate Christian view that our nature is wounded but not corrupted in the Fall and that supernatural grace perfects, rather than supplants, our natural equipment of reason, conscience, and freedom.

The Enlightenment prolonged many themes from the previous century and raised some new issues. Bayle's fideistic skepticism spurred the theistic *philosophes* to find more empirical proofs of God's existence and to be extremely cautious about the perfections attributed to the divine nature. Apart from Wolff, who retained a rationalistic confidence in systematic deductions, they disbarred the ontological proof, looked to mechanics, biology, and moral experience for inductive evidence of God's existence, and reduced His knowable attributes to a bare minimum. Both Voltaire and Rousseau saw in man's moral tendencies a distinctive testimony of God's justice, benevolence, and providence. By viewing nature as the total assemblage of self-moving matter, however, Holbach and Diderot denied that there is any probability of scientific evidence supporting the theistic position. To the theists, the sterility of the idea of God in scientific research meant only the elimination of the rationalist method of studying nature with the help of a functional theism. But to the atheistic naturalists, it signified that nature itself is self-sufficient and furnishes no basis for the inference to God. Both parties would agree with Kant that "we must refrain from all explanation of the ordinance of nature drawn from the will of a highest being, because this is no longer natural philosophy but an admission that we are coming to the end of it."[49] Yet Rousseau would add that the end of natural philosophy and abstract reasoning does not spell the end of all philosophical investigations into the existence and nature of God. From the alliance of reason with moral conscience and feeling, the mind is fitted by natural faith to study personal realities and to acquire certitude about a good and just God.

In a moment of enthusiasm, Kant had once observed that Newton justified God in the physical world and that Rousseau justified Him in the moral order. Nevertheless, the spectacle of the unresolved Enlightenment conflict over the theistic implications of science and the foundations of the moral life raised some perplexing and original afterthoughts in Kant's mind. Both the theists and the atheists might be proceeding upon an unexamined and unjustifiable premise: that Newtonian science is fitted to reveal something about the nature of the real and hence about the ultimate causal source of the material universe. By challenging this presupposition, one could transcend both parties to the dispute, although at the cost of denying that any empirically grounded, speculative inference can be made to God's existence. As for the moral issue, Kant wondered whether one should regard the theistic inference of practical reason or moral faith as the very foundation of morality or provide an autonomous basis for morality and then build one's practical conviction in the reality of God upon the exigencies of ethics itself.

Chapter VI

KANT ON GOD

ALL THE HIGHWAYS in modern philosophy converge upon Immanuel Kant (1724–1804) and lead out again from him. The problem of God is no exception to his historical centrality. To understand his doctrine on God is to see the previous era of theological speculation in summary and the later developments in germ. His early training in Pietism and his enthusiastic reading of Rousseau convinced him of the need for a theistic factor in ethics, as well as of the indelible strength of the individual's affective belief in God. From his university education, his lifelong use of textbooks by followers of Wolff, and his close study of Leibniz, he acquired a certain lasting respect for the systematic approach of rationalism to the nature of God. Yet Kant's equally wide acquaintance with the British empiricists compelled him to inquire critically into the limits of human knowledge, the validity of metaphysics, and, consequently, the philosophical legitimacy of any doctrine on God. As a man of the Enlightenment, he kept his mind open to the views of all parties in the grand debate about God's role in philosophy, ranging from skepticism and naturalism to the defenses based on feeling and common sense.

Nevertheless, Kant was in no sense a merely passive recipient of these various influences. Loyal to the motto he chose for the Enlightenment "Dare to think for yourself!" he scrutinized these positions in the light of a theory of knowledge and belief which was original to himself. His favorite metaphor for the critical philosopher was that of an impartial judge who listens faithfully to all the conflicting testimony and then renders a verdict in the light of his own rational grasp of the law. Kant sat in judgment upon the long dispute, reaching from the Renaissance to the Enlightenment, concerning what the human mind can validly affirm about God in a philosophical way. He felt that Western culture was in the throes of a crisis concerning its traditional adherence to God and that a truly mediating philosophical solution was a prime necessity.

Over the long span of almost half a century of active work, Kant's views on God grew apace with his general philosophical development.[1] There was a reciprocal relation between the two, since his stand on God partly determined his philosophical position at any given stage and in turn reflected that standpoint. During his early or precritical period (the years 1755–1770, before he began work on his three great *Critiques*), he was reluctant to concede entirely to Hume that we have no strict demonstration of God's existence. He attempted to defend the validity of one or two speculative arguments while, at the same time, repudiating the rationalist use of God as a function in natural philosophy. His failure to secure the theistic proofs beyond doubt was a major stimulant impelling him to make a thorough reconstruction of the nature and limits of human knowledge as set forth in the *Critique of Pure Reason* (1781). Here he proposed a theory of knowledge which eliminated the rationalist version of metaphysics and, at the same time, disqualified any demonstrations of God's existence which were based on such a metaphysical foundation. Nevertheless, Kant was careful to find a rightful place in speculative philosophy for the systematic use of at least the concept of God.

In the *Critique of Practical Reason* (1788) and other allied ethical writings, the need for a rational belief in God was explored. Kant's purpose was to defend, against the claims of naturalism, the ethical importance of a belief in God and yet prevent any theological ordering of our conduct. He achieved this double aim by admitting that God is one of the postulates of ethics and, at the same time, denying to Him any normative influence as a basis and motive of moral action. The new Kantian synthesis can be termed a moral functionalism. It contained three major propositions: God Himself does not serve any systematic purpose in speculative philosophy; the idea of God does fulfill a function in this part of philosophy, but only with respect to the ordering of our thoughts and inferences, not with respect to real things; in ethics, the moral aspects of God's own being perform a necessary postulatory function, not as the source of obligation, but as a means for rendering intelligible certain consequences of our moral obligation. In his very old age, however, Kant found it necessary to rethink his moral functionalism. He retained all the major tenets but made it unmistakably clear that moral need and practical belief in God do not open a back door for the speculative exploitation of God Himself, as the new idealist thinkers were beginning to maintain. Thus the intellectual experience of Kant brings us from one era to another in the history of Western theories about God.

1. TESTING THE BASES OF THEISM

A study of Kant's early development is indispensable for understanding his final position on God. More than is usually recognized, his precritical writings stabilized many of his permanent views on God even before he was able to formulate the problem of knowledge and experience satisfactorily for himself. Indeed, the formulation of that problem was largely determined by difficulties which he encountered in trying to deal with the question of whether God's existence is knowable and how far the philosopher has a right to use a theory of God in building up a system of natural truths.[2] Kant's standpoint during the precritical years was characterized by four basic commitments. He sought to bring theism in line with current natural science. This entailed the rejection of the previous rationalist modes of proving God's existence and using God as an explanatory principle in philosophy of nature. Still, Kant claimed that a sound basis can be found for demonstrating God's existence and determining a few things about His nature. And yet he admitted, toward the end of this period, that everything depends upon the validity of metaphysics and that the doubt which can be cast on this supposed science renders all efforts in natural theology suspect until the issue is settled. These four landmarks provide sufficient guidance for exploring the crucial early thoughts of Kant in the domain of natural theology.

(1) The first impression one gains from a synoptic view of all of Kant's treatments of theism is that he began with a firm personal conviction of God's transcendent reality and never wavered from it during a lifetime of the most intense speculation. True enough, he found it increasingly difficult to give an adequate philosophical justification for his acceptance of God and other things-in-themselves. But from the outset of his philosophical career, he took the attitude that no technical investigations into the ways of proof could destroy his personal belief in God, even though they might render its philosophical defense more hazardous. He regarded metaphysics and, later on, critical philosophy as the arena for testing the validity of theistic proofs. Yet the ordinary man need not venture into this ground and need not be disturbed by its findings, just as the philosopher who does engage in the work may exercise complete critical freedom. All of Kant's inquiries were undertaken with the possibility that a wide split might develop between the mind's natural theism and its theoretical analyses. He was convinced, however, that the former was not to be sacrificed to the latter and that some philosophical settlement besides fideistic skepticism could be found.

Kant's first discussion of God occurs, significantly enough, in his *Universal Natural History and Theory of the Heavens* (1755), a scientific treatise in which he outlines a nebular hypothesis similar to Laplace's theory of the formation of the solar system. He stipulates as a necessary condition of any vital philosophical theism its wholehearted acceptance of the Newtonian world-view. His insistence upon elaborating theistic doctrines within the scientific framework, or at least not in opposition to scientific mechanism, is closer to the spirit of Locke, Newton, and Voltaire than to classical rationalism. The agreement between religion and mechanistic science cannot be based on any outmoded assumption that the scientific outlook is dependent upon a metaphysical theory of God and first principles. Kant regards the empiricist emancipation of science from a deductive metaphysics and natural theology as a definitive accomplishment, so that the scientific explanation is an independent achievement to which we must conform our speculations about God.

As a good Newtonian, Kant rules out chance as the genetic principle of the present universe. Since matter enjoys no freedom and is always bound by the inherent necessity of its natural laws, it follows that our orderly, physical system arises through natural necessity. Kant recognizes that the elimination of chance may only open the route for a naturalism of the Holbach-Diderot variety, in which the self-sufficient mechanism of nature dispenses entirely with God. But this danger does not lead him to accept the view of some religious apologists that we should therefore question the universal mechanical laws of Newton (which Kant interprets in an efficient, causal sense). Instead, Kant takes the stand that mechanism and theism can be reconciled only by removing a covert premise shared in common by both the timid religionist and the overbold naturalist. The former

confesses distinctly that if natural causes could be discovered for all the order of the universe, and that if these causes could bring forth this order from the most general and essential properties of matter, it would be unnecessary to have recourse to a higher government at all. The advocate of naturalism finds his account in not disputing this assumption.[3]

But it is precisely this joint assumption which has to be called into question by any intellectually alert theist, thus undercutting the inference to naturalism.

Two simultaneous admissions must be made: that the universal laws of the action of matter have no other destiny than to work inherently and necessarily for cosmic order and that these laws are nevertheless the effect of divine providence. If the harmony of the universe were attributed to some extrinsic intervention on God's part, beyond the natural laws, it would make God the producer of cosmic order as such, but not the author of matter itself, and hence not the creator of the world as this has been understood in Christian times. Kant explicitly admits the influence of revelation upon philosophical concepts when he remarks that the notion of a total production of the material world by God was unknown to the Greeks and was first introduced by Christian thinkers. But his main point is that anyone who restricts the operation of mechanical laws also endangers the universal causality of God as creator. God is reduced to the status of a finite tinkerer by the qualms of some religious minds concerning the reign of necessity in the material world. As soon as this finite God appears upon the scene, naturalism can dispense easily with such a deity by pointing to the forces inherent in nature.

In his *Universal Natural History,* Kant also maintained that there is sufficient evidence to show the dependence of matter and its intrinsic laws upon God. Matter could not have precisely those laws which achieve general order and unity, along with the well-being of living organisms, were there not a common origin for all material forces. This original cause "must have been a universal supreme intelligence, in which the natures of things were devised for common combined purposes. . . . Since [matter] is thus subject to a supremely wise purpose, it must necessarily have been put into such harmonious relationships by a first cause ruling over it."[4] God's existence is thus assured, not by weakening the necessities in natural process, but by acknowledging their universal sway and tracing them to their ultimate source. Although in his later period Kant found it impossible to reach the infinite God from the evidences of cosmic order, he always regarded this argument as a natural and persuasive one.

(2) Kant now had to face the rationalist contention that the main demonstration of God's existence does not start from a study of the universe but is a wholly a priori affair. He made a critical examination of this claim by investigating its basis in the rationalist theory of sufficient reason, causality, and existence. In recent years, these aspects of the Kantian critique of rationalism have been signalized by several historians of philosophy. But what has seldom been noted is the theistic context within which Kant conducted his investigation of these problems. It was a preoccupation with the problem of God that led him to consider these issues and thus, eventually, to reconstruct his theory of knowledge and make a new evaluation of metaphysics.

The theme of *A New Exposition of the First Principles of Metaphysical Knowledge* (1755) is that the term "sufficient reason" conceals a significant ambiguity. It confuses two types of determining reasons and two sorts of relations. There is an undeniable contrast between the reason which determines the actuality or existence of a real thing (*ratio existentiam determinans*) and the reason which determines only our knowledge of the truth about something existent (*ratio existentiae cognitionem determinans*). The former is a real ground and gives rise to the cause-and-effect relation in the actual order. But the latter is a logical ground and gives rise only to the ground-and-consequent relation in the order of knowledge. Rationalism has flourished by merging the former sort of sufficient reason with the latter in cases where a deduction of real being is at stake.

In natural theology, such rationalist philosophers as Spinoza and Leibniz have surreptitiously introduced a real ground of existence into God, whereas their argument permits them to affirm only a logical ground. While it is true that God has a logical reason of existence, to the extent that His existence is intelligible, He does not have a real reason or cause of existence from which that existence itself can be demonstrated in a priori fashion.[5] Taken by itself, the idea of the divine essence is a logical abstraction which exercises no real causality and permits no real, existential inference. Kant always appeals to the limited application of determining reasons to God as evidence that there is no universal, deductive principle of sufficient reason having metaphysical or existential significance. This principle has a purely logical import in its universality and applies only to analytic judgments about abstract, nonexistential relations.

Through this attack on the rationalist principle of sufficient reason, Kant broke down the exact parallelism between the real and ideal orders, thus rendering impossible any ontological proof based on the idea of God. The idea of God as the infinitely perfect being is a logical ground which determines nothing but an ideal sort of existence. Hence it can be employed neither to demonstrate God's real existence in an a priori way nor to determine anything of existential significance about the finite universe. The rationalist appeal to God as cause of Himself or as infinite power rests on an elementary confusion between the ideal and the real grounds determinative of being.

Kant reinforced this criticism with an analysis of existence set forth at the beginning of his treatise on *The Only Possible Basis of Proof for a Demonstration of God's Existence* (1763). Granting that existence is too elusive to be given a formal definition, Kant nevertheless suggested three identifying marks. First, existence is not a predicate or essential determinant of anything. One may know the fully determinate essence of a thing, along with all its predicates, and still not know whether the thing exists or not. It follows, secondly, that existence is posited of a thing in a different way than are its predicates. The properties and other predicates are posited relatively or solely with respect to determining the essence in its logical structure. But existence is posited absolutely, i.e., it determines both the essence and its set of predicates with respect to real being. Neither the essence nor its predicates achieves the actuality of an existing thing without the new and radical positing gained from existence.

The final elucidation concerns whether there is more in the existing thing than in the essential possibility, together with its predicates. As far as the "what," or essential content, is concerned, the existing thing adds nothing to the possible essence precisely because existence is not a perfection added in the line of essence. In respect to the "how," or mode of being, however, there is a decisive difference. The possible essence consists only in a set of mutually compatible relations which *can* exist, whereas the existing thing *does* exist. The former can be ascertained by appeal to the principle of contradiction, as Wolff saw, but the latter requires something else as an adequate criterion. Precisely what the "more" of the existent thing might be and what sort of criterion could determine our knowledge of it remained unanswered during Kant's precritical phase. At least he had already achieved the negative result that existence does not satisfy the Leibnizian and Wolffian definition of it as the complement or fulfillment of essence, since this supposes that existence is generated by the essential principles themselves. Whatever the further actuation may be, it cannot be derived a priori from analysis of the essential constituents and the principles upon which Wolffian ontology depends.

Kant now makes an immediate application of his findings about existence to the problem of natural theology. Since existence is not a predicate, it can never be inferred from a requirement of the essence. Even in the case of the divine essence, the only derivable predicates are those of possibility and logical being, not existence and real being. No amount of a priori analysis of the notion of the infinite essence will reveal to us the absolute sort of positing required for an existent thing. No degree of application of the principle of contradiction or identity alone can establish more than the compatibility among God's essential notes, united in a possible essence. Hence the rationalist method of demonstration is congenitally unfit for the task of proving God's real existence.

Kant adds, somewhat obscurely, that the notion of an existing thing is an empirical concept which is ascertained not by inspecting our concept of the essence but by turning to the origins of our knowledge in experience. Rationalism cannot derive the empirical factor in knowledge, which is to say that it cannot derive the existential truth about God's existence through its proper procedure. At this stage, however, Kant does not inquire too closely into the meaning of experience or into the question of whether existential knowledge gained from experience can lead us to God's transcendent existence. The example which he furnishes about affirming the existence of a sea unicorn depends upon our ability to see such an animal or at least to evaluate the testimony of those who claim to have seen it.[6] Obviously, God is not a direct object of human perception, and hence His existence is not verifiable in the way that a sea unicorn's is. But Kant is not yet prepared to maintain that knowable existence is confined to perceivable objects, determined in space and time, and that therefore we cannot know God's existence in a speculative way. He is still buoyed up by the hope that the experienced world can furnish something that will lead metaphysics to God's existence.

Before attempting this proof, however, the Königsberg philosopher points out that his critique of sufficient reason and existence also applies to the use of God in deducing the world. Kant brings to completion the empiricist attack upon a functional deity in the speculative parts of philosophy. He agrees with Hume that just as the attribute of divine power cannot assure us of the existence of God, so is it unable to provide a basis for deriving the existing world. Between the real cause and its existing effect, there is a real distinction between one thing and another, so that the causal bond cannot be ascertained solely by an essential analysis or by application of the principles of contradiction and sufficient reason. Analyze the concept of the divine will or power as much as you please, Kant challenges, but you will never find our world contained therein by way of necessity or essential entailment from God.[7] Since God is a real ground and free cause, the relation of cause and effect between Him and the world cannot be determined by the standard rationalist procedures. The latter rest on the confusion between real causation and logical implication. Such a confusion seems plausible only within the context of Spinoza's pantheism and divine determinism, where to have divine power is the same as to spill over necessarily into the production of the world and where the world consists of modifications of the divine substance.

(3) In *The Only Possible Basis of Proof,* Kant makes a classification of all the ways of demonstrating God's existence and then reduces them to one valid way.[8] There are two points of departure for the proof: the rational concept of the purely possible and the empirical concept of the existent. Each of these points of departure supplies two bases of proof. In the first proof, the rational concept of the possible is taken as a ground, from which God's existence is then derived as a consequent. The second proof begins with the possible as a given consequent and works back to God as its necessary cause. Starting from an experienced existent, the third proof leads to a first, independent cause, by the analysis of which concept it then infers the attributes of God. The final proof begins in the same way but makes an immediate ascent to both the existence and the attributes of God. Kant holds that the first and third bases of proof are evidently fallacious, that the fourth one has a certain limited value, and that only the second one is a genuine demonstration. Nothing further need be said about his handling of the first proof, since it rests on the discredited assumption that existence can be derived, by analysis, from essential possibility. In the *Critique of Pure Reason,* he labels this the ontological argument and reduces all other speculative proofs to it as their common yet invalidating basis.

Of the third proof, Kant remarks that it is both famous and entirely impossible. He takes its content directly from the Wolffian school's formulation of the argument from contingency, which is even more vulnerable in the popular textbook presentation than in Wolff himself. If something exists, there must also exist one being, or perhaps several beings, not caused by something else. It is not evident, however, that the necessary being is unique and supremely perfect. To establish this point, the Wolffians analyze the concept of the necessary being. Not being able to find the notes of unity and perfection in this concept, they are obliged to fall back on the notion of complete perfection in order to insure the identification of the necessary being with the one, all-perfect God. To do this, however, is to revert to the first proof and thus to deprive the inference of any existential significance concerning God. In the *Critique of Pure Reason,* Kant calls this line of reasoning the cosmological argument and repeats his contention that, to become demonstrative, it must appeal secretly to the ontological argument and thus destroy itself.

It is perhaps easier to see in this earlier formulation why the cosmological argument, as Kant knew it from the Wolffian textbooks, cannot avoid reduction to the ontological argument. Its starting point is not the contingent thing as existent but the abstract idea of contingency, to the neglect of the finite, concrete act of existing. It begins with a purely logical view of contingency, which implies the idea of a necessary ground. Since the necessity of the ground is also considered quite apart from the act of existing of a real being, the inference never reaches the actually existing being of God. It goes as far as the concept of a necessary being and then falters for lack of any existential content. The entire inference is a conceptual one up to this point, so that, inevitably, support must be sought in some other concept: that of the supremely perfect being.

Kant gives an accurate description of the entire procedure, but he does not note that the reversion to the ontological argument is predetermined by the nonexistential way in which the contingent existent is originally considered. His strictures apply to an argument from abstract contingency, but they do not take account of an argument from contingently existing, composite beings. The starting point of this cosmological argument is the definition of contingency as an abstract capacity to think consistently of something as nonexistent, whereas the starting point of a realistic argument is the experienced being of some composed and therefore contingent existent.

Kant's remarks about the fourth proof prefigure what he says in his first *Critique* about the physicotheological argument. He regards the appeal to order and harmony in the universe as a natural and captivating one which common sense can scarcely doubt. It leads to an inconceivably great cause having much perfection and power, but not strictly to the infinitely perfect and omnipotent God. Starting with finite order, we can arrive with considerable probability (but not perfect certainty) at the existence of a very exalted, finite maker (but not the infinite God). In the *Critique,* Kant adds that when the attempt is made to reach the infinite God along this path, it must have recourse to the other proofs and thus share in their defective character.

Like Hume, Kant takes this argument as he finds it in Newton, Derham, Clarke, and some of the deists. These sources are not examining the internal finality of a being which tends toward its own perfection but rather the extrinsic harmony between different parts of the universe. Hence their analysis is not made in metaphysical terms of the relation between regular action, definite ends, and causal intelligence but by means of the metaphor of human craftsmanship. This metaphorical analogy can never yield more than a probability, as both Hume and Kant perceive. They also see that the presence of a finite amount of order does not coerce one to affirm the existence of anything more than a finite maker of the harmony of the universe. What they fail to notice, however, is that the problem of order can also be approached as the tendency of existing agents toward their proper perfection or intrinsic end. Only from the latter perspective can the difference be brought out between an agent which produces a finite order in some given material and an agent which produces this finite order from nothing or without presupposing any given material. The former sort of agent may perhaps be only finite, but the latter must be infinite. Kant himself remarks on the difference between a maker-God and a creator-God, but he establishes no point of departure for making the philosophical inference to God as creating ordered, material things out of nothing and hence having infinite power.

Kant has now narrowed down the several arguments to the second proof, which he adopts as his own. He states this proof in several ways, but never to his complete satisfaction. It begins with the given, internal possibility of all things. There is no contradiction involved in saying that nothing whatever exists. But there is a contradiction in the complex proposition that nothing exists and yet that there is the real internal possibility of things. For the constituent elements in real possibility are always furnished by some actually existing thing. Against rationalism, Kant affirms the primacy of the actual over the possible and thus maintains the necessary foundation of every real possibility in some actual existent. Either the possible factors are capacities residing in the actual existent itself or they are its effects. Hence, given the real internal possibility of our universe, we can conclude that there must exist some actual being as its principle.

That this actual being is the absolutely necessary existent is the crux of Kant's reasoning. He devises one sole test to prove this point: A being exists with real, absolute necessity if its nonexistence would involve a real contradiction by removing the real ground for the intrinsic data which render all things possible. "If you take away God, not only all existence of things, but even the internal possibility of them, is also absolutely abolished."[9] The nonexistence of God would put an end to our coherent thinking and the internal constituents of all things. Since such a consequence is incompatible with our actually experienced situation, Kant concludes that God's necessary existence is proved with all the rigor and certainty of a mathematical demonstration.

At least it "seems" to be a demonstration having mathematical cogency. Kant now introduces some qualifications which indicate his dissatisfaction with his proof, even in its best formulation. He notes that he is concerned only with establishing a basis of proof and not with making the actual demonstration of God's existence. All that he can conclude is that either there is no sound basis or else it is to be found in the direction he has suggested. The whole discussion is concluded with the observation that while it is quite necessary to *convince* oneself of God's existence, it is not equally necessary to *demonstrate* His existence. The gulf between spontaneous belief and tested knowledge of God is not bridged, and Kant is therefore reluctant to make the former in any way dependent upon the latter. The later distinction between rational belief and scientific knowledge is definitely anticipated in Kant's early hesitations about the basis of proof of God's existence.

There are three major weaknesses in Kant's proposed basis of proof. The first concerns how we come to know about the internal possibility of things. Kant speaks vaguely about this possibility as "obtaining" or as "being present," but he does not specify how it is presented to the human mind and how we know that it really obtains. Without falling into the rationalist position of an a priori insight into possible essences, he would have to allow that the possible is presented basically through the actual, which, for us men, means that it is presented through our experience of actually existing, sensible things. Kant recognizes, however, that his notion of experience is not yet sufficiently developed to take care of the objection that the contingent actualities of our experience can never supply the foundation for the demonstration of the absolutely necessary being. Hence, in spite of his polemic against the Wolffian tradition, he is still infected by a deep strain of rationalism, leading to an unexplained relation between the internal possibility and the actuality of experienced things. Secondly, his method of healing the breach between the possible and the actual is unsatisfactory. He does so by virtue of the axiom that the possible is always founded upon the actual. But this axiom is drawn from the air and is not shown to be founded upon our experience of actual beings and their exigencies.

Finally, Kant's test for establishing the absolute necessity of the first actual being, in terms of thinkability and coherence, is a thoroughly rationalistic criterion. On all three scores, Kant fails to respect his own pioneer distinction between the logical and the real ground, in which the moment of experience is indispensable. The experiential factor is slighted everywhere: in the starting point of the proof, in the axiom about the primacy of actuality, and in the test of God's absolute necessity in being. The appeal to internal possibility compromises Kant's own findings concerning cause and existence.

(4) These internal difficulties led Kant to take a more critical view of metaphysics. He now began to doubt seriously whether anything that heretofore went under the name of metaphysics was really an instance of knowledge. "Metaphysics is without doubt the most difficult of all human insights—but a metaphysics has never been written."[10] Whereas Wolff had modeled his ontology and natural theology after the mathematical ideal of clarity, distinctness, and deductive rigor, Kant was becoming convinced that these sciences would have to follow the path of Newtonian physics to become fruitful. This meant a shift from the purely mathematical to the mathematico-physical method. A start had to be made with the relatively obscure concepts delivered by experience, and care had to be taken not to overstep the limits of the human mind and the implications of the sensible data. It even occurred to him that just as physics is the science of the outer world, so may a metaphysics conforming to the requirements of physical knowledge be nothing more than the science of the inner world. If metaphysics be a sort of internal Newtonianism, then its proper study is the ultimate grounds of knowledge and not the ultimate grounds of being.

Kant's *Critique of Pure Reason* is a response to this suggestion that the measurement of metaphysics by the standard of physical knowledge reduces its legitimate sphere to the epistemological order and makes metaphysics the science of the general conditions of knowledge. Any metaphysical analysis of real things and any attempt of natural theology to ascertain the real being of God will now be automatically disqualified.

2. THE DISSOLUTION OF NATURAL THEOLOGY

Kant carried out his attack upon the natural theology of his day in three carefully planned stages. The first move was to determine the general conditions of knowledge which made possible the science of mathematics and the general principles of physics. These requirements provided the universal criteria for every sort of knowledge in the strict sense. In the second place, there was furnished a description of general metaphysics and its application in natural theology as these sciences were presented in the Wolffian tradition. The aim was to show that neither discipline meets the requirements of knowledge and hence that neither is a genuine science. Finally, a closer examination was made of the structure of the arguments for God's existence, since natural theology could thereby be shown to rest upon a footing of sand.

(1) All of the crucial decisions in the prolonged Kantian siege of natu-

ral theology were made at the very outset, when the critical problem was formulated. In the most restricted terms, Kant wanted to find out how the concepts and laws in mathematics and general physics establish a perfect conformity with the objects of these sciences, granted that the concepts are originally drawn from the mind and not from the empirical world. It seemed obvious to him that the concepts and rules of judgment operative in the sciences must have a purely a priori origin in the structure of consciousness-in-general, since they are expressive of the necessary and universal factors in knowledge. Being far removed from any realistic derivation of these factors from the principles of being in existent things, Kant could not find a basis for them in the given sensuous materials; he found it only in the formal structures of the knowing subject. A matter-form theory of the constitution of scientific knowledge suggested itself as a way of preserving both the empirical, progressive side of scientific research and the aspect of universality and necessity embodied in the broadest scientific propositions.[11] There is a given sense manifold of impressions, but, taken in isolation, it remains purely subjective, contingent, and scientifically indeterminate. In order to attain scientific objectivity, the sense materials must be submitted to various formal determinations inherent in the general nature of consciousness.

The object of science is thus the constructural product of this marriage between the material and formal elements. There is conformity between our mental forms and the objects simply because objectivity itself is not something given but something made. There is nothing arbitrary about this construction of the object, since the formal factors belong to the general structure of consciousness and are not peculiar features of the individual mind. Moreover, the given sensuous manifold is indispensable. Still, the conformity in question is not one in which the knower submits himself to the independent being of the thing known but one in which the given raw materials achieve objectivity only by submitting to the informing principles which the knower contributes. In Kant's own epigram, the mind knows only what it puts into nature. Thus it has a priori certainty about its object, but, at the same time, the scope of its knowledge is severely constricted.

The real being of things remains an unknown and unknowable territory, since none of the general determinants of knowledge are known to be originally received from existent things. In his private capacity, Kant assumes that the sense materials do come from things-in-themselves, but from the systematic standpoint, nothing can be affirmed about them. What we know in a scientific way are the appearances, that is, the constructed sensible objects conforming with the general conditions of knowledge. Indeed, there is a strict correlation between the appearances or objects of knowledge and the range of possible experience, at least as determined by speculative criteria. The object of experience and the object of knowledge are the same: the unified world of sense appearances organized by the universal and necessary laws of Newtonian science. Other aspects of reality may be grasped by opinion and belief, but experiential knowledge cannot overstep the boundaries of this world of sensuous objects.

For purposes of his eventual critique of natural theology, it was important for Kant to specify all the elements required for reliable knowledge.[12] Basically, knowledge results from a synthesis between sense intuitions and the rules of judgment or categories of the understanding. Sense intuition is the reception of empirical materials and their organization under the forms of space and time. Without the intuitive content, the categories would be mere empty forms. And yet without the categories of the understanding, our sense intuitions would be lacking in those universal and necessary traits which characterize the world of scientific statement. To bring about this union between sensuous content and intelligible structure, there must be a mutual adaptation between the intuitions and the categories. This is the work of imagination or the inner sense of time, which supplies the schematic patterns for grouping our sense intuitions and concretizing our general concepts. And lest the contrast between intuitions and concepts prevent a synthesis of knowledge, Kant added that the entire formal structure of consciousness is contained within the unity of apperception or the reference of all objects and conditions of knowledge to the knowing subject. Unless all of these factors are present, experience is lacking, and, consequently, objective knowledge remains unachieved by us.

Kant does not cultivate epistemology for its own sake. He sketches the anatomy of scientific knowledge only so that he can have a meaningful basis for his theory of experience. What he calls the great discovery of critical philosophy is the equation between the general conditions for the possibility of experience and those for the possibility of the knowable object. The same requirements that enter into the constitution of objectivity also enter into the constitution of experience and define the scope of our knowledge. Knowledge extends only as far as experience reaches, and experience is regulated by the material and formal conditions of objectivity. Since these conditions lead only to the appearances or sensuous objects, Kant concludes that *only sensible objects are experienceable and hence knowable.*[13] In speculative philosophy, which concerns our knowledge of objects, the human knowing powers are validly occupied only when they concern themselves with sensuous objects or with the a priori, formal structures of consciousness which bear upon knowledge of such objects. Otherwise, the mind is directed away from experience and objectivity and so can issue only in illusions.

Kant is equipped with an effective weapon against the current conceptions of metaphysics and natural theology, once he establishes the proposition that only sensible objects and their formal conditions fall within the range of human knowledge. How he arrives at this proposition should be kept clearly in mind, however, in any attempt to understand and evaluate its polemical use. It follows from a twofold initial decision: to follow Hume in regarding Newtonian physics as the univocal prototype of all real speculative knowledge and to follow Leibniz in assigning a purely mental or a priori origin to our universal and necessary concepts. This dual decision achieves the synthesis between empiricism and rationalism, but it does so at the cost of narrowing down the import of the Kantian analysis of knowledge to the problems and data admitted by these two schools, to the exclusion of other approaches.

Thus the Newtonian postulate dictates the starting point and the scope of Kant's theory of experience. His analysis must begin with the *object of physics,* the object precisely as already submitted to the methodological limitations of physics. A start is not made with the *sensible thing,* grasped precisely as an existing sensible being, so the data of our ordinary acquaintance with things and the data of a realistic metaphysics are not included within the initial starting point. Working back regressively from the physical construct, Kant is able to discover only those factors required to explain such a starting point. What he arrives at is not a theory of human experience and its objects in the comprehensive meaning but a theory of the type of experience and objectivity proportioned to the propositions in Newtonian physics.

Similarly, the Leibnizian postulate imposes a serious qualification upon Kant's use of the matter-form schema to explain knowledge. Knowledge can be treated as a making process, in which all the general formal determinants are structures of consciousness and the sense materials reveal no principles of being, only if one agrees with Leibniz that the human mind must bring forth all its intellectual forms or concepts from its own nature. Only if the a priori origin of concepts and judgmental rules is assumed can the intelligible aspects of objects be traced entirely to the forms of consciousness-in-general. Knowledge is limited to the appearances if we grant these underlying assumptions.

Hence the statement that the only objects of experience and human knowledge are sensuous objects and their formal conditions has to be qualified by the context within which Kant develops his position. A more modest, but also a more precise, epistemological conclusion is that the Kantian aim of explaining the objectivity of propositions in classical physics is achieved by defining experience solely in terms of sensible appearances and formal constructions. This limitation of experience is a consequence of the method employed and the propositions analyzed, not of an integral analysis of the human ways of knowing. It does not warrant the general principle Kant seeks to establish about human experience and knowledge, since the latter are not exhaustively described in terms of the a priori form, the constructural concept, and the object of physics.

(2) Kant's next task was to define metaphysics and natural theology in a way that would clearly show their discrepancy with the conditions for experience and knowledge. His work was facilitated by the fact that the only flourishing metaphysics in his day was the system of Wolff, who never clarified the relation between his reasoning and sense experience. Kant gave an accurate enough description of what the Wolffians meant by ontology, or general metaphysics, and natural theology, or the special application of metaphysical principles to the reality of God. These rationalist sciences were peculiarly vulnerable to Kant's criticism because of their deductive procedure and their inability to show the philosophical significance of sense experience. Kant won his victory over them with ease. His triumph was more limited in historical significance than he claimed, however, since he failed to come to grips with any metaphysics of an experiential sort or any natural theology built squarely upon the deliverances of the sensible world to the senses and intellect of man. Nevertheless, it is understandable why he did not seriously consider the latter alternative. During his day, no competent attempts were being made to develop the theory of being experientially— from an analysis of the world of sensibly existent beings—or to work out the causal implications about God from such a basis.

Kant defines the reigning metaphysics in terms of its aim, method, and real content.[14] Its aim is stated in the very term "metaphysics": it is a *trans-physicam*, or movement of the mind going beyond all knowledge of sensuous objects to the purely suprasensuous realm. And since there is an equation, for Kant, between sensuous objects and experienceable objects, metaphysics is the attempt to transcend all objects of possible experience. This is the same as saying that by its very aim, metaphysics is engaged in a hopeless task. It seeks to gain knowledge of that which can never come within our experience or become an object of knowledge for us. The situation is in no way relieved when we consider the metaphysical method, which is adapted to its aim. A nonexperiential discipline is committed to the use of reason alone. By "reason" is meant here a power which determines its objects through a priori concepts alone, without having any recourse to sense experience. Rationalist metaphysics does not try to go beyond the sensible world by working out *its* implications but rather by laying down some purely a priori concepts and principles and then working out *their* implications. From the procedural standpoint, this metaphysics is the system of all pure rational knowledge through a priori concepts. The criterion for this nonempirical approach can only be inner consistency among the concepts, not agreement with the traits of experience. But Kant has established that concepts by themselves are empty forms and that they can gain objective significance only in alliance with sensuous intuition. Unless the concepts are rendered empirical or are schematized by imagination, in view of sensuous data, they cannot yield any knowledge of objects.

In terms of its content, metaphysics claims to be a system of theoretical principles which can be applied deductively to the sensible world. These principles are the unconditioned totalities of world, soul, and God, which lie beyond experience and yet condition it. A deductive derivation of the entire order of experience is deemed possible by the application of these totalities in a series of contracting inferences. Above all, metaphysics relies on the originative concept of the highest totality: God as the most perfect being *(ens realissimum, omnitudo realitatis)*. By application of the principles of contradiction, sufficient reason, and causality to this supreme concept, finite things can be derived as negations and determinate parts of this "All," or absolute totality.

But Kant observes that metaphysical reason is working only with its own ideas, which may extend our thought but not our knowledge of the real. The human mind is confined to finite appearances and hence cannot really know the unconditioned totalities of rationalist metaphysics. They remain empty concepts whose deductive use is not determinative of any real objects of experience and knowledge. Also, Kant notices a tendency toward pantheism in the deductive explanation of the relation between the most perfect being, or whole of reality, and finite things. The transition is imperceptible from Wolffian ontology to Spinoza's view of natural things as modal determinations of the divine substance.

Whether it be in terms of aim, method, or content, therefore, metaphysics so described fails to fulfill its claim to be a theoreticodogmatic science giving knowledge about real beings. Kant is now prepared to explain this failure by appeal to his own systematic position. He does so by giving prominence to the fundamental distinction between understanding and reason. Understanding works in close harmony with sensuous intuition, whereas reason concerns itself solely with the intelligible forms of thought which are devoid of intuitive content. The categories of understanding are adapted to the conditions of sense perception and thus yield knowledge of the physical laws of sensible objects. But reason deals with the logical meaning of our concepts entirely apart from any adjustment to empirical data. Kant does not claim that reason is inherently fallacious in this open usage of concepts apart from sensory conditions. The ideas of reason do have some logical significance inherent in them.

Nevertheless, reason is able to use its leading ideas of world, soul, and God in two radically different ways: regulatively and constitutively.[15] The regulative use of these ideas is purely subjective: they are helpful in systematizing our thoughts and bringing our explanations to ever increasing unity and comprehensiveness. The regulative use of the ideas of reason is not only a legitimate employment but comprises a *transcendental* metaphysics, which is the only valid metaphysics recognized by Kant. It does not concern itself with real beings but with the understanding and the other formal conditions of knowledge.

Yet reason is never satisfied with exploring the a priori conditions and limits of knowledge. It tries to use its ideas in a constitutive way in order to gain knowledge of real beings without having any recourse to sense intuition. This constitutive use leads to a *transcendent* metaphysics which is essentially empty and illusory. Kant regards the ontology of Wolff, along with Lessing's and Herder's new versions of Spinoza's theory of nature, as belonging in the class of transcendent metaphysics. Reason has overstepped its bounds here in attempting a constitutive or ontological use of its ideas. Since these ideas are purely formal unities and since man has no intellectual intuition which can give them real content, every sort of transcendent metaphysics results in a confusion of the forms of thought with the modes of being. Kant's own transcendental metaphysics has the lucidity to avoid this confusion, but it does so only by foregoing the study of real modes of being and by confining itself to the modes of thought. Either metaphysics is the same as a general theory of knowledge or else it is a dialectical tangle of illusions about world, soul, and God.

This indictment of transcendent metaphysics, or ontology, was now extended by Kant to include natural theology, or that portion of special metaphysics dealing with God. Since the Wolffians conceived of natural theology as a deductive prolongation of ontological principles into a special portion of real being, it was not difficult for Kant to show that this science lacked a sound basis. He regarded natural theology as the supreme instance of fetter-free thinking or the constitutive use of rational ideas entirely apart from the limits set by the only intuition man enjoys: sensuous intuition. Lacking any real content, the inferences about God are "merely a magic lantern of phantoms" having no bearing upon the being of God in the real order.[16] The special Kantian analysis of the proofs for God's existence was intended not only to refute these particular arguments but also to expose the impotence of natural theology as a whole.

(3) Kant reduces all speculative proofs of God's existence to three major types: the ontological argument from the idea of the most perfect being, the cosmological argument from contingency, and the physicotheological argument from evidences of order in the universe. Drawing upon the findings of his precritical period, he shows the impossibility of establishing anything about God's existence from an analysis of the idea of His essence, which the ontological proof attempts to do. He then maintains that our effort to reach God by starting with contingent things and

cosmic order is bound to fail unless we have eventual recourse to the idea of the most perfect being. But this means that the second and third proofs must fall back upon the first one and hence must share its intrinsic defect. To establish with rigor that the necessary being is an infinitely perfect being and that the orderer of the world is an infinite mind, we have to establish a purely ideal link with the idea of the most perfect being. Hence the ontological argument underlies the other ones and radically vitiates them. There is no speculatively valid demonstration of God's existence.

What has happened to Kant's earlier proof from the internal possibility of all things to the existence of the absolutely necessary being? It is disposed of in the most original portion of Kant's treatment in the first *Critique*, namely, his description and criticism of the general procedure of demonstration followed by the mind in mounting from something given in the world to God.[17] Now that he is in possession of a definite theory about experience and the limits of knowledge, Kant is able to detect the weaknesses in his own previous proof from internal possibility. He also thinks that his findings can be generalized for every speculative proof of an ostensibly a posteriori sort. This is where he comes closest to joining issue genuinely with the realistic approach to God.

Kant's principal objections to his previous proof bear upon its starting point and the process of inference to absolute necessity. His phenomenalism now obliges him to deny that we can start off with the real, essential notes of things-in-themselves. He recognizes only two valid meanings for possibility in the speculative order. It may refer to a purely logical possibility, but this can be sufficiently explained through the logical postulation of definitions and the application of the principle of contradiction apart from any ontological basis. Or it may refer to a real possibility, which Kant severely restricts to the real possibility of phenomenal objects, the only ones speculatively knowable by us. He now brings out the polemical significance of his previous enumeration of the elements of knowledge. That enumeration is a complete one and therefore includes all the factors required for explaining the possibility of phenomenal objects. Such objects must have their ground of possibility in the same conditions that render our experience of them a possibility. All of the formal elements of experience and objectivity are immanent to the structure of consciousness-in-general, and the material aspect of sensuous intuition is simply a given element which cannot be traced back to a noumenal source with any speculative certainty. Since all the constituents of the possibility of phenomenal objects refer to the finite phenomenal order, there is no coercive, speculative reason for seeking the basis of possibility in the infinite being of a God who transcends all phenomena.

Even if the inference is made from internal possibility to absolute necessity, Kant questions whether this proves the existence of God. In order to clinch the point, one must identify absolute necessity with the notion of the most perfect being. Kant does not contest the appropriateness of this identification, but he does deny that it is demonstratively established without covert use of the ontological argument. Pure speculative reason has no way of determining, through its own resources, whether the necessary being is finite or infinite, since there is no contradiction in the concept of a necessary but finite being. That the necessary being is also the infinite God can never be shown through sheer conceptual analysis and invocation of the principle of contradiction.

Kant certainly established his point against a procedure which starts from a possibility, rather than from finite actuality, and which relies upon a purely conceptual analysis of the notions of necessity and infinity. But his success in disposing of what he had previously termed the only basis of proof tempted him to generalize beyond the ambit of rationalism, within which his own thinking on God had continued to operate. He now claimed that every speculative effort to move from contingent beings to God is bound to fail. It is this universal claim which must be examined and criticized in the light of a realistic theism.

The realist maintains that a close inspection of finite, sensible existents leads to the existence of God, without any break in the existential continuity of inference. Kant flatly denies this in his description of the three steps required in the general pattern of a posteriori demonstration. We go from contingent things to a necessary existent; then we notice that the idea of the necessary existent must be further determined as an unconditioned necessity; finally, we identify the idea of unconditioned necessity with that of *ens realissimum,* or the most perfect being, and so establish the existence of the infinite God. Kant has already noted the fallacy of ontological argumentation involved in the third step of this proof. At present, his main concern is to show that this third step must indeed be taken. It is mandatory only if every a posteriori inference must also involve itself in the second stage as Kant describes it. He brings all the resources of his epistemology to bear upon this issue in order to establish the inevitability of this second step in every kind of a posteriori inference to God.

There are two notable features about the second phase of the argument: (a) It deals with an idea. (b) It qualifies this idea as being unconditioned. Apparently, the first step of the argument terminates in a necessary *existent,* but the mind soon finds itself to be in possession only of the *idea* of a necessary existent. Why does the necessary existent get transformed so quickly into the idea of a necessary existent? Kant replies that this is the unavoidable consequence of trying to make a transcendent inference from empirical things to an unconditioned reality beyond our experience. The very direction taken by the proof makes it issue not in a real, determinate existent but in an indefinite concept, totally lacking in real content and existential significance. The mind discovers that the very nature of the project of proving God's existence empties out the existential meaning, leaving only a vague, formal concept of necessity to which the nonempirical note of being unconditioned can then be added. But the mind must appeal next to the notion of the most real or perfect being, both to endow the concept of unconditioned necessity with some real reference and to insure its identification with the infinite being of God. Hence the very structure of the second step in the proof dictates the need to take the third one and thus to become involved in the ontological argument.

According to Kantian epistemology, necessity and existence undergo a radical transformation when they function in the a posteriori proof of God's existence. These categories are de-empiricized, deschematized, deactualized. The movement of reason from contingent things toward God is a denuding process, a stripping off of the empirical conditions for knowing an object. The farther the inference moves away from the terrain of experience, the more it sloughs off the only conditions under which the human mind can gain speculative knowledge of objects. Thus the internal dynamism of the theistic inference forces reason to convert the necessary existent into the mere idea of necessity, which is lacking in any reference henceforth to the order of experience and knowable actuality. The very distinction between real necessity and logical possibility collapses, so that reason is left with nothing more than a purely logical idea of the unconditioned being. "The necessity of the underived being is nothing more than the *representation* of its unconditioned existence."[18] There is no way of telling whether any real existent corresponds to this representation, and therefore, in desperation, reason abandons the a posteriori approach to God and settles for the a priori way of rationalism.

Kant concludes that the existence of God is speculatively unknowable. He reinforces this conclusion by applying to God the conditions required of all objects of experience and hence of all knowable realities. The judgments constitutive of philosophical knowledge are only possible "when we relate the formal conditions of *a priori* intuition, the synthesis of imagination and the necessary unity of this synthesis in a transcendental apperception, to a possible empirical knowledge in general."[19] Those things alone are knowable which are temporal, subject to some finite, concrete pattern of imagination, included within the order of appearances, and given through empirical, sensuous intuition. On all four counts, God (as conceived by Western theists) lies patently outside the scope of speculative knowledge. He is eternal and not temporal; His being is infinite and unimaginable; He is not an appearance but the supreme intelligible reality or thing-in-itself; He lies beyond all sensuous intuition, and man is endowed with no intellectual intuition for grasping His intelligible reality. Not only His existence but also His nature and causal relation with the world remain intrinsically impenetrable to our speculative gaze. Natural theology has no possibility of providing us with true knowledge about God and should be abandoned.

(4) The first critical observation to be made on Kant's analysis is that it derives all its strength from his theory of knowledge. This remark would be superfluous, except for the common persuasion that his refutation of natural theology stands, even when one rejects his epistemology. But a direct reading of the text shows that the former is an application of the latter to one particular domain of purported knowledge. The coercive force of the Kantian critique of natural theology depends upon acceptance of his view that the requirements for the knowledge proper to classical physics are the requirements for all knowledge, that the conditions of the object of physics are therefore the same as the conditions for all knowable experience, that experience is confined to sensible appearances and their formal conditions, that the general, formal factors in knowledge derive entirely from the nature of consciousness, and that man has only sensuous intuition. Unless all of these theses are accepted in their full Kantian import, appeal cannot be made to the achievement of Kant in destroying every philosophy of God.

In the history of philosophy, it is deceptive to divorce some particular line of argument from the wider premises and systematic context within which the results are obtained. Furthermore, the historical scope of the refutation has to be determined with precision. The arguments which Kant formulated and attacked were taken from the British followers of Locke and Newton, from the current Wolffian textbooks, and from Kant's own earlier teaching. He exposed the weakness of the empiricist and rationalist methods of dealing with God, but he did not thereby discredit other conceptions of natural theology. Specifically, his description of the general procedure of reason in demonstrating God's existence did not include the experiential-existential inference from sensible beings. His analysis was sharply limited to the types of inference employed in the philosophies of Leibniz and Locke. Leibniz furnished him with an account of how a priori reason operates in a nonempirical way, while Locke and Hume suggested the difficulties involved in attempting to start from sense experience. But both the rationalist conception of the use of reason and the empiricist theory of experience are foreign to a view of knowledge founded on our grasp of sensible, existent beings. To be genuinely universal, Kant's examination of natural theology would have had to take account of this conflict in the epistemological area and its consequences for demonstrating God's existence. The only kind of natural theology upon which he was entitled to declare a moratorium was one which accepted the conception of reason and experience which his criticism supposed.

The Kantian explanation of the three stages in any a posteriori demonstration of God's existence rests upon his theory of experience and his conception of existence. The steps in the process impose themselves upon human intelligence not through any necessity inherent in the human intellect itself or in God's own being but only on condition that the intellect is operating within the framework of the Kantian view of experience and existence. What has been described, then, is the way an a posteriori inference to God must adapt itself to the exigencies of this view, not the way in which such an inference must always develop. Thus the analysis has a sharply limited scope.

Kant's four empirical criteria (temporality, synthesis in imagination, limitation to appearances, and presence through sensuous intuition) are determinants of the objects studied in classical physics. It does not follow that they are the defining marks which characterize everything we can either know experientially or infer from experience. They constitute the *empirical* principle operative within Newtonian physics, but they are not identical with the *experiential* principle operative within our ordinary acquaintance with the existing world and our metaphysical analysis of this world.[20] Human experience and its existentially based causal inferences are not restricted to the factors required for the construction of the physical object of Newtonian mechanics. Kant's fourfold empirical principle is a univocal rule for testing the validity of scientific reasoning. By its nature, it can extend only to objects which already belong to the world of the physicist's investigation. Hence it cannot be used to answer the question of whether experience contains causal implications, leading to the existence of a being distinct from the world of physics. It can settle nothing about whether our inferences, which start with the sensible world, must also terminate with this world and its immanent formal conditions. Hence Kant's use of the empirical principle to rule out the a posteriori demonstration of God's existence is unwarranted. Granted that the starting point is found in sensible things, it cannot be concluded, by the deductive application of such a principle, that these objects are the only things we can know from causal analysis of experience.

Even with respect to the starting point itself, Kant's physicalism did not permit him to do full justice to his own insight into the existential aspect of experienced things. Having shown negatively that rationalism misses the significance of existence, he was unable to find in empiricism an adequate positive explanation of its proper reality. Just as Hume found no meaning for existence other than the entertainment of a perception, so did Kant find no meaning for it other than the conditions for knowing objects in physics. Not the sensible, existing being of our experience but the objectivity of a statement in physical science guided his view of existence. Hence he described the noetic conditions for having an object in physics rather than the act of existing of the sensible thing. It is because Kant failed to grasp the precise starting point of the realistic argument from changing and composite sensible existents that his account of the general procedure of a posteriori demonstration is inapplicable to the realistically ordered inference. The radical divergence between these two approaches to God crops out in the very first stage of the argument; it does not wait for the second stage, where Kant thought that his disagreement with natural theology began.

Kant has a contextual and systemic theory of existence. Capacity for integration within the system of empirical requirements is his criterion of knowable existence. This theory sensualizes Leibniz's view of existence as a harmonious relation among essences by making it a harmonious relation among the factors in the network of space and time. Simultaneously, the Kantian position intellectualizes or injects scientific objectivity into Hume's approach to existence as a perception of ideas by making the act of perceiving conform with the conditions of universality and necessity in scientific judgment. Knowable existence becomes a category or rule of judgment determining the insertion of a phenomenal object within the finite, temporal context. An object can be affirmed as existent when it satisfies the requirements of experience and secures its contextual position within the world of sensible appearances.

The first comment on this theory is that it fails to meet one of Kant's own earlier objections. He had urged that even if an object were totally determined with respect to space and time and described in all its sensible qualities or appearances, it might still remain within the realm of the possible. For even the empirical context of space and time does not assure us that something which has these relations actually exists. The purely relational approach does not lead us to the being which exercises the act of existing but only to a nodal point in a network of general conditions for possible experience. Hence it does not radicate the possibility of scientific constructs in some actually existing, sensible things.[21] Scientific contextualism does not save Kant from beginning his description of the a posteriori demonstration with the idea of contingency; he is in the purely ideal or possible order at the very outset. Far from having existent reality torn from its grasp at the second stage of the demonstration, Kantian reason is never in possession of the existential act of the sensible thing. The ontological argument is inevitable, not only for rationalism, but also for any position which begins with Kant's description of the object of knowledge and the criterion of knowable existence.

In the second place, it is a circular procedure to employ the Kantian conception of existence as a test of the a posteriori demonstration of God's existence. Kant's categorial view of existence is exclusively adapted to objects which are finite, temporal, and phenomenal. Like the empirical principle of which it is a function, this theory is thoroughly univocal and applies only to the homogeneous world of physical objects, which admits no implications beyond its own defining conditions. The critical use of this notion of existence does not establish that our world contains no knowable implications beyond itself but only that the study of such existential implications cannot be made in terms of this notion. Kant has so framed his theory of existence that it leaves out of account any aspects of existing, sensible things that lead to a nontemporal, nonfinite, nonphenomenal being. All that an application of his existential criterion establishes is that a rigorous inference to the truth of God's existence cannot be made from the phenomenalist starting point. It must begin with the act of existing of the composite, finite being if it is to discover the causal implications demanding affirmation of the existence of the infinite act of existing.

The first two steps in Kant's description of the a posteriori demonstration of God's existence depend, respectively, upon his theory of existence and that of experience. But no reckoning is made with the realistic analysis of existence and experience. Hence the Kantian refutation does not hold for a philosophy of God which grounds its inference upon the realistic findings. There are only two types of theistic reasoning which are vitally affected by Kant's dialectic. One grows out of the rationalist metaphysics, which treats the existential and experiential world in a deductive way. The other depends on an empiricist metaphysics, which is only the highest development of physics and hence does not discern the distinctive act of existing, as such, in sensible things. Thus the major targets of Kant's dissolution of natural theology are Leibniz and Wolff, Locke and Mendelssohn, with the lesser rationalists and deists providing illustrative materials.

3. THE SPECULATIVE USE OF THE IDEA OF GOD

Kant did not postpone his reconstruction of theism until the ethical portion of his thought but made a start in speculative philosophy itself. Up to this point, he was in agreement with Hume about the impossibility of a speculative demonstration of God's existence. This was sufficient to remove the functionalism of the rationalists, who thought that they could exploit the reality of God Himself for their systematic purposes. But Kant refused to go the whole length with Hume in denying any speculative role even to the idea of God. On the contrary, Kant

now proposed a mitigated rationalist theism in which the idea of God
has an important function for speculative thought, even though the real
being of God escapes our knowledge.

Throughout his criticism of the use of the idea of God by transcendent
metaphysics to demonstrate His existence, Kant is careful not to claim
that the idea of God is intrinsically contradictory, misleading, or meaningless. It is not this idea but the constitutive use made of it by pure
reason which he rejects. Like the other ideas of pure reason, it has a
basic logical meaning of its own which can improve the quality of our
thinking, even though it cannot give us any objective knowledge. Indeed, this idea expresses the supreme unification of thought around an
unconditioned principle, so that it is rightfully called the ideal of pure
reason. The regulative use of this ideal as an aid to our thought is a
legitimate one and, indeed, constitutes an important phase of Kant's
own transcendental metaphysics.

Regulatively employed, the idea of God has the negative purpose of
preventing certain false inferences from being made and the positive
one of fostering the systematization of our scientific knowledge. Three
instances of the functional use of the idea of God in speculative philosophy figure prominently in the *Critique of Pure Reason*. They concern
the distinction between appearances and things-in-themselves, the nature of human intuition, and the systematic expansion of knowledge.

Although the mind can know nothing speculatively about things-in-
themselves, it can at least think coherently about the logical meaning
they have as something transcending the sensible appearances. This
meaning is contained in the noumenal concepts, which are empty as
far as objective knowledge goes but which nevertheless serve an important purpose. The noumenal concepts have a limiting function, since
they prevent the application of the conditions governing the phenomenal world to the realm of things-in-themselves. When we are tempted
to make the unwarranted generalization that everything is somewhere
and in some time, for instance, the idea of God cautions us against
applying to things-in-themselves the forms of space and time belonging
to our own sensibility.

Again, when naturalism and theism lock horns over the need for a
transcendent being, the idea of God recalls to mind the crucial distinction between the phenomenal and the noumenal aspects of things.[22] It
warns naturalism not to conclude to the nonexistence of God simply
because His noumenal reality is not contained within the sense appearances. Yet it also serves notice on theism not to attempt any demonstration of God's being from a study of these same sense appearances. The
axiom *quae supra nos nihil ad nos* (things above us are nothing to us)
cannot be universalized beyond the sphere of scientific research, where
it means that such things are unknowable by us. As far as demonstrative

knowledge goes, it is also axiomatic that *noumenorum non datur scientia* (there can be no strict knowledge of suprasensuous realities). Thus in its negative role as a limit-concept, the idea of God is one of Kant's major tools for maintaining the rigid distinction of aspect between the sensible appearances and the intelligible things-in-themselves, as well as for eliminating the antinomies and false inferences resultant upon a violation of this distinction.

Kant cannot construct his fundamental thesis about human sensuous intuition without constant recourse to the limit-concept of a divine understanding. He requires a series of strategic contrasts with the noumenal notion of the divine way of understanding in order to determine the need for and the nature of man's intuition. The divine understanding is conceived as having a creative intuition, since its forms are the creative principles of things in the real world. Kant calls this an intellectual intuition and infers that there can be no intellectual intuition except that of the divine understanding, since no finite mind is creative of the real being of things. This enables him to conclude that the human understanding is entirely nonintuitive and that its forms are empty or nonobjective in themselves. Since the divine intuition is totally active and intellectual, it follows that human intuition is totally receptive and sensuous. Man has only a sensuous intuition, and it does not convey to him any distinctively intellectual content. The forms of thought are drawn from the operations of the understanding, but they must compose with sensuous intuition in order to give knowledge of appearances. Latent in this theory of sensuous intuition as confining the mind to sensuous objects is the conclusion that metaphysics and a knowledge of God are beyond the capacity of man.

Although Kant claims that he is making a merely problematic use of the divine intellect as a limit-concept, he verges toward a rationalist type of deduction in this instance. For in his hands, the notion of the divine intellect is extremely determinate and positive, permitting him to set up a real polar contrast between the divine and human ways of understanding. By drawing upon his nonphilosophical conviction about the creative character of the divine exemplar ideas and by equating intellectual intuition with the divine creative intuition, he effectively rules out in advance any sort of human intellectual intuition. It is this a priori reasoning, rather than a direct inspection of how the human intellect co-operates with sensation, that determines the Kantian theory of sensuous intuition. Even by this method, however, Kant is able to show only that the human intellect is noncreative and dependent upon sensation and not that it is barred entirely from grasping the principles of being of the existent, sensible thing. The human cognitive condition is best described as an integration of sensuous intuition with an intellect that is both dependent and intuitive in its basic act of knowing.

A final instance where the idea of God performs an important service is in the theory of scientific inquiry itself.

The *speculative* interest of reason makes it necessary to regard all order in the world *as if* it had originated in the purpose of a supreme reason. Such a principle opens out to our reason, as applied in the field of experience, altogether new views as to how the things of the world may be connected according to teleological laws, and so enables it to arrive at their greatest systematic unity. The assumption of a supreme intelligence, as the one and only cause of the universe, though in the idea alone, can therefore always benefit reason and can never injure it.[23]

Kant terms this use of the idea of God a necessary and beneficial illusion. An element of natural, doctrinal faith in theism gives the scientist confidence in the intelligibility and unity of the world he is investigating. It also spurs him on toward increasingly more complete and unified theories of the universe by holding up the ideal of the plan which the creator may be assumed to have had in mind. The idea of God thus furnishes a sort of concrete symbol of the scientist's goal of a unified and comprehensive theory, and thus this idea can be used validly to prompt the effort at improving our scientific explanations of nature. We do not make a symbolical use of the idea of God in order to determine anything about the being of God Himself but to provide a spur to our scientific inquiries, which require a working belief in the intelligible unity of the world under investigation. This is the sole proper, regulative use to which the idea of God can be put in the speculative order.

In the *Prolegomena to Any Future Metaphysics* (1783), Kant observes that his systematic, regulative employment of the idea of God in the study of nature is one way of distinguishing his theism from the two extreme positions of rationalistic functionalism and Hume's neutralizing of God. He steers a middle course between the claim of rationalism to have strict knowledge of the divine reality as a principle for the study of nature and the inoperative theism of Hume. Kant disclaims any knowledge of the divine attributes in their own being, and yet he finds a legitimate role for the idea of God as an intelligent, good, and just ruler of the material universe. In speculative philosophy, the idea of God's metaphysical and moral attributes can serve a regulative, symbolical, and as-if function in the interests of an always further systematization of our knowledge of sensible appearances and their laws. But the import of this speculative idea of the divine intelligence, justice, and causal action is purely immanent in its reference to our study of empirical objects and manifests nothing about God's own being.

Kant refers to his theory of the immanent, speculative significance of the idea of God as "a *symbolic* anthropomorphism" in opposition to any dogmatic or knowledge-yielding claim for this idea.[24] Ultimately, the idea of God is justified within the context of theoretical knowledge because of what it reveals concerning the conditions for our human inquiry into the sensible world. Our need to employ the idea of an intelligent and just maker of the universe casts symbolical illumination upon the nature of our mind and its formal requirements for gaining knowledge of appearances. This is the analogical function of the speculative idea of God.

Kantian analogy is quite at odds with the kind which operates within a realistic metaphysics. Realism grounds analogy basically upon the causal relation among existents and therefore employs a causal analogy for an existential inference to God. But Kant regards analogy as a *substitute* for causality, as taking the place of causality in cases where the latter cannot function. Hence his use of analogy is fundamentally noncausal and is for the sake of facilitating our symbolic thinking but not for obtaining inferential knowledge of another existent. The analogical role of the idea of God is not to lead us to inferential knowledge about the divine being but only to supply a noetic condition for increasing our knowledge of the natural world. Analogy divorced from a causal foundation has only a symbolical import in speculative matters, giving access to the structure of human subjectivity rather than to the existential act of God's being.

4. GOD AND MORALITY

It is in his ethical philosophy, as contained in the *Critique of Practical Reason,* that Kant endeavors to rehabilitate the real being of God in at least its moral aspects. From this standpoint, a fresh and precise meaning can be assigned to the oft-cited dictum that he "found it necessary to deny *knowledge,* in order to make room for *faith.*"[25] Taking "knowledge" in the Kantian sense of a scientific understanding of phenomenal objects and their laws, it is advantageous to theism to deny that we can know God. For a knowable God would be a sensible appearance rather than the supreme intelligible ground of being, a determined and caused event rather than a free, causal principle, a conditioned and limited object rather than the infinitely intelligent and just ruler. Whereas Augustine and Aquinas maintain that He would not be God if we could *comprehend* Him, Kant amends their position to read that He would not be God if we could, in any rigorous way, *know* Him. To safeguard God's transcendence in the face of his own finitizing and phenomenalizing conception of the knowing process, Kant must deny that God can be known and hence must appeal to a natural sort of faith as the cognitive bond between man and God.

Instead of the usual dualism of knowledge and opinion, Kant proposed a trichotomy of the modes of cognition into: knowledge, opinion, and belief.

Opining is such holding of a judgment as is consciously insufficient, not only objectively, but also subjectively. If our holding of the judgment be only subjectively sufficient, and is at the same time taken as being objectively insufficient, we have what is termed *believing*. Lastly, when the holding of a thing to be true is sufficient both subjectively and objectively, it is *knowledge*.[26]

Natural belief in God is better founded than an opinion, even though it falls short of being knowledge. The attitude of believing is found in both speculative and practical philosophy. In the speculative order, it requires a doctrinal belief in God to make the idea of God operate, in a regulative way, for the efficacious unifying of our knowledge. I postulate the existence of God by way of doctrinal belief so that I may make effective use of the idea of an ordering intelligence in my study of the order of nature. But the perfection of the attitude of belief is found only in the practical sphere. Whereas speculative belief in God is essentially unstable, moral belief in Him is regarded as certain and unshakable, despite the absence of objectively cogent evidence. The informed moral agent is aware that no speculative arguments can disprove God's existence and that the moral life cannot be fully developed without a practical belief in God. Hence Kant's philosophical acceptance of God is a matter of believing and not merely of opining.

Rational, moral belief in God can be expressed metaphorically as a manner of orientating oneself in respect to suprasensuous reality. Although the objective evidence for determining assent to suprasensuous reality is lacking, a subjective principle can be found. The subjective means for determining assent is a *felt need of reason* as such, and the rational belief in God rests upon such a felt need. Kant was anxious, however, to dissociate this ground of assent from mere sentimentalism or an exaltation of private feelings such as he feared could result from a reading of Rousseau's confession of religious faith. Reason itself does not feel but produces the moral feeling after recognizing a certain lack or need within itself.[27] The need itself results from the moral law and hence from reason as subject to a stringent and universal determining ground in the practical order. Belief in God does not stem from private whim or an emotional urge in the individual but from a universal need that is inherent in practical reason as such to the extent that it is subject to the moral law. Hence Kant always referred to this assent as a rational belief, in order to emphasize its foundation in the very demands of the moral law and practical reason. Nevertheless, he also sought to avoid the other extreme, represented by F. H. Jacobi, who identified rational belief with a direct, intellectual intuition of God. Kantian belief remains objectively insufficient and therefore never gives us strict knowledge or vision of God in Himself.

Kant also characterized rational moral faith in God as a postulate of practical reason, along with the companion postulates of freedom and immortality. As a postulate, it is something more than a mere hypothesis and something less than the principle of morality. In our moral life, the existence of God does not present itself as a possible option; it must be postulated. And yet morality does not rest upon belief in God as its proper foundation or motivating principle; Kantian morality is autonomous or self-founded. The moral belief in God constitutes a moral theology, i.e., it recognizes the need of God in moral life.[28] A moral theology is critical of the Humean contention that belief in God is purely speculative and should be kept apart from our conduct. Quite to the contrary, the speculative belief in God is imperfect, whereas moral belief in Him is firm and indispensable to practical existence. Nevertheless, Kant was opposed to any theological ethics, by which he meant any attempt to build ethics upon the existence of God and to regard God as the basis of obligation and the motivating source of moral action. God is a postulate of morality, but He is not its determining ground. The basis of morality is located in practical reason itself, whereas God is postulated only because of a need arising from the independent moral law.

Kant's moral functionalism can now be defined with reference to these aspects of the moral belief in God. In the speculative realm, it is the idea of God rather than the divine reality itself which is made to serve a systematic function. But in the region of morality, a functional role is assigned to God in His own being, or at least in the moral aspects of His nature. These two phases in Kant's functional theism are not related as basis and superstructure, however, since in speculative thought there is no assured knowledge of God's existence. The moral belief in God is based entirely on the exigencies of the moral law, expressed by practical reason as a felt need to have a conviction of God's existence, even in the absence of speculative demonstration. This belief is an instance of moral functionalism, since assent to God's existence is determined by man's moral need and subordinated to its fulfillment. Rational faith in God does affirm the reality of God Himself, but only for the sake of preserving the coherence and reality of the moral ideal. The speculative use of God by Spinoza and Leibniz is no more rigorously functional than is the practical use made of Him by Kant. In referring to his ethics as a moral theology, in contradistinction to a theological ethics, Kant emphasizes the point that God is recognized for the sake of morality and that the moral life is not founded upon the recognition of an obligation to God.

There are two outstanding reasons for Kant's reluctance to base ethics upon an independent doctrine on God. Such a project can only come to grief within the Kantian system, since no provision is made there for any speculative knowledge of God. Having eliminated natural theology, Kant recognizes no speculative teaching that can serve as an independent basis for determining man's moral obligation. Furthermore, he has in mind the way in which the Pietist writers invoked God, in the sense of grounding moral law upon the commands of the divine will, as known through revelation and reason. This is wholly inacceptable to Kant, both because he reduces the content of revelation to practical reason and because he denies that we have speculative insight into what God commands. If the content of revelation is really contained in our practical moral reason, then it is morality which must supply the foundation for belief in God and not the converse. Otherwise, Kant fears that the moralist will try to read into the will of God his own selfish passions in order to give them an absolute sanction. What is missing from Kant's treatment of the problem, however, is any analysis of the nonvoluntarist ways of basing moral obligation upon the relation of man to God. When God is considered precisely as the creator and ultimate end or good of man, no pretense of knowing the private decisions of God is made.

The felt, moral need to postulate the existence of God can be established both indirectly and directly.[29] Kant's indirect method is to indicate its connection with the other postulate of immortality and thus, mediately, with the moral law. We must believe in immortality because the moral law requires us to become holy or bring our will into perfect conformity with the law itself. Hence man must enjoy immortality or the prospect of an endless progression toward the perfect coincidence between his will and moral law. Yet even in a future life, every distinct stage of the progress will be marked by a certain disconformity or lack of complete harmony with the moral standard. Both the moral law and immortality would be meaningless were there not a really existing intelligent being in whose infinite vision can be gathered together all the phases in a man's struggle toward holiness. God must exist in order to assure us of at least the gracious equivalent of bringing our will into perfect conformity with the moral law and thus achieving holiness. This aspect of God's moral function is to gather together our scattered moral efforts and to bridge the gap between intent and achievement of a good will.

There is also a direct connection between the moral law and belief in God. As far as its obligatory force is concerned, the moral law is self-founded. Yet it does direct the will with unconditional authority toward a definite object: the highest good. Although we cannot regard attainment of this good as the motive of moral action, we are certainly entitled to the rational expectation that the highest good can be realized or is a practically possible object. Kant does not deny that man is naturally led to seek a real end beyond the moral law itself. However, an analysis of the components in this object of moral action raises a doubt. For the highest good consists of both a moral virtue or worthiness-to-be-happy as its principal part and an actual happiness in proportion to virtue. Now happiness depends upon the harmony of the course of natural events with the moral will. We ourselves are not the creators of nature and hence cannot assure ourselves of this harmony, much less assure it in precise proportion to our virtue.

> The acting rational being in the world is not at the same time the cause of the world and of nature itself. Hence there is not the slightest ground in the moral law for a necessary connection between the morality and proportionate happiness of a being which belongs to the world as one of its parts and as thus dependent on it. . . . If, therefore, the highest good is impossible according to practical rules, then the moral law which commands that it be furthered must be fantastic, directed to empty imaginary ends, and consequently inherently false.[30]

There now arises an imperative need on the part of reason to look beyond the moral law and happiness to the real existence of an infinitely intelligent, powerful, and just being who can assure the ultimate harmony between nature and virtue. Belief in the existence of God is thus not an option but an absolutely necessary postulate which must be made by anyone who recognizes the force of moral obligation and the felt need which it generates in us. The real facts of freedom and the unconditional moral law compel us, in a rational way, to give the assent of faith to the reality of God, the omnipotent and just ruler of nature and the moral world.

After stating the case for rational belief in God, Kant then felt it advisable to point out the limitations of the argument. His purpose was to rule out two positions with which he disagreed: Enlightenment deism and absolute idealism. Some of the deists used the moral argument to establish the existence of God precisely as a speculative truth, but Kant pointed out that it led to a moral belief and not to knowledge in the speculative order. Moreover, Fichte and the new idealist leaders were also attempting to exploit the moral argument for speculative, systematic ends. Kant placed an incisive qualification upon the scope of his moral argument and thus questioned the validity of these efforts on the part of the new idealism in Germany.

> Now, this [moral order] is an argument to prove God's existence as a moral being adequately for the reason of man, in so far as it is moral-practical, i.e., for its acceptance, and to found a theory of the supersensuous, but only as a practical-dogmatic transition to the supersensuous. Therefore, it is not really a proof of His existence simply *(simpliciter)*, but only in a certain respect *(secundum quid)*, namely, in respect to the goal which moral man has imposed and ought to have imposed. . . . The moral argument could be called, therefore, an *argumentum kat'anthropon* [argument according to man], valid for men as rational natures in general, and not solely for this or that man's accidentally adopted manner of thinking. And it would have to be distinguish from the theoretical-dogmatic *argumentum kat'aletheian* [argument according to speculative truth], which asserts as certain more than man can indeed know.[31]

No absolute, speculative system can be erected on the basis of our moral assent to God's existence, since its origin and total import are in the moral order of human conscience and the moral law.

Kant devoted a long appendix of his *Critique of Judgment* (1790) to a vigorous limitation of the scope of the moral argument. We must admit "that such an argument only establishes the Being of God sufficiently for our moral destination, i.e., in a practical point of view, and that here speculation neither shows its strength in any way nor extends by means of it the sphere of its domain." Only an argument from physical order could make this extension, but such reasoning cannot show with sufficient determinateness that the source of purposiveness and order is the supreme and unlimited intelligence of God. The proof from our moral need does have a dogmatic and universal significance, since it leads to a rational belief in God's own reality and not merely to the idea of God as a private persuasion. But this dogmatic significance is wholly moral and nonmetaphysical, since it is a matter of belief and not, in any way, of speculative knowledge. When the righteous man says "I will that there be a God," his *ego volo* is for moral purposes alone and cannot sustain a cosmic doctrine. Here is the precise point of conflict between Kant's moral-functional theism and the absolute idealism of his successors in German philosophy. They converted his moral postulate of God's existence into a primary speculative truth about the absolute and its generation of the universe.

Kant maintained that Christianity furnished the solution to the chief problem left unsettled by the Greek moral philosophers: the highest good of man. The Epicureans were right in regarding happiness as an ingredient in the highest good, but they were wrong in making it the supreme motive and end. The Stoics saw in virtue the principal part of the highest good, but they exaggerated man's ability to achieve virtue and to attain happiness within the context of nature. Only the Christian concept of the Kingdom of God made the proper synthesis of virtue and happiness, since it combined rigorous adherence to the law with dependence upon the justice and mercy of God. Kant explicitly traced the failure of Greek moralists to the fact that "they made the rule of the use which the human will makes of its freedom the sole and self-sufficient ground of its [the highest good's] possibility, thinking that they had no need of the existence of God for this purpose."[32] To this extent, the Kantian emphasis upon the autonomous moral will must be tempered by the postulate of theism as required for achieving the object of all moral striving, even though it cannot motivate this striving.

But in his own explanation of the Kingdom of God and other Christian doctrines, such as the Fall and the Redemption, Kant gave a naturalized ethical interpretation. In *Religion within the Limits of Reason Alone* (1793), he admitted no distinctive supernatural revelation but equated Christianity with the religion of pure practical reason. For him, religion was an aspect of morality, a way of regarding our moral duties as if they were divine commands. What religion contributed to his ethics was the hope that happiness can be realized. Kant saw in the Christian dogmas nothing more than moving symbols or natural existential myths which encourage the moral agent to continue his struggle against sensuous urges and to remain loyal to the ideal of moral holiness.

Kant's rejection of a speculative natural theology exercised a profound influence upon his conception of God and morality. Taken in conjunction with the practical antinomy between virtue and happiness, it simultaneously required him to attain certainty about God's existence and yet derive this certainty from the moral law alone. This situation led to two important consequences for Kantian ethics and moral theology. First, the unshakable, subjective certainty of rational belief in God could only be obtained by absolutizing practical reason or the moral will. Belief in God would be a mere speculative hypothesis and not an unconditionally necessary postulate were not the moral will considered as absolutely autonomous and the sole source of moral obligation. Precisely because he could not draw upon any speculative knowledge of God's existence and creative causality, Kant had to accept the moral autonomy of self-legislating practical reason as an absolute norm.

The second implication was that a permanent fissure opened up between the ground and the object of moral action, ruling out a morality based on the relation of the finite will to the infinite good. If the principle of morality had to be completely constituted *before* postulating God's existence, then the motive and foundation of moral obligation had to be located in moral reason itself rather than in God as creator and final end. To avoid circular reasoning, Kant was compelled to erect a dualism between the ground and the object of morality, anchoring the need for God directly in the object of moral action. The attainment of ends could not be the basic determinant of morality in this system without admitting that ethics presupposes some independent knowledge of God and our dependence upon Him.

Thus the characteristic autonomy and formalism of moral action, as motivated solely by respect for the law, were forced upon Kant by his position on natural theology. He could not countenance any metaphysical basing of moral obligation upon the bond between man and God, our creator and ultimate good, for this would involve either an arbitrary assumption of God's existence or the restoration of the speculative demonstration of this truth. Kant's ethics assumed its special shape as soon as he joined the elimination of metaphysics and natural theology with the equally intense conviction that a morality of strict duty cannot function without some acknowledgment of God's existence. This double position could lead only to a moral formalism in which God served a functional purpose.

5. LAST THOUGHTS ON GOD

Even in his seventies, after completing his critical trilogy, Kant continued to ponder the problem of God in an original and instructive way. One of the major themes of his last years was that "the concept of God is one which belongs originally not to physics, i.e., to speculative reason, but to morals."[33] Not only is the moral belief in God not founded on speculative knowledge, but even the idea of God which speculative reason uses in a regulative way owes its determinate content to the moral conception of God. Speculative belief in the idea of God is nourished by our moral belief in God's moral reality. Only the latter source can fill out the vague notion of the most perfect being, by specifying God as infinite intelligence, will, and justice.

Another preoccupation of Kant's old age was the definitive repudiation of the theodicies of Leibniz and Wolff. His article *On the Failure of All Philosophical Essays in Theodicy* (1791) helped to clear the atmosphere by exposing the presumptuousness of rationalism in seeking to plead the case for God.[34] Kant compared these lawyers for the defense with the adept theodicists who surrounded Job and interpreted the divine intent behind each of his miseries. The transcendent and all-holy God cannot be hauled before the tribunal of human reason either to be convicted or to be vindicated. Along with expressing the repugnance of a theodicy to one's religious sensibility, however, Kant also ruled out any philosophical discussion of divine providence and justice. He failed to note the difference between the way that these themes are treated in a deductive theodicy and in a realistic philosophy of God. The latter restricts itself rigorously to the bare proposition that God produces the world through wisdom, justice, and mercy and does not attempt to deduce the divine purposes or set up a calculus of divine choices.

The most significant engagement of Kant's closing years was with the new currents in German idealism. During the last quarter of the eighteenth century, there was a vigorous revival of interest in Spinoza. Influential writers like Lessing, Goethe, Herder, and Lichtenberg developed a somewhat romanticized version of his philosophy, stressing an immediate union of man with the divine principle in nature.[35] Even more arresting for Kant was the attempt of Fichte and Schelling to combine Spinozism with Kantian critical philosophy in order to demonstrate the presence of God in the moral and natural worlds. Kant labeled this new trend a "cosmotheology." Its main tenets stated that all things are to be viewed in God, that God is the unique substance in the cosmos, that there is a reciprocal relation between God and the world within the one substantial whole, and that the moral relation between God and finite minds rests on this pantheistic cosmotheology. Although the notes gathered together in his *Opus Postumum* (*ca.* 1796–1803) showed the ravages of old age, Kant managed by a supreme effort to define the relation of his system to these idealist doctrines.

Kant's fundamental criticism marked a return to one of his earliest convictions, namely, the absolute primacy of the existential issue. This was ignored by the idealists, who asked first about the nature of God and only later about His existence. The sum of the idealist conclusions about God and His relation to the world fell within what Kant regarded as the sphere of logical possibility. Although the pantheistic explanation might be logically consistent, it had no demonstrable reference to an existing God and a real order of existing things.[36] The appeal to a pure intellectual intuition or vision of God struck Kant as being a fantastic notion without basis in our experience of man and the capacities of his mind. God is *non dabile sed mere cogitabile*. He cannot be given in any sensuous intuition, and consequently, in speculative philosophy, we have only the concept of God for regulative use in our thinking and not for knowing Him.

Kant also denied the substantialism of the young idealists. By the category of substance, Kant understood a rule of judgment concerning the permanence of sensible appearances. For him, therefore, it would be degrading to call God a substance. This would be equivalent to making Him an easily known sensible appearance or perhaps a physical hypothesis, like the ether of Newtonian science. Furthermore, the substantialist view of God led straight to a pantheistic identification of God with the natural order and the human mind. "The spirit of man is Spinoza's God (what concerns the formal aspect of all objects of sense), and transcendental idealism is realism in its absolute significance," i.e., it reads the purely formal conditions and principles of human knowledge into the structure of nature or the real order.[37] By denying any metaphysical and existential significance to the idealist deductions from the ideas or absolute totalities of pure reason, Kant sought to prevent the identification of God's own being with the natural world. Safeguarding the transcendence of God seemed, to him, to depend upon a renewed denial of the metaphysical or constitutive use of the idea of God. We can assent to the proposition "God exists" only for moral purposes and not for the elaboration of a pantheistic cosmotheology.

In the *Opus Postumum*, Kant states that the idea of God is the sentiment of the presence of divinity in man. Yet it should not be concluded that Kant is thereby repudiating his own moral argument for a transcendent God, since his intention is quite the reverse. He insists in many ways that the *idea* of God is one in substance with man precisely in order to bring out the utter transcendence of God's own *being* to any rational idea we have of Him. Similarly, he declares that we may regard the categorical imperative *as if* it were God, but this only emphasizes the real otherness of God, even to the moral law and the conception of Him which we obtain from moral sources.

Human reason does not reach God's mode of being in itself. Only the (moral) relation characterizes Him, so that for us His nature is unsearchable and perfect *(ens summum, summa intelligentia, summum bonum)*—distinctly moral [properties] which, however, leave His nature unattainable. *God* is a *spirit*, i.e., not in any way the world-soul.[38]

This means that the idealists are fundamentally mistaken in thinking that they can convert the rational, moral belief in God into a speculative premise which will place God within nature as its animating, internal principle. Kant is openly calling a halt to an abuse of his own moral-functional theism. The only function which God's own being can serve in a Kantian context is a moral one, and this is not capable of sustaining any of the speculative inferences of the new idealistic metaphysics of man and nature when they are treated as aspects of God.

In order to understand it, the distinctive manner in which the nineteenth century posed the problem of God must be viewed in the Kantian perspective. The new developments were partly a continuation of Kant's approach and partly a rebellion against it. His criticism of earlier rationalism and empiricism was regarded as definitive, so that no serious attempt was made to revive the pre-Kantian views of God in their original form. Moreover, the Kantian plan of finding a new synthesis for the rationalist and empiricist factors was accepted, although his own critical philosophy was not considered to be the final word. The idealists were profoundly dissatisfied with Kant's solution of the problem of God in terms of a moral functionalism. His bifurcation between the speculative idea of God and the moral conviction about God's own being seemed to them still to lie within the framework of Enlightenment deism, thus blocking the path of further inquiry. It thwarted the desire of the idealists for a comprehensive, systematic explanation of reality.

To overcome this obstacle, they felt obliged to merge our idea and the being of God. This enabled them to develop a metaphysical knowledge of God in which the moral belief in Him is absorbed into the speculative certainty, thus permitting a dialectical derivation of the natural and moral worlds. But they also had the historical and doctrinal perspicuity to see that the idealistic absolute being was not simply identifiable with either the God of the Christian philosophical and theological tradition or with the residually Christian God of Kant himself. The idealistic absolute transformed the transcendent God into something new for the sake of achieving a total knowledge and morality.

Subsequent thinkers in the nineteenth and twentieth centuries have engaged in prolonged controversy over whether this sea change from God to the absolute is intellectually justified and humanly beneficial.

Contrasting answers have been given by atheism, finitism, and existentialism. Behind this continuing discussion lies the perplexing legacy of Kant, who asked the germinal question of whether strict knowledge of God must not be denied in order to preserve the divine transcendence, the autonomy of the natural sciences, and the integrity of the moral law. The Kantian rational faith in God versus the idealist science of the absolute—this is the way in which most of these recent philosophies have formulated the problem of God. The second half of this historically decisive alternative must now be examined in its most impressive statement: the philosophy of Hegel.

Chapter VII

GOD AND THE HEGELIAN ABSOLUTE

PERHAPS no period in modern philosophy compares with the fourteen years between 1794 and 1807 for sheer concentrated brilliance of speculation about God. This short span opened with Fichte's presentation of the absolutist basis for knowledge, included his own investigations of ethics and religion, as well as Schelling's transcendental idealism, and reached a climax in Hegel's *Phenomenology of Spirit*.[1] The transition was thus made from the atmosphere of the Enlightenment and Kant to the romanticism and idealism which dominated German thought during the first third of the nineteenth century and then spilled over into the rest of Europe and America. There was no neat linear succession of outlooks, however, both because the idealistic leaders were deeply affected by the earlier viewpoint and because they were engaged in an intense internecine warfare. Furthermore, some notable contributions were made by thinkers who stood at the philosophical periphery: Goethe and Herder, Schleiermacher and Jacobi. Yet the discernible trend of philosophy during these years was to vindicate metaphysical knowledge against Kant, to synthesize Kant's free moral agent with Spinoza's divine substance of nature, and thus to attain the absolute, in some determinate way, through philosophical knowledge.

That the theory of God was at the storm's eye of the entire movement of German idealism was evident to the main participants, but they disagreed violently with each other about God's precise relationship to their own absolute principle. G. W. F. Hegel (1770–1831) reflected most deeply and consistently on this relationship, so that his explanation achieved a systematic thoroughness and historical influence unparalleled by the other idealistic positions on God. One of his permanent convictions was that no philosophy is worthy of the name until it can answer this question: What does the approach to God mean? As an aid in formulating his own reply, he was able to consult and criticize the theories of Fichte and Schelling (at least Schelling's earlier philosophy). But he also did independent research into the social, religious, and philosophical aspects of the problem of God. The young Hegel somewhat slowly and painfully disengaged his distinctive stand on God from that of orthodox Lutheran Christianity, the Enlightenment, and his German philosophical predecessors while yet retaining some transformed elements from all these sources.

It was not until he forged the doctrine of the absolute as spirit that he possessed an autonomous basis for his philosophical system. To make that system perfectly certain and comprehensive, he had to absorb ontology into a new conception of logic. This could be done only by positing an absolute spirit that is totally immanent to, and developing in, the consciousness of humanity. Hegel saw quite clearly that such an absolute differs not only from the God of Christian tradition but also from the neutralized deity of empiricism and the functional deity of rationalism. In contradistinction to the empiricist deity, the Hegelian absolute had a supremely effective task to perform in philosophy. Yet it had to bear a relation of identity with the total system of knowledge and morality rather than serve a purely instrumental function in respect to them, as did the speculative deity of rationalism and the moral postulate of Kant. Under these conditions, Hegel developed his master theme of *absolute-spirit-as-totality,* which is a unique type of dialectical monism. He met the challenge of the Kantian critique of proofs of God's existence by reformulating them, in his own meaning, as proofs of absolute spirit. In the same vein, he substituted for the providential Lord God of history his own conception of the absolute as the internal developing principle of historical process.

Everywhere, he made a clear differentiation between his absolute spirit and the God of religious theism, not by eliminating the latter entirely, but by treating it as an imperfect, symbolical way of viewing absolute spirit itself. Ironically enough, however, most of his successors forgot about the cardinal distinction between God and the Hegelian absolute, thus giving rise to grave and potent misunderstandings concering man's relation to God.

1. THE THREEFOLD ESTRANGEMENT

The significance of Hegel's apprentice years (until his first university appointment in 1801) is still a matter for dispute. The traditional picture is that of a philosopher occupied solely with the metaphysical and epistemological issues inherited from his German antecedents. Some scholars are fascinated, however, by the mass of manuscripts he composed on religious themes, and hence they present Hegel as a theologian in the throes of laicizing himself. A few others concentrate upon his social and political interests, thus conjuring up the image of a young Hegel who may easily be mistaken for the young Marx. All of these profiles have some foundation, since his fertile mind reached out in many directions.[2] Yet throughout these diversified studies there ran a common thread of meaning, for Hegel found the modern world to be suffering from a threefold estrangement, or dualistic conflict: social, religious, and philosophical. He also diagnosed the root trouble to lie in an inadequate notion of God and hence prescribed a radical revision of the speculative and practical ways of viewing the relation between the finite and the infinite. In his philosophical theory of life as a divine totality, he proposed a remedy for the dislocations of modern existence.

(1) *The social estrangement.* From the days of his undergraduate enthusiasm for the nascent French Revolution down to his last critical appraisal of the English Reform Bill, Hegel took a constant professional interest in economic, social, and political affairs. This was consonant with his claim that systematic idealism does not flee from the harsh realities of the world but endeavors to comprehend and master them. Although he did not go as far as Marx in stressing the determining influence of productive relations upon the entire structure of thought, he did underline the mutual causal connection between material conditions and the prevailing religious and philosophical doctrines of an era.

It was Hegel, indeed, rather than the later atheistic materialists, who took the two decisive steps of relating the concept of God to certain social circumstances and of emphasizing the historical connection between philosophical theism and Christianity. Although there were some anticipations of this approach, Hegel's early writings first gave it a broad basis in social history and related it to the philosophical theory of estrangement. The seventeenth-century skeptics had insisted upon the bond between theism and Christianity because the latter provided their only foundation for accepting a personal, transcendent God. Rousseau and Kant had regarded their theism as Christian in the sense that true Christianity was reducible to a purely natural, moral-religious doctrine. But Hegel understood the relationship, in a converse sense, to mean that the philosophical elements in theism can be reduced to Christianity as a historical movement. The advantage of this interpretation was that he could thereby render the philosophical doctrine on a personal God vulnerable to the same social critique devised for Christianity as a positive, historical religion.

The social argument contains two phases. In the first part, the rise of Christianity and theism is explained in terms of the social circumstances of the Roman Empire. The second part uses a description of contemporary social life as a means of testing the practical efficacy today of the theistic view of God and man and of pressing the case for a new theory of the absolute.

As a young man, Hegel shared the philhellenic enthusiasm of his classmate, Hölderlin, and of such leading literary figures as Herder, Goethe, and Schiller. He formed an idealized picture of the Greek folk religion as a natural moral union of the human community with a divine principle, conceived as the immanent, harmonizing power of rational law. This was the religion of free, happy men and well-integrated citizens of the Greek city-state (with a few anachronistic overtones borrowed from

Rousseau's description of the civil religion for Utopia). How a transition could be made from this fortunate condition to Christianity posed a grave dialectical problem. Instead of locating the reason in the new Christian message as such, Hegel sought it primarily in the social changes leading from the city-state to the Roman Empire. The increase of wealth and the grand scale of military adventure disrupted the close-knit polity, destroyed the sense of dedication to a social whole, and turned the individual inwards upon himself and his private interest. Freedom and self-respect were lost in this situation, since laws were received passively from the alien power of the state and human value was calculated in competitive utilitarian terms alone.

Hegel's inference from this highly selective account is that theism and the Christian pattern of salvation are the proportionate response to this universal devaluation of man and his social life. The idea of a personal, free creator and transcendent source of moral law is exactly adapted to the dehumanization of man in the ancient world.

Thus the despotism of the Roman emperors had chased the human spirit from the earth and spread a misery which compelled men to seek and expect happiness in heaven; robbed of freedom, their spirit, their eternal and absolute element, was forced to take flight to the deity. [The doctrine of] God's objectivity is a counterpart to the corruption and slavery of man, and it is strictly only a revelation, only a manifestation of the spirit of the age. . . . The spirit of the age was revealed in its objective conception of God when he was no longer regarded as like ourselves, though infinitely greater, but was put into another world in whose confines we had no part, to which we contributed nothing by our activity, but into which, at best, we could beg or conjure our way.[3]

This text brings out the essential points in Hegel's indictment of theism, which he criticizes to the extent that its doctrine claims to be independently true and not a preliminary sketch for his own absolutism of the spirit. Theism is an expression of our eternal need for religion, but only when that need is operating under the frustrating conditions of man's social alienation from himself and his infinite spiritual nature. When the individual finds his earthly life to be of little worth and satisfaction, he readily projects his divine nature entirely outside himself and locates it safely in a supramundane zone. Hegel seeks to reduce every theistic effort at distinguishing a transcendent God from the world to a process of "objectifying" the absolute, making it a remote thing set over against us as are other things and thus depriving us of any vital communion with the divine. He presumes that the only way to distinguish God and man irreducibly is to regard them as alien things or, at most, to treat God as a high official, accessible only to a sly bribe and a magic password. This is a caricature, but one not easily rectified by consulting the average Enlightenment manual in theology and natural religion.

Hegel also makes skillful use of contemporary economic and social reports in order to establish that social estrangement is even more acute in our capitalistic and industrial age than in the ancient world. He traces the inhumanity of modern social life directly to the dichotomy which theism and Christianity foster between God and the world, interior consciousness and material demands. The religious relationship is made so private, world denying, and self-abasing that social responsibility is sapped and no foundation is left for moral control of political and social forces. Christian theism is helpless to master the conflicts of capitalist civil society, since this conception of God rests on the very dualism of moral man and immoral society which also nourishes the worldly growth of power.

It is the fate of Christian theism that "church and state, worship and life, piety and virtue, spiritual and worldly action, can never dissolve into one."[4] A true harmonization of all these factors depends upon the restoration of the divine principle to the world through what Hegel calls "a nonpersonal living beauty," i.e., through the depersonalizing of God and the assimilation of temporal processes into the very nature of the absolute. Since Christian theism refuses to take this path of depersonalizing God in favor of a totally immanent absolute, its fate as a distinctive body of doctrine and practice is to remain impotent before life's scissions, and even to intensify them, rather than achieve a reconciliation.

Hegel's method of claiming special insight into the spirit of an age and then judging a philosophical and religious doctrine by its association with that age eludes the effort to apply the ordinary canons of historical evidence. He imagines a Greek life conformable to his social ideal and then, by way of dialectical opposition, envisages Christianity as the counterpart of the wretched conditions prevailing in the Roman period. This historicist argument does not distinguish sufficiently between the time of origin of a doctrine and the grounds of its claim to validity. It also remains silent about the Christian aim of penetrating society and history with its principles of social justice and charity. The distinction between a religious and a worldly way of acting refers to the kind of motive and not to the kind of activity or its objective sphere. All our interests and goods are open to a theistic and religious orientation. Acceptance of God does not estrange us from any human area, but it does affect the motivating principles of our action. Not *that* the world must be refashioned by man but *how* this transformation should be achieved and for what purposes is the real ground of difference. Hegel's quarrel with theism results fundamentally from its refusal to convert God into an absolute, which is the same as the internal unity of the social whole, not from its refusal to bring its principles to bear in any way upon modern society. The extreme conservatism of the "Christian Prussian monarchy" of Hegel's own day cannot be generalized into a universal statement about the social incapacity of the Christian and theistic mind.

(2) *The religious estrangement*. Hegel gives a vivid phenomenological description of the Jewish and Christian outlooks as the purest representatives of theism.[5] He characterizes the Jewish conception of God as a completely objective one, that is, one in which God and man are totally foreign to each other, like objects at opposite poles of the world. Man is declared to be worthless in himself and to be capable of only an extrinsic, servile relation with God. To make it seem more plausible that men would voluntarily accept this grim arrangement, Hegel reshapes the stories of Noah and Abraham so that they portray God as the answer to man's need for dominating natural forces in a nontechnological age. This correlation between a transcendent God and the condition of prescientific man resembles the explanations of Holbach and Comte, except that Hegel never doubts the presence of some spiritual absolute. He presents the Jewish patriarchs as reifying their ideal of mastery over nature into an infinite but real and particular being, God, who has the world beneath His sway. By submitting to this object-on-high, man assures himself of indirect control over natural forces.

Thus the transcendence of God generates the master-slave relation, which marks every type of theism. The theistic mind is constantly harried by an "unhappy consciousness," by a sense of its separation from the infinite reality combined with a yearning after perfect union. Hegel keeps the philosophical and theological issues bound together, by treating Jesus as the supreme effort to abolish the master-slave relation, while still remaining within a genuine theistic context. The doctrine of mutual love and friendship between man and God is the farthest point to which theism can go in ameliorating the situation. But Hegel criticizes Jesus Himself and the Christian church for their insistence upon His unique divine person and His kingdom as a community set apart from the world.

By virtue of his definition of how infinite and finite spirit should unite, Hegel automatically classifies as an instance of the master-slave relation any explanation that conflicts with his norm. He defines religion as the self-elevation of man from finite to infinite life, as man's aspiration to transcend himself by becoming the divine. The infinite life is not distinct in nature from the finite but includes the latter within itself. It is the absolute, living whole, containing within itself all the oppositions between finite and infinite, nonliving and living, object and subject, thought and reality. This divine whole is the one-and-all of Father Parmenides but is instilled with all the contrasts and articulations of finite, changing being. If the infinite life is of this nature, then the only genuine way of participating *in* it is to be a mode or form *of* it.

Hegel is forced to consider the Judaeo-Christian, theistic account of God and man as a master-slave doctrine because it defends a way of sharing in the divine life without becoming a mode of this life. The theistic view rests upon a different metaphysical theory of participation, one that regards God as the supreme, personal existent and cause of finite beings. There can be a community of life between God and man within the theistic perspective, but it is always regulated by the causal bond between them. In undramatic language, then, the master-slave relation applies necessarily to theism only in the strained sense that caused beings, including finite persons, do not exist as forms or configurations of the infinite, existing cause of them.

The theistic conception of religion permits a man to lift up his heart to God without becoming an aspect of God or discovering the absolute to be his own innermost nature. But Hegel defines religion as man's self-elevation or aspiration to transcendence, in the sense of being a recognition and expansion of the divine life which is his own wider nature. For Hegel, then, there will always remain an oppressive estrangement, a devaluation of humanity, in *any* position which accepts God and man as irreducibly distinct beings, however intimate their union. What the theist deems to be the proper distinction required for the personal union of God and man is adjudged a master-slave relation or an inhumane separation by the standard of this monism of infinite life.

(3) *The philosophical estrangement.* After an initial period of keen admiration for the Kantian ethic, Hegel finally regarded its contrast between duty and pleasure, imperative and impulse, as a philosophical variation of the same estrangement already encountered in the social and religious fields. He singled out for special attack the Kantian moral argument for God's existence.[6] An appeal to a harmonizer of the natural and moral orders would lend support to the doctrine of a personal, transcendent God, quite at odds with the impersonal totality of life which Hegel was proposing. Furthermore, the Kantian proof rested upon the primacy of natural moral faith over knowledge, whereas Hegel wanted a speculative knowledge of the absolute which would render superfluous, and even suspect, any independent appeal to moral faith as a proper access to God. He made still another objection, on the humanistic grounds that a proof of God taken from our need of an external power is nothing less than a confession of our moral impotence and a violation of the autonomy of reason. These criticisms were reinforced by the use to which the rationalist theologians at Tübingen were putting the Kantian argument. After granting that Christian dogmas were not susceptible to speculative demonstration, they nevertheless sought to establish them philosophically, as requirements of man's practical nature and hence as proper objects of moral faith. Hegel feared that this theological extension of practical reason would undermine his own rehabilitation of speculative metaphysics.

He agreed with his fellow idealists, Fichte and Schelling, upon a minimal program for reviving metaphysics in the wake of Kant's criticism. The properly human intuition is not sensuous but intellectual; this intellectual intuition is directed toward the self as the only noumenal reality, thus eliminating any phantom thing-in-itself behind sense objects; the noumenal self is known in its absolute nature and not merely as a finite subject; out of the primary intuition of the absolute self can be developed the entire system of philosophy, whose ideal categories are also constitutive of real things. There was sharp disagreement among the idealists, however, with respect to the precise interpretation of these basic theses. The strength and consistency of Hegel's position derived in some measure from his relating of these propositions against Kant to his own preoccupation with estrangement. In the baldest terms, he contended that Kant lacked a speculative metaphysics because he failed to revise the traditional notion of God sufficiently and hence failed to surmount the dualisms inherent in that notion.

Even before working out the details of his system, Hegel was sure that his new speculative metaphysics could not be developed within a theistic context. It would have to be explicitly a metaphysics of the absolute rather than of God, since all of Kant's objections against metaphysics were based upon a comparatively orthodox, theistic conception of God and man. Thus his refusal to allow any intellectual intuition in man stemmed from his restriction of this intuition to the archetypal or creative mind of God, from which the ectypal or derived mind of man was sharply differentiated. The Kantian insistence upon receiving a sense manifold, upon confining our knowledge to sensible appearances, upon regarding the ideas of theoretical reason as purely regulative—all these cardinal arguments against metaphysics supposed an unbridgeable chasm between the divine and the finite minds. Hence the transcendent God provided a barrier against Hegel's project of making an affirmative answer to the Kantian question of whether metaphysics is possible.

Instead of criticizing Kant's conception of metaphysics and his way of formulating its possibility, Hegel sought to vindicate it within the given historical framework. Hence he had no other alternative than to remove the irreducible otherness of God and man, and in order to do this, he had to substitute for the transcendent God his own immanent absolute. For this purpose, Hegel exploited in a novel way the distinction between understanding and reason. They are not two completely different powers; rather, the understanding is one functional aspect of reason. More precisely, the understanding is that aspect of reason which views everything in terms of sharp contrasts and finite limits; it is the finitizing phase of reason. The apparently hard-and-fast distinction between the finite and the infinite mind is drawn by the understanding, and hence it is not an ontological barrier but only a provisional, noetic one. Here we can detect the distant echoes of Bruno and Spinoza.

Kant's difficulty was that he operated only with the understanding and mistook its self-produced contrasts and limits as being due to the very structure of infinite and finite modes of being. "The entire task and content of this [Kantian] philosophy is not the knowledge of the absolute, but the knowledge of this [human] subjectivity. . . . What such a philosophy can reach is not the knowledge of God but the meaning of man."[7] But the definitive standpoint is that of *reason,* which does yield the knowledge of the absolute, as well as of human subjectivity. In its reflective operation, reason recognizes and transcends the limitations of the finite understanding. It overcomes the provisional barrier between the infinite and the finite mind, recognizing the latter to be a phase and shape within the life of the former. Once we grasp the infinite life of reason within ourselves, we are in possession of an intellectual intuition of the only genuine noumenal being and are thus on the road to restoring speculative metaphysics as a rigorous science.

To give metaphysical import to the Kantian ideas of pure reason, two paths can be followed. The realistic way is to challenge whether the ideas are a priori structures of the knowing subject and then search for their inferential foundation in the beings of our sensuous-intellectual experience. Hegel does not make this challenge; hence the only path available for him is to absolutize the reason in which these ideas are present. We do not have to replace God with the immanent absolute reason in order to have a metaphysics, but we must do so if we are to have a metaphysics erected on the very ground of Kantian thought itself.

Hegel's proof that reason is infinite is that it can reflect upon the boundaries or barriers of the understanding, recognize them for what they are, and thus transcend them. But he covertly inserts a being-aspect into the transcending process, whereas it requires only that our reason be able to know the existence of an infinite actuality without being that actuality. Here again, the source of this fusion between transcendence as a form of knowing and transcendence as a form of being can be traced to the Kantian background. Kant does not permit the causal bond between God and the world to come within the range of our knowledge, and he restricts the category of cause to phenomenal sequences. Hegel is thus compelled to substitute a monistic dialectic for the causal relation as the way of explaining the connection between finite and infinite. The presence of the infinite actuality within our reason is not established on causal grounds but through an appeal to the dialectical monism of being. Transcendence is a relative function within the immanent totality of spirit. Hence in its Hegelian sense, one does not transcend the finite order by arriving inferentially at God as the distinct, causal existent but rather by viewing one's own consciousness dialectically in order to discover the infinite spirit as its innermost heart and substance. Kant is thereby overcome, but only at the steep price of transforming the human person into a determinate facet of the absolute. Thus both God and man are undermined in their integrity of being in order to pave the road for Hegel's speculative metaphysics.

Hegel found definite support in Fichte and the early Schelling for the project of depersonalizing God and incorporating finite things into the system of modal expressions of the impersonal absolute. But he criticized Fichte for retaining some traces of the same dualisms that had plagued Kant. Fichte identified the absolute with the moral world order, thus exposing himself to the charge of atheism.[8] Yet his absolute remained an ideal limit toward which the finite self was always striving, so that the gap was never entirely closed between them. From the Hegelian standpoint, the main defect in Fichte was his failure to subordinate moral to speculative reason and thus bring the infinite actuality within the scope of our metaphysical knowledge. The young Schelling, on the other hand, was all too avid to overcome all finite contrasts by engulfing them in the absolute as the point of their confluence and total indifference. Hegel admired Schelling's search for a unifying principle of mind and nature, as well as his teaching that the absolute self is an impersonal whole, but the danger here was that finite things might disappear entirely rather than take their place in the complicated structure of the absolute. Schelling's example warned Hegel that the argument from various sorts of estrangement should not be pushed to the extreme point of destroying the determinations of the finite world instead of supplying them with an absolute basis. A median course had to be found between the estrangements of theism and moralism and the invertebrate unity of absolute indifference.

2. ABSOLUTE SPIRIT AND PHILOSOPHY

Hegel organized his own philosophy around the doctrine of the absolute as spirit. He gave to "spirit" a distinctive systematic meaning and defended its application to the absolute. In support of his theory, he made a special analysis of the autonomy of reason, the nature of life, and the exigencies of philosophy. In each instance, his purpose was to show the need for absolute spirit as the constitutive principle.

Despite the sharp criticism of his predecessors, Hegel regarded himself as their legitimate heir with respect to the autonomy of reason. He set out to show that a philosophy organized around the autonomy of reason is also obliged to accept his own notion of the absolute in order to remain self-consistent. Throughout the modern era, there has been a continuous movement toward progressively extending the sphere of reason's exclusive competence. However antagonistic the Reformation and the Enlightenment were on other issues, at least they agreed upon the supremacy of the appeal to individual, rational appraisal of matters affecting human destiny. What the French Revolution added was the dimension of social reason, as a critical instrument for testing the actual customs and institutions of society. Kant brought the entire modern trend to formal philosophical expression in his doctrine on autonomous reason versus heteronomous reason, but, unfortunately, he restricted it to the moral order. In principle, however, no legitimate restriction can be placed upon autonomous reason without destroying the uncondi-tioned nature of its claim to sufficiency.

Hegel maintains that Kant's appeal to moral faith in God (as well as F. H. Jacobi's appeal to a nonrational intuition of Him) violates the au-tonomy and unity of reason. One cannot split apart the theoretical and practical aspects of reason, or the finite and infinite ways of being, with-out causing the death of philosophy. Reason is an integral whole: What it can attain practically, it can also attain speculatively through rational concepts. It is contradictory to uphold both the autonomy of reason and the need for a separate, moral faith in a being which lies beyond reason and freedom.[9] Instead of the Kantian relationship between moral faith and a transcendent God, Hegel proposes one between the finite specula-tive mind and the absolute rational whole, of which this mind and its concepts are a reflective part. Since reason is both speculatively and prac-tically autonomous, it coincides in its essential nature with the absolute itself. And philosophical reflection is nothing more than the resolute process of giving conceptual form to the truth that reason in man is only a determinate expression of absolute reason.

Whereas Kant treated autonomy in a moral and procedural way, Hegel gave it the metaphysical meaning of aseity, or reason's complete independence in being and knowing. He transferred the Kantian dictum about freedom, as being uncoercible from without, into the order of speculative knowledge and thus excluded any radical receptivity and dependence of reason upon something else. In this sense, reason could only be autonomous if it were fundamentally the same as the creative mind, bringing forth its own content and forms of knowledge. Hence Hegel enclosed finite reason within the infinite and merged human speculation within the divine. He assured the competence of human reason only by coalescing it with infinite reason and not by vindicating its peculiar resources as a finite power belonging to a dependent but in-violable human person. The Hegelian defense of autonomy is made on absolutistic grounds rather than on grounds that are properly humanis-tic and theistic.

The integrally immanent absolute which founds human reason and philosophy is given the distinctive name of "spirit" by Hegel. This term does not simply invoke the biblical saying that God is a spirit; it is a technical way of referring to the inclusion of relative or finite things in the absolute. Absolute spirit has two leading traits: It is substantial, and it is a subject or self.[10] Hegel approves of Spinoza's teaching that in the most pregnant sense, being or substance belongs only to the absolute. In comparison with it, everything else is an inessential modification of the one divine reality: The finite world is only the shadow of the spiritual whole. The substantiality of absolute spirit means that it retains its nature and identity amidst all its changing phases and expressions. Hegel does not want to fall into acosmism or a denial of the actuality of the world, but he does insist that its actual being is that of a field of transient determinations of the unique, absolute substance.

Lest this absolute be treated as a dead, immobile thing, Hegel also regards it as a subject or self. It is not a particular self or person but the concrete universal whole ("pure personality"), which includes within itself all the modes of individual being and all the aspects of universal truth. Hegel deems it the special glory of German idealism to have impenetrated Spinoza's absolute substance with all the rich perfection of consciousness and subjectivity. Yet the absolute spirit is not an abstract or one-sided subject to which is opposed an independent object. Rather, it is the primal ground, developing and containing within itself all the finite contrasts between subjects and objects. The entire distinction between the subjective and objective poles of consciousness arises within itself as the underlying whole. Absolute spirit is called subject or self, however, to bring out the primacy of reason and reflective consciousness over the entire world of objects, which are only phases of the absolute in its state of otherness from, or externality to, its conscious self-possession.

To the extent that absolute spirit synthesizes the content of infinite substance and the activity of infinite subject, it is designated as pure thought or absolute knowledge. Hegel intends these names to cover not only cognition but also all the conative strivings of will, life, and even inanimate forces. All these modes of being are only manifestations of the power and agency of absolute spirit. By "manifestations," he does not mean any substantially distinct, caused likenesses or participants, but determinate ways in which absolute spirit itself is found in being. The absolute as pure thought furnishes its own content precisely by releasing itself in the form of the natural world and then recovering itself through the instrument of human consciousness and philosophy. Hegel regards the religious and theistic doctrine of a creation out of nothing as a metaphorical way of stating that absolute spirit is "the infinite form, or the free creative activity, which can *realise itself* without the help of a matter that exists outside it."[11] The world and man are stages in the self-realization of absolute spirit; this is the radical significance of Hegel's doctrine on the autonomy of reason and the self-furnishing of content by pure, metaphysical thought.

As Hegel proceeds with this description of absolute spirit, he uncovers the extremely acute problem of reconciling the eternal perfection and the temporal becoming of the absolute. He stresses the former as assurance of the dominance and unconditioned truth of the rational totality and the latter as a means of including all finite modes of being within the philosophical system. His theory of absolute spirit rests upon what he himself calls "the resolve that wills pure thought," that is, upon the sheer *will-to-hold-together* these two meanings in a single concept or act of synthesis.[12] This gripping-together is a constructural operation, a decision on Hegel's part to unify eternal perfection and temporal process in a single construct for the sake of endowing his philosophy in advance with the twin attributes of certainty and comprehensiveness.

Hegel has sometimes been called the greatest irrationalist in the history of thought, but perhaps for the wrong reason. His fundamental irrationalism does not consist in a recognition of the tragic separations of life and the antagonisms in existence, for these are viewed by him as aspects in the development of the rational absolute itself. The precise point where arbitrary decision outstrips insight is in his primordial act of constructing the concept of absolute spirit itself. And yet unless he makes the resolve, he cannot develop a speculative metaphysics within his own historical context. Even in the act of including his particular horizon within an absolute whole, he falls victim to its limiting conditions.

In order to induce others to perform the same gripping-together, which alone permits acceptance of the doctrine of absolute spirit, Hegel appeals to an example and proposes a motive. The example supporting this doctrine is the living organism; the motive inducing one's assent to it is the resultant system of philosophy.

Hegel gives a dramatic description of the conditions for life at various levels. Unless the seed die to itself, it remains unfruitful. Only when a living principle submits to change and splits off from itself does it grow and bring forth due fruit. The universal law of life is to submit the content of a given nature to change and painful separation, to undergo a process of diremption or passage into the opposite, and then to achieve a new vital unity in which all the preceding stages are recovered, with added richness of experience. In terms of human character, the timid or falsely prudent man who tries to wrap his talents in a napkin to prevent risk and expenditure soon finds himself hugging an empty cloth from which the life of personality has fled. Only he who generously loses his life out of concern for others shall save it. Stated in more formal logical terms, life is a dialectical development from an implicit state (thesis), through a process of separating, negating, criticizing, and working (antithesis), to a recuperation of energies and growth in self-possession (synthesis). The synthesis overcomes the other two factors, in the threefold sense of negating, preserving, and elevating them to its own higher plane. The law of dialectical logic is identical with the law of life.[13]

Treating this description as an essential and univocal requirement of all being, Hegel then applies it to the absolute. On pain of being regarded as a dead thing, absolute spirit must also undergo development, allowing its content to become enriched through self-estrangement and final recovery. The absolute lives in and as the processes of finite being: the vital movement from the logical categories to the things in nature and thence through human history and conscious reflection to the perfect realization of pure thought. Whereas in his earliest writings Hegel had indicted the social, religious, and philosophical traditions for permitting estrangements to persist, he now acknowledges the positive significance of these separations, not precisely in themselves, but as moments in the life-process of the absolute. Yet he also admits that there is an ineffable sense in which the absolute spirit's life is a thoroughly motionless calm of total perfection. He appeals to the individual's identity throughout its changing career, as well as to the unifying power of purpose and reflection in an intelligent agent, without inquiring too closely into the distinction between a temporal steadfastness of purpose and an eternally complete perfection.

The Hegelian analysis of life is circularly related to the theory of absolute spirit and does not provide independent confirmation of it. Unless one already agrees to conceive of the relation between the finite and the infinite in the prescribed way, one is not obliged to conclude that the pattern of becoming is the graven law essential to all being. The process of self-splitting and recovery of unity characterizes the finite living being, not precisely as living, but as realizing the perfection of life under some limiting conditions. Hence there are two ways in which this process can be absent from a thing: by way of defect or by way of perfection. In the former instance, the inanimate thing lacks the ability to perform the immanent functions of life. In the case of the living God, however, the immanent operation of life is present in its full actual perfection, without the finite conditions which require change. Hegel must inject the process of becoming into his absolute only because he previously characterizes everything finite as an aspect of the absolute. It is not so much to assure the living nature of absolute spirit as to assure the absolutist basis for his statements about finite forms of life and becoming that he makes the absolute undergo development. The dialectical identity between absolute spirit and finite living beings is of crucial importance for him, since this is the only way to insure an indubitably certain knowledge of the realm of becoming.

Hegel's ultimate argument is, therefore, that the fate of philosophy hinges upon acceptance of his theory of absolute spirit. He lays down certain ideal requirements for the philosophical system and then observes that they can be satisfied only by this theory.[14] A thoroughgoing system is perfectly coherent and comprehensive, reflectively complete or self-sufficient for the truth about both the subjective and objective spheres, endowed with completely adequate categories for the knowledge of being, and therefore itself constitutive of experience and actuality. These exalted demands can be met only if our philosophical thinking coincides ultimately and essentially with the pure creative thinking of absolute spirit, as it develops in both the natural world and human consciousness. Hence Hegel defines philosophical science as spirit knowing itself reflectively as spirit through its own development. The truth, certainty, and comprehensiveness of the philosophical system can be achieved with one stroke, provided that its logical categories are identical with the laws of actual being. The identification between logic and metaphysics is carried out in the doctrine of absolute spirit. It enables us to regard logical categories as determinations of the pure thought of the absolute and to regard the beings of nature and human history as the same self-determinations of absolute spirit in another stage of its development. Through the medium of absolute spirit, the complete system of logical forms is also the complete system of the pattern of becoming in the actual world of experience.

There is no doubt that the Hegelian requirements for the philosophical system would remain unrealizable without the doctrine of absolute spirit. This fact does not render the doctrine itself any more likely but simply focuses attention upon whether the requirements in question need to be accepted at all as an attainable goal for the human mind. We are only begging the issue if we speak about the requirements for *the* philosophical system, since there are other views of what a system of philosophy should be. Hegel's conception of system is conditioned by his effort to ontologize the Kantian notion of pure reason and its ideas, but there are other approaches to the problem of systematic thinking.

The realist conception of a system stresses our concern to make explanations as consistent, well organized, and comprehensive as possible for our limited knowing powers and our genuine dependence upon experiential sources not subterraneanly predetermined by the categories of logic. From this viewpoint, it is idle to set up a systematic ideal for its own sake if the aim of the system is not a purely logical one but that of grasping the real order under the conditions of human inquiry. For in the latter case, systems remain human tools for the exploration of being, and hence their requirements must be intrinsically specified by the capacities of man and his actual mode of experiencing beings. Hence the realist type of systematic thinking does not strive for a closed and completed explanation but contents itself with remaining constantly open to a nonabsolutized experience of existing things and persons. A philosophy adhering to this systematic ideal is not compelled to will the construct of absolute spirit. Since the theistic distinction between God and the human knower is congenial to this more modest notion of a system, however, Hegel sees here an added reason for advocating the primacy of absolute spirit over God.

3. REFORMULATING THE PROOFS OF GOD'S EXISTENCE

Hegel is peculiarly open to misunderstanding when he begins to mention God favorably in his major systematic works. In doing so, he does not withdraw his original criticism of the God of theism or his aim of assimilating God to the absolute. Nor does he adopt theistic language in a move to confuse or mollify influential conservative minds of his day. Rather, his favorable references signify his confidence in a method for dethroning God without completely banishing Him from philosophy. The method is to locate the concept of God in a subordinate stage within the entire dialectic of absolute spirit. The God of theistic philosophy and religion is a symbolical way of representing Hegel's own philosophical absolute, and, conversely, absolute spirit is the adequate truth which is veiled under the concept of God. The doctrine on absolute spirit is "that which should express God in the meaning and in the form of thought," or in its proper conceptual truth.[15] Only after the concept of God is deprived of any distinctively theistic meaning, stripped of any claim to be a demonstrated philosophical truth in form as well as content, and dialectically subordinated to the theory of the absolute does it find constructive admission into Hegelian philosophy. Although these conditions are somewhat cumbersome to bear in mind, they are operative in every one of Hegel's systematic references to God. It is only through an ignoring of this elaborately qualified meaning of "God" that Hegel is sometimes reckoned a theist and his philosophy treated as the common patrimony of every subsequent theistic position.

The key to Hegel's very special attitude toward God is provided by his treatment of the proofs of God's existence, a subject which he mentioned in most of his systematic writings and upon which he was working more in detail at the time of his death.[16] His manner of handling this theme enables us to understand what Hegel meant by calling his philosophy a "wisdom of God," a "service and knowledge of God," and even a "theology." By these designations he meant that what the theistic and religious mind grasps under the shadowy and imprecise form of God is only an intimation of absolute spirit. It receives its proper scientific formulation only in his dialectical monism of the absolute. The philosophical wisdom about God involves a process of disenchantment and disillusioning; it is a wisdom about the inadequacy of the concept of a free, personal, transcendent cause of the world to express the true nature of absolute spirit.

Hegel painted a desolate picture of the status of natural theology in the early nineteenth century. The proofs of God's existence were almost universally abandoned as cogent reasoning. Advanced thinkers referred to them only from the historical standpoint—as antiquated procedures which Kant had completely refuted. Theologians used them only for purposes of edification, for shoring up the buttresses of belief, but without any pretense of achieving scientific rigor. Inspired by romanticism and the theology of feeling, many religious people shunned philosophical inferences to God as profane and presumptuous attempts to invade a sacred region which opens itself only to faith and the heart. Believers in God feared or despaired of a rational approach, whereas philosophers were veering toward agnosticism and even atheism.

Prescinding from the work of other idealists and from strictly theological complications, Hegel reduced the situation to three main factors: Jacobi's appeal to natural faith in God, the original rationalist proofs of God's existence, and the Kantian criticism of these proofs. A resolution of the conflict could not be reached simply by rejecting all these positions or defending one of them against the rest. Following his own maxim that the best way to refute a philosophy is to elevate its positive contribution into a higher totality, Hegel sought to criticize and yet find a place for each of these standpoints within his own synthesis. The latter was embodied in a revised version of the ontological argument.

(1) *Jacobi.* Hegel found it easiest to deal with F. H. Jacobi (1743–1819), since his view was relatively uncomplicated and drew its strength from a passionate reaction to the Wolff-Kant debate. Jacobi argued that if the inferential means to God can be doubted, then the mind must turn to an immediate intuition of God, a natural act of faith that is not a piece of rational knowledge. Without conceding that every rational inference is affected by the Kantian criticism, Hegel nevertheless agreed about the right and duty of man to elevate himself somehow to God. One expression of man's native orientation toward God is certainly the report of individual feeling or, more generally, the witness of the heart. Hegel did not challenge either the existence or the legitimacy of this approach, favored as it was by Rousseau and Schleiermacher, as well as by Jacobi. Indeed, behind his own construction of absolute spirit lay a warm, intuitive belief, which Hegel expressed in the poem "Eleusis," which he composed for Friedrich Hölderlin:

> What I called "mine" disappears,
> I surrender myself to the incommensurable,
> I am in it, am all, am only it.[17]

However, Hegel conceived it to be the business of philosophy to reflect critically upon our immediate convictions and thus render them rationally established or mediated truths. Natural faith and feeling have a place, but a subordinate one, since they must submit to a philosophical test to determine whether or not they are nourished upon the true substance of things. Otherwise, we must accept the Hindu's sincerely venerated cow and the Egyptian's cat as authentic expressions of the divine.

Somewhat the same evaluation must be made of the argument from common consent of peoples to God's existence. Hegel views it at two levels: the empirical one, at which it is usually proposed, and as a prolegomenon to his own position. As an empirical claim to unanimous agreement about God, it cannot withstand the objections of the skeptics. It is impossible to make a comprehensive survey of the actual opinions of all peoples at all times and places, and in any case there is absence of belief in God on the part of some peoples and individuals. Nevertheless, Hegel perceives a kernel of truth in the common-consent argument, in that it signifies the need to pass from a fact of individual consciousness to a necessary truth for all minds. It is not the counting of heads but the recognition of what every free mind must hold about the absolute that gives this argument some significance. To penetrate the necessary structure of human thought, however, requires a metaphysical method and a systematic outlook.

(2) *Pre-Kantian rationalism.* Wolff certainly used a metaphysical method, but it was one that was riddled with defects. Despite his broad knowledge of the history of philosophy, Hegel effectively restricted his analysis of pre-Kantian arguments for God's existence to those contained in Wolff's natural theology.[18] This historical limitation fitted in with Hegel's plan of converting the entire content of natural theology (conveniently summarized in Wolff) into a moment within his own dialectic of spirit. He invariably referred to Wolff's arguments as "the so-called proofs of God's existence." His purpose was not to condemn Wolff by a phrase but rather to alert his readers to the distinctive meaning he was about to propose for every word in this common phrase.

There are several meanings of "proof" which Hegel regards as illegitimate in the present context.[19] Although every immediate apprehension of God must submit to some rational reflection and inferential activity, the inference cannot be such that it destroys the unconditioned nature and truth of the absolute. Thus Hegel rejects any empirical arguments patterned after physical inquiries, such as the proofs offered by the Newtonian theists. The empirical method can yield only a hypothetical proposition about the absolute, one that is open to future revision and possible rejection. Neither Voltaire nor Hume gives us more than a probabilist theism, whereas Hegel is in search of absolute certainty about the being of infinite spirit. Similarly, he criticizes Kant's moral postulation of God as being only a practical hypothesis, unsuited to the being of the absolute and too closely bound up with a finite-personal conception of God.

Still, Hegel was reluctant to go as far as Jacobi, who would eliminate every type of inference. Jacobi advanced two serious objections against any inferential activity: (a) If God is proved from finite things, then He is made dependent upon them and conditioned in His nature. (b) In any case, proof is a cold, external process which cannot win our real, practical assent to God. On both scores, Hegel admitted that the older natural theology of the Wolffians was vulnerable. In one place, he tried to answer the first objection by distinguishing between the order of being and that of knowing. Our knowledge of God depends on our prior knowledge of finite things, but the being of God Himself does not depend on that of finite things. But this distinction militated against Hegel's own fundamental contention that the logical and the metaphysical orders are ultimately identical. Hence his definitive answer was that the valid inference does not begin with the bare finite thing but rather with the finite thing considered precisely as a phase in the self-development of the infinite spirit. A properly conceived proof does not make either our knowledge or the being of the absolute dependent upon anything except the absolute spirit itself, in a finite form.

The problem of relating cold objectivity of proof to subjective assent required a more complicated treatment. Hegel's solution was not to abandon reason for feeling but to rethink the finite-infinite relationship, specifically the remote transcendence of God. Here he located a genuine weakness in the empiricist and rationalist theologies of the Enlightenment. While very few of these accounts conformed with the popular notion of deism as completely isolating God from the world, they were extremely vague about the nature of His general providential presence in things. Since they were lacking in an existential metaphysics of God's being and causation, the Enlightenment theists were unable to found the bare assertion of divine providence upon a doctrine of God's causal immanence to finite things. Hence they failed to provide any philosophical basis for the religious sense of God's closeness to us, so that their arguments for God's existence took on the air of unreal and humanly unmoving exercises in barren speculation.

Hegel had the sound plan of amending both transcendence and immanence, since they are correlative notions. But he did not inquire how these notions might be modified in the light of a metaphysics which regards God as transcendent in His unique act of subsisting existence and as immanent through His causal communication of existing being to dependent things. Instead, he denied a creator totally distinct in being from finite things. Whereas God is immanent in virtue of His creative causing of limited beings, the Hegelian absolute is immanent in virtue of its own process of becoming the limited forms of being. Thus Hegel formulated a theory of radical immanentism within which there is a relative transcendence. The absolute spirit is relatively transcendent because it produces the finite things which are its self-determinations and because these things do not constitute its total realization. But it is unconditionally immanent to the extent that finite things are only transient, self-collapsing phases within the absolute's development of its own essence. This position is a *dialectical monism,* which permits a plurality of finite entities and their relative distinction from the infinite whole only because they are limited, modal forms within the all-encompassing being of absolute spirit itself.

How does dialectical monism combine a proof of the absolute with a feelingful assent to the absolute? Hegel insists that there is no valid proof of the absolute which is not also an elevation of finite to infinite spirit. What we ordinarily call proofs of God's existence are only objective expressions of an internal raising of the mind to the absolute; they are conceptual ways in which we become consciously aware of this process. Far from being cut off from our interior life and vital interests, the ordinary inferences have no content except that which is furnished by the upsurge of the human soul. But this lifting of human consciousness is itself a portion of the infinite spirit's own dynamism; the elevation of the finite is actually a self-elevating of the infinite to itself, a return of the divine to the divine, under the form of human consciousness.

Man knows about God only in so far as God-in-man knows about Himself. This knowledge is God's self-consciousness, but it is also God's knowledge of man, and this God's knowledge of man is man's knowledge of God. The spirit of man knowing God is only the spirit of God Himself.[20]

Hegel adds quietly that religion is identical with the actual elevation of the finite and that philosophy alone interprets this act in its proper rational meaning. Thus his eventual subordination of religion to philosophy is clearly foreshadowed in his account of how interior feeling provides the content for our inference to the absolute.

If to prove God's existence means to become aware of the arrival of absolute spirit at self-consciousness within the finite mind, then clearly the term "God" is also being employed in a quite distinctive way. What the proofs really arrive at is the actuality of absolute spirit. For the inference is not completed until we learn "to know God as our true and essential self. . . . But God can only be called spirit in so far as He is known as undergoing mediation with Himself and in Himself. Only thus is He concrete, living, and spirit. Thereby, the knowledge of God as spirit includes mediation within itself."[21] Mediation is the process whereby the infinite subject says nay and yea to itself, undergoes the process of vital movement, explicates itself as the finite world, and then achieves its perfect self-awareness. The so-called proofs of God's existence are in fact directed to the establishment of the truth about absolute spirit, the mediating principle of our spiritual life.

Finally, Hegel cannot agree unqualifiedly that the proofs are aimed precisely at establishing the "existence" of this absolute spirit. Wolff had leveled existence to the plane of the other realities of essence, and now Hegel levels it to the plane of the other determinations of the absolute concept. It is only one in a dialectical series of thought-determinations of absolute spirit, but it enjoys no pre-eminent role, since there are many other and richer modes of the divine idea in its temporal march. In Hegel's logic of absolute spirit, existence fits into a very modest pigeonhole, as signifying that stage in the progress of the absolute concept when the latter stands immediately related to itself and appears as a self-grounded thing. But pure thought produces many subsequent relations, all of which are directed toward determining it more fully as rational spirit.

Existence is only one phase in the course of development of the absolute spirit, and, at that, it is too fixed and finite to be worthy of designating the supreme actuality of the absolute. Hence the proof of absolute spirit is not finalized toward existential truth but is directed toward showing that the absolute is the living, self-finitizing, spiritual whole of being. The existential "that" becomes only a transient incident in the Hegelian procedure of manifesting "what" the absolute is in its own nature. Hegel has the great perspicacity to see that unless he removes the act of existing from the primary significance of being, his criticism of God will not be thoroughly conclusive. As a precautionary measure, then, he establishes his chief metaphysical proportion not between actuality and the act of existing but between actuality and spirit as a self-developing infinite subject. In the Hegelian system, the existential act falls far short of the perfection of actuality as absolute spirit in process. It is the actual being of the absolute spirit, in this special sense, which the proofs seek to establish.

(3) *Kant.* Having thoroughly transformed the meaning of "proofs of God's existence," Hegel is now in a position to meet the Kantian criticism. He distinguishes between the form and the content of the Wolffian proofs, conceding to Kant only that they are defective in their form. As presented by Wolff, the proofs fail to rise above the perspective of the finite understanding, and hence they make easy targets for Kant, who is speculating at the same level. But their content is sound enough and needs only to be recognized for what it is: the rational affirmation of the actuality of absolute spirit.

Wolff and Kant reach a hopeless deadlock, since they mutually accept a defective, pictorial way of envisaging the problem of God. Let us draw a straight, thick line down the entire sphere of real beings. Here, on this side, we will locate all the finite beings, and there, on the farther side, we will place the infinite being. The aim of the cosmological and teleological proofs is to get from this side to the other, from finite things and over the line (which now becomes a wall) to the infinite reality. We start with finite things having an independent being in their own ontological realm, quite without reference to the infinite and quite unaffected by the inferential process itself. Our terminal point is the infinite being, which again has its being in a completely separate way, without involving finite things in any way. Kant's criticism amounts to saying that no amount of analysis of finite beings as such will construct the ladder leading over the wall to the infinite. As for the ontological proof, it seeks a passage from a purely subjective concept of God to His real being. Kant's point here is that the subjective nature of the starting point provides no basis for making an affirmation about a real counterpart.

The objections of Kant fall to the ground, however, as soon as one learns to repudiate the imaginative framework of the dividing line between finite and infinite being, conceptual and real being. To erase this line, Hegel submits the finite to a dialectical analysis. Finitude is the most stubborn and stiff necked of all the categories, since it clings tenaciously to the pretense of irreducible, subsisting ways of being. Transposed within the context of absolute spirit, however, finitude is finally made to confess its purely ideal and dialectical nature. Once it is located within the life-circuit of infinite, self-limiting spirit, the finite becomes a mere shadow, a perpetual perishing, and (if it persists in asserting its own existential act and substantial nature) an illusion. The finite is simply the absolute spirit in the state of negativity, externality, or separation from its original infinite condition. "The finite has no truth; the truth of the finite spirit is the absolute spirit. The finite is no veritable being. There is in it the dialectic to sublate itself, to deny itself," and thus to pass over into its affirmative opposite, which is nothing more than the infinite spirit itself.[22] Penetrate deeply enough into the nature of finite things, Hegel says in effect, and you will find them negating their own claim to subsistence and affirming that their whole truth and actuality consist in being moments in the self-actualizing of absolute spirit. Instead of merely reducing material things to the finite mind, absolute idealism converts the entire finite order into a dialectical aspect of the infinite mind, embracing both material things and finite minds.

With this theory of the finite in his possession, Hegel can now show the groundlessness of the Kantian objections. The starting point of the cosmological and teleological proofs does not consist in a purely phenomenal object, which has its being quite apart from any ascertainable reference to noumenal reality. If the entire being of the finite is that of a determination of the absolute, then we are already installed at the very heart of noumenal reality, even at the outset of the inference. Furthermore, the matter and form of the finite thing constitute an integral whole or joint expression of absolute spirit. In knowing the finite thing, our knowledge contains both the formal and the material element, thus satisfying Kant's requirement for an inference that is based on intuitive content. Since the starting point of the proofs is not a pure phenomenon but a concrete, matter-form expression of absolute spirit, it can yield true metaphysical knowledge about the nature of the infinite being.

This conclusion is strengthened if we consider the nature of the transition and connection involved in the proofs. We do not pass from the finite as one separate kind of being, by means of a purely extrinsic connection and relation, to the infinite as another entirely separate kind of being. Actually, the inference passes from the infinite-in-a-finite-form to the infinite-grasped-as-absolute-spirit, with the one totality of spiritual being as the common floor of the entire movement. It is by the intrinsic movement of its own content that the finite refers to, and indeed passes over into, the infinite considered as absolute spirit.

Taken in this light, finitude retains the advantage, so to say, of being prepared so far ahead [by the Hegelian logic] that it points by itself toward the transition in its truth, toward necessity. . . . The being of the finite is not its own being, but is rather the being of its other: the infinite.[23]

There is no need to appeal to Kant's moral faith in God, once one recognizes that the finite thing furnishes not only the point of departure for the inference but also the solid bridge into the domain of the infinite, necessary being. Or, rather, the infinite itself furnishes this bridge by producing, revoking, and elevating the finite aspects of its own actuality. The connection between the finite and the infinite is not only an intrinsic, essential one but is founded on the dialectical identity between them.

In defense of the ontological proof, Hegel observes that the dividing line between the concept of the absolute and its objective being appears only when the finite understanding pictures this concept as merely a subjective representation. Speculative reason assures us, however, that the absolute concept is the same as the infinite spirit and hence is the productive source of all actual determinations. And on the map of Hegelian logic, being is only the first and emptiest step taken by the absolute spirit in its journey of self-actualization. But although being is the poorest of all determinations, the absolute concept is not so poor that it does not contain it or, rather, that it does not bring itself forth initially in the form of objective being. Far from there being a great leap from the concept of the absolute to its being, the latter is only an internally contained moment in the living growth of the absolute concept.

Once the human mind is elevated to the eminence of this concept, it can see the necessary, intrinsic connection which the absolute nature establishes with being. Hegel's minimizing of being and the act of existing is aimed at making the transition seem not only obvious but jejune. The real weight of the proof is centered around showing not that the absolute has being and exists but that it has precisely the spiritual nature described by Hegel. This preoccupation with its essential traits agrees with the constructural character of the doctrine on absolute spirit.

(4) *The Hegelian ontological proof.* Concerning whether the three proofs enumerated by Kant can be further reduced, Hegel wants to discover an element of necessity in the threefold division and yet also satisfy his systematic urge toward unification. Therefore, he distinguishes sharply between two aspects of the problem: the *descriptive elevation* of the finite mind to the absolute and the strict *demonstration* of the truth of absolute spirit. From the descriptive standpoint, there are three irreducible proofs; from the demonstrative standpoint, there is one comprehensive proof.[24] The three descriptive approaches are irreducible to each other, and yet they are jointly reducible to their common demonstrative basis. There is only one true proof, one path of demonstration, and this is the ontological proof (in the demonstrative sense). But there are three different starting points for the human mind to grasp the force of this demonstration, and thus there are three descriptive proofs: the cosmological, the teleological, and (in the descriptive sense) the ontological argument. The cosmological proof, starting from the contingency of the world, tells us only about the necessity and power of the absolute. Far richer in import is the teleological proof, since it moves onward from the evidence of conformity of action to laws and ends to the rational and purposive nature of the absolute. The ontological description is in one way the least informative of the arguments (since it leads to the objective being of the absolute, stripped, as it were, of any other determinations), and yet in another sense it is the apex of the descriptive process (since it formally identifies this objective being with the absolute concept or infinite spirit).

Hegel formulates three leading questions about the descriptive proofs. Why are separate proofs required? How do they all depend upon a common underpinning of demonstrative thought? What operates within them to bring about their reduction to, and unification in, the more fundamental demonstrative inference?

If it were not for the initial distance between the actual consciousness of men and the truth of the Hegelian system, there would be no need for the separate descriptive proofs. They are only interpretative aids toward understanding the significance of our spiritual efforts at elevation. Since we have to make a beginning in our quest of the absolute, it is bound to be one-sided, abstract, and hence pluralized in several descriptive approaches. The human mind must begin partially, following now the lead of contingency, now that of purpose, and now that of the unconditioned concept. All these arguments are necessary, and yet neither individually nor together do they provide the speculative basis which makes the ascent cogent and scientific.

Separate analysis of the descriptive proofs shows that in each case the validity of the argument is presupposed from an independent source. The cosmological argument from contingency is directly dependent upon the Hegelian theory of finitude, since contingency is only the most concrete form of finitude. The inference does not "go" from contingency but simply follows out the inner movement of contingent being as such, observing it overcome its negative condition and pass over into its affirmative opposite: absolute necessity. What lies behind this magical power of negativity is the impetus of absolute spirit, which only becomes contingent in order to recover, at a higher level, its infinite necessity of being. To bring out unmistakably this logical reduction of the cosmological argument to the general doctrine on absolute spirit, Hegel makes a striking reversal of the usual inference from contingent things to God:

> In an ordinary inference, the being of the finite appears as the ground of the absolute: the absolute *is* because the finite *is*. The truth, however, is that the absolute *is* just because the finite is self-contradictory opposition—just because it *is not*. . . . Not because the contingent *is*, but rather because it is a *non*being, only appearance, its being *not* veritable actuality, [therefore] absolute necessity *is*. This is [contingency's] being and its truth.[25]

One does not grasp why the contingent must manifest itself eventually as the absolutely necessary being without already knowing that the unique meaning of contingent, finite being is to be a self-negating appearance of the necessary and infinite spirit. The same logical pattern obtains for the teleological argument, the nub of which is that finite purposes are but manifestations of the purposive striving of absolute spirit, which seeks its own actuality through the organism and human history.

The relation of dependence is even more manifest in the case of the ontological description. Hegel lists two conditions that would make it insuperably difficult to argue from the concept of the absolute to its real being. The first condition is if the sensuous, temporal, perishing things of experience were regarded as true beings; the second is if the concept were taken as an abstract thought, which would be distinct from existing being. The only sure way to remove these obstacles is to assess experiential things and the concept of the absolute by the standard of absolute spirit. From this standpoint, true being is identified not with sensuous appearances but with the absolute, and the latter is taken as pure thought or concept, which productively generates all actuality from its own resources. "The transition from the concept of God to His being must be regarded as an application of the logical course of the objectification of the [absolute] concept."[26] The ontological description merely applies the logical truth of the self-generating power of absolute spirit to give itself objective being and other perfections. If men had a perfect grasp upon the truth of Hegelian logic, they would see that this logic is itself the true ontological proof of the absolute, obviating any need for the descriptive applications.

In answer to the question of what reduces the descriptive proofs to a unified speculative demonstration, Hegel replies that their own inner dialectic brings about the common reduction. Each description is driven by its own partial nature to open the road for the others, and together they bear joint witness to their own logical insufficiency and dependence upon the truth of absolute spirit. Hegelian logic furnishes the unique demonstration, therefore, in its ontological proof of the actuality of absolute spirit.

Hegel is not suggesting the commonplace that proofs of God's existence rest upon a basis in metaphysics. Instead, he maintains that what we ordinarily call proofs of God's existence are not demonstrations at all but only interpretative descriptions and that what they really arrive at is the actuality of absolute spirit, clothed under the religious guise of God. This spells the elimination of natural theology, to the extent that it claims to be a demonstrative philosophy of God and the culmination of a metaphysics distinct from idealistic logic. Its functions are taken over descriptively by Hegel's philosophy of religion and demonstratively by his ontological logic of the absolute. "Logic is thus the metaphysical theology, which considers the evolution of the idea of God in the aether of pure thought" and hence in its philosophically true significance as absolute spirit undergoing development.[27] Hegel allows the traditionally phrased proofs to stand as long as they claim to be no more than hermeneutic exercises or interpretations of our religious mode of elevation to the absolute and hence to belong only to a philosophy of religion. Genuine demonstration does not establish the existence of the transcendent God but the dialectical actuality of absolute spirit.

Thus Hegel's reply to Kant is even more challenging and radical than it seems at first glance. Hegel denies that the other two proofs are simply reducible to the ontological one, taken in a descriptive sense. Yet he defends the validity of them all, to the extent that they permit a common reduction to the central principle of his own logic, which is itself the ontological proof in the demonstrative sense. However, this manner of vindicating the proofs means that their real cogency comes from and refers to the distinctively Hegelian doctrine on absolute spirit. Even Wolff's minimal acknowledgment of God's transcendence and freedom must be eliminated in order to make the case against Kant watertight. Hegel removes the Kantian speculative objections without restoring either a speculatively or a morally grounded theism. His defense is really a substitution of the logic of absolute spirit for any attempts to prove the truth about God's existence.

(5) *Evaluation.* Because the proofs of God's existence must give way before the absolutism of spirit, Hegel does not refute Kant so much as evade him and prove something else. This substitutional approach is governed by his transformation of metaphysics. Hegel makes a radical shift from a metaphysics of being as existent to a metaphysics of absolute spirit and thus to a metaphysics identical with logic. Actuality is no longer proportioned to the act of existing as the supreme perfection of being but to the articulations of pure thought or absolute spirit. Being and existence are only subordinate moments in the course of conceptual development. Hence instead of regarding spiritual actuality as the *supreme* sort of being, Hegel treats it as the *only* true and actual being. Conversely, everything else has truth and being only to the extent that it is a moment or phase within the total process of self-actualizing spirit. Within this ontological logic, there is no firm basis for a nature having the act of being in any other way than as a determination of the absolute. The only kind of participation in being is that of moments within the monistic totality of spirit.

It is this antecedent theory of actuality and participation which leads Hegel to frame the theological dilemma: either retain the God-world relationship and endure the Kantian criticism or accept the Hegelian absolutism. Either there are no relations between the finite and the infinite upon which to build a speculative philosophical knowledge of God, or the relation is specified by dialectical monism and yields knowledge of absolute spirit. If the absolute spirit and its aspects alone constitute genuine actuality and knowable connections, then theism is tantamount to placing finite things beyond the pale of actual being and placing God beyond the range of knowledge. The theist must draw the straight, thick line down the orbit of being and then admit, with Kant, that the line has reared itself into an unscalable wall, preventing any speculatively valid inference to the infinite being.

Yet instead of either accepting the dividing line or wiping it out with a dialectical stroke, one can altogether refuse the tyranny of this misleading metaphor and make a fresh approach to the relation between God and finite things. They are not distinct from each other in the same external, spatial way that bodies in different places are distinct. Where actuality and existential being are proportioned, a finite thing can have the act of existing in itself, as actuating its nature in its own distinctive way rather than being a phase of the one absolute spirit. The finite existent is both distinct in being from God and totally dependent upon His causal activity and intimate presence for its entire being. The distinction of the finite being from God is based neither upon a barrier between them nor upon the function of finitude as the absolute's own state of otherness. It is grounded in the fact that the finite thing receives its act of existing in a causal way, as composing with its nature, whereas in God the act of existing is uncaused and is simply identical with His nature.

It is this reception of the existential act into a distinct nature which constitutes simultaneously the actual being of the finite thing, its distinction from the infinite being, and its need for a constant causal dependence upon God. The finite thing is not actual by reason of any separation from God or any modal determination of God but precisely by causal dependence for its nature and its act of existing upon the creative action of God. Its own distinctive actuality is our chief assurance of God's causal presence within it. In this discovered causal immanence, our reasoned knowledge of God finds a foundation. The finite existent raises no wall and hence demands no dialectically changing absolute. It only solicits us to seek the source of its being in an unlimited, existing cause, which is intimately and constantly operative within it.

The inadequacy of Hegel's theological alternative is also apparent from his remarks about the nature of proof. He notes that proof renders explicit certain connections. They are of four sorts: a purely external connection, such as the accidental union of bricks in a wall; an empirical bond, resting upon probable, scientific hypotheses; an essential and necessary one, which is nevertheless distinguished from the actual order, such as the mathematical relations; and a connection that is essential, necessary, and also regulative of actual being. Hegel constructs the fourth type of relation out of his theory of infinite spirit, as determining the finite moments of actuality within itself.

But none of these connections covers the dependence-in-being which is established by the causal communication of existence from the infinite, subsisting existent to finite beings. It is not an external relation, since the finite thing depends, in its most intimate, constitutive principles of being, upon its primary cause. It is indeed a bond which can be ascertained from our experience of finite things, but it reveals itself through a causal demonstration from their existent being and not through a physical hypothesis. Finally, the connection is based neither upon ideal mathematical relations nor upon a movement within the infinite being. It concerns actual beings, whose composite and caused way of existing indicates that they are not the same as the infinite being rather than that they are aspects of its own state of otherness. This existential-causal connection cannot be subsumed under the ontological type of proof proposed by Hegel, and neither can it be reduced to the other connections which come under Kant's criticism. Hence this connection is grasped only through an experiential and nonontological proof. By the same token, it leads the human knower to the truth about the existence of God rather than to the desperate resolve upholding the theory of absolute spirit.

Hegel calls finitude a stubborn category, yet the real stubbornness lies not in the category of finiteness but in the finitely existing beings. They resist reduction to the status of developmental phases within absolute spirit, since their entire actuality signifies a distinct-but-dependent way of existing. Hegel's purifying and long-range preparing of finite things is, in fact, a substitution of a logical determination for an existential act. What renders finite existents so stiff necked in the face of the Hegelian logicizing and relativizing process is nothing less than their own intrinsic principles of being, which refuse to be transmuted into ideal categories. Hegel's dialectic about finitude is poles removed from the way of existing of the finite things themselves. The two conditions enumerated by Hegel himself as subverting his ontological proof—actual existence under temporal, sensuous, contingent conditions and distinctness of the act of being from the act of knowing—are fulfilled by finite beings, with superb indifference to the resulting inconveniences for his system. The subversion of the Hegelian theory of absolute spirit coincides with the very act of existing of the composed, finite things.

The internal integrity of finite things is respected by the a posteriori theistic inference, since it does not proceed by way of dissolving finite existents or relativizing them into collapsing moments in the career of absolute spirit. The Hegelian contrast between the absolute and the relative is solidary with his dialectical monism and cannot be transferred to a philosophically alert theism. Not the shadowy, illusory, untrue, and negative character of the finite being but its own true and actual being, its own positive act of existing, leads the human mind to the truth about God's existence. There is no need to relativize the finite world and smuggle in the absolute spirit as its only true being, once the composite and caused way of existing is firmly acknowledged as the genuine, distinctive actuality of limited things. Instead of being relativized away into determinations of the absolute, these things refer causally to their independently existing source. Between a monistic relativizing and a causal referring, there stand all the differences which Hegel himself recognizes between the doctrine of absolute spirit and that of the existence and causal action of God.

4. PHILOSOPHY OF HISTORY AS "THEODICY"

Hegel's conception of history is philosophical in a double sense. It is not the same as the empirical study of human events but is a reflective reconstruction of the empirical findings. Yet it does not receive its interpretative principles from divine revelation and hence is not a theology of history in the tradition of Augustine and Bossuet. Neither an empirical nor a theological approach, the Hegelian philosophy of history is, rather, an extension of the general theory of absolute spirit into the realm of human, temporal happening. It is a reflection upon the pattern and goals which absolute spirit must follow at that critical stage in its progress when human consciousness is being organized under the social forms of a people, a state, and an age.

Hegel admits that his treatment of history is a priori in a threefold sense.[28] It supposes that the historical process has an essential and actual end, that this end is operative through a necessary law of events, and that the aim and law of history are rational or philosophically accessible. Such apriorism does not mean that the philosopher of history can be tolerant of shoddy research, arbitrary judgment, or a purely subjective partiality resting on personal bias. However, there is a partiality for the truth about history which the philosopher cannot banish without also abjuring his own proper function. Yet the task of establishing the actual nature, pattern, and goal of historical process does lie beyond the competence of the historian, and even the philosopher of history, who comes to his task unequipped with Hegelian logic. Hegel's philosophy of history is a priori in the sense that, for its truth and demonstrative cogency, it depends on the basic logic of absolute spirit.

The doctrine on absolute reason in history takes the form and rank of a "theodicy."

Our intellectual striving aims at recognizing that what eternal wisdom *intended* it has actually *accomplished,* dynamically active in the world, both in the realm of nature and that of the spirit. In this respect our method is a theodicy, a justification of God, which Leibniz attempted metaphysically, in his way, by undetermined abstract categories.[29]

Leibniz ultimately failed because he kept the being of God distinct from the historical process, from the finitude, evil, and error in history. Hegel's absolute spirit does not merely hover over history and finite frailty; it lives and develops by means of them. In the doctrine of divine providence, the religious mind has a dim perception of this truth but misinterprets it by retaining the unconditioned transcendence and freedom of God. To make the passage from a theology to a philosophical theodicy of history means primarily to view historical process as the self-realizing of absolute spirit through human consciousness and social life. In philosophical perspective, history is not the autobiography of God but the autobiography of absolute spirit: *historia sive spiritus infinitus in fieri.* Hence, literally speaking, Hegel's philosophy of history is not a "theo-dicy," or justification of God, but a "pneumato-dicy," or justification of absolute spirit in its natural and historical growth.

The consequences of this view of history can be seen in the special problems of freedom, evil, and time. Hegel wants to present history as the growth of freedom without sacrificing the rigor of his demonstrative science. Hence he redefines freedom, with Spinoza, to consist in the necessary self-determination of the absolute concept. Historical process promotes freedom, in the peculiarly Hegelian sense that historical becoming is regulated wholly internally by the necessary laws of absolute spirit and tends toward the total actualization of the essence of spirit. This sort of freedom is the internal spontaneity of absolute reason as it works out the exigencies of its own nature without any alien hindrances. Historical actions are carried out by human individuals, but the latter are historically effective only as being the living instruments of infinite spirit and the unwitting victims of its cunning. While individuals pursue their private interests with passionate intensity, the real substance of history is determined with perfect necessity and foresight by rational spirit. This conception of freedom still permits a demonstrative philosophy of history, since it rests on the spontaneous necessities of the absolute rather than on divine and human free choice.

A pneumatodicy justifies the absolute spirit's development in the world, especially in view of the presence of evil. Taking a point of departure in Schiller's statement that world history is the world's court of judgment, Hegel offers a principle for justifying every historical event.[30] If one grants that world history is the same as the self-actualizing of absolute spirit, then every event is an aspect in the total process. All historical happenings are judged to be phases in the march of the absolute, and this judgment is also their justification. At least they are partially justified, since their inner significance is to contribute in some measure to the development of infinite reason in its historical dialectic.

But the justification is never a complete vindication of an event, precisely because of its particular and one-sided character, its only partial contribution to the actuality of freedom. Hegel does not want his pneumatodicy to mean a surrender of ethical standards but, rather, their more rigorous and comprehensive use. Full justification belongs only to the historical process as a whole, and in this judgment a perfect reconciliation is made with all the defects, errors, and evils of our historical experience. They are all aspects of finitude, necessary negative moments in the dialectical growth of reason. In Hegel's hands, the older theodicy is converted into philosophy of history because the latter definitively replaces the opposition between God and moral evil by a totality, within which evil is a justified episode in the temporal evolution of the absolute.

Time undergoes a similar transformation within this absolutism of history. The certainty and completeness of the philosophical judgment on history are guaranteed by the knowledge that infinite reason is purposive and that its purpose is already actualized and not merely intended. Yet Hegel also holds that real progress is made in the realm of the human spirit, as distinguished from nature, and hence that temporal events are in the genuine process of realizing the divine plan. Here, at the historical plane, he is again encountering the abiding problem of how to combine meaningfully the complete actuality of absolute spirit and its development as our historical experience. "The final purpose of the world is accomplished, no less than ever accomplishing itself. . . . It need not wait upon us, but is already by implication, as well as in full actuality, accomplished."[31] Our interest and passion, as finite agents, are nourished upon the illusion that the historical plan still remains unaccomplished. For the Hegelian philosopher of history, however, the purpose of historical striving is both present in complete actuality and ever seeking to realize itself through the imperfect events.

Having replaced the Lord God of history by history itself as the absolute spirit in temporal consciousness and social forms, Hegel had to accept the attendant paradoxes. Human agents are free and justified and yet they are also victimized in their work; time is real and yet it is an illusion; history makes genuine progress and yet its task is already accomplished, in actuality as well as intention. Whether these statements express the dialectical structure of the actual in its temporal dimension or only the bitter consequences, for history, of an explosive logical concept depends upon one's prior appraisal of the doctrine of absolute spirit, of which they are the fruit in this area. In any case, Hegel's philosophy of history is a theodicy and vindication of providence only in the sense that the justice and the foreknowledge being defended are qualities of absolute spirit in its own temporal unfolding.

5. FROM RELIGION TO PHILOSOPHY

In one of his earliest fragments, Hegel described Greek religion as the hand of beautiful, free imagination, strewing flowers over the impenetrable veil which shields divinity from our gaze. Although he subsequently came to rank Christianity (or his philosophical restatement of it) higher than Greek religion, he never modified his opinion that the religious viewpoint essentially fails to remove the veil concealing the nature of divinity. Only philosophy can make this ultimate penetration and gaze upon the godhead in the splendor of its own form of being. For only philosophic thought grasps the absolute as pure spirit, reconciling within itself all the dualisms of concept and being, finitude and infinity, temporal change and eternal actuality.

In his mature system, Hegel explains the philosophic annulment of the religious outlook along two main lines. Phenomenologically, or in function of human experience, his main clue is found in "the death of God." Ontologically, or in reference to the systematic stages of the absolute concept, he formulates it as the problem of giving adequate formal expression to the content of absolute being.

Hegel never tires of reflecting upon the famous line from Luther's choral announcing the Good Friday message that God is dead.[32] He develops this recurrent theme at three levels of meaning: cultural, dialectical, and speculative. The cultural import of the death of God is that effective belief in God is withering away in the Western world. Hegel points to the predominance of economic motives in modern society, to the universal discrediting of proofs of God's existence, and, above all, to the way in which both pietists and deists have isolated God from the world. Dusk is rapidly falling upon the Christianly inspired culture of the West, which has made the idea of God abstract, ineffective, and unreal. Where belief in God still lingers, He is regarded as an estranged God, literally a stranger to the concrete regions where all our interests lie. This banishment of God from the experienced world is the root of our cultural malaise, our sense of despair, abandonment, and absurdity, as Nietzsche and some of the later existentialists will also describe it.

In dialectical terms, Hegel seeks to secularize the Christian evangel, which proclaims the creative worth of suffering and death. Philosophically interpreted, the Christian appreciation of God's death on the cross means that the dialectical process always includes the antithetic moment of negation, separation, estrangement from oneself and that the outcome is a richer form of life. But that which Christian theology reserves for Christ is extended by Hegel into the essential law of the absolute. The death of God is an obscure, religious presentiment of the properly philosophical truth that absolute spirit must undergo self-diremption and externalization in finite forms before it can achieve its full self-possession.

The most radical meaning for God's death is that the God of religion must finally give way before the absolute of Hegelian philosophy. The death of God is a speculative Good Friday—a crisis affecting the metaphysical foundations of philosophical and religious theism—and the resurrection which it heralds is the new life of Hegel's own speculative system. The human mind must pass through and beyond the stage of belief in the personal, transcendent God, moving onward to the philosophy of absolute spirit, where human life is absorbed into the divine totality. This surpassing of the theistic position is inherent in the dialectical movement of the absolute itself, since it cannot complete its total return to itself through human consciousness as long as that consciousness persists in retaining the theistic distance between man and God.

The circle of vital development is not completely rounded out until men come to recognize that absolute knowledge "is not merely [our] intuition of the divine, but the self-intuition of the divine [spirit] . . . spirit knowing itself in the shape of spirit," and hence until men overcome the theistic repugnance to a dialectical identification between the finite and the infinite.[33] Only the Hegelian philosophy embodies this absolute knowledge in its proper scientific form, since it alone identifies man's highest knowledge *about* the absolute with the absolute spirit's own perfect *self*-knowledge. Since theism stands in the way of the essential identity between consciousness and its highest object, philosophy must regard God as forever a dead God and must seek the living actuality only in the one absolute self or spiritual totality of finite and infinite being. Only then is the religious impulse toward self-transcendence given a thoroughly immanent interpretation and realization free from all illusions of theistic personal distinctness.

The same conclusion can be reached in terms of the dialectical system. The highest stages in the spirit's effort at self-recovery are art, religion, and philosophy.[34] They constitute the final triad, in which art and religion are elevated and transformed into the philosophical system. Their agreement consists in having the same content and goal: absolute spirit as the supreme actuality. Despite the common content, however, these disciplines are sharply differentiated and hierarchically ordered by virtue of their form or way of embodying the absolute. Art seeks to express it in a sensuous form, while religion uses the medium of pious feeling and representative-pictorial thought. These are inferior ways of apprehending and expressing the absolute, and they are therefore subordinated to philosophy. The latter builds upon art and religion, but it also transforms them in accordance with its own dominating conception of spirit. Only philosophy grasps the absolute under the perfectly adequate form of pure thought or the rational concept, since here alone the content and the form of the absolute completely coincide. That which the artistic and religious minds present in a symbolic and veiled way is manifested in its true nature by philosophy. The gap between content and form is closed only by the philosophical doctrine that the absolute is the one living spirit and true being. It alone assures us that the absolute has its being in and through thought and that the absolute spirit is our own true self.

Hegel is not merely remarking that religion uses metaphor to communicate its ideas. His point is that there is a complete identity of content between religion (including its highest state, Christianity) and philosophy. Christianity as the religion of revelation does not use metaphor to convey a distinctive knowledge surpassing, at least in part, the scope of philosophical reason. On the contrary, Christianity is itself a metaphorical way of expressing the unique philosophical truth, and that alone. At all levels, religion is an exoteric metaphysics for the masses of people who cannot appreciate philosophical concepts but who need the content of philosophy in digestible, albeit essentially unsatisfactory, form.

Philosophy of religion performs a dehusking operation on the religious elevation of soul to God, revealing its kernel to be the wholly immanent relation of the finite determination of absolute spirit to the living totality. Hegel's attitude toward religion, especially toward Christianity, depends upon whether or not it submits gracefully to the proposed transmutation. To the extent that it resists dialectical purification, the antipathy between religion and philosophy remains in full force. What Hegel incorporates into his system is a philosophical surrogate for Christianity, a figurative way of using dogmatic terms to express his own systematic concepts. For instance, divine personality is allowed, but only on condition of connoting the concrete, universal spirit of dialectical monism. Creation is treated as a symbolic representation of the eternal production of thought-forms and material contents, as a popular way of stating that the absolute wills the world by becoming it. The bond of love unites the finite with the infinite spirit, but the infinite spirit is itself the community of finite agents in their dialectical identification.

The great stumbling block to the complete philosophical reinterpretation of religion is the religious mind's stubborn adherence to God. This is correlative to the stubbornness of finite beings concerning their own distinctive, nontransmutable actuality. As long as the finite individual stresses its irreducible nature and its nonidentity with the purely actual being, it remains at the level of unpurified religion and unreconstructed theism. God is nothing more than the inadequate religious version of the absolute, the way in which the finite mind pictorially represents the absolute and its own relation to the absolute. The transition from religion to philosophy requires one to forego any claim that the doctrine of a transcendent, freely creating God is unconditionally true in form, as well as content. Since the whole fabric of his system is at stake, it is understandable why Hegel should be so intensely preoccupied with showing that God is simply the symbolic expression for absolute spirit, in that the finite mind has not yet reached the philosophical plateau of rational or dialectically monistic knowledge about the relative and the absolute.

Hegel often denies that his philosophy is pantheistic. He distinguishes between a vulgar pantheism and a more sophisticated sort.[35] The popular type of pantheism simply identifies God with the empirical world of things taken in their ordinary being. Hegel ridicules this position as an "all-godism," since it divinizes finite things without first relating them to the absolute. As for the philosophical pantheism of Spinoza and the German idealists, Hegel criticizes the way in which it unites the absolute with finite things. His opposition is aroused, not by the pantheists' identification of the finite world with the absolute, but by the manner in which they explain the identification. Since none of his predecessors apprehend the absolute precisely as a dialectically developing spirit, they give only a static account of its unity with finite things and of our knowledge of it..Hegel opposes pantheism precisely as a static, nondialectical identity between the world and the absolute and as encouraging a merely intuitive faith in the absolute. Moreover, "*pantheism*" retains too many overtones of the theistic premises about God and the world to permit Hegel to accept the name for his system. His monism of absolute spirit and its dialectical identity with finite things, as the partial determinations of infinite life itself, is a distinctive position. It makes a much more radical departure from theism than do the vulgar and philosophical forms of pantheism.

Whether the absolute spirit enjoys the perfection of consciousness, apart from the conscious strivings of the finite spirit, remains an unclarified issue in Hegel.[36] The entire reason for determining itself in finite shapes lies in the need of the infinite spirit for achieving consciousness through human rational reflection. Finite consciousness, developing in all its cultural, societal, and scientific forms, provides the material for realizing absolute spirit, the living instrument whereby infinite spirit grasps its own nature as rational thought. The systematic, reflective actuality of the absolute is achieved in and through the purposive growth and aspiration of human consciousness to surpass its present finite condition. Yet the absolute is also in eternally complete possession of its own nature as pure thought.

In the single concept of absolute spirit, Hegel tries to join Aristotle's description of the prime mover, as pure thought thinking itself in an eternally self-sufficient act, with the modern idealist stress on the immanence of all living process in the absolute. He even appeals to the Christian dogma of the Trinity, which he interprets as identifying the eternal generation of the Word with the temporal creation of the finite world. But he fails to provide reasonable grounds for ruling out the persistent subsequent inference that one member of the proposed synthesis between the eternal and the temporal is superfluous and illusory. Either eternal consciousness is sufficiently actual in itself and reduces the temporal process of nature and man to an illusory play of forms, or there is a total reduction of the absolute to the human spirit, which alone is truly actual in its natural setting. Upon this dilemma of an absolutism of infinite spirit versus an absolutism of man-in-nature, the Hegelian system founders and splits asunder. The story of this shipwreck is, at the same time, the history of the problem of God during the last century and a quarter.

The paradox of post-Hegelian speculation about God has been the rapid appearance of atheist, finitist, and personalist philosophies. Following so closely on the heels of an idealism which exalted the divine, the infinite, and the impersonal, these new movements seem to involve a complete reversal of the previous trend and, indeed, to furnish a genuine instance of historical discontinuity. However, a closer inspection reveals that these fresh conceptions depend in part upon other intellectual movements of the nineteenth century and in part develop some of the conflicting strains in Hegel's own thought. The Left Wing Hegelians are certainly encouraged by Hegel's ambivalence about the absolute actuality to eliminate infinite spirit and to absolutize human nature and social life in its stead. Atheism is also provoked in response to the threat against ordinary human values contained in the Hegelian analysis of time and finitude. Similarly, the germ of a finite God, subject to becoming, is already contained in the Hegelian theory of the life-process of the absolute, even though it also requires the soil of evolutionary thought in order to flourish. By way of specific opposition, Hegel has also influenced the subsequent emphasis upon a faith-approach to God and upon free, personal, and existential relations between God and man. His shift from God to absolute spirit overshadows more than a century of investigation into the problem of God and man, even though his successors often attribute to God the consequences of Hegel's absolutism of spirit.

Chapter VIII

THE EMERGENCE OF ATHEISM

ATHEISM has had a long and venerable history. It is one of the intellectual and practical possibilities permanently open for adoption in making one's general interpretation of the universe. Yet this outlook is one of the most elusive to define, since it usually has a quite relative signification. Perhaps the broadest meaning assignable to atheism is: *a denial of the prevailing conception of God or the divine*. But since this conception can shift from age to age, there can be a corresponding shift in the meaning of atheism. Sometimes the relative atheist is secretly moved by an awareness that the accepted view of God is unworthy of designating the highest value or that it entails consequences running contrary to his experience and sense of human dignity. Such an attitude is not too far removed from a critical and reconstructive theism, which seeks to replace a thoroughly misleading view of God with one that is relatively adequate. Indeed, the term "atheist" has been applied to Anaxagoras for criticizing the Greek religious notion of the gods, to the early Christian Fathers for attacking pagan polytheism, and to Spinoza for relating God to the world in an unorthodox fashion. The term is being used inappropriately in such instances, since they concern a question of conflict between different conceptions of God rather than a total denial of God.

Historical attempts have been made, however, to achieve an unequivocal and absolute type of atheism, to eliminate God under whatever form of doctrine that may be proposed. In studying these attempts, it is helpful to employ the distinction between the philosopher's intention of establishing an absolute atheism and the actual extent of his rejection of God. For although the absolute atheist aims in principle at discrediting every theory of God, his criticism rests in fact upon a consideration of a few prominent theories about God which are in the forefront during his lifetime. The present chapter deals with a group of post-Hegelian thinkers whose intention is to undercut the concept of God in an uncompromising way and thus to secure an absolute atheism. The extent to which this ambitious aim is actually conditioned by, and restricted to, the special climate of empiricism and absolute idealism represents the margin of discrepancy between intent and achievement of a universal critique of God and hence the opportunity for a fresh consideration of the issues.

The nineteenth century marked the full-bodied emergence of an atheism which aimed at the unconditional elimination of God from our accepted convictions.[1] In previous ages, atheism was rarely espoused in public by major thinkers and was regarded as a destructive position. During the post-Hegelian era, however, it was explicitly and openly held by several leading minds, who gave it a measure of intellectual respectability and even popular currency. This they succeeded in doing by associating atheism with certain major trends in our scientific, cultural, and moral life. Instead of remaining a negative and sterile position, atheism was presented as a constructive component in the scientific and humanistic trend of modern society. Obviously, such a striking reversal was not the singlehanded work of a few philosophers. Even within the philosophical tradition there were some long-range preparations for atheism in certain aspects of skepticism, the Enlightenment, and other currents. There were also some strongly favoring conditions in the scientific, cultural, and social spheres. Nevertheless, it required the technical contributions of a group of philosophers to interpret the tendencies in other fields and to provide a detailed theoretical basis for atheism.

The present attractiveness of the atheistic outlook is not the product of a single massive system; it is the convergent effect of several philosophies. Despite rather sharp disagreement on other issues, these philosophies all concur in regarding absolute atheism as a liberating doctrine for both speculative inquiry and the management of practical affairs. They make common appeal to the dominant motives of humanism and naturalism in defense of the article of belief that there is no God. However, each of the atheistic thinkers presents his position with a unique accent. Feuerbach draws up a humanistic indictment of the Hegelian absolute, inviting all friends of our finite, sensuous mode of being to remove God as a disintegrating principle. Marx's stress is laid upon the necessary opposition between belief in God and effective control over the forces of nature and society. With Nietzsche, the ontological implications of evolutionary theory are combined with a totally immanent set of moral values, so that theism takes on the aspect of an unreal and fundamentally immoral stand. Dewey and the school of American naturalism offer methodological and metaphysical reasons for simply withdrawing interest and energy from any illusory realm beyond nature and for concentrating exclusively upon our this-worldly tasks and goals. Apart from these four main tendencies selected for analysis here, one must also recognize the contributions to the common cause made by Comte, the atheistic wing of existentialism, and logical positivism.

1. FEUERBACH'S HUMANIZING OF THE HEGELIAN ABSOLUTE

A few years before his death, Hegel counted among his students in Berlin a young ex-theologian, Ludwig Feuerbach (1804–1872). Feuerbach had turned to Hegel in 1824, after having been disappointed by the compromises which theologians like Schleiermacher were making between human freedom and dependence on God, the canons of reason and the demands of faith. Even in the leader of German idealism, however, Feuerbach was unable to find a satisfactory resolution of these tensions. In fact, the more he heard Hegel discourse about the manifestations of the absolute idea in human reality, the more he wondered how this idealistic view of man could be reconciled with the biological and physical reports on man. Out of the deeply skeptical mood which this difficulty generated, Feuerbach gradually evolved a philosophy which he recommended as being more in conformity with the scientific spirit of the nineteenth century, even though for that very reason it was also highly critical of Christian theology and Hegelian philosophy.

In the short span between 1839 and 1843, Feuerbach produced four basic works defining his position toward Christianity and Hegelianism, as well as charting a new course of philosophy in a scientific age.[2] He estimated with shrewd perceptiveness that the philosophical future belonged to a standpoint combining humanism with naturalism. But he added the qualification that, to open the way for a naturalistic humanism, the God of Christianity and the absolute of Hegel had to be removed. It is chiefly because of Feuerbach's way of posing the problem of mind and nature that atheism has become a defining characteristic of many humanisms and naturalisms during the past one hundred years. Although this negative defining note eventually came to be regarded as a universally valid, even unquestionable, point of departure, it was, in its original formulation, closely dependent upon the special set of intellectual difficulties inherited by the first generation of Hegelians of the Right and Left.

Feuerbach advances the historical thesis that the main work of modern thought is to humanize God. Protestantism concentrates upon God's significance for human salvation; pantheism encloses God completely within nature; empiricism judges God by the standard of human practicality; idealism treats both God and nature as aspects of a single spiritual whole. Hegel is the apex of this humanizing tendency, but, unfortunately, he lacks the courage to spell out the inevitable conclusion, which would consist in reducing everything superhuman to man and everything extranatural to nature. His system falls short of this ultimate reduction by retaining absolute spirit. Feuerbach regards his own special vocation to be the thorough humanization and naturalization of absolute spirit.

To carry out his project, Feuerbach accepts Hegel's position up to a certain point and then inverts the dialectical relations which he has temporarily conceded. Thus it is indispensable for him to allow Hegel's claim of being the culmination of the entire history of philosophy of

God. Through this tactical admission (in which he is followed by the other exponents of atheism),. Feuerbach can avoid the troublesome problem of philosophical pluralism on the part of positions claiming to resist incorporation into the Hegelian system and can then regard his critique of Hegel as a definitive critique of every other way of viewing God, man, and nature. Another important issue, where he is extremely anxious to admit the Hegelian reasoning as conclusive, is the relation between God and absolute spirit. Acceptance of their fundamental identity enables Feuerbach to visit upon theism and every form of Christianity the inconveniences which he will point out in the theory of absolute idealism.

Assuming the sameness of content between theism and the philosophy of absolute spirit, it follows that "the secret of speculative philosophy [is] theology."[3] In Hegel's hands, this identity means that the doctrine on God is a preliminary phase of the controlling doctrine on absolute spirit, but in its Feuerbachian form, it means, conversely, that there is an essential dependence of the doctrine of the absolute upon that of God. Historically and genetically considered, the Hegelian system is nothing more than the ultimate refuge and rationalizing support of theism and Christian theology, the last great attempt to restore Christian dogma under a philosophical guise. Although Hegel does remove the separateness of the Neo-Platonic One and the personal transcendence of the Christian God, he still tries to engulf the finite in the infinite, the human in a suprahuman spiritual nature. If Hegel depreciates time, history, and sensuous being, it is only a sign of the theological origin which vitiates his thought.

Clearly enough, the focus of criticism must shift from the philosophical absolute to the theological God and its basis in human needs, in accordance with Feuerbach's complementary principle that "the secret of theology is anthropology." Here he employs the psychogenetic method to break down the claim of Christian theology and theistic philosophy (which he always couples together as "theology") to be concerned with independent reality. Psychogenesis is a technique for tracing the doctrine on God back to certain drives of human nature itself. The theistic mind thinks that it is dealing with the real order, whereas it is only engaged in objectifying the human aspirations and images which constitute the stuff of religion. Thus Feuerbach makes a twofold reduction: first, of absolute idealism to theism; second, of theism to our subjective religious dispositions. His point is that speculation about God or absolute spirit is not merely in harmony with our subjective wishes but is nothing more than a hypostasization of them.

In investigating the essence of religion, Feuerbach seeks to illuminate the mental process which provides the entire content of doctrine about God. He admits that the trail was originally blazed by Hegel when the latter explained the proofs of God's existence in terms of a religious elevation of soul. The germ of atheistic humanism was latent in the Hegelian philosophy to the extent that it remained curiously ambivalent about the nature of the pure thought or spirit underlying theistic inference and religious aspiration. Although Hegel himself insisted upon surpassing man in the march toward self-conscious absolute spirit, he also referred to historical development as manifesting the essence and freedom of humanity, as realizing the universal divine nature of man. Feuerbach simply radicalizes the anthropological implication of spiritual and historical life by removing its reference to anything beyond the human essence.

> If, therefore, the old [Hegelian] philosophy said: "only the rational is true and actual," then contrariwise the new philosophy says: "only the human is true and actual." For only the human is the rational: *man the measure of reason....* The *absolute* to man is his own nature.[4]

It is from Feuerbach that Marx will learn the lesson of identifying the peak of self-consciousness, not with absolute spirit, but with the social self-awareness of men. Far from being destined for incorporation in a richer context, man's nature defines for Feuerbach the *ens realissimum,* the highest reach of being and the solid bottom of all philosophizing.

With this as his criterion, Feuerbach can then explain both religion and God entirely in function of human nature and its tendencies. That which distinguishes man from the brutes is his ability to grasp in reflection not only the individual but the entire species. Man's mind is so filled with his own essential nature that he comes to regard himself as an infinite being. When religion is defined as the awareness of the infinite, this can be understood as an awareness of the infinity of man's own essential being. But at first, the religious mind does not see that the proper object of its worship is the unlimited essence of man. "Man first of all sees his nature as if *outside of* himself, before he finds it in himself. His own nature is in the first instance contemplated by him as that of another being."[5] God is nothing more than this alienated way of viewing the human essence as though it were another being. He is the ideal human essence, which we abstract from empirical individuals and then set apart as a real depository of all the attributes and perfections of human nature. Religion is the very process of projecting our essential being into the ideal sphere of divinity and then humbling ourselves before our own objectified essence. In worshiping God, men are really paying homage to their own relinquished essence, viewed at an ideal distance.

From this analysis, Feuerbach draws the paradoxical conclusion that a fully self-conscious, religious mind must be atheistic. *Homo homini*

Deus: Man is the only true God for himself. As soon as a man pierces the real significance of religion, he can dispense with God or the absolute spirit and devote himself to cultivating the potentialities of his own essential being. The only reason for which he ever splits up his being into the empirical individual and the ideal maximum is that the perfections of human nature are jeopardized by actual conditions in nature and society. The miseries of actual existence lead him to yearn after a more perfect condition, to picture this condition as an ideal essence, and, finally, to objectify that essence as an independent, infinite God.

Feuerbach wants to perform a delicate piece of moral surgery, excising the idea of God and retaining the religious attitude to the extent that it fixes our mind and heart upon the perfections of human nature. Having exposed the illusory character of God and absolute spirit, he nevertheless wishes to keep religion within the atheistic framework. Along with the French positivist Auguste Comte, Feuerbach is a pioneer advocate of a purely humanistic and social religion without God. The valid (since it is completely anthropocentric) meaning for religion is to devote oneself to the improvement of interpersonal relations of I-and-Thou among men, based on the exclusively immanent motive of mutual love and sharing in the same essential nature.

Evaluation of the Feuerbachian critique depends in large measure upon one's view of Hegel. The reconstruction of religion on an atheistic foundation depends on the soundness of Feuerbach's two preliminary assumptions: that the Hegelian philosophy recapitulates all others and that the Hegelian absolute spirit is the same in content as God. The acceptance of these two historically questionable premises enables Feuerbach to infer the impossibility of reconciling God with a fully developed humanism and naturalism.

The charge of antihumanism is distilled in Feuerbach's apothegm: "To enrich God, man must become poor; that God may be all, man must be nothing."[6] It is presumed that theism can relate the infinite and the finite only in an antithetic or mutually rivaling way, one in which the divine nature can be glorified only at the expense of human nature. This consequence does indeed follow from the Hegelian dialectic of the relative and the absolute—whenever anything relative is considered in itself and as resisting identification with the absolute—as well as from the estrangement theory of religion. But neither of these theories is to be identified with the theistic view of man and God. Where the infinite being and finite beings are related causally as creator and created, rather than dialectically as absolute and relative, the relationship is not one of rivalry or incompatibility but of diverse ways of realizing the act of existing and other actual perfections of being. God's actuality is manifested not in withdrawing anything from man but in communicating to man his own distinctive actuality. The relation between them is not one of affirmation versus negation but of the diverse actualities proper to causally related existents.

Curiously enough, Feuerbach quotes a well-known sentence from the Fourth Lateran Council of 1215 to the effect that however great the likeness between creator and creature, their unlikeness is all the greater. This does not mean, however, that finite beings are bereft of actual perfections or are utterly lacking in similarity to God. The sense of the proposition is that the distinction between the first cause and its effects is never wiped out by the likenesses admittedly present between them, since God has His being in an uncaused way and finite things always have their being in a caused, derived way. The differences between God and man are founded precisely upon the very perfection in which they are similar, namely, upon their existent actuality, so that the relation between them always remains a causal and analogous one. It is just this permanent retention of both the likeness and the unlikeness between God and man, with respect to their actual perfection, which enables theism to avoid the dire alternative of vindicating human dignity, either through Hegel's dialectical identification of man with the life of the absolute or through Feuerbach's absolutizing of the human essence and destruction of the bond with the transcendent God. A theistic and Christian defense of man's integrity and worth, without requiring a sacrifice of either our finite and intrinsic way of being or our reference to the personal God, is concretely expressed by John Donne.

Man is not onely a contributary Creature, but a totall Creature; He does not onely make one, but he is all; He is not a piece of the world, but the world it selfe; and next to the glory of God, the reason why there is a world. But we must not determine this consideration here, That man is something, a great thing, a noble Creature, if we refer him to his end, to his interest in God, to his reversion in heaven; But when we consider man in his way, man amongst men, man is not nothing, not unable to assist man, not unfit to be relyed upon by man; for, even in that respect also, God hath made *Hominem homini Deum,* He hath made one man able to doe the offices of God to another.[7]

There is a sacred character about the human person and human social relations, considered in their own finite and temporal dimensions, as well as in relation to God. Hence Donne can use the same phrase, *homo homini Deus,* in a usage which both corrects Hobbes' lupine view of interpersonal relations and renders Feuerbach's recourse to antitheism unnecessary on humanistic grounds. In the post-Darwinian era we must inquire more closely into man's relation with nature, but this does not disturb Donne's point about the theistic basis for man's mundane vocation and dignity.

It is worth while to examine the various senses in which Feuerbach claims that man is absolute and infinite in nature. He argues that if finitude is only a euphemism for nothingness, then man is infinite. This conditional argument tells against the Hegelian dialectic of finitude. Outside that restricted context, however, the only warranted conclusion to be drawn is that man is not nothingness or sheer appearance in himself and, consequently, that his being is a thoroughly finite actuality and not a phase within the absolute spirit.

As an extension of the previous thought, Feuerbach sometimes calls man an absolute, in the sense that he is not dialectically deducible from another principle and is not a mere tool of some all-enveloping agency. We are aware that our human powers are perfections and that our actions contribute to our own well-being. This is essentially a protest against any rationalist deduction of man from God and against any idealistic monism of action. Both the protest and the defense offered by Feuerbach are shared by a realistic theism, which also rejects the deducibility and impoverishing instrumentality of finite existents. But Feuerbach thinks that these consequences must flow from every type of theistic philosophy and religion. "Religion of itself, unadulterated by foreign elements, knows nothing of the existence of secondary causes; on the contrary, they are a stone of stumbling to it. For the realm of secondary causes, the sensible world, Nature, is precisely what separates man from God. . . . God alone is the cause, He alone is the active and efficient being."[7] This description is an incautious generalization, which Feuerbach makes on the basis of some reading he had done in the theological controversy over God's concurrence, especially in Bayle's criticism of Malebranche. The denial of efficacy to secondary causes is characteristic of Malebranche's occasionalism, which regards God and man as competitors for the privilege of claiming causal agency and power.

Secondary causes furnish a stumbling block for only two positions, occasionalism and atheistic humanism, since neither can endure the scandal of agents which are both genuinely causal and genuinely dependent upon God. Yet it is this twofold affirmation which realistic theism clearly makes. This theistic approach does not treat natural causes and human agency as barriers but as manifestations of the generosity of the first cause. Since the doctrine of secondary causality upholds the intrinsic power and perfection of finite agents, without being obliged to absolutize the latter, it provides a philosophical means for *deatheizing* naturalistic humanism and preserving its sense of human dignity.

Feuerbach offers several reasons for applying a qualified sort of infinity to man. He repeats almost verbally the Aristotelian formula that the human mind can somehow become all things through a cognitive union. Man is infinite and universal, in the sense of being capable of endless increase in his knowledge, which is not bound down entirely to the initial limits of sensation. This openness of our mind to new truth does not justify Feuerbach's inference, however, that our religious awareness of the infinite is simply an awareness of our own infinite nature. The sort of qualified infinity applicable to us is that of capacity and becoming, not that of perfect actuality, which belongs to God as the goal of our religious search and worship. From the fact that *only man* is a religious animal and has God as an object, Feuerbach argues sophistically that *God is only* an objectification of human nature in its desire for perfection. A comparison is made between God and the proper object of any human power, but from this comparison, it follows only that God retains his own actual being and specifies, rather than explicates, the nature of our mind. What distinguishes us from other animals is the capacity of our mind and will to search after the infinite God, but this is not the same as building our own nature into something infinite in actual perfection.

In a desperate attempt to rule out the ordination of our mind to an infinite reality distinct from ourselves, Feuerbach even risks a tactical dilution of his basic realism of knowledge. He suggests as a general principle that the only object for the human mind is its own subjective nature, treated in objective fashion. In this case, philosophy is only a monologue of reason, discoursing about man's own nature and not about the infinite and independent God. But since the general principle skirts on idealism and undermines the rest of Feuerbach's epistemological attack on Hegel, he qualifies it by observing that at least we begin with subjective imagery and only gradually work out to real sensuous things. Yet if subjectivism is eventually overcome with respect to a knowledge of sensible nature, there is no truly rigorous principle preventing us from extending our knowledge beyond human nature and the sensible world to some assurance of God's existence. In the degree that Feuerbach attacks idealism with an insistence upon our knowledge of real sensuous being in the natural world, he also unavoidably opens a wedge for an experientially founded theism, however disconcerting such a theism appears to a thinker trained to view God only through the spectacles of the Hegelian dialectic.

Feuerbach cements his charge of antinaturalism against a philosophy of God with the help of some fundamental metaphysical propositions.

Truth, actuality, sensuousness are identical. Only a sensuous being [*Wesen*] is a true, an actual being. . . . Space and time are the existential forms of all being. Only existence in space and time is *existence*. . . . All real existence, i.e., all existence which is truly such, is qualitative, determinate, [and hence finite] existence. . . . That which has no effect upon me, has no existence for me. . . . If God is the negation of everything finite, then logically the finite is also the negation of God.[8]

To obtain these definitions of being as being, Feuerbach absolutizes the traits of man and nature. Employing the motto *duce sensu philosophandum esse,* he takes his philosophical lead from what the senses tell us about the natural world. They reveal this world to be finite, spatio-temporal, sensuous, and open to our affective and practical relations. These traits belong inherently to the sensible world and thus provide us with criteria for real being. And since these same traits are not predicated of God, we can conclude both that He is antithetically related to the finite world and that, in fact, He does not enjoy real being. One must choose between nature as a reality and God or absolute spirit as a reality, but the alternative is a perfectly exhaustive one.

This dilemma is forced upon Feuerbach by his own method of constructing a philosophy on a basis of inverted Hegelian propositions. Because Hegel says that only infinite spirt is actual and engaged in temporal process, Feuerbach must counter by saying that only a finite, temporally developing being is actual. Against theism he maintains the infinity of man, but against Hegel he maintains that finite being is the sole reality. The moderate view which our experience recommends, however, is that man is a finite being, with an indefinite capacity for further knowledge and a desire for union with the infinite being.

Feuerbach finds it difficult to avoid exaggeration, since he allows his thought to proceed by way of counterabsolutizing anything which is assigned a subordinate function in the Hegelian dialectic. He does not recognize the difference between vindicating the reality of finite things by showing them *not* to be moments in the dialectical growth of absolute spirit and doing so by *making* them the sole and absolute content of being. The latter procedure is an instance of the fallacy of definition by initial predication; because the real beings which we initially know through sensation are finite and spatiotemporal, actuality is defined as consisting only of finite, spatiotemporal beings. Whether all knowable, real things have these traits cannot be decided by our initial acquaintance with the world but only by the actual outcome of our causal inquiry. On this issue of a metaphysical generalization, Feuerbach permits himself to be distracted by his anxiety that the only way to preserve the integrity of the directly experienced world is to render it a counter-absolute against the Hegelian infinite spirit.

One final trait of Feuerbach's thought is big with significance for the spread of atheism: his exploitation of two aspects of empiricism. He seeks to shift the emphasis of philosophy from idealism and theology to empiricism and the natural sciences. This shift accounts for two aspects of his atheistic argument: its psychological approach and its practical bent. In the Humean tradition, he hails psychology as the first and universal science, of which metaphysics is the secret objectification. This psychologizing of metaphysics leads Feuerbach to reduce the problem of God to that of the psychogenesis of the idea of God. It also underlies his definition of real being exclusively in terms of the defining traits of the direct objects of our experience. Feuerbach even tries to convert the artist's strong feeling for the reality of our sensuous, finite world into the metaphysical principle that this world is the only actual sort of being and that an infinite, spiritual God is incompatible with natural things and our esthetic attitude toward them.

As for the practical orientation of empiricism, it supplies him with an additional argument for atheism. Referring to the focusing of our ordinary practical life and of empiricist analysis upon the finite world, he observes:

It [empiricism in theory and action] does not refuse being to God, i.e., dead, indifferent being, but it does refuse Him the being which proves itself *as being*: active, affective, vital being. It admits God, but denies all consequences which are necessarily bound up with this affirmation. It opposes and gives up theology, yet not on theoretical grounds but out of opposition to, repudiation of, the objects of theology, i.e., from a dark feeling of their unreality. . . . He who concentrates mind and heart solely upon the material, the sensuous, in actual fact refuses its reality to the suprasensuous. For that alone is actual, at least for man, which is an object of real, effective activity.[9]

Feuerbach is arguing that the speculative assent, whether demonstrative or probable, which some empiricist philosophers had previously given to the existence of God is pale, unreal, and incompatible with their working criterion of being. In the theoretical order, we usually demand of a purported reality that it have some active, practical consequences for us and the world. Similarly, we devote our active life to the things we regard as eminently real and worth striving for. But on both of these counts, the affirmation of God's existence is a groundless one and should be withdrawn, out of consistency and honesty.

Feuerbach's reasoning on this score can be taken in the jejune sense that the practical atheist ought to have the courage of his actual commitments and refuse to accord his intellectual assent to a spiritual being whose reality he contradicts with every practical decision. It can also be construed, in a philosophically more significant way, to mean that existential judgments depend completely upon the discovery of practical consequences flowing from a postulated being and that God's existence should be denied for lack of any such observable consequences. In the latter interpretation, Feuerbach is anticipating the pragmatic and instrumentalist conception of truth, which is also invoked by naturalistic atheists and some exponents of a finite God.

Feuerbach is sure that the heart of man is atheistic and that our practical life is essentially the story of man's *Verloren-sein-in-die-Welt*, his total absorption and forlornness in worldly being (a theme which has been richly suggestive to the existentialists). Yet he does not establish the precise point at issue—that practical philosophy must build upon the empiricist attitude as so described and hence that practical engagement in the world is incompatible with a real ordination toward God. Problems concerning the integration of finite goals with a permanent, practical commitment to God inevitably arise for any practical philosophy which does not simply postulate a mutual exclusion between them. But the presence of such difficulties within man's pluralistic experience of goods is not equivalent to an essential antagonism between God and finite values. Our concern with finite projects and controllable things need not rule out a genuine recognition of God as the transcendent, infinite person to whom we must practically relate our freedom, even though there is no question of subjecting Him to our control. The heart which Feuerbach deems to be essentially atheistic is lodged within his own absolutized image of the human essence, not in finite, striving men whose practical freedom can include their relation with God.

2. MARX'S SOCIAL ATHEISM

Writing in 1888, more than forty years after the appearance of Feuerbach's *The Essence of Christianity* (1841) and his other naturalistic treatises, Friedrich Engels still vividly recalled their enthusiastic reception by Left Wing Hegelians. These programmatic statements came just at the opportune moment when Engels needed intellectual assurance about his break with his religious background and when Karl Marx (1818–1883) needed firm guidance toward a naturalistic humanism.[10] Marx possessed by far the keenest speculative mind among the Young Hegelians of the 1840's. He quickly assimilated Feuerbach's arguments against absolute spirit but was disappointed with his predecessor's religious humanism and vague, emotional conception of social activity. Marx brought his own philosophical position rapidly to maturity in a number of manuscripts composed before 1848, that is, before he became fully absorbed with economic problems and the political maneuvering in the international communist movement. It is to the vision of man set forth in these early works that Marxists of all varieties still turn for inspiration and from which they draw an atheistic outlook.

From his study of Epicurus, Feuerbach, and a naturalized Hegel, Marx derived the primary postulate of his thought: the dynamic self-sufficiency of man-in-nature (*das Durchsichselbstsein der Natur und des Menschen*). He indifferently called his standpoint a naturalistic humanism or a humanistic naturalism, depending upon whether he wished to stress the containment of human activity and aspiration within finite nature or the distinctive contribution of human intelligence and work to the natural order. In either emphasis, however, the real coincides completely with the relational totality of man and nature. To insure their dynamic union and mutual ordination, Marx highlighted the crucial function of labor, which is the chief means for humanizing nature and also for naturalizing man. Marx pointed to the transforming power of labor in history as providing ocular proof of finite self-sufficiency. Through his work with others and in a natural environment, man becomes social man, and "here for the first time his natural existence is his human existence and nature has become human for him. Thus, society is the complete essential unity of man with nature, the true resurrection of nature, the achieved naturalism of man, and the achieved humanism of nature."[11] The dialectical meaning of history is a purely immanent and this-worldly one, since all social revolutions tend ultimately toward the realization of the social whole of man-laboring-in-nature. This, then, is the new absolute which Marx offered as a replacement for Hegel's diversion of man to infinite spirit and as a means of rendering Feuerbach's naturalism more sharply social and historical in import.

Granted this social absolute, Marx was bound to seek to eliminate God from philosophy and practical life. He agreed heartily with Feuerbach that the more a man attributes to God, the less he attributes to himself. The God thus indicted was the Hegelian absolute spirit, which was conceived as the only genuine subject in being. In that case, man and nature would be nothing more than mere predicates of this unique, spiritual subject. The entire natural world of things and social relations would be unessential in itself, an objective realm which only expresses absolute spirit in an alienated way. If everything objective were identified with this alienated condition, however, then the only way for this absolute being to remove the alienation would be to subvert the entire objective order. For the Hegelian absolute spirit to overcome its self-estrangement would mean to revoke any distinctive meaning in natural, sensuous being and in objective, social relations. Hence Marx appealed to men's piety toward nature and their humanistic reverence toward cultural achievements as sufficient reasons for the atheistic attitude. His verdict was that henceforth only the halfhearted naturalist or humanist can admit any divine actuality beyond nature and any spiritual principle distinct from human intelligence and labor.

This criticism of God rests on two unspoken premises: that Hegel has reduced the doctrine on God entirely to his dialectic of the absolute and that Feuerbach has reduced God or absolute spirit to a mode of alienation of the human mind and desiring power. In this dual reduction is contained the nerve of Marx's denial of God. The extent of the dependence of his atheistic position upon the intellectual circumstances of the 1840's is not always recognized by those who take Marx, in turn, as a point of departure. Marx often warns against wasting energy upon attacking God and religion, since he regards the antitheistic critique as having been completed in principle by Feuerbach. His own remarks on the subject are intended as mere footnotes to the main text, as a postscript to a critique already achieved in its main points by his predecessor. Marx does not experience any need for a fresh appraisal of God and the religious attitude, since he accepts as almost definitive the exposition and criticism made by Feuerbach. The limiting influence of this special historical situation upon the validity of Marx's atheistic position can be measured by examining his views on the proofs of God's existence and religious alienation.

One notable feature is the paucity of references to the proofs of God's existence. Marx deals formally with them in only two places, both of them in early manuscripts written before his attention turned completely toward the critique of political economy. In notes set down in preparation for his doctoral dissertation, he makes several polemical thrusts at the current vogue for Schelling's version of theism. Against this he quotes, with obvious relish, some of Schelling's earlier pronouncements about the incompatibility between a transcendent God and the moral autonomy and freedom of man. And if the idealists try to shift their acceptance of God back to Hegelian grounds, Marx is ready to point out the weak features in the Hegelian proofs of God's existence.

Specifically, Marx notes four vitiating factors in these proofs. First, he signalizes the paradoxical reversal of the older cosmological arguments: "Hegel has completely reversed these theological proofs, i.e., [he] has rejected them in order to justify them."[12] Whereas theologians used to argue from the real presence of the contingent world to God, Hegel bases his inference upon the unreality of the contingent and accidental traits of experience. This reversal does not rejuvenate the a posteriori proofs; it is their deathblow in an age that is learning to prize finite, contingent things. Second, Hegel's favorite ontological argument is tautologous: *Whatever I represent to myself is an actual representation for me.* If having an effect upon oneself is an index of objective truth, then the most fantastic pagan deity has a good claim upon real being. The only sort of existence involved in the ontological proof is an imaginary one or a conventionally determined one. In the third place, this ontological proof is simply a reflection of human consciousness, since the only thing which exists somehow immediately, upon being thought, is a modification of one's own mind.

Finally, Marx suggests that if his second and third objections are valid, then the proofs manifest only the existence of aspects of human consciousness. "The proofs for God's existence are nothing but *proofs for the existence of the essential human self-consciousness, logical explications of it.*" More precisely, therefore, one should call them proofs of God's nonexistence, since analysis reveals them to be only illusory projections of man's own ideas of himself. One might possibly rescue them by denying that they bear any reference to positive, finite entities, but this would mean proving God from the emptiness, unreasonableness, and badness of man and the world—a mode of inference which any humanistic and naturalistic mind would find intolerable.

In *The Economic-Philosophical Manuscripts* (1844), Marx returns briefly to the same issue, adding a fifth criticism. This one singles out the causal proof, in its popular deistic presentation. The believer in God asks: Who produced the first man and nature as a whole? Marx attacks the very validity of the question, thus anticipating the independent approach of such American naturalists as Woodbridge and Lamprecht.

Whenever you ask about the creation of nature and man, you abstract from man and nature. You presuppose them as not existing and yet you demand that I prove them to you as existing. I now say to you: abandon your abstraction and you will give up your question. Or if you hold fast to your abstraction, accept the consequences. Whenever you think of man and nature as non-existent, regard yourself as non-existent, you who are natural and human. Think not, ask me not—for as soon as you think and ask, your abstraction from the existence of nature and man makes no sense. Or are you such an egotist that you posit everything as nothing, and will yourself to exist?[13]

Hence the question about God as first cause involves a self-refuting process, which relieves one of the responsibility of providing an answer. The very problem of God's existence is impossible to pose, since it entails either the annihilation of the inquirer himself or the abandonment of the abstractive act and thus the silencing of the question about a first cause.

These criticisms afford precious insight into how the problem of God presented itself to Marx's mind. He was acquainted firsthand only with the Enlightenment statement of the causal argument and with the Hegelian proofs. He was also aware of Hegel's transmutation of the argument from contingency, but he failed to correlate this "reversal" with Hegel's subordination of God to absolute spirit. Hence he also failed to see that Hegel's reversal of the inference literally involved a rejection of theism, not an indirect justification of it, according to theism's own meaning and principles. Along with Feuerbach, Marx overlooked the paramount issue of whether God is synonymous with absolute spirit, whether the theistic and absolutistic proofs are simply interchangeable by a reversal process, and hence whether a careful theist can properly base a doctrine of God upon the same nihilating basis required for proof of absolute spirit. A fresh appraisal would stress the incompatibility between theism and an idealism of the absolute and hence would permit recognition of a naturalism and humanism which are not obliged to make a postulatory denial of God.

The central group of Marxian objections concerned the ontological proof, since this was given prominence in the Hegelian philosophy. Marx rightly rebelled against the notion that human self-consciousness is significant only as providing material for the realization of an absolute consciousness. He seconded Feuerbach's appeal to the distance between the dialectical notion of being and real beings, as well as between the concept of absolute spirit and its actuality. His defense of the inalienably finite nature of the human mind and the integrity of sensible, contingent things effectively undermined the ontological proof of absolute spirit. That it did not also furnish Marx with a new perspective on God was due partly to the failure of contemporary theists to understand that the finite world is given sharply opposing valuations by a theism of efficient causation and a dialectical monism.

Unfortunately, the only sort of causal argument familiar to Marx did nothing to clarify this opposition. Any attempt to think away the finite universe, by proceeding backwards over the generations until one reaches the first moment of producing nature and man, is bound to fail. Such a hopeless enterprise stands in contrast to the realistic inference to the first efficient cause. The latter argument does not employ an accidentally ordered series of causes which are in temporal and contingent antecedence to the presently existing things. Hence it does not rest upon a temporal beginning of the world, nor does it require the great feat of visualizing the first moment of creation. We do not argue to a beginning but to a present complete dependence in being. The realistic inference seeks to explain not a series of events trailing away into the vague past but a presently real thing, in the sense that it is finitely existing, changing, or producing change in another present thing. The here-and-now being of the composite existent requires causes that are presently acting in their dependence upon a completely actual and presently existing first cause. As far as the causal inference goes, God is called the "first" cause with respect to His independent existence and activity, not with respect to an initial moment of a time series.

Marx's dilemma is irrelevant for a theistic proof which does not consist in transporting oneself by imagination to the dawn of creation. Instead of either annihilating himself or suppressing the causal question, the individual engaged in the realistic inference to God must ask the question, precisely because he maintains steadily before his mind the present existence of himself and other experienced finite things. The question about God's existence is possible only when the inquiring mind exists, but then this question is not only possible but unavoidable, in view of the given characteristics of the existing man and other beings within his direct acquaintance. The truth of the proposition concerning God's existence depends upon preserving the finite existent in *its* own integrity of being and penetrating into the actual requirement of the first cause of *its* existing actuality.

Revocation of the finite existent would mean the destruction of the evidence for the causal inference to God, just as much as it would mean the elimination of the inquirer. Such a revocation is demanded in the dialectical proof of absolute spirit because of the chasm separating the latter from a causal proof of the existing God. Whereas the beginning of the finite world is an essential part of the absolutist proof, in a theistic philosophy the questions of a beginning through creation and a beginning through a first temporal moment are kept distinct from each other. They are also subsequent to the problem of God's existence as first cause.

In claiming that the inquirer must "be there at the creation of man and the universe," Marx was led astray, both by Hegel's dialectic of a beginning and by Feuerbach's very special use of the term "abstraction."[14] Feuerbach took Plotinus and Proclus to be the prototypes of all theistic reasoning, thus ignoring the historical line of persistent theistic criticism of this school for failing to appreciate the existential significance of God. In Feuerbach's reckoning, however, the Plotinian religious ecstasy, or flight of the alone to the Alone, is one with the speculative proofs of God's existence. Hence Feuerbach interpreted such proofs as requiring an "abstraction" from self and world, an ecstatic annihilation of oneself and everything finite, in order to reach the ineffable One. As further warrant for this interpretation, he pointed to the Hegelian fusion between elevating the soul and proving the absolute, as well as to the idealistic search for a presuppositionless beginning of philosophy. One must empty out the entire content of the finite, sensuous world in order to make such a beginning with the absolute as Hegel demands in his logic and his ontological proof of absolute spirit. Once more, an evacuating "abstraction" of the finite existent is a necessary condition for reaching the absolute.

Taken in these two historically specified senses, an evacuating act of abstraction is indeed required in order to make practical contact with the Plotinian One, lying beyond being and existence, and to make a systematic start with the Hegelian absolute spirit. But neither of these two processes can be identified with what theistic realism does in demonstrating the truth of the proposition about the existence of the transcendent God. This demonstration is a speculative operation and not an ecstatic practical union; it is a culminating phase within a metaphysics of existing being and not a presuppositionless beginning of a system of spiritual monism; it retains finite being in its own actuality rather than dissolving it in an ecstatic or dialectical flight. Hence the Marxian dilemma, based upon the consequences of the abstractive act, does not join proper issue with a demonstration of God's existence as distinct from a flight to the One and a self-recognition of the absolute.

On the theme of religious estrangement, Marx appropriated a good deal from Feuerbach, but he showed a more critical spirit than in the question of God's existence. He was dissatisfied with Feuerbach's attempt to retain a distinction between theology and religion and to construct a humanistic sort of religion without God. Marx forthrightly closed the breach between the theological and religious outlooks, declaring that every sort of religious attitude is an estrangement of some portion of the human essence and hence is detrimental to mankind.

Because of this broadened meaning for religious estrangement, it has been suggested that Marx's philosophy is more precisely antireligious than atheistic and that its antireligious nature stems from the methodological ground of opposing abstract hypostasization rather than from a metaphysical commitment about being.[15] But one cannot say that Marx is antireligious rather than atheistic, as one might well say of Hume that he opposes any distinctive practical religion and yet admits the probability of God. Marx is atheistic in the incisive sense of denying the real existence of any supremely perfect being distinct from the finite world. But he does include his atheism within the wider context of his opposition to religious estrangement, and hence he is atheistic not only because of God's unreality but also because he thinks that acceptance of God alienates a man from himself and nature.

Even stronger, Marx regards belief in God as the most typical and extreme sort of speculative religious estrangement, and for this reason he singles it out for attack. It is true that he also accuses Feuerbach, Bruno Bauer, Arnold Ruge, Max Stirner, and other Young Hegelians of sharing in the religious spirit, even though none of them admit God. Yet this is not because the question of God is unimportant or neutral but because Marx sees in Feuerbach's human essence, Bauer's self-consciousness, Ruge's humanistic state, and Stirner's egoistic individual the lineaments of a cryptodeity and the seeds of a religious worship of God. In Marx's mind, religiousness is specified not only by the method of abstract objectification but also by degrees of kinship with the religious God and the Hegelian absolute spirit. The Marxian critique of religious estrangement must include, as its most characteristic stand, a denial of God and the idealistic absolute (which he never succeeds in keeping distinct).

Still, Marx did not intend merely to reproduce the atheisms of Holbach and Feuerbach. His chief criticism of the former was its purely negative character. Holbach paid so much attention to past belief in God and allowed his thought to be specified so closely by this determinate opposition that Marx referred to Holbachian atheism as merely a negative recognition of God. He approved of Feuerbach's genetic approach to the idea of God but was dissatisfied with his predecessor's vague references to the miseries and wishes of individual man as the birthplace of the idea of God. Marx sought more specific reasons why men have had to project their ideals into another world, and he found these reasons in the oppressive social and economic conditions of life. "Feuerbach therefore does not see that the 'religious temperament' itself is a social product and that the abstract individual whom he analyses belongs to a particular form of society. All social life is essentially *practical*. All the mysteries which urge theory into mysticism find their rational solution in human practice and in the comprehension of this practice."[16] Theism and other manifestations of the religious spirit are nourished by the inhumane conditions of economic, social, and political existence and by the practical desire to shake them off and find peace in a realm which is free from everyday miseries. Man engages in religious estrangement and worship of God as a protest against social tyranny and the inhumane use of material power. It is the method of social, rather than psychological, genesis which finally uncovers the basal motive for abstractly positing and worshiping a God.

At this point, Marx's antitheistic and antireligious position merges into, and subordinates itself to, his critique of political economy. He draws a strict parallel between religion and private property, the former constituting man's theoretical estrangement and the latter constituting his practical estrangement or split with his own reality. That the practical sort of separation of man from his proper nature is the more fundamental and determining "in the final analysis" is one of the major theses in Marx's dialectical and historical materialism. Since theism and religion belong to man's theoretical estrangement, they are not the unconditionally primary issues for Marx.

Marx does not say this to water down his opposition to God and the religious attitude, however, since he regards their removal as essential to any critical and revolutionary movement. Tracing the origin of the idea of God back to our human social needs is an indispensable lesson in the anatomy of estrangement, but it is not sufficient to remove this idea definitively. The complete abolition of every doctrine on God and religion cannot be achieved until there is a practical transformation of society in such a way that none of the conditions which foster belief in a transcendent being remain. Only the revolutionary transformation of society can bring to its full conclusion the process of overcoming human alienation which began with Feuerbach's speculative criticism of God and religion.

The abolition of religion, as the illusory happiness of men, is a demand for their real happiness. The call to abandon their illusions about their condition is a call to abandon a condition which requires illusions. . . . The immediate task is to unmask human alienation in its secular form, now that it has been unmasked in its sacred form. Thus the criticism of heaven transforms itself into the criticism of earth, the criticism of religion into the criticism of law, and the criticism of theology into the criticism of politics.[17]

Hence within the Marxian perspective, theism finds its basic refutation not in speculative analysis but in the practical critique of law and politics and, more precisely, in the social changes consequent upon the latter.

Actual social change will render theism and the religious outlook meaningless and needless within an equitable social order, where life is humanely and naturally ordered.

Marx entertained the lively hope that in the social whole of men-laboring-in-nature, which he envisioned as the goal of historical change, religion would wither away and the question of theism versus atheism would simply become irrelevant. This hope was reasonable enough, granting that man is related to God in the same way that the relative appearance is related to the absolute spirit and that an absolutely necessary dialectic is working itself out in and through human consciousness and history. What was not so reasonable was the uncritical way in which Marx accepted the equation between God and the absolute, as well as the operation of a necessary historical law, even after he had repudiated its mainspring: absolute spirit. Hence his explanation of God in function of the theoretical and practical estrangements constituted a neat dialectical reversal of Hegel's absolute spirit, but it missed coming to grips with the aspects of finite existence which lead men to God. The Marxian method of counterabsolutizing social man-in-nature did not rest upon a thorough reconsideration of the other ways in which human dignity can be defended but only upon an inverted Hegelian "theodicy." For history as the autobiography of absolute spirit, Marx substituted history as the justifying autobiography of absolutized social man.

But Marx's humane insight that man is a root-being, that human existence and acting are not modifications and materials of some wider process, is detachable entirely from the myth of a social absolute and the misleading metaphor of reversing or inverting Hegel's immanent totality. Men can sustain in full intensity the work of humanizing nature and the social world without having to resort to a Marxian reductionism of being and method, without curving their intelligence and desire inward in a closed circle. Human freedom has sufficient strength to remain creatively open and loyal both to our obligations in nature and society and to our venture toward a faithful, loving God.

3. NIETZSCHE AND THE EVANGEL OF GOD'S DEATH

A mighty impetus toward espousing atheism as the noblest human creed came from the pen of Friedrich Nietzsche (1844–1900). He served as the turbulent channel for conveying into our own age the atheistic implications of certain new trends in nineteenth-century science and culture. His interpretations convinced the atheistic wing of existentialism that this is a godless world and induced the other existentialists at least to be very wary of making philosophical statements about God. His influence in this matter reached far beyond professional philosophical circles, just as did the impact of Marx's attack on God and religion.

As a youth, Nietzsche was encouraged toward atheism by reading the books of Arthur Schopenhauer (1788–1860). The latter had argued that the principle of sufficient reason, upon which rested the rationalist proofs of God, applied validly only to particular kinds of reasons and only to particular sensible objects within the infinite series of phenomena. On several counts, Schopenhauer concluded that both the rationalist and the Hegelian use of the principle of sufficient reason to establish the existence of God or absolute spirit was unwarranted.[18] God is supposed to be a nonsensuous being and an absolute or general reason for things, whereas the principle of sufficient reason applies only to sensuous objects and has its real basis only in particular sorts of reasons. Furthermore, we cannot ask about the sufficient reason of the world taken as a whole or about a first reason of becoming for the infinite series of phenomena, since any definite formulation of such questions exceeds our limited capacity. Schopenhauer also blocked off the Kantian access to God by means of practical reason, on the ground that practical reason is without any distinctive content and, in any case, must conform with the general limitations of the principle of sufficient reason. Thus Schopenhauer was professedly atheistic, since he denied the God of Wolff, the moral postulate of Kant, and the absolute reason of Hegel.

Still, he admitted one noumenal entity, the blind and restless cosmic will-to-live, which we can grasp only through an irrational intuition. Since this will is the source of all striving and pain, Schopenhauer counseled men to quell its power, either through esthetic contemplation and altruistic acts or, more radically and permanently, through the ascetic attitude recommended by the Eastern religions and Christianity. He held that the essential message of Christianity is the denial of the world, both in its sensuous aspects and in its inner will toward the increase of life. However, Schopenhauer was curiously reluctant to conclude unqualifiedly that the denial of the will-to-live leads to utter nothingness. He left a loophole open for maintaining that this denial is only the converse side of a new act of affirming the existence of a completely transcendent being. Because of the restriction of the principle of sufficient reason and the evil consequences of the will-to-live, however, Schopenhauer taught that it is beyond the philosopher's competence to make this new affirmation of being. Only the mystics could perhaps do that, but there would be no philosophical means for verifying their assertions.

Although Nietzsche endeavored to seal off even the extraphilosophical possibility of a genuinely transcendent reality, he welcomed Schopenhauer's negative arguments. They gave him the courage to break with his religious past and openly advocate atheism. He hailed Kant and Schopenhauer as supplying the first radical challenge to the optimism of Western culture, with its theistic conviction. The Kantian theory of knowledge effectively questioned whether the human mind can penetrate to the noumenal essence of things and employ the principle of causality to reach God, the supreme noumenal principle. A delaying action in favor of theism was carried on by Hegel, but it was Schopenhauer's glory to topple over the Hegelian system of absolute reason with the opposing view of a purely formal reason and an irrational, cosmic will. What especially aroused Nietzsche's admiration was the bold way in which Schopenhauer took the ungodliness of existence— *die Ungöttlichkeit des Daseins*—to be a palpable, obvious fact requiring no labored defense in our age of positive science and Kantian epistemology. "Herein lies his [Schopenhauer's] complete honesty: unconditioned, frank atheism is precisely the *presupposition* of his setting the problem, as a final and dearly won victory of the European conscience, as the most consequential act of a two-thousand-year training for truth, which ultimately forbids itself the *lie* of belief in God."[19] Nietzsche would like to persuade us to embrace atheism out of sheer honesty and courage to face the truth about being and to see the harsh but unavoidable implication of all the healthy advances in Western culture. When he stated that he himself was an atheist by instinct and taste, he did not mean to rule out all antitheistic arguments but rather to lend them the added weight of scientific inevitability and humanistic liberation.

Like Karl Marx, Nietzsche was fascinated by the myth of Prometheus, hurling his defiant hatred at all the gods. He described his own Promethean atheism as stemming from *hybris,* or an overbearing, passionate pride in human freedom and a resolve to remain true to the earth at all costs. Because this attitude went against the grain of the theistic religious and intellectual traditions, its successful propagation among other minds required a criticism of these prevailing traditions. Nietzsche's antitheistic program was carried out in two stages: an experimental revision of our view of being and knowledge and a dramatic announcement of God's death.

(1) *An experiment concerning the world and truth.* Nietzsche followed the customary pattern of modern atheism, as set by Feuerbach and Marx, by supplying a prophetic image of the philosopher of the future age. According to the outlines limned in *Beyond Good and Evil* (1886), the coming philosopher is to be a tripartite mixture of skeptic, critic, and experimenter. He is to be skeptical about all traditions and absolutes of the past, applying a fearless scalpel to the unexamined convictions favoring the existence of God. Yet he is not to be paralyzed by the indecisiveness of the complete skeptic but is to be a critical moralist using a definite method and standard of values. Above all, however, the philosopher of the future is to engage in intellectual and moral experiments, in harmony with his conviction about the total fluidity of every-

thing. He must be prepared to take a radically new stance toward the world, himself, and God. It is only through introducing a "dangerous perhaps" about the nature of things that the hold of God and a theistically grounded morality can be loosened and finally broken.

To render his metaphysical experiment quite plausible and inescapable, Nietzsche depicts it as the latent consequence of the philosophical and scientific findings of the nineteenth century. In the remote background lies the heritage of Descartes and Hume, both of whom bring man back to the bleak rock of his individual self. Modern man has no choice but to interpret the rest of things through the subjective sampling provided in the individual's probing of himself. Precisely what he finds there is ascertained in the theoretical sphere by Kant and in the practical by Schopenhauer, even though neither thinker fully exploits his discoveries. The only intuitively given factor in the Kantian description of knowledge is the matter of sensation. It is inherently devoid of any definite structure and presents itself merely as a constant flux of impressions, a sheer sensuous manifold lacking in any intrinsic unity, meaning, and value. That this chaotic mass has primarily a striving and desiring character is the main testimony of Schopenhauer. What is given as the stuff of individual experience is not simply a formless flow of sensations but, even more fundamentally, a whirling storm of passions and drives.[20]

Anyone sensitive to the achievements of modern philosophy is obliged to describe the given aspect of individual life as a ceaseless becoming and striving of a sensuous-passional manifold, unregulated by any prior structure and innocent of any inherent, intelligible law or value standard. Judging from our own subjective grasp of the given situation, there is no backdrop of noumenal essence or intelligible world for us to reach. The really real world is nothing more than the sea of becoming with which we are confronted, the undifferentiated and indifferent morass of passional energy which sluices through us. The only general trait it exhibits is the trend toward enhancing its own energy or what Nietzsche calls the will-to-power.

In order to justify his generalization from the individual subject to the whole of nature, Nietzsche appeals to two areas of scientific study. Scientific method recommends economy and uniformity of explanatory principles. Unless there is definite evidence about a quite different state of affairs elsewhere, we can safely assume that the given factor in individual experience also manifests the general character of reality. Indeed, the most significant achievement of biological science in the latter part of the nineteenth century is the Darwinian theory of evolution, which testifies to the pervasive becoming, struggle, and transiency of structures. Despite some sharp criticism of the Darwinians, Nietzsche accords to evolution a general metaphysical significance, going far beyond the biological findings, in order to gain scientific warrant for the universal change in the universe and the wholly immanent significance of the drives of life. He also invokes the sciences of history and classical philology, in which he had been trained, as added witness to the constant fluidity in the realm of human institutions, concepts, and languages. Since man is caught up in the evolutionary flow of life under all these aspects, the evidence is overwhelming for regarding the monism of becoming and the will-to-power as the fundamental description of reality.

There are structures and relations in our human world, of course, but they are contributions of man's own formal, ordering activities or projects. These constructural principles are not universal a priori forms (as Kant supposed) or mysterious Platonic ideas (as in Schopenhauer); they are products of the cosmic will-to-power in its distinctively human mode. Man cannot bear to dwell in a featureless, transient, humanly unoriented cosmos. He craves to harness the torrents of becoming, to stabilize and render them humanly significant. He forges concepts like "thing," "law," and "value" as pragmatic tools for introducing meaning and purpose into his part of the great sea of becoming. Thus knowledge is not a relation of conformity but a perspective taken by the will-to-power and by the esthetic judgment of what will enhance human power and significance in the world. For the honest philosopher of the future, to know means to create, to legislate the order and rank of things, and hence to set values.[21] Underlying all cognitive acts is the practical act of esteeming or endowing becoming with some value for man. Because of their purely human origin, all genuine meanings and values are rigidly circumscribed within the boundaries of becoming and refer only to the polarity set up between this cosmic flow and the human valuator. The structures and relations of our world are wholly immanent in origin and import.

Nietzsche now has an answer to Pilate's question. One cannot properly speak about "the" truth but only about humanly founded truths. There is no absolute truth corresponding to some region of permanent essences because there is no evidence of such a region in being. Hence it is meaningless to proclaim the absolute truth of God's transcendent reality. Human truths are perspectives taken on a particular situation for a particular purpose: they remain many, revisible, and confined to human projects. This also applies, with equal rigor, to moral truths. There is no universal moral world order or absolute good—only the plural goods of human aims and the finite sanctions they impose.

Nevertheless, the Nietzschean experiment never loses its strictly hypothetico-deductive character. It spells out some consequences that might follow the decision to develop certain implications of the Kantian and Schopenhauerian views of phenomenal experience into a full-fledged metaphysics of natural being. But a description of these consequences does not furnish sufficient confirmation of the adequacy of this restricted hypothesis as a point of departure, since phenomenalism leaves out of account man's other ways of becoming directly related to the natural world. The speculative approach to nature through the existential judgment about sensible beings, as well as the approaches to it through symbol and work, bring out aspects other than those which can be accommodated within the postulate of a flowing sense manifold and will-to-power. For they manifest structures, relations, and acts of being which man discovers and does not sheerly produce. Our knowledge of nature cannot be narrowed down to those which are regulated by the Kantian analysis of physical knowledge and the Schopenhauerian universalizing of will.

Even within Nietzsche's given context there are considerations pointing in other directions than the immanent sea of invertebrate becoming and recurrent human projections of meaning. From the fact of our human ability to take perspectives and determine a scale of values, it does not follow that our knowing and valuing consist solely in creating our own meanings and values. Our acts of knowing and estimating involve a definite factor of recognition and respect for the real texture of their objects, for the ways of things and of other men as they become disclosed to us and as they affect our practical operations. Scientific procedures include the indispensable moment of empirical confirmation or disconfirmation, based on public testing, the actual occurrence of events in nature, and the presence of determinate structures which are not entirely reducible to our frame of reference and our mode of measuring. In Charles Peirce's contemporaneous philosophy of science, for instance, attention is given to the real, objective, and social aspects of scientific inquiry. Even Nietzsche's metaphysical statement that the cosmic will-to-power functions in man as a structure-endowing agency is itself a determinate pronouncement about the nature of this agency. There is no reason why the human intelligence cannot expand this capacity for discerning some of the pervasive and definite traits of the real into a structural study of other areas of inquiry. Unless the doctrine of the cosmic will is to be regarded only as a poetic instrument of cultural criticism, it opens the route for a more realistic use of our mind in knowing and valuing the natural realm of things.

When criticism becomes this specific, however, Nietzsche will treat his monism of becoming and the will-to-power as an original metaphysical insight which is only indirectly illustrated by other philosophic and scientific positions. But then there is no obligation in intellectual honesty for men of our generation to adopt his metaphysical hypothesis. The "perhaps" upon which Nietzsche's outlook is erected does, no doubt, enjoy a certain allure and exhilarating quality because of its bold and inclusive demands. But this dramatic quality is not a sufficient reason for converting the hypothesis into a necessary presupposition which modern man cannot question without impugning his loyalty to the earth and his respect for the actual human situation and its evidence.

(2) *The hammer-blow of God's death.* In announcing the death of God, Nietzsche does much more than simply echo a theme already elaborated by Hegel. Instead of making it the prelude to the truth about absolute spirit, he makes it the outcome of the error about absolute spirit. Whereas Hegel interprets God's death in terms of a becoming which is already precontained within the absolute, Nietzsche divorces becoming entirely from the context of absolute spirit and then takes God as a synonym for the illusion about the absolute. Thus God is dead precisely because the absolutism of infinite and eternal spirit is exposed as a mortiferous creation of the human mind.

In the now familiar Feuerbachian pattern, Nietzsche submits the doctrine of God to a thorough psychologizing process. Within his monism of becoming, there can be no serious question about the independent *reality* of God. The whole issue concerns only the origin and value of the *idea* of God, taken without any metaphysical possibility of having a real, suprahuman referent. Hegel had suggested the decline of effective belief in God as one meaning for the death of God. Nietzsche's resolute psychologism on this point requires this meaning to be the only tenable one: *The cultural decay of the idea of God spells the decline of the only kind of being God has ever enjoyed.*

Nevertheless, Nietzsche does not want to imply that the removal of this idea is a painless and insignificant event, like the banishing of the idea of hobgoblins. God's death raises the essential question of whether worldly existence has any intrinsic meaning by itself. Using the figure of the madman who tries to spread the news of God's death, he castigates what might be called the frivolous and nonaggressive way of receiving this news. The everyday atheists joke about God as getting lost, going into hiding, or fleeing away, since they fail to perceive the connection between His death and the collapse of all our Western values. Hence the madman sharply reminds them of their responsible part, both in creating the idea of God and in letting it die out: *"We have killed him— you and I. All of us are his murderers."*[22] It is in much the same vein that Thomas Hardy speaks of "God's funeral" and makes the now receding Deity cry out to man:

> I dwindle day by day
> Beneath the deicide eyes of seers
> In a light that will not let me stay,
> And to-morrow the whole of me disappears.

The death of God means the deliberate extirpation of the idea of God and the downfall of the entire system of standards and conduct hinging upon the acceptance of that idea. Men who no longer adhere to it are deicides, murderers of God, and must bear personal responsibility for the deed and its incalculable repercussions upon our culture.

Nietzsche's favorite image of himself as the philosopher of the future is Zarathustra, the wise man who comes down from his mountain retreat to preach the awful yet glad tidings of God's death. He finds one saintly hermit in the forest who is exceptional in not knowing this evangel and hence in keeping to traditional ways. The crowd in the market place is obliquely aware of the loss of faith in God, but it prefers to be distracted from the consequences. Only a few choice spirits (including the last pope) grasp, in varying degrees, the true significance of the European crisis of theistic belief. To these latter, Zarathustra proclaims the death of God as the greatest recent event, one whose shadow is gradually covering the whole cultural landscape. We are a generation of men living in the shadow of the dead God and fearing the resultant nihilism of intellectual and moral values.

Nietzsche insists that the essential message of modern atheism is neither the speculative impossibility of demonstrating God's existence nor the purely factual cultural report that God is no longer widely believed. The real core of Nietzschean antitheism is that God is not believed because he is no longer believable, no longer worthy of enlisting human assent and support.

That we find no God—either in history or in nature or behind nature—is not what differentiates *us*, but that we experience what has been revered as God, not as "godlike" but as miserable, as absurd, as harmful, not merely as an error but as a *crime against life*. We deny God as God. If one were to *prove* this God of the Christians to us, we should be even less able to believe in him.[23]

This revealing text shows the passionate depth of Nietzsche's antitheism, its voluntaristic aspect which would refuse to accept a demonstration, its recognition of Christian theism as the supreme enemy, and its indictment of God on vitalistic, moral, and humanistic grounds. God is dead in the emphatic sense that the idea of God no longer represents the highest value but is at last rejected as the supreme disvalue or antithesis to human life and ideals.

In order to substantiate this charge, Nietzsche employs what he likes to call the sixth sense of nineteenth-century man: the historical sense. By this he does not mean the capacity for grasping history in the usual meaning of a scrupulously exact and balanced account of past events and convictions but, rather, an intuitive divining of what the essential meaning of an age and its leading concepts "shall be" in order to promote human values.[24] His use of the historical sense or "the poetic lie" in describing the content of the idea of God is a strict application of his general theory that the knower is a legislator of values, not only about the future, but also about the past and present content of men's minds.

He reads history backwards, starting with some miserable or hypocritical features of his own century and tracing them to the idea of God. By this retrospective method of psychogenesis, he constructs a notion of God as the source and depository of all that is inimical to human integrity and freedom. Like the atheistic predecessors in his century, Nietzsche regards Christianity as Platonism for the vulgar and Hegel as the theoretician of Christian theology. He makes a strategically dictated reduction of all doctrines on God to one uniform mold, which is divined to be, somehow, a synthesis of Platonism, Christianity, Kantian dualism, and Hegelian absolutism. The God whose death is to be used as a mighty hammer against all existing institutions and moral systems is this synthetic idea, which is obtained by using the historical sense in the valuational way prescribed by Nietzsche's metaphysics and theory of knowledge.

Examination of *Twilight of the Idols, or How to Philosophize with a Hammer* (1888), one of his last but most lucid writings, shows that Nietzsche's hostility toward God arose from his identification of God with a noumenal, "true" world which, by definition, contradicts our phenomenal, "apparent" world. "To invent fables about a world 'other' than this one has no meaning at all, unless an instinct of slander, detraction, and suspicion against life has gained the upper hand in us. . . . God [is] the counter-concept and condemnation of life."[25] Nietzsche could see only one theistic imperative for distinguishing between the temporal and the eternal: Depreciate the former and cast doubt upon its reality. He understood anyone who maintains that nature does not comprise all reality to be claiming that the natural world is unreal, worthless, and to be abandoned. In this interpretation, Nietzsche remained all too faithful a disciple of Schopenhauer and Wagner, since he unquestioningly treated their world-denying portrayals of God and Christianity as authentic expressions of the essential position of theism. Anyone who accepted this idea of God was a deserter from temporal history, a betrayer of the scientific method based on sense knowledge, and a diverter of moral energy from the immanent, life-promoting aims of the will-to-power to a goal that is enervating and suicidal.

When he considered the moral consequences of regulating one's life by devotion to such a God as he had defined, Nietzsche's furious denunciation burst all bounds. In *The Antichrist* (also 1888), he assailed "God as the declaration of war against life, against nature, against the will to live! God—the formula for every slander against 'this world,' for every lie about the 'beyond'! God—the deification of nothingness, the will to nothingness, the will to nothingness pronounced holy!"[26] As Nietzsche once told Frau Overbeck (wife of his colleague, the church historian, Franz Overbeck), he had committed himself so completely against this conception of God that he was unable and unwilling to consider whether it should be revised and corrected by men's actual views of God. The moral horror which the idea of God, stipulated as a hostile other world, aroused in him was too strong to permit self-criticism to operate on this issue. The death of God had to be proclaimed, as the necessary prelude to the rebirth of man as a responsible agent in the natural world.

In weighing these death tidings, we must scrutinize four features of Nietzsche's approach: its hypothetical starting point, its voluntaristic theory of knowledge, its historical reductionism, and its reversal-criterion of truth and value. First, the thought-experiment about the universe as a vast sea of becoming, governed by the will-to-power, is too quickly converted by Nietzsche into a metaphysical standard for judgments about God. As long as this metaphysics remains a "perhaps," however, it cannot be used to demonstrate that a recognition of God as the eternal reality necessarily entails a devaluation of the finite world. Nietzsche charges that God has been the great objection against existence and the destroyer of the innocence of becoming. Outside the courtroom, this means that his original hypothesis imprints the trait of self-sufficiency upon temporal existence and finite becoming and that Nietzschean innocence consists in strategically forgetting that one has done the imprinting in a hypothetical way. Yet this settles nothing about whether one is warranted, in the first place, to stamp the character of absolute self-sufficiency upon the world of process.

Secondly, Nietzsche celebrates the joy of begetting that he always feels in knowledge, since it is a creation of values and a will to be the *causa prima*. He declares that the situation would be unendurable if there were gods and he could not be one of them through his legislating will. He presumes that there is something humiliating about acknowledging the real existence of a being which does not come within one's own self-creative power. This is a moving description of how the attitude of *hybris* shapes the human mind, but it does not establish that this attitude is well founded with respect to man. The issue with theism concerns whether man's situation in nature permits him to will to be a first cause or whether it furnishes grounds requiring him to acknowledge God as the independent first cause, in whose eternal life we may freely and personally seek to share. Nietzsche's voluntarism of knowledge is a special case of his metaphysics of cosmic becoming and power, and it is only within this framework that human freedom is violated by the acknowledgment of God as the transcendent, causal existent.

A third question is raised by Nietzsche's monolithic approach to the various philosophies of God. His "historical sense" about what the meaning of God must and shall be amounts to a monistic reduction of all the human philosophical efforts to clarify, correct, and improve our propositions concerning God. They are all flattened down to conform with a single prescribed notion. This accounts for the somewhat fantastic air about his description of God as the spider-deity and the thinnest concept of the human mind. His image of God as the eternally spinning cosmic spider is in the tradition of Diderot's dream dialogues, but it is not frankly acknowledged to be a fantasy. A realistic theism can only add that the death of such a notion of God is well deserved and can serve to clarify what the living God does not mean. The main constructive purpose served by Nietzsche's evangel of the death of God is to induce an examination of philosophical conscience on the part of theists and to bring out clearly one way of distinguishing God from the world which a historically enlightened theism cannot support.

The final criticism concerns Nietzsche's use of the reversal-criterion, as expressed ironically in his statement that "whatever a theologian feels to be true *must* be false: this is almost a criterion of truth."[27] In practice, the qualifying word "almost" is dropped from sight, at least as far as the formal question of the existence and nature of God is concerned. Nietzsche boasts that his special gift is that of reversing perspectives, but this is a perilous way of constructing a philosophy. The antipodal mind does succeed in being provocative by reversing current views, but it invariably narrows down the entire history of human thought to the present convention it seeks to overturn. The impoverishing effect of such a procedure has been observed in the case of the Marxian conception of God, and it recurs in Nietzsche. The reversal method compels him to propose a perfect dilemma between eternal being and temporal becoming, between the transcendent God and the order of nature. It also forces him to interpret every instance of distinguishing among ways of being as a suppression of the reality of all but one way and every instance of ordering among values as a subversion of the subordinate values. God is a counterconcept to life only if life is restricted in advance to temporal becoming or if eternal life can be supreme only by denaturalizing and devaluating the finite forms of life. Nietzsche's antipodal logic of terror is an excellent hammer against corruptions and idols of the day, but it lacks the analytic precision and historical range demanded of a philosophical instrument for sustained inquiry about God.

Nietzsche's positive doctrines of the superman and the eternal recurrence of the same events were his deliberate substitutes for theism. His aim was to make a godless existence endurable and meaningful, through an artistic overevaluation or "poetic lie" about the temporal world, and thus to divert the human tendency to transcend nature. In his myth about temporal becoming, there can be gods or particular manifestations of the will-to-power but no transcendent God; there can be a sempiternal cycle of recurring events but no distinctive eternal existent; there can be self-legislating supermen, who stand above the herd of common mortals, but no opportunity for all men to share in the eternal life of God. The result was a substitutional situation in which Nietzsche willed passionately that the great ring of natural becoming should support all our meanings and values. But this legislated compensation was no better founded in the available evidence than was the idea of God, against which he rightly rebelled. Both in his polemic against this description of God and in his myth of the eternal return, Nietzsche remained a wanderer toward the unknown God, to whom he had composed a youthful poem:

> I want to know you, Unknown One,
> You who are reaching deep into my soul
> And ravaging my life, a savage gale,
> You Inconceivable and yet Related One!
> I want to know you—even serve.[28]

But the savage gale of his protest against a noumenal threat to our earth never permitted him to explore the clearer air and calmer seas where the relations between the world and God could be investigated apart from the distracting extremes of absolute spirit versus the will-to-power.

Along with Kierkegaard, Friedrich Nietzsche is one of the main sources of contemporary existentialism. That is why the existentialists have always showed a consuming interest in the question of God and human existence. Their sharply divergent interpretations of Nietzsche's thought reflect the great contrasts among them concerning the role of God. Since the atheistic existentialism of Sartre and Camus represents only one side of this controversy, however, a study of the existentialist theories of God will be postponed until the chapter on the ways of the heart and natural faith in God.

4. AMERICAN NATURALISM AS A METHODOLOGICAL ATHEISM

The standpoints of Feuerbach, Marx, and Nietzsche are instances of atheistic naturalism, but not all varieties of naturalism are atheistic. In the minimal descriptive sense, a naturalism makes the study of the natural world central in philosophy. It stresses the reality of nature against acosmism and defends the importance of the natural context in opposition to an exclusively humanistic view. A philosophy may accord full weight to natural being in these ways without pitting itself against God. During the modern period, however, the predominant types of naturalism have usually opposed anything supernatural and extranatural.[29] An epistemological naturalism excludes any revealed truth and economy of grace beyond that which our natural powers can attain, and yet it may admit God as a being who is distinct from nature and knowable by us in a natural way. The most constricted form of naturalism is the metaphysical sort which, in addition to ruling out a supernatural revelation, also denies that God exists as an extra-natural being or as distinct from its own definition of nature. No one of these meanings of "naturalism" has a pre-emptory claim upon that term, and no historical or dialectical law seems to be operating in favor of only one type.

Nevertheless, the emergence of modern atheism in Europe and America was bound up with a methodological and metaphysical denial of any being beyond nature. One major exponent of this antitheistic naturalism was Auguste Comte (1798–1857). His positivism rested on the postulate that nothing real can transcend the universe of sense events and their laws and, consequently, that the only absolute is this finite world of ours. Comte sought to replace the worship of God with the worship of humanity, but his religion of humanism was too bizarre in detail to attract many subsequent naturalists.[30] Yet they did owe him a vigorous impetus toward detaching the religious sentiment from God and justifying atheism on the methodological ground that we can only assert as real those objects which are verifiable through the scientific method.

A scientifically oriented naturalism took firm root in America through the fundamental work of Santayana and Dewey, Woodbridge and Cohen. These widely diverse thinkers are more unified in their negations than in their affirmations. Perhaps the most cohesive bond among the American naturalists is their rejection of God and personal immortality. As one contributor to the authoritative symposium on *Naturalism and the Human Spirit* remarks: "Even the new naturalism has at least one reductionist or liquidationist thesis: There is no 'supernatural.' God and immortality are myths."[31] In liquidating these myths, however, this school insists that it is being less dogmatically a priori than Holbach, less emotionally aggressive than Nietzsche, and quite a bit closer to the actualities of scientific method than Feuerbach and Marx, whom they nevertheless most closely resemble.

Like their predecessors, the American naturalists stress that theirs is the philosophy of the future, the postmodern path for thought. Yet they also accept from the nineteenth century certain positions which seem to be permanently valid. The essential points in this heritage are precisely catalogued by John H. Randall, Jr.:

Contemporary naturalism thus represents at once the culmination of the idealistic criticism, and of the natural sciences of man and human culture. It carries on the idealistic emphasis that man is united to his world by a logical and social experience. But it rephrases the idealistic scheme of man's activities and environment in biological and anthropological categories. While like the idealists it makes them all amenable to a single intellectual method, it reformulates that method in experimental terms. . . . It can be described equally as the concern to treat the total subject-matter of idealistic metaphysics, with all its sensitivity to the complex range of human culture, in terms of a scientific and experimental method; or as the carrying of scientific methods into all the areas of human experience.[32]

This conforms to the general pattern of post-Hegelian naturalism, which derives some basic philosophical considerations from idealism but inverts or reformulates them in terms of the natural sciences. The chief debt to Hegel is for the correlative theses that there is a single whole of being and that it is knowable through one continuous general method. In scientific language, the whole of being is called nature, and the method is identified as the general logic of science. Although frequent references are made to actual scientific practice, the principles for interpreting this practice in terms of being and method are still rooted in the Hegelian soil.

Once these most general postulates are accepted, naturalism subjects the remaining portions of the idealistic position to intense criticism, with the aid of present-day scientific tendencies. Nature is to be viewed as having an actuality and significance of its own, liberated from the theory that it is only an appearance and self-estrangement of absolute spirit. Similarly, objects in nature are to be studied according to the specific procedures established by physics, biology, and anthropology, without any reliance upon the dialectical method. In this sense, the naturalists will allow as many methods as are needed in the various sciences.

This differentiation, however, is not permitted to disrupt the unity of the methodic continuum. There is a plurality of scientific techniques and procedures, but they retain their distinct validity as paths of knowledge only within the comprehensive unity of the general logic of the sciences. We may experience the world in many different ways, but the only assured way of knowing it is through conformity with the general canons of scientific inquiry, as defined by naturalistic analysis. On this basic issue, the naturalists do not challenge Hegel's contention that there is a radical unity of method, but they identify this method with their conception of the general scientific logic underlying the several disciplines. There is also agreement between Hegel and the American naturalists on the strict correlation between the range of this general method of inquiry and that of warrantably assertible reality. The only knowledge-yielding statements about reality are those which can be publicly verified according to the canons of scientific inquiry, interpreted to support the analytic continuum of method and nature.

This does not mean that all naturalists follow Hegel uncritically in identifying the real with that which can be attained through the underlying method of knowledge. Sidney Hook and others do grant that there may be aspects of man and of other things which we can experience in some noncognitive ways but which cannot be apprehended as cognitively experienced through the scientific method. They add that this method is not excluding any other reliable method of knowing but is simply the best one presently available to us. Nevertheless, this admission is weakened by several qualifications usually attached to it. For one thing, any aspects of being that do remain unamenable to the general logic of the sciences are also strictly unknowable by us, however deeply we may feel about them and experience them in a noncognitive fashion. There is no knowable or cognitively experienceable reality that escapes the scope of this method. Furthermore, to qualify as a genuine advance in the reliable human ways of knowing, any additional or newly discovered approach must first adjust itself to the naturalistic thesis about the continuity of method and the totality of nature. The latent premise is that no matter how they are experienced, all facets of the real are included by definition within the totality of nature and are rendered cognitively accessible to us only through the comprehensive logic of the sciences. These qualifying points are not entirely free from circularity of relationship between the theory of method and that of nature. Without such a relationship, there would be no way of eliminating the cognitive experience and analytic inference which claim to establish some truths about God as the being whose existence is really distinct from the things in nature.

American naturalism emphasizes that its two distinguishing notes are antireductionism and antidualism. The first of these traits signifies its opposition to the crude effort of Holbach and Enlightenment materialism to level all things downward to the mechanical causes and conditions responsible for them. A reductive naturalism or materialism maintains that all the higher developments of human life are "nothing but" matter and mechanical motion. Profiting by the previous inquiries of idealism into the distinctive configurations of organic life and human culture, the new American naturalists refuse to make this simple reduction to the level of material causes and conditions, which are common requirements but which are not sufficient as specific principles of the various levels and values in nature. To this extent, they defend a nonreductive materialism which maintains the existential and causal primacy of matter and yet allows for higher forms of organization.

However, naturalism is antireductionist only up to a point. It will not recognize any reality which is not contingently, intrinsically, and causally dependent upon the material foundation. It permits distinctive forms and functions in the higher levels of human experience, but only on condition that they are never more than functionally and organizationally distinct from bodies. Naturalism accommodates a pluralism of forms and functions, but not a pluralism of beings existing without intrinsic dependence upon matter. It remains radically reductive with respect to any sort of being whose existential act would be distinct in kind from, and causally unreducible to, the material thing. Thus there is a naturalistic reduction of every existential act to intrinsic dependence on matter.

It is in this sense that the key word "nature" is used as the equivalent of "real being," as comprehending everything real rather than designating one region of real beings. Naturalism is reductionist in the philosophically most pregnant sense of refusing to grant the status of reality to anything which challenges the assumption of nature's inclusive self-sufficiency. As one exponent of American naturalism expresses it:

Nature is not itself a problem for the naturalistic philosopher; rather, nature constitutes the subject-matter of all genuine problems (except those of the formal sciences). Hence the grand (indemonstrable) assumption underlying any naturalistic position: *Nature is all there is.*[33]

The counterabsolutizing move of American naturalism does not consist in a crude inversion of Hegel in favor of nature as the absolute; it consists in a postulatory identification of the totality of the real with nature and of genuine problems with those accepting this context for inquiry. When the attempt is made to render problematic the grand naturalistic belief, authentic philosophical questions are stipulated to be those presupposing that nature is all there is and those specified by the methodic continuum corresponding to this presupposition.

The antidualist thesis of naturalism is that no evidence supports the real existence of a transcendent God and an immaterial soul in man. This negative position also involves the same sort of historical reductionism already encountered in earlier representatives of atheism. The Cartesian dualism of mind and body is taken as the prototypal way of conceiving an immaterial principle in man, whereas the standard for God's relation to the world is a vague and shifting "transcendentalism" for which it is difficult to find any precise historical counterpart. In any case, the integrity of nature and the competence of scientific method are defended by naturalism against the threat posed by what it colorfully but obscurely calls the holy jungle of transcendental metaphysics.

The chief contribution of John Dewey (1859–1952) was precisely to insist upon the dual threat of God to nature and method. He took the well-marked route of giving a psychological account of the idea of God or the absolute. The theistic mind is lacking in nerve. It is shaken by the change, contingency, and relativity of our universe, which it calls an inferior realm of being. It yearns after an ideal sphere of immutable, necessary, absolute being where man can be safe from the dangers of worldly existence. Then the theist deludes himself by converting this transcendental goal into an actuality, by mistaking an eventual ideal for an independently existing divine being. God is the outcome of this

abstraction of our hopes from their natural context and this hypostasization of an ideal into an actual, extranatural being.

Underlying Dewey's many scattered references to the problem of God
is a fourfold critique which has built the framework in America for
most of the recent naturalistic thinking about God.[34] There are two
major metaphysical reasons for refusing to admit the reality of a transcendent being: such an admission constitutes a breach in the continuity
of nature, and it also entails a sharp devaluation of everything finite
and contingent and changing. The third basic objection is the epistemological consideration that belief in God rests upon an appeal to a special
knowing power which gives an intuitive vision of Him but which, at
the same time, destroys the continuity of scientific method and the respect for our ordinary means of knowledge. Finally, Dewey links the
acceptance of God with what he calls the "spectator" or purely speculative attitude toward knowledge: In order to contemplate God, the
theist withdraws his energies from the everyday world and its urgent
practical tasks. Thus if the theist is consequential about his conviction
in the reality of a transcendent or extranatural God, he must become
a despiser of our finite world, an obstacle in the path of scientific inquiry,
and a deserter from our human responsibilities in the realm of active
control over nature and society.

These results are indeed disastrous for the character of the individual
and the health of society. And, unfortunately, such a combination of
traits is sometimes found among theists and even justified by them on
the grounds of their adherence to the real being of God. The philosophical question, however, is to determine whether such consequences are
necessarily entailed by all the major routes employed by theists in developing their doctrine on God. At least in the case of a realistically
grounded theism, there is no such necessary connection between assent
to the being of God and the outcome which Dewey has sketched.

The objection drawn from the continuity of being supposes that such
continuity is the same as the homogeneity, or basic oneness in kind, of
being. On this assumption, the only differences admissible into the
realm of reality are those of functional levels and structural organiza-
tions which remain intrinsically dependent upon the common stuff. But
the functional varieties within this homogeneously continuous universe
would represent only one type of continuity. There are other ways of
securing the continuity of being which do not sacrifice the difference in
kind among various actual things. The doctrine on God does not entail
the abandonment of the unity and continuity of being; it specifies them
in a manner different from that of Deweyan naturalism. In a theistically
conceived world, there are causal connections between God and finite
things of different kinds. Hence there is a continuity based on the causal
relations between beings that are analogically similar. Theism suggests

that the continuity among the various kinds of beings is causal and analogical, so that acceptance of God does not disrupt nature but relates it in all its ways of being to the common causal source.

In the second place, not every way of distinguishing between God and the finite world involves a denigration of the latter. Dewey's position on this issue is not sufficiently critical of the commonplace arguments found in the post-Hegelian tradition of atheism. He accepts at face value the identification between the Hegelian absolute and the God of theistic philosophy. Hence he overlooks the sharp and radical difference between the idealistic *contrast* of the absolute and its relative modes and the theistic *distinction* of God and finite things. The absolutist way of contrasting reality and appearance, truth and illusion, rests upon the theory of an immanent absolute and its shadows or phases. There is a devaluation of finite things here to the degree that they stubbornly exist and embody values in their own nature and not as moments of anything else. But this distinctive way of existing, acting, and valuing on the part of finite things lies at the heart of the realistic view of their causal dependence upon God and their analogical relation to Him. Such a dependency and relationship would be meaningless unless finite things had an actuality and value-status proper to themselves. The significance and integrity of finite beings are neither erased nor watered down in order to establish the perfect actuality of God. The realistic causal inference to God owes its strength and import to the presence of finite existents, enjoying their own way of being and their own hold on value. Just as Dewey establishes a subsequent valuation of the fuller and the less rewarding experiences, the more and the less pervasive traits in nature, without depriving the less pervasive of their proper reality or initial equal footing in description, so does theistic realism distinguish between the purely actual being of God and the limited actuality of composed beings, without thereby entailing any depreciation of the latter. Causal differentiation among the kinds of being requires one to remain open to every actual event and to respect the proper integrity of every mode of existing.

For the problem of methodology and knowledge, it is significant that a realistic theism lays claim to no special intuitive insight into God. Our knowledge of God is the outcome of an inference and is not an instance of an intuition. Furthermore, this inferential knowledge of certain truths about God is achieved through the use of our ordinary cognitive powers and does not involve any appeal to a privileged means of knowledge. The evidence upon which the inference rests is drawn from the public zone of sensible things that move, act causally upon each other, and exhibit various dependencies. Our ordinary ability to perceive, analyze experience, and make causal inferences is employed in making this approach to God. Not the invoking of some a priori intuition but the examining of implications of our experience of the sensible world and our own human life provides the means for reaching knowledge about God. Whether the theistic inference is conducted according to the scientific method depends upon how broadly or how narrowly the method in question is conceived. If it is taken to mean observance of the sound canons for making a reliable a posteriori inference of causal relations, then these requirements of scientifically disciplined reasoning are respected in the inference to God. But if a theory of scientific method is restricted to functional relations among sensible events, then to that extent the theistic inference is concerned with the causal relation in a distinct sense and must preserve its own kind of rigor. In neither of these instances is there any denial of the validity and need for scientific method. Opposition arises between theism and the naturalistic claim that inference cannot take us beyond the functional correlations among sensible events. But here there is question of conflicting philosophical interpretations of the scope of scientific method in its restricted meaning rather than a simple case of acceptance or rejection of scientific method.

Finally, the causal inference to God does indeed terminate in speculative knowledge, but this is not to be taken in the pejorative sense of antipractical knowledge. The truth about God is sought for its own sake, as a perfection of the mind in its search for knowledge about causal principles. Yet theistic speculative inquiry proceeds not by fleeing from the finite, changing world but by continuing to examine this world and to wring from it every ounce of its precious significance, including the truth about its causal dependence upon the infinite God. That this finding is vitally important for the conduct of human life is recognized in a philosophy of God, but it also tries to preserve the distinction between two functions of our mind: establishing conclusions in a sound way in order to yield speculatively reliable knowledge and working out the practical implications of such knowledge. Recent naturalists have had to modify Dewey's instrumentalist theory of inquiry sufficiently to permit a speculative consideration of the findings without cutting off the results from their eventual bearing upon practical life. And a similar modification to permit a speculative recognition of God as the causal source of the natural world is long overdue. This speculative phase in theistic inquiry is neither divorced from nor prejudicial to the practical concerns of human life. The philosophy of God is sometimes called a wisdom, not in the sense of an esoteric vision, but precisely because of the relevance of its causal findings for our practical ways of knowing and acting. The acceptance of God does not mean a diversion of interest and energy from our world and its tasks but, rather, a renewed concern for our responsibility in the practical affairs of the natural world and human society. Only this balanced continuity between the speculative and practical aspects of the knowledge of God enables us to obtain truths about God that are humanly important without reducing God to the status of a function within our scientific and moral projects.

One major naturalistic contention is that causal inquiry leads only to further stretches of spatiotemporal events and hence never attains to God. The most persuasive statement of this argument was made by Frederick Woodbridge (1867–1940). He conceived of a naturalistic metaphysics as being primarily an analytic determination of the given structure of existence. Our causal discoveries must terminate absolutely with a grasp of the structure of given things.[35] Granted that these existents raise the question of their ultimate causal source, they never provide an answer leading back to the faraway time and ultimate principle of their production. Our philosophical wonder should prudently be suppressed once we lay bare the given structure of the world. We have neither the instrument nor the incentive to make any further inference to a transcendent God or first cause of nature.

One reason for this naturalistic restriction of causal inference is to prevent the idealistic reincorporation of nature within an absolute spiritual totality. In order to engulf finite things within this totality, however, Hegel had to substitute the dialectical relation of absolute and relative for the existential relation of cause and effect. It was precisely the causal bond between God and finite existents which idealism had to remove from its path in order to make nature an alienated expression of absolute spirit. Hence the revindication of finite, contingent things in nature does require the removal of the absolute-relative dialectic but not a suppression of the question about God. Setting aside the dialectic of the absolute is the preliminary step toward reactivating the theistic problem in its proper import as an inquiry into the primary causal principle of finite things. A realistic theism of both the infinite cause and finite causes does not set up a deductively necessary chain but rests on an a posteriori study of the causal requirements for an experienced, finite existent, whose own act of existing does not become any less real, contingent, and finite for our having recognized its infinite first cause. The deductive and dialectical theories of necessity do revoke the contingency of the finite existent, but that is because they fail to employ the a posteriori inference to God from the composite, existing things in nature.

The restricted scientific meaning of causal connection is certainly met by the establishment of certain functional correlations between events and conditions within the spatiotemporal world. But there is no further scientific proviso that its meaning for causality is undermined, unless it be taken as the sole valid one for all philosophical inquiry. This proviso is a residue of the methodological monism which naturalists have inherited from Hegel despite their criticism of what he took to be the scientific method. Hence when Woodbridge states that existents raise the question of their causal origin without providing an answer, he is accurately reporting the limits of his method of interrogating them. This is not due to the intrinsic opaqueness of a finite thing with respect to dependence on an infinite cause, however, but arises from the fact that the meanings he inquires about do not include the problem of the present dependence of the finite being's act of existing upon a cause.

Without being textually indebted to Feuerbach and Marx, Woodbridge arrives at much the same insight: that descriptive analysis terminates in basic natural structures which we cannot revoke by a dialectical move or by an imaginary journey backwards in time. Yet he also resembles them in failing to see that a given structure which is *descriptively ultimate,* as being actually present in nature, can also be *causally implicative,* as yielding knowledge about a distinct, causal existent, from which it receives its composing and participating principles of being. To seize upon these implications is not to disintegrate the finite structure but to appreciate it in a further dimension of its meaning, that is, in the aspect of its causal sharing in existing being.

Among contemporary naturalists, Sterling Lamprecht and Ernest Nagel have made the most intensive formal investigation of proofs of God's existence. Five of their main objections are mentioned here, along with a few remarks in countercriticism.[36]

(1) They insist that their *horror supernaturae* is not motivated by any emotional animus against theism but simply by the lack of empirical evidence showing God's existence or His relevance to our world. Atheism can be unemphatic rather than polemically and passionately opposed to God. They agree with Dewey in supposing that the empirical argument in favor of theism would be drawn from religious and mystical experience. They rightly point out that although a type of experience which is termed "religious" does occur, its occurrence does not thereby specify which proposition about the nature of the real is supported by such an experience. Theists who do depend on the appeal to religious experience admit that some further analysis must be made of the special characteristics of this experience in order to determine whether or not it does require a reference to a reality distinct from finite things. The realistic demonstration of God's existence is experiential, however, in a somewhat different sense. It does not rest upon the specifically religious type of experience or upon a claim to have a direct experience of God. Rather, its experiential foundation is in our ordinary grasp of finite, sensible things and of human existence, on the basis of whose definite traits a causal analysis is made and an inferential conclusion reached about the truth that God or the infinitely actual being exists.

(2) Unlike classical agnosticism, contemporary naturalism does not lean very heavily upon Kant's refutation of the three rationalist proofs. The naturalists are suspicious of both the Kantian dualism between

phenomenal and noumenal being, upon which the refutation rests, and the subsequent Kantian appeal to moral faith. They merely note that the ontological argument is completely nonempirical and that the teleological one confuses purpose as adaptation with purpose as the planned intent of mind. It is noteworthy that these criticisms are also made by realistic theism in its examination of the arguments circulated by both rationalists and empiricists during the Enlightenment. Admittedly, there is need for a fresh consideration of the meaning of a proof of certain propositions about God, but this need is not the same as discharging the philosopher from his obligation to study the issue with all the tools and evidence presently available.

(3) Against the cosmological argument and every other appeal to contingency, Lamprecht urges that although every particular object is contingent, the world as a whole need not be contingent. The proof from contingency may be vitiated by the fallacy of composition or by arguing from a property of the parts of a thing to a property of the whole thing. He does not press the objection too emphatically, however, since the reply might then be made that the contingent character of a particular thing does not designate some special property flowing from its essence. Because its entire nature is composite, the contingent thing which actually exists does not exist in such a way that it excludes the dependence of its being upon a presently operating cause. A realistic inference to God has its basis in our experience of some particular contingent existents rather than in the concept of contingency or that of the world-as-a-whole. This approach to God does not deduce the properties of a conceptual whole from properties of its parts but infers the existent cause of the composite, material being of certain given contingent things. The concept of the world-as-a-whole is either empirically meaningless, and hence cannot be treated as a superbeing which has or does not have certain properties, or else it refers to the composed existents which do need a cause distinct from themselves and existing through the necessity-in-being of its own nature alone.

(4) Another recurrent naturalistic criticism is that if everything needs a cause, then we must ask about what caused God. John Stuart Mill—and the same can be said of Bertrand Russell—was troubled throughout his life by the consideration that the causal question cannot be ruled out in God's case without making an arbitrary exception or admitting that the question of ultimate origin is unanswerable by us and hence need not be raised. In confronting this difficulty, theism does not rule out the causal question in God's case, but it does propose that the distinction be maintained between the problem of what the causal principle means and the problem of whether God has and needs a cause. The meaning of the causal principle develops out of the need which we discover in some composed and finite existent for an actual source or sources

of being distinct from itself. It is the composed and finite way of having being which provokes particular causal inquiries and hence provides determinate meaning for the causal principle. In its experiential foundation, therefore, this principle does not state that everything needs a cause but that everything existing in a composed and limited way needs a distinct, existing, causal source. The import of the theistic causal inference is that there exists a causal agent whose own being is uncomposed and hence free from any limitation upon its actuality. The causal question can then be asked about this being in order to obtain a definite result. It is not a matter of arbitrarily closing off the causal inquiry but of persisting in it within the achieved context of having established the truth about the existence of a purely actual cause whose being is not subject to composition and limitation. It can then be known that the conditions for requiring a cause do not hold for this being. The causal interrogation has to be carried to the point of assenting to the existence of God as the uncomposed and infinite being and then understanding that God or the uncomposed being is not a caused being. Thus the causal question is not to be suppressed in regard to God, but the reply must be shaped by the distinctive actuality about which it is asked. To use Schopenhauer's colorful figure, when we come to God we cannot dismiss the causal principle, as we might dismiss a hired cab after reaching our destination. But neither can we fail to wait for the appropriate reply when we ask the causal question precisely about the uncomposed existing being to which the causal inference leads us.

(5) A particularly interesting objection is raised by Morris Cohen (1880–1947), whose thought is paralleled closely by Nagel. The following text is a composite drawn from both these naturalistic philosophers.

The postulation of an "absolute cause" or an "ultimate reason" for the world and its structure provides no answer to any *specific* question which may be asked concerning any particular objects or events in the world. On the contrary, no matter what the world were like, no matter what the course of events might be, the same Ultimate Cause is offered as an "explanation." . . . But just what does an "explanation" explain when it explains nothing in particular? . . . Any attempt, for instance, to explain physical phenomena as directly due to Providence or disembodied spirits, is incompatible with the principle of rational determinism. For the nature of these entities is not sufficiently determinate to enable us to deduce definite experimental consequences from them. The Will of Providence, for instance, will explain everything whether it happens one way or another. Hence, no experiment can possibly overthrow it. An hypothesis, however, which we cannot possibly refute cannot possibly be experimentally verified.[37]

This argument would rule out any discourse about God as empirically meaningless, since we cannot deduce from God anything specific which can then be publicly tested and verified.

What the objection shows is that the proposition about God's existence does not belong among those statements established through the hypothetico-deductive method. The warrant for the theistic position comes from an a posteriori inference from experienced, finite existents, a type of argument which remains distinct from the logic of the sciences analyzed by Cohen and Nagel. To maintain the distinctive character of this sort of inference is the antireductionism proposed by realistic theism. The proposition about God's existence does not serve any deductive function, either in the rationalist sense or that of a scientific procedure of hypothetical reasoning. It is not that this proposition pretends to be deductively fruitful and then fails to meet its promise but rather that it makes no such promise. In not doing so, does it cut itself off from all fruitful connection with our world? This would follow only if the connection with experienced things could be secured solely by suggesting deductive consequences about things. But the a posteriori causal inference begins with particular experienced things just as actual existents and not precisely as furnishing the materials for a deductive reconstruction. This is a distinctive yet experientially grounded treatment of the things of our ordinary world. And the cause it establishes is not a hypothetical correlate to the thing's structure but the actual cause of the thing's own act of existing and its other internal principles of being. In this causal sense, the proposition about God is clearly open to confirmation or disconfirmation in our experience of definite, existing beings.

Our assent to God's existence is not based upon His being a possible deductive principle of innumerable worlds but upon the need for His actual causation of things existing in our world. Hence the direct and proper conclusion of the theistic inference is not that God exists as having universal compatibility with all events but that He exists as actually causing the existent being of some actual things of our experience. It is this causal relation with experienced things which constitutes the truth-claim of the theistic proposition and which is subject to the type of verification that tests claims of actual causality of existent things.

Whether the truth about God's existence or nonexistence would make any observable difference in our experience must be determined by the kind of inference in question. Since it is not a deductive process of any kind, the theistic inference is not intended to alter or achieve a logical priority over our initial experience of things. Our direct cognitive acquaintance with things does not depend in the order of knowing upon our philosophical theory of God. The purpose of the inference to God is not to suggest a hypothesis about why things have this or that feature but to work out the causal basis of their actually existing at all as composed beings. The theistic argument does affirm that the composed finite being owes its actual presence to a causal production by the existent first cause, upon which the experienced thing is dependent for its own act of being. This makes a significant, determinate difference, not between several possible arrangements of the universe, but in our full human understanding of the being and causal reference of the things which do exist and enter into our experience. In the cognitive order, there is the speculative consequence of joining the affirmation of the existence and causal action of God to that of finite beings, which are now understood in this aspect of their causal dependence upon and reference to God. This also points toward some practical implications of the relation of causal dependence of ourselves and other finite existents upon God. For the understanding of experienced things and the eventual shaping of human conduct in our world of dependent beings, the establishment of the truth about God's existence makes a definite impact and has fruitful consequences.

The question of what *can* come within the divine will and providence is subsequent to that of God's existence, which concerns what *does* result from His creative causation as the ultimate explanation of certain actual existents. That such an explanation is distinct from the logic of hypothesis and deductive verifiability indicates the quite properly nontheological nature of this logic and the quite properly nondeductive character of the theistic verification. God's existence and attributes are supremely relevant to our experience of actual things and events, but not in the same way that physical theories are relevant. This pluralism of kinds of explanation and experiential relevance is pivotal for establishing the import and the validity of those inferences to God which are based upon existential-causal evidence. This pluralism cannot be ruled out by the reductionist device of being equated with a world-negating dualism without suppressing the issue.

Dewey once proposed that the word "God" might be used by naturalists to signify "the ideal ends that at a given time and place one acknowledges as having authority over his volition and emotion, the values to which one is supremely devoted, as far as these ends, through imagination, take on unity" and promote social action.[38] Most of the American naturalists have accepted this as a description of religious experience but have been reluctant to give it the name "God." They allow the reality of religious experience, in the sense of high dedication to scientific and social ideals, but they divorce it from any transcendent reference to God. Similarly, they detach morality from any foundation in God and look to scientific appraisal of values for a guide to conduct. Naturalistic ethics is seeking a factual basis for obligation, but it looks for it elsewhere than in the causal relation of man to God. That which distinguishes the ethical philosophy of naturalism from that of realistic theism is not the search for a natural, factual ground of morality but the search for it within a view of nature from which the assent to God is excluded.

Finally, mention must be made of the elimination of knowledge of

God on the part of logical positivism or empiricism. This program has been stated in classical form by Rudolf Carnap and Alfred Ayer, who have claimed to be able to show the impossibility of metaphysical knowledge of God and even the meaninglessness of the problem. They have found it difficult actually to execute this program, however, because of their inability to settle upon a satisfactory formulation of the principle of verifiability underlying the critique. In one place, Ayer proposes to determine meaning by the following rule: "A statement is held to be literally meaningful if and only if it is either analytic or empirically verifiable."[39] The statement about God's existence is not included among the nonexistential, analytic statements of logic and mathematics. For this statement to be empirically meaningful, one would have to show by metaphysical reasoning that it entails some observation-statement about the occurrence of some sense-content. But Ayer adds: "I take it to be characteristic of the metaphysician, in my somewhat pejorative sense of the term, not only that his statements do not describe anything that is capable, even in principle, of being observed, but also that no dictionary is provided by means of which they can be transformed into statements that are directly or indirectly verifiable." The conclusion is that statements about God are neither analytic nor empirically verifiable and that therefore they are cognitively meaningless. We have no speculative means for establishing God's existence; neither can we demonstrate God's nonexistence or even show the cognitive meaningfulness of the question of whether He exists or not. It may be that statements about God have a subjective and emotive meaning, but they have no rigorous cognitive import.

More recently, logical empiricists themselves have come to see the inadequacy of this a priori, decisional way of excluding the problem of the meaningfulness and validity of theistic inferences to God. Perhaps the most notable revision of the original position is made by Herbert Feigl, through whom logical empiricism has been modified by the pragmatic and realistic trends in America.[40] He grants that all particular formulations of the criterion of factual meaningfulness are either too indeterminate or too narrow, that this criterion is a practically adopted proposal which can be justified by use but never strictly validated, and that its chief function is to distinguish factual statements from formal ones and those having only emotive meaning. He also admits that Ayer's description of metaphysics is an arbitrarily legislated meaning which does not do justice to the actual varieties of metaphysical thinking. A cardinal distinction must be made between an inductive metaphysics and natural theology, which make some reference to experience, and a transcendent metaphysics and natural theology, which permit no kind of test by experience. The meaning-criterion applies exclusively to the latter sort of metaphysical and theistic reasoning and does not settle the question of an inductive doctrine on being and God. Feigl allows that the latter is cognitively meaningful and that objections to it must rest solely upon Newton's first rule of reasoning in natural philosophy or the principle of parsimony. A theory of God is to be regarded as a meaningful but superfluous hypothesis which we eliminate on the basis of formal simplicity or logical expediency.

This modified attitude of logical empiricism toward the philosophy of God is not far removed from that of American naturalism, with its deliberately unemphatic removal of God. Newton's rule states that we need "admit no more causes of natural things than such as are both true and sufficient to explain their appearances."[41] This rule can be taken in either a broad sense or a restricted way. The general counsel of parsimony or economy of causal explanation is respected by every rigorously constructed philosophy; monotheism appeals to it against a theory of many gods and first causes. To be invoked against every inductive philosophy of God, however, it must be taken in the narrower sense specified by phenomenalism or by current scientific practice. When the rule of parsimony is thus restricted, it does not apply to the kind of inference employed by an existential-causal theism. This inference does not proceed by way of hypothesis and deductive verification of appearances, so it cannot be eliminated on the grounds of being a superfluous hypothesis. Since it does not compete with other hypothetical explanations of the sense appearances, it is not affected by the decision to accept the simplest explanation of a hypothetico-deductive sort. After a relatively sufficient causal explanation of the latter sort has been given, there still remains the question of the actual cause of the act of existing and the other principles of being within the composite, sensible existent. This is the distinctive ground in experience for an inductively developed philosophy of God, whose validity therefore cannot be determined simply by appeal to the formal simplicity or logical expediency of explanations intended to answer questions about other aspects of the sensible world.

Modern atheism has a distinctive quality which is derived from the special intellectual circumstances surrounding its origin. Three marked trends in the period from Descartes to Kant—the mathematicizing and technical manipulation of nature, the emphasis upon God's transcendence at the expense of His immanence, and the phenomenalizing of sensible things—conspired to make the natural world seem entirely devoid of divine significance. In the face of this removal of God from the familiar region of experience, two courses lay open for the nineteenth-century intelligence: Either divinize nature itself or exclude the divine entirely. The first path was taken by transcendental idealism and Hegel, the second by atheism. But the atheistic choice was not made independently of the Hegelian synthesis. Indeed, what rendered modern atheism initially so strong and attractive was its protest against the submergence of man, nature, and the natural arts and sciences into the absolute spiritual whole. From Feuerbach onward, a persuasive case for atheism was built around its defense of the natural and the human against an encroaching absolute spirit. Instead of distinguishing the latter from the transcendent God and thus seeing things and persons in relation to God, however, the atheistic philosophers enclosed themselves in nature and sought terrestrial values alone. They justified a total elimination of God by appealing to both philosophical empiricism and the findings and methods of the sciences. The limits of empirical knowledge, the evolutionary nature of the cosmos, the natural genesis of man, the technological view of man and nature as objects to be calculated and controlled, the guidance of society and interpretation of history by human aims—all these aspects of the modern world were invoked in support of an atheistic outlook. Yet in order to lead to the atheistic conclusion, these aspects had to be interpreted by a set of philosophical principles inherited partly from Humean empiricism and partly from absolute idealism.

Even in its most empiricist and pluralistic form, modern atheism has depended, for its exclusion of God, upon a reductive conception of method and a purely immanent conception of being. The definitive liberation of man and the rest of nature from every sort of reductive monism cannot be achieved within the framework of the atheistic tradition. Once the idealism of absolute spirit is countered and the distinctive ways of finite being and empirical reasoning are vindicated, the defense of nature and man has no further use for either the emphatic or the discreet forms of atheism. Natural methods and humane values can be nourished within a postatheistic philosophical context which also permits men to inquire about the being of God and our human relations with Him.

Chapter IX

GOD FINITE AND IN PROCESS

IF WE WERE to concentrate exclusively upon the emergence of atheism, the trend of post-Hegelian philosophy would seem to be a steady recession from any acceptance of God. But historical movements are seldom so incomplex that they lead in only one direction, and the last century of speculation about God is no exception to the pluralism of intellectual history. For the same period has also seen the rise of several philosophies which admit God's existence with varying degrees of conviction but which describe His nature in terms usually reserved for created things. Instead of regarding finitude and process as the distinguishing marks of a universe radically distinct from God, such philosophies treat them as elements of likeness which bind God and the universe together in a common reality. There is just as impressive a convergence of finitist varieties of theism as there is of types of atheism. Even more striking is the fact that the finitist theories of God spring from much the same background of ideas as the atheistic systems and, in some instances, are definitely conceived as responses to the atheistic challenge. One of the chief ways of replying to contemporary atheism is to adjust the nature of God in order to meet certain objections which might otherwise support the total denial of His existence. If finite, developing, pragmatic traits are the marks of actual being, then their attribution to God is one predictable method for vindicating His reality.

Finitism usually maintains that God is limited in some of His attributes, even though He may be unlimited in other respects. Certain attributes of God are regarded as finite, but without prejudice to the infinite perfection of other sides of His nature. Sometimes, when finitism is joined with an evolutionary viewpoint, God is held to have a relative and provisional infinity, by comparison with lower forms of life. But this is always a temporary and comparative consideration: God is an ideal limit always receding before actual things, or He designates the highest degree presently reached by the evolutionary flow. Often, the introduction of finitude into the divine nature is combined with the admission of a process-factor, or becoming in God. There is a wide range of opinion concerning the ground and character of this becoming, reaching from simple frustration of the divine purpose and its adjustment in the face of obstacles to positive growth in God's knowledge, experience, and power. The ways of conceiving God as subject to limitation and change are just as many as the individual thinkers who develop their positions within this perspective.

The theory of a finite God is not a recent invention but is adumbrated throughout the history of philosophy.[1] The Platonic demiurge, the Aristotelian prime movers, and the Averroistic first cause are more remote examples in the finitist tradition, and the problem becomes a steady concern during the modern period. Locke was well aware of the finitist implications of the rationalistic, deductive approach to God, providing him with one of his strongest reasons for rejecting the a priori method in philosophy. Within the empiricist line itself, Hume and Voltaire deemed a finite Deity to be probably the safest inference from the order in nature. A finite God was repugnant to Kant, who based his argument against speculative knowledge of God precisely upon His unconditioned nature. Yet the Kantian critique at this point furnished a direct impetus toward finitist thinking. God's knowability might be vindicated either through a pantheistic importing of the finite world within the life of God or by showing that God does have finite aspects whereby He comes within the range of our speculative knowledge. One reason for the German revival of interest in Spinoza was the latter's view of finite things as being expressive modes of the divine substance itself, with nature being conceived as a grand totality embracing both infinite and finite aspects of the divine being. Fichte's pantheism viewed God sometimes as the inner law and system of finite entities and sometimes as an ideal limit for moral striving. Schelling introduced a limiting factor into the divine nature itself, in order to account for evil in the world and the travail of history. Finally, Hegel accustomed a whole generation to accept the presence of development in the absolute, one of whose essential phases is the finite realm of nature and human consciousness. A finitizing, changing aspect in the absolute spirit came to be regarded as the surety of divine life and actuality.

Despite these important anticipations, there was a noticeable quickening of the tempo of finitist theories of God after the mid-nineteenth century. Some of the older empiricist and humanist reasons, based upon the problems of knowledge and evil, were reaffirmed by John Stuart Mill. Yet what made his position both unique and intriguing was the suggestion that a finitist theism is only a temporary way station, destined to be replaced eventually by a thoroughgoing cult of humanity. In William James, one can observe some of the pragmatist motives favoring the notion of a finite God. He recommended an unvarnished finitism, both as a quite effective way of overcoming the idealist view that the finite world is only a phase within an infinite, all-inclusive spirit and also for its stimulating moral effect upon human conduct. The impact of evolutionary theory upon the question of God was not pointed exclusively in the direction of atheism but was also in favor of importing the evolutionary process into God's own life and denying that God is strictly a creator. A systematic, evolutionist approach to the finite aspects of the divine nature became a central theme in A. N. Whitehead's philosophy of the organism. He took a speculative view of the issue, showing that the basic description of actual entities entailed the ascription of finitude and process to God under several aspects.

1. MILL'S THEORY OF INTERIM FINITISM

John Stuart Mill (1806–1873) once remarked that he was one of the very few Englishmen of his day whose lack of religious belief was due rather to his never having had it than to his having discarded it in rebellion. He had been raised in the strict, antireligious covenant of his father, James Mill, who himself was indeed in full rebellion against the Calvinist "Omnipotent Author of Hell." The younger Mill had been taught that the origin of the world and oneself must remain unknown, both because it lies beyond our experience and because any given statement of origins always generates the further question about who made God. The parental training was strengthened by Mill's readings in Hume and Comte. To one of his early correspondents, he admitted that he agreed entirely with Comte's negative program of eliminating God from religion and that he had a lively hope in the eventual realization of the positivist religion of humanity.[2]

Nevertheless, there were some intellectual complications which troubled Mill and prompted him to reopen the theistic question from a fresh and personal angle. Both Saint-Simon and Comte himself had called the nineteenth century an age of transition and criticism, in which conflicting views and institutions were simultaneously present and partially justified. Comte had been willing enough to make a strategic compromise with Catholicism, in order to insure the more rapid triumph of positivist institutions, but Mill now argued that this mixed condition applied to beliefs, as well as to institutions, and that a rigid exclusion of theism was neither timely nor well founded. He criticized Comte for closing the philosophical debate about God prematurely and for not allowing intellectual freedom in this many-sided question.[3] It became one of Mill's permanent concerns to explore how far a phenomenalist and positivist thinker was justified in entertaining some sort of conception of God, at least during the transitional age which Matthew Arnold so aptly described as wandering between two worlds, one already dead and the other powerless to be born.

The type of theism which Mill came to regard as having at least a certain temporary validity was that of a God who is limited in power and perhaps also in knowledge. This recognition of a finite God, on an interim basis, constituted his chief amendment of the Comtean religion of humanity. He agreed heartily with his French mentor that the cult of humanity *can* (has the intrinsic capacity to) appropriate all the functions of religion after the complete removal of belief in God. What he questioned, however, was whether the present condition of intellectual evidence overwhelmingly required one to reject God and whether the present condition of social power assured the immediate, practical transition to the humanistic religion. On both the logical and the practical counts, he felt obliged to give a negative answer. The interim position which he proposed was denounced as a timid compromise by some of his positivist followers but was recommended by Mill himself for its integrity and practicality.

In setting forth his interim theism, Mill was careful to surround it with sufficient qualifications to prevent it from consolidating itself as a permanently valid position and thus from thwarting the ultimate historical goal of social and religious humanism. His main safeguards consisted in a distinction between factual belief and imaginative hope and in a set of criteria for the entertainment of an imaginative hypothesis.[4] He never conceded that our acceptance of God can validly attain the status of an inductive belief, since the latter state of mind is reserved for adherence to matters of fact which are quite firmly established through the inductive logic of the physical and social sciences. Nevertheless, in the realm of imagination and hope (the importance of which for coherent, unified thought and for effective human action Mill had learned from reading Wordsworth and Coleridge), a hypothesis can be entertained legitimately and usefully, as long as it satisfies three conditions. It must be consistent with our experience, internally consistent, and morally beneficial to mankind. Mill maintained that acceptance of a finite God is an act of imaginative hope, that it meets the three criteria satisfactorily, and hence that it is provisionally allowable, even for someone whose ultimate purpose is the positivist organization of society and human convictions. A finitist theism is illegitimate in the theoretical order only when it claims to be an inductive belief, in the full sense, and is socially detrimental only when it fails to give way before the positivist organizing activity once that activity is historically mature enough to shape effectively our social outlook and institutions.

All of Mill's speculations about God concentrate upon showing that imaginative hope in a finite God meets the requirements for this kind of mental conviction. His treatment of the proof from design shows that there is at least a minimal consistency between the existence of God and our experience of the world. The criterion of internal self-consistency is invoked against the infinity of divine power, since Mill thinks that an analytic consequence of infinite power is the impossibility of there being any evil. Finally, his defense of the moral utility of finitism is to show that it promotes sound tendencies in conduct by heightening our service to mankind.

(1) *The existence of God.* Mill describes his position as a rational skepticism which includes within itself a theism of the imagination and feelings. Its content can best be appreciated by comparison with the three other doctrines on God to which it is opposed: unconditioned belief in God, atheism, and agnosticism. Mill does not allow a place for any supernatural faith in God or any special organ for intuiting His existence. Even the tentative acknowledgment of God cannot properly base itself upon a claim to special revelation or intuition of His being. One special meaning for belief in God which Mill wants to rule out is that proposed by his contemporaries, Sir William Hamilton and Henry Mansel, whose theism is a strange melange of Scottish common sense, Kantian criticism, and German idealism.[5] Their attempt to work up to God by means of a dialectic of antinomies, compounded by an act of belief that runs in the face of the ordinary meaning of terms, is subjected to long and severe criticism by Mill. He concludes that the only reliable way of reaching God is by analysis of finite perfections and by a posteriori inference. But even this procedure cannot yield strict belief, either in the sense of direct factual acquaintance or an inductive inference of a very strong sort.

Nevertheless, the denial of well-founded belief in God need not lead to a dogmatic kind of either naturalistic atheism or agnosticism. Since his phenomenalism is perhaps even more rigorous than Hume's, Mill is suspicious of the dogmatic, metaphysical pronouncements of naturalistic atheism, even when they are couched in methodological language. He sees nothing intrinsically inconceivable in the notion of an intelligent agent, superior to nature, and nothing therein essentially derogatory to nature, considered as the sum of phenomenal events and causal laws. Hence he is disinclined to identify reality with nature in a way that will rule out, in principle, the possibility and desirability of an extranatural being. Doctrinaire atheism goes far beyond the phenomenalist premise that we can know things only relatively to ourselves and hence that we do not have any absolute, metaphysical definition of what the real can and cannot include.

Mill is not thereby excluding every atheistic attitude but only the sort based upon a general theory of method, nature, and being rather than upon a lack of evidence of God's existence. He makes a similar distinction between an agnosticism which claims to be a necessary inference from principles and one which rests simply upon the present-day limits of our knowledge. Doctrinaire agnosticism either gets entangled in the contradiction of discoursing very knowledgeably about the Unknown or else sheerly assumes that phenomenal objects refer only to intramundane forms of being. Despite his own phenomenalism, Mill is willing to look into the grounds for holding God's existence rather than insulate himself in the dogmatic negations of atheism and agnosticism. In this respect, he is being followed by some of the more recent American naturalists, who prefer to speak about the inevidence of God's existence rather than its absurdity.

His own median position of rational skepticism is in the Humean tradition. Just as Hume asserted that both atheism and theism can agree vaguely upon some sort of remote principle of events, so does Mill hold that the positivist explanation of determined events within the world is compatible with a causal origin of the world from God. Whether one actually joins a theistic doctrine with positivism depends not upon any strictly necessary principles but simply upon the amenability of theistic argumentation to scientific canons and the actual weight of the evidence as presently known.[6] Mill readily concedes that the scientific outlook is incompatible with a God who controls the world through variable laws, subject always to the whim of His will. The purely a priori proofs of God's existence are also disqualified, since they presume to determine existential fact by our ideas alone, whereas scientific inference is thoroughly a posteriori. A general-consensus approach is weak on the side of the evidence, which also supports animism and polytheism, and this proof usually falls back for its cogency upon an intuitive theory or a circular appeal to God's veracity.

There remain, however, the proofs from causation and design. Mill does not grant the validity of any causal proof which is distinct from the appeal to design. His view of causation is completely molded by his phenomenalism and the world-model proposed by the then current physical science. According to the latter, the real objects making up the universe are constituted by solid bits of matter and energy, both of which are eternal and uncaused. Mill never questions this scientific hypothesis of the uncreated, substantial stuff of things, since his theory of knowledge does not permit him to determine anything about real physical objects as distinct from their appearances. But he does use it strategically to eliminate any knowable kind of causation which would be a creation or total origination of being. At most, an active will may produce order in an already existing matter and its properties. Causal agency may account for the cosmos or order of the universe, precisely as it appears to us, but not for the being of the universe. The phenomenalist theory of knowledge deals with appearances, or physical events as they appear to us, but not with material objects in their own being. The only causes knowable by us are orderers of an already given matter, and their ordering activity can reach only to this or that particular appearance and not to the world as a whole. On the basis of his physical and epistemological position, Mill concludes that a causal inference to God cannot have any valid foundation distinct from the ordering activity, upon which the design-argument is based.

When Thomas Carlyle was told that at least the proof from design may still hold water in the scientific nineteenth century, he waxed mightily enthusiastic about Mill's researches in natural theology. Mill had to remind the truculent Scottish seer that a cautious phenomenalist can treat God's existence only as a hypothesis, the strength of which depends entirely upon experience and the canons of induction. At the very most, inductive reasoning from design can yield only a probable conviction or imaginative hope about His reality.

The argument from design can be taken in either an indeterminate or a determinate way. In its indeterminate formulation, it appeals to the general resemblance between the human artifact and the natural world, inferring the presence of a divine artisan with a mind not entirely unlike the mind of the human artisan. But Mill follows Hume in pointing out that since we have no direct observation of the designing activity of God, we cannot determine the precise degree of resemblance or difference. Such an indeterminate appeal to resemblance-in-general is a mere analogy (which Mill takes to be the equivalent of an uncontrolled surmise about a likeness), not a genuine induction.

But when we attend to a determinate aspect of the resemblance—namely, the design-factor, or working of components toward an end on the part of some natural thing—then a real, inductive argument for God can be made. According to his canons of logic, Mill classifies this proof as an instance of the method of agreement among phenomena. Although this method is the least cogent inductive procedure, nevertheless, the determinate argument from design is one of the strongest instances of induction by agreement. The way in which the otherwise disparate parts of the eye join in the unified act of vision indicates that the formation and the unification of these parts were both guided by the idea of seeing and not by the (as yet inexistent) physical act of seeing. The probable conclusion is that the idea of seeing exists originally in the mind of an intelligent, willing designer who is far superior to man in these perfections. This cosmic designer accounts for the order present in that part of the universe with which we are acquainted. It need not be supposed, however, that the orderer of our cosmos produces everything about it (the matter and energy as such) or that his intellectual foresight is universally operative in regions beyond our knowledge.

Mill advances over the previous Enlightenment version of this reasoning in his careful measurement of its logical worth and its relation to evolutionary findings. Although it is an inductive argument attaining a degree of probability, it is not sufficiently well founded to produce full inductive belief. Writing approximately a decade after the publication of Darwin's great *Origin of Species* (1859), Mill notes that the Darwinian hypothesis is not intrinsically absurd and that the evidence so far advanced in its support renders it a plausible explanation of biological order.[7] He recognizes that future research may well render it highly probable that the inherent energy and laws of living matter account for purposive organisms and even for minded beings. The evolutionary explanation is not incompatible with the concept of an ultimate divine agency, but the trend of biological findings may undercut the inductive ground for accepting God as an existential fact. Hence Mill refuses to regard the argument from design as a firmly established inductive belief. Since it is not merely open to revision in the way that all inductive conclusions are open but is liable to definitive replacement by an ongoing tendency in scientific research, the conviction of God's existence is no more than an imaginative hope, yet one that violates no logical canons and rests on some inductive evidence.

Mill never sought to find a nonphenomenalist conception of causality and hence a causal inference which is not reducible to the design-argument or dependent upon biological research. Yet he did indicate his opposition to the Kantian criticism of all speculative arguments for God's existence. Kant had claimed that such arguments must become entangled in the dialectic of the unconditioned and must employ the idea of the most perfect being. But the proof from design conforms to neither of these requirements, for it is an instance of the inductive method of agreement, going from the order given in our sensations concerning the world to an orderer having sufficient foresight and power of will to fashion the order. Faced with Kant's objection that the finite design in the world can lead only to a finite cosmic designer, Mill simply accepted the consequence. But he observed that at least his inductive argument did not have to rely on the concept of the unconditioned or make any covert deduction from the idea of the most perfect being, since the reasoning went directly to a sufficiently intelligent and powerful orderer and stopped right there. Thus finitism appealed to Mill as an effective way to overcome the Kantian criticism and still keep within the framework of inductive reasoning.

(2) *God as finite power.* Hume had once suggested that when we call God "perfect," we may only mean "finitely perfect" or intelligent and powerful enough to fashion our world of phenomena in its orderly aspects. Mill agreed that the inductively established God is not creator but demiurge or fashioner of order in our cosmos. Hence limitations in the experienced order may reflect corresponding limitations in the inferred source of that order. Especially when we are confronted with physical and moral evil, it seems likely that God is finite in some basic aspects. His power is certainly limited, and His intelligence may also have boundaries and defects. Mill recommended finitism as a means of replying not only to Kant but also to Bayle's famous dilemma that, in

the face of evil, we must conclude either that God is omnipotent and hence malevolent or else that He is benevolent and hence limited in power. Mill simply accepted the latter horn of the dilemma, which was consistent with his version of the design-argument. In one of his infrequent historical asides, he noted that Leibniz' own attempt to answer Bayle led him to place a certain limitation upon God. To explain evil through an abstract set of possible essences, to which the divine intellect and will must submit as to an independent law, is implicitly to insert a limiting factor into the divine nature.

The one proposition about God which Mill categorically maintains to be established is that He is not omnipotent. He supports this denial by setting down the consequences which should follow from the hypothesis that God is omnipotent.

It is not too much to say that every indication of design in the kosmos is so much evidence against the omnipotence of the designer. For what is meant by design? Contrivance: the adaptation of means to an end. But the necessity for contrivance—the need of employing means—is a consequence of the limitation of power. . . . If the creator of mankind willed that they [men] should all be virtuous, his designs are as completely baffled as if he had willed that they should all be happy: and the order of nature is constructed with even less regard to the requirements of justice than to those of benevolence. If the law of all creation were justice and the creator omnipotent, then in whatever amount suffering and happiness might be dispensed to the world, each person's share of them would be exactly proportioned to that person's good or evil deeds; no human being would have a worse lot than another, without worse deserts; accident or favouritism would have no part in such a world, but every human life would be the playing out of a drama constructed like a perfect moral tale.[8]

Since the adaptations in nature do require the use of determinate means, since many of our motives and deeds do run contrary to good moral intent, and since happiness and suffering are not nicely proportioned to moral worth, Mill rejects the hypothesis of divine omnipotence. Moreover, he does so not merely in a speculative manner but with a deep fervor which shows his moral abhorrence for the idea. He finds it morally more helpful to picture God as a well-meaning cosmic craftsman, who is not completely powerful and perhaps not fully competent, than as an all-powerful agent who can, but does not, abolish all evil at His mere word.

The finitist position derives much of its appeal from this way of saving God's goodness at the expense of His power. It must be noted, however, that Mill conceives of the divine power in a very special way in reference to the problem of evil. His treatment of divine power presupposes three points: that God is not strictly a creator or total first cause but a maker; that divine power can be isolated adequately from the other divine attributes; that there is no personal freedom and immortality for man. Each of these presuppositions determines the way in which the question of divine power and evil is resolved.

What Mill establishes is the limitation of power in a maker rather than in the creator or total cause of the finite being. He argues from the limited order in the given material world to a limited orderer. This is a perfectly valid inference; no more than a limited power is required to produce such an order, considered just by itself. The crucial issue concerns the materials already "given," in the sense that the physical sciences are not required to explain them. If philosophy can show that these materials have a causal origin through a creative act or a producing of them from nothing, then some grounds are present for maintaining the infinity of divine power. We are led to affirm the infinite power, not because of the intrinsic nature of the product (whether it be the basic materials or some particular order), but because of the manner of its production by the first cause. Although the effect itself is finite, the producing of it from nothing can only be accomplished by an agent who is in no way dependent or circumscribed in causal power.

Mill leaves a shadowy realm of basic matter and energy beyond the pale of the divine causal power. Hence he must conceive of God as a demiurge, pitting His limited skill against alien materials and wringing from them a partial but progressive victory. A designing but noncreating power is a sort of engineering skill, in which the maker is really dependent upon his materials. When Mill appeals to contrivance or adaptation as proof of limited power in God, he is visualizing the contriving activity on the part of a maker, who shapes but does not causally originate his materials. It is not the presence of adaptation as such but the confining of adaptation to the special sort proper to such a maker which provides an argument for limited power. Where the entire means-end relationship is the outcome of a creative act and where the agent himself is not using the means to perfect his own nature, the power is not limited.

Mill isolates the divine power entirely from the other attributes of God and then inquires whether this completely isolated power can be infinite and still bring forth a world of evil and inequality. Like the other finitists, Mill is not sensitive to any special problem raised by this procedure, since he does not concern himself with the nature of the distinction among the attributes or between the divine essence and its perfections. That is why he is in no way disconcerted about holding that God is infinite in some of His attributes and finite in others. The divine simplicity is not a real problem for Mill, and therefore he can isolate power and adjudge it to be finite without having to reckon with any metaphysical consequences. His approach to God is a nonmetaphysical one, in the sense that he deals directly with divine intelligence and power as manifested in the world, and does not have to reckon with any demonstrative inference of God's existence and simplicity as a basis for treating these attributes.

It is this fully isolated sort of infinite, divine power which arouses Mill's moral loathing, not the divine power considered integrally, as carrying out the plan of the divine wisdom and goodness. When Mill asks whether such an isolated power is good, the very way in which this power is being conceived compels a negative answer. This hypostasized divine power has but to nod and all evil will disappear, and yet the nod is never forthcoming. Its relation to the world is that of playwright to script, and the script contains absolutely nothing more than the author's embodied intent and skill. Given this conception of what the infinite power of God would be and what relation the finite world would bear toward it, Mill can only conclude that an infinite power is not good. The power of a good God must be limited.

Mill failed to scrutinize critically his hypothetical assumption that in a world made by an infinitely powerful God, "every human life would be the playing out of a drama constructed like a perfect moral tale." Here he took advantage of the occasionalist and determinist view of God as the master playwright-puppeteer and then pointed out how woefully this life of ours falls short of being a nicely rounded tale or what Poe once called a perfect plot of God. Since he was arguing hypothetically, however, he had the obligation to present the theory of an infinitely powerful and good God in the strongest form. This would have meant a recognition of the bearing of secondary causality, individual freedom, and personal immortality upon our view of human life. Although Mill mentioned the two latter concepts in the course of his argument, he did not accord them full weight precisely at that point where they were most relevant. He did not bring them in as incisive correctives of the playwright metaphor, but only as separate and subsidiary considerations.

In the problem of suffering and evil, however, where man and God are being considered formally in relation to each other, there is a conjunction and causal ordering of the factors of divine power, human freedom, and immortality. Viewed in the perspective of an ordering of free causes, the metaphor of the author-and-his-tale breaks down and fails to convey, with any precision, the complexity of the problem. Mill relied upon the force of the contrast between an infinite God, who simply dictates His morality play, and the evils and tragedies of our life. But the conclusion flowing from this comparison is not that God is working under limitation in divine power but that the conception of a playwright-God is a misleading way to view the infinite cause with respect to finite, free agents. Not only our humanistic tradition, but also a doctrine on divine causality, shows that our temporal life cannot be treated as a perfect morality play. From both sides, then, the comparison between the moral tale and the actual conditions of life ignores some relevant factors and hence fails to decide the issue of divine power.

(3) *The moral utility of finitism.* The major advance which Mill makes over Hume is to remove the latter's restriction of theism to a bare speculative assent to an intelligent agent. Hume's primary reason for setting this limit was his fear of the corrupting effects of an alliance between a few "elect" men and what they might be pleased to regard as the ordinances of an infinite, divine will. But within Mill's context, the will of God is finite and stands in need of human co-operation, while the task of interpreting that will coincides with the reasoning of Mill's own utilitarian ethics, which is an independent rational discipline.[9] Hence he permits the assent to God to be practical, as well as speculative, and to include a recognition of God's moral attribute of benevolence. There is a slight, inductive basis for holding that the divine will and power aim at the temporal duration and happiness of man, even though our happiness may not be God's sole or chief purpose in ordering the cosmos. However slim the indications, they are enough to stimulate our imaginative hope in a good God, and such hope is bound to have practical repercussions.

The readmission of the moral attribute of benevolence, even as a quite tenuous possibility, spelled the end of the total neutralization of God in British empiricism. Mill was confident that the empiricist theory of knowledge had broken the strength of the classical rationalist use of God in a deductive system and that it was quite capable of undermining any dialectical absolute. Hence it was safe enough to acknowledge an intelligent and benevolent God, although only under the conditions of probabilism, finitism, and an interim hope. What Mill was ready to restore to philosophy was the weak probability of the existence of a limited but benevolent demiurge, with the proviso that this probability could not solidify itself but was eventually scheduled for replacement by a definitive, certain belief in humanity. It was not as a speculative natural theology but as a practical instrument, transitional to the positivist religion of humanity, that the inquiry into God figured in Mill's philosophy. Instead of a functionalism ordained to the rationalist and idealist systems, he proposed a functional theism which would serve the purposes of a utilitarian and positivist type of empiricism.

One advantage of the theory of a finite God was to enable Mill to criticize the sheerly equivocal way in which Hamilton and Mansel predicated the moral attribute of goodness to the absolute. They characterized the absolute as the infinite point of coincidence for all attributes and antinomies and claimed that the goodness of this absolute was utterly different from, and contradictory of, our experiential notion of moral good. Yet, as Mill observed, it might then turn out that God is not good in any humanly recognizable sense but includes elements of what we regard as evil. In that case, we should not apply the name "good" to this infinite absolute at all, nor should we give it worship.

Mill located the intellectual difficulty in two points: starting off with an abstract absolute rather than a concrete God and claiming that this absolute is infinite rather than finite. He was keenly aware of the contrast between the dialectical absolute and God, but the only way he could devise for retaining the contrast was to finitize God and establish a continuity of degrees between divine and human attributes.

Language has no meaning for the words "just," "merciful," "benevolent," save that in which we predicate them of our fellow-creatures; and unless that is what we intend to express by them, we have no business to employ the words. If in affirming them of God we do not mean to affirm these very qualities, differing only as greater in degree, we are neither philosophically nor morally entitled to affirm them at all.[10]

One may call God infinitely good and benevolent, but this means the highest degree of the same quality as is found in man.

This controversy over moral goodness throws some further light on the motives for Mill's finitism. The kind of infinite power which he criticized for its demoralizing effect is that of an indeterminate absolute, which embraces all contradictories and is equivocally related to human values. Mill countered this view with the phenomenalist principle that God cannot be known noumenally, or in His own being, but only as related to our sensations. Hence the predications about God can only be extrinsic and univocal ones, admitting at most a difference in degree between human and divine perfections. The distinction which Mill made between the infinite and the finite attributes is thus only a relative one; even the infinite attribute of benevolence signifies no more than the maximum degree of human moral perfection within a universe whose first cause cannot be known certainly to exist. Without any causal and analogical basis for his inference to God's existence, Mill could not replace an equivocal infinite absolute by anything but an imaginative hope in a finite orderer. Since this hope rested upon an expansion of human qualities, Mill concluded that finitism must function as a transitional means to an admittedly man-centered outlook and social order.

During the interim period, however, it is morally stimulating to entertain the idea of siding with the good principle in the cosmos and making a real contribution toward its struggle for human happiness.

A virtuous human being assumes in this theory [of a God finite in power] the exalted character of a fellow-labourer with the Highest, a fellow-combatant in the great strife. . . . According to it, man's duty would consist, not in simply taking care of his own interests by obeying irresistible power, but in standing forward a not ineffectual auxiliary to a being of perfect beneficence; a faith which seems much better adapted for nerving him to exertion than a vague and inconsistent reliance on an author of good who is supposed to be also the author of evil.[11]

It is by this purely pragmatic measure, in final analysis, that Mill justifies the retention of imaginative hope in God. It accustoms men to the vocation of working with others for the good of humanity. Hope in the finite God has no other pragmatic meaning than dedication to the needs of men, and hence it can be held, alongside a humanistic positivism, until social conditions permit the discarding of any reference beyond the totality of man-in-the-cosmos. Mill looks forward to the fulfillment of Goethe's prophecy of a new age of belief, one which will rest not upon the theism of a finite God but upon the ideal of humanity in a completely immanent line of progress. Whereas the theistic hope will pass away, the positivist hope will be transformed into a firmly established, socially organized belief.

2. THE PLURALISTIC THEISM OF WILLIAM JAMES

The intellectual influence of Mill upon the religious formation of William James (1842–1910) is directly traceable through the latter's letters and occasional printed references. Although he found his predecessor's logical and psychological views too atomistic and mechanistic in an evolutionary age, James gave a sympathetic response to Mill's position on moral and religious matters. Even here, however, there was a significant reversal of perspectives. Whereas Mill held that the direction of creative advance went from an interim belief in a finite God to humanitarian ethics, James started with the latter position and gradually moved forward to a belief in the finite God. His eye was first caught by the secular morality of utilitarianism, and only later on did he come to recognize the merits in finitism.

As a young medical student and physiologist, James was an uneasy exponent of a materialistic and utilitarian standpoint.[12] He had been forced into this position by the inadequacy of the theistic arguments of the Scottish common-sense school (which gained a new lease on life in America until the advent of evolutionism) and by his own father's curious mixture of Swedenborgian religion and American transcendentalism. The elder Henry James explained the relation between God and the world in such fashion that the distinctive reality of the latter was seriously threatened. Finite things are manifestations of divine power that appear and are revoked at will. This led William James to fear that the doctrine of creation always meant the dissolution of finite things and the exchange of rational explanation for magical origins. So deep a mark did his father's teaching make upon his mind that even after rehabilitating some aspects of the divine nature and activity, James never afterwards regarded God as the creative cause of the universe. The association between creative power and an illusionist conception of the universe was never dispelled for him, so that the deity which he eventually accepted was a noncreative and finite agency.

His readings in Büchner and Spencer made James skeptical about any proofs of God founded on causality and design. Like Holbach and the naturalistic atheists, he saw in the scientific merging of matter and force an argument for the self-sufficiency of the world, blocking any inference from caused and contingent things. As for the appeal to design, James was deeply impressed with the naturalistic position of Chauncey Wright (a fellow member at Harvard of the so-called "Metaphysical Club," which fathered pragmatism), who liked to refer to events in nature as so much cosmic weather. Like our ordinary weather, things on a cosmic scale are constantly doing and undoing themselves, without achieving any generally recognizable aim. And since Darwin was highlighting the chance factors and the huge amount of waste and carnage in the biological sphere, James concluded that nature as a whole shows no sure indications of benevolent design. He never gained confidence in a distinct, causal inference or in a design-argument covering the whole of nature, although he eventually held that the limited amount of beneficial design perhaps betokens a limited but good God.

Typically enough, the occasion for quickening theistic belief in James' mind was not a metaphysical or scientific argument but a personal, moral crisis. In a revealing letter addressed to Oliver Wendell Holmes, Jr., later a distinguished justice of the United States Supreme Court, James outlined the practical attitude flowing from the sensationalist-utilitarian philosophy which they shared during the 1860's.

If God is dead or at least irrelevant, ditto everything pertaining to the "Beyond." If happiness is our Good, ought we not to try to foment a passionate and bold will to attain that happiness among the multitudes? Can we not conduct off upon our purposes from the old moralities and theologies a beam which will invest us with some of the proud absoluteness which made them so venerable, by preaching the doctrine that Man is his own Providence, and every individual a real God to his race, greater or less in proportion to his gifts and the way he uses them?[13]

Despite the Nietzschean boldness of this passage, James could find no basis for individual, human freedom within the sensationalist-utilitarian context. His search for such a basis led him to criticize the older empiricist theory of mind for failing to take account of the active, purposive, and selective character of our mental life. And unlike Mill and the later American naturalists, he experienced no ultimately compelling attraction in the ideal of scientifically controlled social progress. The welfare of future generations seemed to be too vague a goal to provide a determinate obligation in the moral present. Indeed, during the first stage of his emancipation from Mill and positivist morality, James insisted that it is precisely the finite nature of humanity that prevents it from placing the maximum demand upon our moral action. An "infinite demander" is required to cement our loyalty to our earthly tasks, especially in the face of egoism, discouragement, and tragedy.[14]

James recovered his living conviction in God in much the same way that he regained confidence in human freedom: through a voluntary act of belief. Encouraged by the French phenomenalist and personalist Charles Renouvier, he took the decisive step of willing to believe in freedom. Similarly, he agreed with Renouvier that the only foundation for theism is an act of will and belief. Replying many years later to a questionnaire sent out by J. B. Pratt, he noted emphatically that his own acceptance of God rested in no way upon the arguments from cause and design and not even upon a personal experience of God in direct or mystical union. The source of his theism lay in his personal sense of a need to have God as a corroborator, consoler, and stimulator to moral ideals, as well as in his professional observation of the religious experience of other people. He saw in his own moral need of God a sufficient motive for adopting the theistic hypothesis and in the testimony of religious experience a definite degree of empirical confirmation of this hypothesis. He confined his own theistic belief to this approach, leaving other ways to God for men having other outlooks.

One of James' chief preoccupations was to explain and defend the will to believe in God and to show that the object of this act is a finite God. This led him also to criticize the doctrine of idealistic monism and to reject any speculative, natural theology. Thus his finitism was inter-woven with the most fundamental aspects of his philosophy.

(1) *Pragmatic belief in a finite God.* By locating his assent to God entirely in the domain of practical faith, James intended to dissociate it not only from any speculative claim of knowing God but also from Mill's restriction of theism to imaginative hope. He urged that the business of philosophy is practical as well as theoretical and that the scope of inductive belief must be broadened to include the acceptance of God which Mill had reserved for imaginative hope. Private, practical interest in ultimate matters is not a region apart but is open to regulation by the same logic of action which governs all other instances of inductive belief.

Despite the misleading connotation of "will to believe" and other all too popular slogans taken from his books, James does distinguish the act of natural faith from reckless assertion and dreamful wishing.[15] We have recourse to belief in situations where we are faced with living options, which we cannot resolve by our intellect alone, since the object escapes us either entirely or in reference to our present condition. If we cannot gain direct perceptual access to a purportedly real and practically important object, then at least we can form a hypothesis whose testing will empirically confirm or disconfirm it. Belief means the willingness to act upon a hypothesis in a case where there is room for theoretical doubt and where an option must be made between alternate hypotheses. James regards the existence of God as a hypothesis proposed for an individual's practical belief, in the absence of complete objective cogency of evidence and in a case where the individual is not in direct, mystical contact with God. The theistic hypothesis involves the option of excluding such other explanations as atheism and absolutism; it also entails the willingness to act irrevocably in conformity with what the hypothesis requires concerning man's practical relation to God. Belief in God is a working hypothesis, in the double sense of invoking our active response and of testing itself by its practical consequences.

The pragmatic testing is the crucial consideration for James, since it sets off a responsible from an irresponsible option. The theist gives his assent to God and acts accordingly only because of his primary loyalty to the search for truth. He is in a situation where the refusal to believe may result in the loss of an important, practical truth or in the failure to bring this truth into being. The theistic hypothesis is risked, lest one run the more serious risk of failing to provide the sole conditions under which the truth about God can be ascertained by the nonmystical mind. Acting on this hypothesis is not foolhardy and arbitrary, since the only way to put it to the test is through analysis of the believer's actions. The psychological and moral *motive* of theistic belief is simply our human need for a powerful ally in the universe. The Promethean attitude of defiant self-sufficiency, such as James had outlined to Holmes and such as Bertrand Russell has made popular, fails us in those long stretches where our endurance depends upon living in awareness of a personally responsive, cosmic agent. But the logical *argument* in favor of the objective reality of this ally comes from examining the quality of our acting in conformity with belief in an existent God.

Bringing his pragmatic method to bear upon this issue, James distinguished between the meaning and the truth of the idea of God. Its pragmatic *meaning* consists in the concrete consequences it engenders in the individual believer's outlook and conduct. The shortest expression of this meaning is to say that henceforth certain fears are banished; the theist need no longer fear that the moral order will completely perish and that the good ends in life lack a champion more effective than ourselves. "In saying 'God exists' all I imply is that my purposes are cared for by a mind so powerful as on the whole to control the drift of the universe."[16] In order to stress the practical and forward-looking nature of pragmatic theism, James held that in a world standing on the brink of annihilation, it would be quite indifferent whether we attribute its origin and past history to God or to the motion of physical particles. What would count as a meaningful alternative is the practical difference between facing a future which holds only the prospect of entropy and facing one which contains the hope of an eternal moral order and a personal recognition of our actions. The determinate, pragmatic meaning of the idea of God consists precisely in that difference.

Indeed, after reconsidering the question, James came to admit a meaningful difference between God and matter, even with respect to the past. He likened the individual's response to a godless universe to our attitude toward an "automatic sweetheart" or a "mechanical bride," which would supply all our affective wants through electronic means, but with no accompaniment of free, personal interest in our individual lives. However subtle its organization, matter cannot provide a satisfactory substitute for God, since we value outward activities for the sake of the accompanying consciousness, which can give a personal evaluation of our moral efforts.

As for the *truth* of the idea of God, it must also be ascertained through the ordinary pragmatic course of verification.

Pragmatism is willing to take anything, to follow either logic or the senses and to count the humblest and most personal experiences. She will count mystical experiences if they have practical consequences. She will take a God who lives in the very dirt of private fact—if that should seem a likely place to find him. Her only test of probable truth is what works best in the way of leading us, what fits every part of life best and combines with the collectivity of experience's demands, nothing being omitted. If theological ideas should do this, if the notion of God, in particular, should prove to do it, how could pragmatism possibly deny God's existence?[17]

Except for the mystic, there cannot be full certainty about God resulting from a direct verification which leads the individual to a perception of God. But there can be an indirect or potential verification (verifiability), giving us some probability for entertaining the theistic belief. In this type of verification, the idea is seen to lead at least in the direction of a perceptual conjunction with the object. We can judge indirectly about the truth or satisfactory leading of the idea of God, by finding whether it fits coherently with our past experience, with already verified propositions, and with the needs of action (all of which, taken together, constitute "the collectivity of experience's demands"). If it satisfies these tests, then belief in God probably sets us on the road toward a perceptual fulfillment of our basic needs.

James uses a threefold pragmatic yardstick to measure the probable truth of belief in God.[18] First, the evidence of religious and mystical experience contains—despite a bewildering conflict over the details—a hard core of common conviction in the reality of eternal life, as a "something more" which exists and acts effectively for the better. Even those who (like James himself) have no direct communion with God can at least respect the testimony of others and discern their common ordination to a superhuman consciousness. A second test is provided by the coherence of theism with our other views about the world. James observes that practical theism surpasses the scientific outlook but does not conflict with it. Atheistic naturalism is not the necessary logical outcome of any scientific conception but is itself a practical option and counterbelief against theism. Finally, he recommends theism for its maximal stimulation of the moral will and hence for being better for our active life. From the standpoint of a melioristic ethics, our constant effort at a fuller transformation of reality is sustained by the thought that we have a champion, or powerful superhuman consciousness, working with us toward the realization of the same moral order.

Up to this point, James has been trying to establish the probable truth of theism in general. In order to defend specifically the idea of a finite God, he now distinguishes between verification as the active transforming of one's personal outlook and verification as the active contribution to the very reality and aim of the object of belief. Although admitting that God Himself cannot be used as an instrument, James nevertheless maintains that activity inspired by theistic belief can somehow contribute to God's limited and developing perfection.[19] This perfecting of God through our active belief can be understood either as a furthering of God's purpose in the world, through our loyalty to the divine moral ideal, or as an enrichment of the divine being itself. James accepts both meanings of the perfecting of God through human belief in Him. He finds it morally more invigorating to conceive of ourselves as God's helpers than merely to consider God as our helper. Like Mill, he regards our partnership with God as a two-way affair, in which both the human and the divine agents can be of mutual assistance toward realizing each other's potentialities and common aim.

Thus the pragmatic basis of James' theism leads him to embrace the "overbelief" that the nature of God is finite and developing. All that is required for the minimal pragmatic meaning of God is a real, superhuman consciousness and cosmic power. But if it is a moral stimulant to view this God as limited in power, struggling with evil, and needing our help for His own development, then there is warrant enough for adding that God is finite and in process.

This conclusion is open to criticism from several quarters. For one thing, even within the Jamesian theory of indirect verification the inference to a finite God remains provisional, until it is shown to be coherent with all other relevant truths about the world and its implications. James recognizes that the overbelief in a finite God-in-process is irreconcilable with any demonstration of God's infinite perfection and actuality. Hence he denies that there is any valid natural theology or speculative doctrine on the infinite being of God with which our practical beliefs have to square themselves. Just as his minimal practical belief in God supposes that there is no cogent speculative evidence of the divine existence, so does his overbelief in a finite, developing God suppose that there is no speculative truth of the infinitely actual perfection of God. Whether or not the idea of a finite God can be pragmatically verified depends upon the soundness of James' refutation of every speculative philosophy of God, a question which will be separately examined.

Secondly, after making all possible allowances for James' personal and stylistic exuberance, there is an undeniable remainder of irrationalism motivating his pragmatic belief in God. Merely to designate his position as irrational is not in itself a criticism but only a description, indeed, a description in James' own language. Criticism can rightly intervene, however, by inspecting the structure of this irrationalism in regard to our way of reaching God. It is not based upon recognition of the limits of speculative reason, the value-aspect of knowledge, the distinctive function and influence of will, or the presence in things of an individual, fluent aspect escaping complete conceptual expression. All these features of man and the world can be acknowledged without leading to irrationalism. But James makes a breach between speculative and practical reason with respect to God and answers skepticism simply by countering one voluntary act against another. He founds the rights of practical belief upon skeptical despair in ultimate matters and upon voluntarism rather than upon the need to supplement speculative reason. His doctrine on God is not primarily a defense of our natural, informal inference to God and our practical adhesion to Him. Rather, it is a natural fideism which regards our practical needs as the only positive route to God, apart from religious experience and mysticism. What makes this viewpoint irrational is not its respect for what our practical life and beliefs testify about God but its insistence that speculative reason is thoroughly nonexistential, nonexperiential, and hence inherently incapable of yielding any reliable knowledge of God.

In the third place, James did not fully work out his theory of indirect and practical verification. This is not to say that he was ignorant (as some later American naturalists have claimed) of the distinction between those practical consequences which merely occur simultaneously with adoption of a working hypothesis (and which may nevertheless logically confirm some other view) and those consequences which are logically entailed by the given hypothesis and hence which precisely confirm it as true. To say that religious experiences *may* perhaps be explained otherwise than through the divine reality does not justify the implicit inference that these experiences *cannot* be founded upon God. In his theory of the subliminal self, acting as an alien power and control over conscious life, James provided his own naturalistic explanation of religious experience. He did not regard this explanation as a refutation of theism but as a valid yet inadequate account of some of the factors involved in the religious situation. In addition, he emphasized that the hopeful, religious outlook is something precisely *un*attainable through a naturalistic hypothesis.[20] This indicates his awareness of the problem of securing the determinate, logical entailment of a certain practical attitude from the hypothesis of God and of showing that certain states of consciousness are not only present but also truly indicative of the reality of their object.

Nevertheless, James did underplay both the attractiveness of a morality based upon the technical imperatives of the natural sciences and the scope which a naturalistic morality may allow for a certain secular hope and fellow feeling. On purely pragmatic grounds, many people today find the moral stimulus of a scientifically controlled, social development much stronger than ; n appeal to their loyalty toward a struggling, superhuman consciousness. That is why John Dewey was even willing to attach the name "God" to the former ideal without any special connotation of a finite God. The absence of any speculative doctrine on God prevented James from completing his verification. He failed to show that realizing a certain moral ideal is precisely realizing a moral order intended by his deity, let alone that this deity genuinely improves as the result of human endeavors at upright living. James would reply that his practical belief in a finitist theism is a matter of individual commitment on his own part, but then its relevance to the rest of us remains obscure.

(2) *The critique of absolutism.* The lifelong duel which James fought with such absolute idealists as Bradley and Royce left a deep mark upon his notion of God. For instance, his refusal to admit that speculative reason gives us any access to God had in view the idealistic conception of speculative reason as the source of its theory about the divine nature. The irrationalist tendency in James' theism arose from his conviction that every demonstrative, rational approach to God must terminate in idealistic monism. Another example of the effect of this polemic upon his thought was the way in which he distinguished between limitations in the finite God and limitations in the idealistic absolute. The former was limited externally by alien conditions, which God's power could not wholly master, whereas the latter limited itself internally and by means of its own infinite power. Indeed, James underlined, with even more insistence than did Mill, the disparity between the monistic absolute and God, whether God be regarded as infinite or finite. In both his Hibbert and his Lowell lectures, he asked his audience

to distinguish the notion of the absolute carefully from that of another object with which it is liable to become heedlessly entangled. That other object is the "God" of common people in their religion, and the creator-God of orthodox Christian theology. Only thoroughgoing monists or pantheists believe in the absolute. . . . I trust that you see sufficiently that the absolute has nothing but its superhumanness in common with the theistic God.[21]

James added the pertinent historical remark that Kant remained a theist and should not be considered an exponent of the absolute spirit. The idealistic absolute had a Kantian lineage, but only to the extent that the idealists converted Kant's unity of apperception into a concrete universal or world-self.

The special target of James' criticism was his colleague and friendly opponent for a quarter-century at Harvard, Josiah Royce (1855–1916). The latter sought to accommodate the individual and voluntary aspects of things within absolute idealism and even to find a place in his system for the pragmatic view of cognition. Royce's main argument was that the successful leading of ideas to perceptual objects requires an absolute mind which actively intends the relation of the idea to the object and which encloses both idea and object within its own infinite system of consciousness. After struggling for years with this audacious exploitation of pragmatism for idealist ends, James finally concluded that the force of the reasoning could be dissipated through a historical explanation and an epistemological revision.[22]

Historically, James traces the appeal of absolute idealism to an understandable reaction against the excesses of classical British empiricism. In Hume, the analytic, empirical approach to experience led to the atomizing of discrete ideas, to skepticism concerning real relations, and to a divorce between subjective appearances or meaning and objective reality. The only way to restore a fruitful relation between ideas and real objects seemed to be through importing them both into an absolute mind. Thus when Royce urged the need for a sufficient ground in the absolute for the pragmatic leading of ideas to perceptual objects, he was presupposing the Humean notion of a discrete, subjective idea.

But James now points out that his own radical empiricism criticizes the basic points in Hume's theory of knowledge, showing that relations are really given in experience and that ideas provide their own leadings toward a perceptual terminus. Because of this epistemological reform, the intentional function of ideas and the verifying process can be seen to be wholly intraexperiential or within finite, human experience. This eliminates the need to suppose the monistic absolute as the immediate, epistemological condition for pragmatic verification. The intermediaries between the initial state of ideal meaning and its satisfactory termination are themselves part of our finite experience, obviating the idealist absorption of human cognition within an all-inclusive absolute spirit. We can describe the human knowing process adequately, without requiring the absolute to enter in as a guarantor of its objective reference.

Moving into the offensive, James then takes a critical look at Royce's claim to preserve individuality, contingency, and freedom within his revised idealism. In a private memorandum sent to Royce and later incorporated into book form, he comments on the striking difference between the way up to the absolute and the way down from the absolute to other things. When Royce is making his ascent to the absolute, he stresses the indivisibility of all reality, the impossibility of considering any term apart from all its relations to the whole universe, and the necessary coimplication of all facts in a single lock-step system, which James calls "the block-universe." From this perspective, there is no room for individual integrity of beings, contingent relations, or freedom. These qualities heave into sight only after one concedes the absolute mind and begins moving downwards from it again to the finite order. But the world from which the absolutist demonstration begins is not the same world with which it indulgently terminates the logical movement. If the world of contingent, individual existents were the starting point, it could never lead to the absolute. Hence there is a deep, logical cleavage in the Roycean vision of the finite world, indicating that either the absolute or the contingent existent must be sacrificed. Since James finds no empirical reason in the nature of human cognition or in observable relations for giving up the integrity of finite things, he concludes that it is the absolute spirit which must go.

As a result of this controversy, James is able to clarify for himself the main differences between God and the absolute. God respects the individuality and subjective existence of finite selves, whereas the absolute accords to them no other reality than that of objects in and for itself. But we have the experience of being subjects and having our own perspective. Our *to-be* is something other than *to-be-an-object* of howsoever inclusive a cosmic consciousness. If we were objective points within the implicatory system of the absolute mind, we could only think and act for this mind and as it determines. This consequence would render inquiry and free choice inexplicable and would transmute evil into a dissonant harmony. Whether God be regarded as infinite or finite, however, He is the being who brings us forth to live our own existence, to stumble ahead toward genuine discoveries in knowledge, to experience evil as treasonous allurement and real disruption of order, and to exercise freedom as personal responsibility rather than as dialectical play.

Summarizing the empirical meaning for God in more technical terms, James states that God represents a substitution of the "each-form" of a pluralistic universe of many individual selves for the "all-form" of an absolute mind and its objective phases.[23] But does the each-form apply to God Himself in such a way that the divine being shares somehow in our finitude and changingness? James gives an affirmative answer to this question, since he thinks that otherwise the all-form of absolute monism will be reinstated as a necessary principle. As a consequence, he is led to reject explicitly the intellectual foundation for acceptance of the infinite God, whom he regards as an impossible compromise between the each-form and the all-form of being.

(3) *The critique of philosophical theology.* In *The Varieties of Religious Experience* (1902), there appears a chapter on philosophical theol-

ogy which seems incongruously placed among the sometimes bizarre psychological reports abounding in that book.[24] Its strategic relevance soon becomes plain, however, since James engages in psychological description in order to further a certain philosophical viewpoint. His purpose is to show not only that the common core of religious experience provides verification of the theistic hypothesis but also that this type of evidence *alone* (along with one's personal moral needs) supports the hypothesis of God's existence. Hence he inserts the chapter on philosophical theology as a negative test of his fideism and as a means of removing any speculative grounds for challenging the overbelief in a finite, developing God.

The first step is to introduce a wedge between the theism of ordinary people and that of the theologians. James identifies the religious position of Judaeo-Christian revelation, mystical experience, and ordinary theism with his own concept of a finite God, accepted on natural faith and religious emotion alone. There can be an intellectual description of religious theism, and this is the province of James himself. But the religious attitude repudiates any effort to give it a demonstrated, rational basis, and this is the claim made by Scholastic natural theology. Hence the latter cuts itself off from any vital contact with religious life and seeks to develop a doctrine on God through the resources of logical reason alone. It proceeds, in a purely a priori way, to construct a closed system of self-warranting propositions about God, and it does so in perfect disdain for probable truth, informal inference, private conviction, and the religious sentiments of the heart. (Ironically enough, James quotes a passage from Cardinal Newman as documentation on this monstrous conception of a philosophy of God.) James adds that this approach to God leads inevitably to idealistic monism, so that the Scholastics are the secret progenitors of the modern absolute.

To determine whether current Scholastic natural theology is logically cogent, James proposes a simple empirical test: "Theology based on pure reason must in point of fact convince men universally."[25] But since this is far from the actual case, natural theology must withdraw its claim to be a distinct, demonstrative science. It is, in fact, nothing more than a by-product of the religious sentiment, whose convictions it merely verbalizes and interprets. The arguments of natural theology convince those who already possess religious faith, and they leave other people perfectly cold and unmoved. Hence there is no independent, speculative criterion by which to judge the natural belief in a finite God.

Following the order of topics in such widely used nineteenth-century Scholastic manuals as Stöckl and Boedder, James considers first the existence of God and then His metaphysical and moral attributes. Although he brings forward the objections he had formulated in his youth against the usual proofs from causality and design, he emphasizes his intention of refraining from any detailed analysis. Instead of making any particular examination of the inferences, he gives a new turn to the commonplace remark that most thinkers since Kant have repudiated them. He uses this observation as palmary evidence that the traditional proofs fail to pass the test of being universally convincing, even to trained intellects. There is no need to go into the details of the proofs because their pragmatic consequences do not bear out their claim to be self-sufficient elaborations of pure reason, extortive of everyone's assent.

Passing on to the nature of God, James asks whether philosophical theology can deduce God's other attributes from His aseity, or independence, solely through the use of logic. Even more fundamental for him is whether these attributes are at all meaningful according to the pragmatic test of making an observable difference in our conduct. In the case of such metaphysical attributes as God's pure actuality, simplicity, necessity, immateriality, infinity, and self-love, James confesses that they make no definite impact upon our practical attitudes. It is quite indifferent to us whether they are true or false, and hence from the pragmatic standpoint they are meaningless. This whole tract in natural theology leaves James with the impression of its being only a mechanical shuffling of laudatory adjectives, entirely divorced from our vital concerns.

Unlike the metaphysical attributes, however, God's moral perfections of holiness, goodness, power, and knowledge do enjoy a determinate empirical significance. It means something to our practical attitude that there should be a benign and powerful person furthering our moral aims. But even these attributes are not demonstrated through any logical deduction from a privileged attribute. Their entire power over our assent derives from our religious experience of God or from our recognition of a moral need for a God so qualified. Thus James entirely strips the meaningful content of natural theology of its speculative basis and significance, locating it wholly within the region of natural belief, moral exigency, and religious experience. Henceforth, he need not regulate his ideas about God by the pretended demonstrations of Scholastic natural theology, any more than he should do so by the logic of absolute monism.

It is evident that a natural theology constructed along the lines described by James is a desiccated thing, cut off from its human springs and incapable of substantiating its claims. James' criticism is salutary, since it brings out how much the Scholastic manuals in question were influenced by the rationalist current in modern thought and also how far they departed from a realistic philosophy of God. In noticing the latter discrepancy, however, we must also observe the narrow basis for James' examination of the question. The manuals which he employed are by no means representative of the realist conception of a philosophical study of God, and hence they do not warrant his conclusion that every sort of speculative, philosophical doctrine on God is groundless.

In contradistinction to both the rationalist and the absolutist notions of a speculative theology, the realist approach does not claim to supply the only valid natural knowledge of God. Instead, it distinguishes carefully between the knowledge of God gained through speculative demonstration and that gained through the mind's informal inference, apart from the philosophic mode of thought. The speculative demonstration is not intended to supplant the other ways of gaining cognitive access to God but is simply aimed at satisfying our interest in having a knowledge of God that is rigorously established and critically possessed. In order to engage in the philosophical inquiry about God, the individual is not required to divest himself of his informal ways of reaching God or to purge his mind of all probable grounds, practical interests, and emotional inclinations. But he is asked to become reflectively aware of them and then to assess all the relevant evidence in the light of the canons of existential demonstration. By acquiring a philosophical sort of knowledge of God, he does not thereby eliminate or discredit the other natural ways of knowing Him but simply adds the perfection of a demonstratively founded knowledge.

Because of the speculative character of natural theology, James inferred that it must employ self-sufficient reason, must reach its conclusions deductively, and must coerce every mind to an actual assent to its doctrine. These are the familiar conditions of the rationalist conception of speculative reason, but they do not serve as determinants of a realistically developed philosophical study of God. The latter enterprise employs reason, not in a pure and self-sufficient state, but in its actual human condition, operating, along with the senses, in the interpretation of experience. Moreover, this interpretation is more than a description of the structures already given in experience; it is also a nondeductive, a posteriori inference based on the implications which experienced things furnish about their causal sources. James himself had some appreciation of the need for philosophy to move beyond descriptive analysis to causal inference when he acknowledged that "perception has given us a positive idea of causal agency. . . . May not the flux of sensible experience itself contain a rationality that has been overlooked, so that the real remedy would consist in harking back to it more intelligently?"[26] A realistic, speculative philosophy of God answers this question in the affirmative and hence always retains the method of a causal inference from the "rationality" or demonstrable implications of experienced being.

The speculative character of this approach to God no more requires that it be divorced from practical and affective data than from sense experience. Psychologically viewed, the philosophical theist often receives initial stimulus, continuing encouragement, and significant leads from the practical meaning and value of God in his life. This influence does not destroy the speculative quality of the inquiry itself, since even the evidence supplied by the individual's practical and affective orientation toward or away from God must be submitted to critical scrutiny, from the standpoint of its relevance for an ultimate, causal account of finite reality. Whatever the origin of the data, their validity for a speculative study of God is determined by the common canons of existential-causal inference. Furthermore, their precise significance here is determined by the speculative aim of knowing about God for the sake of having true propositions concerning Him. This aim does not mean, however, that such knowledge of God can have no practical consequences or that it is inimical to these considerations. Indeed, what the speculative philosophy of God establishes about the creative causality, goodness, and providence of God provides a realistic foundation for moral obligation and for the central significance of God in man's practical thinking and action.

Again, it is no part of the realistic conception of the philosophy of God to claim that everyone is automatically forced to give philosophically grounded assent to the philosophical demonstration of God's existence. This demonstration is universally cogent, in the sense that its evidence, method, and inferential operations are available for public inspection and are not intrinsically restricted to some private, incommunicable zone. But to examine the data precisely for their existential-causal significance, to grasp the formal nature of the method of causal inference, and to carry out the actual reasoning are highly specialized and difficult operations presupposing a thorough intellectual formation. Apart from this preparation, the individual mind does not have the requisite means for following and evaluating the reasoning, considered precisely as a philosophical demonstration.

Yet this does not imply that only those who are philosophically trained can gain a reliable knowledge of God. We all share a common basis in the ordinary grasp of existing things and causal relations. Thus men can make an informal, causal reasoning to God's existence and thus acquire genuine knowledge of Him even though such knowledge is not in the mode of a philosophical demonstration. Because of the presence of this common foundation in human experience, the informal inference and the philosophical demonstration are related to each other as distinct ways of attaining the same truth about God's existence. Everyone need not become a philosopher in order to reach this truth, and yet not everyone is proximately prepared to make the philosophical inference to God. The fact that most people who know that God exists do not rely upon the philosophical demonstration does not make the latter a mere verbalization of religious belief. Neither does it make everyone immediately capable of judging the validity of the philosophical demonstration.

James' principal concern is with the disagreement among trained philosophers. There is a notable difference, however, between his treatment of his conflict with Royce over absolute monism and his treatment of the conflict between the rationalistic theists and the Kantians over proofs of God's existence. In the former case, he is quick to recognize the importance of historical influences in accounting for the acceptance or rejection of a doctrine and to use historical clarification as a means of gaining assent to his own finitist theism. However, with respect to the post-Kantian repudiation of rationalistic proofs of God's existence, James suppresses all historical considerations and gives a purely abstract analysis and unqualified conclusion. This use of a double standard beclouds the fact that in the case of God's existence, as well as every other issue, the trained philosopher's assent and dissent are concrete functions, deeply influenced by the particular historical way in which the evidence is presented to him.

Assent to inferences in the philosophy of God cannot be wrung from a philosopher, *regardless* of how he views the nature of human knowledge in general, the problem of the theistic proof, and the relevance of the existential-causal evidence advanced in its support. Any claim to universal convincingness which ignores the concrete historical context within which any act of philosophically grounded assent is bound to operate is chimerical. Historical analysis must be patiently employed even to understand the import of Kant's criticism and the several senses in which subsequent thinkers have accepted his objections. The specific nature of the rationalist proofs of God's existence, the contribution of the empiricist limitation of knowledge, the meaning of existential demonstration for Kant and his successors—all these factors belong, by right, in any adequate discussion of the issue. The failure of the Wolffian arguments to convince Kant and subsequent philosophers involves too many complex and historically conditioned factors to permit James merely to point to the fact and directly conclude that there can be no demonstrative inferences concerning God. These arguments are also inacceptable to the realist mind, which nevertheless maintains that the telling points in the Kantian critique do not affect an existentially based doctrine on God.

Another instance of the impoverishing effect of dispensing with historical analysis is found in James' treatment of the divine attributes. He merely accepts, as he finds it, the distinction between God's metaphysical and moral attributes without inquiring into the special origin of this distinction. In its eighteenth-century usage, this distinction begged the question of the "metaphysical" perfections of God as having no bearing upon our moral life and as being derived in a wholly deductive, mathematical way from some privileged, divine attribute. Some nineteenth-century Scholastic manuals adopted this distinction just as uncritically as they did the corresponding conception of proofs of God's existence. A theory of the divine attributes which is not governed at every moment by the a posteriori truth about God's existence and by an analogical-causal study of finite things is bound to become philosophically sterile and humanly insignificant. But James does not recognize that there are definite philosophical correctives for this approach to the divine perfections and that these correctives can operate within a metaphysical study of God and not by way of denying this knowledge.

Unfortunately, James did not make as patient and thorough a study of the varieties of philosophical theology as he did of the varieties of religious experience. He was so eager to emancipate his own thoughts on a finitist theism from the control of any speculative doctrine on God that he hastily erected a few manuals into the exemplar for every sort of natural theology. But his stimulating criticism of what he found in these sources raised problems whose resolution can only be found in taking the long, historical journey through the several phases in the modern philosophical approaches to God.

(4) *A pluralistic pantheism.* In one of his last publications, *A Pluralistic Universe* (1909), James seems to reverse many of his previously stated positions. He divides spiritual philosophies into the less intimate, or dualistic theism (an infinite creator-God and the world), and the more intimate, or pantheism, and then subdivides pantheism into the two varieties of monistic absolutism and his own pluralistic finitism.[27] According to this division, a theism of the infinite God is criticized for being excessively dualistic, whereas previously it had been taxed with spawning monistic absolutism. And James now relaxes his attack upon monistic absolutism sufficiently to include it, along with his own position, within the common class of pantheism.

Yet this reversal is not so unexpected and inconsistent as it may appear. He always qualified his attacks on the monistic absolutism of Royce and Bradley by noting that he objected to their doctrine precisely as pretending to be a logically coercive, necessary demonstration. He formed a temporary alliance with a creator-theism in order to destroy this claim, but once he had removed it to his satisfaction, he became much more hospitable toward absolutism and less cordial toward a theism of an infinite, creative God. As he stated in a letter to Borden Bowne (who was an exponent of a creator-theism on a personalist basis), his own philosophy was theistic, but not essentially so. Its most fundamental trait was a *finite pluralism* stressing the finitude and manyness of beings. Although James' own moral needs and the testimony of religious souls convinced him of the existence of a superhuman, benign power, he refused to regard God as infinite or uniquely perfect. For this would seem to introduce a breach into the universe and to threaten the reality of the many, finite things of daily experience.

Although he was equally opposed to restoring monistic absolutism as a demonstrated system, James admired its sense of the unity and likeness of all things. After rejecting the monistic formal totality, based upon the all-form of being, he did admit an identity of material content between his pluralism and absolutism. He characterized this material identity as the pantheistic conviction that reality consists somehow in one spiritual substance or kind of being. Having gone this far, James felt strongly attracted toward G. T. Fechner's panpsychism and even toward a polytheism of many superhuman powers in the universe. None of these imaginative excursions fully satisfied him, however, since he saw that the problem of preserving the integrity of finite things is just as acutely present in a vague pantheism as in the more rigorous, formal dialectic of Royce's absolutism.

James wrestled with the ancient problem of the one and the many throughout his life, but he could never reconcile his pluralism completely with either creator-theism or absolutism. The difficulty was that he hinged his entire case against a logically coercive absolutism upon showing that we are not formal, constituent parts of a universal self. To reach this conclusion, however, he made *not being a part of* the equivalent of *not being caused by and derived from*. The theistic view that God is the infinite first cause and creator of things would then seem to him to entail, as a logical consequence, the further admission that finite things are entitative parts of the cosmic self. James could discover no way of avoiding the latter conclusion except by denying creative causality to God and locating Him within some limiting environment of hostile forces.

His difficulty was that in abandoning both the historical and the metaphysical treatment of the problem of God, he had no means left for distinguishing the absolute from God except by finitizing the latter. He failed to attend to the full significance of the substitution of dialectical monism for a causally based theism. This substitution had to be made by the absolute idealists precisely because the relation of cause-and-effect is not equivalent to, or reducible to, the relation of whole-and-parts. Because he had forsworn both a speculative philosophy of God and the philosophical history of the problem of God, James could not reconcile his finite pluralism with God as the infinite, causal existent. With considerable misgivings about the unavoidable compromise, therefore, he was obliged to classify his own pluralistic finitism as a variety of pantheism, hoping that the fragile distinction between the form and the content of the universal stuff would preserve the finite articulations he prized above everything else.[28] From James' own over-all standpoint, this was bound to be an unsatisfactory solution, since it overlooked the close solidarity between a causally based theism and what he himself called the pluralism of each-forms or finite actual beings.

3. WHITEHEAD'S BIPOLAR GOD

During the twentieth century, theories of a finite, developing God have been proposed from various standpoints by Max Scheler, Samuel Alexander, E. S. Brightman, and Charles Hartshorne.[29] But, undoubtedly, the most systematic and influential recent exposition of finitism is that made by Alfred North Whitehead (1861–1947), who includes it as an integral part of his speculative philosophy, or cosmology. Using the method of descriptive generalization, he works out a general scheme or system of ideas for interpreting every element in experience. From a description of the complete, concrete fact or structure of actual entities, he derives certain necessary characteristics that must be present in every actual fact. Because of the universal application of these categories, the speculative philosophy, or cosmology, is also the only genuine metaphysics. If God is to be understood anywhere in philosophy, it must be within this cosmological metaphysics.

Like the great rationalists in the seventeenth century (which he once dubbed "the century of genius"), Whitehead requires a theory of God in order to understand nature more fully. "The secularization of the concept of God's functions in the world is at least as urgent a requisite of thought as is the secularization of other elements in experience."[30] By a secularizing of the concept of God he means that the primary warrant for any philosophical propositions about God must be found in His connection with, and implication in, the general structure of actual entities and the principles of experience. This is a thoroughly functional approach to God, since it is precisely His function as a factor implicated in the world which makes Him philosophically relevant, as well as knowable. Whitehead sees no good reason for limiting the study of God to moral philosophy, in the Kantian fashion, since he finds a use for God in his theoretical interpretation of nature. And without depreciating the deliverances of religious and moral experience about God, he also vindicates a speculative treatment of God against the attack of William James. But to know God speculatively means, for Whitehead, to know Him for the sake of understanding nature in a cosmological system.

In charting the course of his doctrine on God, Whitehead wishes to steer clear of three extreme positions: an impersonal immanentism of nature, pantheistic monism, and what he calls "the Semitic concept of God."[31] Under the latter term, he includes the God of the Old

Testament and of the Christian and Mohammedan theologies (as distinguished from the religion of Jesus and St. John). Whitehead characterizes this position as an extreme transcendentalism, which leaves God outside all metaphysical rationalization and therefore establishes His existence only through the ontological proof. The Semitic God cannot be rationalized, since He is not an exemplification of something more fundamental in being and does not stand in a relation of mutual dependence with other actual entities in the world. Whitehead combines the rationalist principle of sufficient reason with the relativity principle, so that his God must be an instance of a general set of principles and must be involved in the world by way of mutual dependence with the other actual entities. He takes the Semitic God's transcendence to mean that God has no real bond with the universe. From this he concludes that the only way of proving the actuality of this transcendent God would be through the ontological proof. Hence he rejects the teaching that God is the creative first cause of the world. The Whiteheadian God does not create the world but saves it by presenting it with persuasive ideals. This position is admittedly closer to the Platonic demiurge, the Aristotelian first mover, and the evolutionary vital nisus than to the Creator of the Christian tradition.

Whitehead maintains that the very conditions required for an experiential proof of God also demand that His transcendence be a purely relative one, based upon a special way of His inclusion within the universe.

Any proof which commences with the consideration of the character of the actual world cannot rise above the actuality of this world. It can only discover all the factors disclosed in the world as experienced. In other words, it may discover an immanent God, but not a God wholly transcendent. The difficulty can be put in this way: by considering the world we can find all the factors required by the total metaphysical situation; but we cannot discover anything not included in this totality of actual fact, and yet explanatory of it.[32]

In this text, "world" and "totality of actual fact" are used synonymously, but the crux of the problem is whether "world" should be taken initially in a narrower sense, which would include only experienced actual entities, or in the broader sense, as embracing everything actual. If the actual world is the full totality of actual fact, then by definition an actual God must be included *somehow* in the world. But, for Whitehead, the difficulty about starting with this broader meaning is that it does not specify the way in which God belongs to the world but only notes that He is an actual being along with others. This usage does not rule out a transcendent creator, since the latter can be said to form a causal unity of order, or total metaphysical situation, along with created things. Moreover, the unity constituted by the relation of creative causality permits an a posteriori proof from the actual things of experience. The starting point in experienced actualities can lead only to the actual being of those things which are somehow implied and included in the world, but the mode of inclusion may turn out to be that of primary, causal production of finite existents by a transcendent-immanent creator. The issue cannot be decided at the outset, and hence the precise relation of the world and God cannot be determined simply by one's acceptance of the a posteriori starting point of proof and the wider meaning for the totality of actual fact.

Whitehead's famous remark about European philosophy being a series of footnotes to Plato has overshadowed his equally noteworthy acclaim of Aristotle as the greatest metaphysician and last dispassionate student of the question of God.[33] Although repudiating the Aristotelian cosmology and metaphysics of substance, Whitehead nevertheless admired the Stagirite's method and central problem in treating of God. The method is that of starting with the experienced world and affirming nothing of God which is not required by the general character of actual things. The seminal problem in the study of God is to seek an explanation for the becoming of things and the orderly arrangement in the universe. Although Whitehead lists our notion of God as one of the derivative concepts in his system, its very derivative character is a clear sign that the actual being of God is arrived at as something required by the structure of the actual things of our experience.

The most generalized analysis of the actual, temporal world shows the presence of at least these three universal factors: creativity, the individual temporal occasions or actual entities in process, and the eternal objects.[34] Although he rejects a divine creation from nothing, Whitehead retains the term "creativity" to signify the tendency to become, to cause oneself in decision, to order objects, and to pass on. Creativity is that whereby the actual world is a passage to novelty, a constant advance toward new modes of being. But creativity is not itself an entity, and hence it keeps its foothold in reality only through the actual beings which exemplify it. These beings are the actual entities or temporal occasions, in which creativity has its definite routes of becoming. Since he rejects any substance-attribute theory, Whitehead identifies the entity and its process in every respect. The actual entity appropriates the past, realizes its own peculiar, subjective form of feeling and evaluating, and eventually perishes and becomes an objective datum for some future entity. Becoming is an orderly affair and is not chaotic. A particular entity is something definite in its own structure and excludes other possible kinds of realization. It comes to be and perishes in orderly relation with other temporal entities, thus constituting a universe. To account for the determinate, related, and ordered character of temporal reality, there must also be eternal objects. They are not esoteric ideals but, rather, the real potentialities, definite patterns, determinate relations of inclusion and exclusion, grades of relevance, importance, and value which are displayed in our experienced world. They are entities, but in the mode of potentiality rather than of actuality.

The chief concern of a given group of actual entities is to incorporate creativity and eternal objects in certain valuable and fruitful ways of individual becoming, which can then lead toward still fuller actualizations. In addition to the three metaphysical components already indicated, however, the metaphysical situation also requires the active presence of a nontemporal but actual entity, God. By itself, creativity is not an entity and cannot account for the actual paths of becoming which comprise the world. The eternal objects are entities, but only in the mode of potentiality, so that they have no actuality and causal efficacy in their own right. They cannot float into the actual world from nowhere; they require an actual foundation, which is immanent in all temporal process and yet distinct from it. In order to make the entire realm of potentialities or eternal objects relevant to every particular temporal occasion, the actual ground of eternal objects must itself be intemporal. God is this nontemporal, actual entity which "prehends," or actively relates itself to, the eternal objects in such fashion that it grounds them in actuality, renders them available to the creative advance of all temporal entities, and achieves their actual ingression into the order of nature.

Whitehead calls God the principle of limitation, concretion, and relevance. As the principle of limitation, He envisages the eternal potentialities in their relatedness and unity, so that some particular temporal entity can carve out its own determinate kind of being. The divine limiting function enables the individual temporal event to be of this sort rather than another, to acquire a definite relation of inclusion and exclusion, and thus to have its own proper career within the universe. God is also the principle of concretion, since He contributes to the growth or concrescence of the temporal entity. In this function, He provides the initial, conceptual determination and aim for the concrete actuality, thus enabling it to develop according to its own subjective being, valuation, and purpose. Furthermore, God unifies and gradates the eternal objects according to their relation to His own ultimate aim. This operation establishes an order of relevance and value among the eternal forms, thus permitting temporal entities to make a wise and fruitful choice for their future course of action. As the principle of relevance, God is the efficacious source of ideal standards of value and progress.

Human experience explicitly relates itself to an external standard. The universe is thus understood as including a source of ideals. The effective aspect of this source is Deity as immanent in the present experience. The sense of historic importance is the intuition of the universe as everlasting process, unfading in its deistic unity of ideals. Thus there is an essential relevance between Deity and historic process.[35]

Although God does not create the eternal objects or make new ones, He does make available to temporal agencies new ways of combining and realizing them in future practice. History is hopeful, creative, and important by reason of the ideal possibilities which God makes available to actual entities.

The Whiteheadian inference to God depends chiefly upon the theory of eternal objects. They are given a real status as potential entities, distinct from temporal things, because Whitehead repudiates substance and identifies the temporal thing with its process. Although he refers critically to Aristotle's view of substance, the only theory which he seriously considers is the Cartesian conception of substance as that which exists in such a way that it needs no other thing for its existence. Whitehead fears that a multiplicity of such substances would destroy the unity of the universe and prevent any rational explanations, except by reversion to monism. Hence he regards the general structural pattern of the temporal thing as an objective potentiality, having its ground in God's nontemporal actuality. Despite his antipathy toward bifurcations in nature, he retains an unyielding bifurcation between the temporal entity or process and the general kind of a structure which it embodies. Were he to admit that the general aspect is founded upon the substantial nature of temporal entities and brought out through the activity of human thought, he would not be able to make an immediate inference to God from the need for an actual and eternal basis for the eternal objects.

Whitehead's theory of the divine nature or natures depends upon his conception of metaphysical method. In calling that method one of descriptive generalization, he means quite literally a search for generic traits and categories which must belong to all actual entities. Since Whitehead's metaphysics is a cosmology, he is committed to looking for pervasive, univocal, generic characteristics present everywhere. A purely descriptive and categorial method must view actuality as univocal and treat God as an instance of the generic unity of principles of actual being. God is simply a test case for the universality of metaphysical principles understood in this way. "God is not to be treated as an exception to all metaphysical principles, invoked to save their collapse. He is their chief exemplification."[36] Unless God does exemplify the same sort of nature found in temporal entities, Whitehead has no assurance that his analysis of these entities is an ultimate description of concrete facts or basic generic traits. This position closely resembles the functional role of God in classical rationalism.

Generalizing from introspection and his analysis of physical objects and events, Whitehead maintains that every actual entity consists of a physical pole and a mental pole. From the former pole arise the physical prehensions, or physical feelings, whereby an actual entity actively relates itself to other actual entities. By means of its mental pole, an actual entity conceptually prehends and feels all the eternal objects in their unity and graded relevance to its own subjective aim. Such mental or conceptual prehensions need not involve conscious activity, however, since consciousness springs up only from a comparison between the physical feeling of concrete actuality and some general form or eternal object.

A direct transfer of this bipolarity is now made to God. In Him, the mental pole is termed His primordial nature, the physical pole His consequent nature. Whithead also distinguishes a third nature in God, His superjective nature, to correspond with the tendency of other actual entities to make themselves available as objective data in the career of future agents. Taken together, the primordial, consequent, and superjective natures constitute God as an actual entity functioning within the universe. But since very little is said about the superjective nature, Whitehead's fundamental doctrine concerns the bipolarity of primordial and consequent natures.

The functions of God which lead to the proof of His actuality are aspects of His *primordial* nature, or mental pole. This nature is a unity of pure conceptual feelings, which have the eternal objects as their data. It organizes, gradates, and adjusts the eternal objects, both to attain the full esthetic satisfaction of God's own subjective aim and to render them accessible to temporal entities. Although He is complete or infinite in His conceptual prehension, God, in His primordial nature, is subject to a dual deficiency in actuality. First, "His feelings are only conceptual and so lack the fulness of actuality. Secondly, conceptual feelings, apart from complex integration with physical feelings, are devoid of consciousness in their subjective form."[37] Since the data of the mental pole are eternal objects and not other actualities, this pole has only conceptual prehensions and is lacking in physical feelings. In His primordial nature, God remains impersonal and unconscious. With Whitehead, this conclusion is required by the definition of consciousness, although many of the activities assigned to the divine primordial nature would seem to require some sort of conscious life in any other context than this system.

Physical feelings and consciousness come to Him only through the operations of the *consequent* nature, or physical pole. In this respect, God is finite and in process. Through His physical prehensions, God is continually receiving new objective data from the temporal actualities, which now react upon Him. God constantly comes to be in His consequent nature, along with the becoming of other actualities in process. From them He selects and transmutes materials for physical feelings in accord with His own eternal envisagement of a harmonious order of the universe, in which His esthetic satisfaction lies.

The sense in which God saves the world, without having created it from nothing, now becomes clear. Temporal occasions perish, but in doing so, they furnish data for God's prehensive selection and incorporation into His consequent nature. Thus the perishing entities achieve an objective immortality, or at least those aspects which are transmuted into the divine consequent nature become immortal. Whatever God receives from other actualities will never fade away into a past but will be carried along in an everlastingly vivid present. Finally, there is a renewed effort of God to share His own developing experience with the temporal occasions. Through His *superjective* nature, He pours back fresh depths of significance into the world, enabling actual entities to gain a new facet of ideal vision for meeting their future. Religiously, this final phase in the divine functions is symbolized as the providence, love, and fellow suffering of God with mankind.

A few concise remarks can be made in criticism of this theory of the divine nature. From the standpoint of internal consistency, Whitehead does not adhere strictly to his program of making no exception of God in respect to metaphysical principles.[38] Although he introduces the three natures into God, in line with this program, his actual description of these natures leads to some sharp differences between God and temporal entities. God alone (in His primordial nature) has a complete grasp of the eternal objects; He alone (in His consequent nature) can incorporate objective data without permitting them to fade into a past; He alone (in His superjective nature) can make His experience accessible to other actual entities without perishing Himself. Hence He is the only actual entity which is not a temporal occasion achieving objective immortality as a component within something else. God is unique in that His conceptual prehensions are in no way dependent upon physical feelings. Indeed, although there is becoming in His consequent nature, the latter is not temporal but a transmutation of time.

Since these admitted exceptions are not superficial but essential to this theory of the divine nature, they indicate a partial breakdown of Whitehead's speculative principles. The divergences cannot be explained simply by the relativity principle, since they imply the presence not merely of reciprocal adjustments but of radically opposed modes of actual being. Whitehead's struggle to reconcile time and eternity is intrinsically handicapped by a method which permits categorial description but not causal inference. Hence he cannot avoid importing some finite traits into the eternal God and yet admitting some exceptions.

The reason for Whitehead's ability to notice most of these contrasts between God and other actual entities, without amending his claim to one generic sort of being, is his use of the polarity metaphor. But, like every other metaphor, it has intrinsic limits and cannot be extended to all beings without losing determinate significance. Especially in a metaphysical study of God, metaphors have to be subjected to rigorous tests of negative and analogous predication. No metaphorical reasoning is strictly demonstrative, compelling us to conclude that the physical and mental poles must be present in God as an actual entity.

Furthermore, Whitehead fails to note that the bipolar theory can be criticized, not only from a one-sided or monopolar standpoint, but also from the standpoint of a deliberately *non*polar approach to God. John Dewey once protested against the method of interpreting the whole of nature through extrapolation of an introspective description of the physical and mental poles in man. Whitehead's procedure of building his account of the human structure into a prototype for all actual entities is just as unwarranted in the study of God as in the study of nature. In a universe of analogous causes, the validity of one's description of finite things need not depend upon injecting all of their elements into the divine nature. Since a nonpolar approach to God need not presume that either polarity or any other generic trait of finite things must be present pervasively and universally among all beings, it can take its start in a causal analysis of finite entities and yet infer the unqualifiedly infinite actuality of God.

A final remark concerns the sort of union which man is permitted to have with the Whiteheadian God.[39] This is an important question for Whitehead himself, both because he criticizes Aristotle for not providing a God that is available for religious purposes and because he regards the application of his theory to the religious sphere as one of its indispensable tests. Certainly the impersonal, unconscious, and deficiently actual primordial nature of God affords no soil for a religious bond between man and God. As for the divine consequent nature, it incorporates data from actual entities which have perished and become objectified for it. The conditions for such a prehension do not permit a relationship to spring up between God and the living human person. It is not even the integral human person who becomes immortal in God; only those selected aspects which can be transmuted into the divine esthetic experience become immortal. Communion and transmutation are unsimilar relations. The most likely locus for a personal meeting of God and man is in terms of the former's superjective nature. Whitehead does speak very movingly about the loving concern of the divine companion and cosufferer. In systematic terms, however, it is difficult to see how the search for His own esthetic satisfaction makes God good. Whitehead uses the language of the Incarnation, but without accepting an immanent-transcendent creator or the doctrine of the Man-God. The theory of bipolarity trails off just at the point where the question of whether God is good, personal, and personally related to man can be posed.

Apart from the influence exerted by previous philosophies, there seem to have been two major impulses animating the finitist movement:

naturalistic and humanistic. The naturalistic consideration was that
the doctrine on God must be brought into conformity with what we
know about the world of our experience. The overwhelming message of
the several sciences during the past century has been that nature is
undergoing evolution at various levels and paces. For the finitist philosophers, this meant that the universality of continuous change must
be posited throughout the duration and range of real things. There
could be no creation from nothing, with a first beginning of time, and
there could be no exemption of God from the universal reign of becoming. Mill, James, and Whitehead agreed in denying that God is
strictly the creative cause of the world: He is its orderer and adjuster,
but He does not give it existential act and all the other principles of
being. They also agreed upon the presence of some change and struggle
transpiring in the divine nature, although this stress upon process in
God became more pronounced in James and Whitehead, for whom the
concept of God is not provisional.

The humanistic and moral preoccupation leading to finitism was centered upon the problem of suffering and evil. For Mill and James, mere
mention of the presence of evil seemed to be a strong enough argument
against the divine omnipotence. Whitehead regarded this attitude as
overly facile but granted that evil at least testifies to the factor of process
in God's consequent nature and to His superjective concern for the
gradual triumph of His ideal aim. Another humanistic motif was the
use of a pragmatic norm for determining whether or not God is finite
and in process. Once more, Mill and James were in substantial agreement that the moral stimulus derived from viewing God as striving
under limiting conditions is sufficient ground for affirming the finitude
and development of God. Against Mill's argument that we can eventually dispense with even this sort of God, in favor of a total dedication to
humanity, James recoiled instinctively, but without much philosophical
basis. The systematic grounds for the permanent retention of God were
advanced by Whitehead, and in doing so he had to revive the speculative
treatment of God against the attacks of William James on the philosophy of God. His restoration of the speculative doctrine on God was
intrinsically limited, however, by his view of metaphysics as being the
equivalent of cosmology-as-speculative-philosophy. The methodological
implications of this view of the speculative study of God led unavoidably
to the position that God is somehow deficiently actual, limited, and
continually in process.

Finitists such as James and Whitehead have called attention to an important aspect of the problem of God, namely, how the individual gives
his assent to God and how he can lead others to accept the reality of
God. Whether the act whereby a given individual reaches God is called
an imaginative hope, a practical belief, or a metaphysical inference,

there remains the difficulty of convincing other individuals to make a similar adhesion to God. Beyond the intrinsic weight of the theistic arguments there lies the further aspect of perceiving their strength and conveying their cogency to other minds. Should this be done by appealing primarily to emotional inclinations, to practical needs, to religious experience, or to metaphysical principles? The social aspect of the study of God—the responsibility which the reflective individual theist bears toward his fellow men—is recognized by the finitists, especially since most of them require that God be personal, good, and concerned for man's personal relations with Himself. William James suggests that there is a special problem involved in relating philosophical inferences to our ordinary ways of reaching conviction about God. We usually approach this problem as a moral question rather than a purely speculative one, and in the comparison of moral worths, "we must consult not science, but what Pascal calls our heart."[40] On this issue, therefore, it may be well worth while to examine a line of modern thinkers whose views on God have gravitated around the individual's response and the ways of eliciting it.

Chapter X

THE HEART'S WAY TO GOD

THE TASK of this chapter is to bring to focus the contributions of three men—Pascal, Kierkegaard, and Newman—who do not belong in the main stream of modern philosophy but who have markedly influenced its flow from a tangential position. None of these men is a philosopher in the professional and exclusive sense, and yet each has developed some important philosophical themes directly relevant to the study of God. Pascal brings to this discussion the equipment of a practicing scientist, Kierkegaard the gifts of a literary craftsman, and Newman the background of a theologian. Despite their widely diverse intellectual training and historical milieu, however, they can be classed together as personal religious thinkers who see the problem of God as pivoting around the relation between the individual mind and the personal God. In this sense, they represent a prolongation of the Augustinian tradition into the modern world.

Each of these thinkers achieves his relevance by making a critical response to some major moment in the modern philosophical inquiry about God. Pascal always keeps in view the state of mind of the well-meaning seventeenth-century freethinker, who has felt the brunt of the skeptical criticism and yet has been left unconvinced by the Cartesian reconstruction of theism. Kierkegaard's critical analysis is aroused by the Hegelian subordination of God and the human individual to the absolute system of thought. In the case of Newman, the challenge is provided by both the surviving forces of Enlightenment rationalism and the new trends of scientific naturalism in the nineteenth century.

A common pattern becomes discernible when these efforts are viewed together. There is a noticeable shift from nature to man, as providing the principal point of departure for the search after God. This transfer of emphasis from an impersonal to a personal starting point is due to several factors. These three men are convinced that the ordinary systematic approach overlooks the problem of securing assent from the individual mind and that it is precisely here that the entire philosophical quest of God meets its crucial test and reaps its proper harvest. Hence they pay special attention to the interpretation of the human situation and the existential data peculiarly significant for man's recognition of

God. They are also more than commonly sensitive to the difficulties facing the individual mind, especially the influence of custom, emotions, and the will upon the act of intellectual assent to God. Hence they insist upon the need to move the heart, as well as the mind, if theism is to be a real and effective conviction. Their sympathetic concern is for the ordinary individual, whose problems are often neglected in technical philosophical works. A further reason for their concentration upon the human situation and the personal factors is their common aim of reaching God precisely as the good, just, and personal reality who is the term of the religious approach. It is the God of personal, religious attachment whom they seek to bring into relation to man and to the joint movement of mind and heart.

Pascal, Kierkegaard, and Newman are Christian thinkers and apologists who keep their religious faith in close contact with all their philosophical investigations. This influence does not automatically insure their mutual agreement on the key issues, however, precisely because their views on Christianity are not identical in every respect. Although they all accept the Incarnation in its orthodox meaning, they do not take the same position on the relation between faith and reason. In part, their respective conceptions of reason are determined by the specific philosophical climate in which each of them found himself. Their differences are also theologically grounded, however, and serve as a reminder that adherence to the Christian faith may still permit a wide range of views concerning what can be established and what cannot be established about God through philosophical means.

Most modern philosophers have either followed the lead of Bruno, Bacon, and Descartes, in drawing a sanitary cordon around religious faith and isolating it formally from any philosophical theism, or they have accepted Hegel's dialectical identification of Christianity with a phase of philosophical reasoning about God. But the men with whom we are presently concerned have sharply challenged this simple alternative of mutual disparity or identification between the Christian faith and the philosophical study of God. Instead, they have brought out the several modes of relevance of the individual's religious and theological standpoint for his evaluation of the various philosophical paths leading toward or away from God.

Brief mention of the existentialist positions on God is also made in this chapter. There is a sharp division here between the atheistic and theistic forms of existentialism. However, they all frame the problem of God in a way that stresses its significance for the individual, his freedom, and his concrete relations with the world and the moral community of men. Existentialism thus provides a crossroad for bringing the theism of the heart into contact and dialogue with tendencies which in the contemporary world lead to atheism.

1. PASCAL ON THE HIDDEN GOD

Several formidable obstacles stand in the way of forming a just estimate of the mind of Blaise Pascal (1623–1662). Into his thirty-nine years he crowded a host of researches on mathematical and physical problems, theological controversy, and philosophico-religious questions. His views in the latter field were never systematically presented but were scattered throughout a number of treatises on scientific subjects, a wide correspondence, and, above all, in that collection of fragments called the *Thoughts.* Successive editors have constantly rearranged this unfinished work, trying to find an orderly framework for linking the *pensées* together. Only during the past quarter-century, however, have scholars succeeded in identifying Pascal's own broad plan, but even the most faithful redactions have remained only approximations to his detailed order.[1] In any event, the materials never received from their author that final reworking which alone could insure us definitive access to his mature standpoint.

It is at least clear that most of the fragments were intended for an *Apology for Christianity* addressed to the French libertines, with whom Pascal was always on an intimate footing. Yet he never made a final decision upon the precise literary form to employ but experimented with letters, discourses, dialogues, and pithy maxims. Many sections formerly regarded as direct expressions of his own view are now recognized to be explorations of the internal attitudes of his skeptic, Stoic, and libertine friends. Another hindrance to a firm interpretation of his thought is the elusive character of his theological stand. Entirely apart from the question of his deathbed submission to the Catholic church is that of how closely he followed the Jansenist theology during his active years. His Jansenism seems to have been sometimes more rigorous than that of the Port-Royal leaders, Arnauld and Nicole, and on other occasions discreetly Catholic and critical of Jansenist tenets. During his own lifetime, it was difficult for anyone to draw sharp lines of theological demarcation on the main issues, and this radical ambiguity affected many of his remarks on our knowledge of God.

Despite these difficulties, it is possible to ascertain the chief traits of Pascal's approach to God with some surety. Pascal himself laid down the interpretative principle that the proper order is to make whatever natural digressions may be dictated by the interests of the particular individuals involved in the discussion and yet also to keep clearly in view the final goal of the entire inquiry. The individuals to whom he addressed his *Apology* were freethinkers like his friends, Méré and Miton, intelligent but religiously indifferent members of Parisian society; his underlying purpose in discussion was to convert them to the

Christian religion.[2] All of his *pensées* were regulated by the concrete outlook of his interlocutors and by the aim of an eventual conversion of their minds and hearts to Christianity. He was also convinced that indifferent minds have to be shocked out of their apathy concerning ultimate issues, so he followed a definite strategy of extreme and antithetic presentation of his views. All of these conditions affected the content and manner of his thoughts, and they must be kept in mind in determining their import and value for us.

There are three major themes in the Pascalian treatment of God. The first consists in a concentrated study of the proofs of God's existence prevalent during the seventeenth century. Pascal exposes their insufficiency and thus paves the way for his second topic, which is an analysis of the grandeur and misery of man, as well as the incapacity of various philosophies to explain this duality. Finally, he brings in the so-called wager argument and thus carries his readers to the point of actual belief in the Christian message. It is just as important for Pascal, in advancing his practical aim, to respect the proper ordering of these issues as it is for Descartes, in building his house of human wisdom.

(1) *The proofs of God's existence* which come under Pascal's criticism are drawn mainly from the Cartesian philosophy and the current manuals of Christian apologetics. Three statements summarize his attitude toward such proofs.

Metaphysical proofs of God are so remote from man's range of reason and so involved that they fail to grip; and even if they were of service to some it would only be during the moment of demonstration; an hour afterwards men fear they have been wrong. . . . The Christians' God is not a God who is simply author of mathematical truths and of the order of the elements; that is the lot of the heathen and of the Epicureans. . . . Seekers after God apart from Jesus Christ, who do not get beyond nature, either fail to find sufficient light, or else manage to find a way to know God and serve Him without a mediator; and so they fall into either atheism or deism, two things which Christianity holds in almost equal abhorrence.[3]

Concerning the metaphysical arguments of Descartes and the Scholastics, Pascal observes that they cannot be followed without a special training and hence that they are alien to our ordinary ways of reasoning. Even when they are understood, their demonstrative force is apt to slip from our grasp as soon as we complete the very complicated course of reasoning, so that they fail to give us habitual certitude about God's existence. Such proofs fail to reckon with the actual conditions under which men normally acquire their permanent convictions. Therefore they are psychologically useless, especially in practical, apologetic work.

In the second statement quoted, Pascal advanced some objective reasons for refusing to follow the usual type of inference. As a youth he had been introduced by his father to the circle of Father Mersenne, who drew theistic arguments from mathematical truths and natural phenomena. Pascal felt a certain attraction toward the Augustinian and Mersennean inferences from the immutable truths of mathematics to a subsistent and eternal mind, but he did not make personal use of them. They seemed to lead only to a divine mathematician, and perhaps only to a cosmic calculator, just as sheerly impersonal and unresponsive as the calculating machine which Pascal himself had invented. He had a similar objection against the physical inference which Gassendi and the Neo-Epicureans made to God, viewed as the orderer of the elements. Starting from the constitution of material things, the freethinker might arrive at God as a cosmic orderer, but not necessarily at the creative, infinite God of love who is the proper term of the religious relation. Proofs based on the philosophy of nature would not lead directly to the living God as a personal, existing reality but only to a necessary mover. Pascal feared that his freethinking friends might remain content with an impersonal mover and thus refuse to take the additional step to the personal and transcendent God of religious devotion. His famous contrast between the God of the philosophers and scholars and the God of Abraham, Isaac, and Jacob sprang from his awareness of the drawback of proofs based on a physical description of nature, as well as from his desire to have a way to God which leads formally to the truth of His own transcendent and personal existence.

In Pascal's eyes, many physical arguments suffered from an additional handicap if the freethinker in question were not simply indifferent but a convinced atheist and scientifically trained. An aggressive mind could easily detect the weak inductive basis for an appeal based upon nature's abhorrence of a vacuum, for instance, or its desire to achieve an extrinsic ordering of beings. His own experiments on air pressure had made Pascal suspicious of any animistic language, which would attribute to nature something analogous to the passions of abhorrence and desire.[4] He could not appeal abstractly with Leibniz to plenitude or the great chain of being, and he could not rule out what Sir Thomas Browne called the empty cantons and the grotesques of nature which might fill them. His experience with the atheistic mind also convinced him that the evidence of design is not perfectly obvious for everyone to see. The movements of the planets and the birds in the air might testify to God's intelligence and providence in the case of someone already holding for His existence, but they were powerless, by themselves, to remove the basic denial that God does exist. Furthermore, what "hardened" a man in atheism was not primarily the weakness of evidences in the visible world but a decision of will and the passions. The chief deficiency of a theism built solely upon mathematical and physical considerations was that it paid no attention to the human problems and motives which ultimately counted for so much in shaping a man's position concerning God.

Up to this point, Pascal's critique is mainly philosophical and psychological, but there is also a theological undercurrent in his strictures. To appreciate his somewhat complex and unique teaching, we must first take note of his fundamental admission that "we can indeed know God without knowing our misery.... The veil of nature which hides God has been penetrated by several infidels who, as St. Paul said, have recognized an invisible God through visible nature."[5] Pascal does not deny either the intrinsic possibility of a natural knowledge of God or its actual achievement on the part of those who do not have the Christian faith. Yet in avoiding a rigorous fideism, he himself never makes use of the metaphysical proofs, nor does he analyze in detail how the natural knowledge of God is obtained. He seldom mentions this knowledge without adding a word of warning about the attendant moral and religious dangers. Instead of approving of such knowledge as supplying a solid groundwork for the life of grace, he invariably treats it as an obstacle to the reception of faith.

Two leading considerations prompt what can be called, not unfairly, Pascal's antipathy toward a natural theism. The first is his apologetic preoccupation, which prevents him from appreciating a speculative knowledge of God as an intellectual good in itself. Without denying the existence of such knowledge, he simply fails to see its value as a proper perfection of man. He immediately translates it into a practical attitude, identifying it exclusively with the position of those freethinkers who accept God and natural morality but not the Christian revelation. From his purely practical perspective, natural theism is a deistic substitute for the Christian faith and the life of supernatural virtues. Hence, by way of applying shock to his libertine friends, he remarks that Christians abhor deism almost as much as atheism. Significantly, he uses the qualifying word "almost" but refuses to explore its meaning.

The second reason for his antipathy is a special theological one: the Jansenist doctrine of the intrinsic corruption of human nature after original sin and the consequent opposition between grace and our natural operations of reason and will.[6] Pascal is by no means wholly committed to this doctrine, but it leads him to judge our knowledge of God entirely in terms of whether it does or does not issue in a supernatural love of God. The fall of man does not destroy his capacity to love God, but it does take away his actual love of God and inverts all operations of love back upon the self in idolatrous fashion. As Calvin and Jansen had also noted, pride attaches to all of fallen man's accomplishments, not even excepting his knowledge of God. The latter leads him only to admire his own intellectual prowess and to forget his sinfulness and need for redemption. Hence Pascal concludes in a priori fashion that natural theism always results in prideful idolatry and blocks the road to Christianity.

As a consequence of this abstract theological inference, Pascal now fuses the two questions of knowing God and knowing Him in a morally upright and religiously salvific way. This is apparent in his remark that "we cannot really know God unless we know our sin. . . . Without the necessary Mediator [Christ] who was foretold and who came, it is simply impossible to prove God."[7] We only "really know" God when we gain the meritorious knowledge of Christ as our divine redeemer from sin— a type of knowledge which St. Augustine recognized as coming only through charity or supernatural love. Pascal is here measuring theism not by any natural, metaphysical standard but by the norm of Christian faith and charity. It is perhaps for this reason that his criticism of Descartes, on the ground of requiring God only to give the first flick to the mechanical system, makes vivid satire but bad history. The profound and continual need for God in the Cartesian philosophy of nature escapes Pascal's notice; the functionalism which preoccupies him is not the elucidation of nature but the introduction of man to the life of grace. Descartes' philosophical functionalism and Pascal's theological functionalism slip by each other without making proper contact and also without resolving the problem of developing a philosophical theism simply for the sake of having a measure of strict knowledge about God.

There is one recurrent theme in Pascal, however, which does provide at least an indirect answer to both the functional theism of the contemporary rationalists and to skepticism. He constantly quotes the Old Testament sentence *Vere, tu es Deus absconditus* ("Verily, Thou art a hidden God").[8] God neither manifests Himself to us in nature and human life with perfect lucidity nor keeps us in total darkness about His reality. The divine presence is not manifest enough to use God as a deductive principle in a rationalist theory of nature or to sustain the facile arguments from design in nature. Nevertheless, God's absence is not total enough to justify the atheistic negation or the skeptical suspension of judgment about His reality. What we are faced with is neither total absence nor manifest presence but, rather, the presence of a hidden God.

Instead of making a metaphysical analysis of this situation and suggesting the sort of philosophical inference which can establish something about the hidden God, as St. Thomas does, Pascal makes only a moral-religious interpretation. He observes that the chiaroscuro is not a total midnight in which we would despair of ever finding God, for then we would stop looking for a mediator. Yet God's presence is not so obvious and accessible to our natural powers that faith and charity become superfluous. From the theological standpoint, God is hidden from us in our misery, resulting from sin, and present to us in our grandeur, or life of grace, since our original nature is not unworthy of uniting with Him through Christ's redemptive act. Thus there corresponds to the dialectical relation of God's absence and presence a dialectical tension within man between his misery and his grandeur.

(2) The best-known portion of Pascal's thought is his account of *man's actual condition*. He furnishes what would today be termed an existentialist exegesis of the human situation, but he is not composing a philosophical anthropology for its own sake. His study of man remains within the apologetic context and is strictly regulated by the purpose of orienting the individual toward God. Starkly put, his aim is to show that man without God is a wretched and unbearable paradox to himself and that man is happy and lovable only in religious union with God.

In a dramatic interview with the spiritual director at Port-Royal, Monsieur de Saci, Pascal justified his philosophical readings on the ground that they highlighted man's predicament in the world and thus prepared the mind for Christianity.[9] As a faithful student of Montaigne, he accepted the old-fashioned division of all philosophical schools into dogmatists and skeptics. The former group holds tenaciously to our common-sense convictions about the sensible world and our grasp of elementary, mathematical notions. But the skeptics retort that we are ignorant of the origin of these beliefs and hence are uncertain about their truth. They insinuate that life may be a consistent dream, even an intersubjective one, but one which prevents us from distinguishing between being and seeming. Pascal pointed out that man is hopelessly strung between these two extremes; he cannot validate his convictions, and yet he cannot surrender completely to skepticism, since he has to act promptly and with assurance in practical affairs. Not even on such intimate questions as human immortality, the sovereign good, and the relation between soul and body is there any agreement among philosophical schools.

Pascal depicts man as a being cast adrift on an uncharted sea, feeling that nothing is stable, that everything is slipping through his grasp, and that the only certainty is the abyss of uncertainty yawning beneath him.[10] Caught somewhere between the infinity of nothing and the infinity of being, man feels grotesquely disproportioned to the universe and absurdly incapable of ascertaining the meaning of existence. Yet in the midst of this bewildering life, we are still able to construct a noble view of human existence. Epictetus and the Stoics assure man of his noble and even divine nature, his duties toward other men and toward God, and his destiny of union with the divine principle in nature.

What purpose do these diverse readings of human existence serve in furthering the work of Pascal's *Apology*? One might expect him to use the evidence of our contingency and imperfection as an argument for the existence of God. He does, in fact, mention the Cartesian inference which moves from the fragility of the human mind to the eternal and necessary being. But once more, Pascal fails to adopt it as his own and make it a cornerstone of his outlook, since he sees deism in the offing of any rational argumentation to God. Instead, he insists upon taking the skeptic and Stoic views together, so that they generate a dialectical tension. Its outcome is not to prove God's existence but, rather, to expose the inadequacy of all philosophical attempts to resolve the mystery of man and thus to direct attention upon the Christian revelation.

Both Stoicism and Pyrrhonism contain fragmentary portions of the truth about man, but there is no philosophy available to combine their findings into a unified vision. What Stoicism sees is the grandeur of man, as he was in his original condition and as he is now, at least in his nobler aspirations. We need the Stoic spirit, both to disturb ourselves from preoccupation with the external world and to remind us of where our actions ought to lead. But the skeptical spirit is equally indispensable, since it is a realistic warning about the actual state of fallen man and the limits of his native powers. Taken in the round, man is neither unmixed baseness nor unmixed greatness; his nature is a double one, partaking of both elements. Pascal outrivals Montaigne and Shakespeare in his dramatic exclamations about this human duplicity. Man is a prodigy and a contradiction, the glory of the world and its offscouring, the universal judge and the worm.

In his description of our human plight, Pascal is not the "sublime misanthrope" depicted by Voltaire. He is aware of the deep crevices in human nature, but he retains both poles of the antithesis. His purpose is still the apologetic one of showing that the philosophers have no way of overcoming the destructive clash between certainty and doubt, greatness and baseness. He looks to the Christian faith alone for a synthesis of all the warring factors in our complex nature, one that will avoid both the judge's pride and the worm's despair.

It is the truth of the Gospel which reconciles these contradictions through a skill which is truly divine; by uniting everything which is true and dispelling everything false, it makes of them a veritably celestial wisdom in which the opposites, that were incompatible in human doctrines, are reconciled. Now the reason for this is that the wise men of this world place these opposites in a single entity; for some would attribute greatness to human nature, and others would attribute weakness to this same human nature. Yet that is impossible. On the other hand, faith teaches us to attribute them to different entities: all that is infirm belongs to human nature, but all that is powerful derives from grace. This is the astounding and novel union which God alone was able to teach, and which He alone is able to achieve.[11]

This is the climax of the Pascalian description of man, since it invokes the Jansenist theological teaching on the fallen state of man and the order of grace. Only in the light of this version of the doctrine of original sin and redemption can the paradox of human nature be understood and the self-annihilating opposition be replaced by a positive reconstruction of human reality.

It is noteworthy that just as Pascal had previously depreciated philosophical theism in discussing the proofs of God's existence, so here does he depreciate every sort of philosophical humanism. His fear of deism prompts him not only to disparage philosophical theism but also to rule out any satisfactory philosophy of man. He is all too ready to accept as definitive Montaigne's classification of philosophies into the sheerly dogmatic and the sheerly skeptical ones, without exploring new philosophical alternatives. He oversimplifies the problem of attributing diverse aspects to human nature and sees contradictions present when it is only a case of reporting the complex features and tendencies of man. In seeking to formulate the problem of man as a simple clash between the prideful and the despairing views, he gives it too exclusively a moral-religious interpretation and thus overlooks the epistemological and metaphysical roots of these diverse evaluations.

Pascal's refusal to remain for very long at the speculative plane of a philosophical anthropology stems ultimately from the influence of the Jansenist theory on the opposition between corrupted man and grace. This theory dictated the method of assigning only weakness and corruption to our nature in the present state and of locating everything sound and great exclusively in the supernatural order. On this conception, there is still a wide area for the exercise of reason in the service of faith, but only on condition of first securing the humiliation of reason in its natural and philosophical modes. Pascal does not distinguish sufficiently between the limitation and the corruption of our natural knowing powers, since his examples often imply our capacity to know some aspects of being in an imperfect but quite reliable way. Man, or the "thinking reed," is not sheer weakness in his natural being, for thought and free action are the natural roots of his unquenchable strength and dignity. Unfortunately, from Voltaire and Holbach to Marx and Nietzsche, Pascal's expression of the Jansenist doctrine on faith and reason has been taken as the typical Christian attitude toward human nature.

(3) The so-called *wager argument* requires separate analysis because of its own complexity and the misunderstandings it has generated. Pascal himself does not give the fragment this title but simply heads it with the words, signifying man's position between two abysses, "Infinite nothing."[12] In two subsequent sections, he presumably refers back to this fragment as "the incomprehensibility" and "the proofs by the machine." There is a long history of wager arguments, starting with Arnobius and coming down to about a dozen apologists in Pascal's own century, although most of them are concerned solely with the human soul's immortality. What makes his contribution unique is the concurrence of four factors determined by the context of the *Apology:* the audience, the preparatory work, the precise purpose of the argument, and the use of a mathematical theory of probability.

334

Pascal does not address himself to all men, only to those having the same mentality as the freethinkers within his own circle. His audience does not consist of what he calls hardened atheists but of men of the world who are initially open minded, but also practically indifferent, about affirming God's existence and embracing the Christian religion. Their relation with Pascal is not so much that of a passive audience as an actively participating group of friends, since he employs the dialogue form in this place and deliberately involves them in the discussion. Moreover, they do not come cold to the wager but have been carefully prepared, by the earlier parts of the *Apology*, to give it serious consideration.

The timing is most crucial, since the argument's whole force depends upon its being proposed at a certain point in the order of thoughts, just as does the theistic discourse made by Rousseau's Savoyard vicar. Pascal broaches the subject only after having shown his libertine friends that man is a prodigy, an incomprehensible but concretely real union of the infinite and the nought, greatness and baseness. He has circumspectly suggested that the riddle of man can be solved only by viewing him in relation to God and the Christian teaching on sin and grace. The free-thinkers are now definitely intrigued by the possibility that within this theistic and Christian perspective, they can make some sense out of our absurd situation. Yet they are reluctant to commit themselves to it, partly because of their being impressed by Pascal's frequent admonitions that the holy God is just as incomprehensible as man and partly because of their native caution about taking any practical steps where some uncertainty is involved.

Precisely under these circumstances, Pascal intervenes with a new tack. His purpose is neither to effect a direct conversion (for only God can give the power to believe) nor to prove God's existence (for Pascal is suspicious of whether any theoretical demonstrations can make headway against the practical difficulties felt by the libertines). Rather, his aim is to show the patiently prepared freethinker that it is reasonable to risk acting on the chance that God does exist, as well as to indicate a way of overcoming the real obstacle against acceptance of God. Pascal is not so much interested in proving God's existence as in establishing the reasonableness of acting on the supposition that He does exist and in pointing out the best practical way to open up one's mind and heart to actual belief in God.

The friendly libertine is not an utter skeptic but admits to having some knowledge of physical and mathematical objects. This knowledge is included under Pascal's ample conception of the heart, which provides sufficient sense perception of the material world and sufficient intellectual grasp of mathematical and other primary truths to confute a consistent Pyrrhonism. But this knowledge cannot be expanded sufficiently to provide any mathematical demonstration of God's existence, such as the Cartesian proof from our idea of the infinite. Starting from the libertine's own presuppositions, Pascal observes that we know the existence and nature of finite, extended things only because we ourselves are finite and extended. And we know that there is a mathematical infinite, without knowing its nature, because it shares extension with us but not limits. From this line of thought, Pascal concludes:

We know neither the existence nor the nature of God, because He has neither extension nor limit. . . . If there is a God, He is infinitely incomprehensible, since, having neither parts nor limits, He has no relation to us. We are therefore incapable of knowing what He is, or whether He is. This being so, who will dare to solve the problem? Not we who have no relation to Him.[13]

Granted the freethinker's ideal of mathematical knowledge through commensuration, there is no way to bring God and man into a strict cognitive relation, as Cusanus had previously shown.

On Pascal's part, the argument is not intended to settle the question about all proofs of God's existence but only to wean the freethinker away from expecting any natural, philosophical demonstration of God through the mathematico-Cartesian type of reasoning he chiefly respects. But whereas Pascal would like to suggest that faith is the only recourse for such a mind, the freethinker himself concludes that perhaps the safest thing is to remain cautiously noncommital about God's existence. A way must be found for prying the indifferent mind loose from this last refuge.

In the present dialogue, it is noteworthy that the libertine himself expresses his neutralism as a refusal to wager either heads or tails on the existence of God. In point of fact, Pascal's friend Méré was an enthusiastic gambler and had asked him to investigate the mathematics of chance games, for the very practical purpose of calculating how much to indemnify a dice player who is deprived of a throw or has to leave the game. Pascal now addresses the Mérés of this world in their own language, suggesting that a wager concerning the existence of an infinite source of our happiness is on, since reason cannot settle this issue. He invites them to remain consistent in all departments of their practical life and hence to let the theory of games decide their course with respect to God, as well as in other cases where some practical uncertainty is present.

Pascal spells out the conditions under which this wager is being made. Reason cannot demonstratively answer the question; the human individual is already embarked upon existence and must make some interpretation of his life; both the stake of one's temporal happiness and the number of chances of loss of eternal life are finite; the gain itself is an infinite possession of eternal life. In the human situation, we cannot avoid interpreting the significance of our temporal existence with respect to God as our eternal happiness. The stake is the finite one of our own temporal life and happiness, and there is only a limited number of chances of loss in making the wager that God exists. The other side of the risk consists of one definite chance of a gain, which is the infinite win of eternal life with God. In wagering that God exists, the finite stake and risk can bring an infinite win of happiness in the case of God's real existence, while a loss does not result in missing anything at the level of eternal happiness. By implied contrast, the one who wagers against God's existence balances his finite stake and chances of loss against the risk of incurring a real loss of infinite happiness, whereas a win in his case obtains nothing of such happiness. Under these precise circumstances, the searcher after happiness has the backing of the mathematics of probability behind wagering for the real existence of God. This choice is both a reasonable one and also in conformity with the interest of the human will to obtain maximum happiness.

The freethinker is now brought to the very edge of decision. He sees that in prudence, he ought to place his life on the side of God and Christian living, and yet he confesses that his very constitution makes him reluctant and prevents him from taking the practical step. Adverting to his original description of man, Pascal then reminds the freethinker about his composite nature and the concurrence of bodily habits and feelings in shaping his beliefs and working convictions. What prevents the choice of a religious way of life is his second nature, the set of habits imposed by the bodily machine and inclining him in another direction. Hence Pascal advises the interested freethinker to follow at least the external example of other men who have committed themselves to a Christian sort of existence. "This will quite naturally bring you to believe and will stupify you [*vous abestira*]."[14] By this deliberately shocking phrase, Pascal means that the bodily machine has to be bent in a new direction in order to break down gradually the previous set of habits and make an opening for new ones. Only when one's external actions, bodily habits, and passional responses are remolded can the human heart open itself to practical acceptance of God. The individual's own rational appraisal of the wager for God and his reorientation of the bodily habits and passions provide the ordinary occasion for God to confer the gift of faith. The dialogue ends with an enthusiastic approval of this prospect on the interlocutor's part and with Pascal's grave reminder that he has prefaced and followed up the whole argument with a personal prayer to God.

From Voltaire onward, the Pascalian argument has been subjected to severe criticism.[15] The main charges are: that the gambler's attitude toward God is degrading and blasphemous, that a good deal is presupposed about God, that the appeal to external action is literally brutalizing, and that a man might find it more to his interest *not* to believe in the existence of the Jansenist God, who offers happiness to only a few men. Concerning the last objection, Pascal himself remains silent about whether he accepts this portion of the Jansenist theology. But on the other points, he would remind us about the context and general purpose of his *Apology*. He cannot very well appeal to the freethinker's sense of the holy, since the point at issue is the reasonableness of acting on the supposition of the existence of the holy God. Moreover, the discussion is confined to the antecedent logic governing our human choice rather than extended to the consequent relationship of devotion which would result from making a theistic choice. The freethinker naturally views his situation in terms of risk and surmises about how the faces of the cards of life really look. Hence the apologist is addressing him at the most effective level, bearing in mind the precedent in scriptural references to the loss of one's soul and the gain of eternal life as a priceless pearl.

On the question of brutalization, Pascal regards the habit-forming power of the body and the influence of external actions upon our working beliefs as belonging among the hard facts of human nature. His "proofs by the machine" do not require the freethinker to forswear reason and act like a brute, but they do help the individual to understand the somatic and neural basis for his reluctance to make a decision recommended by rational analysis of the probability situation. They also indicate to him the means of creating a new bent which will arouse the heart to choose a life oriented toward God.

In making a defense of this sort, however, Pascal would also be narrowing down his argument so much that its main features *cannot* be taken from their particular context and given a valid generalization. This applies with special force to the first part of the proof from God's "incomprehensibility." Pascal's agreement with his interlocutor concerning the philosophical unknowability of God fits the present occasion and any argument from man's idea of the infinite. But elsewhere he admits some sort of natural knowledge of God and makes it clear that what our natural powers cannot attain is a meritorious knowledge of God as redeemer. Within the context of the wager, he presupposes that like is known only by like and that there must be some direct proportion between the mind and its object. This rests upon the geometrical ideal of knowledge as a commensuration, such as is found in Cusanus. God's lack of extension and bodily limits renders Him entirely unknowable to natural reason only on the premise that "whatever transcends geometry transcends us" and that all demonstrative reasoning conforms with the model of geometry.[16] Pascal is not entitled to generalize the wager argument beyond the given circumstances, since he does not place his epistemological premises on a sufficiently reflective and universal basis. He also fails to explore the distinction between the incomprehensibility and the unknowability of God, even though the latter is not entailed by the former.

Throughout his writings, Pascal remains strangely silent about causality. Yet his reasoning in the first part of the wager argument depends upon showing that there is no knowable relation between ourselves and God. His implicit meaning is that there is no geometrically formulable relation from either side and that natural demonstrations depend upon such a relation being present. When it is not a question of convincing the libertine to abandon philosophy, Pascal is eager to regard God as the creative cause of the visible universe and of man, but he does not analyze the kind of relation which this causal act establishes and the kind of natural, inferential knowledge of God which it can engender. The one pointed reference to causality is a rephrasing of Montaigne's view that all things are reciprocally related as cause and effect within the unified system of nature.[17] This is causality in the sense of a physical reaction within a closed system rather than an existential production of being.

Pascal does not inquire whether a causal inference based on the latter sort of causal relation will enable us to know the truth that God exists without making us coinfinites with God. A philosophical knowledge of God based upon the existential-causal relation does not violate His uniquely infinite and hidden being and hence does not necessarily minister to an idolatrous human pride. It is a knowledge of God derived precisely from a recognition of our caused and finite way of being, including our limited intellectual ability. The causal approach to God finds its cogency in definitively retaining the distinction between God and man, together with the constant dependency in being of the latter upon the former. It dispels rather than cultivates any illusory pride and thus promotes an openness toward God's initiative which need not lead to deism. Pascal's antipathy toward philosophical theism does not rest upon a thorough consideration of the various ways of reaching God but upon an eagerness for a dialectical apology moving forward from the hopeless antitheses in the human philosophies about God and man.

The attractiveness of Pascal does not come from his special dialectic but from the broad themes which he sets forth. He explores with sympathy and delicacy both the soul of the religious individual and that of the man for whom God is totally absent. The hidden God manifests Himself sufficiently to ground the hope of the former, and yet His hiddenness makes the position of the latter at least understandable. It is noteworthy that the religious individual addresses the hidden God as *Thou,* emphasizing that the search for God is a personal one which leads eventually to a personal relationship of the I-and-Thou sort.

There is a lapidary phrase in which Pascal summarizes how the personal God is disclosed to the individual: "This is Faith: God felt by the heart, not by reason."[18] Pascalian faith is not a purely sentimental and blind act. The heart is a complex focus for cognitive acts, having the immediacy, certainty, and obscurity of sense perception and intellectual apprehension of first principles, as well as for the appetitive acts of desire and love. That the heart, rather than reason, attains to God means that a religiously vivifying relation with God engages the will and the feelings, along with the factor of knowledge, so that the union will be permanent, dynamic, and practically operative. This union is termed a feeling, both because the darkness is never fully removed from our view of God and also because it is achieved through faith. The logic of the heart includes both the habits of the bodily machine and the reflections of reason, but above all, it consists in the supernatural faith from God.

Pascal's *Apology for Christianity* seeks fundamentally to elucidate the conditions under which men can normally expect to receive faith and charity as divine gifts. If this leads him to become suspicious of the philosophical study of God, it is because some of his acquaintances did use this study as a diversion from Christian faith and because the Jansenist theory of faith and reason encouraged an antithetical approach to the issue.

2. GOD AND THE KIERKEGAARDIAN SPHERES OF EXISTENCE

There is some analogy between the position of Pascal in the late seventeenth century and that of Søren Kierkegaard (1813–1855) in the early nineteenth century.[19] Both men are primarily moralists and Christian apologists, using their critical powers and literary gifts to induce people to think seriously about Christianity and to distinguish Christian faith from various natural kinds of belief and philosophical systems. They lay joint stress upon the human individual and his act of choice, as well as upon the influence which the emotions and will exert over beliefs. Common to both is a sharp criticism of the current philosophical theories about God, but here the effect of different historical situations is to lead each man to take a distinctive stand. Pascal is confronted with deism at a time when it is rising to the ascendancy, whereas it is a spent force during Kierkegaard's lifetime. Whereas the French thinker is suspicious of philosophical theism as a diversion away from Christianity, the Dane has to reckon with the monistic tendency which embraces Christianity so closely that the distinction between philosophy and Christian faith disappears. Kierkegaard does not attack philosophical theism but simply despairs of ever seeing its resurrection in the era of Romantic pantheism and the Hegelian philosophy of absolute spirit. He concentrates upon re-establishing some frontier between these philosophical conceptions of God and the way in which natural religion and the Christian faith view God.

The weak backwash of the Enlightenment debate over God was felt in the Copenhagen lecture halls of the 1830's. An attempt was still being made to demonstrate theism and Christianity after the mathematical fashion of Wolff, but it was becoming painfully evident that this whole method depended on the validity of the ontological proof of God's existence. Although the Hegelian divines were trying to revive this proof, Kierkegaard returned to Kant for objections against it in its specifically theistic form. His criticism centered around the contrast between *ideal* being and *factual* being. The former is confined to the realm of conceptual essences, as far as our human inferences are concerned, but the latter concerns the zone of really existing things. We can argue from factual being to some ideal structure, but we can never use ideal being as the starting point for determining anything, with certainty, about a real existent. From Descartes and Spinoza onward, the attempt to derive the divine existence from the notion of the infinitely perfect being has foundered upon the intrinsic limitations of the order of ideal being. The latter does not include within its range existence as the act of factual being but only existence as an ideal form within our human thought about an essential structure. In concluding to the latter, the ontological proof leaves untouched the only pertinent question of whether God's being is an actual perfection, distinct from every conceptual determinant of the ideal essence.

This distinction also enabled Kierkegaard to meet Wolff's reformulation of the ontological argument in terms of the greater degree of perfection found in the divine essence. There may be grades of ideal being, since this refers to differences in essential perfections or modes of possibility, but there is no gradation with respect to factual being. "For factual being is subject to the dialectic of Hamlet: to be or not to be. Factual being is wholly indifferent to any and all variations in essence," at least in the sense that there is no gradual shading, which goes from existing a little bit to existing a great deal more.[20] There is something quite definitive about the difference between enjoying factual being and not enjoying it, so there is no point at which we can infer from a graduated series of essences or ideal modes of being that one of them must actually exist. One reason for Kierkegaard's stress upon the human individual was to drive home the point that existential inference is performed by finite minds, for whom the contrast between factual and ideal being is insuperable, and not by an impersonal series of essences which can automatically and impersonally establish its own claim upon actuality.

The other alternative for Enlightenment theism was to reach God inductively from the design in nature. Kierkegaard conceded that once we have assured ourselves by other means about God's actuality, then we can use this truth as an interpretative principle in the study of nature. But physicotheology is a consequence of accepting God, not a primary source of our conviction about His actual being. The mind and heart must be previously prepared by some other type of evidence before we can discern God's providential work in nature and history. On this question, Kierkegaard was influenced not so much by Kant as by J. G. Hamann and the skeptical arguments of Bayle and Hume, who stressed the power of evil and the thorough ambivalence of all natural and historical events. Whereas in the face of such skeptical criticism a Voltaire was still able to argue probably from the world-machine to a transcendent God, Kierkegaard had to reckon with the changing conception of nature in the Romantic age, which tended to view nature as an organic whole having a purely immanent, divine principle. He did not want to make the appeal to design in nature too fundamental, lest it lead to a nature-pantheism.

Although his central teaching on the esthetic, ethical, and religious spheres of existence is primarily a description of human attitudes and ways of disposing freedom, it also concerns the manners in which the individual existent relates himself to God. Each of the spheres of existence is specified, at least in part, by its distinctive view of the individual's bond with God and his way of attaining knowledge of God. In his analysis of the esthetic stage, Kierkegaard includes a discussion of Romantic pantheism. His critical evaluation of the ethical standpoint revolves mainly around the problem of Kant's moral theism. Finally, access to the religious mode of existing depends upon distinguishing both the natural and the Christian conceptions of God from the Hegelian theory of absolute spirit. One cannot appreciate Kierkegaard's view of religious existence apart from his careful, preparatory critique of the pantheistic, moralistic, and absolutist approaches to God.

For a while, Kierkegaard himself was fascinated by the Romantic, or *esthetic*, view of nature.[21] The Enlightenment difficulty about making a transition from an impersonal world-machine to a personal, somewhat distant God was seemingly erased by Fichte's equation of God with the moral laws of the universe and the universal impulse toward eternal life. Similarly, the warm, poetic vision which Schelling and the Schlegels had of the ideal, divine principle holding together the tensions of the world of man and nature brought God much closer to us and gave us intuitive certainty about His being. The same could be said for Schleiermacher's method of building religious conviction upon one's inner feeling of dependence and spontaneous gratitude for life. All these currents tended to make nature instinct with divine activity and benevolent purpose, thus silencing the skeptical objections and replacing Voltairean and Humean probability with an immediate intuition of the divine actuality.

In making nature revelatory and alive with a divine principle, however, the Romantics gave an immanentist interpretation of the relation between God and man which Kierkegaard came to regard as destructive of the nature of both. The human individual is beguiled into thinking that his relationship with God is easily achieved, on the basis of an ultimate identity of finite and eternal being. This has a disintegrating effect upon our moral effort and the discipline of free choice. The esthetic mind never fully unifies and controls its life-pattern because of the predominance of imaginative play over a definite use of will. The tendency to drift and remain enclosed in possibilities is fostered by the pantheistic persuasion that we are already one with the infinitely various spirit of the cosmos. Our distinctive personal existence is thus threatened and the fabric of temporal duties unraveled. A further consequence noted by Kierkegaard is that faith in God is always treated as a primitive conviction which, like animism, has to be subjected to analysis and transformed into a higher philosophical doctrine.

There is a strict correlation between our conceptions of man and God, so that inadequacies regarding the former are inevitably communicated to the latter. Just as pantheism undermines the individuality and freedom of man, so does it misconceive the nature and effective action of God. The fusion of man with the divine principle in nature also means that God's eternal being is identified with the vital forces and temporal sweep of nature. For Kierkegaard, this tampering with the divine transcendence does not make God more intimate to us but only obscures His distinctive way of being and reduces His providential freedom to spontaneous ratification of whatever does occur.

The main objection against pantheism and finitism is that the mutual dissolution of human temporality and divine eternity prevents a personal union between man and God. Hence Kierkegaard is critical of any appeal to the heart and feelings which wipes out the distinction between temporal existence and God's eternal being. Goethe has his Faust exclaim:

The All-Embracer, the All-Sustainer, doesn't He embrace and sustain you and me and Himself? . . . Fill your heart to the very brim with all this, and when that feeling makes your bliss complete, then name it as you will, call it Happiness! Heart! Love! God! I have no name for it. Feeling is everything; a name is sound and smoke, befogging heavenly fire.[22]

Against this pantheistic conception of the heart, Kierkegaard insists upon the need to retain firm distinctions between different modes of being and hence to use words with a meaningful discrimination between the human and the divine. For him, the function of the heart is to insure the practical and permanent commitment of the individual to God but not to dissolve them both in a warm stew of cosmic sentiment.

The function of the *ethical* mind is to recall men to the stern reality of their situation as finite agents whose actions must be brought into conformity with an independent and exacting norm. The standpoint of Kantian morality dispels a cosmic pantheism and yet, in so doing, it generates its own special set of problems concerning God. For it relates the individual directly and primarily to the categorical imperative and only secondarily to God Himself. If a man shapes his existential attitude by the Kantian dictum that God is not the foundation of moral life but a postulate implied by it, then he is displacing God from the motivating center of action. A God who is not the ultimate basis of obligation is no longer supremely relevant to the quality and motive of our moral choice. Kant's moral functionalism is just as detrimental to the sovereign actuality of God in the moral order as the rationalist functionalism is in the speculative order. In an effort to eliminate every sort of functional theism, Kierkegaard disavows the Kantian moral proof of God as the harmonizer of happiness and moral worth; like the ontological proof of the rationalists, it makes the eternal actuality of God follow from knowledge of a prior ideal principle. The Kantian universal moral law corresponds to the infinitely perfect essence of the ontological proof, and in neither instance are we placed in firm possession of anything more than an ideal mode of being.

Kierkegaard's inquiry, in *Fear and Trembling* (1843), about a suspension of the ethical is not a recommendation of moral nihilism and self-creating morality. He does not advocate that the real ordering of man toward God be placed in brackets but only that we take a critical look at the ethical doctrine of Kant concerning the categorical imperative.[23] This ethical system relates us to God only by reason of a more primary relation to the moral imperative, which is autonomously grounded in self-legislating, practical reason. Kierkegaard is not concerned with the practical, moral attitude of the conscientious man, who follows the dictates of his conscience as being immediately binding upon him. His criticism is reserved for the formal, philosophical explanation of the ultimate basis of moral obligation. Kant specifies the objective determining ground as the moral law itself and the subjective ground as respect for law. God enters, not as the ultimate ground of morality, but as a reasonable postulate for harmonizing the formal dedication to duty with our search after a proportionate happiness. Kant stresses the autonomous moral will, lest unscrupulous people read their own aims into the divine will when it is considered as a source of moral obligation. But Kierkegaard is searching for an unambiguously postfunctional approach to God, one that does not read off the details of morality from the divine will, just as it does not read off the details of physical nature from the divine reason. Hence he sees no valid reason for continuing to refuse to view the moral law in its adequate foundation, as expressing the personal concern of God for us and our obligation toward Him.

At this juncture, however, Hegel is prepared to intervene with the remark that both the moral law and the individual conscience must be synthesized in a higher ethical totality and that, for the success of this synthesis, a transcendent God must eventually be sacrificed. Kierkegaard's opposition to this suggestion is one facet in his broad assault upon the popular Hegelianism of his day. He appeals to the biblical examples of Job and Abraham as showing that the man who combines a sensitive conscience with an awareness of God as the last source of moral law does not have to yearn after a dialectical confluence of conscience and law in order to relieve his situation. The responsible individual learns to remain before God and to respect both the transcendence of God and the demanding character of His moral law. The moral situation requires freedom or a "possibility-relationship" between man and God in their irreducible, personal modes of being. Moral personalism on a theistic foundation supplies Kierkegaard with a means of resisting Hegel without returning to the Kantian view of God and the moral law.

Since Kierkegaard breathes the intellectual atmosphere of his own times, his arguments have an unmistakably Hegelian ring to them. In their own significance, however, they point toward a new scene of thought. This combination of conventional and original elements is apparent in his fundamental thesis that "(A), a logical system is possible; (B), an existential system is impossible."[24] The first part of this proposition repudiates any irrationalist plan to erect our conviction in God and Christianity upon the ruins of logic and natural reason. Within well-defined limits, Kierkegaard admits the proper competence of abstract thought and systematic reasoning. Questions in the realm of formal logic, mathematics, and the natural sciences can be given an abstract, systematic explanation. But this is possible only because they concern the ideal or essential order and prescind from existence.

In the second part of the thesis, Kierkegaard opposes Hegel's attempt to treat essential and existential questions in the same way, by including them within a single method and system of pure thought. The Hegelian postulate of the identity between pure thought and pure being, far from correcting the defects of the ontological proof, rests upon the same failure to respect the intrinsic difference between ideal and factual being, between the representation of existence and the existential act itself. The latter displays itself both in sensation and in our reflection on man. Both sensible things and the human person are irreducible to the concept, even in its alienated condition, and hence they are unassimilable to the Hegelian system of absolute spirit. Being in the existential mode shows itself in real sensible change, which is something different from the concept in its state of otherness. It is also present in our personal attitudes and free decisions, which never turn out to be the same as an acceptance of the impersonal necessities of the dialectical absolute. Thus the individual, existing man is himself the primary evidence that an existential system is impossible, in the Hegelian sense of including human existence within the internal development of the absolute idea.

But if the existential being of man escapes through the apertures of the Hegelian system, then neither the system itself nor its method is all inclusive of finite reality. In that case, however, it is all the less likely that this dialectical system can include the eternal and infinite being of God within its scope. The theory of absolute spirit and of dialectical movement breaks down at both ends when it pretends to be something more than a logical construction. It is unable to embrace either man as a temporal existent or God as the eternal being.[25] The human individual has his existence before God and toward God, but not as a moment *within* any developing, absolute spirit. God maintains His transcendence, not by withdrawing at a distance, but by the very act of being in an unchangeable, personal, and free way. Similarly, His immanence does not consist in a dialectical unfolding in finite form but in His intimate knowledge, personal love, and creative power with respect to temporal existents.

As Kierkegaard views it, a merger of man and God in the totality of absolute spirit would not bring them into closer union. It would simply suffocate them by destroying the conditions under which there can be a personal relation between a free, finite individual and the infinite creator. Since both human existence and divine actuality elude the categories of the absolute spirit, the latter has only an ideal form of being in the mind of the Hegelian systematist. Most of Kierkegaard's satirical descriptions are reserved for evoking an awareness of the significant discrepancy between the claims of the system of absolute spirit and the actual modes of human existence, both secular and sacred.

In his private journals, Kierkegaard reveals himself to be a close student of Feuerbach's writings against Hegel and Christianity.[26] Quoting the maxim that one should take counsel from the enemy, he admits the force of Feuerbach's criticism, in that it establishes the capital difference between the orthodox Christian teaching and the version of Christianity being popularized by the Hegelian divines. Yet he observes that Feuerbach himself fails to appreciate the precise significance of this contrast, which is that the Hegelian system does not genuinely incorporate the reality of God and Christianity within itself and is not dialectically reducible to them. Instead of trying to defend God and Christianity on the basis of the idealistic theory of absolute spirit, Kierkegaard takes the radically new course of contrasting them both with absolutism, on the basis of a view of *religious* existence. The effect of his refusal to assimilate God to the absolute spirit is to undercut Feuerbach's plea for an antitheistic humanism. By anticipation, then, the Danish thinker is suggesting that the tremendous surge of atheism in the period from Marx to Nietzsche and beyond rests upon the indefensible premise that God and the Hegelian absolute are identical. Kierkegaard's doctrine on the modes of existing moves entirely beyond the clash between Hegelian and naturalist forms of absolutism to an existential view, which does not confuse either the existing man or the eternal God with any absolutist postulate.

Whereas Feuerbach formulated the central problem as the saving of human reality from God or the absolute spirit, Kierkegaard used all the resources of concrete description to reformulate it as the recovery of God, as well as man, from the doctrine of the absolute. He admitted that the latter was an inhumane concept, but he added that it is just as deeply incompatible with the personal, creative God as with the human existent. The alienation of man comes not from acknowledging God but from confusing God with the absolute spirit and then trying to conform human existence to the latter as a dialectical totality. Hence the restoration of man to his real mode of being cannot come about through the Feuerbachian and Marxist method of attributing to him, in inverse form, all of the properties of the absolute. Human self-estrangement is overcome only by making the *double* movement of recovering the finite, personal existent and recognizing the infinite, personal actuality of God. In eliminating pure thought as the systematic explanation of man, we are also liberated from regarding it as the explanation of God's eternal being. Only through this twofold clarification can we shake ourselves free from the idealistic absolute and its inhumane consequences.

Kierkegaard does not follow up his concrete descriptions with a new philosophical account of man and God. He provides no detailed explanation of the natural world or the means by which the unaided human mind attains to God's eternal being. It is not that he attempts such an explanation and fails at it but rather that he has no confidence in finding a presently available philosophical path which leads anywhere except back into absolute idealism. The realism and theism which he discovers in his own experience of men and in his reading of the Greeks are never developed in a comprehensive, philosophical manner. After uncovering their actual presence, Kierkegaard becomes overwhelmed by the task of giving them a rigorous, philosophical formulation. He regards his own peculiar vocation as that of warning against any confusion of the human individual and the eternal God with the Hegelian absolute, and then of concentrating his poetic and dialectical energies upon the main work of leading men toward the plane of religious existence and Christianity.

Kierkegaard's stress upon the paradoxical quality of Christian faith is an emergency measure, dictated not by any enmity toward our finite understanding but by a resolve not to permit religious faith to be transformed once again into a preliminary stage in the growth of Hegelian reason. By its paradoxical nature, he also means that it is not simply a continuation of natural religion but depends on the initiative and free gift of God. Christian faith also has a passional aspect, since it is not purely an intellectual act but engages the heart as well, as expressed in the life of prayer. Once its distinctive nature is respected, Christian faith works co-operatively with human, existential reflection in bringing the several modes of human existence to their proper fulfillment in the personal love of God.[27]

All of Kierkegaard's analyses of the spheres of existence are incidental, in his own estimation, to the work of preparing our emotions, will, and intelligence for the free act of love for God. Yet that which is incidental for him belongs philosophically at the center of the post-Hegelian discussion on whether man can again acknowledge God without crushing himself as a free individual. Kierkegaard's contribution to the philosophy of God is his concrete affirmation of the solidarity between individual human existence and the eternal actuality of God.

3. NEWMAN AND THE ASSENT TO GOD

At the height of the Victorian age, T. H. Huxley declared, half in irony and half in accusation, that if he were composing a primer of infidelity, he would draw generously from the writings of John Henry Cardinal Newman (1801–1890). He could not comprehend how Newman combined an unswerving faith in God with deep sympathy for the doubting mind or a basic respect for intellectual inquiry with a vivid recognition of the limitations of formal logic. Yet it was just this original mingling of mental traits which set Newman apart from other Victorian divines and permitted him to contribute something unique to the theistic tradition, especially to the *philosophia cordis,* or heart's way to God.

Both as a leader of the Oxford Movement and as a priest of the Oratory, his chief concern was for the practical religious life. But since Newman always conceived of religion as being based upon the dogmatic principle and hence as embodying a definite intellectual content, he gave a major share of his attention to the routes whereby the human mind comes to give its assent to God and Christianity or to withhold it from them. A purely sentimental approach, in which the feelings are the primary determinants, was foreign both to his experience of individual cases of the process of believing and to his conception of historical Christianity. His watchword was that there is no sound devotion without the known fact of God and hence that in matters of theism and religion, the imagination and feelings must be kept under the vigorous discipline of concrete reason.[28] His purpose was to achieve a balanced ordering of all these factors involved in the heartful assent to God rather than to stress any one of them out of all due proportion.

Although cut off almost completely from the Continental philosophical movements favoring the emergence of atheism in the nineteenth century, Newman was nevertheless extraordinarily sensitive to the cultural tendencies at home which pointed in the same direction. He saw that it was becoming increasingly difficult to furnish intellectual justification of one's acceptance of God and that the tendency was toward atheism in the absolute sense rather than toward a piecemeal denial of some aspect of God or some article in the Christian creed. He attributed this drift toward a radical repudiation of God partly to the ethos, or general cultural atmosphere of the day. With an increase in historical and sociological knowledge, it was more difficult to discern God's presence in the realm of history and human society. Concurrently, the increasing prestige of the natural sciences and technology disposed many people to view nature solely as a field for human exploitation and not also as a manifestation of divine intelligence and power. Yet he counted as another primary reason for the weakening of theism the failure of theists themselves to appreciate the strength of the challenge and to meet it effectively upon the ultimate terrain of the individual's act of assent to God.

Both at Oxford and at Rome, Newman was disappointed in his search for assistance in grappling with this problem.[29] Oxford during the 1820's and 1830's was still dominated by the so-called Noetic, or Evidential, school, under the leadership of Richard Whately, at Oriel College, where Newman served as fellow and tutor. This school prolonged the rationalistic defense of natural religion and Christianity made during the previous century by Clarke and Paley. It stressed the criterion of mathematical clarity and cogency, maintained that no one can validly assent to a proposition without proving it through formal logic, favored the argument for God from design, and applied to the Christian doctrines the same procedure as that for natural religion.

Although Newman praised this school for teaching him to think independently and with logical rigor, he soon became aware of its major deficiencies. Both his own experience and the writings of the British empiricists convinced him that the mathematical conception of reason cannot sustain its claims in the zone of matters of fact, where the question of God's existence and nature properly belongs. Furthermore, it was an artificially stringent requirement to demand that every valid assent to God be the outcome of a formal, logical demonstration. This would doom the great majority of theists and Christian believers either to perpetual uncertainty or to unreasonableness of belief—a consequence that ran in the face of Newman's experience of minds which did have reasonable grounds but not the formal demonstration. He also considered it too rationalistic to suppose that logical proof ineluctably issues in assent on the individual's part without any preparation of his heart. The emphasis upon design in nature and upon deductive proof of Christianity sprang from this same disregard for the actualities of the human mind and for the differentiation of methods in treating different objects.

When he went to Rome in the 1840's for theological studies, Newman was astonished by the lack of interest, not only in the Patristic sources, but also in the great syntheses of Aquinas and other Schoolmen. Even though his own mind never acquired a Scholastic cast, Newman did independent readings in the current manuals and the great theologians. He granted that from these sources "he could obtain the various formal proofs on which the being of a God rests, and the irrefragable demonstration thence resulting against the freethinker and the sceptic."[30] His own approach never called into question the objectively necessary demonstrations but moved onward to explore certain issues which he found nowhere else properly treated or even recognized. Newman regarded his investigations as standing in complementary relation with the metaphysical inference to God, as meeting a distinctive and urgent need of the modern world, where diversity of opinions about the being of God is the prevailing condition.

To Newman, the basic problem is that there is no syllogistic device able to extort assent from a mind not personally prepared to grasp the argument and that most people who arrive at genuine certitude about God do so by paths other than the formal proofs. Confronted with this massive situation, Newman devotes himself to four primary tasks bearing upon the philosophy of God: an elucidation of the difficulty of knowing God, a critique of the argument from design, a description of the theistic inference from conscience, and a defense of the certitude of theistic assent by comparison with scientific probability. Beyond this point, his work becomes properly theological and directed toward examining the relations between Catholicism and the modern world. He regards the acceptance of God as the initial step in a steady growth of the mind toward the Catholic faith and hence, in this clearly specified sense, maintains that there is no permanent position between atheism and Catholicism.

(1) *The difficulty of knowing God.* There is a paradox concealed beneath Newman's familiar reference to himself and his creator as the only two luminously self-evident beings. His apprehension of God's reality shares in the strength and intimacy of his grasp of his own existence, and no other real assent enjoys the same inevitability and importance for his mind. By virtue of its direct attachment to the truth of one's own existence, the truth of God's existence is luminous and self-evident (evident through the self), but this is not to say that there

is any facile intuition of Him. On the contrary, natural knowledge of God is acquired by some sort of inference and is justified only after a careful reflection on its grounds. Newman expresses this nice balance between the spontaneity, intimacy, and practical power of the belief in God and the arduous character of its rational defense in his autobiographical remark that "the being of a God is, to my own apprehension, encompassed with most difficulty, and yet borne in upon our mind with most power." It is, he adds, "as certain to me as the certainty of my own existence, though when I try to put the grounds of that certainty into logical shape I find a difficulty in doing so in mood and figure to my satisfaction."[31] One can be certain of God's existence and still recognize the depth of the difficulties and the inadequacy of the syllogistic proofs. It is this twinned vision of both the surety and the obscurity of our knowledge of God which enables Newman to maintain the conditions of dialogue between theists and God-seeking atheists in the modern community.

The two parties in the dialogue do not always recognize the ambiguity contained in the common phrase "God's existence is a demonstrable conclusion." Newman distinguishes between the logical meaning of "conclusion," as that which follows objectively with formal consequence from the premises, and the psychological meaning of one's apprehension and acceptance of the outcome of a course of reasoning.[32] Whereas logicism stresses only the former meaning and psychologism only the latter, the human situation requires both of them for a satisfactory explanation. There is no substitute for the individual's grasp of the weight of an argument. It cannot be forced upon him without any personal insight on his part, and in this sense there is no irresistibly demonstrated conclusion. The objectively demonstrated truth is an inoperative conclusion until it is brought home and appropriated in an act of recognition or concluding. Newman would agree with Kierkegaard that a hiatus remains until the individual mind sees that a conclusion is a concerned truth or one that counts for himself.

On the basis of this distinction, Newman criticizes two interpretations of the fact that some people do not accept the philosophical demonstration of God's existence. One extreme view combines a purely impersonal notion of demonstration, divorced from the need for personal response, with a rigoristic moral judgment that every failure to accept the philosophical conclusion is a willful blotting out of the truth. Newman points out the impossibility of doubting the sincerity of many searchers after the truth about God who nevertheless fail to see the probative force of the formal argument for His existence. Among his own correspondents were lifelong friends who continued the inquiry without ever reaching certitude on this matter.

The other extreme position matches the sincerity of most inquirers against the claims for an irresistible demonstration and concludes that there is no coercive proof of God's existence. This is the type of objection already met with in William James. For his part, Newman observes that the demonstrative quality of an inference does not hinge upon its winning universal, actual agreement, since the act of concluding or accepting the demonstration depends upon more than a logical statement of the premises. When the theist engages others in dialogue, his aim must also be to stimulate in them "a mode of thinking and trains of thought similar to our own, leading them on by their own independent action, not by any syllogistic compulsion."[33] Irresistibility, in the sense of automatic coercion of the individual's judgment, does not properly belong among the traits of a demonstrative argument. When due consideration is paid to the distinctive nature of personal recognition of the evidence, one cannot *necessarily* infer from the fact of diversity over theism either a moral imputation against those who withhold acceptance of the formal proof or a logical objection against the validity of the proof itself.

Further light is cast on the significance of sharp disagreements over the worth of the theistic proofs by distinguishing between the formal and the informal kind of inference to God. The formal inference is a technical effort to cast our reasoning about God into the mold of the abstract logical requirements for syllogistic demonstration. Newman grants that there are always difficulties surrounding this attempt to make our inferences to God conform with the canons of syllogistic logic. Yet he warns against drawing the simple conclusion that the natural basis for acceptance of God is evidentially defective. At least four qualifying considerations have to be kept in mind. The syllogism is not the only kind of reasoning that yields certitude, so the conditions of syllogistic form are not coterminous with those for obtaining certitude about God. Furthermore, the modern rationalistic tradition compounds the theory of syllogism with the model of mathematical reasoning. But neither syllogistic inference nor mathematics is fitted to give demonstrations of things lying beyond the abstract order and the definitions framed by our mind. The problem of God concerns a concrete existential starting point in natural things and man, as well as a terminus in the really existing being of God, who does not get encased within our abstract definitions. In the third place, the evidence for God is drawn largely from our experience of the moral life of man. Here the chief requirement is not the formal schema but the discernment of the common significance of the many aspects of our personal freedom and moral decision. More is required than skill in the logical moods and figures in order to grasp the grounds of certitude about God's existence.

Finally, Newman points out that in most of the issues in life which are not determinable through any abstract deduction, we rely upon an informal inference which does yield some reliable conclusions. Far from being an incipient or imperfect version of formal inference, this informal inference functions precisely in those concrete areas where more than the formal canons is required. Hence informal inference retains its own nature and reaches certainty in a distinctive way. In the case of our ordinary search after God, we rely basically upon an informal kind of inference. This is a question concerning the actual existence of God, for which we especially find a witness in the concrete moral life of conscience. To carry out a direct test of the validity of this inference, we must make an analysis of the mode of reasoning and the evidence we actually use in reaching our natural conviction about God. The informal theistic inference does not depend, for its validity, upon the success of its translation into syllogistic form. Indeed, it is essentially irreducible to syllogistic demonstration and mathematical proof, so that its certainty does not rest upon the formal inferences. Difficulties encountered in trying to prove God's existence through formal inference therefore cannot weaken the informal inference to God. The diversity of estimates concerning the formal proofs does not render our informal inference uncertain and doubtful, but it does remind the theist to use the sort of reasoning which is adapted to reaching certitude in concrete issues pertaining to our moral experience and the real being of the transcendent God.

Newman marshals his further reflections on the question of diversity around his general doctrine that inference (formal, as well as informal) is open at both ends and hence is not a self-sufficient whole. At the initial point, inference depends upon the common acceptance of some relevant factors and principles. Most disagreements over the worth of an argument which is not formally inconsistent resolve into a conflict concerning the original data and the general truths bearing on the issue. The theistic inference is no exception to this rule; most controversy over it does not concern the argumentation as much as the precise facts and guiding truths determining the starting point and procedure. There is indispensable preparatory work which must be done in order to insure acceptance of these qualifying factors. Sometimes the obstacles to agreement at this basic level are due to personal, psychological differences, which have to be patiently analyzed and met. Attention must also be paid to the ethos, or prevailing cultural viewpoint of a society, which unconsciously supplies the individual with many of his fundamental principles and evaluations of fact. The dominant intellectual climate and the steady process of acculturation dispose our minds toward accepting as obvious a particular image of things, even though the standard outlook may differ widely from one age to another.

Nevertheless, Newman also maintains that there is a common pattern of human nature, discernible in the midst of personal and intercultural differences in such a way that it serves as a footing for agreement about the data and general truths upon which a theistic inference grounds itself.

> There is a certain ethical character, one and the same, a system of first principles, sentiments and tastes, a mode of viewing the question and of arguing, which is formally and normally, naturally and divinely, the *organum investigandi* given us for gaining religious truth.[34]

Thus we have a reasonable basis for expecting that the preparatory disposition of a man's mind and heart will often bring about sufficient agreement on fundamentals to permit the inference to God to be made. There are many occasions, however, when the individual either deliberately refuses to accept the primary findings about facts and principles or else cannot withdraw himself from some conventional position. In such instances, it is futile to attempt to convince the mind by formal argumentation and we can only resume the subsurface work of trying to reach personal agreement on man's actual condition in our world.

At the terminal side of the theistic inference, Newman distinguishes between the intellectual act of inferring or concluding and the final assent to the truth of what is so inferred.[35] Inference proper, or the act of concluding from premises, is conditional, i.e., dependent upon viewing the proposition precisely as an outcome of an argumentation. But the assent itself is an indivisible and unconditional act, since it accepts the proposition in itself and not merely as a result following from premises. Sometimes the individual fails to give his assent to the proposition about God's existence because he remains passive and makes no personal examination of the evidence supporting it. In another case, he may admit God's existence and nevertheless find the formal proofs too recondite and difficult, so that he will never assent to the proposition in a notional or philosophical way. Again, the individual may follow the reasoning through to the very act of concluding and yet never relate the result to his personal conception of God, where his real assent centers. He may admit the validity of the argument and draw the conclusion in an abstract way, without relating it practically to his own conduct and moral concern. He sees where the argument leads, but he never gives it his personal assent. Thus there are innumerable variations at the individual level, so that there is no uniform explanation of the absence of universal assent to the philosophical proofs.

In the actual world, Newman likens our predicament to that of men looking down a deep well or milling together on a dark plain (somewhat as Matthew Arnold conceives the situation) rather than to a clear-cut division of the hosts of heaven and evil at noonday. Even under the best conditions, when a person appreciates the scientific proofs and also relates them to himself, the obscurity is never completely removed from our finite knowledge of God. "After all, you do not know, you only conclude that there is a God; you see Him not, you but hear of Him."[36] God remains the hidden and unknown God, even when the truth of His existence and infinite actuality is borne home inferentially by the existence of oneself and the world.

There is a technical meaning in Newman's phrase that ten thousand difficulties do not make one doubt in matters concerning God. By doubt he means the state of mind which does not give assent to the being of God. This is quite distinct from the standpoint of the convinced theist, who does assent to God and yet who remains keenly aware of the limits and inadequacy of his knowledge. The difficulties encountered by the theist do not concern an intrinsic defect in the evidence for the divine reality but, rather, our inability to penetrate God's infinite perfections and fully understand His presence to creatures and their individual relationship with Him. These difficulties not only coexist with the certitudinal assent to God's infinite being but are generated precisely by our reflective hold upon this truth.

Newman deems it a mark of the proper humility of the human intelligence to acknowledge both the surety and the arduousness of our knowledge of God. This intellectual humility differs considerably from the humiliation prescribed for natural reason by Pascal and rejected so violently by Nietzsche. Since Newman couples the certain assent and the recognition of difficulties firmly together as the only balanced and natural attitude of man concerning his knowledge of God, he does not have to follow the Calvinist and Pascalian view that natural knowledge of God always generates an idolatrous pride of self. Hence he is relieved of the necessity to be suspicious of philosophical inferences to God and to evaluate them by moral-religious norms alone.

Ordinarily, Newman distinguishes between two ways of conducting the philosophical study of God: inquiry and investigation. By the former he means a study of God on the part of one who entertains doubt or does not actually give assent to His being. This approach is contrasted with the way of investigation, which is the procedure of the theist who does assent to God and yet finds it within his vocation to probe into the difficulties surrounding our human knowledge of Him, as well as to enter sympathetically into the mind of the doubter and the atheist. Newman formally designates his own work as a continual investigation. Its mainspring is not any failure of his own assent to God but a lifelong sense of responsibility for examining the difficulties in his mind, for helping other theists to strengthen their hold on God, and for remaining open and responsive to the problems of inquirers after God.

(2) *Critique of physical theology.* In making his investigations, Newman did not tone down the difficulties but presented them in full force. He was especially severe with any facile appeals to human history and to design in the visible world. There is a descriptive passage in the

Apologia Pro Vita Sua (1864), for instance, which rivals any unblinking naturalistic account of man in his evolutionary, social, and historical dimensions.

The world seems simply to give the lie to that great truth [about God's existence], of which my whole being is so full; and the effect upon me is, in consequence, as a matter of necessity, as confusing as if it denied that I am in existence myself. If I looked into a mirror, and did not see my face, I should have the sort of feeling which actually comes upon me, when I look into this living busy world, and see no reflexion of its Creator. . . . [To consider] the tokens so faint and broken of a superintending design, the blind evolution of what turns out to be great powers or truths, the progress of things, as if from unreasoning elements, not towards final causes, the greatness and littleness of man, his far-reaching aims, his short duration, the curtain hung over his futurity, the disappointments of life, the defeat of good, the success of evil, physical pain, mental anguish, the prevalence and intensity of sin, the pervading idolatries, the corruptions, the dreary hopeless irreligion, that condition of the whole race, so fearfully yet exactly described in the Apostle's words, "having no hope and without God in the world,"—all this is a vision to dizzy and appal; and inflicts upon the mind the sense of a profound mystery, which is absolutely beyond human solution. What shall be said to this heart-piercing, reason-bewildering fact? I can only answer, that either there is no Creator, or this living society of men is in a true sense discarded from His presence.[37]

A look at human history in its natural, evolutionary perspective brings one up abruptly before the alternative of godlessness or original sin, with the need for some further illumination from sacred history.

In this text, there are distinct overtones of Pascal, whom Newman sometimes quotes. However, there are also some capital differences, showing that the English cardinal does not share his predecessor's pessimistic view of our natural knowledge of God. In Newman's description, that which causes dismay is precisely the frustration of the theist's expectation that the divine power will be manifested unambiguously in nature and human society. His bewilderment supposes that he has already found good grounds in informal inference for accepting the existence of a good and infinitely powerful God. Whereas Pascal uses his account of the human situation to cast moral opprobrium on any natural approach to God, Newman suggests that our very certainty of God's existence can predispose us to admit the further truth of some original moral disaster and the need for a redeemer. Ultimately, this divergence is traceable to the fact that Newman does not share in Pascal's Jansenist heritage concerning nature and grace. He has neither a theological reason for depreciating natural knowledge of God nor a philosophical reason, such as the Hegelian system which Kierkegaard was combating. Instead of specifying his position along Jansenist or anti-Hegelian lines, Newman appeals to the example of St. Paul preaching to the Athenians on the Areopagus.[38] One should always respect the natural truths about God already present in the human mind. Christian revelation is not something totally alien to human nature, and its purpose is not to abrogate our natural knowledge of God but to purify it and bring it to a new fulfillment.

Once this basic issue is settled, Newman is prepared to agree with Pascal and Kierkegaard on three major points: that a speculative assent to God is morally and religiously barren without the agreement of the heart, that God is truly a hidden God, and that the actual drift of natural reason is often toward unbelief and atheism. Yet on each of these scores, he makes an independent interpretation. He does not seek to promote the way of the heart to God at the expense of other routes. The religious barrenness of a purely speculative assent to God does not mean that the inference upon which it is based is logically invalid or morally vitiated, but only that it has not yet borne its full fruit in a practical, as well as a speculative, assent. Newman suggests that the argument from conscience fosters a practical assent, but this does not hinder it from being integrated with a speculative factor and does not exclude other ways to God.

Furthermore, God's hiddenness is not a total withdrawal of His being from all natural inferences, since it is our very assurance about His infinite perfection which also leads us to respect the transcendence of His being to any results of human reasoning. Our reasoning to God is all the more reliable when it includes a recognition that we cannot gain any natural vision or exhaustive knowledge of Him. In this sense, Newman is in agreement with St. Augustine that if the human mind comprehends God to the point of removing His hidden nature, then that which it comprehends is not God Himself.

There is a special aspect of this theme of the hidden God which Newman employs in studying the cultural drift toward atheism and the inadequacy of the argument from design. Since God is not a massive physical fact, He never completely manifests Himself through any created thing or natural event, so that on earth the shadow and the mystery will always remain.[39] The material world both reveals and conceals God: It provides some evidence of its creator, but it also encourages us to remain at its own level and forego the search after God. Similarly, human society and history furnish hints about the divine presence, but they combine this testimony with a story of pointless activity and evil. Since God's existence and goodness are not emblazoned upon nature and history, the search for Him requires genuine personal effort, and the circumstances permit a genuine turning away of the human mind from the evidence leading to Him.

Hence Newman is careful to refrain from attributing the tendency toward atheism in his century to any intrinsic corruption of our knowing powers or any essential defect in the evidence. Rather, it is due to the fact that the evidence does permit the human mind, in its *interpretative* activity, to concentrate upon only one aspect of the constant pressure exerted by the material mode of being and by the historical order. Among the ways in which we can view nature and man, there is one powerful and wearing conception which isolates certain features of material and social existence in order to block the way to God. It is this particular interpretation, and not the philosophical investigation of God as such, which arouses Newman's opposition. But he also sees that the possibility of the atheistic outlook is bound up with the hidden nature of God and hence that as a historical tendency in our age, atheism cannot be conquered by any easy appeal to design in nature.

From his earliest journals down to his most mature statements on God, Newman never failed to express serious reservations about the proof from design, which was the favorite argument of the Enlightenment and the Noetic school. He did not rely upon it for his own theistic conviction, and he would not admit its cogency or even its properly theistic significance except under sharply restrictive conditions. For this reason, he was almost alone among the great Victorian churchmen in being quite unterrified by, and unhostile toward, the evolutionary theory of Darwin.[40] In a long correspondence with the biologist St. George Mivart, he kept abreast of the latest scientific advances and their theoretical interpretation. He made some quiet comments on the hypothetical character of natural selection and wondered whether there might be any biological analogue for the principles established in his own theory of the development of Christian doctrine. Newman's constant attitude was that Darwinism added further difficulties to conceiving nature as a mechanistic design but that it left untouched the nonmechanistic approaches to God from nature and man.

There was also a theological motive present in Newman's mind, not precisely for eliminating the proof from design, but certainly for refusing to take it as the fundamental inference to God. The data upon which it rested were cosmic in scope. They were not especially bound up with man's moral career, and hence they remained unaffected by original sin and the work of redemption. To found our knowledge of God primarily upon this basis would be to reach a God who has no direct relevance to our personal nature and religious needs. The evidences of design might lead to a cosmic power having great (but not necessarily infinite) power, skill, and beneficence, but they remained silent about the God of justice, mercy, and holiness, about particular providence and the need of redemption.

Newman's chief theological criticism, then, was that a design-centered theism generates a deistic outlook and even a species of finitism. The only way to break the hold of Enlightenment deism and empiricist finitism upon the European mind was to dislodge the proof from design as the primary approach to God and to show that *the God who made the heavens* is also *the God of our hearts*. Newman's own proof from conscience was explicitly intended by him to displace the design argument from the mid-point of the theistic outlook and to secure the link between God as creator of the cosmos and as lord of the human heart. In this way, he sought to overcome Pascal's antithesis between the God of philosophers and scholars and the God of Abraham, Isaac, and Jacob.

To pave the way for his own approach, he drew a sharp distinction between *physical* theology and *natural* theology.[41] The former is a doctrine on God grounded in the design argument and attributing to Him only such perfections as are exhibited in the physical world. This is the familiar standpoint of English deism, of William Derham's *Physico-Theology* (1713), and of the standard treatises of Clarke, Paley, and the Noetic school. Even conceding the soundness of the appeal to design, Newman noted that a physical theology can make only an indirect and quite enigmatic approach to God as a personal, just, and moral being. For a more inclusive doctrine, we must have recourse to a natural theology. It is "natural" in the twofold sense of using our native knowing powers and of drawing upon all our natural sources of evidence rather than concentrating upon the physical world. Those which Newman called the three *natural informants* about God are: the material world, the individual human soul and its acts of conscience, and human history. All three sources must be used in an adequately grounded philosophy of God. The method of natural theology is inductive inference, but this includes within itself the special techniques of metaphysical demonstration, probable reasoning, and historical testimony in order to adapt itself to the various kinds of natural evidence about God.

Newman himself never attempts to develop a natural theology in this plenary sense. But the conception of such a science provides him with a common framework within which he can locate both his own analysis of conscience and the metaphysical arguments. It also enables him to specify that the only type of design argument which may profit some minds is one which operates within this wider context, retains a vital relation with the data of man's spiritual life, and hence occupies a subordinate position within the whole field of natural theology.

Furthermore, Newman does not regard the argument from design as the only kind of inductive inference that can be made, even from the physical world to God. He contrasts design with the order of nature.[42] Although this is potentially a most crucial distinction, he does not develop it with sufficient thoroughness. Newman simply observes in passing that the proof from design is closely bound up in intellectual history with the Newtonian scientific conception of nature as a mathematically regulated machine and hence cannot be confused with the broader idea of the order of nature or uniform sequence of events. No matter what the prevailing scientific framework, order leads philosophically to law, purpose, and causal mind. He does not work out the detailed implications of this contrast, yet it seems to underlie his position that evolutionary findings bear upon the question of design but not upon the general order and finality of events. Instead of illuminating the meaning of order through a direct metaphysical analysis, however, Newman remains content with his general correlation between design and mechanistic science and between order and a philosophical study of nature.

Newman's chief concern is to show that despite their historical connection, the design-proof of God does not flow with strict logical necessity from the Newtonian view of the world.[43] He agrees with Francis Bacon (as explained in Macaulay's essay) that a radical separation can be made between efficient and final causes so that the scientific investigator can concentrate exclusively upon the proximate, physical components and efficient causes. If to the Baconian emphasis upon the efficient and material causes is added the empiricist notion of physical causation as a sequence of finite phenomena, then a consistent and methodically self-contained account can be given of the material world without adverting to a cosmic designer. The outlook of classical modern physics is neutrally *a*-theistic, not in the sense of denying God or establishing anything inconsistent with His being, but simply in the sense of carrying out its proper tasks without requiring mention of Him. Within the scientific context alone, one cannot force a decision about whether the motions of the solar system are reducible entirely to Laplace's formula or require the agency of a divine mind. One can read nature either backwards, in terms of physical antecedents and components, or forwards, in terms of design. But there is no "smart syllogism" which can coerce the mind to accept the argument from design merely from the explanations of Newtonian science. This proof is not a necessary consequence of any scientific position, and hence it need not be made central even in an age which prizes scientific findings and inferences so highly. The design proof is both nondemonstrative and nonprimary from the standpoint of natural theology and science alike. Newman would agree with the American philosopher Chauncey Wright (against the "scientific" theism and atheism of the Enlightenment) on the essential neutrality of scientific method in respect to any theistic inference.

That nature can be regarded either as a machine to be approached with scientific curiosity or as a work of intelligence to be studied with religious awe is only the counterpart of the fact that God both hides and reveals Himself in nature. He does not blatantly advertize His presence in nature and history, and yet He does provide us with a trail, which is sometimes faint and circuitous, leading to the truth about His existence and providential governance.

This is the law of Providence here below; it works beneath a veil, and what is visible in its course does but shadow out at most, and sometimes obscures and disguises what is invisible. . . . The visible world is the instrument, yet the veil, of the world invisible,—the veil, yet still partially the symbol and index: so that all that exists or happens visibly, conceals and yet suggests, and above all sub- serves, a system of persons, facts, and events beyond itself.[44]

Along with Clement of Alexandria and Bishop Butler, Newman affirms that ours is a sacramental universe in both its physical and its socio- historical aspects. To regard it only as a concealing veil is the extreme view of agnosticism and atheism, whereas to regard it solely as symbol and index is the weakness of theosophy and deism. Newman recognizes the difficulty and the tension in preserving the complex relation between veil and symbol, between nature as concealing and nature as suggesting the reality of the eternal, providential God. One cannot integrate these two aspects without some previous disposition of the mind and heart and hence without giving more importance to the human factors in our acceptance of God than is possible within a physical theology.

Newman does not permit atheism to profit by his critique of physical theology, since his argument holds equally for any attempt at denial of God's existence on the basis of the scientific mode of prescinding from ultimate causality. Underlying both atheism and design-based theism is a certain interpretation or view of nature.[45] Atheism and design-based theism are not primary determinants of our conception of the world but are derivative positions resulting from some special philosophical prin- ciples. Neither one follows necessarily from the scientific, empirical con- ception of nature. Both can be grafted onto this scientific outlook, but the grafting process is a separate operation requiring the intervention of philosophical considerations and is not an unavoidable logical entail- ment of the scientific account itself. Newman is suggesting that scientific naturalism is valid within its sphere but that it does not supply the premises which lead men inevitably to either atheistic, philosophical naturalism or to physical theology. No one can avoid the responsibility of looking within himself for the God of our hearts simply by saying that science rules out God or that science tells him all that need be known about God. If there is no impersonal, syllogistic bridge from the prevailing scientific world-view to either atheism or a design-cen- tered theism, then the individual must still reflect upon the metaphysi- cal demonstrations and upon the witness of his own conscience.

(3) *The inference to God from conscience.* Newman provides scant guidance in one's inspection of the metaphysical arguments. In his ser- mons, he does occasionally refer to the proofs from motion in the world, from the internal order of beings, and from the need for a first cause.[46] He admits their cogency, but he does not devote himself to an analysis of difficulties in this area. One reason for his reticence is his acceptance of Locke's view that our internal acts of will provide the only experi- ential source of our knowledge of causation. We have no experience of

causation in material nature, but we infer its presence from our observation of uniform sequence and relation of events. But precisely what grounds we have in ordinary data for an analogy between volitional acts and external sequence remains unanswered in Newman. He does not explore the meaning of secondary causality on the part of nonhuman agents but simply states that material sequence must ultimately be due to some will and yet is patently independent of the human will. Hence the spiritual agency of God is required as the ultimate causal principle of the natural world. These points are rapidly sketched rather than scrutinized with Newman's ordinary care, since he does not move beyond Locke and Butler to a more metaphysical treatment of causality and the kind of existential demonstration adapted to real causal inference from sensible existents, rather than to logico-syllogistic inference.

Newman justified the restricted scope of his own theistic investigations with the remark that in this sphere, egoism is the true modesty. He found the argument from conscience to be not only the most intimate and compelling for himself but also the one most commonly employed by men in their informal inference to God and assent to His real being. Newman's constructive approach in natural theology was guided entirely by the plan of examining the popular, personal, and practical sort of evidence upon which ordinary men rely in forming their conviction about God's existence. It was in the region of conscience that he looked for the strongest informal argument which gives a reasonable basis to their assent to God. He did not propose it as the only valid one but simply concentrated his own study upon the real, certain assent to God in which it terminates. His main intent was to show that the informal inference from moral facts is an irreducible and reasonable way to God.

In his private notes, Newman lists four main reasons for his choice of the proof from conscience.[47] First, it is a proof common to all conditions of mankind, to pagans as well as Christians, to the unlearned as well as the learned. It is present to us from our childhood, taking its root in the abiding experience of being under law. Informal reasoning based upon conscience is nontechnical and truly portable; it does not require special training to grasp and is not bound down to books or laboratories. Second, the proof from conscience is not a purely theoretical process and does not stop at a purely abstract truth. Instead, it makes us aware of God at the center of our freedom. It is personal, not only in its point of departure, but also in apprehending God precisely as a personal judge and providential guide. Hence this inference ordinarily yields both a speculative truth and a practical commitment of the finite person to God as a person. It is the source of a moral and religious relationship with God and thus overcomes the deficiencies of the proof from design. In the third place, Newman approves the argument from conscience as forming a basis for belief in the senses, since they can then be regarded as God-given instruments. Although in his later writings he personally accepts sense perception on its own grounds, he always sees in conscience a way of reaching God which is available even to those who are unsure about the external world.

Newman's fourth reason deserves separate treatment. He states rather cryptically that the argument from conscience explains and refutes what the Scholastic manuals refer to as the "philosophical sin." He finds a concrete meaning for this term in the tendency of some philosophical minds to transform conscience from being the voice of a directing and rewarding God into being a mere taste. This is part of the resolute warfare against regarding conscience as the internal witness to God's existence and to His natural, moral law. Newman's own view is that conscience is a unique constituent in our intellectual nature, one which cannot ultimately "be resolved into any combination of principles in our nature, more elementary than itself."[48] But he recognizes several philosophical systems which do try to dissolve it into something else. Among these reductionist explanations are the utilitarian, esthetic, anthropological, sociological, and psychological accounts. They seek to equate conscience with, respectively, an estimate of utility or long-sighted selfishness, a sense of the fitting, a twist in the mind of primitive man, a product of social conditioning and teaching, and the offspring of determined, associative bonds.

Against these various forms of moral reductionism, Newman relies upon what he terms a direct inspection of the meteorological phenomena of the human mind, or what would today be roughly called a phenomenological description of human attitudes. His famous portrait of the gentleman is a concrete way of establishing the decisive contrast between conscience as a moral command and its esthetic counterpart. Drawing upon the writings of Shaftesbury and Hume, Burke and Goethe, he shows how the moral-sense approach substitutes good taste for a practical dictate and self-approval for the reference to a superior norm. In reply to Matthew Arnold's prediction that literature and culture will replace religion, Newman analyzes conscience as a personal act, quite distinct from a culturally generated response, and as terminating in a specifically moral relationship which cannot be reduced to any esthetic equivalent. He takes special care to understand and criticize the phenomenalist and associationist view of John Stuart Mill, whose logical system replaced that of the Noetic school at Oxford shortly after Newman's departure. Conscience is found too early in the individual to be simply accounted for by association, and it is found too uniformly and interculturally among pagan Greeks and Christians alike to be the result of accidental and socially determined bonds. Both Hume and Mill make large drafts upon the principle of association, which nonetheless remains an unknown cause within their phenomenalism. Their theory does not square with our experience of reflective deliberation, of bringing to bear imperative principles upon new particular circumstances, and of free choice—traits which characterize the actual operation of conscience in men.

The concrete acts or moral imperatives of the individual's own conscience supply the relevant data which he imperceptibly generalizes into the principle that conscience imparts commands binding upon our will. Like our other first principles, this one is not generated in an a priori and impersonal way but arises inductively out of our personal experience. In the presence of repeated judgments of moral commanding, the mind gradually forms the conception of conscience. This is a complex conception, since conscience can be regarded either as an awareness of a rule of morality, in respect to particular conditions, or as an awareness of duty or moral obligation bearing upon particular actions. It is the latter aspect of conscience which is especially relevant for the theistic inference. Taken as an apprehension of duty in respect to our practical decisions in concrete matters, it has the two primary functions of commanding-and-forbidding and praising-and-blaming. Conscience manifests itself, therefore, in dictates and sanctions, together with the accompanying feelings of satisfaction and shame. Under the aspect of its dictates, or judgments of commanding and forbidding, it has an imperious character which casts a special light upon the natural, moral law. It enables us to view this law not only as *being* an intimate inclination of our own nature but also as *coming from* a superior, personal source of our own being and moral tendencies.[49] The conscientious man becomes aware of himself as existing, choosing, and acting in the effective presence of, and demanding reference to, the personal and transcendent God. He is known to exist precisely as the personal source and ultimate basis of moral law and obligation.

Newman does not pretend that this argument can coerce everyone or that its force can be appreciated without personal effort and experience of the moral situation he is describing. He does suggest, however, that it illuminates the rational grounds upon which the ordinary man relies in giving his assent to God's existence. The informal theistic inference from conscience is just as reasonably founded as our ordinary inference to the existence of the external world. In both cases, there is an experiential foundation which cannot be further resolved: the presence of sensations in the mind and the presence of moral commands. From our grasp of sensations, as being aroused in us by another source, we make a spontaneous, wholly unreflective inference to the existing, material world. And we use the same inductive principle of a real causal source to proceed from the experience of moral commands, as coming from a superior moral person, to the existence of God. The commands of my conscience are seen to convey the intention-to-oblige on the part of an intelligent, moral agent distinct from, and superior to, myself. Given the irreducible nature of the moral command itself and the internal experience of causation as effective will, the individual moves surely to assent to the existence of God, His transcendence, and His moral goodness.

There are epistemological and metaphysical issues involved · here which Newman himself does not investigate. He does not examine the difficulties entailed by comparing the inference to God to an inference to the real, material world. He presumes that most people hold a type of mediate realism and that the problems connected with this theory are not sufficiently serious to doubt the reliability of other existential inferences using a similar procedure. His previous failure to establish the meaning of causality in the nonhuman, material order finds a counterpart here in a reluctance to consider formally whether the internal experience of volition applies beyond the realm of finite, spiritual agents. But in his descriptions of the imperative quality of the dictates of conscience, he does indicate that in the moral command, we discover the intention of an authoritative person transcending all finite agents. The stress upon causality as effective action of the will opens the way for interpreting moral command as the real authoritative presence of God, the infinite and personal agent.

There were two special advantages which Newman hoped to reap from the argument from conscience. First of all, he was aware that both the atheistic tendency and Mill's finitism were coalescing the problem of God's existence and that of His moral goodness. They were laying down the condition that one does not prove God to exist unless one shows directly the existence of a good God. Instead of examining this premise on metaphysical grounds, Newman recommended the way of conscience as a means of meeting the requirement. To the atheistic naturalist, he observed that one must take man rather than the physical world as the proper point of departure if one expects to reach a morally qualified God at once. The way of conscience is located within a moral context and leads to God precisely as the good and just provider and judge. Similarly, to the finitist, Newman's reply was that the situation of conscience manifests God as the holy and perfect person who rightfully transcends and commands all finite agents. The presence of pain, evil, and pointless events is a trial for one's conviction in the infinite power and goodness of God, but it is not a directive for abandoning the infinitude of either His power or His goodness.

Newman discerned a second valuable result from including the testimony of conscience among the primary grounds of adhering to God. The data in this instance are not only in the personal order but are specifically moral, so that they address us in a practical way. The normal outcome of the theistic inference from conscience is a practical assent to God, not in the sense of being deprived of any speculative significance, but of adding to it a firm adhesion of our will and loyalty to an existential truth. This practical commitment to God as infinitely good and holy enables us to experience the savagery of evil and to explore the immanent system of events, without concluding either that the divine power is lamed and limited or that there is no transcendent, good God who creates man and his natural world. Indeed, a practically oriented, theistic assent supplies a positive impetus toward opposing the evil and mastering the natural and historical forces for humane ends.

(4) *Scientific probabilism and certitudinal assent to God.* The argument from conscience was not only Newman's answer to the Noetic school, which had tried to confine everyone's reasonable approach to God to formal demonstrations and the appeal to design, but was also his way of meeting an important objection proposed from the standpoint of the logic of science. This objection was framed by a friend, William Froude, during the course of a lifelong correspondence. Froude's elder brother had been Newman's closest associate in the Oxford Movement, and William himself had a distinguished scientific career in hydrodynamics and naval engineering. Through him, Newman kept in touch with the actual methods in nineteenth-century physics and was informed about the same trends in the logic of science which interested Charles Peirce in America. Froude was struck by the similarity between the view of Sir Charles Lyell and other scientists that the methods of modern science lead only to probable conclusions and declarations in Newman's *Apologia* that probability is the guide of life and that his belief in God is based on grounds of probability. Putting these two sources together, Froude concluded that every inference to God must remain probable and subject to doubt and hence can never yield absolute certainty about His existence.

For many years this difficulty deeply troubled Newman, both because it seemed to be an inescapable implication of his own position and because it was recommended by the current view of scientific thinking. Froude maintained that in no subject is the human mind "capable of arriving at an absolutely certain conclusion. That though of course some conclusions are far more certain than others, there is an element of uncertainty in all. That though any probability however faint, may in its place make it a duty to *act as if* the conclusion to which it points were absolutely certain, yet that even the highest attainable probability does not justify the mind in discarding the residuum of doubt."[50] Like Charles Peirce, Froude stressed the attitude of fallibilism, or acceptance of the essential fallibility of all scientific reasoning and the duty to remain prepared for revision and rejection of present probabilities. The exigencies of action should not be permitted to deceive us about the

speculative uncertainty of even our most promising and practically fruitful views.

Newman's response to this argument is hammered out both in private
correspondence and in *A Grammar of Assent* (1870). This is one of the
purposes for his distinction between the act of inferring and concluding
and the act of assenting. Since inference and assent are specifically different mental acts, the assent to God can be reasonable and certain apart
from a formal demonstrative inference. Furthermore, Newman's statement about the probable grounds for our natural belief in God is to be
strictly construed, so that the probability refers to some of the separate
theistic arguments and the act of concluding from them rather than to
the ultimate assent. The act of concluding is conditional in the sense
of looking toward and depending upon the premises of the argument
but not in the sense of being essentially revisable. Yet the theistic assent
is unconditional because it accepts the truth of God's existence as being
in itself a fully warranted proposition. Moreover, Newman does not
use "probable" as synonymous with "uncertain," "doubtful," or "relatively weak in evidence." In designating an argument as probable, he
seeks to set it off from the only kind of demonstration admitted by
rationalism and the Noetic school. A line of reasoning is probable to
the extent that: (a) it is not a mathematical demonstration; (b) it receives
its data and premises from experience rather than from pure reason
and a priori postulation; and (c) it is concerned with a concrete, existing
being rather than an abstract concept.[51] The moral argument for God's
existence is probable in this threefold Newmanian sense. It is not a
formal, mathematical proof; it draws its strength from our experience
of the acts of conscience; it concludes to the real existence of a personal
God and not to some abstract truth. But none of these circumstances
prevent the subsequent assent to God's existence from being a certain
and unconditional one, although it is not the same sort of certain assent
as that given to a mathematical truth.

The assent which we give to God's existence, consequent upon the
informal inference from conscience, enjoys a moral certitude. Newman's
usage must be distinguished carefully from that of Descartes and many
modern Scholastic authors, who regard moral certitude as being quite
weak and as standing in contrast with metaphysical and physical certitude. For Newman, on the contrary, moral certitude is primarily opposed to the mathematico-logical sort resulting from abstract, nonexistential reasoning. It is not a quasi-certitude or one of a lesser breed
but is the certitude genuinely proportioned to the concrete and informal
reasoning which leads inductively to God's existence and to other truths
of fact. The morally certain proposition is not a pragmatic convenience
but contains a speculative truth. It does indeed bear a practical reference to our subsequent conduct, but this does not reduce it to an as-if

requirement of action. The proposition about God's existence is a moral certitude not because of any lack of speculative truth in it but because of its foundation in concrete, moral evidence and its pertinence to our active life.

Moral certitude is characterized not only negatively by its contrast with mathematical certitude and positively by its practical reference but also by the contribution made to it by what Newman calls the illative sense. This does not refer to a separate power of the mind but to a distinctive function of our ordinary intellectual power. The illative sense signifies the capacity of our intellect to undertake an informal inference in order to discern a unified pattern of evidence in a group of independent but converging arguments. It does not add up the probabilities, in the scientific sense of probability, but searches by informal inference after a speculatively certain truth, which may or may not be contained in such a group of arguments. If it does discover a speculative certainty in the unified import of several sources of evidence, some of which may not be fully convincing in their separate condition, it leads to an intellectual and certain assent to this complex truth. The function of the will in the operation of the illative sense is not to convert a likelihood into a certainty but simply to insure a unified consideration of the totality of evidence, whether the outcome be opinion or certitude. The certain assent given to God's existence on the basis of all the complex data of our moral life is a moral one, not because it is of a weak degree, but because it rests upon an illative assessment of the meaningful unity of the data of conscience and leads to an adhesion of will, as well as intellect, to the truth of the proposition.

Is the certitudinal assent to God a simple or a reflex one, a notional or a real one? Newman seeks to combine the values of all four types of assent in the mature and complete acceptance of God.[52] The heart's acknowledgment should have the immediacy and force of simple assent, as the fruit of our informal inference to God, together with the assurance about the grounds of evidence which comes with a reflex assent. Spontaneous conviction and reflective analysis are not incompatible but are complementary aspects of one's plenary assent to, or complex certitude about, God. The certitude of the philosopher about why he accepts the existence of God is continuous with the knowledge gained by the ordinary man. Newman's synthesis of simple and reflex assent prevents any permanent opposition between the philosophical, the religious, and the everyday approaches to God.

Similarly, Newman maintains that we can have both notional and real assent to God's existence. They are not related as an imperfect and a perfect act of the mind but as assent to a notional object and assent to a real thing, without there being any necessary difference in the certitude itself. There can be a notional assent to God's existence, in the sense of accepting the truth of the theistic proposition as such. The inference from conscience issues initially in such a notional or perfect speculative assent to the truth that God exists. But one can also give a real assent to this truth, to the extent that one is aware that the basis of the proof consists in one's own moral being and that its significance concerns the moral and personal being of God Himself. Real assent adds the reference of the validated proposition to particular, personal data and to the indirect consequences in action. Our notional assent to God from conscience is quite natı rally conjoined with a real assent when we succeed in habitually integrating the truth about God with the particular acts of our conscience and our practical affections, thus realizing that this truth concerns a personal, practical relation between the human person and the divine personal reality. Real assent does not wipe out the speculative truth about God and its informal inferential foundation, but it adds the perfection of a practical attachment of our heart to His own personal being.

There is a special historical significance in Newman's insistence that our plenary assent to God should include the peculiar contributions of all four sorts of assent. In an age when theism is under attack from atheism and agnosticism, simple assent needs the support it can gather from a reflex assent to the foundations for knowing God. Yet even our reflective hold on God is not enough when it remains in the speculative mode of a notional assent. The speculative truth about the God-proposition needs to be integrated with a real assent of our mind to God, apprehended as a personal reality. Newman's phrase about the luminous self-evidence of oneself and God thus refers to the intimate bond which the argument from conscience knits between one's experience of the moral self and the intellectual act of notional-real assent to the infinitely good, personal being of God.

In the synthesis between the informal inference from conscience and the four kinds of assent, Newman finds his fundamental, natural answer to the problem of modern atheism and philosophical naturalism which he so vividly appreciates and which underlies all his investigations.

"There is a God," when really apprehended, is the object of a strong energetic adhesion, which works a revolution in the mind. . . . To a mind thus carefully formed upon the basis of its natural conscience, the world, both of nature and of man, does but give back a reflection of those truths about the One Living God, which have been familiar to it from childhood. . . . It interprets what it sees around it by this previous inward teaching, as the true key of that maze of vast complicated disorder; and thus it gains a more and more consistent and luminous vision of God from the most unpromising materials. Thus conscience is a connecting principle between the creature and his Creator.[53]

If our plenary assent of heart to God contains both the speculative sinews of a reflex assent and the practical endurance of a real assent, we will have light enough and patience enough to grapple with the actual difficulties encountered in our experience of the natural and historical worlds. Attention to the significance of conscience does not dissipate the problem of evil, but it does enable the individual to develop an adequate personal basis of interpretation for grappling with this problem. Our integral assent to God includes the true affirmation that goodness, justice, and mercy are really present in the infinite being even though it does not enable us to grasp in an essential vision the infinite way in which God is good, just, and merciful. The revolution toward which Newman is working is to maintain a real and certitudinal assent to the personally good God, without ceasing to remain sensitive to the difficulties of our human condition, and to work actively toward rendering our natural situation more humane and more responsive to God. That the goal of our reflection on God should be to accept the conditions of personal dialogue and friendship between God and men is the import of Newman's motto: "Heart speaks to heart."

4. THE EXISTENTIALIST QUARREL OVER GOD

The contemporary stand of the existentialists on God can only be understood against the background of the clash between the personal theism of Pascal and Kierkegaard and the antitheism of Marx and Nietzsche. Although the existentialists regard the question of God as central for philosophy and culture, as well as for human transcendence, they offer no uniform answer to it. They represent a continuation of the contrast between Kierkegaard and Nietzsche, and, indeed, they prefer to formulate the issue in this dialectical way.[54] The range of existentialist positions reaches from the declared atheism of Sartre and Camus to Jaspers' acceptance of a transcendent God and from Heidegger's refusal to speak about God in philosophy to Marcel's view that philosophy is a reflective quest of the relation of communion between God and finite persons.

Profiting by the Nietzschean view of the world as a chaos of becoming in which there are no inherently inscribed meanings, Jean-Paul Sartre reduces the problem of God to that of the idea of God. Like every other idea, it is the product of man's creative consciousness, and yet there is something about this particular idea which is not entirely optional. It is an inevitable one for the human mind to bring forth, since it expresses a necessary tendency of our nature, albeit in a deceptive way. We strive incessantly to combine, in a single reality, the fullness and solidity of material being with the openness and agility of consciousness. The idea of God signifies the point of confluence where these two modes would meet. But it is a juncture which we can only dream about and strive after, without ever realizing, since inert, opaque being and active, translucent consciousness are at constant war with each other. Hence the idea of God is intrinsically contradictory, even though we cannot help framing it and seeking to become what it signifies.

The real tragedy of Sartrean man is a theistic one. His alliance with both being and the nihilating power of consciousness drives him toward transcendence, so that the most radical passion of his life is to be a God who does not and cannot exist. This is the very essence of the human structure: "Man fundamentally *is* the desire to be God."[55] The touchstone of sincerity is our readiness to face up to this truth and to abide by its moral consequence, which is that man must create his own values without any sanction from an already existing divine standard.

Despite his emphasis upon freedom and the responsible production of one's moral values, Sartre has not been able to elaborate an ethical philosophy because of the difficulty of reconciling his metaphysical statements about the individual's primordial determination with the free choice of goals and the demands of the common good. No such metaphysical handicaps prevent the passionate mind of Albert Camus from developing the moral side of atheistic humanism. Instead of offering metaphysical reasons for the impossibility of God, he begins with the cultural fact of widespread rebellion against the idea of God. He agrees with Nietzsche that this repudiation is not a complete nihilism but the beginning of an absolute affirmation of the earth and all things finite. Yet Camus himself remains suspicious of the will to pure immanence and the absolutizing of the finite world, since this may result in a total submission to the inevitable, including "the unreserved affirmation of human imperfection and suffering, of evil and murder."[56] As an atheistic moralist, Camus advises us to refuse to try to become gods or to expect history to produce an absolute, although we must hope and strive for happiness and the heart's desire. We should moderate our aims in accord with the intrinsic limits of human nature and yet remain universally concerned for other men in view of our common humanity.

Camus' stand is a notable and unique one, in that it does not rest upon a counterabsolutizing of finite being against God. Its weakness arises from a failure to analyze the idea of God with any precision and to move beyond Nietzsche's psychological criticism of the Hegelian absolute into an independent study of the grounds for the being of God Himself. Camus gives us a sociological portrait of the full-bodied rebel as one who casts his lot with the masses of people whose sufferings have made them feel at first Godforsaken and then godless. The atheistic rebel sympathizes with the masses in regarding the Christian teaching on providence and eternal life as an intolerable postponement of happiness in which our grinding form of present existence prevents us from hoping. Thus Camus substitutes for the metaphysical determinism of

Sartre's individual project a cultural determinism of the mass mind against accepting the reality of God. He endows his conception of the mass mind with an ideal necessity, so that anyone who would ally himself with suffering humanity must take the nonexistence of God as a first principle.

This imperative of Camus is exposed to two critical observations, one based upon the consequences of acknowledging God and the other based upon the influence of the cultural situation. A careful distinction is needed between opinions which are sometimes associated with belief in God and the consequences logically entailed by such belief. Acceptance of God does not necessarily lead one to judge that suffering is well merited by an individual, that suffering and evil are just as normal conditions for men as is the change of weather, or that evil actions are easily explained and even exculpated by reference to our common guilt. Such attitudes owe their presence to a combination of insensitivity, hypocrisy, and theological haziness rather than to the assent to God and the Christian gospel. Moreover, the argument from sympathy with the plight of the ordinary man depends upon regarding the condition of widespread godlessness as a fatality to be accepted. But this social condition can be traced to certain quite specific conditions and causes, none of which are inevitable for the individual or the group. Our human freedom can be developed to the point of criticizing and overcoming the intellectual and social circumstances which do foster an atheistic outlook. This requires a willingness to examine our intellectual and religious history carefully and apart from the prejudices of a cultural determinism.

Martin Heidegger offers a new interpretation of the ascendancy of the world of technology and mass movements, in which God finds no part. He regards this age of the eclipse and absence of God as only the latest stage in a centuries-long process in Western thought, in which the nature of being as such has been overlaid and forgotten. Philosophers have concentrated upon particular beings and the whole order of things-that-are, while ordinary people have busied themselves with the tools and projects in this practical world of things. In taking this orientation, men have also been led to conceive of God after the pattern of particular beings and to explain Him simply as the supreme instance of the things-that-are. Such a view is degrading to God and dangerous to finite things. Hence Heidegger regards the atheism of Nietzsche and Marx as a salutary attempt to purge us of idols in the speculative and practical orders. On their nihilistic side, they have brought an end to the previous Western tradition in metaphysics and the organization of life. It is no longer possible to identify God with our finite categories of cause, perfection, and value or to mistake Him for the apex of the realm of things-that-are.

Heidegger's own interest is not to study God, however, but to distinguish being as such from any of its particular expressions and even from the totality of things-that-are, with which the metaphysicians have always confused it.[57] Being is powerfully present in its particular modes, which are its means for both revealing and concealing itself. The philosopher's work is to recognize this ambiguity and to listen for the word of being itself amid the particular voices and interests of things-that-are. But being can manifest itself only by reference to the existential reality of man and his freedom. From the horizon of human existential reality, then, being is itself finite. This consideration leads Heidegger to separate an infinite God not only from the realm of things-that-are but also from the entire meaning of being as such and hence from all philosophical discourse. As far as the philosopher is concerned, God cannot come within the range of our reflective thought. He may perhaps be grasped by religious and poetic minds in symbol and myth, but He escapes all philosophical efforts to understand Him by reference to being itself and the things-that-are. Even the philosophical exegesis of religious and poetic testimony must confine itself to the significance of the divine and the holy for human freedom and being as finite, without inferring anything therefrom about the question of God Himself. Precisely because the man of prayer addresses himself to God as utterly transcending the human and the finite order, the philosopher must remain totally silent about God.

Although he approves of the purgation effected by nineteenth-century atheism in our idolatrous conceptions of God, Heidegger himself places his philosophy beyond the issue of atheism and theism. Starting with the Kantian view of the finitizing effect of the human cognitive structure upon the knowable aspects of being, he goes far beyond Kant in closing off even the relation of moral freedom to the transcendent being of God. There is no open horizon within which the philosopher can legitimately approach God, even though he cannot be satisfied with any atheistic denial of His existence. Working out from much the same background in Kant, however, Karl Jaspers does suggest a way in which there can still be a philosophical theism. He grants that the issue between atheism and theism cannot be settled on either side through demonstrative reasoning. The reason for this is that the infinite God lies beyond the boundaries of objectively knowable being and the objective methods of demonstration. But the alternative is not to exchange rigorous thinking for an arbitrary sentiment of divinity or an equally arbitrary sentiment of godless heroism. There is still available the way of reflective awareness of the data which human freedom discloses but which do not belong to the world of objects. Theistic existentialism maintains a pluralism of methods, not just of specialized techniques, in order to permit a study of the evidence proper to our interior human mode of being and acting.

373

God, or the encompassing reality, lies beyond the confines of objectively determinable being. He manifests Himself ambiguously in the world and cannot be grasped through an objective metaphysics. We can make an approach to Him only by becoming aware of the ultimate direction taken by human freedom and by reaching its theistic significance through an act of rational or philosophical faith.[58] We have to assume responsibility for interpreting the ciphers of His presence in the world, for understanding why metaphysics is always shipwrecked when it takes the objective route to God, and for following the dynamism of our freedom beyond the forms of worldly being and human existence. Philosophical faith in the one, transcendent being of God is founded upon the basic human attitude of transcending, or straining beyond the limits of the finite world and man to His encompassing reality. Unlike Newman and Marcel, however, Jaspers does not admit any supernatural act of faith in God along with this natural commitment to Him. Anything valid in the Christian conception of God is reducible to the philosophical faith, which finds the fullest meaning for human existence in its natural orientation toward the transcendent God.

Although he does not pretend to furnish a demonstrative refutation of atheism, Jaspers does evaluate it by its intellectual presuppositions and consequences. What he says about Nietzsche also applies to atheistic existentialism. Sartre's dialectical argument against theism assumes that we must try to ascribe objective being to God and that we must regard Him as a unity of consciousness and thinghood. Neither assumption is acceptable to Jaspers, who observes that the idea of God involves a contradiction only when we try to think of God as an objective thing. The contradiction in the Sartrean idea of God does not affect the divine reality itself, and hence it does not rule out a philosophical theism which approaches God in a nonobjectifying way. In both Nietzsche and Sartre, the atheistic outlook results in a breakdown of friendly communication among men. In Nietzsche's case, the atheistic postulate makes him the prisoner of his own myths about the superman and the eternal recurrence and thus introduces sharp divisions between kinds of men and kinds of moralities. Sartre finds a counterpart of our futile effort to realize God in our equally futile effort to establish social relations among men on any other basis than mutual hatred and aggression. On the contrary, Jaspers' own theism is under no pressure to read into God the composite factors in our own nature. It establishes our mutual relation of transcendence toward God, providing a basis in reason and freedom for humane communication among men and a practical attitude of respect.

The chief reason why Jaspers terms our acceptance of God a natural act of faith, rather than an instance of reasoned knowledge, is his Kantian correlation between knowledge proper and the world of finite objects. Gabriel Marcel also maintains the nonobjective nature of the divine reality and of our grasp thereof, but he does so apart from the Kantian and idealistic theories of knowledge. He is even more critical than Pascal and other philosophers of the heart about attempts to reach God from a study of the objective world or to justify His ways through a rationalistic use of sufficient reason. He goes so far as to state that theodicy is inverted atheism. There is a perfect correlation between justifying and denying God, since both approaches presume that there is a problem of God, in the same sense in which there is a problem about any other object or third party, who may or may not exist. The methods employed in theodicies and atheologies are adapted only for dealing impersonally and problematically with things in the world. They can determine nothing about God, who is a personal reality and not an object, a Thou and not an impersonal something.

In this sense, Marcel denies that there is any *problem* of God. There is the *mystery* of God, but His reality does not submit to being made a problematic object. The upsurge of modern atheism was prepared philosophically by the attempts to deal problematically with God, since this was equivalent to excluding any distinctive consideration of His personal presence to us in our personal region of being. Marcel follows all the philosophers of the heart in stressing that the human self is the surest point of departure for gaining knowledge of God. The drama of the self begins with an act of freedom, in which I either acknowledge my participation in being or pretend to complete autonomy. An act of free, natural faith or one of refusal specifies my primary relation with being. By means of recollection or nonobjectifying reflection (which Jaspers calls reflective awareness), I can discover in my original acceptance of being the implication of an absolute Thou or transcendent person as the source of my participated personal being.[59]

All so-called proofs of God's existence are convincing only to the extent that they acknowledge this original relation of personal, free commitment of myself to the unlimited Thou. Atheism rests either upon a confusion between inquiring about God as an objective problem and as a personal mystery or upon a refusal to remain open to our participated mode of being. But the refusal itself is often encouraged or prolonged by a failure to use the method of recollection in exploring the basic attachment of our heart and expression of our freedom. Marcel asks that our open attitude include the access of Christian faith and hope in God.

Existentialism serves as the common ground for a meeting and open clash between the theistic proponents of the heart and the atheistic thinkers. The former are uniformly critical of the argument from design, of any easy claims for syllogistic knowledge of God, and of theodicy. They are too keenly aware of the transcendence and hiddenness of God, as well as the difficulties provided by the natural and moral world, to exaggerate the extent of our knowledge about God. However, they do suggest that when the goodness and power of God are called in question, special attention must be paid to the personal relation between the human self and the personal God. The method of reflection and concrete description fits this investigation. Pascal and his successors regard this interior approach not as a flight from the objective world and its scientific methods but as a way of adapting the theistic inquiry to the human reality which furnishes some of the relevant evidence.

These representatives of a personal way to God agree upon some sort of natural knowledge of Him but not upon whether it can and should be expanded into a philosophy of God. They are unanimous, however, in appealing to the heart as the most effective way of acquiring truths about the personal reality of God. They do not conceive the heart as some special and privileged instrument, such as an intuition, an irrational feeling, or a conative projection of our wishes and needs. Instead, it signifies a distinctive manner in which to use our ordinary cognitive abilities. The heart's way to God means undertaking the theistic investigation as a personal responsibility, keeping oneself alert to the difficulties and deliverances of the individual mind, paying careful attention to the concrete data supplied by human freedom and moral conscience, and following through with the practical response implied in the findings about God as personally related to oneself.

At least in the case of Newman, this approach is not intended to exclude other human modes of inference to God or to depreciate the use of intelligence in other areas of study. In contrast to William James, Newman sets up no opposition between the moral argument and a more speculative method but envisages them both as belonging within an integral philosophy of God. He scrutinizes the problem of suffering and evil just as closely and frankly as do Hume and Mill, but he includes within the total assent to God an acknowledgment of His infinite and morally good nature. Finally, he suggests that the conventional opposition maintained by atheistic naturalism between the scientific outlook and the assent to God be subjected to critical revision so that the scientific study of nature and man will both retain its autonomy and also permit man to make informal inference and causal demonstration leading to some truths about God. In Newman's hands, the way of the heart secures its own access to God, without infringing upon the metaphysical avenue to God or the integrity of scientific and historical research.

Chapter XI

TOWARD A REALISTIC PHILOSOPHY
OF GOD

THE HISTORICAL investigation of the problem of God in modern philosophy results in some findings which are significant not only for the history of thought but also for our contemporary philosophizing about God. We are now in a position to specify some of its contributions in the latter sphere.

1. THE RELEVANCE OF THE HISTORICAL APPROACH

Perhaps its first service is to furnish the data required for a sound historical induction concerning the status of a theory of God in philosophy. Comte's hypothesis of the three stages of human thinking (theological, metaphysical, and positive) made it plausible to suppose that philosophy began with an overwhelmingly theological preoccupation and then gradually whittled down the doctrine on God until it finally disappeared from the vital center of thought. According to this account, the modern period is the story of the steady recession of critical intelligence from acceptance of, and concern with, God as an important issue in philosophy. But examination of the actual evidence reveals quite a different situation. It shows that the leading modern philosophers have been no less focally occupied with questions about God than were their predecessors. Granted that their theories have often differed sharply from earlier ones, they have nevertheless recognized, both formally and in practice, the basic importance of these questions. Indeed, on such issues as the significance of the starting point of inferences to God, the deductive use of God in a philosophical system, and the relation between one's notion of God and one's view of human values, the modern systems have been unsurpassed in their steady exploration of the possible explanations. A genuine advance has been made by modern thinkers in the understanding of these points.

There is continuity of interest at the problem level even when there is violent disagreement about where the philosophical truth concerning God lies. This holds for our own day as well, when analytic thinkers are taking pride in not philosophizing after the grand manner, when naturalists are declaring the death of the absolute or at least its inevidence, and when some existentialists and phenomenologists are placing God beyond the legitimate range of philosophy. All of these positions are meaningfully related to specific modern traditions, which both illuminate the reasons for declaring a moratorium on the philosophy of God and also render them less cogent and universal than is often recognized. The modern history of the problem suggests the following relevant points: that one can make inferences about God other than in the grand style of the rationalist system-builders, that there is a cardinal distinction between God and any kind of absolute, and that the descriptive study of finite things can be integrated with a method of causal inference and still respect the integrity of the descriptive results. A study of the modern theories of God clears a path for certain fresh approaches which have not yet been explored in sufficient depth. Here, as well as in other regions of philosophy, the effect of historical studies is not to render the mind effete and discouraged about the contemporary prospects but to give it useful guidance about the consequences of certain ways already taken and to help it realize how much of the work still lies ahead.

The philosophy of God is no exception, of course, to the skeptical interpretation of our intellectual history. This position maintains that the only thing perennial about the modern study of God is a series of persistent attempts which fail to yield any reliable knowledge of the divine. But this view of the situation concentrates too exclusively upon general systematic results, without taking adequate account of the achievement in terms of specific theories and methods put to the test. Whitehead's remark that philosophy has its criterion not in complete uniformity and finality of results but in making some reflective progress in the controlled use of methods and ideas is completely pertinent. Philosophy does not advance by totally abandoning the wreckage of past systems but by patiently discovering the limits of a proposed starting point or procedure and taking a firm hold upon the positive findings which do come within view by this means. There is some penetration into the nature of the philosophical study of God when the pattern and consequences of a functionalizing or neutralizing viewpoint are thoroughly worked out.

2. GOD AND FUNCTIONALISM

The functionalist notion of using the conception of God to develop or shore up one's philosophical system has exercised a profound and steady attraction over the modern rationalists. As the analysis of pre-Kantian philosophy shows in classical outline, God must be invoked in a functional role as soon as one takes a certain view of philosophy itself. This role is required for the theory of God when philosophy is treated primarily as a deductive system aiming at a complete body of truths, obtained in an a priori and purely intellectual fashion. Such a view of philosophy provides an emergency answer to the disturbing challenge of the skeptics. God must then be called in to guarantee the objectivity of ideal constructs, the continuity of deduction, the comprehensiveness of the results, and their necessary generation of human happiness. Functionalism always tends to compromise the transcendence and freedom of this guarantor-God, but it measures the sacrifice by the benefit of strengthening the philosophical system and satisfying the philosopher's aspirations.

One way of viewing the rise of modern functionalism is in terms of a transposition to the philosophical plane of certain characteristics of sacred doctrine or theology based on Christian revelation.[1] The order, evidence, and method of reasoning previously regarded as proper to such a theology are transferred to the philosophical order by thinkers who are isolated from the Christian faith as a source of truth. This can be seen from the distinction which St. Thomas makes between sacred doctrine and philosophy. The former science takes its point of departure in God, deals with God as its proper subject, and considers other things only in their unified relation with God. When these conditions become the constitutive principles of the rationalist notion of philosophy, they must inevitably transmute the whole conception of philosophy itself and reduce the doctrine on God to an instrumental status. A philosophy which takes an unqualified, natural start from God, rather than from finite, sensible things, is bound to depreciate sensation and the finite self in their own mode of being, to claim for itself an intuitive knowledge of God, and then to use its constructural notion of God as a springboard for making a complete and continuous deduction of the visible world and man. Such a philosophy cannot avoid eventually claiming to have direct insight into the divine essence or some privileged divine attribute and using the latter as an explanatory and system-generating principle of knowledge.

Functionalism secularizes the mode of reasoning which a theologian like Aquinas regarded as being reserved for sacred doctrine, namely, argumentation that a thing "conduces to God's glory, or that God's power is infinite."[2] An appeal to the divine glory or power need not entail any functional conception of God in the sphere of sacred doctrine, which is regulated by faith in the revealed word of God. But when God's power and perfection are expanded into primary deductive principles in philosophy, the entire theory of God must be subordinated to the demands of the rationalist system and hence given a functionalist treatment. The pantheistic outcome in Spinoza is only the most rigorous formulation of this position, which ultimately requires an identity of substance underlying the modes of thought, the visible expressions of nature, and the divine power itself.

Criticism of this functional theory of God can be of an empiricist or a realist sort, and during most of the modern period, the former type of criticism has predominated. It draws strength partly from its direct analysis of human reasoning, partly from the failure of the rationalist deduction to account for the world of physics (even with the presumable aid of a knowledge of the divine plan), and partly from our human repugnance against ambitious claims to know and exploit the mind of the Creator. On this last score, William James voices the ordinary reaction with typical candor and vigor: "It is a curious thing, this matter of God! I can sympathize perfectly with the most rabid hater of him and the idea of him, when I think of the use that has been made of him in history and philosophy as a *starting-point,* or premise for grounding deductions."[3] Implied in this observation, however, is the distinction between God and the rationalist idea of God, as well as the distinction between the deductive use to which the idea of God is put in a functionalist philosophy and other ways of gaining philosophical truths about God. By itself, a program of antifunctionalism cannot achieve any positive doctrine on God. The dead end of the purely critical approach is reached in Hume's minimal theism, which not only removes every instrumental appeal to the divine power but also confines the mind to a barely noticeable and purely speculative probable assent to God. Simply to accept sense-phenomenalism from scientific method and then to oppose a functional deity removes the latter without giving due consideration to other philosophical ways of viewing the problem of God.

Realism operates today as a *postfunctional* sort of theism, one which ponders the historical example of rationalism without accepting the latter's premises or specifying its own doctrine on God solely by way of its opposition to functionalism. It suggests a way of defunctionalizing theism without, at the same time, evacuating all demonstrative knowledge of God. This it does by stressing three points in an approach to God which is irreducible either to the functionalist method or to the Kantian critique of the rationalist types of proofs in natural theology.

The first step is a methodological recognition that even in the philosophical search after God, there is no exception to the need for beginning with an analysis of sensible beings, including man. The question of the starting point of the inference to God is a prime instance of the clarification of an issue in the course of modern speculation. Given a knowledge of the modern experiments with other types of starting points, one can never afterwards look with indifference upon this crucial issue or place all proposed points of departures on the same level. If one expects to develop a truly human philosophy of God, it must be based unequivocally upon the sensible existents of ordinary experience. The lesson of functionalism here is that there is something illusory about beginning with an intuitive, philosophical knowledge of God's existence or with a self-generating idea of God's essence and power.

A second feature in the realist project of disentangling the study of God from functionalism is its refusal to regard the divine essence as the constitutive subject matter of metaphysics or any other part of philosophy. The human intellect cannot capture and exploit God's nature for any systematic aim in philosophy. Realistic theism thus involves a radical refusal to put God to work for any a priori and deductive conception of how philosophical knowledge is acquired. This refusal stems both from the way in which we attain the truth about God's existence and from the consequences of this way for our knowledge of His attributes. It is through causal inference from sensible beings that we establish the truth that God exists. In gaining true knowledge that God exists, we can never remove the inferential way of founding this knowledge or the need for the proposition expressing its ultimate conclusion. In this life, the theistic philosopher must be especially careful not to pretend to be able to exchange inference for vision or demonstrative assurance that God exists for a direct perception of the divine act of existing. If he has the honesty and modesty to retain his dependence upon the causal inference, then he will not be led to claim to have direct access to the divine essence, either as a principle for reaching God's existence in a priori fashion or as a deductive principle for constructing the knowledge of finite things. The heart is extracted from the functionalist standpoint when the divine essence is reserved from our intuitive vision and assigned no role as the source of a deductive system of propositions. Only within a pantheistic functionalism does the divine nature fuse with the substantial nature of finite things in order to constitute the definable subject matter of a philosophical science.

The third realistic safeguard against a functional deity consists in its criticism of any method which employs the divine attributes as a set of premises for filling out the system of philosophy. We can ascertain that certain perfections must be attributed to God, not only because of His causal activity, but also because of His own unlimited actuality. Yet we do not see the unlimited actuality of God in His own being, and hence we can never detach our predications about the divine essence from the inferential and analogical way in which we know that God is the subsistent act of existing. The consequence is that the theistic philosopher cannot convert the theory of the divine attributes into an essentially known set of deductive principles for generating a systematic knowledge of the universe.

With the aid of these three marks of a realistic philosophy of God, some evaluation can be made of the argument advanced by French phenomenologist Maurice Merleau-Ponty for removing the question of God entirely from philosophy.[4] Together with Heidegger, he regards the issue of theism versus atheism as a purely theological dispute, in the sense of belonging to sacred doctrine and not at all to philosophy. Philosophy can treat psychologically of the human idea of God, but it must forsake all problems involving the real being of God, in which respect philosophy remains neutrally *a*-theistic. For Merleau-Ponty, every theory of God is based upon the always supposed notion of the necessary being. It must claim to install man within the metaphysical functions of God, considered as some all-powerful emperor of the world, and hence must derive man's contingent being through a deductive process which destroys both the contingency in question and our philosophical sense of wonder. To preserve the wonder and integrity of contingent things and the historical process, one must deliberately restrict philosophical inquiry to a description of man in his historicity, freedom, and intrafinite relations.

This description of a theory of God and its implications is drawn from the tradition of functionalism. The emperor-of-the-world metaphor is native to a philosophy of God built around the a priori analysis of the essential idea of a necessary, all-perfect being, but it is foreign to the atmosphere of a philosophy of God centering around the causal inference from sensible existents. The latter approach to God both begins with finite things and prevents any revocation of their contingent existence precisely because it never has the delusory aim of installing man within the mind and power of God. Because it respects the twofold mystery of finite existents and the infinite God, this realistic theism acknowledges the inexhaustible wonder of the existential act of all contingent beings, especially man in his free and historical mode of existing.

In Merleau-Ponty's case, there is an additional complication. He maintains that God is inevident in philosophy and that philosophy simply detours around the theism-atheism issue because of his conviction that phenomenology provides the only valid method for philosophy. When phenomenology is taken as a purely descriptive and noncausal study of the intentional structures binding human consciousness with the world, there is indeed no room for raising the problem of God's own being and no horizon upon which the evidence leading to our affirmation of His being can come within range of philosophical analysis. In his methodological exclusion of the question of the divine actuality and his foreshortening of the inquiry at most to the genesis of the idea of God, Merleau-Ponty is not far removed from the naturalistic standpoint. Two aspects of his position call for further examination. The first is concerned with whether a descriptive method is adequate to treat of every philosophically significant aspect of human experience. It is certainly a potent instrument for analyzing the detailed features of presently given structures of human consciousness and its world of perception. But there are causal implications of these structures which require an inferential type of analysis, co-operating with the descriptive process but also taking account of the meanings and dependencies in being which lead from the polarity of consciousness-and-world to God. The second issue is concerned with whether the causal inference to God can be made without revoking the integrity of man's intentional reference to the world. Here the circular procedure of assuming that God can only serve as a principle of necessary deduction of contingent beings and hence that every sort of inference to God is inimical to our finite, contingent, and historical world cannot be followed.

From the history of the modern rationalist speculation on God, it can only be concluded that some philosophers have unwarrantedly exploited the concept of God, not that every doctrine on God exploits and destroys the contingent and finite existent. The trouble does not lie in the fact that philosophers concern themselves with God but, rather, in the manner in which some of them formulate the problem and make the theory of God instrumental to their own system. Hence the historical evidence does not suggest that philosophers should refrain from seeking the truth about the being of God but only that they should refrain from trying to make God a mere tool for rounding out their special view of things. Existential knowledge about God is itself the peak of philosophical wisdom and is not instrumental to any wonder-destroying conception of the perfect system of knowledge.

3. GOD AND PHENOMENALISM

One firm methodological rule to emerge from the historical investigation is that one should always deal *jointly* with the rationalist and phenomenalist theories of God. If one remains satisfied merely with stressing, against rationalism, the impossibility of an intuitive grasp of God and a deductive use of His attributes, one runs the danger of eliminating all knowledge of Him. Hence, simultaneously, there must be a critique of the empiricist neutralization of God and the Kantian view of natural theology. The purpose of this joint treatment is not to achieve a symmetrical compromise between rationalism and phenomenalism. Such a compromise would consist in nothing more than a restless oscillation between exaggerating our human knowledge of God and underestimating it. Rather, its purpose is to keep the extremes clearly in sight while trying to develop a philosophy of God on a basis which is independent of both functionalism and phenomenalism. As a result of this synoptic treatment, realistic theism can learn to avoid making extreme claims for a philosophy of God in the face of Hume and Kant and then minimizing it beyond due measure in the presence of Spinoza and Hegel.

A reflective study of Kant and the empiricists brings the discussion about God back to the fundamentals. Instead of letting controversy expend itself peripherally upon questions involving the divine attributes, these thinkers force the philosophical theist to consider whether there is any demonstrative knowledge at all about God. They raise this question, moreover, in connection with their general attack upon the rationalist view of metaphysics, with which its theory of God is inextricably joined. It is insufficient to show that not every philosophy of God rests upon the rationalistic type of metaphysics. The dissociation must indeed be made between a realistic theism and such a metaphysics, but there also has to be a distinctive and thorough metaphysical study of God along experiential-causal lines. The realist is unable to accept the usual post-Kantian alternative of either reconstituting the philosophy of God as a theory of the idealistic absolute or recasting it as an empirical psychology of religious experience. Hence the salutary effect of the phenomenalistic critique is to force attention to be paid to the basic points in a realistically founded metaphysics.

Ours is the age of philosophical sandhogs working far below the surface at the foundations of the theory of being, not the age of steeple jacks and decorators who put finishing touches on an already erected metaphysical edifice. The neutralizing of all speculative knowledge of God helps to focus the major work of realistic theism upon four underlying issues: the substantial nature of a given sensible thing, its distinct and composing act of existing, the received character of the existential act, and the causal inference leading to a knowledge of the first cause of this composite being. These themes keep recurring in the historical and critical study of the British empiricists and Kant and help to keep the inquiry about God close to its roots in man's experience of sensible existents and our human reality.

Phenomenalism itself does not give us this rooting, however, since it is unobtainable either from the analysis of ideas or from the Newtonian model for speculative knowledge. Analysis of sense-data ideas as the direct terminals of cognition does not yield a knowledge of the act of existing or the real causal dependence of sensible beings, and neither does this knowledge flow from the conditions determining scientific statements. To bring the existential act and the causal bond within our intellectual range, we must have recourse beyond the way of ideas to the way of existential judgment and the analysis of the principles of being in the sensibly given existent. This is where the resources are available for a metaphysics of finite things in their composed way of being and their causes, in counterdistinction to both the rationalist system and the phenomenalist critique. Only within the context of a metaphysics so founded can realistic theism establish an inference to God which is irreducible to the three kinds of proof of God's existence formalized and criticized by Kant. A reflective study of the composing principles of being in the finite, sensible existent leads to a causal inference to God and also provides assurance that this inference is radically differentiated from even the so-called cosmological proof advanced by Wolff and rejected by Kant.

In our own century, logical positivism was aware that its attack upon metaphysics entailed a denial of metaphysically founded knowledge of God. To carry this denial beyond the stage of a program for future work, however, three tasks had to be performed. The first was to establish a definite formulation of the criterion of meaning, which could then be used to show the cognitive meaninglessness of sentences about God. The actual attempts made in this direction only resulted in a progressive weakening of the principle of verification, which was successively construed in terms of verifiability, confirmability, and an indeterminate conceivability of reference to sense experience or vital needs. Precisely what the manner and content of this reference must be has remained an open question, so that a simple appeal to the criterion of cognitive meaning has been indecisive for the problem of our knowledge of God.[5]

The second requirement was to show that metaphysics can consist solely of nonempirical sentences having no foundation in the basic thing-language of science and common sense. The difficulty encountered here was that of making a generalization about the necessary structure of every kind of metaphysics on the basis of too narrow a sampling of the various kinds of metaphysical discourse. Apart from the Hegelians and Heidegger, no further sources were used as instances of metaphysical kinds of statements about God. This had the circular effect of showing the a priori and nonexperiential character of metaphysics from a restricted group of instances which, in any case, did not profess to be making an a posteriori approach to metaphysics and God from experience.

Finally, the logical empiricists should have considered some specific ways in which theistic philosophers do discourse about God and do attempt to provide an experiential, nonanalytic basis for such discourse. But the typical attitude was expressed in a summary way by Otto Neurath: "We can start from everyday language after dropping some expressions, derived from magical, theological, or metaphysical speculations."[6] This prejudicial purge of everyday language was a convenient way of cutting the cloth of language to fit physics and behaviorism exclusively, but it arbitrarily impoverished the language of all those ordinary statements which are significant for an experiential theism. That which Morton White has called the doubtful strategy of legislative decisions about what is cognitively meaningful and meaningless has been substituted for an inductive analysis of the actual varieties of human discourse, including our discourse about God.

Among more recent exponents of the analysis of language and the elucidation of concepts, however, certain theistic problems are being studied. Thus the contributors to *New Essays in Philosophical Theology* cautiously admit that God-propositions are somehow significant to many people.[7] Some analytic writers are still content with assigning only an emotive meaning, whereas others grant, at least hypothetically, that the question may be more complex and may involve some properly cognitive factors. One suggestion is that the significance of statements about God has a dual source: Christian faith and ordinary experience. There is a concurrence between some analysts and some theologians in treating all proofs of God's existence as conceptual elucidations of our faith in God rather than as independently founded inferences which establish, through philosophical demonstration, the truth about His existence. To John Wisdom and the nontheistic analysts, however, such a position is reminiscent of the parable about the garden tended by an invisible and perpetually elusive gardener whom the watchers could never distinguish experientially from no gardener at all.

A reply to this difficulty is sought in the several levels of perspective for looking at human language. From the standpoint of the perceptual language, there is something decidedly odd about the use of perceptual terms in statements we use about God. But the linguistic theists regard this usage as an appropriate and consistent oddness, corresponding to the faith-grounded affirmation of an order of reality distinct from the perceptual world and yet related to it. By tracing out some of the implications of this relation upon the cluster of statements concerning divine omnipotence, human freedom, and evil, recent analytic philosophers have revived the Bayle-Leibniz discussion in the form of a linguistic theodicy. In doing so, they have also assumed that the language of theodicy is the prototype for every philosophical discourse on God.

In the main, the linguistic approach is continuous with classical phenomenalism and logical empiricism. The chief issue concerns the experiential element which may be present in statements about God, over and above the contributions which may come from revelation and tautologous definition. This is part of the problem of a translinguistic reference of at least some of our statements to the actual world rather than to another level of statements. The language of ordinary perception contains ground-floor statements and words whose determination is not drawn from a syntactical rulebook but from actually experienced things. Such sentences may state facts, but they are about things. The so-called linguistic oddness of theistic propositions will be treated as nothing more than a consistent illusion or a quirk in the discourse of fluent fideists unless it can be shown that experienced beings provide a basis for a causal interpretation distinct from the system of physical constructs.

The theistic use of language is not self-validating, no matter how consequential and intriguing it may be. Its correspondence with an act of faith does not make it any better founded from the standpoint of those analytic philosophers lacking the Christian faith. A reliable basis must be shown in our experience of things for making the separative judgment that not all actual beings are material. Linguistic usage alone cannot establish this point, but a metaphysical analysis must be made of the change and manyness of sensible things and the distinctive being of the human inquirer, viewed in his reflective operations and freedom.

Even then, however, many analytic and naturalistic philosophers are prevented beforehand from inquiring about inferences concerning God's existence because of the Humean view that all necessary propositions are nonexistential and that all existential propositions are contingent and nondemonstrative.[8] Hume's analysis sets up this dichotomy, however, only in view of that sort of necessity which belongs to analytic statements in logic and mathematics. Even granting the distinctiveness of such analytic statements, their formal necessity does not entail the stipulation that every other sort of necessity must be reduced to an analytic basis. On the side of existential fact, a distinction is needed between the contingency of the being in its own act of existing and the contingency of propositions concerning that act of existing and its implications. To take one's start with contingent things need not mean to start only with contingent premises. There can be propositions stating a necessary truth about the composite contingent existent and its causal dependence upon the purely actual existent. Here the necessity does not come from a formal analytic relation among the terms or from any physical rules of translation but from the composite manner in which some experienced thing has its act of existing. The causal demonstration of the truth about God's existence is not grounded upon the analytic necessity of a relation in logic or mathematics but upon a causal necessity found to be required for an actual, sensible existent within our experience.

4. GOD AND HUMANISTIC NATURALISM

Charles Peirce once remarked that Hegel's and Royce's "Absolute is, strictly speaking, only God in a Pickwickian sense, that is, in a sense that has no effect" upon the being of God Himself.[9] But that it has had a profound effect upon many human conceptions about God is evident from the actual consequences of absolutism during the past century and a half. Viewing the historical rise of naturalistic atheism out of the Hegelian absolute, prophetic thinkers like Nicholas Berdyaev and Martin Buber have interpreted it as a providential scourge for perverting the Judaeo-Christian conception of God. They remark that nothing is easier than to transmute one's best view of God into something else. This can be done all the more facilely if there is encouragement from a philosophy employing religious language and aiming at spiritual goals. Hegel's philosophy has attracted many theists who have failed to recognize how radical a transformation it demands of the notion of God and how the latter is emptied of its distinctive meaning. Historically considered, those who accepted Hegelianism as a defense of the reality of God have reaped a whirlwind. Whether one regards humanistic naturalism as the essential message of Hegel or as the subversion of his doctrine, the outcome is the same for the knowledge of God's actuality. Absolute idealism is the solvent which hastens the death of the idea of God among many philosophically trained minds. They rightly refuse to forget that Hegel never waxed more ironical than when he was referring to Kant's attachment to his well-beloved humanity and that this irony was generated by a theory of the absolute.

According to the previously mentioned providential interpretation of the rise of modern atheism, however, one should look upon Feuerbach, Marx, and Nietzsche, as well as their counterparts today, as passionate minds rebelling against an unworthy conception of God and, at least by implication, vindicating His true existence. This aspect of the theory is not readily confirmed by the available evidence and requires a generous amount of interpolation concerning private aims and latent thoughts. One can at once concede the difficulty of distinguishing, in any particular case, between a relative and an unconditional form of atheism. But one must also bear in mind that there are various ways of extricating oneself from the dialectical absolutism of Hegel, as the contrasting examples of Kierkegaard and Feuerbach illustrate. One can do so either by firmly refusing any kind of absolutism and restoring the personal relation between God the creator and the world of men and things or by retaining the absolutist assumption and yet identifying the absolute metaphysically with the totality of man-in-nature or methodologically with the logic of the sciences. Feuerbach and Nietzsche are instances of metaphysical absolutism, whereas Dewey and certain American naturalists exemplify a methodological absolutism. They all take to heart Goethe's maxim *nemo contra deum nisi deus,* which they translate as saying that one cannot overcome absolute spirit except by positing some sort of counterabsolute. There may be a secret sense of true divinity fermenting within the breasts of these thinkers, but their formal principle of counterabsolutizing the finite modes of being or one conception of inquiry is not compatible with any recognizable conception of God.

The heart of modern atheism does not consist precisely in its rejection of absolute spirit but in its counterabsolutist way of vindicating natural and human values. It claims that a choice must be made between these values and the existence of a transcendent, immaterial being, whatever the precise description of this being. Humanistic naturalism is anti-theistic to the extent that it encloses the cognitively attainable real within the horizon of this universe or within that which can be attained through the logic of the sciences, whether the standard is found in Marx's social whole or Nietzsche's cosmic circle of becoming or Dewey's continuum of inquiry. It is only by reference to these special interpretative principles that human and other natural values are held to prosper only through the effective exclusion of the conviction about a transcendent God. There is no such necessary entailment when one starts with the ordinary and nonabsolutized conception of scientific methods, nature, and man. From this vantage point, it can be seen that the divergence between naturalism and theism arises from their respective philosophical analyses of human experience, not simply from the scientific methods and findings as such.

The modern development of the problem of God suggests that the various historical doctrines on God have affected our view of man and nature in quite different ways and that the prospect remains open for a new theistic form of humanism and naturalism. In order to determine the consequences of a particular conception of God upon the significance of man and nature, this conception has to be examined in its own content and peculiar lines of evaluation. There is no single comprehensive way of stating what the philosophical effects of a given theory on God will be until it is studied in its own right. The nineteenth-century atheists attempted to make a generalization by setting up a necessary opposition between acceptance of God and our common human loyalty to the earth, that is, to sense perception, proximate agencies, and finite actualities. On all these issues, however, the lesson of the modern history of the philosophy of God is a thoroughly pluralistic one, showing that no unqualified inference can be drawn about the consequences of acknowledging the being of God. For instance, sense perception is depreciated both by the skeptics who allow no knowledge of God and by the rationalists who do allow it. Again, personal human freedom is jeopardized by Malebranche's occasionalism and Hume's minimal theism, by Spinoza's pantheistic naturalism and by Marx's atheistic naturalism, whereas it is defended in the moral theism of Kant and in William James' finitism. Moreover, the status and worth of man and other finite things differ considerably in the passage from Locke to Hegel to Whitehead, rendering a simple judgment about the philosophical effects of admitting God's reality too hazardous.

It does not follow from these instances either that the doctrine on God is perfectly indeterminate and irrelevant to the defense of natural, human values or that it is irreconcilable with them but only that each type of theism and antitheism must be studied separately in its own theoretical structure. No completely general and uniform proposition can be established, historically or speculatively, concerning the effect of an acceptance of God upon one's view of man and nature. Just as there are many conceptions of God, so are there many ways of envisaging the bond between finite things and God. There is no dialectical law requiring all of them to converge in the opposition between absolute spirit and its metaphysical and methodological counterabsolutes, since a reflectively disciplined theism moves definitively beyond the polarity among such absolutes. One cannot decide a priori how the doctrine on God must shape one's outlook on finite values, since the human mind does not approach God along a unique and predetermined road. This rules out the a priori argument of antitheism, but it does not dispense us from the work of inspecting the observable differences between various actual philosophies of God as they show themselves in operation.

Thus in the present historical inquiry, each time that realistic theism has been brought to bear upon other theories of God, it has made a joint defense of sense perception, proximate agencies (inclusive of human freedom), and finite actual beings. Far from there being any antithesis between these experiential truths and the realistic philosophy of God, the latter requires their validity and integrity as the basis of its own inferences. No causal inference or existential judgment can be made about God in the realistic context, apart from the contribution of sense perception and the evidence of finite causality and existential act, as these are manifested to man's judging intellect and reflective analysis. This is not a strategy of the moment but the permanent pattern of realistic theism, which it displays consistently in its appraisal of the many varieties of theism, pantheism, monism, finitism, and atheism. Hence this philosophy of God has a distinctive obligation both to defend our loyalty to the earth and to show its continuity with our loyalty to God. Yet this obligation cannot be fully met until the theistic mind recovers from its overwhelmingly defensive preoccupations and develops in full depth a positive, philosophical doctrine on God and finite existents.

In the case of the various naturalistic efforts to settle the problem of God by describing a possible psychological or social origin for the idea of God, for instance, it is not sufficient to appeal to other facts in psychology and cultural anthropology. It is not even enough to warn against the genetic fallacy of seeking to determine the validity of propositions about God solely by tracing the growth of a particular idea about God. A direct study must also be made of whether the motive of fleeing from the contingent, mutable world to an ideal zone, mistakenly taken for actuality, is indeed the dominant pattern for inquirers and searchers after God.

A representative instance of such inquiry is provided by St. Augustine. He testifies that the movement of mind and heart to God is a complex one and cannot be reduced to the simple schema of projective hypostasizing of our wishes. Instead, it consists of a threefold tension between awareness, searching, and finding. All of these components must remain present and fully operative throughout our temporal inquiry in the direction of God. The basal point is our *awareness* of the things in our world and of ourselves. This awareness is not an emotional fear but a steady understanding and affective grasp of the meaning of time and change and valuation as the pervasive traits of things and men. There is no flight from the world, for we do not leave the awareness of ourselves and the visible world behind as a first stage, but, rather, we make the understanding of historical beings a part of our marrow and a center of constant reflection and memory.

Hence the *searching* after God is not powered by repudiation of our own way of being. It does not involve turning away from finite things in fear and negation but exploring them and tracking down their implications. If the search leads to a recognition of God's changeless and eternal being, this is the consequence of tracing out faithfully the indications and pointers furnished by the things of our temporal acquaintance. If we expand our awareness to include the generous source and goal of our being, this is because the traces of God lead our mind and heart to acknowledge God and thus to widen our horizon of values. And the *finding* itself is not a delusion, since it is always correlated with the primary awareness of things and the need for searching. Augustine stresses the dialectic of searching and finding, of testing and acknowledging the outcome and then looking still further. This is the mark of the inquiring, rather than the deluded, mind. The finding of God does not blot out our awareness of the visage of creatures, our responsibility in human affairs, or our attitude of critical inquiry and constant searching. We find God in such a way that we always maintain our close and active fellowship with other temporal beings, always seek for more light from them about the eternal being of God, and always try to acknowledge the radical claim of God upon our devotion and our further pursuit.

On two cognate questions, the study of post-Hegelian naturalisms can be of direct assistance in this work. For one thing, their radically psychologizing approach to God has made imperative a fresh interpretation of that weasel-phrase "the idea of God." In modern philosophy, these words seldom refer to an exemplar present in the divine mind. They usually signify some conception which man has concerning God. During the pre-Kantian period, the aim is to establish the objective validity of a certain idea about God, either by showing its innateness, clarity, and distinctness from every other idea or by tracing its empirical derivation and its connection with other ideas. The former is the rationalist path, which culminates in Spinoza's theory of the idea of God as an expression of the divine power under the attribute of thought and again in Hegel's transformation of the idea of God into the absolute idea or self-apprehension of the absolute in pure thought. It is against this self-founding idea of God that Feuerbach and Marx, Nietzsche and Freud emphasize once more the empirical origin of the idea of God. Their purpose is not to justify it but to expose it as a purely subjective product of our human miseries, aspirations, and search after power.

None of these philosophers challenges the unspoken assumption, however, that the question of knowledge of God's existence is settled definitively in terms of the nature and origin of our idea of God. The modern philosopher who is most sensitive to the distinction between God's own being and our idea of God is Kant. Against both the rationalizing theists and the atheists, he is sure that the speculative idea of God cannot be so analyzed that it determines by itself either the real being or the non-being of God. A genetic description of how we might have formed the idea of God is just as inconclusive for His nonexistence as the ontological argument for His existence. A cultural or psychoanalytic report on the birth and death of a certain idea of God has some relevance for the career of this particular notion, but alone it settles nothing concerning the eternal being of God. Kant rightly locates the question of our knowledge of the latter upon the plane of judgment and inference, even though he finds no speculative way of resolving it.

The causal theory of the inference to God makes a capital difference in a realistic view of the idea of God. Given the existential-causal type of inference, this idea has no independent philosophical standing as a principle of demonstration. It is not determined beforehand in its own nominal content and then applied to the problem of God's existence and nature. On the contrary, in its philosophical meaning and validity, it is completely subordinate to and dependent upon the inferences concerning the first cause and subsistent act of existing. Our conception of God resembles our conception of existence, in that it is always referred to a judgmental act. In the case of our conception of God, however, the judgment upon which it is founded is itself the conclusion of an inference. Hence the conception of God is determined by a complex reference to both the judgment that the purely actual, causal being exists and to the inferential process underlying this judgment. This radical dependence upon a judgmental-inferential source is the decisive reason why the realistic theist cannot employ the idea of God as an aboriginal principle of knowledge. Its content and evidence come progressively from our inquiry about the infinite act of existing and primary cause of being. For our philosophical conception of God to be a living and humanly fitting one, it must always remain open to and dependent upon whatever we can learn inferentially about God from our prolonged study of finite existents.

Another area in which the prodding of naturalism serves as a helpful stimulus to realistic theism is in determining the character of the experiential reference of knowledge of God. This question came to the forefront with the pragmatic theism of William James, who advocated testing the idea of God by its empirically determinable consequences. James himself was confident that there was a determinately entailed empirical consequence of accepting the idea of God, since it gave him a distinctive quality of hopefulness under the trials of life which he, at any rate, could acquire in no other way. His friend Charles Peirce (1839–1914) always looked for universal cognitive consequences of ideas, in conjunction with their effect upon the individual. He found an empirical warrant for the theistic conviction in the fact that the idea of God both shaped his own attitude toward life and served to explain the convergent growth of the three universes of experience: the purely ideal realm of logical truths, the region of brute fact and force, and the semantic functions connecting idea and fact. In meditating or musing upon the way in which these universes conspire and jointly make provision for the future, he found it natural and morally fruitful to entertain the idea that God is the good creator and purposive unifier of all three aspects of human experience.

Meditation upon the Idea of God . . . naturally results in the most intense and living determination (Bestimmung) of the soul toward shaping the Muser's whole conduct into conformity with the Hypothesis that God is Real and very near; and such a determination of the soul in regard to any proposition is the very essence of a living Belief in such proposition. This is that "humble argument," open to every honest man, which I surmise to have made more worshippers of God than any other.[10]

In view of its interpretative significance for the facets of experience and its powerful moral effect in molding our attitude toward chance events, suffering, and evil, Peirce accepted the idea of God as a highly probable hypothesis. He would not grant that we could ever completely determine its objective import, since this would mean submitting the infinite God Himself to our testing operations and our temporal projects.

Naturalists such as Cohen and Nagel have tried to counter this pragmatic defense of theism by stating that the idea of God is so indeterminate that it is compatible with any arrangement of empirical facts and hence is positively confirmed by no definite empirical data. Against James they cite the inspirational effects of certain secular ideals, and against Peirce they object that the passage cannot be made from an effect in the mind to the being of God. On Peirce's behalf, however, it may be noted that the idea of God is suggested in his mind by a very definite sort of convergence in the universe.

It is significant that all these thinkers (and such finitists as E. S. Brightman) take "the idea of God" to mean "a hypothesis proposed for empirical testing." Although they reject a rationalist kind of test and look to the idea's relation with subsequent experience, they make the idea of God once more a primary determinant of whether or not we can know God to exist. In particular, a conflict develops between theistic realism and naturalism over the philosophical status of the idea of God. Basically, it is the difference between regarding experienced, composed beings as the inductive basis for the a posteriori causal inference to God and regarding them as materials for devising a test of an already constituted hypothesis or idea of God. In the realistic philosophy, the conception of God is the reflective outcome of causal reasoning from sensible existents, whereas naturalism treats it as an antecedently conceived possibility which now awaits its empirical verification. When the idea of God is taken in the latter sense, it can appear so remote and protean that it is incapable of any meaningful relation with experience. But in the realist framework, the conception of God is admitted philosophically only as a consequence of having arrived inferentially at the true determinate proposition concerning the existence of the subsistent act of existing and first cause.

This proposition is not indifferent to every empirical state of affairs and determinately related to none. It rests upon an inference, the force of which comes from the given, actual existents of our experience. The proposition which gives meaning and validity to our philosophical conception of God ultimately gets its causal foundation and inferential warrant from our analysis of composite, sensible beings. There is no more radically determinate and relevant a basis for assent than this one, since the inference is made and the assent given to God as a consequence of inspecting some given sensible things in their composing principles of being. In this way, a definite connection is made between our existential knowledge of God and the experienced things, not by verifying a hypothetical idea of God by reference to these things as its supposed deductive consequences, but by accepting some concrete existents as the starting point of an inquiry and discovering the causal implication which leads us to affirm the existence of their fully actual and operating causal source, God. The determinate experiential significance of a realistic theism is established through this causal inference from sensible things rather than through making a deductive conjunction of a hypothesis with its testing situation.

5. PHILOSOPHY OF GOD AND THE MORAL REQUIREMENT

Some analytic and naturalistic philosophers specify that the existence of God is not really established until the transcendent being is shown to be morally good, i.e., to be a just, providential, and merciful God. It is this group of divine attributes which arouses considerable philosophical interest today, particularly among finitists and atheists. The ancient skeptical difficulties about reconciling the divine power and goodness with our world are taken to mean either that there is a limited God or that there is no compelling evidence of the real presence of the only sort of being which the moral person would acknowledge as God. Whereas an Ivan Karamazov wanted to turn in his ticket rather than accept the suffering of innocent children, the contemporary naturalist suspects that there is no ticket-issuer with whom one can remonstrate about the conditions of life. It is assumed that God's existence cannot be proved and that a study of evil will uncover contradictions even in the hypothetical idea of His nature.[11]

As it is actually posed, the question of suffering and moral evil involves many religious, theological, ethical, historical, and psychological questions which lie outside the direct competence of a speculative philosophy of God. The latter does not claim to deal with every aspect under which man is related to God but only with the metaphysically determinable truths about God. In retaining its distinctness and limitations, the realistic philosophy of God is set off from both the older theodicies and the more recent atheologies and philosophies of religion, in which all these different issues are merged. Without denying the need for some synthesis of the several knowledges about the relation between man and God, realistic theism occupies itself with those aspects of the problem which come within the scope of the metaphysics of existent being.

There is some ambiguity in the requirement that one must directly prove that there is a good God. This may mean either that the very first proposition to be established is that there exists a good God or else that the continuous demonstrative effort must eventually show that God, the purely actual being and primary cause, is just and providential. The former demand is an arbitrary one unless some reason can be given why the truth about the existence of the infinite actuality and first cause cannot be established prior to establishing that this being is just. Since this is not required by the way in which finite things exist and have causal power, the latter meaning must be accepted.

In the order of discovery, the causal inference does properly conclude to the existent God, whose very act of existing is really the same as His being good (both in the metaphysical sense and in the sense corresponding to the moral requirement). However, our approach to God is not intuitive or simultaneously comprehensive of all the truths which can be established about God through philosophical means. The human mind must continue its inferential work in order to ascertain which traits are validly predicated of God. The truth that there exists a purely actual being which is distinct from finite things and is their primary cause is determinate to the extent of assuring us that this being really exists and is not nonexistent. But it remains open to further inferential determinations and, indeed, impels the inquiring mind onward toward the discovery of further truths about this being. Both the finite existents constituting the point of departure for the study of God and the pregnant truth of the purely actual and causal being's existence lead the inquirer in the direction of other propositions about God.

The propositions which are progressively ascertained about God, with the aid of causal analysis and the various types of analogical predication, are pertinent for establishing that He is good, just, and providential. There can be no deductive derivation of the divine perfections from some essentially known principle of God's being. But if one can show a posteriori the truth that the purely actual being exists as distinct from the world and as its creative cause, then this knowledge is relevant evidence toward establishing that this being is just and merciful. The demand that one directly show the divine goodness contains this further ambiguity, therefore, of requiring such a demonstration to move from the suffering and evil in the world to God, in total isolation from all other considerations about the world and God. Such an abstraction does not guarantee a rigorous test but guarantees only that no inference at all can be made, since it cuts off the existential and integral consideration of both the basis of proof and its proposed terminus. Thus there is a way of posing the problem of God and the moral requirement which eliminates, in advance, the possibility of establishing that the providentally good God exists.

There is another kind of stipulated isolation which also prevents a realistic theism from bringing all its resources to bear upon this question: the separation often made between the personal and the metaphysical ways to God. Pascal's contrast between the God of the patriarchs and the God of the scholars has had its echo in the personalist opposition between the living God of the I-Thou relationship and the impersonal, necessary essence of the philosophical treatise.[12] There is a valid sense in which some distinction must be maintained between our speculative knowledge of God and our practical relations with Him, but the distinction is often extended to mean that philosophical reasoning can never lead the mind to the personally existing God. This view is based upon either Hegelian absolutism or the rationalist procedure of first establishing a necessary essence or an infinite attribute and then trying to identify the result with the existing God. Neither of these positions supplies the prototype, however, for every metaphysical approach to God.

Realistic theism consistently criticizes the rationalist and absolutist thinkers from the standpoint of a conception of existential demonstration which does terminate properly in the truth about the actual being of God, as the subsistent act of existing. Subsequent inferences do not move from some impersonal essence and abstract attribute to God but simply enable us to realize that the propositions about the personal and providentially good being of God are founded upon the same truth about His infinite act of existing. In the light of this continuous inquiry about the existent cause of our human reality and other experienced things, it can then be validly affirmed that the realistic inference establishes the truth about the existence of the living, just, and good God.

Both in its starting point and in its way of predication, realistic theism respects the speculative basis for a personal relationship with God. In order to achieve the existential inference to God, the philosophical inquirer must reflect upon the significance of his own judgment of existence, his grasp of concrete sensible beings and causal dependencies, and his separative judgment about immaterial ways of being, as indicated by his own reflective intellectual and moral life. The foundation of the existential inference to God is not private, in the sense of being inaccessible to others and unverifiable in our common human condition, but it is personal, in that it requires the individual inquirer to see for himself the significance of the basic human judgments and experiences.

Furthermore, the point of departure for the inference includes man along with other sensible beings, includes him not only in the aspects shared in common with other sensible beings but also in his distinctive way of existing as a personal, free, and reflective being. This indispensable inclusion of the distinctively human mode of reality among the data for inferences concerning God permits us to employ the several types of analogical predication which develop from the basic causal analogy. To show that God is good, in the sense of being just and providential, requires a different sort of analogy than that used to show His unity. The finite analogate from which the former sort of predication proceeds embraces man in his distinctively intellectual and moral aspects, without divorcing them from a fundamental ordination to the sensible world.

One of the tasks of a realistic philosophy of God is to work out more explicitly its relevance for the moral requirement and for the personal relationship. It must do this, however, without losing its own nature as a speculative study of God. It can show that there is doctrinal continuity between the existential inference and the moral and personalist considerations, and it can thus give to the latter a metaphysical foundation. But it must also respect its own organization as a speculative discipline which does not provide a total synthesis of human knowledges about God and which does not do the practical work of uniting men with God. It reaches the border line with Newman's recommendation that our reflective approach to God be both notional and real, both concerned to establish the speculative validity of our propositions about

God and oriented to adherence of the whole person to the personal being of God Himself. Nevertheless, the speculative and inferential work must always remain dominant in a philosophy of God which functions in this world and which sees that the inquiring power has reasons which it is well for the heart to know.

6. GOD KNOWN AND UNKNOWN

Like thinkers in any other age, modern philosophers have felt the attraction of making flat statements that either we have essential insight into the divine being or we know nothing at all about God. Invariably, the function of critical intelligence has been to force qualifications to be placed upon these extreme statements. It is not primarily a question of degree: we can know a little about God, but not everything; rather, it is a question of kind: there are ways in which we can know God and ways in which we cannot know Him.

One way to achieve balance on this question is to clarify the meaning of the elusive words "proof of God's existence." They can mean either that the outcome of the inference is God's own act of existing or that it is the truth of our proposition concerning His act of existing. In order to sustain the former interpretation, the philosopher must proportion his mind to the divine existence itself, either through an immediate intuition of it or through seeing it flow from the divine essence or some attribute. This is the high priori path leading to the ontological argument, whose chief inconvenience for theists is (as Vico once noted) that it makes us gods of God. His existence is treated as the outcome of our process of reasoning, which proves His existence from a plane of metaphysical equality as we might solve an equation, discover an island, or produce a new compound. When this rationalist meaning for a proof of God's existence is also applied to a study of the divine essence, it has similarly disconcerting consequences. Sometimes even those who use the a posteriori proof of God's existence nevertheless approach His essence by way of a deduction from some privileged divine attribute or name. To do so in any fashion except verbally, however, would require a direct ordination of the human mind to some aspect of the divine essence instead of to finite beings.

The results of this kind of discourse about God are bound to be pretentious, despite personal disclaimers, since the method itself supposes a mode of knowing which surpasses our human state. From the older Samuel Butler and Voltaire onward, there has been a steady stream of satire directed against what William James once dubbed "the closet-naturalists of the deity," those who are methodologically forced to claim some familiarity with the divine essence. It is well to let Butler's acid portrait of the all too knowledgeable systematist sink home.

398

He could raise Scruples dark and nice,
And after solve 'em in a trice:
As if Divinity had catch'd
The Itch, of purpose to be scratch'd.[13]

It is just such an attitude toward the study of God which has led the contemporary Calvinist theologian, Karl Barth, to regard any independent, philosophical doctrine on God as blasphemous and destructive of our sense of the divine majesty. And it has led Paul Tillich to seek God as the ground or power of being, lying beyond the idolatrous God of this finitizing and thingifying conception of theism, and to balance off every theistic statement with its atheistic counterpart. Yet the outstanding question which remains is whether there is a kind of philosophical theism that avoids the rationalist position and yet bases assent to its propositions about God formally upon the evidence available to our natural intelligence, even when suggestions from revelation are considered.

To open the trail toward the realist philosophy of God, the other meaning for "proof of God's existence" must be examined. What is proved is not the divine act of existing but the truth of our human proposition affirming that God or the purely actual being exists. The demonstrative work in philosophy of God does not proceed by placing the divine act of existing under the microscope or bringing it within range of some metaphysical telescope but by testing the evidence for or against the validity of our proposition that God exists. This evidence does not come from any direct sight of God's existential act and essential nature. A humanly developed philosophy of God must examine the structure of the existing sensible thing of our experience, discover its intrinsic composition and causal dependence in being for its concrete act of existing, and in this way infer the truth of the proposition that there exists a first, purely actual cause of this being. The causal inference terminates not in a view of the divine act of existing itself but in the humanly concluded knowledge that the proposition "The purely actual being and first cause, God, exists" is well founded and true. The realistic proof gives knowledge *about* the existing God, but not by *using* the divine act of existing as the conclusion of the inference itself. This is the most radical level at which one can see the nonfunctional approach of realistic theism to God.

With the help of the basic inferential proposition about the existing God and a further inspection of the concrete finite existents of our experience, we can discover compelling grounds for inferring the truth of some further propositions about God by way of causal source, negation of imperfect ways of existing and thinking, and the transcendent actuality proper to the infinite existent. But in none of these efforts at obtaining further warranted statements about God does a realistic theism proceed on the basis of making the divine act of existing serve our purposes or by using a claim to direct insight into the divine essence or some special attribute as a middle term of proof. Philosophy of God remains a thoroughly human science in its method, source of evidence, and order of inference. Its propositions about God must base their claim to our assent upon the findings of causal analysis of finite sensible beings and upon the causal analogy and other analogical inferences required both by these things and by the truth of the fundamental proposition that the infinitely actual being and first cause exists.

An integral part of realistic theism is a methodology of how its propositions are meant and what limits they must respect. This is the task of the theory of analogical predication, which requires that our propositions about God respect the difference, as well as the similarity, in respect to the ways in which the infinite being and composed, finite beings exist and have their actuality. The purpose of a doctrine on analogy is not to achieve a studied ambiguity concerning the perfections predicated about God but to render the propositions stating such predications as precise as possible. It is regulated by the analysis of our human condition of inference and discourse about God when the human inquirer is seeking to ascertain the truth or falsity of his propositions about the infinitely actual being through a causal inference from finite existents within his range of experience.

By the very situation and direction of such an inquiry, the underlying sort of analogy must be of a causal sort. Our propositions about God can be determined as true by showing their connection of causal implication with what we know about composed finite beings in our world. The verification of propositions about God is neither purely experiential nor purely inferential. If it were experiential alone, then it would either concern only the finite things of our acquaintance or it would suppose an intuition of the divine actuality. If it were inferential alone, it would proceed from some deductive premise grounded in an intuition of God or it would be purely formal and definitional, thus lacking in existential import. The truth of our propositions about God is determined, on the contrary, in an unavoidably compound way or through a joint process of experience and inference. The verification proceeds in an experiential-and-inferential manner, that is, both by making direct acquaintance with some finite things (by analyzing them in their composing principles of being) and by carrying out the causal inference on this basis. Hence in the order of human inquiry about God, the causal analogy is the fundamental approach for a realistic mode of establishing the truth of our propositions bearing on God. There are other kinds of analogy which can be brought into play once the claim of our proposition that God exists is shown to be an evidenced one. These additional analogical significations are required both because of the complexity and diversity of finite things and because of the truth about the purely actual being of God. In the philosophical order, however, their demonstrative force is owed to these controlling sources in experience and in the primary existential inference about God rather than to any autonomous validity. Precisely because of their intrinsic dependence on the causal inference, they differ from what we ordinarily call loose analogies, comparisons, and metaphors. The kind of analogy considered by Hume and Kant is a comparison which is not grounded in and controlled by a more basic causal inference, whereas in a realistic philosophy of God, the condition for valid employment of every proposed analogical predication is its relation with the true proposition that God exists, as established from intrinsic analysis of, and causal inference from, sensible existing beings.

Just as the philosophy of God must include a theory of analogy, so must it make explicit reference to the limits under which it develops. St. Augustine culminates his quest of God with a *pia confessio ignorantiae*, a humble acknowledgment that God is above everything he can say and think about Him and, indeed, that God is best known by us on earth as being unknown. Similarly, St. Thomas holds that the summit of man's knowledge of God is to know that he does not know God.[14] This is not the same as saying that man knows that God does not exist, or that he knows nothing about God, or that he must remain silent about Him. It means that once a man becomes fully aware of the natural source and mode of his inferences about God, he also recognizes that God, in His infinite actuality, always surpasses anything we can say about Him. To know in a human and philosophical way the truth of our propositions about God includes knowing the truth that the infinite actuality is really other than, and transcendent of, the finite beings which nevertheless constitute our sole philosophical routes to God. These existent things serve faithfully as *viae*, or ways, of knowing about God and do so in a twofold sense. For one thing, they furnish the experiential warrant for the validity of our causal inference leading to the proposition that God exists. Hence acceptance of this proposition as true is the outcome of an inference rather than an intuitive leap from nature to the beyond. Yet precisely in supplying the demonstrative ground for the theistic assent, the composed existents of our experience also yield the truth that God is not submitted in His own unlimited act of existing to our thought, since our philosophical approach to Him never ceases to be causally inferential or dependent upon the finite beings which are under analysis. This guards against the inclination to exploit the very being of God for the human purposes of either a speculative or a practical functionalism.

The theme of the unknown God runs contrapuntally throughout modern philosophy, especially since it is responsive to the Judaeo-Christian tradition. The wide variations in its interpretations indicate, however, that the individual minds have been rethinking and assessing it in keeping with their other philosophical and theological positions. Within the realistic context, it must be correlated with the meaning suggested for "proof of God's existence." God is both known and unknown by us. He is known in that we can determine the truth of certain propositions about Him in an experiential-inferential way; this removes the extreme claim of agnosticism and of atheism, whether of the emphatic or the unemphatic variety. God is unknown in that none of the finite things from which we draw our knowledge gives us a vision of His divine being in its own infinite actuality; this removes the extreme claim of the functionalists and dialectical monists, the ontologists and theosophists.

This conception of the philosophy of God avoids Barth's stricture against a blasphemous and idolatrous approach. In the strict sense, it does not permit us to speak about treating God or proving God but only of proving the truth of certain human propositions about God. To use the language of Gabriel Marcel in a different signification, there is a problem of our propositional knowledge about God, and yet this enables us to appreciate the mystery of God in His own being. This combination of problem and mystery conforms to our human condition, just as does the combination of notional and real assent. The problem of our propositions about God leads eventually to a verified notional assent (founded upon a speculative, experiential-causal inference) to their truth, thus encouraging us to give our real assent to the mystery of God's own infinite act of being or personal identity.

The realistic philosophy of the known and unknown God explores finite existents as far as they can lead men toward a knowledge of God, but it does not confuse the resultant human propositions about God with the infinite God in His own act of being. It agrees with Augustine in distinguishing between discovery and judgment in matters concerning God. Our minds "may rightly know the eternal law but may not judge it."[15] Man can discover the truth that God exists and is eternal, but this knowledge does not make the eternal being of God dependent upon the human mind. Hence our inquiry about God does not submit God Himself to our superior judgment but conforms our mind to the truth concerning His infinite being. The philosophical inference to God enables us to know certain true propositions about Him, including the affirmation of His perfect independence in being.

There is no need to seek, with Tillich, for a God beyond the God of theism but only for a philosophical theism for which God is known to be other than all finite existents and conceptions. Apart from reference to the controlling principles of some particular philosophy of God, it is impossible to determine a priori whether God will be finitized and thingified through the predication of actuality and cause to Him or whether this result will follow from regarding Him as being-itself or as the ground and power of being. There can be no wholesale elimination of certain divine names, since each instance has to be considered on its own merits and within some definite context of principles of inference and predication, where it will receive its determinate meaning and usage. Since realistic theism includes a definite theory of the analogical predication and limitation of human propositions about God among the dominant principles regulating its use of existence, act, and cause, it has its own safeguards for respecting the divine transcendence and uniqueness of being. Tillich cannot simply make a privileged case of regarding God as being-itself and as the power of being, since the tradition of Boehme and Schelling carries its own problems about whether God is made functional to a special conception of human experience and history. To show the philosophical validity of his primary naming of God, he must make use of the common standard of relevance to finite things. But this opens the way for a nonsymbolical basis of causal analogy and hence for a procedure that safeguards the being of God otherwise than by a dialectical counterbalancing of symbolic terms.

7. THE NATURE OF THE PHILOSOPHY OF GOD

There are four widely prevalent views today about the nature of a philosophy of God. The first two are that it is only a memorial surviving from the past, without any footing in the living tendencies of thought, and that it is indeed vital but only as a reflection on the Christian faith and its language. The other two views are that it deals with genuinely philosophical evidence, but only as an integral part of sacred doctrine, and that it is the equivalent of the philosophy of religion. The notion of the philosophy of God which has developed out of the present investigation does not conform exactly with any of these positions. It is only at the end of our study, however, that there is a sufficient inductive basis for showing the differences and thus specifying our historically relevant meaning for a realistic theism.

Those who regard the philosophy of God as a relic of the philosophical and theological past are themselves the heirs of one definite, historical tradition concerning God. Their view is the latest expression of what may be called the *archaicizing* argument, which was forged during the struggle against Hegel and the general recession from the theory of absolute spirit. Although useful for the original polemical purpose, this argument cannot be taken as a definitive judgment about the philosophy of God. For it rests on the assumption that all philosophical approaches to God can be narrowed down historically to the debate between Hegel and naturalism and that every present-day consideration of evidence must find its interpretative principles in the naturalistic explanation of the logic of inquiry. Since the historical part of this premise oversimplifies the data and since the theoretical part is the point at issue in the realist interpretation of existence, the archaizing argument cannot stand permanently in the path of a renewed inquiry into the foundations of human knowledge of God.

The fideistic interpretation is sometimes theologically motivated, sometimes the result of philosophical skepticism, and sometimes the conclusion drawn from the phenomenalistic character of the sciences. The philosopher as such cannot deal with the theological grounds in a particular theory of man's Fall, but he can make a critical examination of the claim that all philosophical theories of God must terminate in some kind of idolatry and confusion of the human and the divine. Furthermore, analysis can be made of the contention that all proofs of the truth about God's existence are reducible to the ontological argument, which, in turn, is only a reasoned explication of faith.[16] Both of these consequences of theological fideism clash with the realistic conception of how the human intellect comes to know something about God. Such knowledge does not rest upon analysis of our idea of God and does not confuse this idea with God's own being. When fideism appeals to the phenomenalism of modern scientific knowledge, it joins company with the empiricist and analytic tendency to limit philosophical inquiry to a study of the ordinary and scientific language, apart from any distinctive metaphysical inference. This significant convergence of fideistic and phenomenalistic positions underlines the twofold need of showing that the philosophical study of God is an aspect of the metaphysics of existent being and of making a careful examination of the meaning and limits of scientific methods and the techniques of analysis.

Some of the fundamental metaphysical aspects of a realistic theism are found in St. Thomas, who did his philosophizing within the context of his theology. While this theological orientation is recognized, there remains the question of whether thinkers in our day can develop, in a Thomistic spirit, their own philosophy of God, which is not formally integrated with, and ordered by, sacred doctrine.[17] This can be done as long as one does not claim to be giving a purely historical presentation of the mind of Aquinas or to be doing the work of a theologian. Both the historical and the theological treatments are indispensable, but they do not exhaust the thought of Aquinas in the area of human inquiry about God, many aspects of which he establishes in terms of the philosophical evidence and with a basic respect for the order entailed by that evidence. Today there is a clear need to proceed deliberately and reflectively in developing this tendency into a doctrine on God that is formally and explicitly philosophical, both in its source of data and in its corresponding order of inference.

The same exigency is found when one's main intention is to establish some speculatively certain truths about God for their own sake and to do so within the intellectual setting provided by the modern history of the problem of God and its contemporary status. Such issues as the possibility of any metaphysical knowledge, the warrant in experience for the analysis of finite beings with respect to their essential nature and existential act, the validity of the causal inference and the causal analogy which reach beyond the finite order to the infinite actuality of God, the functional or nonfunctional significance of knowledge of God for one's whole philosophy and the conduct of life, the relation between a doctrine on the transcendent God and the various forms of pantheistic and atheistic monism, the experiential relevance of a theory of God and the role of the idea of God—all these issues have been confronted in the course of the present inquiry and stated in their peculiarly modern and contemporary urgency. They belong properly in the philosophical domain, both in regard to the determining evidence taken from beings within the range of our natural experience and in regard to the order of reasoning which is required to take full advantage of a starting point in sensible existents. To meet these problems adequately, a realistic philosophy of God must not only base itself upon the evidence of finite things available to our human experience but must also develop its findings by means of the distinctively philosophical ordering of inference which moves from sensible beings to God.

The critical analyses advanced throughout the present study point toward a balanced realistic theism whose method is experiential and causal and hence whose order of discovery of truths about God is specified by its point of departure in sensible beings, including the whole reality of man as disclosed to our experience and reflection. With the aid of the causal inference to God, a renewed study can be made of finite things considered now precisely as produced in their existing being by God. Further light can also be thrown upon the basic instruments of theistic analysis: the essential nature and existential act of limited beings, the causal bond, and the relations of analogy. But all such inquiries are indeed *renewed* studies and cast some *further* light; they do not involve any claim to revoke the finite starting point in experience or to begin with God but belong to the return phase of a theistic investigation which began with experienced things and is now coming back to them as related to the inferred truth about God. These further studies can utilize the inferred truth about the existent God, but they are conducted legitimately only within the context of the primary movement from sensible beings to God and upon the basis laid down by our direct metaphysical inspection of the principles of being, the causal relation, and causal analogy as encountered among experienced beings. This radical dependence of theistic philosophical inquiry upon its founding order of discovery is never wiped out, transcended, or otherwise transmuted, whatever deeper understanding of finite beings and of metaphysical principles we gain from coming into possession of the demonstrated truth about the being of God.

Fidelity to the philosophical order of inquiry does not close off any avenue of instruction for a realistic philosophy of God. The theist who is also a Christian remains alertly open to revelation, especially since it conveys some natural truths about God. He acknowledges the influence of his faith in directing his mind toward regions of evidence and classes of problems that might otherwise be slighted or entirely overlooked. Yet as a philosopher, he also has the responsibility to take a direct look at the data, to follow through the suggestions of revelation to the point of making his own inspection of the condition of finite beings and their bearing on a knowledge of God. His philosophical assent to truths about God has to be regulated by the outcome of his personal investigation of the evidence available to human experience of the sensible world and the life of man. Hence he must avoid any confusion between the various sources of his instruction and the ground of validity for his assent to propositions about God, whenever the latter are intended to constitute a philosophical doctrine on God. In this way, he can avoid the two extremes of a total Cartesian divorce between philosophy and the influence of revelation and the fideistic tendency to regard the contribution of revelation as a substitute for finding the evidential basis of theistic truths in our experience and causal inference. In the hands of a Christian theist, a realistic philosophy of God is both responsive to the testimony of faith and responsible for making its own assay of whatever materials can belong within a philosophical doctrine on God. Both the act of assent and the ordering of inferences in a realistic theism depend fundamentally upon philosophical analysis of our experience of man and the sensible world, whatever the sources that actually influence us to make this inspection for implications concerning God.

There are so many widely varying theories about the nature of a philosophy of religion that at present it does not seem possible to determine precisely how such a discipline stands related to a realistic theism. One negative point seems clearly established. If the aim of a particular philosophy of religion is to be a substitute for all metaphysical knowledge of God, then it cannot be reconciled with realistic theism. But the meaning of philosophy of religion need not be arbitrarily restricted to the tradition which developed in the wake of Kant and which consequently despaired of any metaphysics or else turned in desperation to an absolutism of spirit. On the positive side, there is room for a philosophy of religion as a second-level synthesis of the several primary sciences dealing with God and man's relation to Him. It would bring to a common focus the relevant portions of metaphysics, ethics, psychology, and other studies which deal with the bond between God and man. Precisely how this can be done within a philosophy of religion that remains a cognitive synthesis and not itself a practical way of life or substitute for religious worship remains one of the outstanding questions for exploratory trial by realistic theists.

The historical study of the problem of God furnishes some pertinent suggestions, moreover, on the precise relationship between a philosophy of God, a theodicy, and a natural theology. There are serious historical reasons for refusing to make the realistic philosophy of God equivalent to a theodicy. Taken in its determinate Leibnizian meaning, a theodicy claims to make a demonstration of the justice of God through a special appeal to the divine power, the power of essence, and the principle of sufficient reason as a univocal key to moral motivations. Given the actual historical meaning and consequences of such a discipline, it cannot be taken as synonymous with or even reconcilable with a realistic theism. Classical theodicy also has a theological and practical orientation, mingling questions of grace and Scripture with philosophical issues and having a primarily controversial and apologetic aim. If theodicy is taken broadly as a deductive justification of God's way with the world, then it can only come into conflict eventually with a realistic theism which relinquishes all deductive approaches to God, out of respect for both the divine majesty and the integrity of man.

The case is somewhat different with "natural theology," which in some of its senses is the equivalent of the realistic meaning for "philosophy of God."[18] When St. Augustine came to define the term, he distinguished between three types of theology not based on revelation: mythical, political, and physical, or natural. He classified mythical and political theology together as species of conventional or man-made theology, since they study the gods constructed by the poets and by the state. Opposed to conventional theology is natural theology, or the doctrine on God based upon a philosophical study of nature. A theology is natural both with respect to its object (God in His own being, not as subject to human myth-making or political ordinance) and its source of information (the physical world in its real features). In harmony with his own distinction in kind between philosophy and sacred doctrine, St. Thomas recognized a philosophical theology, which is a metaphysical doctrine on God developed through a study of the evidence available to our natural knowing powers and according to the method and order of philosophical reasoning as it moves from finite things to God. Cardinal Newman also regarded the philosophical doctrine on God as a natural theology, both in view of the natural informants, or sources of fact leading to God, and because both pagan and Christian minds can make the inference and the assent to God. A realistic theism is a natural theology if the latter study is conceived in these ways.

But attention must also be paid to at least four modern meanings for "natural theology" which have quite a different tenor. In Calvin's and Francis Bacon's conception of it, there is no way of establishing a philosophical science of God from the study of finite things. A theology is natural, not by having a basis in the physical or metaphysical study of the finite world, but by reason of applying the teachings of revelation to nature and interpreting the latter in the light of faith. Descartes does have a natural, demonstrative, and metaphysical theory of God, but it is natural in the sense of positively excluding any influence of revelation, and it is metaphysical in the sense of belonging to a science which is deductively prior and functionally ordered to philosophical physics. Wolff also accords demonstrative force to a natural theology and relates it to an ontology, but they are separate sciences related as a special part of metaphysics to general metaphysics. Wolffian ontology, or general metaphysics, does not treat formally of the existential act of finite things or of the existent God, whereas Wolffian natural theology offers demonstrations of God's existence and attributes by appealing to the order of essence and the principles founded thereon. Finally, the deists of the Enlightenment return to the sensible world for their natural theology, but they do so to the formal exclusion of suggestions from revelation, without any metaphysical analysis of finite being, and by means of probable arguments leading to a God who may be finite. Although these interpretations of "natural theology" do not necessitate the outright abandonment of the term, they do indicate difficulties connected with its use today and the need for a very careful demarcation of the precise meaning in which one intends to employ it.

The realistic philosophy of God can define its nature by contrast with some of the viewpoints mentioned in this section. It is not an excursion into the past, as the archaicizing interpretation claims, although it employs historical research to obtain intelligent guidance from the past developments in the problem of God. As a living discipline, it carries on its inquiry in the present and requires the individual theist to make his own study of the evidence of finite existents. Precisely because this evidence comes from experience of finite sensible beings, is available to the human mind, and conveys some significance for determining the truth about God, the philosophy of God is not a fideistic enterprise. It does not found its propositions upon a clarification of the content and language of faith, even though it can receive suggestions from revelation. The influence of the history of philosophy and revelation will be to stimulate the theistic philosopher to make a direct inspection of certain aspects of man and sensible things. Yet it is the outcome of his own examination of things which provides the basis of assent to the propositions constituting his doctrine on God. Moreover, the path of inquiry follows the order, as well as the evidence, of natural, philosophical reasoning, not the order proper to sacred doctrine. It begins with the finite, sensible existents of our direct experience and regulates all of its propositions about God by the requirements imposed by such a starting point and the existential-causal reasoning to Him. Since its foundation is in the speculative judgment of existence and the judgment about nonmaterial existents and causes, the philosophy of God is not the same as an analysis of religious experience or any sort of theodicy. It achieves this distinctive judgmental rooting through an experiential metaphysics of being as existent rather than through a design-analysis of scientific order or through the philosophy of nature.

A realistic theism is not a separate science but the culmination of the metaphysics of being as existent. It is that moment in the metaphysical inquiry when it seeks out the ultimate cause of its proper subject, being, or the experienced things which exist. Hence the philosophy of God shares the experiential-existential basis of this metaphysics, its use of the causal inference and analogical predication, and its speculative, nonfunctional nature. The existential truth about God is significant for its own sake, as knowledge of the subsistent act of existing and primary cause of being. Metaphysical wisdom does order the other philosophical sciences, but not by supplying them with deductive premises or supplanting their own method and evidence. The doctrine on God is relevant for other problems in metaphysics and for the ethical study of man as long as the judgmental-inferential nature of our propositions about God is respected and not suppressed for any functionalist purpose. Beyond their importance within the sphere of philosophical knowledge, however, the propositions about God can be personally assimilated and thus assist the human person to move by knowledge and love toward the living God Himself, known and unknown.

> I kiss my hand
> To the stars, lovely-asunder
> Starlight, wafting him out of it; and
> Glow, glory in thunder;
> Kiss my hand to the dappled-with-damson west:
> Since, tho' he is under the world's splendour and wonder,
> His mystery must be instressed, stressed;
> For I greet him the days I meet him, and bless when I understand.[19]

NOTES

Notes for Chapter I

NEW APPROACHES TO GOD THROUGH FAITH AND REASON

1. See Parts 10 and 11 of E. Gilson's *History of Christian Philosophy in the Middle Ages*, especially 534–40, on Cusanus from the medieval perspective. On the problem of God's existence in the great commentators and more recent Scholastics, consult J. Owens, C.Ss.R., "The Conclusion of the *Prima Via*," *The Modern Schoolman*, 30 (1952–53), 203–15, and G. P. Klubertanz, S.J., "Being and God according to Contemporary Scholastics," *The Modern Schoolman*, 32 (1954–55), 1–17.

2. The nonspeculative character of the "Christian philosophy" recommended by Renaissance religious humanists is seen in two representative works: Petrarca, *Of His Own Ignorance and That of Many Others*, translated by H. Nachod, in *The Renaissance Philosophy of Man*, edited by E. Cassirer, P. O. Kristeller, and J. H. Randall, Jr., 47–133; Erasmus, *The Paraclesis: An Exhortation to the Study of Christian Philosophy*; translated by J. R. O'Donnell, C.S.B., in *The Wisdom of Catholicism*, edited by A. C. Pegis, 520–30. Petrarca (*op. cit.*, 64) quotes the words of St. Augustine in praise of the "learned ignorance" of Christian believers in God, as opposed to the pretended knowledge of pagan philosophers. Cusanus appropriates the phrase but uses it to overcome the opposition.

3. *Of Learned Ignorance*, I, i and iii, translated by G. Heron, O.F.M., 7–8, 11–12. Two useful general studies on Cusanus are H. Bett, *Nicholas of Cusa*, and M. Gandillac, *La philosophie de Nicolas de Cues*. The recent research of L. Sweeney, S.J., "Divine Infinity: 1150–1250," *The Modern Schoolman*, 35 (1957–58), 38–51, shows that the very being of God was not explicitly affirmed to be infinite until about 1250. Thus the problem of ascertaining truths about the divine being becomes more acute after that date, and Cusanus is heir to the difficulties.

4. *Idiota De Mente*, Chapters 4 and 7, edited by L. Baur, 58–62, 73–79. This is in Vol. V of the still incomplete, critical edition of *Nicolai de Cusa Opera Omnia*, sponsored by the Heidelberg Academy of Sciences; all Latin references here are given to this edition, where possible. On the image doctrine, see also *Of Learned Ignorance*, II, ii; III, iii–iv (Heron, 74–75, 134–41).

5. *De Conjecturis*, I, vi–x, in *Nikolaus von Cues, Philosophische Schriften* (Vol. I only), edited by A. Petzelt, 128–38. (Unfortunately, this edition of Cusanus must be used with caution, and only until the Heidelberg edition is completed.) See also *Of Learned Ignorance*, III, vi (Heron, 144–46).

6. *Of Learned Ignorance*, I, x–xi (Heron, 22–27). The mathematical aspects are examined by M. Feigl, "Vom *incomprehensibiliter inquirere* Gottes im I. Buch *De docta ignorantia* des Nikolaus von Cues," *Divus Thomas* [Freiburg], Series 3, Vol. XXII (1944), 321–38. That the stress on knowledge, method, and mathematics is a prefigurement of modern trends is noted by K.-H. Volkmann-Schluck, *Nicolaus Cusanus: Die Philosophie im Übergang vom Mittelalter zur Neuzeit*, 146–90.

7. *Of Learned Ignorance*, I, xii (Heron, 27).

8. *Ibid.*, I, xvi, xxi (Heron, 34, 48). For the definition of the Maximum, see *ibid.*, I, ii, iv (Heron, 9–10, 12–14). On the philosophical consequences of the choice of the mathematical method of limits, read V. Martin, O.P., "The Dialectical Process in the Philosophy of Nicholas of Cusa," *Laval Théologique et Philosophique*, 5 (1949), 213–68.

9. *De Docta Ignorantia*, I, xxii, edited by E. Hoffman and R. Klibansky, 44; *De Beryllo*, 1, edited by L. Baur, 3. These are Vols. I and XI, respectively, of the Heidelberg edition. The *coincidentia* doctrine is studied by J. Hommes, *Die philosophische Gotteslehre des Nikolaus Kusanus in ihren Grundlehren*. Its similarity to Hegel has often been remarked, but the differences are also striking. Cusanus makes a faith-enlivened intellect the highest faculty, imports no opposition and movement as such into God, and admits no essential knowledge of God through his dialectical principle.

10. *Of Learned Ignorance*, I, iv; II, iii–v (Heron, 12–14, 75–86; one word modified).

11. The main references are in *ibid.*, I, vi; II, ii (Heron, 16–17, 71).

12. *Ibid.*, I, xxiv–xxvi (Heron, 51–61).

13. *Ibid.,* I, xvii; II, ii–iii, viii (Heron, 39, 71–79, 95–96).

14. *Of Learned Ignorance,* III, i, ii (Heron, 128, 133); *Apologia Doctae Ignorantiae,* edited by R. Klibansky, 10–11. This is Vol. II of the Heidelberg edition. For a critical discussion of the pantheism question in Cusanus, see J. Neuner, S.J., "Das Gottesproblem bei Nikolaus von Cues," *Philosophisches Jahrbuch,* 46 (1933), 331–43. Although the term "pantheism" has an eighteenth-century coinage, the doctrine of a substantial identity between God and the universe has a much longer history.

15. On the distinction between the magisterial or prideful use of reason, which Luther condemns, and the ministerial or captive use of reason in the service of faith, of which he approves, see H. H. Kramm, *The Theology of Martin Luther,* 109, and R. Bainton, *Here I Stand: A Life of Martin Luther,* 167–73.

16. *Die Heidelberger Disputation* [1518], 21, in *Martin Luther, Ausgewählte Werke,* edited by H. H. Borcherdt and G. Merz, Vol. I: *Aus der Frühzeit der Reformation,* 134. Compare Theses 19–24 (133–36), on the contrast between the theology of majesty and the theology of the cross, and the editors' commentary (476–78). On Luther's Ockhamist training and intellectual growth until 1518, see R. Fife, *The Revolt of Martin Luther,* 32–271. Later theological interpretations of Luther's doctrine on *Deus absconditus* are considered in J. Dillenberger, *God Hidden and Revealed.*

17. *Institutes of the Christian Religion,* I, i, 1, translated by Henry Beveridge, I, 37. A brief sketch of Calvin's doctrine on God is given by A. M. Hunter, *The Teaching of Calvin,* 49–62.

18. The dialectical complexity of Calvin's method is recognized by E. A. Dowey, Jr., *The Knowledge of God in Calvin's Theology.*

19. *Institutes of the Christian Religion,* I, iii, 1 (Beveridge, I, 43). For the historical background of Calvin's conception of God, see F. Wendel, *Calvin: Sources et évolution de sa pensée religieuse,* 110–36.

20. *The Catechism of the Church of Geneva,* in *Calvin: Theological Treatises,* translated by J. K. Reid, 93; cf. *Institutes of the Christian Religion,* I, v (Beveridge, I, 51–63).

21. *Institutes of the Christian Religion,* I, v, 12 (Beveridge, I, 61); *Joannis Calvini Opera Selecta,* edited by P. Barth and W. Niesel, Vol. III: *Institutionis Christianae Religionis 1559 libros I et II continens,* 57. The relevance of man's Fall to the problem of knowing God is stressed by T. F. Torrance, *Calvin's Doctrine of Man,* with special reference to man as the image of God (35–82) and its bearing on natural theology (154–83). On the image of God and the Fall, see *Institutes of the Christian Religion,* I, xv, 3–5; II, i (Beveridge, I, 162–66, 210–20).

22. *Institutes of the Christian Religion,* II, ii, 18, 19 (Beveridge, I, 238).

23. *Ibid.,* I, vi and x (Beveridge, I, 64–67, 87–88). Scripture as the remedy for nature's failure to bring her message through to us is explained by T. H. Parker, *The Doctrine of the Knowledge of God,* 29–40.

24. *Institutes of the Christian Religion,* I, xi, 1 (Beveridge, I, 91). The question of a natural theology has been hotly disputed by such leading contemporary Calvinist theologians as K. Barth and E. Brunner. Consult the review of the controversy in Dowey, *op. cit.,* and a Thomistic critique of Calvin and Neo-Calvinism by E. Gilson, *Christianity and Philosophy,* translated by R. MacDonald, C.S.B., 13–51.

25. *Institutes of the Christian Religion,* I, ii, 1 (Beveridge, I, 40); *The Catechism of the Church of Geneva* (Reid, 91).

26. A close biographical and doctrinal correlation is established by D. W. Singer, *Giordano Bruno: His Life and Thought.*

27. *On the Infinite Universe and Worlds,* V, translation in D. W. Singer, *op. cit.,* 348–450.

28. *Concerning the Cause, Principle, and One,* III, translation in S. Greenberg, *The Infinite in Giordano Bruno,* 136.

29. *Concerning the Cause, Principle, and One,* II (Greenberg, 110).

30. *Ibid.,* Introductory Epistle, poem "Of Love" (Greenberg, 89).

31. See M. Nicolson, *Science and Imagination,* 2–3. The transition from Copernicus to the infinite universe of Thomas Digges and Bruno is outlined by Alexandre Koyré, *From the Closed World to the Infinite Universe,* 28–55. Bruno criticizes the finite horizon presented by the senses in his *On the Infinite Universe and Worlds,* Introductory Epistle and Dialogue I (Singer, 246, 250–51).

32. There is an elaborate metaphysical attack upon Aristotle in *Concerning the Cause, Principle, and One*, II, III, V (Greenberg, 82–85, 118–20, 128–35, 162–66), whereas the entire *On the Infinite Universe and Worlds* undermines the Aristotelian natural philosophy. For a Marxian, materialist interpretation, see I. L. Horowitz, *The Renaissance Philosophy of Giordano Bruno*, who regards Bruno's most original doctrine on the universal form-as-mind as a dialectical aberration.

33. *Concerning the Cause, Principle, and One*, V (Greenberg, 163).

34. *Ibid.*, III, V (Greenberg, 142, 66). That the distinction between God and nature in its substantial constitution is a logical one is shown in Greenberg, *op. cit.*, 21, 24, 75–76, and more at length in E. Namer, *Les aspects de Dieu dans la philosophie de Giordano Bruno*.

35. *Concerning the Cause, Principle, and One*, II (Greenberg, 108–10). The proportionality which Bruno establishes is one between substance and its modal aspects rather than one between substantially distinct existents, and the necessity of inference is based upon an identity between the divine substance and infinite nature rather than upon a known causal relation of dependence. Bruno does not give sufficient consideration to the alternate metaphysical way of reaching God with philosophical rigor through causal inference. Consult St. Thomas, *In Metaphysicam Aristotelis Commentaria*, edited by M. Cathala, O.P., Book VI, Number 1170, p. 355 (also Numbers 398 and 2267), on the identification of philosophy of nature with first philosophy if there were no unchanging and immaterial substance distinct from nature.

36. *On the Infinite Universe and Worlds*, III (Singer, 307–308); cf. *Concerning the Cause, Principle, and One*, V (Greenberg, 169–72).

37. *Concerning the Cause, Principle, and One*, III (Greenberg, 139–40); *On the Infinite Universe and Worlds*, I (Singer, 261–62).

38. *Concerning the Cause, Principle, and One*, V (Greenberg, 166–68); cf. *On the Infinite Universe and Worlds*, Introductory Epistle and Dialogue V (Singer, 244, 377–78), as well as the formally moral dialogues of the London period in Bruno's writing.

39. The medieval theologians had a ladder of being and knowing, but within the context of revelation. Bruno transfers it to a purely philosophical context, from which revelation is positively excluded, and then must found it upon a monistic theory of God and the universe. For a Thomistic approach to Bruno, see L. Cicuttini, *Giordano Bruno*.

Notes for Chapter II

THE SKEPTICAL ASSAULT UPON KNOWLEDGE OF GOD

1. On this connection, see R. H. Popkin, "The Sceptical Crisis and the Rise of Modern Philosophy," *The Review of Metaphysics*, 7 (1953–54), 132–51, 307–22, 499–510.

2. A survey of classical skepticism has been made by M. M. Patrick, *Sextus Empiricus and Greek Scepticism*.

3. See Popkin, Note 1 above; see also E. Gilson, *History of Christian Philosophy in the Middle Ages*, 759, on the medieval Latin translation of Sextus' *Outlines*, which was never effectively circulated. Sir Walter Raleigh translated a portion of the *Outlines* into English. The modern Greek-English edition is in the Loeb Classical Library: [*Works of*] *Sextus Empiricus*, with an English translation by R. G. Bury. All references are to this edition.

4. *Outlines of Pyrrhonism*, I, 12 (Bury, I, 8–9). Cf. V. Cauchy, "The Nature and Genesis of the Skeptic Attitude," *The Modern Schoolman*, 27 (1949–50), 203–21, 297–310.

5. *Outlines of Pyrrhonism*, I, 36–163 (Bury, I, 24–93; the ten major tropes). The aim of this argumentation is to establish that "if the senses do not apprehend external objects, neither can the mind [*dianoia*] apprehend them." *Ibid.*, I, 99 (Bury, I, 59).

6. *Ibid.*, I, 13–14; II, 167–70, 177–82 (Bury, I, 10–11, 258–61, 264–67). See also *Against the Professors (Logicians)*, I, 364–68 (Bury, II, 192–95). In the last of these texts, Sextus argues that nothing existing in itself and apart from our affections can be evident to us.

7. *Outlines of Pyrrhonism*, III, 2–12 (Bury, I, 324–33). *Against the Professors (Physicists)*, I, 13–193 (Bury, III, 8–99).

8. *Outlines of Pyrrhonism*, III, 11 (Bury, I, 333).

9. *On the Nature of the Gods*, III, 39 (in the H. M. Poteat translation, 332). A concise summary of the classical influences on Renaissance skepticism is provided by G. T. Buckley, *Atheism in the English Renaissance*, 1–19. This book analyzes the atheistic and skeptical currents imported into Elizabethan literature, as well as the counter-criticism made with the help of translations of French Calvinist apologetic works. The impact of Continental skepticism upon the seventeenth-century English mind is traced out by L. Bredvold, *The Intellectual Milieu of John Dryden*.

10. The Italian contribution is weighed by J. R. Charbonnel, *La pensée italienne au XVIe siècle et le courant libertin*, especially Chapter 3, on the Paduans. Pomponazzi's chief work, *On the Immortality of the Soul* (W. H. Hay translation), is included in *The Renaissance Philosophy of Man*, edited by E. Cassirer, P. O. Kristeller, and J. H. Randall, Jr., 280–381.

11. On Agrippa, see C. Nauert, "Magic and Skepticism in Agrippa's Thought," *Journal of the History of Ideas*, 18 (1957), 161–82. The early crosscurrents of French skepticism have been charted in H. Busson, *Les sources et le développement du rationalisme dans la littérature française de la Renaissance (1533–1601)*. Montaigne and Charron are located within this movement, 434–59. See also J. Owen, *The Skeptics of the French Renaissance*, a less reliable study.

12. *The Essays of Michel de Montaigne*, II, 12, translated by J. Zeitlin, II, 149. The twelfth essay in Book II is the famous "Apology for Raimond Sebond," which is the main source for Montaigne's philosophical views. Most scholars are now agreed that this was written as an independent expression of skepticism and that the sections of so-called "apology" for Sebond's ultrarationalistic book on natural theology were added as an afterthought. For a fideistic interpretation of Montaigne's religious standpoint, see M. Dréano, *La pensée religieuse de Montaigne*, and D. M. Frame, *Montaigne's Discovery of Man*. For the views of Sebond and Pomponazzi on the study of God, see C. C. J. Webb, *Studies in the History of Natural Theology*, 292–343.

13. *Essays*, II, 12 (Zeitlin, II, 215, 217). Charron is equally outspoken: "The immortality of the soul is the thing most universally, religiously, and plausibly accepted by everyone (I mean by external and public profession, not by an internal, serious, and true belief, of which mention will be made later on), the most usefully believed, [and yet] the most feebly proved and established by human reasons and means." *De la sagesse*, I, xv, 16. This is the first-edition version (1601), printed as an appendix to the third (1607) edition of *De la sagesse* (reprinted at Paris in 1646), 769. All subsequent references are to the 1646 printing of the 1607 edition. The 1729 English translation by G. Stanhope is too free and padded to be useful. For Charron's relationship with Montaigne, see A. M. Boase, *The Fortunes of Montaigne: A History of the Essays in France, 1580–1669*, 77–103. Boase also outlines the criticism of the skeptics by Garasse, Mersenne, and others.

14. *De la sagesse*, II, v, 19 (1646 printing, 394). Charron outlines the probable proofs of God's existence in *Les trois véritez*, I, 6–8, (1593 edition, 27–47). For a general study of Charron, see J. B. Sabrié, *De l'humanisme au rationalisme: Pierre Charron (1541–1603), l'homme, l'oeuvre, l'influence*. The Dryden couplet is from *The Hind and the Panther*, I, lines 104–105, in *Works*, edited by W. Scott and G. Saintsbury, X, 131.

15. *De la sagesse*, I, xiv, 13; II, ii, 6 (1646 printing, 100, 337).

16. *Ibid.*, II, v, 18 (1646 printing, 398–402). On the leading figure in the Christian Stoic movement, consult J. L. Saunders, *Justus Lipsius: The Philosophy of Renaissance Stoicism*.

17. *Essays*, II, 12 (Zeitlin, II, 102).

18. On these men, see R. Pintard, *Le libertinage érudit dans la première moitié du XVIIe siècle*. Pintard includes Gassendi among the erudite libertines and examines his philosophy at length (477–504). His questionable thesis that Gassendi is "a tempted Christian" laboring under "a pathetic duality" of faith and libertinism has been sharply challenged by B. Rochot, *Les travaux de Gassendi sur Epicure et sur l'atomisme, 1619–1658*, 192–95.

19. *Exercitationes Paradoxicae adversus Aristoteleos*, II, vi, 1, in *Opera Omnia*, III,

129a. All references are to the 1658 Lyons edition. The thesis stated in *Exercitatio* vi reads: "Quod nulla sit scientia, et maxime aristotelea."

20. On this project, see Rochot, *op. cit.*, and the brief summary on God and atomism in G. S. Brett, *The Philosophy of Gassendi*, 224–29.

21. For the doctrine in Epicurus, cf. Diogenes Laertius, *Lives of Eminent Philosophers*, X, 33, with English translation by R. D. Hicks, in the Loeb Classical Library, II, 562–63, and N. W. De Witt, *Epicurus and His Philosophy*, 142–50. Gassendi is more faithful to Epicurus than De Witt thinks (356), however, since Gassendi makes sense perception only the stimulating occasion or correlate of the anticipatory ideas.

22. The clearest statement of his natural theology is in *Syntagma Philosophicum*, Part 2 (Physics), I, iv, 2–8 (*Opera Omnia*, I, 287–326). A good account of Gassendi's philosophy is given in G. Sortais, S. J., *La philosophie moderne depuis Bacon jusqu'à Leibniz*, II, 1–269. That Gassendi is the seventeenth-century humanist heir of Montaigne, blending skepticism with moral faith and adding an interest in natural philosophy, is established by G. Hess, *Pierre Gassend: Der französische Späthumanismus und das Problem von Wissen und Glauben*. His scientific contribution is weighed by M. H. Carré, "Pierre Gassendi and the New Philosophy," *Philosophy*, 33 (1958), 112–20.

23. *Syntagma Philosophicum*, I, iv, 2 (*Opera Omnia*, I, 295a).

24. Consult the *Fifth Set of Objections* (by Gassendi) and the *Replies to Objections*, V (by Descartes), in *The Philosophical Works of Descartes*, translated by E. S. Haldane and G. R. Ross, II, 123–233. Gassendi also published his criticism separately under the title *Disquisitio Metaphysica adversus Cartesium* (1644; reprinted in Vol. III of the Lyons edition). Cf. R. Pintard, "Descartes et Gassendi," *Travaux du IXe Congrès International de Philosophie* (12 vols., Paris, Hermann, 1937), II, 115–22.

25. *Traité philosophique de la foiblesse de l'esprit humain*, I, i (1723 edition, 6–21). Huet deduces the imperfection of human certitude from its lack of the supernatural certitude of faith and the beatific vision. All that he proves in this way is that natural reason cannot attain the highest conceivable certitude, not that its certitude is defective in the natural order. His more empirical arguments rest on the principle that the proper and immediate object of the mind is the image or idea, not the real thing. Huet rejects Cartesian innatism for a sensory origin of all ideas (including the idea of God), the resemblance of which to real objects cannot be ascertained with perfect certainty (I, iii; II, iii [1723 edition, 32–36, 194–200]).

26. *Ibid.*, II, xv (1723 edition, 275–80).

27. *De Providentia Numinis et Animi Immortalitate Libri Duo adversus Atheos et Politicos.*

28. *La vérité des sciences contre les septiques* [sic] *ou Pyrrhoniens*, unpaged Preface, 1625 edition.

29. Consult R. Lenoble, *Mersenne ou la naissance du mecanisme*, for his attitude toward modern science.

30. *La vérité des sciences*, I, xi (1625 edition, 134–56).

31. *Ibid.*, I, xv (1625 edition, 195).

32. Mersenne's most orderly and economical treatment of the proofs of God's existence is found in *L'impiété des déistes, athées, et libertins de ce temps*, V (1624 edition, I, 72–120). See R. H. Popkin, "Father Mersenne's War against Pyrrhonism," *The Modern Schoolman*, 34 (1956–57), 61–78, which interprets the phenomenalism of Mersenne as a kind of constructive Pyrrhonism.

33. It is noteworthy that a century later, in his Boylean Lectures (1711–12) on scientific arguments favoring theism, William Derham should appeal to Mersenne as belonging in the tradition of Boyle and Newton. See Derham's *Physico-Theology*, which was first published in 1713, p. viii (see below, Chapter five, note 27).

Notes for Chapter III

GOD AS A FUNCTION IN RATIONALIST SYSTEMS

1. Consult the evaluation by W. J. Ong, S. J., *Ramus, Method, and the Decay of Dialogue*, 306–18.

2. "An Anatomie of the World: The First Anniversary," in *The Poems of John Donne,* edited by H. J. C. Grierson, I, 237. But C. M. Coffin, *John Donne and the New Philosophy,* 90, points out that Donne also gave a religious interpretation to the Copernican system, since it convinces us of man's smallness and his ordination to the spiritual sun, God. On the intertwining of skepticism and faith in seventeenth-century English literature, see M. L. Wiley, *The Subtle Knot,* as well as Bredvold's *The Intellectual Milieu of John Dryden.*

3. *Replies to Objections,* VII, in *The Philosophical Works of Descartes* (Haldane-Ross, II, 334–36); cf. *The Search after Truth* (Haldane-Ross, I, 314–16). Descartes' close acquaintance with Montaigne is established by L. Brunschvicg, *Descartes et Pascal, Lecteurs de Montaigne,* 113–54. Descartes observed that the Fifth Lateran Council of 1512–1517 "expressly orders Christian philosophers to refute their [the Averroists' and libertines'] arguments and to employ all their intellectual abilities to make the truth known." *The Meditations concerning First Philosophy,* Letter of Dedication, translated by L. Lafleur, 4. To the extent that he refuted skepticism and demonstrated God's existence and the mind's immateriality, Descartes claimed to be defending "the cause of God." *Letter to Gibieuf,* November 11, 1640 (*Oeuvres de Descartes,* edited by C. Adam and P. Tannery, III, 238; cf. 240). A thorough investigation of Descartes' religious standpoint has been made by H. Gouhier, *La pensée religieuse de Descartes.*

4. His skillful use of equipollence and his subordination of it to the method of truth are brought out dramatically in Abbé Baillet's account of Descartes' meeting with the papal nuncio in Paris in 1628. The text is given in English by N. K. Smith, *New Studies in the Philosophy of Descartes,* 42–43.

5. *The Principles of Philosophy,* Author's Letter to the Translator (Haldane-Ross, I, 204). Montaigne claimed that only revealed principles are certain, that all philosophical principles are presupposed, and, especially, that metaphysics adopts its principles from physics; cf. *The Essays of Michel de Montaigne,* II, 12 (Zeitlin, II, 202). This forced the rationalists to concentrate upon showing that there are nonhypothetical principles of natural knowledge and that the primary ones are metaphysical. A Thomistic criticism of this concern with principles is given by E. Gilson, "Les principes et les causes," *Revue Thomiste,* 52 (1952), 39–63.

6. The opening chapter of M. Guéroult, *Descartes selon l'ordre des raisons,* stresses the importance of the order in which truths are demonstrated; cf. *ibid.,* I, 154–384, on the proofs of God's existence.

7. *The Meditations concerning First Philosophy,* III, V (Lafleur, 30–47, 58–62); *The Principles of Philosophy,* I, 14–21 (Haldane-Ross, I, 224–28); *Replies to Objections,* II, Appendix (Haldane-Ross, II, 57–58; a geometrical exposition).

8. *Replies to Objections,* V (Haldane-Ross, II, 218). On the distinction between comprehending and understanding the infinite God, consult J. Laporte, *Le rationalisme de Descartes,* 255, 291–92, where it is adduced as an instance of the empirical strain in Descartes. He agreed with Augustine that God is incomprehensible but hastened to add that He is also supremely knowable (understandable) and effable: *maxime cognoscibilis et effabilis* (*Letter to Mersenne,* January 21, 1641 [*Oeuvres,* Adam-Tannery, III, 284]). Unless God were supremely knowable in His attributes, the anchorage for the rationalist deduction would be lost.

9. *The Meditations concerning First Philosophy,* V (Lafleur, 58–59).

10. *Ibid.* (Lafleur, 62–63); cf. *The Principles of Philosophy,* I, 13 (Haldane-Ross, I, 224). On the Cartesian Circle, see M. Versfeld, *An Essay on the Metaphysics of Descartes,* 38–56.

11. The long debate among Cartesian scholars about the respective roles of physics and metaphysics is summarized by S. V. Keeling, *Descartes,* 58–61. The position taken here is that Descartes' prime concern is with the whole body of philosophy, within which a philosophical physics is a systematic outgrowth of metaphysics. He is neither a metaphysician nor a philosophical physicist exclusively, but (to coin a barbarism) a "univocal sapientialist," a philosopher seeking to constitute a total wisdom through a univocal method. All the rationalists are univocal sapientialists.

12. *Replies to Objections,* III, VI (Haldane-Ross, II, 78, 245); *The Principles of Philosophy,* I, 5 (Haldane-Ross, I, 220).

13. *The Principles of Philosophy,* II, 36–37 (in the E. Anscombe and P. T. Geach

translation of Descartes, *Philosophical Writings*, 215–16); *Le Monde*, VII (*Oeuvres*, Adam-Tannery, XI, 36–48). The relevance of God to our world of individual bodies is noted by G. Lewis, *L'individualité selon Descartes*, 52–53, 65. On seventeenth-century attempts to demonstrate the principle of inertia, see J. A. Weisheipl, O.P., *Nature and Gravitation*, 44–64.

14. *Discourse on Method*, VI, translated by L. Lafleur, 41–42. Moral and absolute or metaphysical certitude are contrasted in *The Principles of Philosophy*, IV, 205–206 (Haldane-Ross, I, 301–302). The methodological aspect of physical theory is analyzed by L. J. Beck, *The Method of Descartes*, 230–271; the role of God is emphasized in the unpublished doctoral dissertation of T. P. McTighe, "God and Physics in Galileo and Descartes" (St. Louis University, 1955).

15. The English fideist, Joseph Glanvill, went farther than Descartes by denying that there is any absolute or infallible certainty in physics and affirming that there is only moral or "indubitable" certainty; the laws of physics are hypothetical and pragmatic but arouse no reasonable doubt. He did this explicitly to counteract the tendency of the philosopher of nature "to set bounds to Omnipotence, and to confine infinite power and wisdom to our shallow models." *The Vanity of Dogmatizing*, 211–12; cf. F. Greenslet, *Joseph Glanvill*, 110–11. In *Joseph Glanvill, Anglican Apologist*, 104–26, J. I. Cope stresses his anti-Scholastic and probabilist position.

16. The letters to Mersenne and Mesland on the eternal truths are included in the Anscombe-Geach edition of Descartes, *Philosophical Writings*, 259–63, 291–92. Descartes' suggestion that "God might have made creatures not to be dependent on him" (*ibid.*, 292) contains the seed of the naturalistic development of Cartesianism in the Enlightenment, which effectively cut off the physical and moral worlds from God. The extent to which Descartes' theory of divine power affects his view of certain knowledge is examined by L. Miller, "Descartes, Mathematics, and God," *The Philosophical Review*, 66 (1957), 451–65.

17. In two *Letters to Chanut*, June 15, 1646, and November 20, 1647 (*Oeuvres*, Adam-Tannery, IV, 440–42, and V, 86–88), Descartes grants that he has not yet worked out his ethics, claims that he nevertheless has developed his theory of the passions to the point where it provides certain foundations for morality, and adduces two curious reasons for not setting forth his systematic ethics (it might provide ammunition for his enemies, and in any case only sovereigns have the authority to regulate the conduct of others). The transition from the psychological to the ethical view of man was never achieved in a rigorous way.

18. *Letters VI, LXXIII*, in *The Correspondence of Spinoza*, translated by A. Wolf, 98–99, 343. The alternative is stated by Spinoza as either separation or identification of God and nature, but there is another position of maintaining both God's intimate causal presence in nature and His complete transcendence of it in being.

19. *Ethics*, II, 48–49, the White translation reprinted in *Spinoza Selections*, edited by J. Wild, 195–204. See H. A. Wolfson, *The Philosophy of Spinoza*, II, 164–79. Descartes prepared the ground for Spinoza's identification of intellect and will by teaching that the assent in judgment is an act of will.

20. *On the Improvement of the Understanding*, translated by J. Katz, 28. Consult H. H. Joachim, *Spinoza's Tractatus De Intellectus Emendatione, A Commentary*, 39, on the absolutely individual character of God or nature. As applied here to Spinoza, "monism" means a universe having only one substance although many modes. "Pantheism" means that nature or the unique, impersonal substance is regarded as divine and that the modal things in the world are regarded as affections or determinate expressions of God under a finite form. There is an underlying identity of substance and necessity of action on God's part. These terms have to be adjusted to the given systematic context and cannot be given a univocal definition to cover every historical case. Cf. H. Robbers, S.J., "Wat is pantheïsme?" *Bijdragen der Nederlandse Jezuieten*, 12 (1951), 314–44, and C. E. Plumptre's somewhat uncritical *General Sketch of the History of Pantheism*.

21. *Ethics*, I, Definitions, and Proposition II (Wild, 95, 104). "Perfection" signifies the self-causing power of the infinite essence. It is even more important for Spinoza than for Descartes to hold that God is *maxime cognoscibilis* (cf. Note 8 above). Since we can know some divine attributes, we can obtain a proper and adequate definition

of God's essence and hence can prove His existence a priori, in opposition to Aquinas (*Short Treatise on God, Man, and His Well-Being*, I, 7 [A. Wolf translation reprinted in *Spinoza Selections*, edited by J. Wild, 79–80]). A comparison between the Cartesian and Spinozistic proofs is made by P. Lachièze-Rey, *Les origines cartésiennes du Dieu de Spinoza*, 162–251.

22. *Ethics*, I, 30; II, 11, 45–47 (Wild, 126–27, 155–56, 192–94). On Spinoza's conviction that when the human mind has the idea of God, it is God Himself who has it, see M. Dufrenne, "La connaissance de Dieu dans la philosophie spinoziste," *Revue Philosophique de la France et de l'Étranger*, 139 (1949), 474–85. That Spinoza's definition of God is not existentially self-justifying is noted by G. H. Parkinson, *Spinoza's Theory of Knowledge*, 43–56, and P. Siwek, S. J., *Au coeur du Spinozisme*, 112–41.

23. In studying bodies, Spinoza will "consider those things only which may conduct us as it were by the hand to a knowledge of the human mind and its highest happiness." *Ethics*, II, Prologue (Wild, 143). Hence he defines and analyzes bodies, philosophically, only as modal expressions of God's attribute of extension and as objective correlates of minds.

24. *Ethics*, I, 15, Scholium (Wild, 108–13). Spinoza defended himself against the charge of atheistic materialism by denying that the intelligible extension which is in God is the same as bodily dimensions. But this involved him in an epistemological dualism between the "imaginative" or realistic-theistic way of viewing bodies and the "intellectual" or Spinozistic-pantheistic way—a dualism which remains unaccountable in his system, despite an elaborate theory of imagination and error.

25. *Metaphysical Thoughts*, II, 10, in the H. H. Britan translation of *The Principles of Descartes' Philosophy*, 162; *Letter LVIII* (Wolf, 295); *Ethics*, I, Definitions (Wild, 95).

26. *Letter LXVIIa* (Wolf, 332). The scientific context of Stensen's objection against the geometrical method of deriving the theory of nature is explained by G. Scherz, C.Ss.R., *Vom Wege Niels Stensens*, 107–109. See the exchange between Spinoza and E. W. von Tschirnhaus on whether or not the need to evacuate all empirical meaning from extension as a divine attribute frustrates the deduction of the actual world of bodies: *Letters LXXX–LXXXIII* (Wolf, 361–65).

27. See the fourth and fifth books of the *Ethics* (Wild, 282–400), and A. Darbon, *Études spinozistes*, 135–62.

28. Goethe's "Prooemion" is the introductory poem in his pantheistic series, *God and World* (1816). The lines quoted here were included in Albert Schweitzer's 1932 centennial address, reprinted in his *Goethe, Four Studies*, translated by C. R. Joy (translator's English version of the poem), 49; cf. 66, 107.

29. Substance "is something full and active." *Refutation of Spinoza*, in *Leibniz Selections*, translated by P. Wiener, 487. "The nature of substance consists, in my opinion, in that regulated tendency with which phenomena arise in an orderly fashion." *Further Discussion of Vis Viva* (Wiener, 181). J. F. Mora, "Suarez and Modern Philosophy," *Journal of the History of Ideas*, 14 (1953), 528–47, relates this theory of substance to the *essentia actualis* of Suarez.

30. On Leibniz' first principles and the individual substantial essence, cf. J. Collins, *A History of Modern European Philosophy*, 262–71.

31. *Reflections on Bellarmine*, in *Textes inédits*, edited by G. Grua, I, 301. Leibniz' comments on Bellarmine's *On Grace and Free Choice* are typical of his wide and critical reading in Catholic theologians.

32. Consult the background in the two fragments, *On Freedom*, in Leibniz' *Philosophical Papers and Letters*, translated by L. E. Loemker, I, 404–10, and *De Libertate* (Grua, I, 287–91), as well as the polemical explanation in *Letters to Samuel Clarke*, V (Wiener, 238–39, 264).

33. *The Principles of Nature and of Grace*, 10 (Wiener, 528). As the excellent Geometer of the universe, God spontaneously chooses the mathematically most perfect and economical universe, "the one which is at the same time the simplest in hypotheses and the richest in phenomena." *Discourse on Metaphysics*, VI (Wiener, 297). For Malebranche, this posed the problem of whether a mathematical Deity could ever choose a less perfect and hence mathematically less admirable universe. Chapter 6 of E. Rolland, *Le déterminisme monadique et le problème de Dieu dans la philosophie*

de Leibniz, discusses the ways in which Leibniz and Malebranche tried to reconcile mathematical determinism and divine freedom.

34. *On the Ultimate Origin of Things* (Wiener, 348; italics added). A critical estimate of Leibniz' efforts to save divine and human freedom is given by O. A. Johnson, "Human Freedom in the Best of All Possible Worlds," *The Philosophical Quarterly*, 4 (1954), 147–55.

35. See G. Grua, *Jurisprudence universelle et theodicée selon Leibniz*, 55–72, 530–34, for texts and criticism pertaining to the univocity of rationalist metaphysics. In his *New Essays concerning Human Understanding*, II, xiii, 18, and IV, viii, 9, translated by A. G. Langley, 153–54, 494–96, Leibniz bases natural theology on the laws of being or substance common to God and other things in a generic way.

36. *Theodicy*, Preface, translated by E. M. Huggard, 62. For a philosophical history of the problem of evil, cf. Friedrich Billicsich, *Das Problem des Übels in der Philosophie des Abendlandes*. The second volume includes the period from Eckhart to Hegel, and a third volume will lead into the contemporary discussion on evil and theodicy.

37. *De la recherche de la vérité*, VII, ii, 3, edited by G. Lewis, II, 201. Of the typical Scholastic and the Cambridge Platonist, Malebranche observed: "If his heart is Christian, at bottom his mind is pagan." *Ibid.* (Lewis, II, 198). On Malebranche's extreme position on faith and reason and his consequent oscillation between fideism and rationalism see A. Decourtray, "Foi et raison chez Malebranche," *Mélanges de science religieuse*, 10 (1953), 67–86. For his efforts to avoid the charge that his definition of nature and extension leads to Spinozism, see Malebranche's *Correspondance avec J. J. Dortous de Mairan*, edited, with a highly informative Introduction, by J. Moreau. Mairan was struck by the similarities between the two systems.

38. "Because God is bound to act in a simple and uniform way, he had to make general laws and the simplest ones possible. . . . The efficacy of these [eternal, divine] decrees is determined to action only by the circumstances of those causes which are called 'natural,' and which I think should be called 'occasional.' " *Dialogues on Metaphysics and on Religion*, VII, xii, and VIII, ii, translated by M. Ginsberg, 191, 204. Malebranche's opponent, Bishop Fénelon, argued that the equation between divine perfection and mathematical simplicity leads to a necessary act of creation, despite Malebranche's stipulation of a free intervention of the divine will; cf. H. Leclère, P.S.S., "Fénelon, critique de Malebranche," *Revue Thomiste*, 53 (1953), 347–66.

39. *Dialogues on Metaphysics and on Religion*, II, v (Ginsberg, 90). In *ibid.*, II, i (Ginsberg, 87), the Augustinian argument from the need of eternal truths to have an immutable and necessary foundation in the divine mind is employed. H. Gouhier, *La philosophie de Malebranche et son expérience religieuse*, 312–52, stresses the need to relate the theory of the vision of God to a meditative religious context, as in the case of Augustine and Anselm. For a modern restatement of Malebranche's notion of the idea of the infinite, as an inchoative grasp of the infinite being, see Louis Lavelle's *La présence totale*.

40. *De la recherche de la vérité*, III, ii, 5–7 (Lewis, I, 246–59); *Dialogues on Metaphysics and on Religion*, II (in conjunction with the vision of God), III–VI (in conjunction with sensation and scientific knowledge) (Ginsberg, 86–176). Cf. M. Guéroult, *Malebranche*, Vol. I: *La vision en Dieu*, and R. W. Church, *A Study in the Philosophy of Malebranche*, 116–42, on the vision of other things in God. That Malebranche's theocentrism suffers from its occasionalistic and mathematical elements is shown by A. Bremond, S.J., "Le théocentrisme de Malebranche," *Archives de Philosophie*, 6 (1928), 281–303.

41. A brief exposition is given in *Dialogues on Metaphysics and on Religion*, III, vii (Ginsberg, 102–103). One of Malebranche's earliest critics, Abbé Simon Foucher, complained in his *Critique de la Recherche de la vérité*, 34, 116–23, that Malebranche spoke more like a theologian than a philosopher and that the doctrine on vision in God is either a datum of faith or a remote conclusion of scientific inference, but at any rate not a first principle in philosophy. Foucher anticipated Locke's objection that Malebranche does not establish the conformity between our perceptions and the divine ideas and yet that the entire epistemological problem is concentrated in the question of how the modes of perception come to our soul, where alone human knowl-

edge is found. Foucher's own psychological approach to the problem of certitude, based on a mitigated skepticism of the Academic or probabilist variety, is described by R. Popkin, "L'Abbé Foucher et le problème des qualités premières," *Bulletin de la Société d'Étude du XVIIe Siècle*, Number 33 (1957), 633–47.

Notes for Chapter IV

EMPIRICISM AND THE NEUTRALIZING OF GOD

1. Instruction at the English universities was dominated by the Continental textbooks on natural philosophy, the content of which is described by L. Thorndike, *A History of Magic and Experimental Science*, Vol. VII: *The Seventeenth Century*, 372–425. A description of the Cambridge curriculum is provided in W. T. Costello, S.J., *The Scholastic Curriculum at Early Seventeenth-Century Cambridge*, which brings out the relationship between natural philosophy and the theory of God (79–102). Oxford views on sense, intellect, and substance, as related to Locke, are analyzed in the unpublished doctoral dissertation of W. H. Kenney, S.J., "John Locke and the Oxford Training in Logic and Metaphysics" (St. Louis University, 1959).

2. *Of the Proficience and Advancement of Learning, Divine and Human*, II. All references are to *The Philosophical Works of Francis Bacon*, edited by J. M. Robertson; cf. 89–101, on the division of the sciences. Spelling has been modernized throughout. F. H. Anderson, *The Philosophy of Francis Bacon*, 148–59, gives a good summary of Bacon's theory of the sciences pertaining to God and nature.

3. *Of the Proficience and Advancement of Learning, Divine and Human*, II (Robertson, 93–94).

4. English translation of *De Augmentis Scientiarum*, III, iv (Robertson, 459).

5. "The summits, or universal forms, of nature do *in a manner* reach up to God; the passage from metaphysics to natural theology being ready and short." English translation of *De Sapientia Veterum*, VI (Robertson, 829; italics added).

6. English translation of *De Augmentis Scientiarum*, III, ii (Robertson, 456–57).

7. English translation of *De Principiis atque Originibus* (Robertson, 647–48, 664); English translation of *De Sapientia Veterum*, XVII (Robertson, 840). Translation modified.

8. *Essays*, xvi, "Of Atheism" (Robertson, 754).

9. For Hobbes' theory of God, consult *The Elements of Law*, XI, 2–4, edited by F. Tönnies, 41–42; *Leviathan*, I, xi–xii, edited by M. Oakeshott, 68–72; *An Answer to a Book Published by Dr. Bramhall*, in *The English Works of Thomas Hobbes*, edited by W. Molesworth, IV, 306, 349, 384. See also the exchange of views between Descartes and Hobbes: *Replies to Objections*, III (Haldane-Ross translation of *The Philosophical Works of Descartes*, II, 66–74). Richard Peters, *Hobbes*, 240–65, describes Hobbes' position on God and religion.

10. *Journal entry for February 8, 1677*, in *An Early Draft of Locke's Essay*, edited by R. I. Aaron and J. Gibb, 84–89; see also *An Early Draft*, 38 (Aaron-Gibb, 59–60), on the probability of God's existence. This Draft A, as well as Draft B (Note 15 below), was drawn up in 1671, whereas the final *Essay* was not published until 1690.

11. "All that has been said [by Malebranche] amounts to no more but this, that I have those ideas that it pleases God I should have, but by ways that I know not. . . . That *presence* or union of theirs [ideas with the human mind] is not enough to make them seen, but God must *show* or exhibit them; and what does God do more than make them present to the mind when he shows them?" *An Examination of P. Malebranche's Opinion of Seeing All Things in God*, 25, 30, in *Locke's Philosophical Works*, edited by J. A. St. John, II, 428, 433–34; italics added. For a similar objection against the epistemological appeal to an absolute consciousness by Hegelian idealists, see B. P. Bowne, *Theory of Thought and Knowledge*, 54.

12. *An Examination of P. Malebranche's Opinion*, 23 (St. John, II, 427; cf. 445, 464, against pantheism).

13. *An Essay concerning Human Understanding*, I, iii, 8–18, edited by A. C. Fraser, I, 95–107.

14. *Ibid.*, II, xv, 2–4; xvii; xxiii, 33–36 (Fraser, I, 258–61, 276–93, 418–21); the background is supplied in *An Early Draft of Locke's Essay*, 45, (Aaron-Gibb, 71–73).

15. *An Essay concerning the Understanding, Knowledge, Opinion, and Assent,* 94, edited by B. Rand, 207, 208. This is Draft B (also 1671) of the final *Essay*.

16. *Journal* entry for July 29, 1676, in *An Early Draft of Locke's Essay* (Aaron-Gibb, 81–82). On Locke's reading of the *Pensées* of Pascal during the 1670's, consult Gabriel Bonno, *Les relations intellectuelles de Locke avec la France,* 59–62. The couplet is from Alexander Pope's *An Essay on Man,* IV, 315–16, edited by Maynard Mack, 158. See Mack's Introduction, xxiii–xlvi, on Pope's relation to contemporary theodicy, ethics, and skepticism.

17. *Essays on the Law of Nature,* IV, edited by W. von Leyden, 150–55; manuscripts written *ca.* 1660–1664. See also *An Essay concerning Human Understanding,* IV, x (Fraser, II, 306–24). As preparatory work for his final position in the *Essay,* Locke translated the proof in Pierre Nicole's *Essais de morale* (vols. 1–2, 1671) and transcribed the arguments pro and con in Ralph Cudworth's *The True Intellectual System of the Universe* (1678). (Hume also consulted Cudworth but was mainly impressed by the atheistic arguments; see Note 30 below.) On the historical background, see W. von Leyden, "Locke and Nicole: Their Proofs of the Existence of God and Their Attitude toward Descartes," *Sophia,* 16 (1948), 41–55. Locke's own demonstration was immeasurably strengthened for the eighteenth-century reader after the appearance of Isaac Newton's famous affirmation of theism in the General Scholium appended to the second edition (1713) of his *Mathematical Principles of Natural Philosophy.*

18. *An Essay concerning Human Understanding,* IV, x, 10 (Fraser, II, 315). The hypothesis of a finite God was not taken very seriously until Hume argued for it.

19. *Ibid.,* IV, iii, 6 (Fraser, II, 192–98); see also the relevant sections from the *Controversy with the Bishop of Worcester* (Stillingfleet), in *Locke's Philosophical Works* (St. John, II, 357–77, 386–411). The relevance of Locke's epistemology to the controversy over English deism is examined by J. W. Yolton, *John Locke and the Way of Ideas;* see pp. 148–66 for discussion of thinking matter.

20. *Essays on the Law of Nature,* IV (von Leyden, 157); cf. *The Second Treatise of Civil Government,* XI, 135, in *Two Treatises of Government,* edited by T. I. Cook, 190. Cf. J. W. Lenz, "Locke's Essays on the Law of Nature," *Philosophy and Phenomenological Research,* 17 (1956–57), 105–13.

21. *A Treatise concerning the Principles of Human Knowledge,* I, 156, in *The Works of George Berkeley,* edited by A. A. Luce and T. E. Jessop, II, 113. All references are to this edition of the *Works.*

22. *Ibid.,* I, 91 (*Works,* II, 81); *Three Dialogues between Hylas and Philonous,* III (*Works,* II, 235).

23. *A Treatise concerning the Principles of Human Knowledge,* I, 142 (*Works,* II, 106). On immortality, cf. *ibid.,* I, 141 (*Works,* II, 105–106).

24. Consult the highly critical but accurate study by I. Hedenius: *Sensationalism and Theology in Berkeley's Philosophy,* and M. Guéroult, *Berkeley: Quatres études sur la perception et sur Dieu.* Guéroult maintains that the theistic grammar of nature in Berkeley results from his steady evolution from Locke toward Malebranche. But his theistic view of nature is present from the beginning and requires no abandonment of his theory of sense perception and causality in favor of Malebranche.

25. L. Paul, *The English Philosophers,* 126. For Berkeley's theistic handling of the problems of intermittent existence and reality versus fantasy, consult *A Treatise concerning the Principles of Human Knowledge,* I, 6, 28–36, 45, 48, 146–47 (*Works,* II, 43, 53–56, 59, 61, 107–108). Objects are either actually perceived or at least perceivable by us and are necessarily perceived by God. The meaning of "perception" and "vision," as applied to God's unreceptive mind, is not fully clarified by Berkeley.

26. *Philosophical Commentaries,* 794 (*Works,* I, 95). On the difference between God as causing ideas and as speaking to us through them, cf. D. Grey, "Berkeley on Other Selves," *The Philosophical Quarterly,* 4 (1954), 28–44. The theory of scientific laws is outlined in *A Treatise concerning the Principles of Human Knowledge,* I, 101–109 (*Works,* II, 85–89), and developed at more length in the treatise *Of Motion* (English translation of *De Motu, Works,* IV, 31–52). In the *Philosophical Commentaries,* there are several direct citations of Spinoza, whom Berkeley knew better than did the other

British empiricists and whose pantheistic determinism and impersonalism he was anxious to avoid by taking an inductive, nonintuitive approach to God. The poem quoted in the next paragraph is "Frost at Midnight," in *The Poems of Samuel Taylor Coleridge*, edited by E. H. Coleridge, 242. For the English poetical witness to God, see H. N. Fairchild, *Religious Trends in English Poetry*, from 1700 to 1880.

27. Berkeley's chief present-day follower, A. A. Luce, remarks that "for practical purposes the God-given character of sensible things is an absolute criterion." *Berkeley's Immaterialism*, 111. In strict speculative theory, however, this criterion is inadequate, since it both underlies the New Principle and is its chief conclusion.

28. *Philosophical Commentaries*, 508 (*Works*, I, 63; punctuation modified). In establishing God's personal nature, Berkeley admits that "all the notion I have of God, is obtained by reflecting on my own soul, heightening its powers, and removing its imperfections. I have, therefore, though not an inactive idea, yet in my self some sort of an active thinking image of the Deity." *Three Dialogues between Hylas and Philonous*, III (*Works*, II, 231–32). Berkeley does mention analogy, but his heightening of spiritual qualities (like Locke's enlarging of ideas of quantity) is a matter of degree. The danger in Locke's case is to identify divine infinity with a magnified quantity, whereas Berkeley's pitfall is to depict God as a magnified human self. Although neither thinker will accept this consequence literally, the hypothesis of a finite God does not seem absurd to their philosophical heir, David Hume. A Thomistic evaluation of Berkeley's natural theology will be found in E. A. Sillem, *George Berkeley and the Proofs for the Existence of God*, 184–224.

29. *Passive Obedience*, 6, 7 (*Works*, VI, 20, 21).

30. E. C. Mossner, "Hume's Early Memoranda, 1729–1740. The Complete Text," *Journal of the History of Ideas*, 9 (1948), 492–518; cf. Section II, items 14, 16, 31, 35, 37. Also E. C. Mossner, *The Life of David Hume*, 78–80, on Hume's early readings in theism and atheism (see Note 17 above, on Cudworth). Fénelon's book also strongly influenced Berkeley, in his view of God as a directly perceived personal presence, as indicated by J. Wild, *George Berkeley*, 217–18.

31. *An Enquiry concerning Human Understanding*, II, edited by L. A. Selby-Bigge, 19.

32. *Ibid.*, XII, i (Selby-Bigge, 153).

33. *A Treatise of Human Nature*, I, iv, 5, and Appendix, edited by L. A. Selby-Bigge, 248–49, 633, Note 1.

34. For these doctrines, cf. *ibid.*, I, iii, 1–8 (Selby-Bigge, 69–106); *An Enquiry concerning Human Understanding*, IV–VII (Selby-Bigge, 25–79). The application to proofs of God's existence is made in *Dialogues concerning Natural Religion*, IX, edited by N. K. Smith, 189–90. The direct object of Hume's attack was the set of proofs offered in Samuel Clarke's Boylean Lectures and the theistic interpretation of Newton's system by Colin Maclaurin (see below, Chapter five, Notes 27 and 31). The historical background of Hume's *Dialogues* is treated by A. Leroy, *La critique et la religion chez David Hume*, 113–15, 248–65, and R. Hurlbutt, "David Hume and Scientific Theism," *Journal of the History of Ideas*, 17 (1956), 486–97.

35. *Dialogues concerning Natural Religion*, IX (Smith, 189).

36. *An Abstract of a Treatise of Human Nature*, edited by J. M. Keynes and P. Sraffa, 24.

37. *Dialogues concerning Natural Religion*, XII (Smith, 214–28).

38. *Ibid.* (Smith, 227).

39. *Letter to William Mure*, June 30, 1743, in *New Letters of David Hume*, edited by R. Klibansky and E. C. Mossner, 13; use of capitals modified.

40. *Essays on the Intellectual Powers of Man*, V, vii, in *The Works of Thomas Reid*, edited by Dugald Stewart, II, 358. In Reid's estimation, the only exception to the pervasive Cartesian influence is Claude Buffier, S.J. (1661–1737), who "has the honour of being the first, as far as I know, after Aristotle, who has given the world a just treatise upon first principles." *Ibid.* (*Works*, II, 358–59). In his *Traité des premières véritez et de la source de nos jugemens*, Buffier reached a sort of common-sense fideism, guaranteeing all our inferences in terms of principles held through common sense or the disposition of our own nature. He rejected the Cartesian demonstrations of God's existence on the ground that all demonstration is an ideal geometrical deduction

about essences in our mind. This left him with faith and a probable argument from design as the ways to God's existence—a position not far removed from that of the Scottish school.

41. *Essays on the Active Powers of the Human Mind,* IV, iii (*Works,* III, 187).

42. *Outlines of Moral Philosophy,* II, ii, 1, Articles 1 and 2, and *The Philosophy of the Active and Moral Powers of Man,* III, 1–3, in *The Collected Works of Dugald Stewart,* edited by Sir William Hamilton, VI, 44–68, and VII, 4–160.

Notes for Chapter V

THE ENLIGHTENMENT: BATTLEGROUND OVER GOD

1. In *The Philosophy of the Enlightenment,* translated by F. Koelln and J. Pettegrove, 136, E. Cassirer applies to the religious thought of this era Goethe's remark that the main theme of history is the conflict between belief and disbelief, although Cassirer adds that the Enlightenment experiments with new, secular forms of belief. A prime instance of this conflict centers around the Jesuit editor G. F. Berthier, whose complex relations with the Encyclopedists are examined by J. Pappas in *Studies on Voltaire and the Eighteenth Century,* Vol. III: *Berthier's Journal de Trévoux and the Philosophes.*

2. *Dictionnaire historique et critique,* Éclaircissement III, "Third edition," IV, 3004. In his study, *Pierre Bayle (Sämmtliche Werke,* VI, 158–59), Ludwig Feuerbach calls Bayle "an intellectual ascete, a spiritual flagellant, . . . in contradiction with himself," for accepting both subjective faith and critical reason. The entire problem is reviewed by W. H. Barber, "Pierre Bayle: Faith and Reason," in *The French Mind,* edited by W. Moore, R. Sutherland, and E. Starkie, 108–25; see also R. H. Popkin, "The Skeptical Precursors of David Hume," *Philosophy and Phenomenological Research,* 16 (1955–56), 61–71.

3. *Theses Philosophicae,* IX–XII; *Synopsis Metaphysicae,* II, iii, 2 (*Oeuvres diverses,* IV, 138–44; 516–19). The scattered references to God's existence in the *Dictionary* are analyzed by J. Delvolvé, *Religion critique et philosophie positive chez Pierre Bayle,* 268–71. The most extensive eighteenth-century criticism of Bayle's views on the existence of God was made by J. P. de Crousaz, *Examen du pyrrhonisme ancien et moderne,* 414–51. Hume drew much of his information about skepticism from this treasury and was not highly impressed by Crousaz' defense of the almost universal acceptance of the idea of God, its political usefulness, and its causal basis.

4. *Supplement du Commentaire philosophique,* XV (*Oeuvres diverses,* II, 527). Bayle adds that in practice, this bent of the mind is not so much a great perfection as a great weakness, since it relates us to particular truths only by way of appearance.

5. *Commentaire philosophique,* II, i (*Oeuvres diverses,* II, 396). On the various types of truths and first principles, cf. *ibid.,* I, i (*Oeuvres diverses,* II, 367–70); *Supplement du Commentaire philosophique,* XXIV (*Oeuvres diverses,* II, 546); *Logica,* VI, X (*Oeuvres diverses,* IV, 239, 256).

6. *Dictionnaire historique et critique,* Éclaircissements II and III ("Third edition," IV, 2992, 3005). On the problem of evil, see *Selections from Bayle's Dictionary,* edited by E. Beller and M. Lee, Jr., "Manichees," 157–83. After reviewing the various rational solutions, Bayle concluded that reason "can only discover to man his ignorance and weakness, and the necessity of another revelation, which is that of the Scripture." (Beller and Lee, 177.) On Bayle's system of cross-references, consult H. Robinson, *Bayle the Sceptic,* especially 200–19, on skepticism, evil, and atheism. The eighteenth-century development of theodicy, from Bayle and Leibniz to Kant and Goethe, is traced in Hans Lindau's *Die Theodicee im 18. Jahrhundert.*

7. "The ideas of natural religion, the ideas of virtue, the impressions of reason, in a word, the light of conscience, may subsist in the mind of man, even after the ideas of the existence of God, and the firm belief of a life to come, are extinguished in it." *Selections from Bayle's Dictionary,* "Knuzen" (Beller and Lee, 155). On Bayle's secular morality, cf. P. Hazard, *The European Mind,* translated by J. May, 284–86.

8. *Commentaire philosophique,* I, i *(Oeuvres diverses,* II, 368).

9. See M. Wundt, *Die deutsche Schulmetaphysik im Zeitalter der Aufklärung,* 122–99.

10. *Discursus Praeliminaris de Philosophia in Genere,* II, #29. This essay is placed at the beginning of the first volume in Wolff's Latin series, *Philosophia Rationalis sive Logica* (the edition used for the entire series is: Verona, Moroni, 1779), 7.

11. The theme of a *sanctum connubium* dominates the first two chapters of the *Discursus Praeliminaris de Philosophia in Genere,* in *Philosophia Rationalis sive Logica* (Verona edition, 1–15).

12. *Philosophia Prima sive Ontologia,* I, ii, 3, #168 (Verona edition, 72). On the notion of being, see *ibid.,* #134–39 (Verona edition, 60–61). Wolff's ontology and natural theology are evaluated from the Thomistic standpoint by E. Gilson in *Being and Some Philosophers,* 113–19, and more at length in *L'être et l'essence,* 163–83.

13. *Theologia Naturalis methodo scientifica pertractata, Pars prior . . . et Pars posterior.* The Prefaces and the Prolegomena explain the Wolffian conception of natural theology; cf. *Discursus Praeliminaris de Philosophia in Genere,* III *(Philosophia Rationalis sive Logica,* Verona edition, 15–28), on the place of natural theology in the parts of philosophy. Wolff's conception of God is studied by M. Campo, *Cristiano Wolff e il razionalismo precritico,* II, 573–663.

14. *Theologia Naturalis,* I, i, #24 (Verona edition, I, 13).

15. After giving his definition of sufficient reason *(Philosophia Prima sive Ontologia,* I, i, 2, #56 [Verona edition, 22]), Wolff promises that it will become clearer in his general discussion of being and existence and in the special cosmological and psychological studies of contingent acts. But in his ontological discussion of existence in terms of possibility and actuality *(ibid.,* I, ii, 3, #170–74 [Verona edition, 73–75]), he relies upon non-philosophical, common notions of the relation between existential act and possibility. And his cosmological and psychological treatments of contingent acts still await philosophical grounding in the theological demonstration of the sufficient reason for the existential actuality of the universe.

16. *Theologia Naturalis,* I, 1, #34 (Verona edition, I, 16).

17. *Ibid.,* I, 1, #72 (Verona edition, I, 28).

18. Cf. *ibid.,* II, i, 1, #5, 6, 12–13 (Verona edition, II, 2–3, 5–6).

19. *Theologia Naturalis,* II, i, 1, #21 (Verona edition, II, 8). Consistently, Wolff maintains that the atheist cannot admit that the notion of God is possible but must regard it as contradictory *(Theologia Naturalis,* II, ii, 1, #413–14 [Verona edition, II, 180]).

20. *Ibid.,* II, i, 1, #27 (Verona edition, II, 9).

21. *Ibid.,* II, i, 4, #349 (Verona edition, II, 153). Wolff observes that philosophers have neglected the notion of the divine will *(Theologia Naturalis,* I, 3, #395 [Verona edition, I, 177]).

22. *Ibid.,* #430 (Verona edition, I, 196).

23. *Theologia Naturalis,* I, 3, #390 (Verona edition, I, 175).

24. The (unpaged) Preface to *Theologia Naturalis,* II, advances this claim.

25. See J. Gurr, S.J., "The Principle of Sufficient Reason in Some Scholastic Systems, 1750–1900," (Unpublished doctoral dissertation, St. Louis University, 1955). For penetrating remarks by Maréchal, see A. Hayen, S.J., "Un interprète thomiste du kantisme: le P. Joseph Maréchal (1878–1945)," *Revue Internationale de Philosophie,* 8 (1954), 449–69.

26. Consult N. L. Torrey, *Voltaire and the English Deists.* The English deist movement is described by J. Orr, *English Deism: Its Roots and Fruits.* Chapter VI (179–220) discusses its impact on the French, German, and American Enlightenment. Voltaire and Lessing are regarded as the prototypes, respectively, of French and German deism by P. Hazard, *European Thought in the Eighteenth Century,* translated by J. May, 402–34.

27. The first text is from the General Scholium to the second edition (1713) of Newton's *Mathematical Principles of Natural Philosophy;* the second is from his letter to Richard Bentley, December 10, 1692. These passages may be consulted conveniently in *Newton's Philosophy of Nature,* edited by H. S. Thayer, 42, 48–49. Newton's views on God are presented in Thayer, 41–67; another collection of the sources is *Isaac New-*

ton's Papers and Letters on Natural Philosophy and Related Documents, edited by I. B. Cohen, 271–394 (including Bentley's sermons against atheism and P. Miller's analysis of Newton's reserved mind on the cause of gravity). Newton's thoughts on God are analyzed and compared with other seventeenth-century views by A. Koyré, *From the Closed World to the Infinite Universe,* 159–276. For a popular explanation by the British Newtonian theist Colin Maclaurin, see *An Account of Sir Isaac Newton's Philosophical Discoveries,* 377–92, underlining the implications in favor of theism. Widely popular at the time of Voltaire's stay in England were the two treatises in which William Derham combed the various scientific and folklore sources for physical evidence supporting the orthodox conception of God: *Physico-Theology: or, a Demonstration of the Being and Attributes of God, from His Works of Creation* (1713) and the 1715 continuation, *Astro-Theology: or, a Demonstration of the Being and Attributes of God, from a Survey of the Heavens.* Like Voltaire, Derham accepted the Newtonian system as highly probable, regarded the inference to God from that system as inevitable for the unprejudiced mind, and hence looked upon atheists as odd or prejudiced minds. "For so manifest a Demonstration of a Deity are the Motions of the Heavens and Earth, that if men *do* not see them, it is a sign of great stupidity; and if they *will* not see, and be convinced by them, it is as plain a sign of their prejudice and perverseness." *(Astro-Theology,* 70). Derham's two books were translated into French in 1726 and 1729. For the theistic use of Newton by Derham, Bentley, Clarke, and other British Newtonians, consult H. Metzger, *Attraction universelle et religion naturelle chez quelques commentateurs anglais de Newton.*

28. Joseph Addison, "Ode on the Spacious Firmament," in *The Spectator,* Number 465, August 23, 1712 (A. Chalmers edition, V, 295).

29. *Éléments de la philosophie de Newton,* I, i (Part I is the *Métaphysique de Newton*), reprinted as an Appendix to Voltaire's *Traité de métaphysique,* edited by H. T. Patterson, 71. During his English period, Voltaire wrote in his Cambridge notebook: "God cannot be proved nor denied, by the mere force of our reason." *Voltaire's Notebooks,* edited by T. Besterman, I, 67; cf. I, 74. But a further study of Newton convinced him that attraction "is a real thing, since one demonstrates its effects and calculates its proportions. The cause of this cause is in God's bosom." *Lettres philosophiques,* XV, edited by R. Naves, 89. The early phase of French Newtonianism is outlined by P. Brunet, *Introduction des théories de Newton en France au XVIIIe siècle.* Voltaire's decisive intervention in 1738 and the ensuing conflict between him and the atheistic Newtonians (Holbach and Diderot) are investigated by R. T. Murdoch, "Newton's Law of Attraction and the French Enlightenment" (Unpublished doctoral dissertation, Columbia University, 1950). For an Aristotelian evaluation of the clash between Cartesian and Newtonian physics, see J. A. Weisheipl, O.P., *Nature and Gravitation,* 87–105.

30. The quotation appears in *Questions sur l'Encyclopédie.* This work is printed as Supplementary Notes (pp. 415–628) to the *Dictionnaire philosophique,* edited by J. Benda and R. Naves; cf. "Fin, Causes finales," Supplementary Notes, 542. Voltaire's most ambitious proofs of God's existence are in Chapter II of *Traité de métaphysique* (Patterson, 6–18). For his defense of some natural knowledge of God, in opposition to Pascal, cf. *Lettres philosophiques,* XXV, Supplement (Naves, 275). His doctrine on God is synthesized by I. W. Alexander, "Voltaire and Metaphysics," *Philosophy,* 19 (1944), 19–48, and R. Lauer, "Voltaire's Constructive Deism" (Unpublished doctoral dissertation, St. Louis University, 1958).

31. Manuscript third draft of sections on freedom for Voltaire's *Traité de métaphysique;* printed in full by I. O. Wade, *Studies on Voltaire,* 105. Wade concludes that for Voltaire, "it is less important to know His [God's] being and attributes than the fact of His existence." (P. 112.) Voltaire's chief target was the influential Boylean Lectures (1704–1705) delivered by the leading English Newtonian, Samuel Clarke: *A Discourse concerning the Being and Attributes of God, the Obligations of Natural Religion, and the Truth and Certainty of the Christian Revelation.* In Proposition V, Clarke maintains that *"though the substance or essence of the self-existent being, is itself absolutely incomprehensible to us; yet many of the essential attributes of his nature are strictly demonstrable, as well as his existence."* (38.) He proceeds to offer quasi-mathematical proofs of numerous physical and moral attributes (38–75, 100–109)

and then gives a rationalized account of revelation. Both Hume and Voltaire challenged the demonstrative character of these proofs.

32. *Le philosophe ignorant,* XX (*Oeuvres complètes de Voltaire,* Moland edition, XXVI, 62).

33. *Lettres philosophiques,* XXV, Supplement (Naves, 290). The hypothesis of a limit upon the divine power and presence is advanced in *Le philosophe ignorant,* XVIII (Moland, XXVI, 60–61). Voltaire suggests that only a divine revelation could decisively rule out the hypothesis of a limited and eternally necessitated God.

34. *Dictionnaire philosophique,* "Dieu," Supplementary Notes (Benda-Naves, 518). That God Himself is the author of not only our moral impulses but also the socially effective idea of God is stressed by Voltaire. "Did He not in short inspire all men united in society with the idea of a Supreme Being, in order that the adoration that we owe to this Being might be society's strongest tie?" *The Questions of Zapata,* English translation by N. L. Torrey, *Voltaire and the Enlightenment: Selections from Voltaire,* 91.

35. *Dictionnaire philosophique,* "Théiste," (Benda-Naves, 399). Rousseau argued that God is just as powerful as He is good and hence that His power is as unlimited as His goodness. Both Voltaire and Rousseau acknowledged a natural, divine providence and immanence, a denial of which did not characterize deism as a whole. The deists were solidly opposed only to a special supernatural providence and a revelation not reducible to reason.

36. Hume's reaction to this incident is reported in E. C. Mossner, *The Life of David Hume,* 483–86.

37. *The System of Nature, or Laws of the Moral and Physical World,* translated by H. D. Robinson (continuous pagination); cf. II, 3 (325–27). The earlier undercurrent of atheistic materialism in France is charted by I. O. Wade, *The Clandestine Organization and Diffusion of Philosophic Ideas in France from 1700 to 1750.* For the case of Jean Meslier, the priest who left a widely circulated atheistic testament, see A. R. Morehouse, *Voltaire and Jean Meslier.*

38. *The System of Nature,* II, 3 (227); Clarke's proofs are treated separately, II, 2 (202–25). On Holbach's atheism, read W. H. Wickwar, *Baron d'Holbach,* 62–91, and V. W. Topazio, *D'Holbach's Moral Philosophy,* 117–32.

39. *The System of Nature,* I, 2 (19; modified). Holbach's scientific studies are weighed by P. Naville, *Paul Thiry D'Holbach et la philosophie scientifique au XVIIIe siècle,* especially 181–200, 228–30.

40. *The System of Nature,* I, 6, and II, 2 (43–44, 213–15). Julien Offray de la Mettrie's theories on moving, sensitive matter, sensationalism, and atheism are set forth in *Man a Machine,* translated by G. Bussey, with extracts from *The Natural History of the Soul.*

41. This transition is followed by A. Vartanian, "From Deist to Atheist: Diderot's Philosophical Orientation," in *Diderot Studies,* I, edited by O. E. Fellows and N. L. Torrey, 46–63. Vartanian argues more at length, in his *Diderot and Descartes,* that the naturalism of the Enlightenment is a scientific methodology and not a metaphysical declaration about the real. "Correctly understood, scientific naturalism was not concerned with a denial of the existence of God, the agency of an ineffable Providence, and similar concepts peculiar to metaphysics, ethics, or theology. It sought basically to prevent the use, or more exactly, the abuse of such notions in the investigation of nature. In doing so, it guaranteed to scientific inquiry the maximum degree of autonomy in the explanation of physical phenomena." (314.) Among the Enlightenment theists, there is a continuation of the empiricists' policy of methodologically excluding God from scientific work and natural philosophy, but Holbach, and sometimes Diderot, goes beyond this standpoint to a metaphysical denial of the reality of God. For an atheistic view of Diderot, see M. Wartofsky, "Diderot and the Development of Materialist Monism," in *Diderot Studies,* II, edited by O. E. Fellows and N. L. Torrey, 279–329. Diderot's handling of God, Providence, and freedom in the *Encyclopedia* is discussed by J. E. Barker, *Diderot's Treatment of the Christian Religion in the Encyclopédie,* 58–70.

42. English translation by L. G. Crocker, *The Embattled Philosopher: A Biography*

of Denis Diderot, 320; cf. 63–67, 95–99, 317–47, on Diderot's complex attitude toward God.

43. *Dictionnaire philosophique,* "Dieu," Supplementary Notes (Benda-Naves, 515); against Holbach, consult *ibid.,* 513–18, 539–42 ("Dieu," "Fin, Causes Finales"). This reply supposes, however, that God is all powerful over matter. The contemporary Catholic reaction to Holbach is exemplified in N.-S. Bergier's *Examen du matérialisme* (first issued in 1771); cf. R. R. Palmer, *Catholics and Unbelievers in Eighteenth Century France,* 214–18.

44. *Correspondance générale,* edited by T. Dufour and P. Plan, II, 324; #300, *Letter to Voltaire,* August 18, 1756.

45. See the monograph by R. Derathé, *Le rationalisme de J.-J. Rousseau,* 36–37, 62–73; see also the more strictly Kantian interpretation by E. Cassirer: *Rousseau, Kant, Goethe,* translated by J. Guttmann, P. Kristeller, and J. Randall, Jr., 43–55, and Cassirer's *The Question of Jean-Jacques Rousseau,* translated by P. Gay, 109–12.

46. *Émile, or Education,* translated by B. Foxley; see the major part of Book IV, pp. 216–79, including the educational and esthetic setting. A critical text and historical commentary are provided in *La "Profession de foi du vicaire savoyard" de Jean-Jacques Rousseau,* edited by P.-M. Masson. Other commentaries are made by C. A. Hendel, *Jean-Jacques Rousseau, Moralist,* II, 124–162; E. H. Wright, *The Meaning of Rousseau,* 113–64; F. C. Green, *Jean-Jacques Rousseau,* 242–59.

47. *Émile, or Education,* IV (Foxley, 235, 237, 243). On God and a providential order, see P. Burgelin, *La philosophie de l'existence de J.-J. Rousseau,* 402–28.

48. Rousseau's advice for Émile is "to bear in his heart virtue, not only for the love of order which we all subordinate to the love of self, but for the love of the Author of his being, a love which mingles with that self-love." *Émile, or Education,* IV (Foxley, 279). Since self-love is the root of all virtue, Rousseau faces the problem of *eros* and *agape.* In the opinion of his chief contemporary Catholic critic, N.-S. Bergier, Rousseau resolves the moral and religious question in terms of a theistic but antisupernatural rationalism. The basic principle of Rousseau's philosophy is that *"God can only reveal to us, and we ought only to believe, that which is demonstrated as true* [by natural reason and inner feeling]. Since the Catholic doctrine on the Fall of man and original sin shocks your reason, you have rejected it, to substitute for it this fundamental dogma: *that man is a naturally good being, loving justice and order, and that there is no original perversity in the human heart.* It is on this maxim that you have built your new plan of education." *Le Déisme réfuté par lui-même* (first issued in 1765), I, 7–8. Bergier's popular work thus challenged Rousseau mainly for his theological rationalism or Socinianism, for reducing the content of faith to the natural evidence of moral reason and sentiment; cf. Derathé, *op. cit.,* 142–43, 150–62.

49. Immanuel Kant, *Prolegomena to Any Future Metaphysics,* 44, translated by P. G. Lucas, 95.

Notes for Chapter VI

KANT ON GOD

1. An informative survey is provided in F. E. England, *Kant's Conception of God,* and in J. Kopper, "Kants Gotteslehre," *Kantstudien,* 47 (1955–56), 31–61. The latter shows the persistence in Kant of a nonspeculative conviction about God's supersensuous reality, as the term for the human search for a good which transcends the whole order of nature.

2. This connection was brought out forcibly by M. Stefanescu, *Essai sur le rapport entre le dualisme et le théisme de Kant.*

3. *Universal Natural History and Theory of the Heavens,* or *An Essay on the Constitution and Mechanical Origin of the Whole Universe, Treated according to Newton's Principles,* Preface; English translation by W. Hastie in *Kant's Cosmogony,* 20.

4. *Ibid.* (Hastie, 26).

5. *A New Exposition of the First Principles of Metaphysical Knowledge,* II, vi, scholium; English translation in England, *Kant's Conception of God,* 223–24.

6. "The notion of the sea-unicorn is an experiential concept, that is, the notion of

an existing thing. Wherefore, also, in order to establish the validity of this proposition about the existence of such a thing, one does not search into the concept of the subject, since there one finds only predicates of possibility, but into the origins of the knowledge which I have of it. One says: I have seen it, or I have accepted it from those who have seen it." *Der einzig mögliche Beweisgrund zu einer Demonstration des Daseins Gottes,* I, i, 1, in the Prussian Academy edition of Kant's *Gesammelte Schriften,* II, 72–73. All German references are to this edition.

7. *Versuch, den Begriff der negativen Grössen in die Weltweisheit einzuführen,* General Note *(Gesammelte Schriften,* II, 202).

8. *Der einzig mögliche Beweisgrund,* III *(Gesammelte Schriften,* II, 155–63).

9. *A New Exposition of the First Principles of Metaphysical Knowledge,* II, vii, scholium (England, 225). Cf. *Der einzig mögliche Beweisgrund,* I, ii *(Gesammelte Schriften,* II, 77–81), for the most extensive treatment of this proof.

10. *An Inquiry into the Distinctness of the Principles of Natural Theology and Morals,* I, 4; English translation by L. W. Beck, *Critique of Practical Reason and Other Writings in Moral Philosophy,* 268. In *Dreams of a Spirit-Seer Illustrated by the Dreams of Metaphysics,* II, ii (English translation by E. F. Goerwitz, edited by F. Sewall, 113–14), Kant speaks about clipping off the butterfly wings of metaphysics so that men can walk on the solid ground of experience, common sense, and moral faith. The maxim that one must deny (pseudo-) knowledge of God in order to make room for (genuine) rational faith in Him has a long history in Kant's intellectual growth, reaching back to his early skepticism about transcendent metaphysics and natural theology.

11. The matter-form analysis of knowledge is applied to sense perceptions (involving the forms of space and time) in the inaugural dissertation of 1770: *On the Form and Principles of the Sensible and Intelligible World,* II, 4; English translation by J. Handyside, *Inaugural Dissertation and Early Writings on Space,* 44–45. This approach is extended to the categories or forms of the understanding in *Critique of Pure Reason,* A 84–130: B 117–69; English translation by N. K. Smith, 120–75. Kant allows empirical determinations in the particular propositions of physics and other natural sciences, but from the critical standpoint they can be accommodated only relatively, through the regulative use of the analogies of experience, and hence do not constitute strict knowledge. Empirical generalizations are not constitutive of the entire system of physical knowledge.

12. See Kant's own summary in *Prolegomena to Any Future Metaphysics,* 20–22; English translation by P. G. Lucas, 58–64.

13. "Now all our intuitions are sensible; and this knowledge, in so far as its object is given, is empirical. But empirical knowledge is experience. *Consequently, there can be no a priori knowledge, except of objects of possible experience.* . . . Only our sensible and empirical intuition can give to them [concepts of the understanding] body and meaning." *Critique of Pure Reason,* B 149, B 165–66 (Smith, 163, 173–74). "By 'the sensible' I understand nothing more than that which can be an object of experience. . . . Experience is the knowledge of the objects of the senses as such, i.e., through empirical presentations of which one is made aware (through connected perceptions)." *Welches sind die wirklichen Fortschritte, die die Metaphysik seit Leibniz'ens und Wolff's Zeiten in Deutschland gemacht hat? (Gesammelte Schriften,* XX, 274, 316). This prize essay (written about 1793 and published posthumously in 1804) is a valuable summary of Kant's theory of knowledge in its metaphysical implications and his conception of the nature of the metaphysics and natural theology of the Leibniz-Wolff school.

14. The most concentrated summary is in *ibid. (Gesammelte Schriften,* XX, 316-17). That the Kantian description of metaphysics does not fit Aristotle's conception of that science is brought out by N. Rotenstreich, "Kant's Concept of Metaphysics," *Revue Internationale de Philosophie,* 8 (1954), 392–408.

15. *Critique of Pure Reason,* A 642–48: B 670–76 (Smith, 532–36).

16. *Critique of Practical Reason,* I, ii, 2, Section vii (translation by L. W. Beck, 243).

17. *Critique of Pure Reason,* A 584–90: B 612–18 (Smith, 495–99). The analysis is continued in the discussion of the cosmological argument, *ibid.,* A 604–608: B 632–36 (Smith, 508–10). A clear account of Kant's criticism of natural theology and his constructive, speculative use of the idea of God is given by H. W. Cassirer, *Kant's First Critique,* 312–57.

18. *Welches sind die wirklichen Fortschritte (Gesammelte Schriften,* XX, 330).

19. *Critique of Pure Reason,* A 158: B 197 (Smith, 194). The need to conform speculative reasoning with the fourfold empirical principle is emphasized in Kant's criticism of the ontological proof, *ibid.,* A 597: B 625, Note *a* (Smith, 503), but it underlies
his entire approach. An interesting attempt was made by O. Herrlin, *The Ontological
Proof in Thomistic and Kantian Interpretation,* to determine whether there is a veiled
ontological argument in Aquinas. Unfortunately, the modern Thomists upon whom
Herrlin relied led him to think that for St. Thomas, existence is a predicate and in
God is an essential predicate (*op. cit.,* 31, 37), thus raising some otherwise avoidable
difficulties.

20. From a modified idealist standpoint, A. C. Ewing, "Kant's Attack on Metaphysics," *Revue Internationale de Philosophie,* 8 (1954), 371–91, inquires whether
experience has implications that go beyond the empirical element in experience and
hence whether objects are analyzable only in phenomenalist terms. The overruling
physicalism behind Kant's notion of a valid metaphysics prevents him from acknowledging a distinctive metaphysical study of experienced objects and their implications.
This attitude is apparent in his parenthetical remark that metaphysics "only contains
the pure a priori principles of physics in their universal import." *Critique of Practical
Reason,* I, ii, 2, Section vii (Beck, 240). His transcendental metaphysics would merely
formalize and generalize the findings of physics, in epistemological terms, instead of
securing its own view of the experiential data as such.

21. The purely phenomenal and relational significance of knowable necessary existence is brought out in the following text: "It is not, therefore, the existence of *things*
(substances) that we can know to be necessary, but only the existence of their *state;*
and this necessity of the existence of their state we can know only from *other states,*
which are given in perception, in accordance with empirical laws of causality." *Critique
of Pure Reason,* A 227: B 279–80 (Smith, 248; italics added). This is an a priori, phys-
icalist conception of necessary existence, so that by the very terms of the approach, the
only object whose existence can be known with necessity is some finite, phenomenal effect within the natural order. Even here Kant's theory of knowledge permitted only a
relative, a priori anticipation of the actual perceptions that manifest actual existents.
The actual existence of sense appearances is not subject to strict knowledge but only to
the regulative use of the analogies of experience. The gap between the possible conditions of experience and the actual exercise of the act of existing is never closed by means
of speculative knowledge, since this act escapes the reach of physics and hence also of
critical philosophy. Cf. *Critique of Pure Reason,* A 178–79: B 221–22, A 225–26: B
272–74 (Smith, 210, 243).

22. See *Critique of Pure Reason,* A 559–65: B 587–93 (Smith, 479–83); *Welches sind
die wirklichen Fortschritte (Gesammelte Schriften,* XX, 277, 335).

23. *Critique of Pure Reason,* A 686–87: B 714–15 (Smith, 560; second set of italics
added). See R. McRae, "Kant's Conception of the Unity of the Sciences," *Philosophy
and Phenomenological Research,* 18 (1957–58), 1–17.

24. *Prolegomena to Any Future Metaphysics,* 57 (Lucas, 124; cf. 122–28). G. Martin,
Kant's Metaphysics and Theory of Science, translated by P. Lucas, 158–70, brings out
the analogical use of the idea of God, but without stressing the new meaning for
analogy as isolated from causal relations. E. K. Specht, *Der Analogie-begriff bei Kant
und Hegel,* shows that Kant retains some sort of analogy because of his theistic distinction between the temporal appearances and the eternal, which idealism tries to
overcome and in doing so disintegrates even a noncausal analogy.

25. *Critique of Pure Reason,* B xxx (Smith, 29).

26. *Ibid.,* A 822: B 850 (Smith, 646). For the influence of Hamann and Jacobi on
Kant's doctrine of faith, cf. P. Merlan, "Hamann et les dialogues de Hume," *Revue de
Métaphysique et de Morale,* 59 (1954), 285–89; L. Lévy-Bruhl, *La philosophie de Jacobi,*
174–204.

27. *What is Orientation in Thinking?* (Beck's translation, in *Critique of Practical
Reason and Other Writings in Moral Philosophy,* 290, n.). When Hamann's follower,
Thomas Wizenmann, argued that we can be fooled just as much by the need for God as
by that for love or food, Kant replied by distinguishing between a merely contingent,
subjective, pragmatic need and an objectively (i.e., universally and necessarily) deter-

mined, practical need, expressive of the entire dynamism of practical reason. (*Critique of Practical Reason*, I, ii, 2, Section viii [Beck, 245, n.]). From this latter standpoint, Kant admired Rousseau as the discoverer of order in the moral world, the compeer of Newton in justifying God. Nevertheless, Kant was also aware of the sentimentalism derivable from Rousseau.

28. *Critique of Pure Reason*, A 632–34: B 660–62, A 814–16: B 842–44 (Smith, 526, 541–42).

29. *Critique of Practical Reason*, I, ii, 2, Sections iv–v (Beck, 226–28). For other texts, consult R. Whittemore, "The Metaphysics of the Seven Formulations of the Moral Argument," *Tulane Studies in Philosophy*, 3 (1954), 133–61. Whittemore sees that this inference establishes the real existence of God, but he adds that this gives to God an ontological standing and makes of the moral argument a disguised teleological and cosmological argument. However, Kant explicitly stated that assent is given only to the moral aspect of God's reality and that the view of God as a real cause and just ruler has an exclusively moral origin and significance. Its systematic use can only be regulative outside of the moral sphere, so that no disguised use can be made of it as a speculative argument or a constitutive principle of a system of transcendent metaphysics. Kant wanted to establish the reality of God's moral aspect without entailing any implications for a transcendent metaphysics and hence without covertly reinstating the speculative proofs of God's existence.

30. *Critique of Practical Reason*, I, ii, 2, Sections i and v (Beck, 218, 227–28).

31. *Welches sind die wirklichen Fortschritte* (*Gesammelte Schriften*, XX, 305, 306). The next quotation is from *Critique of Judgment*, Appendix, translated by J. H. Bernard, 336; cf. 325–39. A commentary on Kant's moral argument for God in the second and third *Critiques* is given by K. Marc-Wogau, *Vier Studien zu Kants Kritik der Urteilskraft*, 246–318.

32. *Critique of Practical Reason*, I, ii, 2, Section v (Beck, 229). For a precritical statement of this same view from the standpoint of a naturalized Christian Stoicism, cf. P. A. Schilpp, *Kant's Pre-Critical Ethics*, 111. On the importance of Pietism in Kant's outlook, see pp. 49–52. Kant's naturalization of Christian dogmas is manifest in *Religion Within the Limits of Reason Alone*, English translation by T. M. Greene and H. H. Hudson, especially 110–14, where he establishes the two theses that "ecclesiastical faith has pure religious faith [the religion of pure reason] as its highest interpreter" and that "the gradual transition of ecclesiastical faith to the exclusive sovereignty of pure religious faith is the coming of the kingdom of God."

33. *Critique of Practical Reason*, II, ii, 2, Section vii (Beck, 242).

34. The text of this work (*Über das Misslingen aller philosophischen Versuche in der Theodicee*, 1791) is given in *Gesammelte Schriften*, VIII, 255–71. The only authentic "theodicy" is not a speculative science at all but is found in the human attitude of moral faith in God, together with loyalty and sincerity in confessing our inability to harmonize the workings of God, as creator of nature and as orderer of moral life.

35. The initial documents in the quarrel over Spinoza were collected by H. Scholz: *Die Hauptschriften zum Pantheismusstreit zwischen Jacobi und Mendelssohn*. A representative expression of German Neo-Spinozism is J. G. Herder, *God: Some Conversations*, English translation by F. H. Burkhardt.

36. "These concepts [of the divine attributes and relation to the world] are all contained analytically in the idea of the supreme being which we ourselves fashion. But the task of transcendental philosophy still remains always unresolved: *Does a God exist?*" *Opus Postumum*, I, ii, 1, Entry iv (*Gesammelte Schriften*, XXI, 17).

37. *Ibid.*, I, vii, 4 (*Gesammelte Schriften*, XXI, 99).

38. *Ibid.*, VII, v, 4 (*Gesammelte Schriften*, XXII, 57–58). More reliable than the older commentaries on the *Opus Postumum* by C. C. J. Webb and N. K. Smith is the recent article by G. Schrader, "Kant's Presumed Repudiation of the 'Moral Argument' in the *Opus Postumum*," *Philosophy*, 26 (1951), 228–41. Consult also J. Maréchal, S.J., *Le point de départ de la métaphysique*, Vol. IV: *Le système idéaliste chez Kant et les postkantiens*, 293–301. In the remainder of this volume, Maréchal discusses the relation of Fichte and the other idealists to Kant. Like Pascal's *Thoughts* and Berkeley's *Philosophical Commentaries*, Kant's last writing contains many tentative explorations of other positions and dialectical replies in terms of these positions. This makes the

Opus Postumum difficult to interpret. The guiding principle followed here is that Kant tries to defend the transcendence of God's own real being, in the face of any pantheistic identification of Him either with the substance of nature or with our moral idea of Him. He also tries to retain the dependence of our moral idea of God upon our moral experience of the categorical imperative in order to preclude any theological ethics and any cosmological use of the idea of God in speculative metaphysics. He cannot entirely succeed in these tasks without seeming to weaken the ordination of moral assent to God's own actual moral being, and hence the possibility of pantheistic idealism always looms over Kant's final efforts. He feels the systematic attractiveness of overcoming the bifurcation between the reality of God's being and our speculative and practical ideas of God through an absolutist system, but he also does his best to resist the temptation.

Notes for Chapter VII

GOD AND THE HEGELIAN ABSOLUTE

1. A conspectus of the period is given by R. Kroner, "The Year 1800 in the Development of German Idealism," *The Review of Metaphysics*, 1 (1948), 1–31.

2. A religious interpretation is proposed by W. Dilthey, *Die Jugendgeschichte Hegels*, Vol. IV of his *Gesammelte Schriften*, and a Marxist interpretation by G. Lukács, *Der junge Hegel*. In an article, "Hegel's Early Antitheological Phase," *The Philosophical Review*, 63 (1954), 3–18, W. Kaufmann makes some cautionary historical remarks about one-sided views.

3. *The Positivity of the Christian Religion*, II, 2, in *Early Theological Writings*, translated by T. M. Knox and R. Kroner, 162–63. This translation includes the major pieces from *Hegels theologische Jugendschriften*, edited by H. Nohl.

4. *The Spirit of Christianity*, v, in *Early Theological Writings* (Knox-Kroner, 301). For an informative study of Hegel's early social thought, consult Part I, Chapter 1, of H. Marcuse's *Reason and Revolution: Hegel and the Rise of Social Theory*; see also the political specimens in *The Philosophy of Hegel*, edited by C. J. Friedrich, 523–45.

5. The relevant texts from Nohl, *Hegels theologische Jugendschriften*, are examined by P. Asveld, *La pensée religieuse du jeune Hegel*, 133–83, and by Mother M. C. Wheeler, R.S.C.J., "The Concept of Christianity in Hegel," *The New Scholasticism*, 31 (1957), 338–63. The idealistic interpretations of Christ, as well as the criticism of these interpretations made by Feuerbach and Kierkegaard, are studied in W. Schönfelder, *Die Philosophen und Jesus Christus*, and C. Fabro, C.P.S., "La sintesi idealistica dell' Uomo-Dio," in *Cristo vivente nel mondo*, edited by P. Parente, 341–402.

6. Hegel works out this criticism in his correspondence with Schelling; cf. Letters 7, 8, 14, in *Briefe von und an Hegel*, edited by J. Hoffmeister, I, 13–18, 29–33 (Letters of January and August, 1795).

7. *Glauben und Wissen*, Introduction and Section A ("Kantian Philosophy"), in *Erste Druckschriften*, edited by G. Lasson, 233, 236. Hegel continues his criticism of Kant and his fellow idealists in *Differenz des Fichteschen und Schellingschen Systems der Philosophie*, which is included in Lasson's volume. Cf. J. Maier, *On Hegel's Critique of Kant*; C. Michalson, "The Boundary between Faith and Reason: A Study of Hegel's *Glauben und Wissen*," *Drew University Studies*, 3 (1951), 3–12; J. Hyppolite, "La critique hégélienne de la réflexion kantienne," *Kantstudien*, 45 (1953–54), 83–95.

8. For Fichte's conflict with the authorities at Jena University over the charge of godlessness, see the documents collected by H. Lindau, *Die Schriften zu J. G. Fichte's Atheismus-Streit*. On the two main idealists other than Hegel, see R. W. Stine, *The Doctrine of God in the Philosophy of Fichte*; H. Fuhrmans, *Schellings Philosophie der Weltalter*; W. Schulz, *Die Vollendung des deutschen Idealismus in der Spätphilosophie Schellings*.

9. To the claim that certain truths are above but not against reason, Hegel replies that "one could say that the doctrines as such do not contradict reason, but it is contradictory to reason to believe them" to be above itself. *Volksreligion und Christentum*, 4, in *Hegels theologische Jugendschriften* (Nohl, 54, Note a).

10. See the Preface to *The Phenomenology of Mind*, translated by J. B. Baillie, 80–

88, and the elucidations of J. Hyppolite, *Genèse et structure de la Phénoménologie de l'esprit de Hegel*, 556–60. The centrality of *Geist*, or spirit, for Hegel's entire philosophy is brought out by R. Kroner, *Von Kant bis Hegel*, and T. Steinbüchel, *Das Grundproblem der Hegelschen Philosophie*, Vol. I.

11. *The Logic of Hegel*, translated from *The Encyclopaedia of the Philosophical Sciences*, 163, Addition, translated by W. Wallace, 294 (italics added). This is cited hereafter as *Encyclopaedia Logic*.

12. *Ibid.*, 78 (Wallace, 142). Even the word *con-cept (Be-griff)* connotes an element of dynamic unifying: "The unity which constitutes the essence of the [absolute] concept is recognized to be the original and synthetic unity of apperception, as unity of the 'I think' or of self-consciousness." *Science of Logic*, translated by W. H. Johnston and L. G. Struthers, II, 218. This work is cited only according to the volume and page of the English translation, and throughout, the term *Begriff* is rendered as *concept* instead of *notion*.

13. *Science of Logic* (Johnston-Struthers, II, 400–404); *Encyclopaedia Logic*, 81 (Wallace, 147–48). An explanation of the dialectical method is given in J. Collins, *A History of Modern European Philosophy*, 619–34. For an excellent account of the ontologizing and vitalizing of logic, read J. Hyppolite, *Logique et existence: Essai sur la logique de Hegel*.

14. The Introduction to *Encyclopaedia Logic*, 1–18 (Wallace, 3–29), sketches the nature of philosophy as a system. A penetrating criticism of both absolute systemism and absolute antisystemism is made by P. Weiss, "*Existenz* and Hegel," *Philosophy and Phenomenological Research*, 8 (1947–48), 206–16.

15. *Encyclopaedia Logic*, 85 (Wallace, 157; modified). This is the sense in which Hegel can say: "I am a Lutheran and will remain the same." *Lectures on the History of Philosophy*, Introduction, translated by E. S. Haldane and F. H. Simpson, I, 73.

16. The chief sources for Section 3 are: *Vorlesungen über die Philosophie der Religion*, edited by G. Lasson, and *Vorlesungen über die Beweise vom Dasein Gottes*, edited by G. Lasson. There is an English version of both works: *Lectures on the Philosophy of Religion, together with a Work on the Proofs of the Existence of God*, translated by E. B. Speirs and J. B. Sanderson. All references are to the German editions of *Philosophie der Religion* and *Beweise* because of the critical text and superior arrangement, but the approximately corresponding place in the English translations is also given in parentheses.

17. "Eleusis," lines 31–33, in J. Hoffmeister, *Dokumente zu Hegels Entwicklung*, 381. See J. Hoffmeister, *Hölderlin und Hegel*. On Jacobi's theory of natural faith, see M. M. Cottier, O.P., "Foi et surnaturel chez F.-H. Jacobi," *Revue Thomiste*, 54 (1954), 337–73. Hegel gives a lengthy criticism of Jacobi and the intuitional school in *Encyclopaedia Logic*, 71–73 (Wallace, 133–36).

18. The defects of Wolffian natural theology are set forth in *Encyclopaedia Logic*, 36 (Wallace, 71–75).

19. *Philosophie der Religion* (Lasson, I, 206–24; Speirs-Sanderson, I, 166–72).

20. *Beweise*, Lecture 14 (Lasson, 117; Speirs-Sanderson, III, 303–304). Cf. *Philosophy of Mind, translated from The Encyclopaedia of the Philosophical Sciences*, 564, translated by W. Wallace, 299; this translation is hereafter referred to as *Philosophy of Mind*.

21. *Encyclopaedia Logic*, 194, Addition, and 74 (Wallace, 137, 335; revised). The meaning of mediation is explored by H. Niel, S.J., *De la médiation dans la philosophie de Hegel*.

22. *Philosophie der Religion* (Lasson, I, 218; Speirs-Sanderson, III, 352). There is a long, critical survey of Kant's treatment of the cosmological proof in *Beweise*, Appendix (Lasson, 136–57; Speirs-Sanderson, III, 352). On finitude, cf. *Encyclopaedia Logic*, 81, Addition (Wallace, 150), and *Science of Logic* (Johnston-Struthers, I, 142–44, 149). "The proposition that the finite is of ideal nature constitutes idealism. In philosophy idealism consists of nothing else than the recognition that the finite has no veritable being." *Science of Logic* (Johnston-Struthers, I, 168).

23. *Beweise*, Lecture 10, and Appendix (Lasson, 86, 153; Speirs-Sanderson, III, 236, 259). On this dialectical theory of being, cf. E. Coreth, S.J., *Das dialektische Sein in Hegels Logik*. The Hegelian inference rests on the dialectical identity of the absolute

with finite things, whereas a realistic and theistic inference rests on the causal dependence and analogical likeness of finite things with respect to God, Who is never identified with the finite world. The contrast between the Thomistic "analectic," or analogical similarity seen between the nonidentical finite and infinite acts of being, and the Hegelian "dialectic" is the theme of B. Lakebrink's work, *Hegels dialektische Ontologie und die thomistische Analektik*, especially 86–100, 267–78 (on the proofs of God's existence and the relation between the infinite and the finite).

24. *Beweise*, Lecture 8 (Lasson, 66–74; Speirs-Sanderson, III, 212–20). For synoptic treatments of the three proofs, cf. *Philosophie der Religion* (Lasson, I, 214–24; Speirs-Sanderson, III, 347–59); *Beweise*, Lectures 13–15 (Lasson, 100–123; Speirs-Sanderson, III, 281–312; on the cosmological proof); the Amplifications, dating from Hegel's final year, in *Beweise*, Appendix (Lasson, 158–77; Speirs-Sanderson, III, 328–46, 360–67). A helpful analytic study is made by H. A. Ogiermann, S.J., *Hegels Gottesbeweise*.

25. *Science of Logic* (Johnston-Struthers, II, 70); *Beweise*, Lecture 13 (Lasson, 103; Speirs-Sanderson, III, 285); some italics added.

26. *Science of Logic* (Johnston-Struthers, II, 345). It is noteworthy that Hegel makes his major defense of the ontological proof (as a demonstration) in his logic, which absorbs natural theology as well as metaphysics. Cf. *ibid.* (Johnston-Struthers, I, 98–102; II, 69–70, 343–46); *Encyclopaedia Logic*, 51, 193 (Wallace, 107–109, 329–34).

27. *Beweise*, Lecture 10 (Lasson, 86; Speirs-Sanderson, III, 235–36). Hence I. Iljin, *Die Philosophie Hegels als kontemplative Gotteslehre*, entitles his discussion of Hegel's logical doctrine: "The Divine Logic" (Chapter 9). But Iljin gives a mystical-theosophical interpretation, which is more appropriate to Schelling than to Hegel's speculative dialectic.

28. *Philosophy of Mind*, 549 (Wallace, 275–79). See also, *Reason in History*, I–II, translated by R. S. Hartman, 10–18.

29. *Reason in History*, II (Hartman, 18). See J. Maritain, *On the Philosophy of History*, 19–35, for a criticism of the claim of Hegel and Marx to supply an explanatory philosophy of history.

30. *Philosophy of Right*, 340–48, translated by T. M. Knox, 215–18.

31. *Encyclopaedia Logic*, 212 and 234, Additions (Wallace, 352, 373).

32. *The Phenomenology of Mind* (Baillie, 752–53, 780–82). J. Wahl makes an extensive commentary, *Le malheur de la conscience dans la philosophie de Hegel*, 69–118, relating the theme of God's death to unhappy consciousness and the influence of Boehme and Romanticism.

33. *The Phenomenology of Mind* (Baillie, 795, 798; modified). Hegel was fond of quoting St. Anselm's recommendation: *quod credimus, intelligere studemus*, but he meant that nonthoughtful religious belief must be transformed into philosophical knowledge, at least by men with superior minds.

34. For an outline of this dialectic, see *Philosophy of Mind*, 553–77 (Wallace, 291–316); *Lectures on the History of Philosophy*, Introduction (Haldane-Simpson, I, 61–81). The proper significance of Hegel's dialectical treatment of God and religion is a disputed issue. E. Schmidt, *Hegels Lehre von Gott*, regards Hegel as an orthodox Lutheran in belief but a prisoner of his own dialectic and secularized eschatology in speculative matters. J. McT. E. McTaggart, *Studies in Hegelian Cosmology*, 247–51, calls Hegel the most dangerous rival of Christianity, since he subordinates Christianity to his own philosophical cosmos. G. Dulckeit, *Die Idee Gottes im Geiste der Philosophie Hegels*, asks for a refashioning of the religious idea of God to correspond with the impersonal spirit of the folk or community. Writing from a Marxist viewpoint, A. Kojève, *Introduction à la lecture de Hegel*, maintains that "Hegel is the first to have attempted a complete atheistic and finitist *philosophy*, in respect to man." (525.) The position taken in the present chapter is that Hegel's view is neither Christian nor theistic, neither pantheistic nor atheistic, but a distinctive monism of absolute spirit.

35. *Philosophy of Mind*, 573 (Wallace, 305–15); *Beweise*, Lecture 16 (Lasson, 124–35; Speirs-Sanderson, III, 312–27).

36. Consult F. Grégoire, *Études hégéliennes*, 140–217, on several interpretations of Hegel's absolute idea and the sense in which it leads to an "idealist pantheism" (the absolute subject has no distinctive consciousness but achieves it only through its finite particularizations).

Notes for Chapter VIII

THE EMERGENCE OF ATHEISM

1. Fritz Mauthner, *Der Atheismus und seine Geschichte im Abendlande,* devotes the first three volumes to the medieval and modern antecedents of nineteenth-century atheism. He writes from the atheistic standpoint, includes deism, pantheism, and any other doctrine opposing the ordinary Christian idea of God, and regards atheism as triumphant in our era. For theistic approaches to modern atheism, see H. De Lubac, S.J., *The Drama of Atheist Humanism,* translated by E. M. Riley; J. Maritain, *The Range of Reason,* Chapter 8: "The Meaning of Contemporary Atheism" (103–17); Cornelio Fabro, C.P.S., *Dio,* 39–69. The possibility and modern prevalence of atheism are discussed by P. Descoqs, S.J., *Praelectiones Theologiae Naturalis—Cours de théodicée,* II, 441–524. The atheism analyzed in the present chapter is what Descoqs calls a positive (positively denying), theoretical atheism or dogmatic atheism in the proper sense.

2. These works are: *Toward the Critique of the Hegelian Philosophy; The Essence of Christianity; Preliminary Theses for the Reform of Philosophy; Principles of the Philosophy of the Future. The Essence of Christianity* is quoted here in the English translation by George Eliot (Marian Evans), in the more available reprint edition (New York, Harper Torchbook, 1957). The other works are quoted from Feuerbach's *Sämmtliche Werke,* Vol. II: *Philosophische Kritiken und Grundsätze* (cited hereafter as *Kritiken*). Four recent studies stress his position on God and religion: G. Nüdling, *Ludwig Feuerbachs Religionsphilosophie;* W. B. Chamberlin, *Heaven Wasn't His Destination: The Philosophy of Ludwig Feuerbach;* W. Schilling, *Feuerbach und die Religion;* H. Arvon, *Ludwig Feuerbach ou la transformation du sacré.* Arvon, especially, analyzes his entire philosophy and relates it to Hegel and Marx.

3. *Vorläufige Thesen zur Reform der Philosophie* (*Kritiken,* 244); the complementary principle quoted in the following paragraph is from the same sentence. Most of Feuerbach's liberally sprinkled italics are omitted here. H. N. Fairchild, *Religious Trends in English Poetry,* IV, 6–9, notes Feuerbach's relevance for understanding the affirmation of man's self-sufficiency and man's creation of the idea of God, as these views were represented by the Romantic tendency in Victorian poetry, in contradistinction to the stress of the Christian poets on man's need for God as creator and goal of man.

4. *Grundsätze der Philosophie der Zukunft,* 50 (*Kritiken,* 339); *The Essence of Christianity* (Eliot, 5). See J. Hyppolite, *Logique et existence: Essai sur la logique de Hegel,* 231–47, on the basis which Feuerbach and Marx found in Hegel for interpreting the development of spirit as the deification of humanity and objective nature. See also the interpretation by A. Kojève, quoted above, Chapter 7, Note 34.

5. *The Essence of Christianity* (Eliot, 13; modified). A theological criticism of this book is made by J. C. Osbourn, O.P., and P. H. Conway, O.P., "Pen and Sword versus God," *The Thomist,* 6 (1943), 285–317. See K. Grün, *Ludwig Feuerbach in seinem Briefwechsel und Nachlass,* I, 424–25, where Feuerbach states that he does not deny God, in that he holds that divinity is a real predicate of nature and objectivity. But he does oppose the theistic view that the divine being is a real subject having its own existence, and hence Feuerbach unequivocally denies any God who is actually distinct from man and nature.

6. *The Essence of Christianity* (Eliot, 26). The Lateran Council's statement is: "Inter creatorem et creaturam non potest tanta similitudo notari, quin inter eos major sit dissimilitudo notanda." *Enchiridion Symbolorum,* edited by Denzinger-Bannwart-Umberg-Rahner, Number 432 (p. 202). For Donne's use of the phrase *homo homini Deus,* in a theistic and Christian sense, see *The Sermons of John Donne,* edited by G. R. Potter and E. M. Simpson, vol. VI, Sermon 15, pp. 297–98.

7. *The Essence of Christianity* (Eliot, 189–90; modified). A Thomistic study of the Feuerbachian and Marxian meanings for "universal" and "infinite" is made in C. N. McCoy's "Ludwig Feuerbach and the Formation of the Marxian Revolutionary Idea," *Laval Théologique et Philosophique,* 7 (1951), 218–48.

8. *Grundsätze der Philosophie der Zukunft*, 16, 32 *(Kritiken*, 291, 321); *Vorläufige Thesen zur Reform der Philosophie (Kritiken*, 255); *The Essence of Christianity* (Eliot, 14, 15; modified). For the anti-Hegelian significance, read K. Löwith, "Feuerbach und der Ausgang der klassischen deutschen Philosophie," *Logos*, 17 (1928), 323–47.

9. *Grundsätze der Philosophie der Zukunft*, 15, 16 *(Kritiken*, 289, 292). That this view entails not only the denial of God but also the conception of nature as having its becoming through human history and economic activity, thus preparing for Marx, is brought out by J. Vuillemin, "La signification de l'humanisme athée chez Feuerbach et l'idée de nature," *Deucalion*, 4 (1952), 17–46.

10. Engels' somewhat exaggerated reminiscences are contained in his book, *Ludwig Feuerbach and the Outcome of Classical German Philosophy*, which is included in *Karl Marx, Selected Works*, English edition revised by C. P. Dutt, I, 428–29. For historical and systematic purposes, it is essential to distinguish clearly between Marxism as a loose amalgamation of Marx-Engels-Lenin and Marxism as the personal doctrine of Karl Marx himself. In the former sense, see F. Conklin, "The Marxian Philosophy of God," *The New Scholasticism*, 28 (1954), 38–57. The present chapter restricts itself to the personal views of Karl Marx on God, particularly as stated in the pre-1848 writings, which serve as the common fount of present-day Marxist thinking on God. This early period is analyzed by A. Cornu, *Karl Marx, l'homme et l'oeuvre*; A. Cornu, *The Origins of Marxian Thought*; and H. P. Adams, *Karl Marx in His Earliest Writings*.

11. "Private Property and Communism," in *Three Essays by Karl Marx*, translated by R. Stone, 21. In *Hegel and the Rise of Social Theory*, 273–87, H. Marcuse establishes the continuity of thought with Hegel, as well as the new factors in Marx's *Economic-Philosophical Manuscripts*.

12. This quotation and the next one are from Marx's notes to the Appendix to his doctoral dissertation. The Appendix is: *Kritik der plutarchischen Polemik gegen Epikurs Theologie*, printed in the *Marx-Engels Gesamtausgabe*, edited by D. Riazanov and V. Adoratsky, I, 1, i, pp. 80–81. Marx's attitude toward God and religion is traced by W. Sens, *Die irreligiöse Entwicklung von Karl Marx*, and B. Romeyer, S.J., "L'athéisme marxiste," *Archives de Philosophie*, 15 (1939), 293–353.

13. "Private Property and Communism," *Three Essays by Karl Marx* (Stone, 26; punctuation modified).

14. Cf. Feuerbach: *Vorläufige Thesen zur Reform der Philosophie (Kritiken*, 247–54); *Grundsätze der Philosophie der Zukunft*, 13, 14, 29 *(Kritiken*, 284–89, 313–18). On Marx's intellectual relations with Hegel and Feuerbach, consult S. Hook, *From Hegel to Marx*; F. Grégoire, *Aux sources de la pensée de Marx: Hegel, Feuerbach*; and J. Hyppolite, *Études sur Marx et Hegel*.

15. See S. Hook, *Reason, Social Myths, and Democracy*, 100–101. To emphasize Marx's elimination of God is by no means necessarily to confuse it with a "village atheism" but simply to respect Marx's own specification of speculative alienation in theistic terms. The centrality of atheism in Marx and communist thought is shown by J.-Y. Calvez, S.J., *La pensée de Karl Marx*, 55–102, 536–55.

16. "Theses against Feuerbach," VII, VIII, the version appended to *The German Ideology, Parts I and III*, translated by R. Pascal, 199.

17. "Toward the Critique of the Hegelian Philosophy of Right," in Karl Marx, *Selected Writings in Sociology and Social Philosophy*, edited by T. Bottomore and M. Rubel, 27. Part One of *The German Ideology* (Pascal, 3–78) gives a concentrated philosophical exposition of Marx's dialectical-historical materialism. The naturalistic context of Marxian atheism in general is brought out by H. B. Acton, *The Illusion of the Epoch: Marxism-Leninism as a Philosophical Creed*, 51–71, 116–33 (with reference to the debt of Marx to Feuerbach).

18. *On the Fourfold Root of the Principle of Sufficient Reason*, VIII, 50, 52, translated by K. Hillebrand, 183–84, 186–89.

19. *Die fröhliche Wissenschaft*, 357, in *Gesammelte Werke, Musarionausgabe*, XII, 288. Nietzsche's criticism of Schopenhauer (whom he came to link with Wagner and Christianity as being inimical to life) is examined by F. C. Copleston, S.J., *Nietzsche, Philosopher of Culture*, 142–62; his place in the intellectual history of his century is established by K. Löwith, *Von Hegel bis Nietzsche*.

20. *Beyond Good and Evil*, 36, translated by M. Cowan, 43–45.

21. *Ibid.*, 211 (Cowan, 135). See C. A. Morgan, Jr., *What Nietzsche Means*, 241–65, on revaluing truth.

22. *The Gay Science*, 126, in *The Portable Nietzsche*, translated by W. A. Kaufmann, 95. The poem quoted here is "A Plaint to Man," in *Collected Poems of Thomas Hardy*, 306. On the theme of God's death, see W. A. Kaufmann, *Nietzsche: Philosopher, Psychologist, Antichrist*, 74–81; M. Heidegger, *Holzwege*, 193–247; Paulus Lenz-Médoc, "The 'Death of God,' " in *Satan*, edited by Bruno de Jésus-Marie, O.C.D., 469–96. (See below, Chapter nine, note 11.)

23. *The Antichrist*, 47, in *The Portable Nietzsche* (Kaufmann, 627). Compare K. Reinhardt, "Nietzsche's Godless Universe," *Journal of Arts and Letters*, 3 (1951), 89–96.

24. *Beyond Good and Evil*, 224 (Cowan, 148). Cf. M. Bindschedler, *Nietzsche und die poetische Lüge*.

25. *Twilight of the Idols*, in *The Portable Nietzsche* (Kaufmann, 484, 490). An intensive study of Nietzsche's antitheism is made by G. Siegmund, *Nietzsche der "Atheist" und "Antichrist."*

26. *The Antichrist*, 18 (Kaufmann, 585–86). Karl Jaspers, *Nietzsche*, 426–40, criticizes "the will to pure immanence or thisworldliness," upon which Nietzsche founds his atheism.

27. *The Antichrist*, 9 (Kaufmann, 576).

28. "To the Unknown God" (composed in 1864), translation in W. A. Kaufmann, *Nietzsche: Philosopher, Psychologist, Antichrist*, 371. What Shelley calls "the unknown God" in his later poem, *Hellas*, resembles the impersonal, cosmic power of Nietzsche's own last period, but neither admits a theistic view.

29. For Diderot's influential description of this sort of naturalism, consult the *Encyclopédie*, s.v. "Naturaliste," in *Oeuvres complètes de Diderot*, edited by Assézat and Tourneaux, XVI, 140.

30. For a summary of the positivist conception of religion, cf. A. Comte, *The Catechism of Positive Religion*, translated by R. Congreve, and the critical Hegelian commentary by E. Caird, *The Social Philosophy and Religion of Comte*.

31. H. T. Costello, "The Naturalism of Frederick Woodbridge," in *Naturalism and the Human Spirit*, edited by Y. H. Krikorian, 295. "Myth" is understood here in the sense of a baseless illusion, not in a more constructive sense.

32. J. H. Randall, Jr., "Epilogue: The Nature of Naturalism," in *Naturalism and the Human Spirit*, 373, 374. For a more recent statement, stressing the pluralism of methods or procedures within the context of scientific inquiry and holding for the inevidence of God within a metaphysics centered around the significance of nature for human experience, see S. Hook, "Naturalism and First Principles," in *American Philosophers at Work*, edited by S. Hook, 236–58. A comparison is made between Marx and American naturalism by J. Collins, "Marxist and Secular Humanism," *Social Order*, 3 (1953), 207–32.

33. P. Romanell, *Toward a Critical Naturalism*, 5. Consult the joint statement by J. Dewey, S. Hook, and E. Nagel, "Are Naturalists Materialists?" *The Journal of Philosophy*, 42 (1945), 515–30; see also E. Nagel, *Logic without Metaphysics*, 3–18, for other views.

34. Instances of this recurrent theme can be found in: *Reconstruction in Philosophy*, 16–24, 103–12; *Experience and Nature*, 32–34, 48–63; *The Quest for Certainty*, 3–40. Dewey resembles Nietzsche in giving a historical form to his charge of pernicious bifurcation into real and apparent realms of being. But their historical references are in the tradition of soul-divining and using historical materials for a polemical purpose. Since Hegel, the history of philosophy has been part of the philosophical argument itself. For an evaluation of Dewey's naturalism, see F. Smith, O.P., "A Thomistic Appraisal of the Philosophy of John Dewey," *The Thomist*, 18 (1955), 127–85.

35. F. J. Woodbridge, *Nature and Mind*, 21–24, 41–46, 154–57.

36. S. P. Lamprecht, "Naturalism and Religion," in *Naturalism and the Human Spirit*, 30–37; E. Nagel, *Sovereign Reason*, 29–34.

37. Nagel, *Sovereign Reason*, 30, and M. A. Cohen, *Reason and Nature*, 158–59.

38. *A Common Faith*, 42.

39. *Language, Truth and Logic*, 9; the next quotation is from *ibid.*, 14. Knowledge of God is treated in *ibid.*, 114–20.

40. Herbert Feigl, "Some Major Issues and Developments in the Philosophy of Science of Logical Empiricism," in *Minnesota Studies in the Philosophy of Science*, Volume I, edited by Herbert Feigl and Michael Scriven, 14–15.

41. Isaac Newton, *Mathematical Principles of Natural Philosophy and System of the World*, III, Rules of Reasoning in Philosophy, the A. Motte translation, revised by F. Cajori, 398; italics removed. A convenient collection of recent positivist and naturalist views on God is found in *A Modern Introduction to Philosophy*, edited by P. Edwards and A. Pap. It contains a naturalistic summary of the problems by Edwards (446–63), a short dialogue on "Empiricism versus Theology" by H. Feigl (533–38), and the text of "Logical Positivism—A Debate" by A. J. Ayer and Father F. C. Copleston, S.J. (586–618). The modifications which Ayer has been making in other parts of his philosophy have not greatly affected his position on God, except to force him to consider specific issues of necessity, causation, and analogy instead of relying on any general elimination of the question of God as cognitively meaningless. Feigl's dialogue culminates in the statement that "if between the assertion and the denial of a sentence there is no difference that makes a difference as regards the deducible facts of experience, then the sentence may have logical meaning and/or emotive appeal, but it is devoid of factual reference" and hence is not factually meaningful (536–37). But this supposes that empirical confirmation is obtained *only* by establishing a difference as regards deducible facts, whereas the point at issue (as far as a realistic theism is concerned) is whether the difference concerns the empirical facts as deducible or as involving a starting point in sensible beings.

Notes for Chapter IX

GOD FINITE AND IN PROCESS

1. The closest approach to a historical survey of finitism is the annotated anthology edited by Charles Hartshorne and W. L. Reese, *Philosophers Speak of God*, especially Part 2.

2. *The Letters of John Stuart Mill*, edited by H. S. R. Elliot, I, 183. Mill gives a genetic account of his views on God in *Autobiography of John Stuart Mill*, edited by J. J. Coss, 27–33; also consult Mill's *The Positive Philosophy of Auguste Comte*, 120.

3. *The Positive Philosophy of August Comte*, 15–16. Mill's most persistent Catholic critic, W. G. Ward, *Essays on the Philosophy of Theism*, II, 106–18, noted his compromise on God but maintained that phenomenalism as such is antitheistic.

4. *The Letters of John Stuart Mill*, II, 63–64, 308; *Three Essays on Religion*, II (103–105). Although this latter work was published posthumously, Mill made known his position on God both in his correspondence and in brief references in books published during his lifetime.

5. Throughout *An Examination of Sir William Hamilton's Philosophy*, especially 88–105, Mill criticizes the Hamilton-Mansel teaching on God. On this polemic, consult Leslie Stephen, *The English Utilitarians*, III, 376–452.

6. Mill evaluates the evidences for theism in *Three Essays on Religion*, III (138–75).

7. *Ibid.*, III (152, 172–74).

8. *Ibid.*, I, III (37–38, 176–77; Mill's capitalization is modified throughout). Hume's finitist meaning for "perfect" occurs in *Dialogues concerning Natural Religion*, XI (N. K. Smith edition, 203).

9. *Utilitarianism*, 2; the text is printed in John Plamenatz, *The English Utilitarians*, 183–84.

10. *An Examination of Sir William Hamilton's Philosophy*, 101.

11. *Three Essays on Religion*, I, II (39, 116–17). On the other hand, Thomas Hardy ironically suggests that the presence of suffering indicates a defect in God's knowledge, a forgetting of the world, and that our role is not so much to fight alongside this deity as to inform Him of what we are undergoing on earth. See his two poems, "God-Forgotten" and "The Bedridden Peasant to an Unknowing God," in *Collected Poems of Thomas Hardy*, 112–14. Friedrich Nietzsche once claimed that the only hypothesis

which could block off his theory of eternal recurrence was that a suffering God tossed off the world and then forgot about it. *Thus Spoke Zarathustra*, I, in *The Portable Nietzsche*, 142–43.

12. The pertinent source materials for James' early outlook on God are printed in R. B. Perry, *The Thought and Character of William James*, I, 150–66, 470–71, 492–93, 521–28; II, 707–16.

13. *Ibid., Letter to O. W. Holmes*, May 15, 1868, I, 517. For the constructive influence of Renouvier, see *ibid.*, I, 654–69.

14. *The Will to Believe*, 213. James' reply to the J. B. Pratt questionnaire is printed in *The Letters of William James*, edited by Henry James, II, 212–15. A thorough exposition of the argument for God from religious experience is made by W. E. Hocking, *The Meaning of God in Human Experience*.

15. *The Will to Believe*, 1–31, 59–61, 90–103. An analysis is made by E. W. Lyman, "William James, Philosopher of Faith," in *In Commemoration of William James, 1842–1942*, edited by H. M. Kallen, 192–208.

16. Perry, *The Thought and Character of William James, Letter to Thomas Davidson*, January 8, 1882, I, 737. James added: "This is as much polytheism as monotheism. . . . The only difficulties of theism are the moral difficulties and meannesses; and they have always seemed to me to have flowed from the gratuitous dogma of God being the all-exclusive reality. Once think possible a primordial pluralism of which he may be one member and which may have no single subjective synthesis, and piety forthwith ceases to be incompatible with manliness, and religious 'faith' with intellectual rectitude." (Perry, I, 737, 738.) This early text indicates that James' fundamental commitment was to a pluralism of finite beings, that he saw no metaphysically coercive arguments favoring infinite divine power, that he was led to deny the latter in an effort to exculpate God from moral objections arising from supposed interpretations of His infinite will and unique perfection, and that he did not rule out polytheism or a pluralism even of divine beings. On the problem of assigning a pragmatic meaning to God, in reference to past events, read *Pragmatism*, 96–99, and *The Meaning of Truth*, 189, n. 1.

17. *Pragmatism*, 80.

18. *The Varieties of Religious Experience*, 18. The note of "immediate luminousness," corresponding to ordinary direct perception, is confined here to the religious experience of God.

19. *The Will to Believe*, 61, 141; *A Pluralistic Universe*, 124–26, 294–95. A similar position was adopted by James' friend, F. C. S. Schiller; cf. Reuben Abel, *The Pragmatic Humanism of F. C. S. Schiller*, 132–33.

20. This is the whole drift of the Conclusions to *The Varieties of Religious Experience*, 516–24. There is a critical discussion of this point by D. C. Williams, "William James and the Facts of Knowledge," in *In Commemoration of William James*, 110–12.

21. *A Pluralistic Universe*, 110; *Pragmatism*, 299.

22. Perry, *The Thought and Character of William James*, I, 808–809; II, 386, 726–34; *The Meaning of Truth*, 22, n. 1; *A Pluralistic Universe*, 52–73. Royce's major attempt to reconcile finite selves with the absolute is made in *The World and the Individual*, II, 281–452. For a concise summary and criticism, see J. H. Cotton, *Royce on the Human Self*, 146–56.

23. *A Pluralistic Universe*, 34.

24. *The Varieties of Religious Experience*, 430–48; in the remainder of the chapter (448–55), James rejects any idealistic intellectual justification of theism and puts it on a par with the Scholastic attempt.

25. *Ibid.*, 435.

26. *Some Problems of Philosophy*, 217; *A Pluralistic Universe*, 73. James did not live to expand the experiential basis of causation and causal inference beyond the active, human self.

27. *A Pluralistic Universe*, 23–35. See F. H. Bradley, *Essays on Truth and Reality*, 428–38, for an idealistic defense of the distinction between God and the absolute, as well as a criticism of James' doctrine on a finite God as a religious alternative.

28. Today, his standpoint would perhaps be catalogued as an instance of "panentheism" or the presence of everything in God. When he tried to describe the im-

manence of finite things in God, James conceded that "we are indeed internal parts of God and not external creations." (*A Pluralistic Universe*, 318.) Creation always meant to him a magic ejection and alienation of things from God. To save the unity and intimacy of the universe, therefore, he felt compelled to be sympathetic toward panpsychism and pantheism. Yet these views led back to a partitive relation of other things to God and thus posed a threat to James' pluralism, even when he denied that there was a unique cosmic unity of self or subjective synthesis. The term "panentheism" is meant to signify a medium between theism and pantheism. But the theism in question is still the exaggerated transcendence-ejection conception of God, and the panentheist solution still makes finite things to be components of the one divine self under one of its relational forms. Cf. Charles Hartshorne, *The Divine Relativity*, and R. C. Whittemore, "Prolegomena to a Modern Philosophical Theism," *Tulane Studies in Philosophy*, 5 (1956), 87–93, for a panentheistic finitism.

29. Consult James Collins, "Scheler's Transition from Catholicism to Pantheism," in *Philosophical Studies in Honor of the Very Reverend Ignatius Smith, O.P.*, edited by J. K. Ryan, 179–207; Samuel Alexander, *Space, Time, and Deity*; F. R. Tennant, *Philosophical Theology*; E. S. Brightman, *The Problem of God*; Charles Hartshorne, *Man's Vision of God*. See also the symposium by T. P. McTighe and L. H. Kendzierski, "The Finite God in Contemporary Philosophy," *Proceedings of the American Catholic Philosophical Association*, 28 (1954), 212–36; F. J. Sheen, *God and Intelligence in Modern Philosophy*; F. J. Sheen, *Religion Without God*, books which study the relation between universal becoming, anti-intellectualism, and vitalism, with special reference to Henri Bergson, who was not formally a finitist.

30. *Process and Reality*, 315. See the chapter on God in R. Das, *The Philosophy of Whitehead*, 156–70. Also consult Ivor Leclerc, *Whitehead's Metaphysics*, 189–208, which stresses the need for admitting God in virtue of the ontological principle that there is nothing apart from things that are actual and hence no subjective aim of actual entities without some unique actual entity.

31. *Religion in the Making*, 68–74.

32. *Ibid.*, 71.

33. *Science and the Modern World*, 249. But in *Adventures of Ideas*, 213, he calls Plato the greatest intuitive metaphysician.

34. For metaphysical descriptions leading to the proof of God's actuality, see *Adventures of Ideas*, 250–57; *Religion in the Making*, 88–93; *Process and Reality*, 46–47, 73, 373–74, 377, 521–22. An analytic study is made by Charles Hartshorne, "Whitehead's Idea of God," in *The Philosophy of Alfred North Whitehead*, edited by P. A. Schilpp, 515–59. Nathaniel Lawrence, *Whitehead's Philosophical Development*, 279–85, shows how indispensable the functional concept of God is to Whitehead's system but maintains that Whitehead made an unwarranted constitutive use of the regulative idea of God. For a critical comparison with St. Thomas on God, see L. Foley, S.M., *A Critique of the Philosophy of Being of Alfred North Whitehead in the Light of Thomistic Philosophy*, 59–84, 146–64.

35. *Modes of Thought*, 141–42.

36. *Process and Reality*, 521. On metaphysical method, cf. *ibid.*, 4–26; *Adventures of Ideas*, 283–305.

37. *Process and Reality*, 521. On the three natures and "dipolarity" in God, see *ibid.*, 46–47, 134–35, 521–33, and A. H. Johnson, *Whitehead's Theory of Reality*, 59–69.

38. Whitehead himself notes these exceptions, in *Process and Reality*, 134, 168, 377, 521–32. Yet, unlike some of his interpreters, he regards God as indispensable for his system. God is the reason why there is an orderly world and laws of nature; He makes chaos impossible; He even provides a non-statistical basis of probability (*Ibid.*, 169, 315; *Religion in the Making*, 104). For a critical account of the exceptions which God provides to metaphysical principles, see R. C. Whittemore, "Time and Whitehead's God," *Tulane Studies in Philosophy*, 4 (1955), 83–92. Some of Whitehead's clues on God are developed by P. Weiss, *Modes of Being*, 277–370; cf. 349–51, on God's need of the other modes of being.

39. This topic is investigated by S. L. Ely, *The Religious Availability of Whitehead's God*.

40. *The Will to Believe*, 22.

Notes for Chapter X

THE HEART'S WAY TO GOD

1. This is discussed by Sister Marie Louise Hubert, O.P., *Pascal's Unfinished Apology*, and L. Lafuma, *Histoire des Pensées de Pascal (1656–1952)*.

2. The French intellectual and religious background is described by F. Strowski, *Pascal et son temps*, I, and H. Busson, *La pensée religieuse française, de Charron à Pascal*.

3. The translation is from the bilingual edition of Pascal's *Pensées*, translated by H. F. Stewart, Fragments 10, 12 (pp. 5, 7, 9). For an introductory sketch, see V. Buranelli, "Pascal's Principles of Philosophy," *The New Scholasticism*, 30 (1956), 330–49.

4. *Letter to M. Périer*, November 15, 1647, in *Great Shorter Works of Pascal*, translated by E. Cailliet and J. C. Blankenagel, 56. Pascal explains his conception of physical research in *Fragment of a Preface to the Treatise on the Vacuum*, in *ibid*. (Cailliet-Blankenagel, 50–55).

5. *Pensées*, 12 (Stewart, 7); *Letter to M. and Mlle. de Rouannez*, October 27 [?], 1656, in *Great Shorter Works of Pascal* (Cailliet-Blankenagel, 147).

6. J. Russier, *La foi selon Pascal*, emphasizes the Jansenist factor but concludes that Pascal allows no natural knowledge of God. Actually, he regards deism as nonmeritorious and (in the context of the wager) not mathematically established but still as a natural knowledge of God which furnishes a dangerous rival to Christianity.

7. *Pensées*, 543 (Stewart, 313); see *ibid.*, 285 (Stewart, 161), for the criticism of Descartes. Pascal's biblical orientation is brought out by E. Cailliet, *Pascal: Genius in the Light of Scripture*.

8. *Is.*, 45:15. See *Pensées*, 210b, 246, 247, 514 (Stewart, 101, 133, 289). The Augustinian and Jansenist influences on this theme are noted by N. Abercrombie, *Saint Augustine and French Classical Thought*, 102–104.

9. *Conversation with M. de Saci on Epictetus and Montaigne*, in *Great Shorter Works of Pascal* (Cailliet-Blankenagel, 121–33). On the antitheses among philosophers, compare *Pensées*, 252–287 (Stewart, 145–163).

10. *Pensées*, 43, 210b, 311, 316 (Stewart, 19–29, 101–11, 171, 173). See E. Benzécri, *L'esprit humain selon Pascal*.

11. *Conversation with M. de Saci on Epictetus and Montaigne*, in *Great Shorter Works of Pascal* (Cailliet-Blankenagel, 131).

12. *Pensées*, 223 (Stewart, 115–23); cf. the headings to fragments 236 and 249 (Stewart, 127, 135). A careful reproduction, transcription, and commentary are made by Georges Brunet, *Le pari de Pascal*, who suggests that Pascal's introductory words ("Infiny rien") are equivalent to the contrast: "Infini néant" (54–55). Consult J. K. Ryan, "The Argument of the Wager in Pascal and Others," *The New Scholasticism*, 19 (1945), 233–50, and J.-E. D'Angers, O.F.M.Cap., *Pascal et ses précurseurs*, on apologetic activities during Pascal's century. Although there is no complete surety about where the wager would fit into the *Apology*, the present interpretation tries to take account of recent scholarship on the order of the fragments.

13. *Pensées*, 223 (Stewart, 117). For a mathematical analysis of the wager, consult the Appendix by P. Lambossy, "Ce qu'il faut savoir du calcul des probabilités pour comprendre le pari de Pascal," in C. Journet's *Vérité de Pascal*, 313–17. Journet's own commentary is doctrinal, not historical. Another interpretation of the wager is given by R.-E. Lacombe, *L'apologétique de Pascal*, 72–111, who claims that it will interest only that type of man who seeks an eternal infinite good and requires either absolute truth and justice or none at all on earth. Brunet, *op. cit.*, 75–84, gives a balanced summary, suggests that there is always a finite risk, and stresses the alternatives of winning everything and losing nothing.

14. *Pensées*, 223 (Stewart, 120, 121). There is a note on this phrase in E. Gilson, *Les idées et les lettres*, 263–74.

15. Voltaire, *Lettres philosophiques*, XXV (Naves edition, 141–75); D. Finch, *La critique philosophique de Pascal au XVIIIe siècle*; M. Waterman, *Voltaire, Pascal and Human Destiny*.

442

16. *The Mind of the Geometrician*, in *Great Shorter Works of Pascal* (Cailliet-Blankenagel, 189).

17. *Pensées*, 43 (Stewart, 27).

18. *Ibid.*, 627 (Stewart, 345). Cf. J. Laporte, *Le coeur et la raison selon Pascal*.

19. This is worked out by D. Patrick, *Pascal and Kierkegaard*.

20. *Philosophical Fragments*, translated by D. F. Swenson, 32, n. 2 (modified). For a brief account, see J. A. Mourant, "The Place of God in the Philosophy of Kierkegaard," *Giornale di metafisica*, 8 (1953), 207–21.

21. Cf. James Collins, *The Mind of Kierkegaard*, 50–65, 72–79, on Romanticism.

22. J. W. von Goethe, *Faust, Part One*, translated by B. Q. Morgan, 86.

23. On Hegel, Kant, and the moral end, see *Fear and Trembling*, translated by W. Lowrie, 80, 105; see also, *Journals*, Entry 7, translated by A. Dru, 3.

24. *Concluding Unscientific Postscript*, translated by D. F. Swenson and W. Lowrie, 99. On existence, see T. H. Croxall, *Kierkegaard Commentary*, 10–34.

25. The correlation between one's conception of God and of the human individual permeates *The Point of View*, translated by W. Lowrie, where Kierkegaard discloses his primary aim. For a similar theistic and personalist criticism of Hegel's idealism, see J. B. Siemes, S.J., "Friedrich Schlegel als Vorläufer christlicher Existenzphilosophie," *Scholastik*, 30 (1955), 161–84.

26. *Papirer*, 1849, edited by P. A. Heiberg, V. Kuhr, and E. Torsting, X² A163.

27. James Collins, "Faith and Reflection in Kierkegaard," *The Journal of Religion*, 37 (1957), 10–19. For his religious outlook, see Reidar Thomte, *Kierkegaard's Philosophy of Religion*, and P. D. LeFevre, *The Prayers of Kierkegaard*.

28. *Apologia Pro Vita Sua*, edited by C. F. Harrold, 44–45; *An Essay in Aid of A Grammar of Assent*, edited by C. F. Harrold, 91–92. These works are hereafter referred to, respectively, as: *Apologia* and *Grammar*.

29. The basic story of the years before *Apologia* (1864) is contained in *Newman: His Life and Spirituality* by Louis Bouyer, C.O., and the first volume of W. Ward's *The Life of John Henry Cardinal Newman*, cited hereafter as Ward's *Life*. On the Noetic school, cf. Bouyer, 58–59; Ward's *Life*, I, 37–38. On the Roman experience, see Bouyer, 258–79; Ward's *Life*, I, 135–75. See also, on the Noetic school, A. D. Culler, *The Imperial Intellect: A Study of Newman's Educational Ideal*, 34–45. For the view of God and nature that was popularized by Paley and the British natural theologians of the pre-Darwinian years 1790–1850, see C. C. Gillispie, *Genesis and Geology*.

30. *Discourses Addressed to Mixed Congregations*, 261–62. Cf. *The Idea of a University*, edited by C. F. Harrold, 23–24; *Grammar*, 255, 382–83.

31. *Apologia*, 217, 218–19. Compare *Discourses Addressed to Mixed Congregations*, 261–74.

32. Ward's *Life*, II, 250, 276; the application to diversity is made in *Grammar*, 182–93. On Newman's epistemology, see J. F. Cronin, S.S., *Cardinal Newman: His Theory of Knowledge*.

33. *Grammar*, 235; cf. *ibid.*, 323–24. This theme is developed by A. J. Boekraad, *The Personal Conquest of Truth according to J. H. Newman*, who nevertheless insists, more than does Newman, upon the metaphysical basis.

34. *Grammar*, 382. On the formation of personally realized first principles, see *ibid.*, 46–56.

35. *Grammar*, 119–32, where Newman regards his own theory as empirical, in contradistinction to Locke's a priori view of degrees of assent.

36. *Discourses Addressed to Mixed Congregations*, 276–77. On difficulty and doubt, cf. *Apologia*, 216–17; on investigation and inquiry, *Grammar*, 144. Newman sometimes calls his own work an inquiry, in the broad sense of an intellectual examination of grounds and problems.

37. *Apologia*, 219–20. Compare this passage with Newman's portrait of the "*purus, putus* Atheist," who does accept the alternative of no creator (*Grammar*, 187).

38. *Fifteen Sermons Preached Before the University of Oxford*, 247–49. He puts this point forcefully in "A Letter Addressed to His Grace the Duke of Norfolk," in *Certain Difficulties Felt by Anglicans in Catholic Teaching*, II, 254: "I must not be supposed to be limiting the Revelation of which the Church is the keeper to a mere republication of the Natural Law; but still it is true, that, though Revelation is so distinct from the

teaching of nature and beyond it, yet it is not independent of it, nor without relations towards it, but is its complement, reassertion, issue, embodiment, and interpretation." Newman answers Pascal, deism, and atheistic humanism together and not in separation from each other. His general theological position is examined by E. D. Benard, *A Preface to Newman's Theology*, and his theory of faith and reason is explained by P. Flanagan, *Newman, Faith and the Believer*. See also F. Bacchus, "Newman's Oxford University Sermons," *The Month*, 140 (1922), 1–12. For a thorough exegesis of the incident about St. Paul, see Bertil Gartner, *The Areopagus Speech and Natural Revelation*.

39. On the hidden God, atheism, and the need for revelation, read *Grammar*, 267–68, 301–302.

40. On Darwinism, see Ward's *Life*, II, 342–43; Culler, *The Imperial Intellect*, 266–69; C. F. Harrold, *John Henry Newman*, 76; *Grammar*, 182. Newman's relations with other Victorians are studied in R. Shafer's *Christianity and Naturalism*.

41. *The Idea of a University*, 54, 326–31.

42. *Grammar*, 53–56; Ward's *Life*, II, 269. Even with respect to the order of nature, however, Newman maintained that it should be integrated with the evidence of conscience in order to reach the transcendent God and not merely a Humean cosmic mind, perfectly proportionate to nature, which mind is nothing more than "Nature with a divine glow upon it." (*The Idea of a University*, 35). Newman was always concerned about the naturalistic finitism of Hume, especially as expressed in the speech for Epicurus, in Section xi of *An Enquiry concerning Human Understanding*. On the distinction between design and finality in reference to the Thomistic fifth way of proof, see R. L. Faricy, S.J., "The Establishment of the Basic Principle of the Fifth Way," *The New Scholasticism*, 31 (1957), 189–208.

43. See "The Tamworth Reading Room," in *Essays and Sketches*, edited by C. F. Harrold, II, especially 204–13; *The Idea of a University*, 196–200, 310–13.

44. "Milman's View of Christianity," in *Essays and Sketches*, II, 221, 223. There is a strong Patristic inspiration behind Newman's entire conception of God, yet it is joined with an acute awareness of the outlook resulting from British empiricism and the Noetic school.

45. *The Idea of a University*, 35; *Grammar*, 305.

46. There are two typical passages in *Discourses Addressed to Mixed Congregations*, 264–65, 285–86. On causation, consult *Grammar*, 51–53; Ward's *Life*, II, 258.

47. Newman's unpublished manuscripts at the Birmingham Oratory include a group of papers (MS A46.3) on such metaphysical subjects as proofs of God's existence. This collection is now available on microfilm at Yale University Library and a few other American libraries. The notes on the proof from conscience were published by E. Przywara, *Ringen der Gegenwart*, II, 834, n. 24. H. Fries, *Die Religionsphilosophie Newmans*, gives a balanced account of the role of conscience in Newman's theory of religion.

48. "A Letter Addressed to His Grace the Duke of Norfolk," in *Certain Difficulties Felt by Anglicans in Catholic Teaching*, II, 248. On the various types of moral reductionism, consult *Grammar*, 93; on the theory of the gentleman, within the context of the program of substituting moral sense or taste for conscience, *The Idea of a University*, 169–87; on the weak points in Mill's associationist explanation, MS A46.3, as transcribed by Boekraad, *op. cit.*, 268–69.

49. *The Idea of a University*, 169; *Grammar*, 79–88. Flanagan, *Newman, Faith and the Believer*, 18–22, 184–92, restates the proof from conscience in terms of man's contingency, but this puts the stress on conscience as expressive of a moral rule, whereas for Newman, its function as a dictate is primary in a direct inference to God. The comparison between the theistic inference and that to the existing, sensible world is suggested in *Grammar*, 47–49, and in MS A46.3, as transcribed by Przywara, *op. cit.*, II, 841, n. 1. Elsewhere, Newman suggests that even in self-consciousness there is a certain reliance upon the inferential power of the mind to move from consciousness to the certainty about one's own existence; see C. S. Dessain, C.O., "Cardinal Newman on the Theory and Practice of Knowledge. The Purpose of the *Grammar of Assent*," *The Downside Review*, 75 (1957), 1–23, especially 8. The background in Bishop Butler for the analysis of conscience in its critical and judicial office is described by J. Robin-

son, "Newman's Use of Butler's Arguments," *The Downside Review*, 76 (1958), 161–80.

50. *Cardinal Newman and William Froude, F.R.S.: A Correspondence*, edited by G. H. Harper, 120. See *Apologia*, 180–81, on the probable grounds for belief in God.

51. On probability, moral certitude, and the illative sense, see *Grammar*, 204, 212, 219–29, 261–91; *Cardinal Newman and William Froude, F.R.S.: A Correspondence*, 131–32, 200–209; Ward's *Life*, I, 168, and II, 248–50, 507–508. See also M. C. D'Arcy, S. J., *The Nature of Belief*; Dr. Zeno, O.F.M. Cap., *John Henry Newman: Our Way to Certitude*.

52. *Grammar*, 57, 159–64. For an integration between real assent and the evidential basis of metaphysics, consult G. P. Klubertanz, S.J., "Where is the Evidence for Thomistic Metaphysics?" *Revue Philosophique de Louvain*, 56 (1958), 294–315.

53. *Grammar*, 88, 89, 95. Newman insists that assent be given to the proposition about *Deum esse*, as the intellectual foundation of religious worship of *Dei esse*.

54. See Karl Jaspers, *Reason and Existenz*, translated by W. Earle, 23–55. James Collins, *The Existentialists: A Critical Study*, 217–24, gives a comparative analysis of the various existentialist positions on God.

55. Jean-Paul Sartre, *Being and Nothingness*, translated by H. E. Barnes, 566 (italics added); cf. 89–90, 592, 599, 615.

56. Albert Camus, *The Rebel*, translated by Anthony Bower, 72.

57. Consult the essay, "What is Metaphysics?" in Martin Heidegger's *Existence and Being*, 355–92. For the relation between Heidegger and the God of the Christian and poetic traditions, cf. the two essays by E. Dinkler and S. R. Hopper, in *Christianity and the Existentialists*, edited by C. Michalson, 97–127, 148–90.

58. See Karl Jaspers, *The Perennial Scope of Philosophy*, translated by R. Manheim, 30–46, on philosophical faith; Karl Jaspers, *Nietzsche*, 426–40, for a critical treatment of the atheistic alternative.

59. Gabriel Marcel, *The Mystery of Being*, translated by G. Fraser and R. Hague, I, 77–92, 197–219 (reflective method and mystery), and II, 173–77 (theistic proofs). Additional unpublished sources are used by R. Troisfontaines, S.J., *De l'existence à l'être: La philosophie de Gabriel Marcel*, II, 207–38, on the personal approach to God. A. C. Cochrane, *The Existentialists and God*, studies not only the existentialists but also Gilson, Tillich, and Barth, from the standpoint of a Calvinist theology which seeks to differentiate the theological study of the being of God from the philosophical study of being, which he identifies exclusively with an ontology.

Notes for Chapter XI

TOWARD A REALISTIC PHILOSOPHY OF GOD

1. On the side of the content of the idea of God, this transposition is sketched by Etienne Gilson, *God and Philosophy*, 74–108; for the methodological side, see James Collins, "God as a Function in Modern Systems of Philosophy," in *American Philosophers at Work*, edited by Sidney Hook, 194–206.

2. St. Thomas Aquinas, *On the Truth of the Catholic Faith*, Book II: *Creation*, translated by J. F. Anderson, 35 (*Summa Contra Gentiles*, II, 4).

3. William James, *Letter to Thomas Davidson*, January 8, 1882, in R. B. Perry, *The Thought and Character of William James*, I, 737. For a vigorous historical effort to show that the God of theism, rather than the Hegelian absolute spirit or the Heideggerian existential freedom of man, constitutes the central problem of modern metaphysics, consult Walter Schulz, *Der Gott der neuzeitlichen Metaphysik*.

4. Maurice Merleau-Ponty, *Éloge de la philosophie*, 57–65; Maurice Merleau-Ponty, *Sens et non-sens*, 192–93. Critical studies of Merleau-Ponty's refusal to extend phenomenological analysis beyond the temporal-historical horizon of man in the world are made by A. Dondeyne, "L'historicité dans la philosophie contemporaine," *Revue Philosophique de Louvain*, 54 (1956), 468–76, and R. Jolivet, "Le problème de l'absolu dans la philosophie de M. Merleau-Ponty," *Tijdschrift voor Philosophie*, 19 (1957), 53–100.

5. John Hospers, *An Introduction to Philosophical Analysis*, 192–214, 322–74, criti-

cizes some conventional arguments for God's existence, on the basis of a procedural view of the verifiability principle and a nonempirical definition of metaphysics, but without giving a precise determination of the principle or a criticism of the definition of metaphysics.

6. Otto Neurath, "The Orchestration of the Sciences by the Encyclopedism of Logical Empiricism," *Philosophy and Phenomenological Research*, 6 (1945–46), 499. On the ritualistic character of the legislation of meaning, compare Morton White, *Toward Reunion in Philosophy*, 108–109, 154–63.

7. *New Essays in Philosophical Theology*, edited by A. Flew and A. MacIntyre. The basic linguistic treatment was made by John Wisdom, "Gods," reprinted in *Essays on Logic and Language*, First Series, edited by A. Flew, 187–206. Further developments in the direction of linguistic theism can be found in: *Metaphysical Beliefs*, by S. Toulmin, R. Hepburn, and A. MacIntyre; I. T. Ramsey, *Religious Language;* E. L. Mascall, *Words and Images;* B. Mitchell, editor, *Faith and Logic.*

8. See J. N. Findlay and G. E. Hughes, "Can God's Existence be Disproved?" in *New Essays in Philosophical Theology*, 47–67.

9. Charles Peirce, *Letter to William James*, June 12, 1902, in R. B. Perry, *The Thought and Character of William James*, II, 425. Cf. Nicholas Berdyaev's autobiographical remarks on his early atheism, in *Dream and Reality*, translated by K. Lampert, 91–92; Martin Buber's historical analysis of the nineteenth century, *Between Man and Man*, translated by R. G. Smith, 137–56; Karl Barth's interpretation of Feuerbach, included as an Introductory Essay to the George Eliot translation of L. Feuerbach, *The Essence of Christianity*, x-xxxii.

10. *Collected Papers of Charles Sanders Peirce*, edited by Charles Hartshorne and Paul Weiss, 6. 486.

11. See, for instance, J. L. Mackie, "Evil and Omnipotence," *Mind*, N. S., 64 (1955), 200–212. Christian treatments of suffering and evil are made by M. C. D'Arcy, S.J., *Pain and the Providence of God;* P. Siwek, S.J., *The Philosophy of Evil;* A. Sertillanges, O.P., *Le problème du mal.*

12. For the contrast between the religious I-Thou relation and the modern philosophical I-It relation, consult Martin Buber, *Eclipse of God*, 159–67. Since Buber refers the idea of God primarily to a process of imaging the imageless rather than to the judgmental inference, he cannot specify the philosophical resources for referring our philosophical knowledge, as well as our religious act, to the existent God.

13. Samuel Butler, *Hudibras*, I, i, edited by A. R. Waller, 7 (originally published, 1663–1678). Voltaire praised and summarized this poem during his stay in England: *Lettres Philosophiques*, XXII (Naves edition, 124–25, 251–55). For two major contemporary theological viewpoints which are critical of philosophical theism, see Karl Barth, *Dogmatics in Outline;* Paul Tillich, *Systematic Theology* and *The Courage to Be;* Gustave Weigel, S.J., "The Theological Significance of Paul Tillich," *Gregorianum*, 37 (1956), 34–54, containing a clarifying letter from Tillich. See J. A. Martin, "St. Thomas and Tillich on the Names of God," *Journal of Religion*, 37 (1957), 253–59, for a comparative study, which, however, omits causal analogy. Because of his difficulties about a philosophical theism, Tillich is compelled to deny that there can be a theistic existentialism and must regard Jaspers as having only a religious basis for his doctrine on God: "Existentialist Aspects of Modern Art," in *Christianity and the Existentialists*, edited by Carl Michalson, 141–42. Two conflicting historical interpretations of the relation of revelation to philosophies of God are now in course of publication, in English: Herman Dooyeweerd, *A New Critique of Theoretical Thought*, translated by D. H. Freeman and W. S. Young; Richard Kroner, *Speculation in Pre-Christian Philosophy*, which is Vol. I of *Speculation and Revelation in the History of Philosophy*. Dooyeweerd roots scientific and philosophical theorization ultimately in a religious source, whereas Kroner accords separate origins to speculation and revelation in the different periods, although they are both concerned with the absolute and are in relations of agreement and conflict.

14. In a text which combines the metaphysics of existential act with the metaphor used in revelation, St. Thomas observes that "we remove from Him even this act of existing itself, according as it is in creatures. And thus it [human reason] remains in a certain shadow of ignorance, in accord with which ignorance (as Dionysius says) we

are best united to God, as far as concerns the present life. And this is the certain mist in which God is said to dwell." (*Commentary on Book I of the Sentences*, d. 8, q. 1, a. 1, ad 4). See the commentary by E. Winance, O.S.B., "L'essence divine et la connaissance humaine dans le Commentaire sur les Sentences de Saint Thomas," *Revue Philosophique de Louvain*, 55 (1957), 171–215. The theme is treated in V. White, O.P., *God the Unknown*, 16–61; E. Gilson, *The Christian Philosophy of St. Thomas Aquinas*, translated by L. Shook, C.S.B., 103–10; R. Markus, "A Note on the Meaning of *Via*," *Dominican Studies*, 7 (1954), 239–45; Josef Pieper, "On the 'Negative' Element in the Philosophy of Thomas Aquinas," *Cross Currents*, 4 (1953–54), 46–56. There is a relevant linguistic study by W. P. Alston, "Ineffability," *The Philosophical Review*, 65 (1956), 506–22.

15. St. Augustine, *Of True Religion*, xxxi, 58, in *Augustine: Earlier Writings*, translated by J. H. Burleigh, 255. Cf. *ibid.*, xxxix, 73 (Burleigh, 263).

16. John Hutchison, *Faith, Reason, and Existence*, 149–58, summarizes this view.

17. On the question of the order for a Thomistic philosophy, consult E. Gilson, *The Christian Philosophy of St. Thomas Aquinas*, 21–23, 442–43, n. 33, and J. Collins, "Toward a Philosophically Ordered Thomism," *The New Scholasticism*, 32 (1958), 301–26. On the Thomistic philosophy of God, see Gilson, *ibid.*, 29–143; J. Maritain, *Approaches to God*; R. Jolivet, *The God of Reason*, translated by M. Pontifex, O.S.B.; G. Smith, S.J., *Natural Theology*; H. Carpenter, O.P., "The Philosophical Approach to God in Thomism," *The Thomist*, 1 (1939), 45–61; A. Motte, O.P., "Théodicée et théologie chez S. Thomas d'Aquin," *Revue des Sciences Philosophiques et Théologiques*, 26 (1937), 5–26. The crucial metaphysical question of causal analogy and other types of analogy employed in philosophy of God is treated by G. Klubertanz, S.J., "The Problem of the Analogy of Being," *The Review of Metaphysics*, 10 (1957), 553–79. The objection of W. Kaufmann, *Critique of Religion and Philosophy*, 129, that most statements about God are essentially ambiguous does not take into account two factors: the difference between the several kinds of analogy and the controlling role of causal inference and causal analogy, at least in the realistic theism of St. Thomas, which he is considering.

18. The classical locus is in St. Augustine's *The City of God, Books I–VII*, VI, v–ix (Varro), x–xii (Seneca), translated by D. B. Zema, S.J., and G. G. Walsh, S.J., 314–37. After criticizing poetic and political theology, he concludes: "Thus, both systems are rejected, and there is nothing left for men who can think but to choose the theology of the philosophers," the theology of nature. *Ibid.*, VI, ix (Zema-Walsh, 331). There are further historical and doctrinal remarks in: C. C. J. Webb, *Studies in the History of Natural Theology*, 1–83; Werner Jaeger, *The Theology of the Early Greek Philosophers*, 2–9, 191–95; Joseph Owens, C.Ss.R., "Theodicy, Natural Theology, and Metaphysics," *The Modern Schoolman*, 28 (1950–51), 126–37. Owens is concerned mainly with a natural theology treated as a science distinct from metaphysics.

19. "The Wreck of the Deutschland," *Poems of Gerard Manley Hopkins*, edited by Robert Bridges, 13. For Hopkins' wrestling with *Deus absconditus*, compare the untitled poem, Number 73, "Thee, God, I come from, to thee go," and the poem "*Nondum*" (*ibid.*, 91, 138–40). Two well-selected anthologies of human thought about God are Victor Gollancz, *Man and God*, and C. H. Voss, *The Universal God*.

BIBLIOGRAPHY

BIBLIOGRAPHY

This list contains the books, articles, and unpublished dissertations mentioned in the Notes. Wherever possible, recent reliable translations of the foreign sources are used. The list constitutes the working core of a library for the study of modern philosophies of God.

I. BOOKS

Abel, Reuben. *The Pragmatic Humanism of F. C. S. Schiller.* New York, King's Crown Press, 1955.

Abercrombie, N. *Saint Augustine and French Classical Thought.* Oxford, Clarendon Press, 1938.

Acton, H. B. *The Illusion of the Epoch: Marxism-Leninism as a Philosophical Creed.* Boston, Beacon Press, 1957.

Adams, H. P. *Karl Marx in His Earliest Writings.* London, Allen and Unwin, 1940.

Addison, Joseph. *The Spectator.* Edited by A. Chalmers. 6 vols. New York, Appleton, 1854.

Alexander, Samuel. *Space, Time, and Deity.* 2 vols. New York, Macmillan, 1920.

Anderson, F. H. *The Philosophy of Francis Bacon.* Chicago, University of Chicago Press, 1948.

Arvon, H. *Ludwig Feuerbach ou la transformation du sacré.* Paris, Presses Universitaires, 1957.

Asveld, P. *La pensée religieuse du jeune Hegel.* Louvain, Publications Universitaires, 1953.

Augustine, St. *Earlier Writings.* Translated by J. H. Burleigh. Philadelphia, Westminster Press, 1953.

———. *The City of God, Books I–VII.* Translated by D. B. Zema, S.J., and G. G. Walsh, S.J. New York, Fathers of the Church, Inc., 1950.

Ayer, A. J. *Language, Truth and Logic.* Second edition. London, Gollancz, 1946.

Bacon, Francis. *The Philosophical Works of Francis Bacon.* Edited by J. M. Robertson. New York, Dutton, 1905.

Bainton, R. *Here I Stand: A Life of Martin Luther.* New York, New American Library, 1955.

Barker, J. E. *Diderot's Treatment of the Christian Religion in the Encyclopédie.* New York, King's Crown Press, 1941.

Barth, Karl. *Dogmatics in Outline.* New York, Philosophical Library, 1949.

Bayle, Pierre. *Dictionnaire historique et critique.* "Third edition." 4 vols. Rotterdam, Bohm, 1720.

———. *Oeuvres diverses.* 4 vols. The Hague, Husson, 1727–1731.

———. *Selections from Bayle's Dictionary.* Edited by E. Beller and M. Lee, Jr. Princeton, Princeton University Press, 1952.

Beck, L. J. *The Method of Descartes.* Oxford, Clarendon Press, 1952.

Benard, E. D. *A Preface to Newman's Theology.* St. Louis, Herder, 1945.

Benzécri, E. *L'esprit humain selon Pascal.* Paris, Presses Universitaires, 1939.

Berdyaev, Nicholas. *Dream and Reality.* Translated by K. Lampert. New York, Macmillan, 1951.

Bergier, N.-S. *Examen du matérialisme.* New edition. 2 vols. Tournai, Casterman, 1838.

———. *Le Déisme réfuté par lui-même.* Sixth, revised and corrected edition. 2 vols. Lyons, Périsse, 1822.

Berkeley, George. *The Works of George Berkeley.* Edited by A. A. Luce and T. E. Jessop. 9 vols. London, Nelson, 1948–1957.

Bett, Henry. *Nicholas of Cusa.* London, Metheun, 1932.

Billichsich, Friedrich. *Das Problem des Übels in der Philosophie des Abendlandes.* 2 vols., to date. Vienna, Verlag Sexl, 1936–1952.

Bindschedler, M. *Nietzsche und die poetische Lüge.* Basel, Verlag für Recht und Gesellschaft, 1954.

Bibliography

Boase, A. M. *The Fortunes of Montaigne: A History of the Essays in France, 1580–1669.* London, Metheun, 1935.

Boekraad, A. J. *The Personal Conquest of Truth according to J. H. Newman.* Louvain, Nauwelaerts, 1955.

Bonno, Gabriel. *Les relations intellectuelles de Locke avec la France.* Berkeley and Los Angeles, University of California Press, 1955.

Bouyer, Louis, C.O. *Newman: His Life and Spirituality.* Translated by J. L. May. New York, Kenedy, 1958.

Bowne, B. P. *Theory of Thought and Knowledge.* Cincinnati, American Book, 1897.

Bradley, F. H. *Essays on Truth and Reality.* Oxford, Clarendon Press, 1914.

Bredvold, L. *The Intellectual Milieu of John Dryden.* Ann Arbor, University of Michigan Press Ann Arbor Books, 1956.

Brett, G. S. *The Philosophy of Gassendi.* London, Macmillan, 1908.

Brightman, E. S. *The Problem of God.* New York, Abingdon Press, 1930.

Brunet, Georges. *Le pari de Pascal.* Paris, Desclée de Brouwer, 1956.

Brunet, P. *Introduction des théories de Newton en France au XVIIIe siècle.* Vol. I only. Paris, Blanchard, 1931.

Bruno, Giordano. *Concerning the Cause, Principle, and One.* Translation in S. Greenberg, *The Infinite in Giordano Bruno.* New York, King's Crown Press, 1950.

————. *On the Infinite Universe and Worlds.* Translation in D. W. Singer, *Giordano Bruno: His Life and Thought.* New York, Schuman, 1950.

Bruno de Jésus-Marie, O.C.D., editor. *Satan.* New York, Sheed and Ward, 1951.

Brunschvicg, Léon. *Descartes et Pascal, Lecteurs de Montaigne.* New York, Brentano, 1944.

Buber, Martin. *Between Man and Man.* Translated by R. G. Smith. London, Routledge and Kegan Paul, 1947.

————. *Eclipse of God.* London, Gollancz, 1953.

Buckley, G. T. *Atheism in the English Renaissance.* Chicago, University of Chicago Press, 1932.

Buffier, Claude, S.J. *Traité des premières véritez et de la source de nos jugemens.* Paris, Didot, 1724.

Burgelin, P. *La philosophie de l'existence de J.-J. Rousseau.* Paris, Presses Universitaires, 1952.

Busson, H. *La pensée religieuse française, de Charron à Pascal.* Paris, Vrin, 1933.

————. *Les sources et le développement du rationalisme dans la littérature française de la Renaissance (1533–1601).* Paris, Letouzey, 1922.

Butler, Samuel. *Hudibras.* Edited by A. R. Waller. Cambridge, the University Press, 1905.

Cailliet, E. *Pascal: Genius in the Light of Scripture.* Philadelphia, Westminster Press, 1945.

Caird, E. *The Social Philosophy and Religion of Comte.* New York, Macmillan, 1885.

Calvez, J.-Y., S.J. *La pensée de Karl Marx.* Paris, Seuil, 1956.

Calvin, John. *Calvin: Theological Treatises.* Translated by J. K. Reid, Philadelphia, Westminster Press, 1954.

————. *Institutes of the Christian Religion.* Translated by Henry Beveridge. 2 vols. London, Clarke, 1953 printing.

————. *Joannis Calvini Opera Selecta,* Vol. III: *Institutionis Christianae Religionis 1559 libros I et II continens.* Edited by P. Barth and W. Niesel. Munich, Kaiser Verlag, 1929.

Campo, M. *Cristiano Wolff e il razionalismo precritico.* 2 vols. Milan, Vita e Pensiero, 1939.

Camus, Albert. *The Rebel.* Translated by Anthony Bower. New York, Vintage Books, 1956.

Cassirer, Ernst. *Rousseau, Kant, Goethe.* Translated by J. Guttman, P. Kristeller, and J. Randall, Jr. Princeton, Princeton University Press, 1947.

————. *The Philosophy of the Enlightenment.* Translated by F. Koelln and J. Pettegrove. Princeton, Princeton University Press, 1951.

————. *The Question of Jean-Jacques Rousseau.* Translated by P. Gay. New York, Columbia University Press, 1954.

————, Kristeller, P., and Randall, J., Jr., editors. *The Renaissance Philosophy of Man.* Chicago, University of Chicago Press, 1948.

Cassirer, H. W. *Kant's First Critique.* New York, Macmillan, 1954.

Chamberlain, W. B. *Heaven Wasn't His Destination: The Philosophy of Ludwig Feuerbach.* London, Allen and Unwin, 1941.

Charbonnel, J. R. *La pensée italienne au XVIe siècle et le courant libertin.* Paris, Champion, 1919.

Charron, Pierre. *De la sagesse.* Reprint of third edition. Paris, Feuge, 1646.

————. *Les trois véritez.* Bordeaux, Millanges, 1593.

Church, R. W. *A Study in the Philosophy of Malebranche.* London, Allen and Unwin, 1931.

Cicero. *On the Nature of the Gods.* In the H. M. Poteat translation of *Brutus; On the Nature of the Gods; On Divination; On Duties.* Chicago, University of Chicago Press, 1950.

Cicuttini, L. *Giordano Bruno.* Milan, Vita e Pensiero, 1950.

Clarke, Samuel. *A Discourse concerning the Being and Attributes of God.* Sixth, corrected edition. London, Knapton, 1725.

Cochrane, A. C. *The Existentialists and God.* Philadelphia, Westminster Press, 1956.

Coffin, C. M. *John Donne and the New Philosophy.* New York, Columbia University Press, 1937.

Cohen, I. B., editor. *Isaac Newton's Papers and Letters on Natural Philosophy and Related Documents.* Cambridge, Harvard University Press, 1958.

Cohen, M. A. *Reason and Nature.* Second edition. Glencoe, Illinois, The Free Press, 1953.

Coleridge, S. T. *The Poems of Samuel Taylor Coleridge.* Edited by E. H. Coleridge. New York, Oxford University Press, 1912.

Collins, James. *A History of Modern European Philosophy.* Milwaukee, Bruce, 1954.

————. *The Existentialists: A Critical Study.* Chicago, Regnery, 1952.

————. *The Mind of Kierkegaard.* Chicago, Regnery, 1953.

Comte, Auguste. *The Catechism of Positive Religion.* Translated by R. Congreve. Second edition. London, Trübner, 1883.

Cope, J. I. *Joseph Glanvill, Anglican Apologist.* St. Louis, Washington University Studies, 1956.

Copleston, F. C., S.J., *Nietzsche, Philosopher of Culture.* London, Burns, Oates and Washbourne, 1942.

Coreth, E., S.J. *Das dialektische Sein in Hegels Logik.* Vienna, Herder, 1952.

Cornu, A. *Karl Marx, l'homme et l'oeuvre.* Paris, Alcan, 1934.

————. *The Origins of Marxian Thought.* Springfield, Illinois, Thomas, 1957.

Costello, W. T., S.J. *The Scholastic Curriculum at Early Seventeenth-Century Cambridge.* Cambridge, Harvard University Press, 1958.

Cotton, J. H. *Royce on the Human Self.* Cambridge, Harvard University Press, 1954.

Crocker, L. G. *The Embattled Philosopher: A Biography of Denis Diderot.* Lansing, Michigan State College Press, 1954.

Cronin, J. F., S.S. *Cardinal Newman: His Theory of Knowledge.* Washington, Catholic University of America Press, 1935.

Crousaz, J. P. de. *Examen du pyrrhonisme ancien et moderne.* The Hague, Hondt, 1733.

Croxall, T. H. *Kierkegaard Commentary.* New York, Harper, 1956.

Culler, A. D. *The Imperial Intellect: A Study of Newman's Educational Ideal.* New Haven, Yale University Press, 1955.

Cusanus, Nicholas. *Apologia Doctae Ignorantiae.* Edited by R. Klibansky. Leipzig, Meiner, 1932.

————. *De Beryllo.* Edited by L. Baur. Leipzig, Meiner, 1940.

————. *De Docta Ignorantia.* Edited by E. Hoffmann and R. Klibansky. Leipzig, Meiner, 1932.

————. *Idiota: De Sapientia, De Mente, De Staticis Experimentis.* Edited by L. Baur. Leipzig, Meiner, 1937.

————. *Nikolaus von Cues, Philosophische Schriften.* Edited by A. Petzelt. Vol. I only. Stuttgart, Kohlhammer, 1949.

———. *Of Learned Ignorance.* Translated by G. Heron, O.F.M. New Haven, Yale University Press, 1949.

D'Angers, J.-E., O.F.M.Cap. *Pascal et ses précurseurs.* Paris, Nouvelles Éditions Latines, 1954.

Darbon, A. *Études spinozistes.* Paris, Presses Universitaires, 1946.

D'Arcy, M. C., S.J. *Pain and the Providence of God.* Milwaukee, Bruce, 1935.

———. *The Nature of Belief.* London, Sheed and Ward, 1931.

Das, R. *The Philosophy of Whitehead.* London, Clarke, n.d.

Delvolvé, J. *Religion critique et philosophie positive chez Pierre Bayle.* Paris, Alcan, 1906.

Denzinger-Bannwart-Umberg-Rahner. *Enchiridion Symbolorum.* Twenty-ninth edition. Freiberg i. B., Herder, 1953.

Derathé, R. *Le rationalisme de J.-J. Rousseau.* Paris, Presses Universitaires, 1948.

Derham, William. *Astro-Theology.* London, Innys, 1715.

———. *Physico-Theology.* Ninth edition, London, Innys and Manby, 1737.

Descartes, René. *Discourse on Method.* Translated by L. Lafleur. New York, Liberal Arts Press, 1950.

———. *Oeuvres de Descartes.* Edited by C. Adam and P. Tannery. 13 vols. Paris, Cerf, 1897–1913.

———. *Philosophical Writings.* Translated by E. Anscombe and P. T. Geach. London, Nelson, 1954.

———. *The Meditations concerning First Philosophy.* Translated by L. Lafleur. New York, Liberal Arts Press, 1951.

———. *The Philosophical Works of Descartes.* Translated by E. S. Haldane and G. R. Ross. Revised edition. 2 vols. Cambridge, the University Press, 1934.

Descoqs, P., S.J. *Praelectiones Theologiae Naturalis—Cours de théodicée.* 2 vols. Paris, Beauchesne, 1932–1935.

Dewey, John. *A Common Faith.* New Haven, Yale University Press, 1934.

———. *Experience and Nature.* Chicago, Open Court, 1926.

———. *Reconstruction in Philosophy.* Enlarged edition. Boston, Beacon Press, 1948.

———. *The Quest for Certainty.* New York, Minton, Balch, 1929.

De Witt, N. W. *Epicurus and His Philosophy.* Minneapolis, University of Minnesota Press, 1954.

Diderot, Denis. *Oeuvres complètes de Diderot.* Edited by Assézat and Tourneaux. 20 vols. Paris, Garnier, 1875–1877.

Dillenberger, J. *God Hidden and Revealed.* Philadelphia, Muhlenberg Press, 1953.

Dilthey, Wilhelm. *Gesammelte Schriften,* Vol. IV: *Die Jugendgeschichte Hegels.* Leipzig, Teubner, 1921.

Donne, John. *The Poems of John Donne.* Edited by H. J. C. Grierson. 2 vols. London, Oxford University Press, 1912.

———. *The Sermons of John Donne.* Edited by G. R. Potter and E. M. Simpson. 10 vols. Berkeley and Los Angeles, University of California Press, 1953—.

Dooyeweerd, H. *A New Critique of Theoretical Thought.* Translated by D. H. Freeman and W. S. Young. 4 vols. Philadelphia, Presbyterian and Reformed Publishing Company, 1953–1958.

Dowey, E. A., Jr. *The Knowledge of God in Calvin's Theology.* New York, Columbia University Press, 1952.

Dréano, M. *La pensée religieuse de Montaigne.* Paris, Beauchesne, 1936.

Dryden, John. *Works.* Edited by W. Scott and G. Saintsbury. 18 vols. Edinburgh, Patterson, 1882–1893.

Dulckeit, G. *Die Idee Gottes im Geiste der Philosophie Hegels.* Munich, Rinn, 1947.

Edwards, P., and Pap, A., editors. *A Modern Introduction to Philosophy.* Glencoe, Illinois, The Free Press, 1957.

Ely, S. L. *The Religious Availability of Whitehead's God.* Madison, University of Wisconsin Press, 1942.

Engels, Friedrich. *Ludwig Feuerbach and the Outcome of Classical German Philosophy.* In *Karl Marx, Selected Works.* English edition revised by C. P. Dutt. 2 vols. New York, International Publishers, n.d.

England, F. E. *Kant's Conception of God.* London, Allen and Unwin, 1929.

Bibliography

Fabro, Cornelio, C.P.S. *Dio.* Rome, Editrice Studium, 1953.

Fairchild, H. N. *Religious Trends in English Poetry.* 4 vols., to date. New York, Columbia University Press, 1939–1957.

Feigl, H., and Scriven, M., editors. *Minnesota Studies in the Philosophy of Science.* Volume I. Minneapolis, University of Minnesota Press, 1956.

Fellows, O. E., and Torrey, N. L., editors. *Diderot Studies, I and II.* 2 vols. Syracuse, Syracuse University Press, 1949–1952.

Feuerbach, Ludwig. *Sämmtliche Werke.* 10 vols. Leipzig, Wigand, 1844–1866.

―――. *The Essence of Christianity.* Translated by George Eliot. New York, Harper Torchbook, 1957.

Fife, R. *The Revolt of Martin Luther.* New York, Columbia University Press, 1957.

Finch, D. *La critique philosophique de Pascal au XVIIIe siècle.* Philadelphia, University of Pennsylvania Press, 1940.

Flanagan, P. *Newman, Faith and the Believer.* Westminster, Maryland, Newman Press, 1946.

Flew, A., editor. *Essays on Logic and Language.* First series. New York, Philosophical Library, 1951.

―――― and MacIntyre, A., editors. *New Essays in Philosophical Theology.* London, SCM Press, 1955.

Foley, L., S.M. *A Critique of the Philosophy of Being of Alfred North Whitehead in the Light of Thomistic Philosophy.* Washington, Catholic University of America Press, 1946.

Foucher, Simon. *Critique de la Recherche de la vérité.* Paris, Coustelier, 1675.

Frame, D. M. *Montaigne's Discovery of Man.* New York, Columbia University Press, 1955.

Fries, H. *Die Religionsphilosophie Newmans.* Stuttgart, Schwabenverlag, 1948.

Fuhrmans, H. *Schellings Philosophie der Weltalter.* Düsseldorf, Schwann, 1954.

Gandillac, M. *La philosophie de Nicolas de Cues.* Paris, Aubier, 1941.

Gartner, Bertil. *The Areopagus Speech and Natural Revelation.* Uppsala, Almqvist and Wiksell, 1955.

Gassendi, Pierre. *Opera Omnia.* 6 vols. Lyons, Anisson and De Venet, 1658.

Gillispie, C. C. *Genesis and Geology.* Cambridge, Harvard University Press, 1951.

Gilson, Etienne. *Being and Some Philosophers.* Toronto, Pontifical Institute of Mediaeval Studies, 1949.

―――. *Christianity and Philosophy.* Translated by R. MacDonald, C.S.B. New York, Sheed and Ward, 1939.

―――. *God and Philosophy.* New Haven, Yale University Press, 1941.

―――. *History of Christian Philosophy in the Middle Ages.* New York, Random House, 1955.

―――. *Les idées et les lettres.* Paris, Vrin, 1932.

―――. *L'être et l'essence.* Paris, Vrin, 1948.

―――. *The Christian Philosophy of St. Thomas.* Translated by L. K. Shook, C.S.B. New York, Random House, 1956.

Glanvill, Joseph. *The Vanity of Dogmatizing.* Facsimile of the 1661 edition. New York, Columbia University Press, 1931.

Goethe, J. W. von. *Faust, Part One.* Translated by B. Q. Morgan. New York, Liberal Arts Press, 1954.

Gollancz, Victor, editor. *Man and God.* Boston, Houghton Mifflin, 1951.

Gouhier, H. *La pensée religieuse de Descartes.* Paris, Vrin, 1924.

―――. *La philosophie de Malebranche et son expérience religieuse.* Second edition. Paris, Vrin, 1948.

Green, F. C. *Jean-Jacques Rousseau.* Cambridge, the University Press, 1955.

Greenberg, S. *The Infinite in Giordano Bruno.* New York, King's Crown Press, 1950.

Greenslet, F. *Joseph Glanvill.* New York, Columbia University Press, 1900.

Grégoire, F. *Aux sources de la pensée de Marx: Hegel, Feuerbach.* Louvain, Institut Supérieur, 1947.

―――. *Études hégéliennes.* Louvain, Publications Universitaires, 1958.

Grua, G. *Jurisprudence universelle et théodicée selon Leibniz.* Paris, Presses Universitaires, 1953.

Bibliography

Grün, K. *Ludwig Feuerbach in seinem Briefwechsel und Nachlass.* 2 vols. Leipzig, Winter, 1874.

Guéroult, Martial. *Berkeley: Quatres études sur la perception et sur Dieu.* Paris, Aubier, 1956.

———. *Descartes selon l'ordre des raisons.* 2 vols. Paris, Aubier, 1953.

———. *Malebranche,* Vol. I: *La vision en Dieu.* Paris, Aubier, 1955.

Hardy, Thomas. *Collected Poems of Thomas Hardy.* London, Macmillan, 1920.

Harrold, C. F. *John Henry Newman.* New York, Longmans, Green, 1945.

Hartshorne, Charles. *Man's Vision of God.* Chicago, Willett, Clark, 1941.

———. *The Divine Relativity.* New Haven, Yale University Press, 1948.

———, and Reese, W. L., editors. *Philosophers Speak of God.* Chicago, University of Chicago Press, 1953.

Hazard, P. *European Thought in the Eighteenth Century.* Translated by J. May. New Haven, Yale University Press, 1954.

———. *The European Mind.* Translated by J. May. New Haven, Yale University Press, 1953.

Hedenius, I. *Sensationalism and Theology in Berkeley's Philosophy.* Uppsala, Almqvist and Wiksell, 1936.

Hegel, Georg. *Briefe von und an Hegel.* Edited by J. Hoffmeister. 3 vols. Hamburg, Meiner, 1952–1954.

———. *Early Theological Writings.* Translated by T. M. Knox and R. Kroner. Chicago, University of Chicago Press, 1948.

———. *Erste Druckschriften.* Edited by G. Lasson. Leipzig, Meiner, 1928.

———. *Hegels theologische Jugendschriften.* Edited by H. Nohl. Tübingen, Mohr, 1907.

———. *Lectures on the History of Philosophy.* Translated by E. S. Haldane and F. H. Simpson. Reprint edition. 3 vols. New York, Humanities Press, 1955.

———. *Lectures on the Philosophy of Religion.* Translated by E. B. Speirs and J. B. Sanderson. 3 vols. London, Kegan Paul, Trench, and Trübner, 1895.

———. *Philosophy of Mind.* Translated by W. Wallace. Oxford, Clarendon Press, 1894.

———. *Philosophy of Right.* Translated by T. M. Knox. Oxford, Clarendon Press, 1942.

———. *Reason in History.* Translated by R. S. Hartman. New York, Liberal Arts Press, 1953.

———. *Science of Logic.* Translated by W. H. Johnston and L. G. Struthers. 2 vols. New York, Macmillan, 1929.

———. *The Logic of Hegel.* Translated by W. Wallace. Second edition. Oxford, Clarendon Press, 1892.

———. *The Phenomenology of Mind.* Translated by J. B. Baillie. Second edition. New York, Macmillan, 1931.

———. *The Philosophy of Hegel.* Edited by C. J. Friedrich. New York, Modern Library, 1953.

———. *Vorlesungen über die Beweise vom Dasein Gottes.* Edited by G. Lasson. Leipzig, Meiner, 1930.

———. *Vorlesungen über die Philosophie der Religion.* Edited by G. Lasson. 3 vols. Leipzig, Meiner, 1927–1930.

Heidegger, Martin. *Existence and Being.* London, Vision Press, 1949.

———. *Holzwege.* Frankfurt a. M., Klostermann, 1950.

Hendel, Charles. *Jean-Jacques Rousseau, Moralist.* 2 vols. New York, Oxford University Press, 1934.

Herder, J. G. *God: Some Conversations.* Translated by F. H. Burkhardt. New York, Hafner, 1949.

Herrlin, O. *The Ontological Proof in Thomistic and Kantian Interpretation.* Uppsala, Lundequistska Bokhandeln, 1950.

Hess, G. *Pierre Gassend: Der französische Späthumanismus und das Problem von Wissen und Glauben.* Jena, Gronau, 1939.

Hobbes, Thomas. *Leviathan.* Edited by M. Oakeshott. Oxford, Blackwell, 1946.

Bibliography

————. *The Elements of Law.* Edited by F. Tönnies. Cambridge, the University Press, 1928.

————. *The English Works of Thomas Hobbes.* Edited by W. Molesworth. 11 vols. London, Bohn, 1839–1845.

Hocking, W. E. *The Meaning of God in Human Experience.* New Haven, Yale University Press, 1912.

Hoffmeister, J. *Dokumente zu Hegels Entwicklung.* Stuttgart, Frommann, 1936.

————. *Hölderlin und Hegel.* Tübingen, Mohr, 1931.

Holbach, Paul. *The System of Nature.* Translated by H. D. Robinson. 2 vols. New York, Matsell, 1835.

Hommes, J. *Die philosophische Gotteslehre des Nikolaus Kusanus in ihren Grundlehren.* Munich, Philosophical Faculty of the University, 1926.

Hook, Sidney, editor. *American Philosophers at Work.* New York, Criterion Books, 1956.

————. *From Hegel to Marx.* New York, John Day, 1936.

————. *Reason, Social Myths, and Democracy.* New York, John Day, 1940.

Hopkins, G. M., S.J. *Poems of Gerard Manley Hopkins.* Edited by Robert Bridges. Second edition. New York, Oxford University Press, 1937.

Horowitz, I. L. *The Renaissance Philosophy of Giordano Bruno.* New York, Coleman-Ross, 1952.

Hospers, John. *An Introduction to Philosophical Analysis.* New York, Prentice-Hall, 1953.

Hubert, Sister Marie Louise, O.P. *Pascal's Unfinished Apology.* New Haven, Yale University Press, 1952.

Huet, P. D. *Traité philosophique de la foiblesse de l'esprit humain.* Amsterdam, Sauzet, 1723.

Hume, David. *An Abstract of a Treatise of Human Nature.* Edited by J. M. Keynes and P. Sraffa. Cambridge, the University Press, 1938.

————. *An Enquiry concerning Human Understanding.* In *Enquiries concerning the Human Understanding and concerning the Principles of Morals.* Edited by L. A. Selby-Bigge. Second edition. Oxford, Clarendon Press, 1902.

————. *A Treatise of Human Nature.* Edited by L. A. Selby-Bigge. Oxford, Clarendon Press, 1888.

————. *Dialogues concerning Natural Religion.* Edited by N. K. Smith. Second edition. London, Nelson, 1947.

————. *New Letters of David Hume.* Edited by R. Klibansky and E. C. Mossner. Oxford, Clarendon Press, 1954.

Hunter, A. M. *The Teaching of Calvin.* Second, revised edition. London, Clarke, 1950.

Hutchison, John. *Faith, Reason and Existence.* New York, Oxford University Press, 1956.

Hyppolite, J. *Études sur Marx et Hegel.* Paris, Rivière, 1955.

————. *Genèse et structure de la Phénoménologie de l'esprit de Hegel.* Paris, Aubier, 1946.

————. *Logique et existence: Essai sur la logique de Hegel.* Paris, Presses Universitaires, 1953.

Iljin, I. *Die Philosophie Hegels als kontemplative Gotteslehre.* Bern, Francke, 1946.

Jaeger, Werner. *The Theology of the Early Greek Philosophers.* Oxford, Clarendon Press, 1947.

James, William. *A Pluralistic Universe.* New York, Longmans, Green, 1909.

————. *Pragmatism.* New York, Longmans, Green, 1908.

————. *Some Problems of Philosophy.* New York, Longmans, Green, 1911.

————. *The Letters of William James.* Edited by Henry James. 2 vols. Boston, Atlantic Monthly Press, 1920.

————. *The Meaning of Truth.* New York, Longmans, Green, 1909.

————. *The Varieties of Religious Experience.* New York, Longmans, Green, 1902.

————. *The Will to Believe.* New York, Dover Publications reprint, 1956.

Jaspers, Karl. *Nietzsche.* Third edition. Berlin, Walter De Gruyter, 1950.

————. *Reason and Existenz.* Translated by W. Earle. New York, Noonday Press, 1955.

457

Bibliography

————. *The Perennial Scope of Philosophy.* Translated by R. Manheim. New York, Philosophical Library, 1949.

Joachim, H. H. *Spinoza's Tractatus De Intellectus Emendatione, A Commentary.* Oxford, Clarendon Press, 1940.

Johnson, A. H. *Whitehead's Theory of Reality.* Boston, Beacon Press, 1952.

Jolivet, R. *The God of Reason.* Translated by M. Pontifex, O.S.B. New York, Hawthorn Books, 1958.

Journet, Charles. *Vérité de Pascal.* St. Maurice, Switzerland, Éditions de l'Oeuvre St. Augustin, 1951.

Kallen, H. M., editor. *In Commemoration of William James, 1842–1942.* New York, Columbia University Press, 1942.

Kant, Immanuel. *Critique of Judgment.* Translated by J. H. Bernard. New York, Hafner, 1951.

————. *Critique of Practical Reason and Other Writings in Moral Philosophy.* Translated by L. W. Beck. Chicago, University of Chicago Press, 1949.

————. *Critique of Pure Reason.* Translated by N. K. Smith. Second, corrected impression. London, Macmillan, 1933.

————. *Dreams of a Spirit-Seer Illustrated by the Dreams of Metaphysics.* Translated by E. F. Goerwitz and edited by F. Sewall. New York, Macmillan, 1900.

————. *Gesammelte Schriften.* Prussian Academy of Sciences edition. 22 vols. Berlin, Reimer, and W. De Gruyter, 1902–1942.

————. *Inaugural Dissertation and Early Writings on Space.* Translated by J. Handyside. Chicago, Open Court, 1929.

————. *Kant's Cosmogony.* Translated by W. Hastie. Glasgow, Maclehose, 1900.

————. *Prolegomena to Any Future Metaphysics.* Translated by P. G. Lucas. New York, Barnes and Noble, 1953.

————. *Religion Within the Limits of Reason Alone.* Translated by T. M. Greene and H. H. Hudson. Chicago, Open Court, 1934.

Kaufmann, W. *Critique of Religion and Philosophy.* New York, Harper, 1958.

————. *Nietzsche: Philosopher, Psychologist, Antichrist.* Princeton, Princeton University Press, 1950.

Keeling, S. V. *Descartes.* London, Benn, 1934.

Kierkegaard, S. *Concluding Unscientific Postscript.* Translated by D. F. Swenson and W. Lowrie. Princeton, Princeton University Press, 1941.

————. *Fear and Trembling.* Translated by W. Lowrie. Princeton, Princeton University Press, 1941.

————. *Journals.* Translated by A. Dru. New York, Oxford University Press, 1938.

————. *Papirer.* Edited by P. A. Heiberg, V. Kuhr, and E. Torsting. 11 vols., in 20 parts. Copenhagen, Gyldendalske Boghandel, 1909–1948.

————. *Philosophical Fragments.* Translated by D. F. Swenson. Princeton, Princeton University Press, 1936.

————. *The Point of View.* Translated by W. Lowrie. Princeton, Princeton University Press, 1939.

Kojève, A. *Introduction à la lecture de Hegel.* Second edition. Paris, Gallimard, 1947.

Koyré, A. *From the Closed World to the Infinite Universe.* Baltimore, Johns Hopkins Press, 1957.

Kramm, H. H. *The Theology of Martin Luther.* London, Clarke, 1947.

Krikorian, Y. H., editor. *Naturalism and the Human Spirit.* New York, Columbia University Press, 1944.

Kroner, Richard. *Speculation in Pre-Christian Philosophy.* Philadelphia, Westminster Press, 1956.

————. *Von Kant bis Hegel.* 2 vols. Tübingen, Mohr, 1921–1924.

Lachièze-Rey, P. *Les origines cartésiennes du Dieu de Spinoza.* Paris, Alcan, 1932.

Lacombe, R.-E. *L'apologétique de Pascal.* Paris, Presses Universitaires, 1958.

Laertius, Diogenes. *Lives of Eminent Philosophers.* Revised edition. 2 vols. London, Heinemann, 1950.

Lafuma, L. *Histoire des Pensées de Pascal (1656–1952).* Paris, Éditions du Luxembourg, 1954.

Bibliography

Lakebrink, B. *Hegels dialektische Ontologie und die thomistische Analektik.* Cologne, Bachem, 1955.

Laporte, J. *Le coeur et la raison selon Pascal.* Paris, Éditions Elzévir, 1950.

———. *Le rationalisme de Descartes.* Paris, Presses Universitaires, 1945.

Lavelle, Louis. *La présence totale.* Paris, Aubier, 1934.

Lawrence, Nathaniel. *Whitehead's Philosophical Development.* Berkeley and Los Angeles, University of California Press, 1956.

Leclerc, Ivor. *Whitehead's Metaphysics.* New York, Macmillan, 1958.

LeFevre, P. D. *The Prayers of Kierkegaard.* Chicago, University of Chicago Press, 1956.

Leibniz, Gottfried. *G. W. Leibniz, Textes inédits.* Edited by G. Grua. 2 vols. Paris, Presses Universitaires, 1948.

———. *Leibniz Selections.* Translated by P. Wiener. New York, Scribner, 1951.

———. *New Essays concerning Human Understanding.* Translated by A. G. Langley. Third edition. La Salle, Illinois, Open Court, 1949.

———. *Philosophical Papers and Letters.* Translated by L. E. Loemker. 2 vols. Chicago, University of Chicago Press, 1956.

———. *Theodicy.* Translated by E. M. Huggard. London, Routledge and Kegan Paul, 1952.

Lenoble, R. *Mersenne ou la naissance du mecanisme.* Paris, Vrin, 1943.

Leroy, A. *La critique et la religion chez David Hume.* Paris, Alcan, 1930.

Lessius, Leonard. *De Providentia Numinis et Animi Immortalitate Libri Duo adversus Atheos et Politicos.* Antwerp, Moreti, 1613.

Lévy-Bruhl, L. *La philosophie de Jacobi.* Paris, Alcan, 1894.

Lewis, G. *L'individualité selon Descartes.* Paris, Vrin, 1950.

Lindau, H., editor. *Die Schriften zu J. G. Fichte's Atheismus-Streit.* Munich, Müller, 1912.

———. *Die Theodicee im 18. Jahrhundert.* Leipzig, Engelmann, 1911.

Locke, John. *An Early Draft of Locke's Essay.* Edited by R. I. Aaron and J. Gibb. Oxford, Clarendon Press, 1936.

———. *An Essay concerning Human Understanding.* Edited by A. C. Fraser. 2 vols. Oxford, Clarendon Press, 1894.

———. *An Essay concerning the Understanding, Knowledge, Opinion, and Assent.* Edited by B. Rand. Cambridge, Harvard University Press, 1931.

———. *Essays on the Law of Nature.* Edited by W. von Leyden. Oxford, Clarendon Press, 1954.

———. *Locke's Philosophical Works.* Edited by J. A. St. John. 2 vols. London, Bohn, 1854.

———. *Two Treatises of Government.* Edited by T. I. Cook. New York, Hafner, 1947.

Löwith, Karl. *Von Hegel bis Nietzsche.* Zurich, Europa Verlag, 1941.

Lubac, H. De, S.J. *The Drama of Atheist Humanism.* Translated by E. M. Riley. New York, Sheed and Ward, 1950.

Luce, A. A. *Berkeley's Immaterialism.* London, Nelson, 1945.

Lukács, G. *Der junge Hegel.* New edition. Berlin, Aufbau-Verlag, 1954.

Luther, Martin. *Martin Luther, Ausgewählte Werke,* Vol. I: *Aus der Frühzeit der Reformation.* Edited by H. H. Borcherdt and G. Merz. Third edition. Munich, Kaiser Verlag, 1951.

Maclaurin, Colin. *An Account of Sir Isaac Newton's Philosophical Discoveries.* London, Millar, 1748.

McTaggart, J. McT. E. *Studies in Hegelian Cosmology.* Cambridge, the University Press, 1901.

Maier, J. *On Hegel's Critique of Kant.* New York, Columbia University Press, 1939.

Malebranche, Nicholas. *Correspondance avec J. J. Dortous de Mairan.* Edited by J. Moreau. Paris, Vrin, 1947.

———. *De la recherche de la vérité.* Edited by G. Lewis. 3 vols. Paris, Vrin, 1946.

———. *Dialogues on Metaphysics and on Religion.* Translated by M. Ginsberg. London, Allen and Unwin, 1923.

Marcel, G. *The Mystery of Being.* Translated by G. Fraser and R. Hague. 2 vols. Chicago, Regnery, 1951.

Bibliography

Marcuse, H. *Reason and Revolution: Hegel and the Rise of Social Theory*. Second edition. New York, Humanities Press, 1954.

Marc-Wogau, K. *Vier Studien zu Kants Kritik der Urteilskraft*. Uppsala, Lundequistska Bokhandeln, 1938.

Maréchal, J., S.J. *Le point de départ de la métaphysique*, Vol. IV: *Le système idéaliste chez Kant et les postkantiens*. Paris, Desclée de Brouwer, 1947.

Maritain, J. *Approaches to God*. New York, Harper, 1954.

——. *On the Philosophy of History*. New York, Scribner, 1957.

——. *The Range of Reason*. New York, Scribner, 1952.

Martin, G. *Kant's Metaphysics and Theory of Science*. Translated by P. G. Lucas. Manchester, University of Manchester Press, 1955.

Marx, Karl. *Karl Marx, Selected Works*. English edition revised by C. P. Dutt. 2 vols. New York, International Publishers, n.d.

——. *Selected Writings in Sociology and Social Philosophy*. Edited by T. Bottomore and M. Rubel. London, Watts, 1956.

——. *Three Essays by Karl Marx*. Translated by R. Stone. New York, Pioneer Publishers, 1947.

——, and Engels, Friedrich. *Marx-Engels Gesamtausgabe*. Edited by D. Riazanov and V. Adoratsky. Incomplete edition. Frankfurt a. M., Marx-Engels-Archiv, 1927—.

——, and ——. *The German Ideology, Parts I and III*. Translated by R. Pascal. New York, International Publishers, 1947.

Mascall, E. L. *Words and Images*. New York, Longmans, Green, 1957.

Mauthner, Fritz. *Der Atheismus und seine Geschichte im Abendlande*. 4 vols. Stuttgart, Deutsche Verlags-Anstalt, 1921–1923.

Merleau-Ponty, M. *Éloge de la philosophie*. Paris, Gallimard, 1953.

——. *Sens et non-sens*. Paris, Nagel, 1948.

Mersenne, Marin. *La vérité des sciences contre les septiques [sic] ou Pyrrhoniens*. Paris, Toussainct du Bray, 1625.

——. *L'impiété des déistes, athées, et libertins de ce temps*. 2 vols. Paris, Bilaine, 1624.

Mettrie, J. O. de la. *Man a Machine*. Translated by G. Bussey. La Salle, Illinois, Open Court, 1912.

Metzger, H. *Attraction universelle et religion naturelle chez quelques commentateurs anglais de Newton*. Paris, Hermann, 1938.

Michalson, C., editor. *Christianity and the Existentialists*. New York, Scribner, 1956.

Mill, John Stuart. *An Examination of Sir William Hamilton's Philosophy*. London, Longmans, Green, 1865.

——. *Autobiography of John Stuart Mill*. Edited by J. J. Coss. New York, Columbia University Press, 1948.

——. *The Letters of John Stuart Mill*. Edited by H. S. R. Elliot. 2 vols. London, Longmans, Green, 1910.

——. *The Positive Philosophy of Auguste Comte*. New York, Holt, 1873.

——. *Three Essays on Religion*. London, Longmans, Green, 1874.

——. *Utilitarianism*. Printed in John Plamenatz's *The English Utilitarians*. Oxford, Blackwell, 1949.

Mitchell, Basil, editor. *Faith and Logic*. Boston, Beacon Press, 1957.

Montaigne, Michel de. *The Essays of Michel de Montaigne*. Translated by J. Zeitlin. 3 vols. New York, Knopf, 1934–1936.

Moore, W., Sutherland, R., and Starkie, E., editors. *The French Mind*. Oxford, Clarendon Press, 1952.

Morehouse, A. R. *Voltaire and Jean Meslier*. New Haven, Yale University Press, 1936.

Morgan, C. A., Jr. *What Nietzsche Means*. Cambridge, Harvard University Press, 1941.

Mossner, E. C. *The Life of David Hume*. London, Nelson, 1954.

Nagel, E. *Logic without Metaphysics*. Glencoe, Illinois, The Free Press, 1956.

——. *Sovereign Reason*. Glencoe, Illinois, The Free Press, 1954.

Namer, E. *Les aspects de Dieu dans la philosophie de Giordano Bruno*. Paris, Alcan, 1926.

Naville, P. *Paul Thiry D'Holbach et la philosophie scientifique au XVIIIe siècle*. Paris, Gallimard, 1943.

Bibliography

Newman, John Henry. *An Essay in Aid of A Grammar of Assent*. Edited by C. F. Harrold. New York, Longmans, Green, 1947.

———. *Apologia Pro Vita Sua*. Edited by C. F. Harrold. New York, Longmans, Green, 1947.

———. *Cardinal Newman and William Froude, F. R. S.: A Correspondence*. Edited by G. H. Harper. Baltimore, Johns Hopkins Press, 1933.

———. *Certain Difficulties Felt by Anglicans in Catholic Teaching*. London, Pickering, 1876.

———. *Discourses Addressed to Mixed Congregations*. New York, Longmans, Green, 1919.

———. *Essays and Sketches*. Edited by C. F. Harrold. 3 vols. New York, Longmans, Green, 1948.

———. *Fifteen Sermons Preached Before the University of Oxford*. New York, Longmans, Green, 1918.

———. *The Idea of a University*. Edited by C. F. Harrold. New York, Longmans, Green, 1947.

Newton, Isaac. *Isaac Newton's Papers and Letters on Natural Philosophy and Related Documents*. Edited by I. B. Cohen. Cambridge, Harvard University Press, 1958.

———. *Mathematical Principles of Natural Philosophy and System of the World*. The A. Motte translation, revised by F. Cajori. Berkeley, University of California Press, 1934.

———. *Newton's Philosophy of Nature*. Edited by H. S. Thayer. New York, Hafner, 1953.

Nicolson, M. *Science and Imagination*. Ithaca, Cornell University Press, 1956.

Niel, H., S.J. *De la médiation dans la philosophie de Hegel*. Paris, Aubier, 1945.

Nietzsche, Friedrich. *Beyond Good and Evil*. Translated by M. Cowan. Chicago, Regnery, 1955.

———. *Gesammelte Werke, Musarionausgabe*. 23 vols. Munich, Musarion Verlag, 1920–1929.

———. *The Portable Nietzsche*. Translated by W. A. Kaufmann. New York, Viking, 1954.

Nüdling, G. *Ludwig Feuerbachs Religionsphilosophie*. Paderborn, Schöningh, 1936.

Ogiermann, H. A., S.J. *Hegels Gottesbeweise*. Rome, Gregorian University Press, 1948.

Ong, W. J., S.J. *Ramus, Method, and the Decay of Dialogue*. Cambridge, Harvard University Press, 1958.

Orr, J. *English Deism: Its Roots and Fruits*. Grand Rapids, Michigan, Eerdmans Publishing Company, 1934.

Owen, J. *The Skeptics of the French Renaissance*. New York, Macmillan, 1893.

Palmer, R. R. *Catholics and Unbelievers in Eighteenth Century France*. Princeton, Princeton University Press, 1939.

Pappas, J. *Berthier's Journal de Trévoux and the Philosophes*. In *Studies on Voltaire and the Eighteenth Century*, Vol. III. Geneva, Institut et Musée Voltaire, 1957.

Parente, P., editor. *Cristo vivente nel mondo*. Rome, Coletti, 1956.

Parker, T. H. *The Doctrine of the Knowledge of God*. Edinburgh and London, Oliver and Boyd, 1952.

Parkinson, G. H. *Spinoza's Theory of Knowledge*. Oxford, Clarendon Press, 1954.

Pascal, Blaise. *Great Shorter Works of Pascal*. Translated by E. Cailliet and J. C. Blankenagel. Philadelphia, Westminster Press, 1948.

———. *Pensées*. Bilingual edition, with English translation by H. F. Stewart. London, Routledge and Kegan Paul, 1950.

Patrick, D. *Pascal and Kierkegaard*. 2 vols. London and Redhill, Lutterworth Press, 1947.

Patrick, M. M. *Sextus Empiricus and Greek Scepticism*. Cambridge, the University Press, 1899.

Paul, L. *The English Philosophers*. London, Faber and Faber, 1953.

Pegis, A. C., editor. *The Wisdom of Catholicism*. New York, Modern Library, 1949.

Peirce, C. S. *Collected Papers of Charles Sanders Peirce*. Edited by Charles Hartshorne, Paul Weiss, and Arthur Burks. 8 vols. Cambridge, Harvard University Press, 1931–1958.

Perry, R. B. *The Thought and Character of William James.* 2 vols. Boston, Little, Brown, 1936.

Peters, Richard. *Hobbes.* Baltimore, Penguin Books, 1956.

Pintard, R. *Le libertinage érudit dans la première moitié du XVIIe siècle.* 2 vols. Paris, Boivin, 1943.

Plumptre, C. E. *General Sketch of the History of Pantheism.* 2 vols. London, Deacon, 1878–1879.

Pope, Alexander. *An Essay on Man.* Edited by M. Mack. New Haven, Yale University Press, 1951.

Przywara, Erich. *Ringen der Gegenwart.* 2 vols. Augsburg, Filser, 1929.

Ramsey, I. T. *Religious Language.* London, SCM Press, 1957.

Reid, Thomas. *The Works of Thomas Reid.* Edited by Dugald Stewart. 3 vols. New York, Bangs and Mason, 1822.

Robinson, H. *Bayle the Sceptic.* New York, Columbia University Press, 1931.

Rochot, B. *Les travaux de Gassendi sur Epicure et sur l'atomisme, 1619–1658.* Paris, Vrin, 1944.

Rolland, E. *Le déterminisme monadique et la problème de Dieu dans la philosophie de Leibniz.* Paris, Vrin, 1935.

Romanell, P. *Toward a Critical Naturalism.* New York, Macmillan, 1958.

Rousseau, Jean-Jacques. *Correspondance générale.* Edited by T. Dufour and P. Plan. 20 vols. Paris, Colin, 1924–1934.

——. *Émile, or Education.* Translated by B. Foxley. New York, Dutton, 1911.

——. *La "Profession de foi du vicaire savoyard" de Jean-Jacques Rousseau.* Edited by P.-M. Masson. Paris, Hachette, 1914.

Royce, Josiah. *The World and the Individual.* 2 vols. New York, Macmillan, 1900–01.

Russier, J. *La foi selon Pascal.* 2 vols. Paris, Presses Universitaires, 1949.

Ryan, J. K., editor. *Philosophical Studies in Honor of the Very Reverend Ignatius Smith, O.P.* Westminster, Maryland, Newman Press, 1952.

Sabrié, J. B. *De l'humanisme au rationalisme: Pierre Charron (1541–1603), l'homme, l'oeuvre, l'influence.* Paris, Alcan, 1913.

Sartre, Jean-Paul. *Being and Nothingness.* Translated by H. E. Barnes. New York, Philosophical Library, 1956.

Saunders, J. L. *Justus Lipsius: The Philosophy of Renaissance Stoicism.* New York, Liberal Arts Press, 1955.

Scherz, G., C.Ss.R. *Vom Wege Niels Stensens.* Copenhagen, Munksgaard, 1956.

Schilling, W. *Feuerbach und die Religion.* Munich, Evangelischer Presseverband, 1957.

Schilpp, P. A. *Kant's Pre-Critical Ethics.* Evanston and Chicago, Northwestern University Press, 1938.

——, editor. *The Philosophy of Alfred North Whitehead.* Second edition. New York, Tudor, 1951.

Schmidt, E. *Hegels Lehre von Gott.* Gütersloh, Bertelsmann, 1952.

Scholz, H. *Die Hauptschriften zum Pantheismusstreit zwischen Jacobi und Mendelssohn.* Berlin, Reuther and Reichard, 1916.

Schönfelder, W. *Die Philosophen und Jesus Christus.* Hamburg, Meiner, 1949.

Schopenhauer, Arthur. *On the Fourfold Root of the Principle of Sufficient Reason.* Translated by K. Hillebrand. London, Bell, 1907.

Schulz, Walter. *Der Gott der neuzeitlichen Metaphysik.* Pfullingen, Neske, 1957.

——. *Die Vollendung des deutschen Idealismus in der Spätphilosophie Schellings.* Stuttgart, Kohlhammer, 1955.

Schweitzer, A. *Goethe, Four Studies.* Translated by C. R. Joy. Boston, Beacon Press, 1949.

Sens, W. *Die irreligiöse Entwicklung von Karl Marx.* Halle, Klinz, 1935.

Sertillanges, A., O.P. *Le problème du mal.* 2 vols. Paris, Aubier, 1949–1951.

Sextus Empiricus. [*Works of*] *Sextus Empiricus.* Greek text, with English translation by R. G. Bury. 4 vols. London, Heinemann, 1933–1949.

Shafer, R. *Christianity and Naturalism.* New Haven, Yale University Press, 1926.

Sheen, F. J. *God and Intelligence in Modern Philosophy.* New York, Longmans, Green, 1925.

——. *Religion without God.* New York, Longmans, Green, 1928.

Bibliography

Siegmund, G. *Nietzsche der "Atheist" und "Antichrist."* Fourth edition. Paderborn, Schöningh, 1946.

Sillem, E. A. *George Berkeley and the Proofs for the Existence of God.* New York, Longmans, Green, 1957.

Singer, D. W. *Giordano Bruno: His Life and Thought.* New York, Schuman, 1950.

Siwek, Paul, S.J. *Au coeur du Spinozisme.* Paris, Desclée de Brouwer, 1952.

————. *The Philosophy of Evil.* New York, Ronald Press, 1951.

Smith, Gerard, S.J. *Natural Theology.* New York, Macmillan, 1951.

Smith, N. K. *New Studies in the Philosophy of Descartes.* London, Macmillan, 1952.

Sortais, G., S.J. *La philosophie moderne depuis Bacon jusqu'à Leibniz.* 2 vols. Paris, Lethielleux, 1920–1922.

Specht, E. K. *Der Analogiebegriff bei Kant und Hegel.* Cologne, Cologne University Press, 1952.

Spinoza, Benedict. *On the Improvement of the Understanding.* Translated by J. Katz. New York, Liberal Arts Press, 1958.

————. *Spinoza Selections.* Edited by J. Wild. New York, Scribner, 1930.

————. *The Correspondence of Spinoza.* Translated by A. Wolf. New York, Dial Press, 1928.

————. *The Principles of Descartes' Philosophy.* Translated by H. H. Britan. La Salle, Illinois, Open Court, 1905.

Stefanescu, M. *Essai sur le rapport entre le dualisme et la théisme de Kant.* Paris, Alcan, 1915.

Steinbüchel, T. *Das Grundproblem der Hegelschen Philosophie.* Vol. I. Bonn, Hanstein, 1933.

Stephen, Leslie. *The English Utilitarians.* 3 vols. London, Duckworth, 1900.

Stewart, Dugald. *The Collected Works of Dugald Stewart.* Edited by Sir William Hamilton. 11 vols. Edinburgh, Clark, 1877.

Stine, R. W. *The Doctrine of God in the Philosophy of Fichte.* Philadelphia, University of Pennsylvania dissertation, 1945.

Strowski, Fortunat. *Pascal et son temps.* 3 vols. Paris, Plon, 1907–1908.

Tennant, F. R. *Philosophical Theology.* 2 vols. Cambridge, the University Press, 1928.

Thomas Aquinas, St. *In Metaphysicam Aristotelis Commentaria.* Edited by M. Cathala, O.P. Third edition. Turin, Marietti, 1935.

————. *On the Truth of the Catholic Faith,* Book II: *Creation.* Translated by J. Anderson. New York, Doubleday Image Book, 1956.

Thomte, Reidar. *Kierkegaard's Philosophy of Religion.* Princeton, Princeton University Press, 1948.

Thorndike, L. *A History of Magic and Experimental Science,* Volumes VII–VIII: *The Seventeenth Century.* New York, Columbia University Press, 1958.

Tillich, P. *Systematic Theology.* 2 vols. Chicago, University of Chicago Press, 1951–1957.

————. *The Courage to Be.* New Haven, Yale University Press, 1952.

Topazio, V. W. *D'Holbach's Moral Philosophy.* Geneva, Institut et Musée Voltaire, 1956.

Torrance, T. F. *Calvin's Doctrine of Man.* London, Lutterworth Press, 1949.

Torrey, N. L. *Voltaire and the English Deists.* New Haven, Yale University Press, 1930.

Toulmin, S., Hepburn, R., and MacIntyre, A. *Metaphysical Beliefs.* London, SCM Press, 1957.

Troisfontaines, R., S.J. *De l'existence à l'être: La philosophie de Gabriel Marcel.* 2 vols. Paris, Vrin, 1953.

Vartanian, A. *Diderot and Descartes.* Princeton, Princeton University Press, 1953.

Versfeld, M. *An Essay on the Metaphysics of Descartes.* London, Metheun, 1940.

Volkmann-Schluck, K.-H. *Nicolaus Cusanus: Die Philosophie im Übergang vom Mittelalter zur Neuzeit.* Frankfurt a. M., Klostermann, 1957.

Voltaire. *Dictionnaire philosophique.* Edited by J. Benda and R. Naves. Paris, Garnier, 1954 edition.

————. *Lettres philosophiques.* Edited by R. Naves. Paris, Garnier, 1951 edition.

————. *Oeuvres complètes de Voltaire.* Moland edition. 52 vols. Paris, Garnier, 1877–1883.

————. *Traité de métaphysique*. Edited by H. T. Patterson. Manchester, University of Manchester Press, 1937.

————. *Voltaire and the Enlightenment: Selections from Voltaire*. Translated by N. L. Torrey. New York, Crofts, 1931.

————. *Voltaire's Notebooks*. Edited by T. Besterman. 2 vols. Geneva, Institut et Musée Voltaire, 1952.

Voss, C. H., editor. *The Universal God*. Cleveland, The World Publishing Company, 1953.

Wade, I. O. *Studies on Voltaire*. Princeton, Princeton University Press, 1947.

————. *The Clandestine Organization and Diffusion of Philosophic Ideas in France from 1700 to 1750*. Princeton, Princeton University Press, 1938.

Wahl, Jean. *Le malheur de la conscience dans la philosophie de Hegel*. Second edition. Paris, Presses Universitaires, 1951.

Ward, Wilfrid. *The Life of John Henry Cardinal Newman*. Reprint edition. 2 vols. in 1. New York, Longmans, Green, 1927.

Ward, W. G. *Essays on the Philosophy of Theism*. 2 vols. London, Kegan Paul, Trench, 1884.

Waterman, M. *Voltaire, Pascal and Human Destiny*. New York, King's Crown Press, 1942.

Webb, C. C. J. *Studies in the History of Natural Theology*. Oxford, Clarendon Press, 1915.

Weisheipl, J. A., O.P. *Nature and Gravitation*. River Forest, Illinois, Albertus Magnus Lyceum, 1955.

Weiss, P. *Modes of Being*. Carbondale, Illinois, Southern Illinois University Press, 1958.

Wendel, F. *Calvin: Sources et évolution de sa pensée religieuse*. Paris, Presses Universitaires, 1950.

White, Morton. *Toward Reunion in Philosophy*. Cambridge, Harvard University Press, 1956.

White, Victor, O.P. *God the Unknown*. New York, Harper, 1956.

Whitehead, Alfred North. *Adventures of Ideas*. New York, Macmillan, 1933.

————. *Modes of Thought*. New York, Macmillan, 1938.

————. *Process and Reality*. New York, Macmillan, 1929.

————. *Religion in the Making*. New York, Macmillan, 1926.

————. *Science and the Modern World*. New York, Macmillan, 1925.

Wickwar, W. H. *Baron d'Holbach*. London, Allen and Unwin, 1935.

Wild, John. *George Berkeley*. Cambridge, Harvard University Press, 1936.

Wiley, M. L. *The Subtle Knot*. London, Allen and Unwin, 1952.

Wolff, Christian. *Philosophia Prima sive Ontologia*. Verona, Moroni, 1779.

————. *Philosophia Rationalis sive Logica*. Verona, Moroni, 1779.

————. *Theologia Naturalis methodo scientifica pertractata, Pars prior . . . et Pars posterior*. 2 vols. Verona, Moroni, 1779.

Wolfson, H. A. *The Philosophy of Spinoza*. 2 vols. Cambridge, Harvard University Press, 1934.

Woodbridge, F. J. *Nature and Mind*. New York, Columbia University Press, 1937.

Wright, E. H. *The Meaning of Rousseau*. London, Oxford University Press, 1929.

Wundt, Max. *Die deutsche Schulmetaphysik im Zeitalter der Aufklärung*. Tübingen, Mohr, 1945.

Yolton, J. W. *John Locke and the Way of Ideas*. Oxford, Clarendon Press, 1956.

Zeno, Dr., O.F.M. *John Henry Newman: Our Way to Certitude*. Leiden, Brill, 1957.

II. ARTICLES

Alexander, I. W. "Voltaire and Metaphysics," *Philosophy*, 19 (1944), 19–48.

Alston, W. P. "Ineffability," *The Philosophical Review*, 65 (1956), 506–22.

Bacchus, F. "Newman's Oxford University Sermons," *The Month*, 140 (1922), 1–12.

Bremond, A., S.J. "Le théocentrisme de Malebranche," *Archives de Philosophie*, 6 (1928), 281–303.

Bibliography

Buranelli, V. "Pascal's Principles of Philosophy," *The New Scholasticism*, 30 (1956), 330–49.

Carpenter, H. J., O.P. "The Philosophical Approach to God in Thomism," *The Thomist*, 1 (1939), 45–61.

Carré, M. H. "Pierre Gassendi and the New Philosophy," *Philosophy*, 33 (1958), 112–20.

Cauchy, V. "The Nature and Genesis of the Skeptic Attitude," *The Modern Schoolman*, 27 (1949–50), 203–21, 297–310.

Collins, J. "Faith and Reflection in Kierkegaard," *The Journal of Religion*, 37 (1957), 10–19.

———. "Marxist and Secular Humanism," *Social Order*, 3 (1953), 207–32.

———. "Toward a Philosophically Ordered Thomism," *The New Scholasticism*, 32 (1958), 301–26.

Conklin, F. "The Marxian Philosophy of God," *The New Scholasticism*, 28 (1954), 38–57.

Cottier, M. M., O.P. "Foi et surnaturel chez F.-H. Jacobi," *Revue Thomiste*, 54 (1954), 337–73.

Decourtray, A. "Foi et raison chez Malebranche," *Mélanges de science religieuse*, 10 (1953), 67–86.

Dessain, C. S., C.O. "Cardinal Newman on the Theory and Practice of Knowledge. The Purpose of the *Grammar of Assent*," *The Downside Review*, 75 (1957), 1–23.

Dewey, J., Hook, S., and Nagel, E. "Are Naturalists Materialists?" *The Journal of Philosophy*, 42 (1945), 515–30.

Dondeyne, A. "L'historicité dans la philosophie contemporaine," *Revue Philosophique de Louvain*, 54 (1956), 468–76.

Dufrenne, M. "La connaissance de Dieu dans la philosophie spinoziste," *Revue Philosophique de la France et de l'Étranger*, 139 (1949), 474–85.

Ewing, A. C. "Kant's Attack on Metaphysics," *Revue Internationale de Philosophie*, 8 (1954), 371–91.

Faricy, R. L., S.J. "The Establishment of the Basic Principle of the Fifth Way," *The New Scholasticism*, 31 (1957), 189–208.

Feigl, M. "Vom *incomprehensibiliter inquirere* Gottes im I. Buch *De docta ignorantia* des Nikolaus von Cues," *Divus Thomas* [Freiburg], Series 3, Vol. XXII (1944), 321–38.

Gilson, E. "Les principes et les causes," *Revue Thomiste*, 52 (1952), 39–63.

Grey, D. "Berkeley on Other Selves," *The Philosophical Quarterly*, 4 (1954), 28–44.

Hayen, A., S.J. "Un interprète thomiste du kantisme: le P. Joseph Maréchal (1878–1945)," *Revue Internationale de Philosophie*, 8 (1954), 449–69.

Hurlbutt, R. "David Hume and Scientific Theism," *Journal of the History of Ideas*, 17 (1956), 486–97.

Hyppolite, J. "La critique hégélienne de la réflexion kantienne," *Kantstudien*, 45 (1953–54), 83–95.

Johnson, O. A. "Human Freedom in the Best of All Possible Worlds," *The Philosophical Quarterly*, 4 (1954), 147–55.

Jolivet, R. "Le problème de l'absolu dans la philosophie de M. Merleau-Ponty," *Tijdschrift voor Philosophie*, 19 (1957), 53–100.

Kaufmann, W. "Hegel's Early Antitheological Phase," *The Philosophical Review*, 63 (1954), 3–18.

Klubertanz, G., S.J. "Being and God according to Contemporary Scholastics," *The Modern Schoolman*, 32 (1954–55), 1–17.

———. "The Problem of the Analogy of Being," *The Review of Metaphysics*, 10 (1957), 553–79.

———. "Where is the Evidence for Thomistic Metaphysics?" *Revue Philosophique de Louvain*, 56 (1958), 294–315.

Kopper, J. "Kants Gotteslehre," *Kantstudien*, 47 (1955–56), 31–61.

Kroner, R. "The Year 1800 in the Development of German Idealism," *The Review of Metaphysics*, 1 (1948), 1–31.

Leclère, H., P.S.S. "Fénelon, critique de Malebranche," *Revue Thomiste*, 53 (1953), 347–66.

Bibliography

Lenz, J. W. "Locke's Essays on the Law of Nature," *Philosophy and Phenomenological Research*, 17 (1956–57), 105–13.

Leyden, W. von. "Locke and Nicole: Their Proofs of the Existence of God and Their Attitude toward Descartes," *Sophia*, 16 (1948), 41–55.

Lintz, E. J. "The Unity of the Universe, according to Alfred N. Whitehead," *The Thomist*, 6 (1943), 135–79, 318–66.

Löwith, K. "Feuerbach und der Ausgang der klassischen deutschen Philosophie," *Logos*, 17 (1928), 323–47.

McCoy, C. "Ludwig Feuerbach and the Formation of the Marxian Revolutionary Idea," *Laval Théologique et Philosophique*, 7 (1951), 218–48.

Mackie, J. L. "Evil and Omnipotence," *Mind*, N. S., 64 (1955), 200–12.

McRae, R. "Kant's Conception of the Unity of the Sciences," *Philosophy and Phenomenological Research*, 18 (1957–58), 1–17.

McTighe, T., and Kendzierski, L. "The Finite God in Contemporary Philosophy," *Proceedings of the American Catholic Philosophical Association*, 28 (1954), 212–36.

Marcus, R. "A Note on the Meaning of *Via*," *Dominican Studies*, 7 (1954), 239–45.

Martin, J. A. "St. Thomas and Tillich on the Names of God," *Journal of Religion*, 37 (1957), 235–57.

Martin, V., O.P. "The Dialectical Process in the Philosophy of Nicholas of Cusa," *Laval Théologique et Philosophique*, 5 (1949), 213–68.

Merlan, P. "Hamann et les dialogues de Hume," *Revue de Métaphysique et de Morale*, 59 (1954), 285–89.

Michalson, C. "The Boundary between Faith and Reason: A Study of Hegel's *Glauben und Wissen*," *Drew University Studies*, 3 (1951), 3–12.

Miller, L. "Descartes, Mathematics, and God," *The Philosophical Review*, 66 (1957), 451–65.

Mora, J. "Suarez and Modern Philosophy," *Journal of the History of Ideas*, 14 (1953), 528–47.

Mossner, E. "Hume's Early Memoranda, 1729–1740. The Complete Text," *Journal of the History of Ideas*, 9 (1948), 492–518.

Motte, A., O.P. "Théodicée et théologie chez S. Thomas d'Aquin," *Revue des Sciences Philosophiques et Theologiques*, 26 (1937), 5–26.

Mourant, J. "The Place of God in the Philosophy of Kierkegaard," *Giornale di metafisica*, 8 (1953), 207–21.

Nauert, C. "Magic and Skepticism in Agrippa's Thought," *Journal of the History of Ideas*, 18 (1957), 161–82.

Neuner, J., S.J. "Das Gottesproblem bei Nikolaus von Cues," *Philosophisches Jahrbuch*, 46 (1933), 331–43.

Neurath, O. "The Orchestration of the Sciences by the Encyclopedism of Logical Empiricism," *Philosophy and Phenomenological Research*, 6 (1945–46), 496–508.

Osbourn, J. C., O.P., and Conway, P. H., O.P. "Pen and Sword versus God," *The Thomist*, 6 (1943), 285–317.

Owens, J., C.Ss.R. "The Conclusion of the *Prima Via*," *The Modern Schoolman*, 30 (1952–53), 203–15 (one of a series of articles).

―――. "Theodicy, Natural Theology, and Metaphysics," *The Modern Schoolman*, 28 (1950–51), 126–37.

Pieper, J. "On the 'Negative' Element in the Philosophy of Thomas Aquinas," *Cross Currents*, 4 (1953–54), 46–56.

Pintard, R. "Descartes et Gassendi," *Trauvaux du IXe Congrès International de Philosophie* (12 vols., Paris, Hermann, 1937), II, 115–22.

Popkin, R. "Father Mersenne's War against Pyrrhonism," *The Modern Schoolman*, 34 (1956–57), 61–78.

―――. "L'Abbé Foucher et le problème des qualités premières," *Bulletin de la Société d'Étude du XVIIe Siècle*, Number 33 (1957), 633–47.

―――. "The Sceptical Crisis and the Rise of Modern Philosophy," *The Review of Metaphysics*, 7 (1953–54), 132–51, 307–22, 499–510.

―――. "The Skeptical Precursors of David Hume," *Philosophy and Phenomenological Research*, 16 (1955–56), 61–71.

Bibliography

Reinhardt, K. "Nietzsche's Godless Universe," *Journal of Arts and Letters*, 3 (1951), 89–96.

Robbers, H., S.J. "Wat is pantheïsme?" *Bijdragen der Nederlandse Jezuieten*, 12 (1951), 314–44.

Robinson, J. "Newman's Use of Butler's Arguments," *The Downside Review*, 76 (1958), 161–80.

Romeyer, B., S.J. "L'athéisme marxiste," *Archives de Philosophie*, 15 (1939), 293–353.

Rotenstreich, N. "Kant's Concept of Metaphysics," *Revue Internationale de Philosophie*, 8 (1954), 392–408.

Ryan, J. K. "The Argument of the Wager in Pascal and Others," *The New Scholasticism*, 19 (1945), 233–50.

Schrader, G. "Kant's Presumed Repudiation of the 'Moral Argument' in the *Opus Postumum*," *Philosophy*, 26 (1951), 228–41.

Siemes, J. B., S.J. "Friedrich Schlegel als Vorläufer christlicher Existenzphilosophie," *Scholastik*, 30 (1955), 161–84.

Smith, F., O.P. "A Thomistic Appraisal of the Philosophy of John Dewey," *The Thomist*, 18 (1955), 127–85.

Sweeney, L., S.J. "Divine Infinity: 1150–1250," *The Modern Schoolman*, 35 (1957–58), 38–51.

Vuillemin, J. "La signification de l'humanisme athée chez Feuerbach et l'idée de nature," *Deucalion*, 4 (1952), 17–46.

Weigel, G., S.J. "The Theological Significance of Paul Tillich," *Gregorianum*, 37 (1956), 34–54.

Weiss, P. "*Existenz* and Hegel," *Philosophy and Phenomenological Research*, 8 (1947–48), 206–16.

Wheeler, Mother M. C., R.S.C.J. "The Concept of Christianity in Hegel," *The New Scholasticism*, 31 (1957), 338–63.

Whittemore, R. "Prolegomena to a Modern Philosophical Theism," *Tulane Studies in Philosophy*, 5 (1956), 87–93.

―――. "The Metaphysics of the Seven Formulations of the Moral Argument," *Tulane Studies in Philosophy*, 3 (1954), 133–61.

―――. "Time and Whitehead's God," *Tulane Studies in Philosophy*, 4 (1955), 83–92.

Winance, E., O.S.B. "L'essence divine et la connaissance humaine dans le Commentaire sur les Sentences de Saint Thomas," *Revue Philosophique de Louvain*, 55 (1957), 171–215.

III. UNPUBLISHED DISSERTATIONS

Gurr, J. E., S.J. "The Principle of Sufficient Reason in Some Scholastic Systems, 1750–1900." St. Louis University, 1955.

Kenney, W. H., S.J. "John Locke and the Oxford Training in Logic and Metaphysics." St. Louis University, 1959.

Lauer, R. Z. "Voltaire's Constructive Deism." St. Louis University, 1958.

McTighe, T. P. "God and Physics in Galileo and Descartes." St. Louis University, 1955.

Murdoch, R. T. "Newton's Law of Attraction and the French Enlightenment." Columbia University, 1950.

INDEX

INDEX

Absolute, the, 143, 195, 201, 237, 250, 252 f., 272 ff., 297, 305 ff., 313 f., 387 ff.
Abstraction, 254
Addison, Joseph, 145
Agnosticism, 34, 118, 147, 289 f., 361, 402
Alexander, Samuel, 315
Analogy and univocity, 6, 10 f., 84 f., 109, 120, 186, 190, 244, 273 f., 319 ff., 396 f., 400 ff., 431, 435, 446 f.
See also Sapientialism
Anaxagoras, 238
Anselm, St., 421, 435
Anthropomorphism, 35, 149, 159, 189 f., 424
Arcesilas, 32
Archaicizing, *ix*, 403 f., 408
Aristotle, 4; and Bruno, 23 ff., 415; and Gassendi, 46; and Hegel, 236; and Kant, 430; and Paduans, 39 f.; and Whitehead, 317, 319
Arnauld, Antoine, 327
Arnobius, 334
Arnold, Matthew, 354, 363
Assent, fourfold, 368 ff., 197 f., 402
Atheism, 35, 47, 64 f., 95, 103, 108, 131, 210, 236 f., 238 ff., 289 f., 302 f., 326, 329, 347 f., 357 f., 360 ff., 369 ff., 371 ff., 382, 387 ff., 402, 426, 435, 436 f.; American naturalism, 269 ff.; Feuerbach, 239 ff.; Holbach, 151 ff.; Marx, 249 ff.; Nietzsche, 257 ff.
Atomism, 46 f., 95, 300 f. *See also* Scientic influences on theism
Attributes, divine, 9, 16, 42 f., 68, 74 f., 77 f., 88, 141 f., 147, 159, 381, 395 ff., 427; natural and moral, 120 f., 189, 296 f., 308 f., 312 f.
Augustine, St., 2, 86, 159, 229, 325, 331, 421; and Descartes, 57 ff.; kinds of theology, 97, 407, 447; man and God, 391; unknown God, 41, 190, 357, 401, 413, 418
Ayer, Alfred, 282, 439

Bacon, Francis, 17, 90 ff., 97 f., 104, 114, 120, 326, 360, 408, 422
Barth, Karl, 86, 399, 402
Bauer, Bruno, 255
Bayle, Pierre, 31, 107, 114, 126, 127 ff., 144 f., 157, 160, 425; on evil, 37, 85, 292 f., 342
Belief. *See* Faith, natural
Berdyaev, Nicholas, 387
Bergier, Nicholas, 429
Bergson, Henri, 441
Berkeley, George, 90, 107 ff., 117, 121, 423 f.
Bérulle, Cardinal, 58
Boehme, Jacob, 403, 435
Bowne, Borden, 313, 422
Boyle, Robert, 47

Bradley, F. H., 305, 313, 440
Brahe, Tycho, 54
Brightman, E. S., 36, 315, 394
Browne, Thomas, 329
Bruno, Giordano, 2, 7, 10, 14, 20 ff., 51, 55, 326, 415
Buber, Martin, 388, 446
Buffier, Claude, 424 f.
Buffon, G. L. de, 154
Burke, Edmund, 363
Butler, Joseph, 361, 362, 444
Butler, Samuel, 398 f.

Calvin, John, 2, 11, 12 ff., 21, 28, 92, 96, 128, 160, 408
Camus, Albert, 268, 370 ff.
Cardano, Geronimo, 39
Carlyle, Thomas, 291
Carnap, Rudolph, 282
Cassirer, Ernst, 425
Causa sui, 61 f.
Causality and causal inference, 9, 11, 25 ff., 86, 104, 122 ff., 147 f., 243, 245, 253 f., 290 ff., 299, 310, 314, 316 f., 339, 360 ff., 382 ff., 389 ff., 399 ff., 405; American naturalism, 273 f., 276 ff.; Hegel, 207, 209, 219 f., 227 ff.; Hume, 116 ff.; Kant, 165 ff., 190; Spinoza, 75 f., 77 ff.
Certitude, 49 f, 63 f, 67 ff., 98,, 130 ff., 352 f., 366 ff., 417 ff
Charron, Pierre, 31, 34, 42 ff., 49, 416
Christianity, 2, 4, 7, 11 ff., 20 f., 25, 29, 36 40, 42 ff., 46, 69, 76, 86 ff., 92, 128 ff., 144, 149, 154, 159 f., 165, 195 f., 203 ff., 233 ff., 240 f., 258, 287, 308, 316, 326 ff., 406, 408, 418, 421, 432, 435 f., 443 f. *See also* Faith, Christian
Christian Fate, 82 f.
Cicero, 14 f., 38, 114
Clarke, Samuel, 119 f., 152, 171, 349, 359, 424; and Voltaire, 144 ff., 427 f.
Cohen, Morris, 269, 279 f., 393
Coincidentia oppositorum, 7, 413
Coleridge, Samuel, 112, 288
Collins, Anthony, 144, 147
Common consent about God, 47, 100, 218, 290
Comte, Auguste, 206, 239, 243, 269, 287, 377
Conscience and God, 357 ff., 361 ff. *See also* Moral bearing of God
Contingency, 10 f., 54, 60 f., 81, 137 ff., 146 ff., 169 f., 179 f., 185, 224 ff., 251 f., 278, 299, 382, 387
Copernicus, Nicholas, 22 f., 54
Creator and creation, 7, 9, 13, 18, 21, 28, 39, 60, 75, 82 ff., 88, 99, 147 ff., 159, 165, 171, 235, 254, 281, 293 f., 298, 313 ff., 421, 441
Cudworth, Ralph, 103, 423

471

Index